New Achievements in Evolutionary Computation

Edited by

Peter Korosec

New Achievements in Evolutionary Computation
Edited by Peter Korosec

Republished by InTech
Janeza Trdine 9, 51000 Rijeka, Croatia

Additional hard copies can be obtained from orders@intechopen.com

New Achievements in Evolutionary Computation, Edited by Peter Korosec
p. cm.
ISBN 978-953-307-053-7

For EU product safety concerns:
IN TECH d.o.o., Prolaz Marije Krucifikse Kozulić 3, 51000 Rijeka, Croatia, info@intechopen.com or visit our website at intechopen.com.

Meet the editor

Peter Korosec received the BSc and MSc degrees in computer science from the University of Ljubljana, Slovenia, in 2001 and 2004, respectively. In 2006, he received his PhD from the Jožef Stefan International Postgraduate School. Since Winter 2002 he has been a researcher at the Jožef Stefan Institute in Ljubljana, Slovenia. His current areas of research include combinatorial and numerical optimization with ant-based metaheuristics.

Preface

Evolutionary computation has been widely used in computer science for decades. Even though it started as far back as the 1960s with simulated evolution, the subject is still evolving. During this time, new metaheuristic optimization approaches, like evolutionary algorithms, genetic algorithms, swarm intelligence, etc., were being developed and new fields of usage in artificial intelligence, machine learning, combinatorial and numerical optimization, etc., were being explored. However, even with so much work done, novel research into new techniques and new areas of usage is far from over. This book presents some new theoretical as well as practical aspects of evolutionary computation.

The first part of the book is mainly concentrated on evolutionary algorithms and their applications. First, the influence that diversity has on evolutionary algorithms will be described. There is also an insight into how to efficiently solve the constraint-satisfaction problem and how time series can be determined by the use of evolutionary forecasting. Quantum finite-state machines are becoming increasingly more important. Here, an evolutionary-based logic is used for its synthesis. With an ever increasing number of criteria being used to evaluate a solution, this is leading to different multi-objective evolutionary approaches. Such approaches are being applied to control optimization and phylogenetic reconstruction. It is well known that evolutionary-computation approaches are mostly bio-inspired. So it is interesting to see how they can return to its origin by solving bio-problems. Here, they are used for predicting membrane protein-protein interactions and are applied to different bioinformatics applications.

The second part of the book presents some other well-known evolutionary approaches, like genetic algorithms, genetic programming, estimations of the distribution algorithm, and swarm intelligence. Genetic algorithms are used in Q-learning to develop a compact control table, while flight-control system design is being optimized by genetic programming. A new estimation of the distribution algorithm, using the empirical selection distribution, is being presented and, on the other hand, a classical version is being applied to the video-tracking system problem. The book ends with the recently very popular swarm-intelligence approaches, where they are used in artificial societies, social simulations, and applied to the Chinese traveling-salesman problem.

This book will be of great value to undergraduates, graduate students, researchers in computer science, and anyone else with an interest in learning about the latest developments in evolutionary computation.

Editor

Peter Korosec

Contents

1

Diversity-Based Adaptive Evolutionary Algorithms

Maury Meirelles Gouvêa Jr. and Aluizio Fausto Ribeiro Araújo
Pontifical Catholic University of Minas Gerais
Federal University of Pernambuco
Brazil

1. Introduction

In evolutionary algorithms (EAs), preserving the diversity of the population, or minimizing its loss, may benefit the evolutionary process in several ways, such as, by preventing premature convergence, by allocating the population in distinct Pareto optimal solutions in a multi objective problem, and by permitting fast adaptation in dynamic problems. Premature convergence may lead the EA to a non-optimal result, that is, converging to a local optimum. In static problems, standard EAs work well. However, many real world problems are dynamic or other uncertainties have to be taken into account, such as noise and fitness approximation. In dynamic problems, the preservation of diversity is a crucial issue because EAs need to explore the largest number of regions possible. Standard genetic algorithms (SGA) are not suitable for solving dynamic problems because their population quickly converges to a specific region of the solution space.

The loss of diversity is caused by selection pressure and genetic drift, two factors inherent in EAs. The loss of diversity may lead the EA to a non-optimal result, despite the fact that after a period of time, EA tends to find the global optimum. In static problems, loss of diversity might not be a very critical problem. However in dynamic environments lack of diversity may degrade EA performance. Especially in dynamic problems, the preservation of diversity is a crucial issue because an EA needs to explore the search space aggressively.

One option for reacting to a change of the environment is to consider each change as the arrival of a new optimization problem to be solved. This is a viable alternative if there is time available to solve the problem. However, the time available for finding the new optimum may be short and also sometimes the algorithm cannot identify the environmental change. When the new optimum is close to the old one, the search can be restricted to the neighborhood of the previous optimum. Thus, some knowledge about the previous search space can be used. However, reusing information from the past may not be promising depending on the nature of the change. If the change is large or unpredictable, restarting the search may be the only viable option.

The approaches that handle dynamic environments, addressing the issue of convergence, can be divided into the following categories (Jin & Branke, 2005): (i) generating diversity after a change, (ii) preserving diversity throughout the run, (iii) memory-based approaches, and (iv) multi-population approaches. The first two approaches cover the diversity problem.

In (i), an EA runs in standard way, but when a change is detected, some actions are taken to increase diversity. In (ii), convergence is avoided all the time and it is expected that a more dispersive population can adapt to changes. In (iii), EA is supplied with a memory so as to be able to recall useful information from past generations. In (iv), the population is divided into several subpopulations allowing different peaks in the environment to be tracked.
The preservation of diversity has advantages that can be supported by theory, such as those cited above, and from Nature. The loss of diversity because of the extinction of species may produce irreversible ecological disturbance for an ecosystem. A high diversity level produces abilities which allow populations or species to react against adversities, such as diseases, parasites, and predators. An appropriate level of diversity allows populations or species to adapt to environmental changes. On the other hand, a low diversity level tends to limit these abilities (Amos & Harwood, 1998). From the point of view of the evolutionary process, the loss of diversity also represents serious problems, such as population convergence to a specific region of the solutions space; thus, EA losses its main feature, the global search. In order to preserve the diversity of the population it is necessary to create strategies to adjust one or more EA parameters, such as the mutation rate, selection pressure, etc. These strategies are known as diversity-based algorithms.
This chapter presents a survey on diversity-based evolutionary algorithms. Two classes of models are presented: one to minimize the loss of diversity and another to control population diversity based on the desired diversity range or level. Several methods to measure the diversity of the population and the species are presented as a foundation for diversity control methods. The rest of this paper is organized as follows. Section 2 presents parameter setting and control in EAs. Section 3 describes several methods for measuring diversity. Section 4 presents methods to preserve and control population diversity in evolutionary algorithms. Finally, Section 5 concludes this chapter.

2. Parameter tuning and control in evolutionary computation

The EA parameters can affect population diversity directly. For instance, a larger mutation rate causes disturbances in the offspring and, consequently, increases the diversity of the population in the next generation. On the other hand, the greater the selection pressure is, the fittest individuals tend to survive or generate more offspring. Thus, these individuals tend to be genetically similar, thus decreasing the diversity of the population.
We can set parameter values by parameter tuning and parameter control (Angeline, 1995; Eiben et al., 1999; Hinterding et al., 1997). Parameter tuning finds appropriate values for the parameters before the algorithm is used, and these parameters are fixed during the run. For example, Bäck & Schutz (1996) suggest the following mutation probability

$$p_m = \frac{1.75}{N\sqrt{L}}, \tag{1}$$

where N is the population size and L is the individual length.
Parameter control changes parameter values on-line in accordance with three categories (Eiben et al., 1999; Hinterding et al., 1997): deterministic, adaptive, and self-adaptive control methods. The next three subsections present these categories.

2.1 Deterministic control methods

Deterministic techniques in which the control rule is triggered when a number of generations has elapsed since the last time the rule was activated. For example (Hinterding et al., 1997), the mutation rate may be defined as

$$p_m(k) = 0.5 - 0.3\frac{k}{K}, \tag{2}$$

where k is the current generation and K is the maximum number of generations. This strategy aims to produce high exploration in the beginning of the evolutionary process as a way to seek out promising regions in the solutions space. During the evolutionary process, the mutation rate decreases in order to benefit the exploration continuously. Thus, the diversity of the population tends to decrease throughout the evolutionary process.

2.2 Adaptive control methods

Adaptive techniques consider that the assignment of parameter values is associated with feedback from the evolutionary process. For example, the mutation rate may be defined as in (Srinivas & Patnaik, 1994)

$$p_m(k) = \frac{A}{f^*(k) - \bar{f}(k)}, \tag{3}$$

where f^* is the fitness of the best individual, $\bar{f}$ is the mean fitness of the population, and A is a constant. This strategy increases the mutation rate as the mean fitness of the population approximates to the best fitness of the population. The objective is to avoid the convergence of the whole population to a specific region of the solutions space. This interaction with the environment by adaptive control methods may be an advantage over deterministic methods because the former may overcome some problems during the evolutionary process, such as local optimum convergence. In dynamic problems, even if the population is located around the global optimum, when the environment changes, it is almost always necessary to spread the population. Using Equation (2), it is not possible to modify the mutation rate based on the environmental change. With adaptive methods, if the algorithm has a mechanism to detect the environment change, the mutation rate can be increased. On the other hand, adaptive methods require more computational effort than deterministic methods.

2.3 Self-adaptive control methods

Self-adaptive techniques encode the parameters in the chromosomes and undergo EA operators. For instance (Eiben et al., 1999), the representation of the i-th individual g_i becomes

$$[g_{i1}, \ldots, g_{iL}, p_m],$$

in which both the solution vector and mutation probability undergo the evolutionary process. The self-adaptive methods use the evolution principle on the EA parameters, which are modified and undergo the whole evolutionary process - selection, crossover, and mutation. For instance, an individual with L genes in the standard evolutionary algorithm will have L+1 genes in a self-adaptive method, where the extra gene is an evolutionary factor parameter, such as the mutation rate, crossover rate, type of crossover operator, and so forth. The advantage of this strategy over the other control parameter methods is that the parameters are modified by the effects of evolutions, and tend to persist at all parameter values that produce better individuals. Another benefit of this strategy is its low computational effort because only few genes are added into the individuals, and no extra computation is necessary. The disadvantage of the self-adaptive strategy occurs especially in a dynamic environment where the changes in the environment may not be detected or are detected late. Self-adaptive methods may not be able to avoid premature convergence in the local optimum because, normally, they do not have a direct way to detect it.

3. Diversity measurement

In order to preserve and, especially, to control population diversity it is necessary to measure it. This section presents some of the measurement methods proposed by several authors (Rao, 1982; Weitzman, 1992; Solow et al., 1993; Champely & Chessel, 2002; Ursem et al., 2002; Wineberg & Oppacher, 2003; Simpson, 2004). Rao (1982) created a diversity function based on the probability distribution of a finite set of species. His diversity function uses the distance d(s_1, s_2) between two species s_1 and s_2 defined over a finite set of species, as follows

$$\Gamma = \sum_{i=1}^{n_S}\sum_{j=1}^{n_S} p_i\, p_j\, d(s_i, s_j)\,, \tag{4}$$

where n_S is the number of species and $p_i = \mathrm{P}(X = s_i)$.
Weitzman (1992) created a recursive method to compute diversity, as follows

$$\Gamma(S) = \max_{s_i \in S} \Gamma(S - s_i) + d(s_i, S)\ \forall s_i \in S\,, \tag{5}$$

in which there is a unique solution whether if the condition $\Gamma(s_i) = d_0$ is considered, where $d_0 \geq 0$ is a constant.
Solow et al. (1993) proposed a function, named the preservation measure, to calculate the loss of diversity when a species s_i becomes extinct, as follows

$$\Delta\Gamma = -\sum_{s_i \notin S} d(s_i, S)\,. \tag{6}$$

Based on Rao (1982), Champely and Chessel (2002) introduced a function for diversity using the Euclidean distance between species, defined as

$$\Gamma = \frac{1}{2}\sum_{i=1}^{n_S}\sum_{j=1}^{n_S} p_i\, p_j \left[d(s_i, s_j)\right]^2. \tag{7}$$

Simpson (2004) created a heterozygosity-based diversity function, H_e. When H_e is replaced with Γ, Simpson´s diversity function becomes

$$\Gamma = 1 - \sum_{i=1}^{n_a} (p_i)^2\,, \tag{8}$$

where p_i is the occurrence rate of the i-th allele, individual, or species from the set S, and n_a is the number of alleles, individuals, or species.

In evolutionary computation, normally, the methods that measure population diversity use two different types of models: one as a function of the distance between individuals (Wineberg & Oppacher, 2003) and another as a function of the distance from the individuals to a reference (Ursem et al., 2002), e.g., the population mean point.

Diversity as a function of the distance between all individuals can be measured as follows

$$\Gamma = \sum_{i=1}^{N} \sqrt{\sum_{j=1}^{i-1} d(g_i, g_j)}\,, \tag{9}$$

where $d(g_i, g_j)$ is the distance (e.g., Euclidean or Hamming) between individuals g_i and g_j. The diversity from Equation (9), with complexity $O(L, N^2)$, has the disadvantage of requiring a large computational effort.

Wineberg & Oppacher (2003) proposed a smaller computational effort than Equation (9), with complexity $O(L, N)$, based on allele frequencies, as follows

$$\Gamma = \frac{N^2}{2L} \sum_{i=1}^{L} \sum_{\forall \alpha \in A} f_i(\alpha)\left[1 - f_i(\alpha)\right], \tag{10}$$

where A is the set of alleles,

$$f_i(\alpha) = \frac{c_i(\alpha)}{N}\,, \tag{11}$$

is the frequency in which the allele α occurs in the i-th gene of the individuals in the population,

$$c_i(\alpha) = \sum_{j=1}^{N} \delta_{ji}(\alpha)\,, \tag{12}$$

is the number of occurrences of α and $\delta_{ji}(\alpha)$ is the delta of Kronecker, which becomes 1 if the gene in *locus* i in chromosome j is equal to α; or 0, otherwise.

Ursem et al. (2002) proposed a model as a function of a reference point in the solutions space, which requires a smaller computational effort and complexity $O(L, N)$. This diversity model shows the population distribution with respect to the population mean point calculated as follows

$$\Gamma = \frac{1}{DN} \sum_{i=1}^{N} \sqrt{\sum_{j=1}^{L} \left(g_{ij} - \overline{g}_j\right)^2}\,, \tag{13}$$

where D is the solutions space diagonal, $D \subset \Re^L$, g_{ij} is the j-th gene of the i-th individual, $\overline{g}$ is the j-th gene of the population mean point, $\overline{g}$, where

$$g_j = \frac{1}{N} \sum_{i=1}^{N} g_{ij}\,. \tag{14}$$

The diversity between species and population diversity have different characteristics. In the former, the species are always different, whereas in the latter, two individuals may be genetically equal. In the diversity of species, a new individual added to a set *S* increases its diversity. In populations, a new individual may increase or decrease diversity.

4. Diversity preservation and control

The parameter control methods that aim to preserve diversity can be divided into two classes: diversity preservation and diversity control. The diversity preservation methods use strategies that minimize the loss of diversity (Bui et al., 2005; Herrera et al., 2000; Simões & Costa, 2002a; Wong et al., 2003). The diversity control methods have a value or range of desired diversity (Meiyi et al., 2004; Nguyen & Wong, 2003; Ursem et al., 2002). Thus, diversity control strategies aim to minimize the difference between the population and the diversities desired. The next two subsections present some important diversity preservation and control methods in evolutionary computation.

4.1 Diversity preservation

Most methods that deal with population diversity try to avoid loss of diversity without setting a desired value or range. Cobb (1990) created the trigged hypermutation (THM) method that set the mutation probability to a high value (hypermutation) during periods where the time-averaged best performance of the EA worsens; otherwise, the EA maintains a low level of mutation. THM permits the EA to accommodate changes in the environment, while also permitting the EA to perform optimization during periods of environmental stationariness.

Simões & Costa (2001) created a biologically inspired genetic operator called transformation. The computational mechanism is inspired by the biological process and consists of the capacity of the individuals to absorb fragments of DNA (desoxirribonucleic acid) from the environment. These gene segments are then reintegrated in the individual genome. Simões & Costa incorporated transformation into the standard evolutionary algorithm as a new genetic operator that replaces crossover. The pseudo-code of this modified EA is described in Figure 1.

```
k ← 0
Generate P(k)
Evaluate P(k)
Generate initial gene segment pool
while( NOT stop condition )
{
        Select S(k) from P(k)
        Transform S(k)
        Evaluate S(k)
        P(k+1) ← S(k)
        Generate new gene segment pool
        k ← k + 1
}
```

Fig. 1. Transformation-based GA (TGA)

The foreign DNA fragments, consisting of binary strings of different lengths, will form a gene segment pool and will be used to transform the individuals of the population. In each generation k, a sub-population S(k) is selected to be transformed by the pool of gene segments. The segment pool is changed using the old population to create part of the new segments with those remaining being created at random. In the transformation mechanism there is no sexual reproduction among the individuals. To transform an individual the following steps are conducted: select a segment from the segment pool and randomly choose a point of transformation in the selected individual. The segment is incorporated in the genome of the individual. This corresponds to the biological process where the gene segments when integrated in the DNA cell recipient, replace some genes in its chromosome.

Wong et al. (2003) created a method to adjust the crossover, p_c, and mutation probability, pm, in order to promote a trade-off for exploration and exploitation. The evolutionary process is divided into two phases: the first uses pc and pm with values at random; the second adjusts pc and pm according to the fitness enhancements from the first phase. The diversity of the population is maintained by appending a "diversity fitness" into the original individual fitness. Thus, population diversity contributes to survivor selection as a weighted form, that is, there is a weight to balance the original fitness and the diversity fitness.

Shimodaira (2001) designed a method to preserve diversity, called the diversity control-oriented genetic algorithm (DCGA). First, the population is paired, each one is recombined and their offspring are mutated. After that, the offspring and current population are merged. Then, the survivor selection is made from the remaining population in accordance with the following roles:

1. Duplicate structures in M(t) are eliminated and M'(t) is formed. Duplicate structures mean that they have identical entire structures;
2. Structures are selected by using the Cross-generational Probabilistic Survival Selection (CPSS) method, and P(t) is formed from the structure with the best fitness value in M'(t) and the selected structures. In the CPSS method, structures are selected by using uniform random numbers on the basis of a selection probability defined by the following equation:

$$p_s = \left((1-c)\frac{H_i}{L} + c \right)^{\alpha}, \tag{15}$$

   where H_i is the Hamming distance between a candidate structure and the structure with the best fitness value, L is the length of the entire string representing the structure, c is the shape coefficient the value of which is in the range of [0.0, 1.0], and α is the exponent. In the selection process, a uniform random number in the range of [0.0, 1.0] is generated for each structure.
3. If the number of the structures selected in Role 2 is smaller than N; then new structures randomly generated as in the initial population are introduced by the difference of the numbers.

DCGA has an empirical and theoretical justification for avoiding premature convergence. The duplicated offspring decrease the population diversity. Thus, the crossover and large mutation probability tend to produce offspring that are as different as possible from their parents, and that explore regions of the solutions space that have not been explored. The selection pressure and population diversity should be externally controlled independently of the condition of the population, because the algorithm cannot recognize if the population is in a local or global optimum. If the selection pressure is high, the best individuals near the best one tend to rise and survive in larger numbers, thus causing premature convergence. Shimodaira tried to solve this problem by reducing appropriately the selection pressure in the neighborhood of the best individual to eliminate individuals similar to it. Equation (15) creates a bias between the elimination of individuals with the smallest Hamming distance to the best individual and the selection of individuals with the greatest Hamming distance to the best individual. The greater this bias is, the greater the diversity of the population is.

Grefenstette (1992) proposed an approach based on the flow of population immigrants over generations, called the random immigrants genetic algorithm (RIGA). This approach maintains a population diversity level by replacing some individuals from the current population by random individuals, called random immigrants, in every generation. There are two ways that define how individuals are replaced: replacing individuals at random or replacing the worst ones (Vavak et al., 1996). RIGA inserts random individuals into the population, a strategy that may increase population diversity and benefit the performance of the GA in dynamic environments. Figure 2 shows the pseudo-code of the RIGA.

```
k ← 0
Generate P(k)
Evaluate P(k)
while( NOT stop condition)
{
        Generate a sub-population S_ri(k) of n_ri random immigrants
        Evaluate S_ri(k)
        Replace the worst individuals of P(k) with S_ri(k)
        P'(k) ← select( P(k) )
        Q(k) ← recombine( P'(k) )
        Mutate Q(k)
        Evaluate Q(k)
        P(k+1) ← Q(k)
        k ← k + 1
}
```

Fig. 2. Random immigrants GA (RIGA)

4.2 Diversity control

The control aims to keep the process output within prescribed limits (Narendra & Annaswamy, 2005). Figure 3 shows a simple control model. The objective of the control may be stated as the determination of the process input, u, to keep the error between a desired output, Γ_m, and the process output, Γ, within a pre-determined interval. If Γ_m is constant, the problem is called regulation around this value – also known as a set point. If Γ_m is a function of time, the problem is referred as tracking. When the characteristics of the process are known, the aim becomes to determine a control strategy to stabilize the feedback loop in Figure 3 around Γ_m. Otherwise, when the characteristics of the process are unknown, both regulation and tracking can be viewed as an adaptive control problem.

Diversity control methods have a level or range of desired diversity. Thus, it is possible to define a control strategy based on a desired diversity. Ursem et al. (2002) created the diversity-guided evolutionary algorithm (DGEA) with two evolutionary modes:

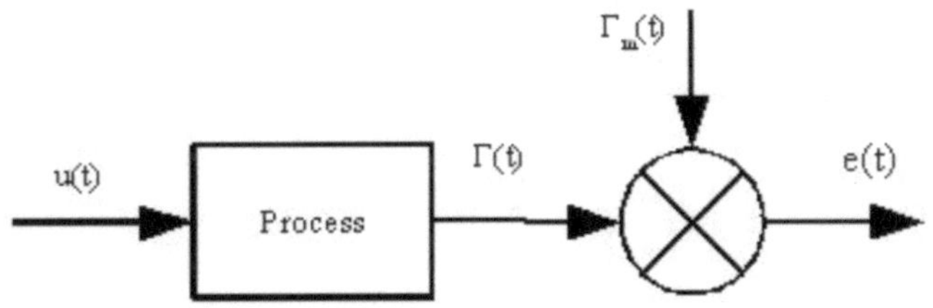

Fig. 3. The simple control scheme

exploitation and exploration. The former applies selection and recombination operators, which tend to decrease population diversity, while the diversity is above a limit d_{low}. When the population diversity drops below d_{low}, DGEA switches to an exploration mode that applies only the mutation operator, which tends to increase the diversity, until a diversity of d_{high} is reached. Ursem et al. used Equation (13) to measure the diversity of the population. Both evolutionary modes, exploitation and exploration, change from one to the other in the evolutionary process as a function of the diversity range. Figure 4 shows the pseudo-code of the DGEA.

```
k ← 0
Generate P(k)
Evaluate P(k)
mode ← 'exploit'
while( NOT stop condition )
{
        if( diversity( P(k) ) < dlow )
          mode ← 'explore'
        else if( diversity( P(k) ) > dhigh )
          mode ← 'exploit'

        if( mode = 'exploit' )
          P'(k) ← select( P(k) )
          Q(k) ← recombine( P'(k) )
        else
          Q(k) ← mutate( P(k) )

        Evaluate Q(k)
        P(k+1) ← Q(k)
        k ← k + 1
}
```

Fig. 4. Diversity-guided evolutionary algorithm (DGEA)

An important issue is to apply a mutation operator that rather quickly increases the distance to the population mean point. Otherwise, the algorithm will stay in exploration mode for a long time. An advantage for a mutation operator is to use the population mean average point to calculate the direction of each individual mutation. A disadvantage of the DGEA is its non-use of selection, recombination, and mutation together, which is the fundamental principle of EA.

Nguyen & Wong (2003) used control theory to adjust the mutation rate in unimodal space. The desired diversity, in generation *k*, was defined as follows

$$\Gamma_d(k) = \Gamma(0)\exp(-k\tau)\,, \tag{16}$$

where $\Gamma(0)$ is the initial diversity and $\tau > 0$ is a constant. Nguyen & Wong model is motivated by the observation that for unimodal search, convergence implies a corresponding reduction in the population diversity and that an exponential convergence rate would need to be accompanied by an exponential reduction of diversity. Nguyen & Wong adopted a diversity measurement based on the radial deviation from the population mean point.

In Nguyen & Wong method, when the current population diversity deviates from the diversity desired, Γ_d, the mutation rate is adjusted as a control problem (Ogata, 1998), as follows

$$p_m(k+1) = p_m(k)\exp\left(\frac{e(k)}{\tilde{e}(k)}\right), \tag{17}$$

where $e(k)$ is the deviation or error between the current and desired diversities, $\tilde{e}(k)$ is the square mean error defined as

$$\tilde{e}(k) = \sqrt{\left[e(1)\right]^2 + \left[e(2)\right]^2 + \ldots + \left[e(k)\right]^2}\,. \tag{18}$$

From the work of Beyer & Rudolph (1997), Nguyen & Wong hypothesized that EAs can be induced to have linear order convergence for unimodal search if the population diversity can be controlled so as to decrease at a matching exponential rate.

We created an adaptive EA named diversity-reference adaptive control (DRAC) (Gouvêa Jr. & Araújo, 2007). Our approach was based on the model-reference adaptive system (MRAS), an adaptive controller in which the desired performance of a particular process is determined by a model-reference (Astrom & Wittenmark, 1995; Wagg, 2003). The implicit assumption is that the designer is sufficiently familiar with the system under consideration. When a suitable choice is made of the structure and parameters of the model-reference, the desired response can be specified in terms of the model output.

In MRAS, the model and process output are compared and the difference is used to yield the control signal. The system holds two feedback loops: the first loop, an ordinary piece of feedback, comprises the process and controller; and the second changes the controller parameter. Given one process, with an input-output pair $\{u, \Gamma\}$, and one model-reference, with an input-output pair $\{u_c, \Gamma_m\}$, the aim is to determine the control input $u(t)$, for all $t \geq t_0$, so that

$$\lim_{t \to \infty} \left|\Gamma_m(t) - \Gamma(t)\right| = 0\,. \tag{19}$$

Parameter updating is based on feedback from the error. Two widely used methods to yield the control signal using MRAS are (Astrom & Wittenmark, 1995): the MIT rule and the stable adaptation law derived from Lyapunov stability theory.

The MIT rule begins by defining the tracking error, *e*, which represents the difference between the process output and the model-reference output, as follows

$$e(t) = \Gamma_m(t) - \Gamma(t), \tag{20}$$

where $\Gamma_m(t)$ and $\Gamma(t)$ are the model-reference and process output, respectively, at time t. From this error, a cost function, $J(\theta)$, is formed, where θ is the controller parameter that will be adapted. A typical cost function is

$$J(\theta) = \frac{1}{2}\left[e(t)\right]^2. \tag{21}$$

If the goal is to minimize this cost related to the error, the parameter θ can be changed in accordance with the negative gradient of J, then

$$\frac{d\theta}{dt} = -\eta\frac{\partial J}{\partial \theta} = -\eta\, e\frac{\partial e}{\partial \theta}, \tag{22}$$

where $\eta \in [0, 1]$ is the step length of the θ adjustment. The partial derivative $\partial e/\partial\theta$, the sensitivity of the system, establishes how the error is influenced by the adjustable parameter.

Thus, the process output has to track the model-reference output. The block diagram of DRAC, Figure 5, has a block called process comprising the evolutionary process and the diversity evaluator so as to determine the current diversity of the population. The controller sends the control signal, u, to the process as a function of the command signal, u_c, and the parameter, θ. The updating of θ is based on the error between the process and model-reference output. The model-reference, as a whole, represents a behaviour to be tracked by the population diversity.

DRAC computes the population diversity based on Equation (8) as a function of the allele occurrence rate for a given gene. In real-coded EA, the number of alleles is calculated by separating the gene length into defined intervals, i.e., the number of alleles, n_a, is the number of intervals. Thus, the allele that belongs to a given interval j is regarded as allele g_{ij}, i.e., allele j from the gene i.

In DRAC, the model-reference represents a crucial feature of behaviour to be tracked by the evolutionary process. Note that while the evolutionary process aims to determine the optimal solution, the control system regulates the population diversity to track the model-reference. The model-reference is expressed by

$$\Gamma_m(k+1) = \Psi(\Gamma_m(k), u_c(k), k). \tag{23}$$

where $\Psi(.)$ is a non-linear function, Γ_m is the model-reference output, and u_c is the command signal (i.e., the model input).

From the Hardy-Wimberg model (Hardy, 1908; Weinberg, 1908), it is possible to assume that there is no evolution without loss of diversity. Regarding this premise, a general model-reference should consider two hypotheses: (i) during the evolutionary process, diversity decreases, and (ii) there is a minimum diversity level to maintain a balance between exploitation and exploration. Thus, after each change in the environment, Γ_m goes from its current value to $\Gamma(0)$, to increase exploration.

DRAC proposes a model-reference that decreases its diversity limited by a determined minimum value. This model also forces a strong growth in diversity after changes in the environment. The modifications to the environment are detected by the decrease of the best

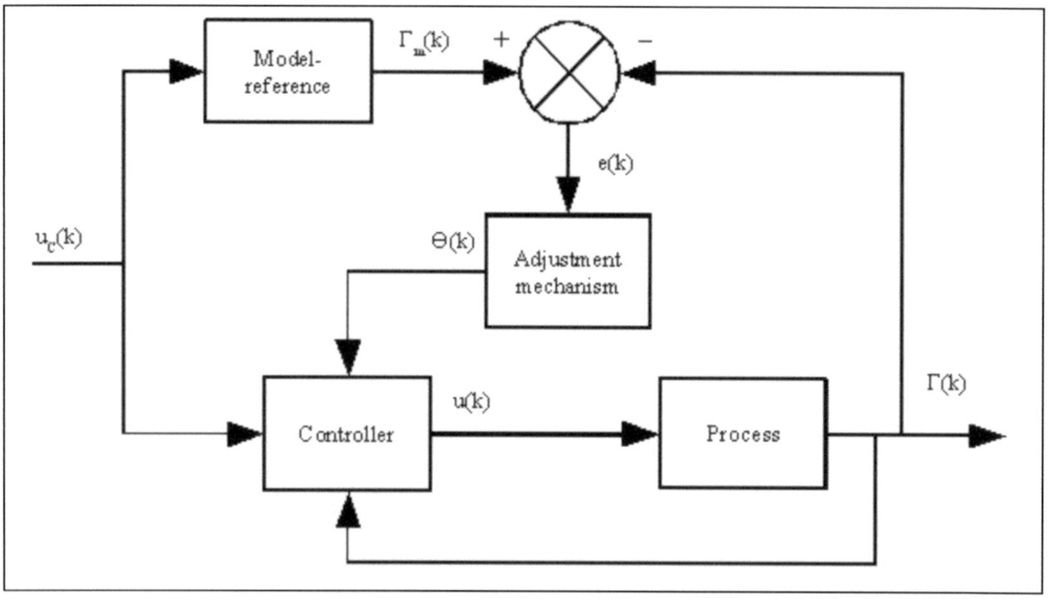

Fig. 5. Block diagram of the DRAC method for EA parameter control

individual. Our model reference is based on heterozygosity dynamics, from an ideal Wright-Fisher population (Wright, 1931; Fisher, 1930), as follows

$$\Gamma_m(k+1) = \Gamma_m(k)\left(1 - \frac{1}{2N_e}\right), \tag{24}$$

where N_e is the effective population size, i.e., the size of the ideal Wright-Fisher population. The command signal, u_c, is the effective population size, N_e,, $\Gamma_m(0)$ is the initial population diversity, $\Gamma_m(0) = \Gamma(0)$, and a minimum diversity value must be defined to avoid zero diversity.

DRAC modifies the selection mechanism, which is conducted in three stages as follows:

1. Selection of the individual with best fitness to assure that the best solution survives to the next generation.
2. Selection of αN individuals based on a standard selection (e.g., roulette wheel or tournament).
3. Selection of $(1 - \alpha)N - 1$ individuals based on their distances from an individual to the population mean point, $\bar{g}$, so as to preserve diversity. This individual fitness is based on the distance, d_i, weighted by the selection pressure, becoming

$$f'_i(d_i) = 1 - \exp(-\beta d_i), \tag{25}$$

where $\beta > 0$ is the selection pressure. The lower d_i is, the lower is the fitness, $f'_i(\,.\,,.)$. Thus, an individual far from $\bar{g}$ is more likely to be selected, thus, preserving the diversity. The selection pressure, β, regulates the influence of the distance d_i upon the selection mechanism, i.e., the larger β is,, the higher the influence of the individual distance d_i is upon the selection, and the higher the diversity in the next generation is.

In DRAC, the selection pressure is the control signal, i.e., $u_c = \beta$, and its parameter θ is adjusted as a function of the error between the current, Γ, and model-reference diversity, Γ_m. DRAC model proposes a control signal as a function of the command signal and the controller parameter. The control law is defined as

$$u(k) = \theta(k) u_c(k) , \quad (26)$$

The method employed to adjust θ is a particular case of the MIT rule. The parameter θ is updated as a function of the error between the process and model-reference output. The discrete version of the adjustment of θ is defined as an approximation of Equation (22), as follows

$$\theta(k+1) = \theta(k) - \eta' e(k) , \quad (27)$$

where $\eta' = \eta\, \partial e/\partial\theta$, $\eta' > 0$, is a constant. This adjustment rule gives no guarantee that the adaptive controller makes the error vanish. Figure 6 shows the DRAC pseudo-code.

```
k ← 0
Generate P(k)
Evaluate P(k)
Γ(k) ← diversity( P(k) )

while (NOT stop condiction )
{
  Select P'(k) from P(k)
  Q(k) ← recombine( P(k) )
  Mutate Q(k)
  Evaluate Q(k)
  Associate P(k) and Q(k)
  Γm(k) ← model-reference( k )
  Adjust θ(k+1) as a function of the error, e(k) = Γm(k) - Γ(k)
  Select the survivors S(k):
          1. Select the best individual
          2. Select αN individuals by tournament
          3. Select the rest to the next population
  P(k+1) ← S(k)
  Γ(k+1) ← diversity( P(k+1) )
  k ← k+1
}
```

Fig. 6. Diversity-reference adaptive control (DRAC)

5. Conclusion

This paper presented a survey about diversity-based evolutionary algorithms. Two sets of models were presented, one to minimize the diversity loss and another to control the population diversity based on a desired diversity range or level. The problem of the inappropriate level of diversity with respect to the environment and its dynamic can be avoided or reduced if the population diversity is controlled. For example, DRAC controls population diversity, which tracks a model-reference. The method provides a model-reference of diversity that decreases according to a control law and increases after the environment changes. In DRAC, the evolutionary process is handled as a control problem, and MRAS is used to adjust the control signal.

The model-reference, tracked by the population in DRAC, is based upon principles: (i) from the Hardy-Weinberg theory that, in a population, it is necessary for diversity to decrease in order that there is evolution; and (ii) it is necessary to have a minimum level of diversity in order to benefit exploitation. The diversity control method proposed can accelerate the speed at which the algorithm reaches promising regions in a dynamic environment.

DRAC reveals several possibilities, such as adjusting the model-reference as a function of the environment and its dynamic, especially for small-sized and chaotic dynamics. Another possibility is to use other EA parameters as the control signal, such as mutation and crossover probabilities, the number of individuals selected for crossover, and the number of individuals selected in Stage 3 of the proposed selection mechanism. These parameters have a significant influence on population diversity and the evolutionary process, and they can be investigated and compared with pressure-based selection.

6. Acknowledgment

The authors gratefully acknowledge the support given by the National Council for Scientific and Technological Development (CNPq) to this research study.

7. References

Amos, W.; Harwood, J. (1998). Factors affecting levels of genetic diversity in natural populations. *Philosophical Transactions of the Royal Society of London – Series B: Biological Sciences*, Vol. 353, No. 1366, pp. 177—186

Angeline, P. J. (1995). *Adaptive and Self-adaptive Evolutionary Computation,* IEEE Press, Piscataway

Aström, K. J.; Wittenmark, B. (1995). *Adaptive Control,* Addison-Wesley

Bäck, T.; Schutz, M. (1996). Intelligent Mutation Rate Control in Canonical Genetic Algorithms, *International Symposium on Methodologies for Intelligent Systems (ISMIS'96)*, pp. 158—167, Springer

Beyer, H. G.; Rudolph, G. (1997). Local performance measures, In: *Handbook of Evolutionary Computation,* Back, T.; Fogel, D. B.; Michalewicz, Z. (Ed.), B2.4:1—B2.4:27, Oxford University Press, Oxford

Champely, S.; Chessel, D. (2002). Measuring biological diversity using euclidean metrics. *Environmental and Ecological Statistics,* Vol. 9, No. 2, pp. 167—177

Cobb, H. G. (1990). *An Investigation into the Use of Hypermutation as an Adaptive Operator in Genetic Algorithms Having Continuous, Time-dependent Nonstationary Environments,* Naval Research Laboratory, Technical Rep. AIC-90-001, Washington

Crow, J. F.; Kimura, M. (1970). *An Introduction to Population Genetic Theory,* Burgess Publishing, Minnesota

Eiben, A. E.; Hinterding, R.; Michalewicz, Z. (1999). Parameter control in evolutionary algorithms. *IEEE Transactions on Evolutionary Computation,* Vol. 3, No. 2, pp. 124—141

Grefenstette, J. J. (1986). Optimization of control parameters for genetic algorithms. *IEEE Transactions on Systems, Man and Cybernetics,* Vol. 16, No. 1, pp. 122—128

Fisher, R. A. (1930). *The Genetical Theory of Natural Selection,* Oxford University Press

Gouvêa Jr., M. M.; Araújo, A. F. R. (2007). Diversity-Based Model Reference for Genetic Algorithms in Dynamic Environment, *2007 IEEE Congress on Evolutionary Computation (CEC'2007),* Singapore, South Korea, September 25-28, IEEE Press

Hardy, G. H. (1908). Mendelian proportions in a mixed population. *Science,* Vol. 78, 49—50

Hinterding, R.; Michalewicz, Z.; Eiben, A. E. (1997). Adaptation in evolutionary computation: a survey, *Proceedings of the 4th IEEE Conference Evolutionary Computation,* pp. 65—69, Indianapolis, USA, Apr 13-16, IEEE Press

Jin, Y.; Branke, J. (2005). Evolutionary optimization in uncertain environments - a survey. *IEEE Transactions on Evolutionary Computation,* Vol. 9, No. 3, pp. 303—317

Magurran, A. E. (2004). *Measuring Biological Diversity,* Blackwell, Oxford

Meiyi, L.; Zixing, C.; Guoyun, S. (2004). An adaptive genetic algorithm with diversity-guided mutation and its global convergence property. *Journal of Central South University of Technology,* Vol. 11, No. 3, pp. 323—327

Morrison, R. W. (2004). *Designing Evolutionary Algorithms for Dynamic Environments,* Springer

Narendra, K. S.; Annaswamy, A. M. (2005). *Stable Adaptive Systems,* Dover Publications, Mineola

Nguyen, D. H. M.; Wong, K. P. (2003). Controlling diversity of evolutionary algorithms, *Proceedings of the Second International Conference on Machine Learning and Cybernetics,* pp. 775—780

Ogata, K. (1990). *Modern Control Engineering,* Prentice-Hall

Rao, C. R. (1982). Diversity and dissimilarity coefficients: a unified approach. *Theoretical Population Biology,* Vol. 21, pp. 24—43

Schwefel, H.- P. (1995). *Evolution and Optimum Seeking,* John Wiley, Chichester

Shimodaira, H. (2001). A diversity control-oriented-genetic algorithm (DCGA): performance in function optimization, *2001 IEEE Congress on Evolutionary Computation (CEC'2001),* pp. 44–51, Seoul, Korea, IEEE Press

Simões A. ; Costa, E. (2001). On Biologically Inspired Genetic Operators: Transformation in the Standard Genetic Algorithm, *Proceedings of Proceedings of the Genetic and Evolutionary Computation Conference (GECCO'2001),* pp. 584—591, San Francisco, USA, July 7—11, Morgan Kaufmann Publishers

Smith, R. E.; Goldberg, D. E. (1992). Diploidy and dominance in artificial genetic search. *Complex Systems,* Vol. 6, No. 3, pp. 251 285

Solow, A.; Polasky, S.; Broadus, J. (1993). On the measurement of biological diversity. *Journal of Environmental Economics and Management,* Vol. 24, No. 1, pp. 60—68

Srinivas, M.; Patnaik, L. M. (1994). Adaptive probabilities of crossover and mutation in genetic algorithms. *IEEE Transactions on Systems, Man and Cybernetics,* Vol. 24, No. 4, pp. 656—667

Ursem, R. K.; Krink, T.; Jensen, M. T.; Michalewicz, Z. (2002). Analysis and modeling of control tasks in dynamic systems. *IEEE Transactions on Evolutionary Computation,* Vol. 6, No. 4, pp. 378–389

Wagg, D. J. (2003). Adaptive control of nonlinear dynamical systems using a model reference approach. *Meccanica,* Vol. 38, No. 2, pp. 227–238

Weinberg, W. (1908). Über den Nachweis der Vererbung beim Menschen. *Jahreshefte Verein f. vaterl. Naturk. in Wurtemberg,* Vol. 64, pp. 368–382

Weitzman, M. L. (1992). On diversity. *Quarterly Journal of Economics,* Vol. 107, No. 2, pp. 363–405

Wineberg, M.; Oppacher, F. (2003). Distances between populations, *The Proceedings of the Fifth Genetic and Evolutionary Computation Conference (GECCO'2003),* pp. 1481–1492, Chicago, USA, July 12–16, Morgan Kaufmann Publishers

Wong, Y.- Y.; Lee, K.- H.; Leung, K.- S.; Ho, C.-W. (2003). A novel approach in parameter adaptation and diversity maintenance for genetic algorithms. *Soft Computing,* Vol. 7, No. 8, pp. 506-515

Wright, S. (1931). Evolution in Mendelian populations, *Genetics,* Vol. 16, pp. 97–159

2

Evolutionary Computation in Constraint Satisfaction

Madalina Ionita, Mihaela Breaban and Cornelius Croitoru
Alexandru Ioan Cuza University, Iasi, Romania

1. Introduction

Many difficult computational problems from different application areas can be seen as constraint satisfaction problems (CSPs). Therefore, constraint satisfaction plays an important role in both theoretical and applied computer science.

Constraint satisfaction deals essentially with finding a best practical solution under a list of constraints and priorities. Many methods, ranging from complete and systematic algorithms to stochastic and incomplete ones, were designed to solve CSPs. The complete and systematic methods are guaranteed to solve the problems but usually perform a great amount of constraint checks, being effective only for simple problems. Most of these algorithms are derived from the traditional backtracking scheme. Incomplete and stochastic algorithms sometimes solve difficult problems much faster; however, they are not guaranteed to solve the problem even if given unbounded amount of time and space.

Because most of the real-world problems are over-constrained and do not have an exact solution, stochastic search is preferable to deterministic methods. In this light, techniques based on meta-heuristics have received considerable interest; among them, population-based algorithms inspired by the Darwinian evolution or by the collective behavior of decentralized, self-organized systems, were successfully used in the field of constraint satisfaction.

This chapter presents some of the most efficient evolutionary methods designed for solving constraint satisfaction problems and investigates the development of novel hybrid algorithms derived from Constraint Satisfaction specific techniques and Evolutionary Computation paradigms. These approaches make use of evolutionary computation methods for search assisted by an inference algorithm. Comparative studies highlight the differences between stochastic population-based methods and the systematic search performed by a Branch and Bound algorithm.

2. Constraint satisfaction

A *Constraint Satisfaction Problem (CSP)* is defined by a set of variables $X = \{X_1, \ldots, X_n\}$, associated with a set of discrete-valued domains, $D = \{D_1, \ldots, D_n\}$, and a set of constraints $C = \{C_1, \ldots, C_m\}$. Each constraint C_i is a pair (S_i, R_i), where R_i is a relation $R_i \subseteq D_{S_i}$ defined on a subset of variables $S_i \subseteq X$ called the scope of C_i. The relation denotes all compatible tuples of D_{S_i} allowed by the constraint.

A solution is an assignment of values to variables $x = (x_1, \ldots, x_n)$, $x_i \in D_i$, such that each constraint is satisfied. If a solution is found, then the problem is named satisfiable or consistent. Finding a solution to CSP is a NP-complete task.
However, the problem may ask for one solution, all solutions, or - when a solution does not exist - a partial solution that optimizes some criteria is desired. Our discussion will focus on the last case, that is, the Max-CSP problem. The task consists in finding an assignment that satisfies a maximum number of constraints. For this problem the relation R_i is given as a cost function $C_i(X_{i1} = x_{i1}, \ldots, X_{ik} = x_{ik}) = 0$ if $(x_{i1}, \ldots, x_{ik}) \in R_i$ and 1 otherwise. Using this formulation, an inconsistent CSP can be transformed into a consistent optimization problem.
There are two major approaches to solve constraint satisfaction problems: search algorithms and inference techniques (Dechter, 2003). Search algorithms usually seek for a solution in the space of partial instantiations. Because the hybrid methods presented in this chapter make use of inference techniques, we present next an introduction to directional consistency algorithms.

2.1 Inference: directional consistency

Inference is the process of creating equivalent problems through problem reformulation. The variable domains are shrunk or new constraints are deduced from existing ones making the problem easier to solve with search algorithms. Occasionally, inference methods can even deliver a solution or prove the inconsistency of the problem without the need for any further search.
Inference algorithms used to ensure local consistency perform a bounded amount of inference. The primary characteristic by which they are distinguished is the number of variables or the number of constraints involved. Any search algorithm will benefit from representations that have a high level of consistency. The complexity of enforcing i-consistency is exponential in i, as this is the time and space needed to infer a constraint based on i variables. There is a trade-off between the time spent on inference and the time spent on subsequent search.
Because of the nature of search algorithms which usually extend a partial solution in order to get a complete one, the notion of directional consistency was introduced. The inference is restricted relative to a given ordering of the variables. Directed arc-consistency is the simplest algorithm in this category; it ensures that any legal value in the domain of a single variable has a legal match in the domain of any other selected variable (Wallace, 1995; Larossa et al., 1999).

2.1.1 Bucket Elimination

Bucket Elimination (Dechter, 1999; 1996) is a less expensive directional consistency algorithm that enforces global consistency only relative to a certain variable ordering. The algorithm takes as input an ordering of variables and the cost functions. The method partitions the functions into buckets. Each function is placed in the bucket corresponding to the variable which appears latest in the ordering. After this step, two phases take place then. In the first phase the buckets are processed from last to first. The processing consists in a variable elimination procedure that computes a new function which is placed in a lower bucket. In the second phase, the algorithm considers the variables in increasing order. It builds a solution by assigning a value to each variable, consulting the functions created during the first phase.

Mini-bucket Elimination (MBE) (Dechter & Rish, 2003) is an approximation of the previous algorithm which tries to reduce space and time complexity. The buckets are partitioned into smaller subsets, called mini-buckets which are processed separately, in the same way as in BE. The number of variables from each mini-bucket is upper bounded by a parameter, *i*. The time and space complexity of the algorithm is *O(exp(i))*. The scheme allows this way adjustable levels of inference. This parameter controls the trade-off between the quality of the approximation and the computational complexity.
For the Max-CSP problem, the MBE algorithm produces new functions computed as the sum of all constraint matrices and minimizes it over the bucket's variable (Kask & Dechter, 2000).

Algorithm 1 Mini-Bucket Elimination(i)

Require: A constraint network R, an ordering $d = (x_1, \ldots, x_n)$
Ensure: The set of ordered augmented buckets, an upper bound on the Max-CSP value, and an assignment.

Initialize: Partition constraints into buckets $bucket_1, \ldots bucket_n$:
for $i \leftarrow n$ downto 1 **do**
  put in $bucket_i$ all constraints whose highest variable is X_i
end for
Let $S_1 \ldots S_j$ be the scopes be of functions (new or old) in the processed bucket

Backward:
for $p \leftarrow n$ downto 1 **do**
  for all functions $h_1, h_2, \ldots h_j$ in $bucket_p$ **do**
    if $bucket_p$ contains an instantiation $X_p = x_p$ **then**
      assign $X_p = x_p$ to each h_i and put each resulting function into its appropriate bucket.
    else
      generate an (i)-partitioning $Q' = \{Q_1, \ldots, Q_r\}$
      for each $Q_l \in Q'$ containing $h_{l_1}, \ldots, h_{l_t}$ generate function $h^l = min_{X_p} \sum_{i=1}^{t} h_{l_i}$
      add h^l to the bucket of the latest variable in
      $U_p \leftarrow \bigcup_{i=1}^{j} S(h_{l_i}) - \{X_p\}$
    end if
  end for
end for

Forward:
for $i = 1$ to n **do**
  given $x_1, \ldots, x_{p-1}$ choose a value x_p of X_p that minimizes the sum of all the cost functions in X_p's bucket
end for

Output the ordered set of augmented buckets, an upper bound and a lower bound assignment.

The mini-bucket algorithm is expanded in (Kask & Dechter, 2000) with a mechanism to generate some heuristic functions. The functions recorded by MBE can be used as a lower bound for the number of constraints violated by the best extension of any partial assignment. For this reason these functions can be used as heuristic evaluations functions in search. Given a partial assignment of the first p variables $x^p =(x_1, \ldots, x_p)$, the number of constraints violated by the best extension of x^p is:

$$f^*(x^p) = min_{x_{p+1},\ldots,x_n} \sum_{k=1}^{n} C_k$$

for the variable ordering $d = (X_1, \ldots, X_n)$.
The previous sum can be computed as:

$$f^*(x^p) = (\sum_{C_i \in buckets(1\ldots p)} C_i)(x^p) + h^*(x^p)$$

where $h^*(x^p)$ can be estimated by a heuristic function $h(x^p)$, derived from the functions recorded by the MBE algorithm. $h(x^p)$ is defined as the sum of all the h_j^k functions that satisfy the following properties:

- they are generated in buckets $p + 1$ through n, and
- they reside in buckets 1 through p.

$$h(x^p) = \sum_{i=1}^{p} \sum_{h_j^k \in buckets_i h_j^k} h_j^k, \; where\ k > p$$

h_j^k represents the function created by processing the j-th mini-bucket in $bucket_k$. The heuristic function f can be updated recursively:

$$f(x^p) = f(x^{p-1}) + H(x_p),$$

where $H(x_p)$ computes the cost of extending the instantiation x^{p-1} with the value x_p for the variable placed on the position p in the given ordering:

$$H(x_p) = \sum_j C_{p_j}(x^p) + (\sum_k h_{p_k}(x^p) - \sum_j h_j^p(x^p)).$$

In the formula above C_{p_j} are the constraints in bucket p, h_{p_k} are the functions in bucket p and h_j^p are the functions created in bucket p which reside in buckets 1 through p -1.

3. Evolutionary algorithms for CSPs

3.1 Existing approaches

Evolutionary Computation techniques are population-based heuristics, inspired from the natural evolution paradigm. All techniques from this area operate in the same way: they maintain a population of individuals (particles, agents) which is updated by applying some operators according to the fitness information, in order to reach better solution areas. The most known evolutionary computation paradigms include evolutionary algorithms (Genetic Algorithms, Genetic Programming, Evolutionary Strategies, Evolutionary Programming) and swarm intelligence techniques (Ant Colony Optimization and Particle Swarm Optimization).

Evolutionary algorithms (Michalewicz, 1996) are powerful search heuristics which work with a population of chromosomes, potential solutions of the problem. The individuals evolve according to rules of selection and genetic operators.

Because the application of operators cannot guarantee the feasibility of offspring, constraint handling is not straightforward in an evolutionary algorithm. Several methods were proposed to handle constraints with Evolutionary algorithms. The methods could be grouped in the following categories (Michalewicz, 1995; Michalewicz & Schoenauer, 1996; Coello & Lechunga, 2002):

- preserving feasibility of solutions

  For particular problems, where the generic representation schemes are not appropriate, special representations and operators have been developed (for example, the GENOCOP (GEnetic algorithm for Numerical Optimization of COnstrained Problems) system (Michalewicz & Janikow, 1991). A special representation is used aiming at simplifying the shape of the search space. Operators are designed to preserve the feasibility of solutions.

  Other approach makes use of constraint consistency to prune the search space (Kowalczyk, 1997). Unfeasible solutions are eliminated at each stage of the algorithm. The standard genetic operators are adapted to this case.

  Random keys encoding is another method which maintains the feasibility of solutions and eliminates the need of special operators. It was used first for certain sequencing and optimization problems (Bean, 1994). The solutions encoded with random numbers are then used as sort keys to decode the solution.

  In the decoders approach (Dasgupta & Michalewicz, 2001), the chromosomes tell how to build a feasible solution. The transformation is desired to be computationally fast.

  Another idea, which was first named *strategic oscillation*, consists in searching the areas close to the boundary of feasible regions (Glover & Kochenberger, 1995).

- penalty functions

  The most common approach for constraint-handling is to use penalty functions to penalize infeasible solutions (Richardson et al., 1989). Usually, the penalty measures the distance from the feasible region, or the effort to repair the solution. Various types of penalty functions have been proposed. The most commonly used types are:

  - static penalties which remain constant during the entire process
  - dynamic functions which change through a run
  - annealing functions which use techniques based on Simulated Annealing
  - adaptive penalties which change according to feedback from the search
  - co-evolutionary penalties in which solutions evolve in one population and penalty factors in another population
  - death penalties which reject infeasible solutions.

  One of the major challenges is choosing the appropriate penalty value. Large penalties discourage the algorithm from exploring infeasible regions, and push rapidly the EA inside the feasible region. For low penalties, the algorithm will spend a lot of time exploring the infeasible region.

- repairing infeasible solution candidates

  Repair algorithms are problem dependent algorithms which modify a chromosome in such a way that it will not violate the constraints (Liepins & Vose, 1990). The repaired solution is used only for evaluation or can replace with some probability the original individual.

- separation of objectives and constraints
  The constraints and the objectives are handled separately. For example, in (Paredis, 1994) a co-evolutionary model consisting of two populations, one of constraints, one of possible solutions is proposed. The populations influences each other; an individual with a high fitness from the population of potential solutions represents a solution which satisfies many constraints; an individual with a high fitness from the population of constraints represent a constraint that is violated by many possible solutions.
  Another idea is to consider the problem as a multi-objective optimization problem, in which we will have m+1 objectives, m being the number of constraints. Then we can apply a technique from this area to solve the initial problem.
- hybrid methods
  Evolutionary algorithms are coupled with another techniques.

There have been numerous attempts to use Evolutionary algorithms for solving constraint satisfaction problems (Dozier et al., 1994), (Paredis, 1994), (Eiben & Ruttkay, 1996). The *Stepwise Adaptation of Weights* is one of the best evolutionary algorithms for CSP solving. The constraints that are not satisfied are penalized more. The weights are initialized (with 1) and reset by adding a value after a number of steps. Only the weights for the constraints that are violated by the best individual are adjusted. An individual is a permutation of variables. A partial instantiation is constructed by considering the variables for assigning values in the order given by the chromosome. The variable is left uninstantiated if all possible values add a violation. The uninstantiated variables are penalized. The fitness is equal with the sum of all penalties.

Another efficient approach is the *Microgenetic Iterative Descent Algorithm* (Dozier et al., 1994). The algorithm uses a small population size. At each iteration an offspring is created by crossover or mutation operator, the operator being chosen after an adaptive scheme. A candidate solution is represented by n alleles, a pivot and a fitness value. Each allele has the variable, its value, the number of constraint violations the variable is involved in and an *hvalue* used for initializing the pivot. The pivot is used to choose the variable that will undergo mutation. If the fitness of the child is worse than the parent value, the h-value of the pivot offspring is decremented. The pivot is updated next: for each allele, the sum of the number of constraint violations and its h-value are computed; the allele with the highest value is chosen as the pivot. The fitness function is adaptive, employing the Morris Breakout Creating Mechanism (Morris, 1993) to escape from local optima.

Another approach for solving CSPs makes use of heuristics inside the evolutionary algorithm. In (Eiben et al., 1994) heuristics are incorporated into the genetic operators. The mutation operator selects a number of variables to be mutated and assigns them new values. The selected variables are those appearing in constraints that are most often violated. The new values are those that maximize the number of satisfied constraints. Another way of incorporating heuristic information in an evolutionary algorithm is described in (Marchiori & Steenbeek, 2000). The heuristics are not incorporated into operators, but as a standalone module. Individual solutions are improved by calling a local optimization procedure for each of them and then blind genetic operators are applied.

In (Craenen et al., 2003) a comparison of the best evolutionary algorithms is given.

3.2 Hybrid evolutionary algorithms for CSP

Generally, to obtain good results for a problem we have to incorporate knowledge about the problem into the evolutionary algorithm. Evolutionary algorithms are flexible and can be easily extended by incorporating standard procedures for the problem under investigation. The heuristic information introduced in an evolutionary algorithm can enhance the exploitation but will reduce the exploration. A good balance between exploitation and exploration is important.

We will describe next the approach presented in (Ionita et al., 2006). The method includes information obtained through constraint processing into the evolutionary algorithm in order to improve the search results. The basic idea is to use the functions returned by the minibucket algorithm as heuristic evaluation functions. The selected genetic algorithm is a simple one, with a classical scheme. The special particularity is that the algorithm uses the inferred information in a genetic operator and an adaptive mechanism for escaping from local minima.

A candidate solution is represented by a vector of size equal to the number of variables. The value at position i represents the value of the corresponding variable, x_i. The algorithm works with complete solutions, i.e. all variables are instantiated. Each individual in the population has associated a measure of its fitness in the environment. The fitness function counts the number of violated constraints by the candidate solution.

In an EA the search for better individuals is conducted by the crossover operator, while the diversity in the population is maintained by the mutation operator.

The recombination operator is a fitness-based scanning crossover. The scanning operator takes as input a number of chromosomes and returns one offspring. It chooses one of the i-th genes of the n parents to be the i-th gene of the offspring. For creating the new solution, the best genes are preserved. Our crossover makes use of the pre-processing information gathered with the inference process. It uses the functions returned by the mini-bucket algorithm, $f^*(x^p)$ to decide the values of the offspring. The variables are instantiated in a given order, the same as the one used in the mini-bucket algorithm. A new value to the next variable is assigned by choosing the best value from the parents according to the evaluation functions f^*. As stated before, these heuristic functions provide an upper bound on the cost of the best extension of a given partial assignment.

Algorithm 2 *multiparent_crossover($P(t)$, k)*

for each set of k parents, $p_1, \ldots, p_k$ **do**
  for each position i in the ordering **do**
    $child_i \leftarrow best(p_{1i}, \ldots, p_{ki})$
    /* use $f^*(p_1^i), \ldots, f^*(p_k^i)$ in *best* */
    parent ← get_worst_parent($p_1, \ldots, p_k$)
    replace(*parent*, *child*)
  end for
end for

This recombination operator intensifies the exploitation of the search space. It will generate new solutions if there is sufficient diversity in the population. An operator to preserve variation is necessary. The mutation operator has this function, i.e. it serves for exploration. The operator assigns a new random value for a given variable.

After the application of the operators, the new individuals will replace the parents. Selection will take place next to ensure the preservation of fittest individuals. A fitness-based selection was chosen for experiments.

Because the crossover and the selection direct the search to most fitted individuals, there is a chance of getting stuck in local minima. There is a need to leave the local minima and to explore different parts of the search space. Therefore, we have included the earliest breakout mechanism (Morris, 1993). When the algorithm is trapped in a local minimum point, a breakout is created for each nogood that appears in this current optimum. The weight for each newly created breakout is equal to one. If the breakout already exists, its weight is incremented by one. A predefined percent of the total weights (penalties) for an individual that violates these breakouts are added to the fitness function. In this manner the search is forced to put more emphasis on the constraints that are hard to satisfy. The evaluation function is an adaptive function because it is changed during the execution of the algorithm.

4. Particle swarm optimization for CSPs

The idea of combining inference with heuristics was also tested on another population-based paradigm, the Particle Swarm Optimization. The method presented in (Breaban et al., 2007) is detailed next.

Algorithm 3 GA-MBE(i)

```
apply MBE(i)
t ← 0
initialize P(t)
evaluate P(t)
while termination condition not meet do
   t ← t + 1
   select P(t) from P(t − 1)
   multiparent_crossover (P(t), k)
   mutation(P(t))
   evaluate P(t)
   if no diversity then
      get the list of breakouts from the best individual
      introduce the breakouts in the fitness
   end if
end while
```

4.1 Particle swarm optimization

Particle Swarm Optimization is a Swarm Intelligence technique which shares many features with Evolutionary Algorithms. Swarm Intelligence is used to designate the artificial intelligence techniques based on the study of collective behavior in decentralized, self-organized systems. Swarm Intelligence systems are typically made up of a population of simple autonomous agents interacting locally with one another and with their environment. Although there is no centralized control, the local interactions between agents lead to the emergence of global behavior. Examples of systems like this can be found in nature, including ant colonies, bird flocking, animal herding, bacteria molding and fish schooling.

The PSO model was introduced in 1995 by J. Kennedy and R.C. Eberhart, being discovered through simulation of a simplified social model such as fish schooling or bird flocking (Kennedy & Eberhart, 1995). PSO consists of a group (swarm) of particles moving in the search space, their trajectory being determined by the fitness values found so far.

The formulas used to actualize the individuals and the procedures are inspired from and conceived for continuous spaces. Each particle is represented by a vector x of length n indicating the position in the n-dimensional search space and has a velocity vector v used to update the current position. The velocity vector is computed following the rules:

- every particle tends to keep its current direction (an inertia term);
- every particle is attracted to the best position p it has achieved so far (a memory term);
- every particle is attracted to the best particle g in population (the particle having the best fitness value); there are versions of the algorithm in which the best particle g is chosen from topological neighborhood.

Thus, the velocity vector is computed as a weighted sum of the three terms above. The formulas used to update each of the individuals in the population at iteration t are:

$$v_i^t = v_i^{t-1} + w_1 \cdot (p_i - x_i^{t-1}) + w_2 \cdot (g_i - x_i^{t-1}) \quad (1)$$

$$x_i^t = x_i^{t-1} + v_i^t \quad (2)$$

4.2 Adapting PSO to Max-CSP

Schoofs and Naudts (Schoofs & Naudts, 2002) have previously adapted the PSO algorithm for solving binary constraint problems. Our algorithm is formulated for the more general Max-CSP problem. The elements of the algorithm are presented below.

An individual is an instantiation of all variables with respect to their domains.

The evaluation (fitness) function counts the violated constraints. Because Max-CSP is formulated as a minimization problem smaller values of the evaluation function correspond to better individuals.

The algorithm uses the basic idea of PSO: every particle tends to move towards his personal best and towards the global best. Updating the particle consists in instantiating its variables by choosing from the values of the two particles or keeping its own values. The decision is made based on the values of the heuristic function described in section 2.1.1. The MBE inference scheme is used as a preprocessing step.

The velocity and the operators must be redefined in order to adapt the PSO formulas to the problem. This technique has already been used in order to adapt the PSO to discrete problems. For example, for permutation problems the velocity was redefined as a vector of transposition probabilities (X. Hu et al., 2003) or as a list of transpositions (Clerc, 2000) and the sum between a particle position and the velocity consists in applying the transpositions.

We define the velocity which results from the subtraction of two positions $\vec{v} = \vec{y} \ominus \vec{x}$ as the vector $\vec{v} = [x_i \to y_i]$ where $\to$ represents as in (Schoofs & Naudts, 2002) a change of position.

The sum $\vec{v_1} \circ \vec{v_2}$ of the two velocities $\vec{v_1} = \vec{p} \ominus \vec{x}$ and $\vec{v_2} = \vec{g} \ominus \vec{x}$ produces the velocity $\vec{u}$ given by

$$u_i = \begin{cases} p_i \ominus x_i, H(p_i) < H(g_i) \\ g_i \ominus x_i, otherwise \end{cases}$$

where H is the heuristic function described in section 2.1.1.

The addition $\vec{p} = \vec{x} \oplus \vec{v}$ of the velocity $\vec{v} = \vec{y} \ominus \vec{z}$ to a position $\vec{x}$ is defined by $p_i = \begin{cases} y_i, x_i = z_i \\ x_i, otherwise \end{cases}$

No parameter is used.

The PSO formulas become:

$$\overrightarrow{v}^t = \overrightarrow{v}^{t-1} \circ (\overrightarrow{p} \ominus \overrightarrow{x}^{t-1}) \circ (\overrightarrow{g} \ominus \overrightarrow{x}^{t-1}) \tag{3}$$

$$\overrightarrow{x}^t = \overrightarrow{x}^{t-1} \oplus \overrightarrow{v}^t \tag{4}$$

Because the first term $\overrightarrow{v}^{t-1}$ in equation (3) is the velocity used to obtain the position $\overrightarrow{x}^{t-1}$ at time t -1 we replace it with the velocity $\overrightarrow{v}^{t-1} = \overrightarrow{x}^{t-1} \ominus \overrightarrow{x}^{t-1}$. In this way the resulted velocity formula selects the particle which has the smaller heuristic function value from the current position x, the personal best p and the global best g.
The pseudocode of the algorithm is illustrated in Algorithm 4.
The step (*) from the pseudocode can be described as:

find $minimum(H(x_i), H(p_i), H(g_i))$
if $minimum = H(p_i)$ then
  $x_i = p_i$
else if $minimum = f(g_i)$ then
    $x_i = g_i$

Algorithm 4 PSO-MBE

order the variables
apply MBE(i)
randomly initialize the population (swarm particles)
evaluate population
find the best individual g in population and set personal best p
while stop criteria not met **do**
  for all particle x in population **do**
    for $i = 1$ to n **do**
      $x_i = x_i \oplus ((x_i \ominus x_i) \circ (p_i \ominus x_i) \circ (g_i \ominus x_i))$ $(*)$
    end for
    if $eval(x) \geq eval(g)$ **then**
      apply mutation to particle x
    end if
    update personal best p
  end for
  find the best individual g in population
end while

In order to explore the search space and to prevent the algorithm from getting trapped in local optima a mutation operator is introduced. This is identical to the one used in GAs: a random value is set on a random position. The role of the mutation is not only to maintain diversity but also to introduce values from variables' domains which do not exist in the current population. To maintain diversity, the algorithm also uses the following strategies: 1. in case of equal values for the evaluation function the priority is given to the current value and then to the personal optimum; 2. the algorithm is not implementing the online elitism: the best individual is not kept in population, the current optimum can be replaced by a worst individual in future iterations.

5. Tests and results

5.1 Data suite

Experiments were conducted only on binary CSPs (each constraint is built over at most two variables), but there is no reason that the algorithm could not be run on n-ary CSPs with $n > 2$.

The algorithms were tested on two well-known models for generating CSPs.

The four-parameter model (Smith, 1994), called **model B** does not allow the repetition of the constraints. A random CSP is given by four parameters (N, K, C, T), where N represents the number of variables, K the domain size, C the number of constraints and T the constraint tightness. The tightness represents the number of tuples not allowed. C constraints are selected uniformly at random from the available $N(N - 1)/2$ ones and for each constraint T nogoods are selected from the available K^2 tuples. We have tested the approach on some over-constrained classes of binary CSPs. The selected classes are sparse ⟨25, 10, 37, T⟩, with medium density ⟨15, 10, 50, T⟩ and complete graphs ⟨10, 10, 45, T⟩. For each class of problem the algorithms were tested on 50 instances.

We investigate the hybrid approaches also against the set of CSP instances made available by Craenen et al. on the Web[1]. These instances are generated using the **model E** (Achlioptas et al., 2001). We have experimented with 175 solvable problem instances: 25 instances for different values of p in model $E(20, 20, p, 2)$. Parameter p takes the following values: {0.24, 0.25, 0.26, 0.27, 0.28, 0.29, 0.30}. All instances considered were solvable.

5.2 Algorithms settings

The variable ordering used in MBE was determined with the min-induced-width heuristic. This method places the variable with the minimum degree last in the ordering. It connects then all of the variable neighbors, removes the node and all its adjacent edges and next repeats the procedure.

Experiments were made for different levels of inference, changing the values of the parameter i in the MBE algorithm. Values 0 and 1 for parameter i means that no inference is used. Value 2 for i corresponds to a DAC (directed arc consistency) preprocessing adapted to Max-CSP: instead of removing values from variable domains cost functions are added for variable-value pairs that count the number of variables for which no legal value match is found. Greater values for parameter i generate new cost functions over at most i -1 variables.

For model B, for each class of problems 50 instances were generated. The problems were first solved using a complete algorithm PFC-MRDAC (Larossa & Meseguer, 1998). This algorithm is an improved branch-and-bound algorithm, specifically designed for the Max-CSP problem. The optimal solution was the solution found by the PFC-MRDAC algorithm.

For each instance, for both PSO-MBE and GA-MBE, five independent runs were performed. The number of parents for the recombination operator in GA-MBE was established to five. The population size was set to 40 in the GA-MBE, while for PSO-MBE the swarm size was equal to 30 particles. A time limit of 30 seconds was imposed for all search algorithms (the time limit is used only for the search phase and does not include time needed for MBE).

For comparison purposes the Branch and Bound algorithm described in (Kask & Dechter, 2000) was implemented.

---

[1] 1http://www.xs4all.nl/ b̃craenen/resources/csps modelE v20 d20.tar.gz

5.3 Results

As measures of effectiveness we use as in (Craenen et al., 2003) the success rate and the mean error at termination. The success rate represents the percentage of runs that find a solution. The mean error at termination for a run is equal to the number of constraints which are violated by the best solution, at the end of the algorithm.

The average number of constraint checks and the average duration of the algorithms until the optimum solution is reached was recorded only for the runs which find the optimum within the time limit.

5.3.1 Results for MBE and Branch-and-Bound

The results concerning the two criteria on model B instances for the inference algorithm and a Branch and Bound algorithm are given in Table 1. Each line of the table corresponds to a class of CSPs.

Obviously, the Mini-bucket elimination algorithm solves more problems when the bound i increases. The Branch-and-Bound algorithm behaves similarly. However, the time needed to find a solution increases too (see Table 2).

Class	MBE B&B SR/ME $i=0$	MBE B&B SR/ME $i=2$	MBE B&B SR/ME $i=4$	MBE B&B SR/ME $i=6$
25-10-37-84	0/ 7.72 0.02/ 5.70	0/ 5.28 0.3/ 2.82	0.48/ 0.78 1/ 0	1/ 0 1/ 0
25-10-37-85	0/ 8.20 0.02/ 6.22	0/ 5.30 0.18/ 3.06	0.3/ 1.16 1/ 0	0.98/ 0.02 1/ 0
15-10-50-84	0/ 7.78 0/ 5.42	0/ 6.32 0.06/ 3.94	0/ 4.60 0.88/ 0.16	0.14/ 2.02 0.98/ 0.02
15-10-50-85	0/ 8.2 0/ 6.02	0/ 5.48 0.06/ 3.14	0.02/ 4.98 0.78/ 0.38	0.14/ 2.24 1/ 0
10-10-45-84	0/ 5.6 0.10/ 2.16	0/ 4.74 0.32/ 1.22	0/ 4.16 1/ 0	0.18/ 2.18 1/ 0
10-10-45-85	0.02/ 5.90 0.14/ 2.48	0.02/ 5.44 0.24/ 1.74	0.06/ 4.28 1/ 0	0.16/ 1.86 1/ 0

Table 1. Results on model B: the success rate and the mean error for Mini-Bucket Elimination (MBE) and Branch and Bound (B&B) algorithms for different levels of inference(i)

The results on model E are given in Figure 1 and Figure 2.

The Branch and Bound algorithm is not influenced at all by the low levels of inference performed (the three curves in Figure 1 and 2 overlap); higher levels of inference are necessary but they require much more time and space resources.

5.3.2 Results for the hybrid evolutionary computation algorithms Model B

The success rate and the mean error measures for the hybrid approaches are given in Table 3.

The search phase of the hybrid algorithms improves considerably the performance of the inference algorithm. For the class of problems 15 - 10 - 50 - 84 the MBE with i = 4 did not find the optimum for any of the generated problems. GA-MBE and PSO-MBE have solved 41%, respectively 52% of the problems.

Class	MBE B&B i=0	MBE B&B $i=2$	MBE B&B $i=4$	MBE B&B $i=6$
25-10-37-84	0.0 25.860	0.001 12.031	0.063 0.013	0.921 0.001
25-10-37-85	0.0 0.609	0.0 10.774	0.061 0.026	0.935 0.002
15-10-50-84	- -	0.0 10.906	0.115 6.250	11.924 1.357
15-10-50-85	- -	0.0 13.531	0.110 8.431	12.292 0.909
10-10-45-84	0.0 15.824	0.0 12.936	0.096 2.199	7.419 0.296
10-10-45-85	0.0 6.555	0.0 7.179	0.095 2.330	7.438 0.286

Table 2. Results on model B: average time in seconds for MBE and B&B algorithms for the runs which return the optimum

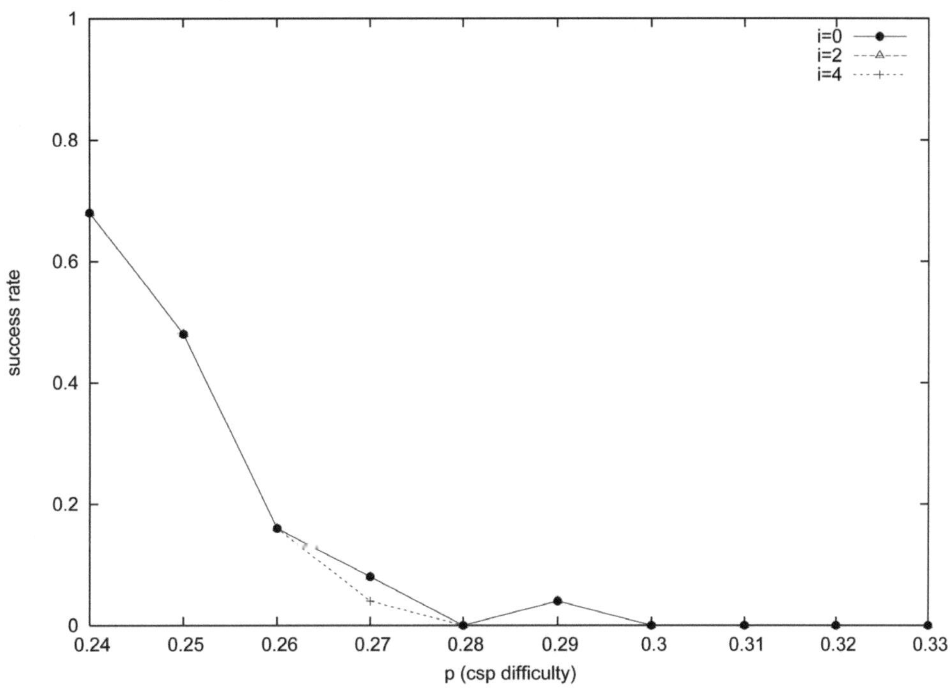

Fig. 1. Results on model E: Success rate for B&B

Even when the optimum solution was not found, the hybrid algorithms return a solution closed to the optimum. This conclusion can be drawn from Table 3 by looking at the mean error values.

We have also used an additional criterium for the evaluation of the hybrid algorithms. The standard measure of the efficiency of an evolutionary algorithm, the number of fitness evaluations is not very useful in this context. The use of heuristics implies more

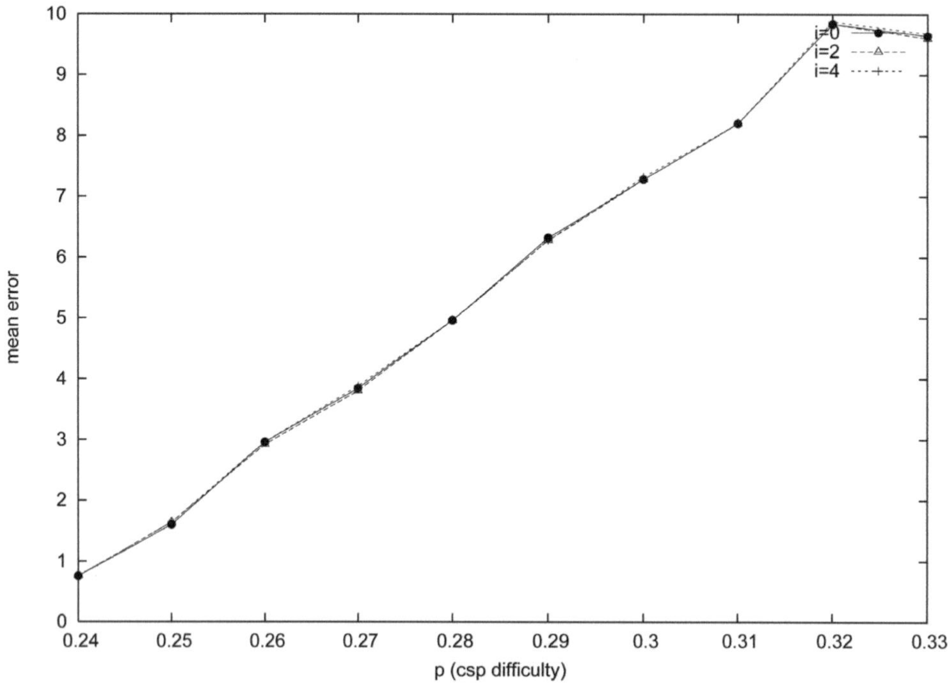

Fig. 2. Results on model E: Average mean error for B&B

Class	GA-MBE PSO-MBE SR/ME $i=0$	GA-MBE PSO-MBE SR/ME $i=2$	GA-MBE PSO-MBE SR/ME $i=4$	GA-MBE PSO-MBE SR/ME $i=6$
25-10-37-84	0.05/ 2.23	0.23/ 1.24	0.88/ 0.12	1/ 0
	0.29/ 1.02	0.32/ 0.95	0.74/ 0.31	1/ 0
25-10-37-85	0.03/ 2.46	0.12/ 1.42	0.79/ 0.22	1/ 0
	0.20/ 1.21	0.27/ 1.10	0.65/ 0.42	0.98/ 0.01
15-10-50-84	0.22/ 1.30	0.13/ 1.82	0.41/ 0.80	0.61/ 0.49
	0.58/ 0.55	0.21/ 1.46	0.52/ 0.70	0.54/ 0.65
15-10-50-85	0.09/ 1.58	0.11/ 1.84	0.30/ 1.18	0.59/ 0.51
	0.58/ 0.58	0.22/ 1.36	0.36/ 1.08	0.52/ 0.70
10-10-45-84	0.65/ 0.36	0.42/ 0.78	0.55/ 0.57	0.64/ 0.40
	0.66/ 0.40	0.43/ 0.83	0.42/ 0.80	0.48/ 0.80
10-10-45-85	0.73/ 0.29	0.42/ 0.91	0.59/ 0.56	0.78/ 0.27
	0.71/ 0.38	0.41/ 1.07	0.53/ 0.83	0.64/ 0.54

Table 3. Results on model B: the success rate and the mean error for GA and PSO hybrid algorithms

computation that is invisible for this metric. Therefore we have computed the average number of constraint checks, for the runs which return the optimum solution (see Table 4). Regarding the number of constraint checks performed by the two algorithms, one general rule can be drawn: the higher the inference level, the less the time spent on search.

Class	GA-MBE PSO-MBE $i = 0$	GA-MBE PSO-MBE $i = 2$	GA-MBE PSO-MBE $i = 4$	GA-MBE PSO-MBE $i = 6$
25-10-37-84	$5.5 \cdot 10^6$ $27.7 \cdot 10^6$	$5.7 \cdot 10^6$ $10.0 \cdot 10^6$	$5.6 \cdot 10^6$ $4.5 \cdot 10^6$	$0.1 \cdot 10^6$ $1.5 \cdot 10^6$
25-10-37-85	$4.7 \cdot 10^6$ $22.0 \cdot 10^6$	$8.6 \cdot 10^6$ $13.8 \cdot 10^6$	$2.5 \cdot 10^6$ $2.6 \cdot 10^6$	$0.1 \cdot 10^6$ $1.9 \cdot 10^6$
15-10-50-84	$22.4 \cdot 10^6$ $16.5 \cdot 10^6$	$17.8 \cdot 10^6$ $23.0 \cdot 10^6$	$5.3 \cdot 10^6$ $10.8 \cdot 10^6$	$4.3 \cdot 10^6$ $6.4 \cdot 10^6$
15-10-50-85	$24.5 \cdot 10^6$ $25.4 \cdot 10^6$	$14.0 \cdot 10^6$ $10.9 \cdot 10^6$	$11.6 \cdot 10^6$ $11.4 \cdot 10^6$	$4.3 \cdot 10^6$ $3.5 \cdot 10^6$
10-10-45-84	$18.5 \cdot 10^6$ $16.6 \cdot 10^6$	$11.8 \cdot 10^6$ $10.8 \cdot 10^6$	$14.5 \cdot 10^6$ $5.26 \cdot 10^6$	$7.6 \cdot 10^6$ $3.5 \cdot 10^6$
10-10-45-85	$10.8 \cdot 10^6$ $9.37 \cdot 10^6$	$16.9 \cdot 10^6$ $9.84 \cdot 10^6$	$11.5 \cdot 10^6$ $4.85 \cdot 10^6$	$6.28 \cdot 10^6$ $1.07 \cdot 10^6$

Table 4. Results on model B: the average constraint checks of the hybrid evolutionary computation algorithms

For sparse instances the efficiency of the preprocessing step is evident for the two algorithms: increasing the inference level more problems are solved. The Genetic Algorithm for medium density cases behaves similarly as for the sparse one. For complete graphs, the genetic algorithm for $i = 0$ (no inference) gives a good percent of solved problems. But the best results are for the larger level of inference. In almost all cases, the performance of the GAMBE is higher when using a higher i-bound. This proves that the evolutionary algorithm uses efficiently the information gained by preprocessing.

When combined with PSO, inference is useful only on sparse graphs; on medium density and complete graphs low levels of inference slow down the search process performed by PSO and the success rate is smaller. Higher levels of inference ($i = 6$) necessitate more time spent on preprocessing and for complete graphs it is preferable to perform only search and no inference.

Unlike evolutionary computation paradigms, the systematic Branch and Bound algorithm has much benefit from inference preprocessing for all classes of problems. When no inference is performed B&B solves only 2% of the sparse instances and 14% of the complete graphs. The approximative solutions returned after 30 seconds run are of lower quality than those returned by the evolutionary computation methods (the mean error is high). When inference is used the turnaround becomes obvious starting with value 4 for parameter i.

Table 5 lists the average time spent by MBE and PSO algorithms for the runs which return the optimum. Similarly, Table 6 refers to MBE and B&B time. These tables are illustrative for the inference/search trade-off: increasing the inference level the time needed by the search algorithms to find the optimum decreases.

An interesting observation can be drawn regarding the time needed by PSO to find the optimum: even if the algorithm is run for 30 seconds the solved instances required much shorter time; this is a clear indicator that PSO is able to find good solutions in a very short time but it gets stuck often in local optima and further search is compromised.

Class	MBE PSO i=0	MBE PSO $i=2$	MBE PSO $i=4$	MBE PSO $i=6$
25-10-37-84	0 8.746	0.003 3.917	0.099 0.824	1.081 0.558
25-10-37-85	0 8.910	0.004 6.087	0.096 0.654	1.115 0.877
15-10-50-84	0 3.467	0.003 5.549	2.384 2.384	12.906 1.123
15-10-50-85	0 4.488	0 3.490	0.176 2.490	13.780 0.963
10-10-45-84	0 2.529	0.019 1.806	0.111 0.986	7.511 0.701
10-10-45-85	0 1.529	0.001 1.703	0.111 0.939	7.774 0.222

Table 5. Results on model B: average time in seconds for MBE and PSO algorithms for the runs which return the optimum

Model E

The results for model E corresponding to GA-MBE are given in Figure 3 and 4. Figures 5 and 6 present the results for PSO-MBE.

Class	MBE BB i=0	MBE BB $i=2$	MBE BB $i=4$	MBE BB $i=6$
25-10-37-84	0.0 25.860	0.001 12.031	0.063 0.013	0.921 0.001
25-10-37-85	0.0 0.609	0.0 10.774	0.061 0.026	0.935 0.002
15-10-50-84	- -	0.0 10.906	0.115 6.250	11.924 1.357
15-10-50-85	- -	0.0 13.531	0.110 8.431	12.292 0.909
10-10-45-84	0.0 15.824	0.0 12.936	0.096 2.199	7.419 0.296
10-10-45-85	0.0 6.555	0.0 7.179	0.095 2.330	7.438 0.286

Table 6. Results on model B: average time in seconds for MBE and B&B algorithms for the runs which return the optimum

The performance of the algorithms decreases with the difficulty of the problem. For smaller values of p (0.24) the percentage of solved problems increases with the inference level. For more difficult problems low levels of inference are useless.

One can also observe that the mean error is small, meaning that the algorithm is stable (Figure 4 and Figure 6). This feature is very important for such kind of problems.

Given that the bounded inference performed on the model E instances has low effect on subsequent search both for the randomized and the systematic methods, GA-MBE and

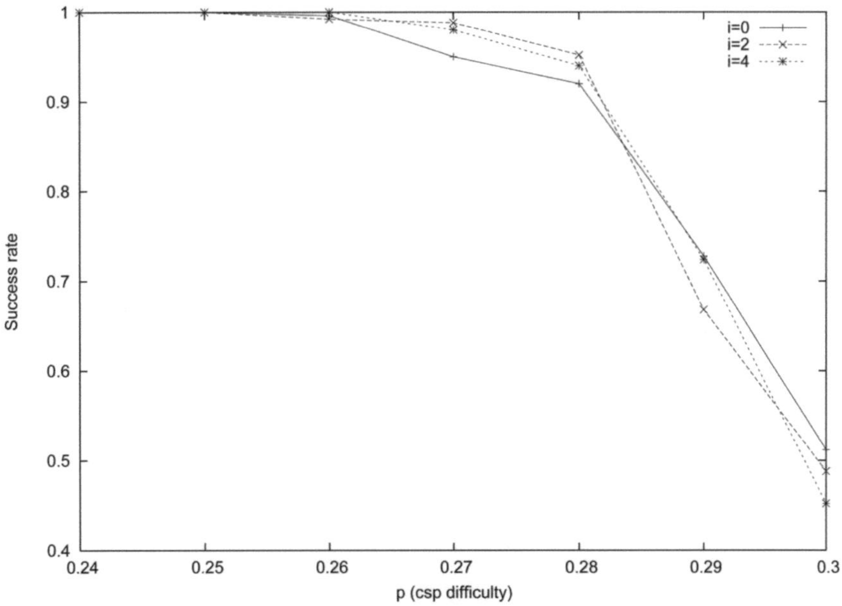

Fig. 3. Results on model E: success rate for GA-MBE

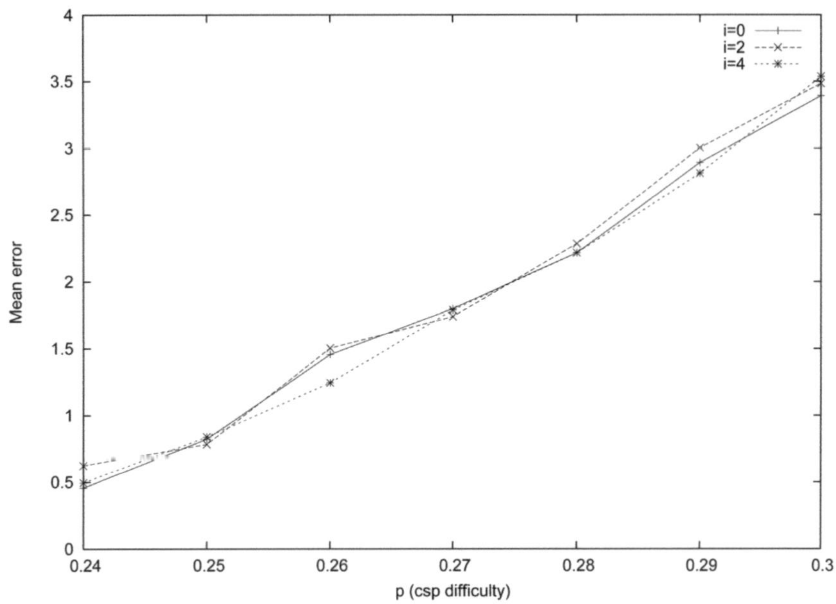

Fig. 4. Results on model E: mean error for GA-MBE

PSOMBE obtain better results than B&B: the percentage of solved problems (SR) is higher and the approximative solutions returned after 30 seconds run are better qualitatively. The average number of constraint checks on model E test instances increases with parameter p from $5 \cdot 10^7$ to $8 \cdot 10^7$ for PSO-MBE and from $9 \cdot 10^7$ to $2 \cdot 10^8$ for B&B. The average time for the runs which find the optimum increases with p from 9 seconds to 13 seconds for PSO-MBE and from 10 seconds to 18 seconds for B&B.

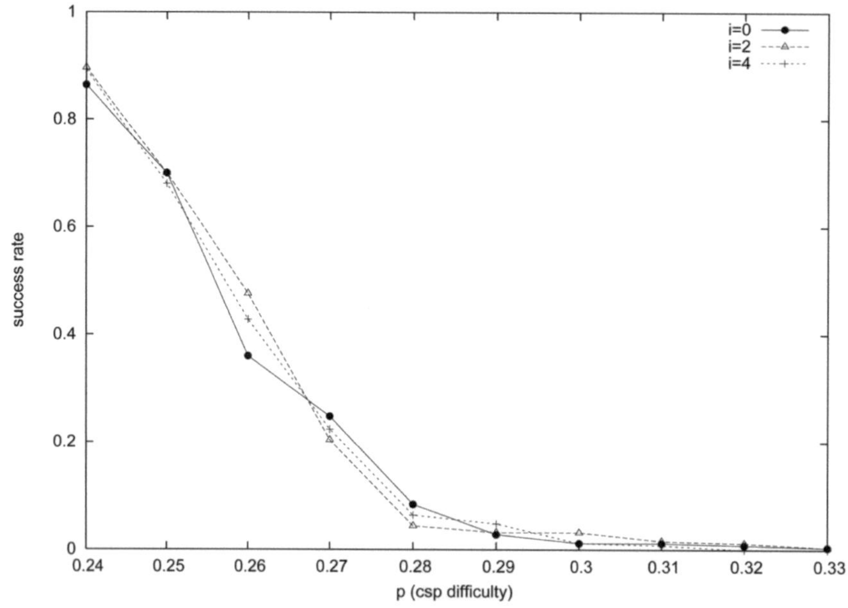

Fig. 5. Results on model E: success rate for PSO-MBE

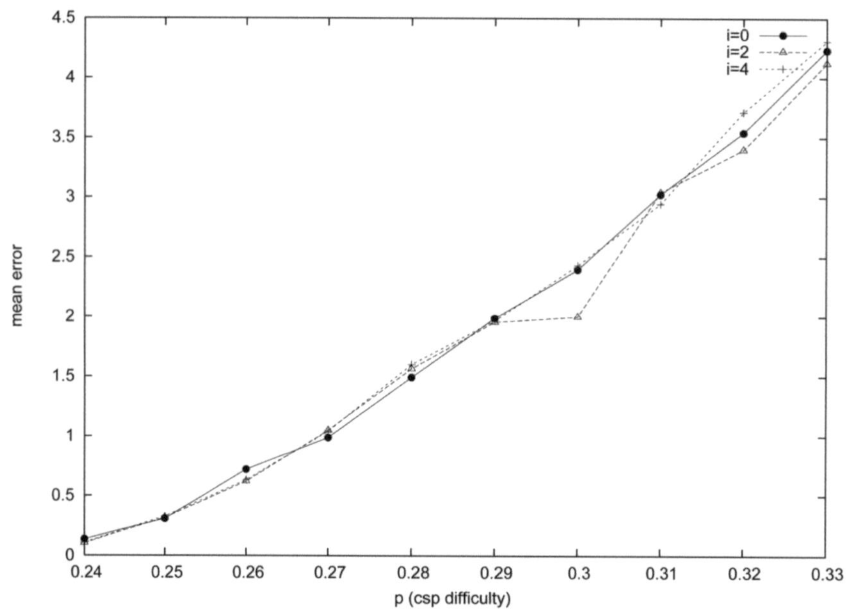

Fig. 6. Results on model E: mean error for PSO-MBE

Using the results from the comparative study of several genetic algorithms made by Craenen et al. (Craenen et al., 2003) we can conclude that the performance of the hybrid algorithms is comparable with that of the best GAs in the CSP field: *Stepwise Adaptation of Weights* and *Glass-Box GA*. Low levels of inference slightly improve the performance of our algorithm on difficult CSP instances; higher levels of inference are needed.

6. Conclusion

The chapter presents some of the techniques based on Evolutionary Computation paradigms for solving constraints satisfaction problems. Two hybrid approaches based on the idea of using the heuristics extracted from an inference algorithm inside evolutionary computation paradigms are detailed. The effect of combining inference with randomized search was studied by exploiting the advantage of adaptable inference levels offered by the Mini-Bucket Elimination algorithm. Tests conducted on binary CSPs against a Branch and Bound algorithm show that the systematic search has more benefit from inference than the randomized search performed by evolutionary computation paradigms. However, on hard CSP instances the Branch and Bound algorithm requires higher levels of inference which imply a much greater computational cost in order to compete with evolutionary computation methods.

7. References

Achlioptas, D., Kirousis, L., Kranakis, E., Krizanc, D., Molloy, M. & Stamatiou, Y. (2001). Random constraint satisfaction: A more accurate picture, *Constraints* 4(6): 329-344.

Bean, J. (1994). Genetic algorithms and random keys for sequencing and optimization, *ORSA Journal on Computing* 6(2): 154–160.

Breaban, M., Ionita, M. & Croitoru, C. (2007). A new pso approach to constraint satisfaction, *Proceedings of IEEE Congress on Evolutionary Computation*, pp. 1948–1954.

Clerc, M. (2000). Discrete particle swarm optimization. illustrated by the traveling salesman problem, *Technical report*. Available at htpp://www.mauriceclerc.net.

Coello, C. & Lechunga, M. (2002). Mopso: A proposal for multiple objective particle swarm optimization, *Proceedings of the IEEE Congress on Evolutionary Computation*, pp. 1051–1056.

Craenen, B., Eiben, A. & van Hemert, J. (2003). Comparing evolutionary algorithms on binary constraint satisfaction problems, *IEEE Transactions on Evolutionary Computation* 7(5): 424–444.

Dasgupta, D. & Michalewicz, Z. (2001). *Evolutionary Algorithms in Engineering Applications*, Springer 1st edition.

Dechter, R. (1996). Bucket elimination: A unifying framework for probabilistic inference algorithms, *Uncertainty in Artificial Intelligence*, pp. 211–219.

Dechter, R. (1999). Bucket elimination: A unifying framework for reasoning, *Artificial Intelligence* 113(1-2): 41–85.

Dechter, R. (2003). *Constraint Processing*, Morgan Kaufmann Publishers.

Dechter, R. & Rish, I. (2003). Mini-buckets: A general scheme for bounded inference, *Journal of the ACM* 50(2): 107–153.

Dozier, G., Bowen, J. & Bahler, D. (1994). Solving small and large constraint satisfaction problems using a heuristic-based microgenetic algorithm, *Proceedings of the 1st IEEE Conference on Evolutionary Computation*, pp. 306–311.

Eiben, A., Raue, P.-E. & Ruttkay, Z. (1994). Solving constraint satisfaction problems using genetic algorithms, *Proceedings of the 1st IEEE Conference on Evolutionary Computation*, pp. 542–547.

Eiben, A. & Ruttkay, Z. (1996). Self-adaptivity for constraint satisfaction: Learning penalty functions, *Proceedings of the 3rd IEEE Conference on Evolutionary Computation*, pp. 258– 261.

Glover, F. & Kochenberger, G. (1995). Critical event tabu search for multidimensional knapsack problems, *Proceedings of the International Conference on Metaheuristics for Optimization*, pp. 113–133.

Ionita, M., Croitoru, C. & Breaban, M. (2006). Incorporating inference into evolutionary algorithms for max-csp, *Lecture Notes in Computer Science. 3rd International Workshop on Hybrid Metaheuristics* 4030: 139–149.

Kask, K. & Dechter, R. (2000). New search heuristics for max-csp, *Lecture Notes In Computer Science. Proceedings of the 6th International Conference on Principles and Practice of Constraint Programming* 1894: 262–277.

Kennedy, J. & Eberhart, R. (1995). Particle swarm optimization, *Proceedings of the 1995 IEEE International Conference on Neural Networks*, Vol. 4, pp. 1942–1948.

Kowalczyk, R. (1997). Constraint consistent genetic algorithms, *Proceedings of the IEEE International Conference on Evolutionary Computation*, pp. 343–348.

Larossa, J. & Meseguer, P. (1998). Partial lazy forward checking for max-csp, *Proceedings of the 13th European Conference on Artificial Intelligence*, pp. 229–233.

Larossa, J., Meseguer, P. & Schiex, T. (1999). Maintaining reversible dac for max-csp, *Artificial Intelligence* 107(1): 149–163.

Liepins, G. & Vose, M. (1990). Representational issues in genetic optimization, *Journal of Experimental and Theoretical Artificial Intelligence* 2(2): 101–115.

Marchiori, E. & Steenbeek, A. (2000). A genetic local search algorithm for random binary constraint satisfaction problems, *Proceedings of the 14th Annual Symposium on Applied Computing*, pp. 458–462.

Michalewicz, Z. (1995). A survey of constraint handling techniques in evolutionary computation methods, *Proceedings of the 4th Anual Conference on Evolutionary Programming*, pp. 135–155.

Michalewicz, Z. (1996). *Genetic Algorithms + Data structures = Evolution programs*, Springer Berlin 3rd edition.

Michalewicz, Z. & Janikow, C. Z. (1991). Handling constraints in genetic algorithms, *Proceedings of the 4th International Conference on Genetic Algorithms*, pp. 151–157.

Michalewicz, Z. & Schoenauer, M. (1996). Evolutionary algorithms for constrained parameter optimization problems, 4(1): 1–32.

Morris, P. (1993). The breakout method for escaping from local minima, *Proceedings of the 11th National Conference on Artificial Intelligence*, pp. 40–45.

Paredis, J. (1994). Coevolutionary constraint satisfaction, *Lecture Notes In Computer Science. Proceedings of the 3rd Conference on Parallel Problem Solving from Nature* 866: 46–55.

Richardson, J., Palmer, M., Liepins, G. & Hilliard, M. (1989). Some guidelines for genetic algorithms with penalty functions, *Proceedings of the 3rd International Conference on Genetic Algorithms*, p. 191197.

Schoofs, L. & Naudts, B. (2002). Swarm intelligence on the binary constraint satisfaction problem, *Proceedings of the IEEE Congress on Evolutionary Computation*, pp. 1444–1449.

Smith, B. (1994). Phase transition and the mushy region in constraint satisfaction, *Proceedings of the 11th ECAI*, pp. 100–104.

Wallace, R. (1995). Directed arc consistency preprocessing, *Lecture Notes in Computer Science. Constraint Processing, Selected Papers* 923: 121–137.

X. Hu, X., Eberhart, R. & Shi, Y. (2003). Swarm intelligence for permutation optimization: a case study on n-queens problem, *Proceedings of the IEEE Swarm Intelligence Symposium*, pp. 243–246.

3

Morphological-Rank-Linear Models for Financial Time Series Forecasting

Ricardo de A. Araújo[1], Gláucio G. de M. Melo[1], Adriano L. I. de Oliveira[2] and Sergio C. B. Soares[2]
[1]*Information Technology Department, [gm][2] Intelligent Systems, Campinas, SP,*
[2]*Systems and Computing Department, University of Pernambuco, Recife, PE,*
Brazil

1. Introduction

The financial time series forecasting is considered a rather difficult problem, due to the many complex features frequently present in such time series (irregularities, volatility, trends and noise). Several approaches have been studied for the development of predictive models able to predict time series, based on its past and present data.

In the attempt to solve the time series prediction problem, a wide number of linear statistical models were proposed. Among them, the popular linear statistical approach based on Auto Regressive Integrated Moving Average (ARIMA) models [1] is one of the most common choices. However, since the ARIMA models are linear and most real world applications involve nonlinear problems, this can introduce an accuracy limitation of the generated forecasting models.

In the attempt to overcome linear statistical models limitations, other nonlinear statistical approaches have been developed, such as the bilinear models [2], the threshold autoregressive models [3], the exponential autoregressive models [4], the general state dependent models [5], amongst others. The drawbacks of those nonlinear statistical models are the high mathematical complexity associated with them (resulting in many situations in similar performances to the linear models) and the need, most of the time, of a problem dependent specialist to validate the predictions generated by the model, limiting the development of an automatic forecast system [6].

Alternately, Artificial Neural Networks (ANNs) based approaches have been applied for nonlinear modeling of time series in the last two decades [7-14]. However, in order to define a solution to a given problem, ANNs require the setting up of a series of system parameters, some of them are not always easy to determine. The ANN topology, the number of processing units, the algorithm for ANN training (and its corresponding variables) are just some of the parameters that require definition. In addition to those, in the particular case of time series forecasting, another crucial element necessary to determine is the relevant time lags to represent the series [15]. In this context, evolutionary approaches for the definition of neural network parameters have produced interesting results [16{20]. Some of these works have focused on the evolution of the network weights whereas others aimed at evolving the network architecture.

In this context, a relevant work was presented by Ferreira [15], consisting of the Time-delay Added Evolutionary Forecasting (TAEF) method definition, which performs a search for the minimum number of necessary dimensions (the past values of the series) to determine the characteristic phase space of the time series. The TAEF method [15] finds the most fitted predictor model for representing a time series, and then performs a behavioral statistical test in order to adjust time phase distortions that may appear in the representation of some series.

Nonlinear filters, on the other hand, have been widely applied to signal processing. An important class of nonlinear systems is based on the framework of Mathematical Morphology (MM) [21, 22]. Many works have focused on the design of morphological systems [21, 23-28]. An interesting work was presented by Salembier [29, 30], which designed Morphological/Rank (MR) filters via gradient-based adaptive optimization. Also, Pessoa and Maragos [31] proposed a new hybrid filter, referred to as Morphological/Rank/Linear (MRL) filter, which consists of a linear combination of an MR filter [29, 30] and a linear Finite Impulse Response (FIR) filter [31]. In the branch of the filters and Artificial Intelligence integration, Pessoa and Maragos [32] also proposed a neural network architecture involving MRL operators at every processing node.

In the morphological systems context, another work was presented by Araújo et al. [33, 34]. It consists of an evolutionary morphological approach for time series prediction, which provides a mechanism to design a predictive model based on increasing and non-increasing translation invariant morphological operators and according to Matheron decomposition [35] and Banon and Barrera decomposition [36].

This work proposes the Morphological-Rank-Linear Time-lag Added Evolutionary Forecasting (MRLTAEF) method in order to overcome the random walk dilemma for financial time series prediction, which performs an evolutionary search for the minimum dimension to determining the characteristic phase space that generates the financial time series phenomenon. The proposed MRLTAEF method is inspired on Takens Theorem [37] and consists of an intelligent hybrid model composed of an MRL filter [31] combined with a Modified Genetic Algorithm (MGA) [16], which searches for the particular time lags capable of a fine tuned characterization of the time series and estimates the initial (sub-optimal) parameters of the MRL filter. Each individual of the MGA population is trained by the averaged Least Mean Squares (LMS) algorithm to further improve the MRL filter parameters supplied by the MGA. After training the model, the MRLTAEF method chooses the most tuned predictive model for the time series representation, and performs a behavioral statistical test [15] and a phase fix procedure [15] to adjust time phase distortions observed in financial time series.

Furthermore, an experimental analysis is conducted with the proposed MRLTAEF method using six real world financial time series. Five well-known performance metrics are used to assess the performance of the proposed method and the obtained results are compared with the previously presented methods in literature.

This work is organized as follows. In Section 2, the fundamentals and theoretical concepts necessary for the comprehension of the proposed method are presented, such as the time series prediction problem, the random walk dilemma for financial time series prediction, linear and nonlinear statistical models, neural network models, genetic algorithms (standard and modified), intelligent hybrid models (in particular the TAEF method). Section 3 shows the fundamentals and theoretical concepts of mathematical morphology and the MRL filter definition and its training algorithm. Section 4 describes the proposed MRLTAEF method. Section 5 presents the performance metrics which are used to assess the performance of the proposed method. Section 6 shows the simulations and the experimental results attained by the MRLTAEF method using six real world financial time series, as well as a comparison between the results achieved here and those given by standard MLP networks, MRL filters and the TAEF method [15]. Section 7 presents, to conclude, the final remarks of this work.

2. Fundamentals

In this section, the fundamentals and theoretical concepts necessary for the comprehension of the proposed method will be presented.

2.1 Time series forecasting problem

A time series is a sequence of observations about a given phenomenon, where it is observed in discrete or continuous space. In this work all time series will be considered time discrete and equidistant.

Usually, a time series can be defined by

$$X_t = \{x_t \in \mathbb{R} \mid t = 1, 2, \ldots, N\}, \tag{1}$$

where t is the temporal index and N is the number of observations. The term X_t will be seen as a set of temporal observations of a given phenomenon, orderly sequenced and equally spaced.

The aim of prediction techniques applied to a given time series (X_t) are to provide a mechanism that allows, with certain accuracy, the prediction of the future values of X_t, given by X_{t+k}, $k = 1, 2, \ldots$, where k represents the prediction horizon. These prediction techniques will try to identify certain regular patterns present in the data set, creating a model capable of generating the next temporal patterns, where, in this context, a most relevant factor for an accurate prediction performance is the correct choice of the past window, or the time lags, considered for the representation of a given time series.

Box & Jenkins [1] shown that when there is a clear linear relationship among the historical data of a given time series, the functions of auto-correlation and partial auto-correlation are capable of identifying the relevant time lags to represent a time series, and such procedure is usually applied in linear models. However, when it uses a real world time series, or more specifically, a complex time series with all their dependencies on exogenous and uncontrollable variables, the relationship that involves the time series historical data is generally nonlinear, which makes the Box & Jenkins' analysis procedure of the time lags only a crude estimate.

In a mathematical sense, such a relationship involving time series historical data defines a d-dimensional phase space, where d is the minimum dimension capable of representing such relationship. Therefore, a d- dimensional phase space can be built so that it is possible to unfold its corresponding time series. Takens [37] proved that if d is sufficiently large, such phase space is homeomorphic to the phase space that generated the time series. Takens' Theorem [37] is the theoretical justification that it is possible to build a state space using the correct time lags, and if this space is correctly rebuilt, Takens' Theorem [37] also guarantees that the dynamics of this space is topologically identical to the dynamics of the real system state space.

The main problem in reconstructing the original state space is naturally the correct choice of the variable d, or more specifically, the correct choice of the important time lags necessary for the characterization of the system dynamics. Many proposed methods can be found in the literature for the definition of the lags [38-40]. Such methods are based on measures of conditional probabilities, which consider,

$$X_t = f(x_{t-1}, x_{t-2}, \ldots, x_{t-d}) + r_t, \tag{2}$$

where $f(x_{t-1}, x_{t-2}, \ldots, x_{t-d})$ is a possible mapping of the past values to the facts of the future (where x_{t-1} is the lag 1, x_{t-2} is the lag 2,…, x_{t-d} is the lag d) and r_t is a noise term.
However, in general, these tests found in the literature are based on the primary dependence among the variables and do not consider any possible induced dependencies. For example, if

$$f(x_{t-1}) = f(f(x_{t-2})), \tag{3}$$

it is said that x_{t-1} is the primary dependence, and the dependence induced on x_{t-2} is not considered (any variable that is not a primary dependence is denoted as irrelevant).
The method proposed in this work, conversely, does not make any prior assumption about the dependencies between the variables. In other words, it does not discard any possible correlation that can exist among the time series parameters, even higher order correlations, since it carries out an iterative automatic search for solving the problem of finding the relevant time lags.

2.2 The random walk dilemma

A naive prediction strategy is to define the last observation of a time series as the best prediction of its next future value ($X_{t+1} = X_t$). This kind of model is known as the Random Walk (RW) model [41], which is defined by

$$X_t = X_{t-1} + r_t, \tag{4}$$

or

$$\Delta X_t = X_t - X_{t-1} = r_t, \tag{5}$$

where X_t is the current observation, X_{t-1} is the immediate observation before X_t, and r_t is a noise term with a gaussian distribution of zero mean and standard deviation σ ($r_t \approx N(0, \sigma)$). In other words, the rate of time series change (ΔX_t) is a white noise.
The model above clearly implies that, as the information set consists of past time series data, the future data is unpredictable. On average, the value X_t is indeed the best prediction of value X_{t-1}. This behavior is common in the finance market and in the economic theory and its so-called random walk dilemma or random walk hypothesis [41].
The computational cost for time series forecasting using the random walk dilemma is extremely low. Therefore, any other prediction method more costly than a random walk model should have a very superior performance than a random walk model, otherwise its use is not interesting in the practice.
However, if the time series phenomenon is driven by law with strong similarity to a random walk model, any model applied to this time series phenomenon will tend to have the same performance as a random walk model.

Assuming that an accurate prediction model is used to build an estimated value of X_t, denoted by $\widehat{X_t}$, the expected value ($E[\cdot]$) of the difference between $\widehat{X_t}$ and X_t must tend to zero,

$$E[\widehat{X_t} - X_t] \rightarrow 0. \tag{6}$$

If the time series generator phenomenon is supposed to have a strong random walk linear component and a very weak nonlinear component (denoted by $g(t)$), and assuming that $E[r_t] = 0$ and $E[r_t r_k] = 0$ ($\forall\ k \neq t$), the expected value of the difference between $\widehat{X_t}$ and X_t will be

$$\begin{aligned} &E[\widehat{X_t} - (X_{t-1} + g(t) + r_t)] \rightarrow 0 \\ &E[\widehat{X_t}] - E[X_{t-1}] - E[g(t)] - E[r_t] \rightarrow 0 \\ &E[\widehat{X_t}] - E[X_{t-1}] - E[g(t)] \rightarrow 0 \\ &E[\widehat{X_t}] \rightarrow E[X_{t-1}] + E[g(t)]. \end{aligned}$$

But $E[X_{t-1}] \gg E[g(t)]$, then $E[X_{t-1}] + E[g(t)] \simeq E[X_{t-1}]$ and

$$E[\widehat{X_t}] \rightarrow E[X_{t-1}]. \tag{7}$$

Therefore, in these conditions, to escape the random walk dilemma is a hard task. Indications of this behavior (strong linear random walk component and a weak nonlinear component) can be observed from time series lagplot graphics. For example, lagplot graphics where strong linear structures are dominant with respect to nonlinear structures [42], generally observed in the financial and economical time series.

2.3 Linear statistical models

The time series prediction process consists of representing the time series features through a model able to extend such features to the future. According to Box & Jenkins [15], classical statistical models were developed to represent the following kind of information patterns: constants, trends and sazonalities. However, there are some variations that occur in such patterns as irregularities, volatility, noise, amongst other.

In this way, it is possible to verify that the statistical models are based on transcendental or algebraic time functions, which can be represented by

$$X_t = b_1 f_1(t) + b_2 f_2(t) + \cdots + b_k f_k(t) + r_t \tag{8}$$

where b_i and $f_i(t)$ ($i = 1, 2, \ldots, k$) denotes, respectively, the constant parameters and mathematical functions of t. Term r_t represents a random component or noise.

However, there are other ways for time series modeling, where X_t will be modeled as a temporally ordered random component function, from the present to the past (r_t, r_{t-1}, r_{t-2},…). This kind of representation is kwon as "linear filter models", which is widely applied when the time series observations are highly correlated [1]. In this way, X_t can be defined by

$$Z_t = m + y_0 r_t + y_1 r_{t-1} + y_2 r_{t-2} + \cdots + y_k r_{t-k}, \tag{9}$$

where m and y_i ($i = 1, 2,\ldots, k$) are constants.

Therefore, the time series prediction process consists of an accurate parameters estimation of the prediction models to build the future behavior of a given phenomenon.

Box & Jenkins Models In the literature, several models were proposed to solve the time series prediction problem. Among these models, it is verified that a wide number of them are linear: Simple Moving Averages (SMA) [43, 44], Simple Exponential Smoothing (SES) [43, 44], Brow's Linear Exponential Smoothing (BLES) [43, 44], Holt's Bi-parametric Exponential Smoothing (HBES) [43, 44], Adaptive Filtering (AF) [43, 44], are some examples of that. However, among these linear models, the Box & Jenkins [1] models receive a special mention, given that, in practice, are the most popular and commonly used to solve the time series prediction problem.

Box and Jenkins [1] a set of algebraic models, referred to as Auto-Regressive Integrated Moving Average (ARIMA) models, where it builds an accurate prediction for a given time series. The ARIMA model is based on two main models:

1. Auto-Regressive (AR), which is defined by

$$\widetilde{Z}_t = \phi_1 \widetilde{Z}_{t-1} + \phi_2 \widetilde{Z}_{t-2} + \cdots + \phi_p \widetilde{Z}_{t-p} + r_t, \quad (10)$$

   where $\widetilde{Z}_k = Z_k - \mu$, being μ defined as the mean of the time series. Terms ϕ_i (i = 1, 2,..., p) denotes the auto-regressive coefficients.

2. Moving Average (MA), which is defined by

$$Z_t = \mu + r_t - \theta_1 r_{t-1} - \theta_2 r_{t-2} - \cdots - \theta_q r_{t-q}. \quad (11)$$

   Assuming that $\widetilde{Z}_k = Z_k - \mu$, it has

$$\widetilde{Z} = (1 - \theta_1 B - \theta_2 B^2 - \cdots - \theta_q B^q) r_t = \Theta(B) a_t \quad (12)$$

   where $\Theta(B) = 1 - \theta_1 B - \theta_2 B^2 - \cdots - \theta_q B^q$ represent the moving average operator.

The union of both AR and MA models build a model known as Auto-regressive Moving Average (ARMA) of order (p,q), which was proposed in the attempt to build the most parsimonious model as possible, given that, with the inclusion of auto-regressive and moving average terms in a unique model can be seen as a possible solution to obtain a small number of model parameters. In this way, the ARMA model is defined by

$$\widetilde{Z}_t = \phi_1 \widetilde{Z}_{t-1} + \cdots + \phi_p \widetilde{Z}_{t-p} + r_t - \theta_1 r_{t-1} - \theta_q r_{t-q}. \quad (13)$$

The ARIMA model basically consists of the application of data to the high-pass filter, which is sensible only to high frequencies of the function, which is applied to the ARMA model. Such a filter is represented by letter "I" (integrated) in the ARIMA notation and this is the main difference among the separated data by a constant distance d. This procedure, known as data differences, is performed to remove the data trends, building the time series as a stationary process, that is, an ARIMA(p,d,q) model is an algebraic study that show as a time series variable (X_t) is related with its past values ($X_{t-1}, X_{t-2}, \ldots, X_{t-p}$) and the past noisy term values ($r_{t-1}, r_{t-2}, \ldots, r_{t-p}$), differentiated d times [15].

In this way, Box & Jenkins [1] proposed a procedure able to find an adequate prediction model to solve the time series prediction problem, as be seen in Figure 1.

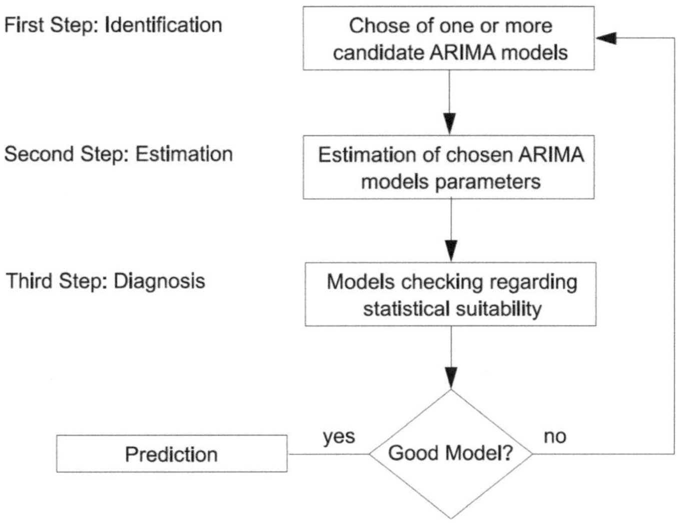

Fig. 1. Box & Jenkins method procedure.

According to Figure 1, it verifies that the first step (identification) uses two graphical devices to measure the correlation among the observations of the data set of the time series. Such devices are the Auto-Correlation Function (ACF) [1] and the Partial Auto-Correlation Function (PACF) [1]. In the second step (estimation), the model coefficients are estimated, and finally, in the third step (diagnosis), Box & Jenkins [1] proposed some checking procedures to determine the statistical suitability of the chosen model in previous steps. Then, the model that fails in these procedures will be rejected.

2.4 Nonlinear statistical models

As mentioned in the previous section, the ARIMA model [1] is one of the most common choices for the time series prediction. However, since the ARIMA models are linear and most real world applications involve nonlinear problems, this can introduce a limitation in the accuracy of the predictions generated, that is, this model assumes that the time series are stationary or generated by a linear process. However, it is not correct to generalize the linearity assumption of the time series due to the nonlinear nature of a given real-world phenomena, where nonlinear structures are found in historical time series data.
n this way, a time series can be modeled by

$$X_t = h(X_{t-1}, \dots, X_{t-p}, r_{t-1}, \dots, r_{t-q}) + r_t, \tag{14}$$

where r_t represents a random component, or noisy term. Terms p and q represent integer indexes that define the time windows of past terms of the time series and noise, respectively. The term $h(\cdot)$ denotes a nonlinear transference function, which build the mapping among the past and future values of the time series.
Therefore, to overcome the linear statistical models limitations, several nonlinear statistical models have been proposed in the literature, such as the bilinear models [2], the exponential auto-regressive models [4], the threshold autoregressive models [3], and the general state dependent models [5], amongst other.

The general state dependent models (GSD) [5] of (p, q) order is defined as an expansion and a local linearization of Equation 14 in Taylor series around a fixed time point, which can be defined by

$$X_t + \sum_{i=1}^{p} \phi_i(y_{t-1})X_{t-1} = \mu(y_{t-1}) + r_t + \sum_{j=1}^{q} \theta_i(y_{t-1})r_{t-1}, \tag{15}$$

where $y_t = (r_{t-q+1},\ldots, r_t, X_{t-q+1},\ldots, X_t)'$ is defined as a state vector, and the symbol "'" denotes a transposition operator.

A special class of such models, known as bilinear models [2], may be seen as a natural nonlinear extension of the ARMA model, making $\mu(x)$ and $\phi_i(x)$ constants and $\theta_j(y_{t-1}) = \theta_j + \sum_{v=1}^{Q} c_{jv}X_{t-v}$ $(j = 1, 2, \ldots$ and c_{jv} the coefficients to be adjusted). The general form of bilinear models of (p, q, P, Q) order is defined by

$$X_t + \sum_{i=1}^{p} \phi_i X_{t-1} = \mu + r_t + \sum_{j=1}^{q} \theta_j r_{t-j} + \sum_{u=1}^{P}\sum_{v=1}^{Q} c_{uv}X_{t-v}r_{t-u}. \tag{16}$$

According to Ferreira [15], it is verified that Equation 16 is linear in terms X_t and r_t and nonlinear regarding the cross term of Z and r. Thus, a bilinear model of first order can be built from the Equation 16 is given by

$$X_t = \alpha X_{t-1} + \beta r_t + \gamma X_{t-1}r_{t-1}, \tag{17}$$

where α, β and γ are the constant parameters to be determined.

Another particular class of such models, known as Exponential Auto-Regressive (EAR) models [4], of p order, is given by using a constant term $\mu(x)$, $\theta_j(x) = 0(\forall x)$ and $\phi_i(y_{t-1}) = \phi_i + \pi_i exp(-\gamma X_{t-1}^2)$ in Equation 15, and is formally defined by

$$X_t + \sum_{i=1}^{p} \{\phi_i + \pi_i exp(-\gamma X_{t-1}^2)\}X_{t-1} = \mu + r_t, \tag{18}$$

where γ denotes the time series scale factor.

Another class of nonlinear models which are used in time series predictions are the Threshold Auto-Regressive (TAR) models [3], where its parameters depend only on past values of its own process, and represent a finite set of possible AR models that a particular process could obey at any time point [15]. However, if the switch on of such models is determined by the data values location regarding thresholds, in this way the TAR model is known as Self-Excited Threshold Auto-regressive (SETAR) model [45].

A first-order TAR model is defined by

$$X_t = \begin{cases} \alpha_1 X_{t-1} + r_t, \text{ se } X_{t-1} < d \\ \alpha_2 X_{t-1} + r_t, \text{ se } X_{t-1} \geq d \end{cases}, \tag{19}$$

where the constant d is defined as the threshold.

The SETAR model can be defined $\mu(x) = \phi_0(j)$, $\theta_j(x) = 0(\forall x)$ and $\phi_i(y_{t-1}) = Á_i(j)$ if $X_{t-d} \in R_{(j)}$ (i = 1, 2,..., p; j = 1, 2,..., l), being d a positive integer and $R_{(j)}$ is a subset of real numbers (the threshold). Thus, Equation 15 can be rewritten in these terms, defining a SETAR model by

$$X_t + \phi_0^{(j)} + \sum_{i=1}^{p} \phi_i^{(j)} X_{t-i} = r_t^{(j)}, \text{ se } X_{t-d} \in R^{(j)},\ j = 1, 2, \ldots, l, \quad (20)$$

where such equation represents a SETAR model of kind (l, p,..., p). Term $r_t^{(j)}$ denotes a white noise, being $r_t^{(j)}$ independent of $r_t^{(j')}$, with $j \neq j'$.

There are several other nonlinear models for time series prediction in literature, such as auto-regressive smooth models [46], auto-regressive models with time-dependent coefficients [46], auto-regressive conditional heteroscedastic models (ARCH) [47], amongst other. However, even with a wide number of nonlinear models proposed in the literature, De Gooijer and Kumar [46] do not find clear evidences, in terms of prediction performance, of nonlinear models when compared with the linear models. Clements et al. [45, 48] also argues that the prediction performance of such nonlinear models is more inferior than expected, and this problem still remains open.

According to Ferreira [15], a general accepted concept is that the environment of a given temporal phenomenon is nonlinear, and the fact that the nonlinear models do not achieve the expected results is due to inability of such models to describe the time series phenomenon more accurately than simple linear approximations. In particular, it is verified that the models applied in real world stock market and finance are highly nonlinear [48]. However, the problem of financial time series prediction is still considered a very di±cult problem due to several complex characteristics that often are present in these time series (irregularities, volatility, trend and noise).

Due to the complexity of the structures of relationships among time series data, there are several limitations of the nonlinear models when applied in real situations. One of these limitations is a high mathematical complexity, a factor that limits the nonlinear models to a performance similar to linear models, as well as the need, in most cases, of a problem specialist to validate the predictions generated by the model [6]. These factors suggest that new approaches must be developed in order to improve the prediction performance. Consequently, it is not surprising the great interest on the development of nonlinear models for time series prediction using new approaches and paradigms applied to the problem previously exposed.

2.5 Neural network models

The Artificial Neural Networks (ANN) are models that simulate biological neural systems behavior, particularly the human brain. The ANNs represent a parallel and distributed system composed of simple processing units, such as neurons, which calculate non linear mathematical functions.

The neurons are contained in a spatial arrangement generally composed of one or more layers interconnected by a wide number of connections. Generally, in most models, such connections are associated with weights, which are responsible for the storage of knowledge represented in the model, used as weights for the signals to be processed by neurons in the network.

Each ANN unit is conditioned to receive a signal, weighted by their respective input unit processing connections (ANN weights), which is processed by a mathematical function, known as activation function or transfer function, and producing a new output signal which is propagated over the network.

In this way, making an analogy to the human brain, an ANN has the ability to learn through examples, as well as perform interpolations and extrapolations of the learned information. In the ANN learning process the main task is to determine the intensity of connections among neurons, which are adjusted and adapted by learning algorithms, which aims to make a fine tuned adjustment of connection weights, in order to better generalize the information contained in the pattern examples.

Therefore, a wide number of ANNs have been proposed in literature, which is worth mentioning,

- MultiLayers Perceptron (MLP) Neural Networks [49];
- Recursive Networks [49];
- Kohonen Networks [50, 51];
- Hopfield Networks [52];

Among the several kinds of ANNs, the MLPs are undoubtedly the most popular due to convenience, flexibility and efficiency, and can be applied to a wide range of problems [9, 49, 53].

2.6 MultiLayer perceptron neural networks

The MLP neural networks are typically composed of several neuron layers. The first layer is known as the input layer, where information is passed to the network. The last layer is called the output layer, where the model responses of a given information is then produced. Among input and output layers, there are one or more layers, which are referred to as intermediate layers.

Each layer is interconnected with the adjacent layer. If each neuron of a layer is connected to all neurons of the next layer, then it haas a fully connected MLP network (illustrated in Figure 2).

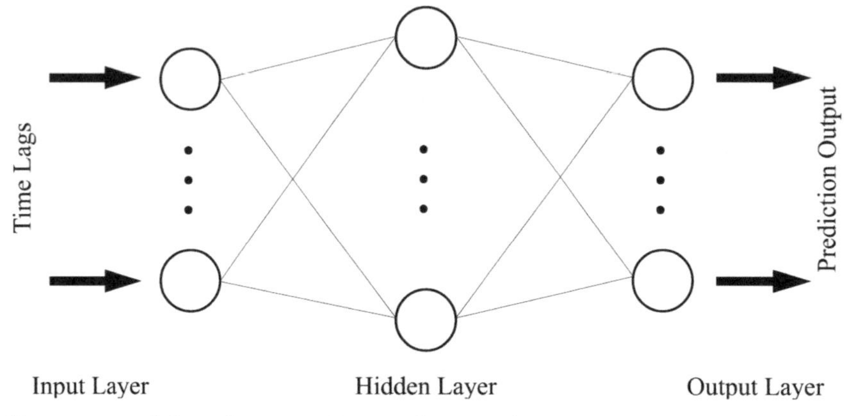

Fig. 2. Fully connected three layer MLP neural network.

An MLP is able to mapp past observations (network input) in their future values (network output). However, before having the capability to perform a given task, it is necessary that the network passes through a training or learning process. The MLP is typically trained by a supervised process and an external supervisor presents the input patterns and adjusts the weights of the network, according to the ANN success degree. For each pair of input-output, the network will be adjusted to make the mapping between input patterns and desired output (output pattern).

The ANN training is usually a very complex process, and according to a given problem, it requires a large number of input patterns. Each pattern of these vectors is presented to a neuron of the network input layer. In the time series prediction problem, the number of processing units in the ANN input layer is determined by the number of time lags of a given time series.

The set of patterns (or historical data) are usually divided into three sets according to Prechelt [54]: training set (50% of the points), validation set (25% of the points) and test set (25% of the points). Thus, the ANN training uses these three sets. Initially, the set of training examples are presented to the network, then the information passed between the input, hidden and output layers, the response is calculated, then a training algorithm is perfomed to minimize the global error achieved by the network, calculating new values for the weights of the network, taking the difference between the desired output and the output obtained by the network, as in Sum of Squared Errors (SSE), given by

$$\frac{1}{2}\sum_{n=1}^{N}(target_i - output_i)^2, \tag{21}$$

where $target_i$ is the real value of the i-th pattern, $output_i$ is the response obtained by the network to the i-th pattern, and the factor $\frac{1}{2}$ is just a term for the simplification derived from the expressions in Equation 21, often calculated in training algorithms such as BackPropagation in [49].

2.7 Genetic algorithms

Evolutionary Algorithms (EAs) are a powerful class of stochastic optimization algorithms and have been widely used to solve complex problems which cannot be solved analytically. The most popular EA is the Genetic Algorithm (GA) [55, 56]. The GAs were developed by Holland [55] motivated by Charles Darwin's Evolution Theory [57], where its main goal was to find ways in which the mechanisms of natural adaptation might be integrated into computer systems. The GAs are used successfully in several kind of real-world applications due to their high search power in state spaces, being widely applied to optimization and learning machine problems. The GAs work with a set of attempt solutions (initial states) for the problem. This set, referred to as population, is evolved towards a sub-optimal or optimal solution to a given problem by performing a search in the multiple trajectory simultaneously.

Standard Genetic Algorithm. In this section, a brief description of Standard Genetic Algorithm (SGA) procedure is presented, which is illustrated in Figure 3. More details will be supplied as follows. For further details see [56, 58-60].

According to Figure 3, the SGA procedure starts with the creation of an individuals' population, or more specifically, the solutions set. Then, each individual is evaluated by a fitness function (or cost function), which is a heuristic function that guides the search for an optimal solution in state space. After evaluating the SGA population, it is necessary to use some procedures to select the individual parent pairs, which will be used to perform the genetic operators (crossover and mutation). There are some procedures to perform this selection, and is worth mentioning the rank-based selection, elitist strategies, steady-state

```
begin SGA
    τ = 0;                  // τ: iteration number
    initialize p;           // p: population
    evaluate f(p);          // f(·): fitness or cost function
    while not termination condition do
        τ = τ+1;
        select individuals parents pairs from p;
        perform crossover operator with the selected individuals parents pairs;
        generate a new population (np);
        perform the mutation operator with the np;
        evaluate f(np);
        p = np;
    end
end
```

Fig. 3. Standard genetic algorithm procedure.

election and tournament selection [16], amongst others. The next step is responsible for performing the crossover genetic operator. Usually, the crossover operator mixes the parent genes for exchanging genetic information from both, obtaining its individual offspring. There are some procedures to perform the crossover operator such as one-point, two-point or multi-point crossover, arithmetic crossover, heuristic crossover [16], amongst others. After crossover operator, all offspring individuals will be the new population, which contains relevant characteristics of all individual parent pairs obtained in the selection process. The next step is to mutate the new population. The mutation operator is responsible for the individual genes aleatory modification, allowing the population diversification and enabling SGA to escape from the local minima (or maxima) of the surface of the cost function (fitness). After that, the new mutated population is evaluated. This procedure is repeated until a stop condition has been reached.

Modified Genetic Algorithm. The Modified Genetic Algorithm (MGA) used here is based on the work of Leung et al. [16]. The MGA is a second version of the Standard Genetic Algorithm (SGA) [56, 58, 59] that was modified to improve search convergence. The SGA was first studied, and, then, was modified to accelerate its convergence through the use of modified crossover and mutation operators (described later). The algorithm is described in Figure 4.

According to Figure 4, the MGA procedure consists of selecting a parent pair of chromosomes and then performing crossover and mutation operators (generating the offspring chromosomes – the new population) until the termination condition is reached; then the best individual in the population is selected as a solution to the problem.

The crossover operator is used for exchanging information from two parents (vectors $\underline{p}_1$ and $\underline{p}_2$) obtained in the selection process by a roulette wheel approach [16]. The recombination process to generate the offsprings (vectors $\underline{C}_1$,$\underline{C}_2$,$\underline{C}_3$ and $\underline{C}_4$) is done by four crossover operators, which are defined by the following equations [16]:

$$\underline{C}_1 = \frac{\underline{p}_1 + \underline{p}_2}{2}, \tag{22}$$

$$\underline{C}_2 = \underline{p}_{max}(1-w) + max(\underline{p}_1, \underline{p}_2)w, \tag{23}$$

$$\underline{C}_3 = \underline{p}_{min}(1-w) + min(\underline{p}_1, \underline{p}_2)w, \tag{24}$$

$$\underline{C}_4 = \frac{(\underline{p}_{max} + \underline{p}_{min})(1-w) + (\underline{p}_1 + \underline{p}_2)w}{2}, \tag{25}$$

```
begin MGA
    τ = 0;                // τ: actual iteration
    initialize population;
    evaluate f(population);      // f(·): fitness function
    while not termination condition do
        τ = τ+1;
        select a parent pair of chromosomes (p_1 and p_2) from population;
        begin crossover operator
            generate the offsprings C_1, C_2, C_3 and C_4 by Equations (22)-(25);
            the offspring with the best fitness function is denoted C^best;
        end
        begin mutation operator with C^best
            generate the mutated offsprings M_1, M_2 and M_3 by Equation (26);
        end
        // generate a new population
        insert C^best in the population;
        if random number < p_mut then
            the one among M_1, M_2 and M_3 with largest fitness value replaces the individual of the population with the
            smallest fitness value;
        else
            if f(M_1) > smallest fitness value in the population then
                M_1 replaces the individual of the population with the smallest fitness value;
            end
            if f(M_2) > smallest fitness value in the population then
                M_2 replaces the individual of the population with the smallest fitness value;
            end
            if f(M_3) > smallest fitness value in the population then
                M_3 replaces the individual of the population with the smallest fitness value;
            end
        end
        evaluate f(population);
    end
end
```

Fig. 4. The modified genetic algorithm procedure.

where $w \in [0, 1]$ denotes the crossover weight (the closer w is to 1, the greater is the direct contribution from parents), $max(\underline{p}_1, \underline{p}_2)$ and $min(\underline{p}_1, \underline{p}_2)$ denotes the vector whose elements are the maximum and the minimum, respectively, between the gene values of $\underline{p}_1$ and $\underline{p}_2$. The terms $\underline{p_{max}}$ and $\underline{p_{min}}$ denote a vector with the maximum and minimum possible gene values, respectively. After offspring generation by crossover operators, the offspring with the best evaluation (greater fitness value) will be chosen as the offspring generated by the crossover process and will be denoted by $\underline{C}^{best}$.

After the crossover operator, $\underline{C}^{best}$ is selected to have a mutation process, where three new mutated offsprings are generated and defined by the following equation [16]:

$$\underline{M}_j = C_i^{best} + \gamma_i \Delta M_i, \; j = 1, 2, 3 \text{ and } i = 1, 2, \ldots, NG, \quad (26)$$

where γ_i can only take the values 0 or 1, ΔM_i are randomly generated numbers such that $p_{min} \leq C_i^{best} + \Delta M_i \leq p_{max}$ and NG denotes the number of genes in the chromosome.

The first mutated offspring (M_1) is obtained according to (26) using only one term γ_i set to 1 (i is randomly selected within the range [1,NG]) and the remaining terms γ_i are set to 0. The second mutated offspring (M_2) is obtained according to (26) using some γ_i, randomly chosen, set to 1 and the remaining terms γ_i are set to 0. The third mutated offspring (M_3) is obtained according to (26) using all γ_i set to 1.

It is worth mentioning that the GA is not directly used for modeling and predicting time series, but it is applied to support other methods and techniques in the search for the optimal or sub-optimal parameters of the predictive model [15].

2.8 Intelligent hybrid models

Humans can be considered a good example of machines that have hybrid information. Their attitudes and actions are governed by a combination of genetic information and information acquired through learning. In genetic information, known as genotype, the information that come with the individual in the form of genetic coding, are the features inherited from your parents. The phenotype is the combination of features given by genotype combined with the environmental influences. The information in our genes ensures the success of our survival, which has been proven and tested over millions of years of evolution. Human learning consists of a variety of complex processes that use information acquired from environmental interactions. It is the combination of these different types of methods of processing information that enables humans to succeed in their survival in dynamic environments that change all the time.

This kind of hybrid information processing has been replicated on adaptive machines generation, where in their main unit processing there are intelligent computing systems and some mechanisms inspired by nature. It is possible to find some examples: neural networks [49, 61], genetic algorithms [56, 58, 59], fuzzy systems [62], artificial immune systems [63], expert systems [64] and induction rules [65]. The IA techniques have produced encouraging results in some particular tasks, but some complex problems, such as time series prediction, can not be successfully solved by a single intelligent technique. Each of these techniques have strengths and weaknesses, which make them suitable for some and not other problems. These limitations have been the main motivation for the study of Hybrid Intelligent Systems (HIS) where two or more AI techniques are combined in order to overcome the particular limitations of an individual technique. Hybrid Intelligent systems are also important when considering a wide range of real world applications. Many areas have many complex components of different problems, each of them may require a different type of processing. Moreover, the HIS being can be combined with different techniques, including conventional computing systems. The reasons for the HIS built are numerous, but can be summarized in three [66]:

1. Intensification Techniques: the integration of at least two different techniques, with the purpose of offsetting the weakness of a technique with the strength of the other;
2. Multiplicity of Applications in Tasks: A HIS is built, with the purpose of a single technique not being applied to many sub-problems that some application might have;
3. Implementation of Multiple Feature: the HIS build exhibits the capacity for multiple processing information within an architecture. Functionally, these systems emulate or mimic different processing techniques.

There are many possible combinations of the various techniques of artificial intelligence for hybrid intelligent systems built, however the discussion outlined here will be limited to a combination of techniques such as artificial neural networks and genetic algorithms.

TAEF Model. The Time-delay Added Evolutionary Forecasting (TAEF) method [15] tries to reconstruct the phase space of a given time series by carrying out a search for the minimum dimensionality necessary to reproduce the generator phenomenon of the time series. The TAEF method is an intelligent hybrid system based on Artificial Neural Networks (ANNs) architectures trained and adjusted by a Modified Genetic Algorithm (MGA) which not only searches for the ANN parameters but also for the adequate embedded dimension represented in the time lags.

The scheme describing the TAEF algorithm is based on the iterative definition of the four main elements: (i) the underlying information necessary to predict the series (the minimum number of lags), (ii) the structure of the model capable of representing such underlying information for the purpose of prediction (the number of units in the ANN structure), (iii) the appropriate algorithm for training the model, and (iv) a behavior test to adjust time phase distortions that appear in some time series.

Following this principle, the important parameters defined by the algorithm are:

1. The number of time lags to represent the series;
2. The number of units in the ANN hidden layer;
3. The training algorithm for the ANN.

The TAEF method starts with the user defining a minimum initial fitness value (*MinFit*) which should be reached by at least one individual of the population in a given MGA round. The fitness function is defined as

$$\text{Fitness Function} = \frac{1}{1 + \text{MSE}} \tag{27}$$

where MSE is the Mean Squared Error of the ANN and will be formally defined in Section 5.

In each MGA round, a population of M individuals are generated, each of them being represented by a chromosome (in Ferreira's works [15] $M = 10$ was used). Each individual is in fact a three-layer ANN where the first layer is defined by the number of time lags, the second layer is composed of a number of hidden processing units (sigmoidal units) and the third layer is composed by one processing unit (prediction horizon of one step ahead).

The stopping criteria for each one of the individuals are the number of epochs (NEpochs), the increase in the validation error (*Gl*) and the decrease in the training error (*Pt*).

The best repetition (the smallest validation error) is chosen to represent the best individual. Following this procedure, the MGA evolves towards an optimal or close to optimal fitness solution (which may not be the best solution yet), according to the stopping criteria: number of generations created (NGen) and fitness evolution of the best individual (BestFit).

After this point, when the MGA reaches a solution, the algorithm checks if the fitness of the best individual paired or overcame the initial value specified for the variable MinFit (minimum fitness requirement). If this is not the case, the value of MaxLags (maximum number of lags) is increased by one and the MGA procedure is repeated to search for a better solution.

However, if the fitness reached was satisfactory, then the algorithm checks the number of lags chosen for the best individual, places this value as MaxLags, sets MinFit with the fitness value reached by this individual, and repeats the whole MGA procedure. In this case, the fitness achieved by the best individual was better than the fitness previously set and, therefore, the model can possibly generate a solution of higher accuracy with the lags of the best individual (and with the MinFit reached by the best individual as the new target). If, however, the new value of MinFit is, again, not reached in the next round, MaxLags gets the same value defined for it, just before the round that found the best individual, increased by one (the maximum number of lags is increased by one). The state space for the lag search is then increased by one to allow a wider search for the definition of the lag set. This procedure goes on until the stop condition is reached. After that, the TAEF method chooses the best model found among all the candidates.

After the best model is chosen, when the training process is finished, a statistical test (*t*-test) is employed to check if the network representation has reached an "in-phase" matching (without a one step shift - the shape of the time series and the shape of the generated prediction has a time matching) or "out-of-phase" matching (with a one step shift { the shape of the time series and the shape of the generated prediction do not have a time

matching). If this test accepts the "in-phase" matching hypothesis, the elected model is ready for practical use. Otherwise, the method carries out a new procedure to adjust the relative phase between the prediction and the actual time series. The validation patterns are presented to the ANN and the output of these patterns are re-arranged to create new inputs that are both presented to the same ANN and set as the output (prediction) target.
It is worth mentioning that the variable *cont* just represents the current iteration of the TAEF method. The maximum of ten iterations of the TAEF method (given by expression *not cont* > 10), was chosen empirically according to previous experiments in order to generate an optimal prediction model.

3. Mathematical morphology

The Mathematical Morphology (MM) is based on two basic operations, the sum and substraction of Minkowski [67], which are respectively given by [68]

$$X \oplus B = \bigcup_{b \in B} X_b; \tag{28}$$

$$X \ominus B = \bigcap_{b \in B^r} X_b, \tag{29}$$

where $X_b = \{x + b : x \in X\}$ represents the input signal and $B_r = \{-b : b \in B\}$ is the reflected structuring element B.
All of MM transformations are based on combinations of four basic operations, which are defined by [68]

$$\text{Dilation: } \delta_B(X) = X \oplus B; \tag{30}$$

$$\text{Erosion: } \epsilon_B(X) = X \ominus B; \tag{31}$$

$$\text{Anti-Dilation: } \delta_B^a(X) = (X \oplus B^{rc})^{rc}; \tag{32}$$

$$\text{Anti-Erosion: } \epsilon_B^a(X) = (X \ominus B^{rc})^{rc}, \tag{33}$$

where $B_{rc} = \{-b : b \notin B\}$ represents the reflected complement of structuring element B.
According to Sousa [68], an operator of kind Ψ: $P(E) \rightarrow P(E)$, where $P(E)$ represents all subsets of $E = \mathbb{R}^N$, may be a translation invariant (Equation 34), increasing (Equation 35), decreasing (Equation 36) or window (Equation 37).

$$\Psi(X_{\underline{h}}) = (\Psi(X))_{\underline{h}}, \tag{34}$$

where $X_{\underline{h}} = \{x + h : x \in X\}$ represents the translation of $X \in P(E)$ by vector $h \in E$.

$$X_{\underline{h}} = \{x + \underline{h} : x \in X\} \tag{35}$$

$$X \supset Y \Rightarrow \Psi(X) \supset \Psi(Y), \forall X, Y \in P(E); \tag{36}$$

$$\forall x \in E \,,\, x \in \Psi(X) \Leftrightarrow x \in \Psi(X \cap L_x), \tag{37}$$

where L_x is the translation of $L \in E$ finite.

3.1 Morphological-Rank-Linear (MRL) filter preliminaries

Definition 1 – Rank Function: the r-th rank function of the vector $t = (t_1, t_2, \ldots, t_n) \in \mathbb{R}^n$ is the r-th element of the vector t sorted in decreasing order ($t_{(1)} \geq t_{(2)} \geq \ldots \geq t_{(n)}$). It is denoted by [31]

$$\mathcal{R}_r(\underline{t}) = t_{(r)}, \quad r = 1, 2, \ldots, n. \tag{38}$$

For example, given the vector t = (3, 0, 5, 7, 2, 1, 3), its 4-th rank function is $\mathcal{R}_4(\underline{t}) = 3$.
Definition 2 – Unit Sample Function: the unit sample function is given by [31]

$$q(v) = \begin{cases} 1, \text{ if } v = 0, \\ 0, \text{ otherwise.} \end{cases} \tag{39}$$

where $v \in \mathbb{R}$.
Applying the unit sample function to a vector $\underline{v} = (v_1, v_2, \ldots, v_n) \in \mathbb{R}^n$, yields a vector unit sample function ($Q(\underline{v})$), given by [31]

$$Q(\underline{v}) = [q(v_1), q(v_2), \ldots, q(v_n)]. \tag{40}$$

Definition 3 – Rank Indicator Vector: the r-th rank indicator vector c of t is given by [31]

$$\underline{c}(\underline{t}, r) = \frac{Q\left((z \cdot \underline{1}) \ - \underline{t}\right)}{Q\left((z \cdot \underline{1}) \ - \underline{t}\right) \cdot \underline{1}^T}, \tag{41}$$

where $z = \mathcal{R}_r(\underline{t})$, $\underline{1} = (1, 1, \ldots, 1)$ "$\cdot$" represents scalar product and the symbol T denotes transposition.
For example, given the vector $\underline{t}$ = (3, 0, 5, 7, 2, 1, 3), its 4-th rank indicator function is $\underline{c}(\underline{t}, 4) = \frac{1}{2}(1, 0, 0, 0, 0, 0, 1)$.
Definition 4 – Smoothed Rank Function: the smoothed r-th rank function is given by [31]

$$\mathcal{R}_{r,\sigma}(\underline{t}) = \ \underline{c}_\sigma(\underline{t}, r) \ \cdot \underline{t}^T, \tag{42}$$

with

$$\underline{c}_\sigma(\underline{t}, r) = \frac{Q_\sigma\left((z \cdot \underline{1}) \ - \underline{t}\right)}{Q_\sigma\left((z \cdot \underline{1}) \ - \underline{t}\right) \cdot \underline{1}^T}, \tag{43}$$

where c_σ is an approximation for the rank function $\underline{c}$ and $Q_\sigma(\underline{v})=[q_\sigma(v_1), q_\sigma(v_2), \ldots, q_\sigma(v_n)]$ is a smoothed impulse function (where $q_\sigma(v)$ is like $sech^2(v/\sigma)$) (where $sech$ is the hyperbolic secant), $\sigma \geq 0$ is a scale parameter and "$\cdot$" represents the scalar product.
Thus, $\underline{c}_\sigma$ is an approximation for the rank indicator vector $\underline{v}$. Using ideas from the fuzzy set theory, $\underline{c}_\sigma$ can also be interpreted as a membership function vector [31]. For example, if the vector $\underline{t}$ = (3, 0, 5, 7, 2, 1, 3), $q_\sigma(v) = sech^2(\frac{v}{\sigma})$ and $\sigma = 0.5$ then its smoothed 4-th rank indicator function is

$$\underline{c}_\sigma(\underline{t}, 4) = \tfrac{1}{2}(0.9646, 0, 0.0013, 0, 0.0682, 0.0013, 0.9646),$$

where $\underline{c}(\underline{t}, 4) = \frac{1}{2}(1, 0, 0, 0, 0, 0, 1)$.

3.2 MRL filter definition

The MRL filter [31] is a linear combination between a Morphological-Rank (MR) filter [29, 30] and a linear Finite Impulse Response (FIR) filter [31].

Definition 5 – MRL Filter [31]: Let $\underline{x} = (x_1, x_2, \ldots, x_n) \in \mathbb{R}^n$ represent the input signal inside an n-point moving window and let y be the output from the filter. Then, the MRL filter is defined as the shift-invariant system whose local signal transformation rule $\underline{x} \rightarrow y$ is given by [31]

$$y = \lambda\alpha + (1 - \lambda)\beta, \tag{44}$$

with

$$\alpha = \mathcal{R}_r(\underline{x} + \underline{a}) = \mathcal{R}_r(x_1 + a_1, x_2 + a_2, \ldots, x_n + a_n), \tag{45}$$

and

$$\beta = \underline{x} \cdot \underline{b}' = x_1 b_1 + x_2 b_2 + \ldots + x_n b_n, \tag{46}$$

where $\lambda \in \mathbb{R}$, $\underline{a}$ and $\underline{b} \in \mathbb{R}^n$. Terms $\underline{a} = (a_1, a_2, \ldots, a_n)$ and $\underline{b} = (b_1, b_2, \ldots, b_n)$ represent the coefficients of the MR filter and the coefficients of the linear FIR filter, respectively. Term $\underline{a}$ is usually referred to "structuring element" because for $r = 1$ or $r = n$ the rank filter becomes the morphological dilation and erosion by a structuring function equal to $\pm\underline{a}$ within its support [31]. The structure of the MRL filter is illustrated in Figure 5.

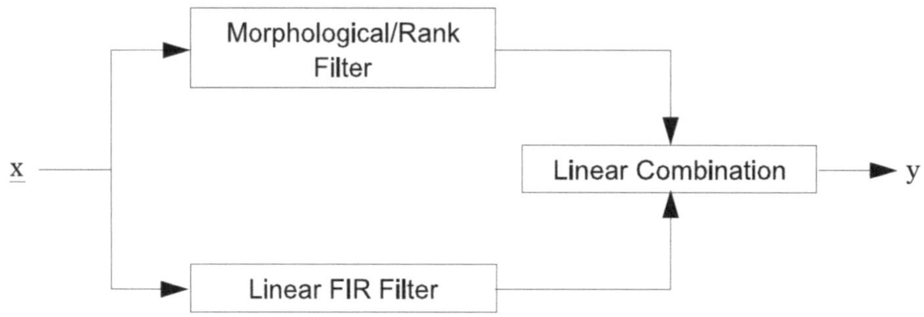

Fig. 5. Structure of the MRL filter.

3.3 MRL filter training algorithm

Pessoa and Maragos [31] presented an adaptive design of MRL filters based on the LMS algorithm [29, 30], the "rank indicator vector"" [31] and "smoothed impulses" [31] for overcoming the problem of nondifferentiability of rank operations.

Pessoa and Maragos [31] have shown that the main goal of the MRL filter is to specify a set of parameters ($\underline{a}$, $\underline{b}$, r, λ) according to some design requirements. However, instead of using the integer rank parameter r directly in the MRL filter definition equations (44-46), they argued that it is possible to work with a real variable ρ implicitly defined through the following rescaling [31]

$$r = round\left(n - \frac{n-1}{exp(-\rho)}\right), \tag{47}$$

where $\rho \in \mathbb{R}$, n is the dimension of the input signal vector $\underline{x}$ inside the moving window and round(·) denotes the usual symmetrical rounding operation. In this way, the weight vector to be used in the filter design task is defined by [31]

$$\underline{w} \equiv (\underline{a}, \underline{b}, \rho, \lambda). \tag{48}$$

The framework of the MRL filter adaptive design is viewed as a learning process where the filter parameters are iteratively adjusted. The usual approach to adaptively adjust the vector $\underline{w}$, and therefore design the filter, is to define a cost function $J(\underline{w})$, estimate its gradient $\nabla J(\underline{w})$, and update the vector $\underline{w}$ by the iterative formula

$$\underline{w} \equiv (\underline{a}, \underline{b}, \rho, \lambda). \tag{49}$$

where $\mu_0 > 0$ (usually called step size) and $i \in \{1, 2, \ldots\}$. The term μ_0 is responsible for regulating the tradeoff between stability and speed of convergence of the iterative procedure. The iteration of Equation 49 starts with an initial guess $\underline{w}(0)$ and stops when some desired condition is reached. This approach is known as the method of gradient steepest descent [31].

The cost function J must reflect the solution quality achieved by the parameters configuration of the system. A cost function J, for example, can be any error function, such as

$$J[\underline{w}(i)] = \frac{1}{M} \sum_{k=i-M+1}^{i} e^2(k), \tag{50}$$

where $M \in \{1, 2, \ldots\}$ is a memory parameter and $e(k)$ is the instantaneous error, given by

$$e(k) = d(k) - y(k), \tag{51}$$

where $d(k)$ and $y(k)$ are the desired output signal and the actual filter output for the training sample k, respectively. The memory parameter M controls the smoothness of the updating process. If we are processing noiseless signals, $M = 1$ is recommended [31]. However, when we use $M > 1$, the updating process tends to reduce the noise influence of noisy signals during the training [31].

Hence, the resulting adaptation algorithm is given by [31]

$$\underline{w}(i+1) = \underline{w}(i) + \frac{\mu}{M} \sum_{k=i-M+1}^{i} e^2(k) \frac{\partial y(k)}{\partial \underline{w}}, \tag{52}$$

where $\mu = 2\mu_0$ and $i \in \{1, 2, \ldots\}$. From Equations (44), (45), (46) and (48), term $\frac{\partial y(k)}{\partial \underline{w}}$ [31] may be calculated as

$$\frac{\partial y}{\partial \underline{w}} = \left(\frac{\partial y}{\partial \underline{a}}, \frac{\partial y}{\partial \underline{b}}, \frac{\partial y}{\partial \rho}, \frac{\partial y}{\partial \lambda}\right) \tag{53}$$

with

$$\frac{\partial y}{\partial \underline{a}} = \lambda \frac{\partial \alpha}{\partial \underline{a}}, \tag{54}$$

$$\frac{\partial y}{\partial \underline{b}} = (1 - \lambda)\underline{x}, \tag{55}$$

$$\frac{\partial y}{\partial \rho} = \lambda \frac{\partial \alpha}{\partial \rho}, \tag{56}$$

$$\frac{\partial y}{\partial \lambda} = (\alpha - \beta), \tag{57}$$

where

$$\frac{\partial \alpha}{\partial \underline{a}} = \underline{c} = \frac{Q\left((\alpha \cdot \underline{1}) \ - \underline{x} - \underline{a}\right)}{Q\left((\alpha \cdot \underline{1}) \ - \underline{x} - \underline{a}\right) \cdot \underline{1}'}, \tag{58}$$

$$\frac{\partial \alpha}{\partial \rho} = 1 - \frac{1}{n} Q\left((\alpha \cdot \underline{1}) \ - \underline{x} - \underline{a}\right) \cdot \underline{1}', \tag{59}$$

where n is the dimension of $\underline{x}$ and $\alpha = \mathcal{R}_r(\underline{x} + \underline{a})$.
It is important to mention that the unit sample function Q is frequently replaced by smoothed impulses Q_σ, in which case an appropriate smoothing parameter σ should be selected (which will affect only the gradient estimation step in the design procedure [31]).

4. The proposed morphological-rank-linear time-lag added forecasting (MRLTAEF) model

The approach model in this work, referred to as Morphological-Rank-Linear Time-lag Added Evolutionary Forecasting (MRLTAEF) model, uses an evolutionary search mechanism in order to train and adjust the Morphological-Rank-Liner (MRL) filter applied to financial time series prediction. It is based on the definition of the four main elements necessary for building an accurate forecasting system [15]:

- The underlying information necessary to predict the time series;
- The structure of the model capable of representing such underlying information for the purpose of prediction;
- The appropriate algorithm for training the model
- The behavior statistical test to adjust time phase distortions

It is important to consider the minimum possible number of time lags in the representation of the series because the model must to be as parsimonious as possible, avoiding the overfitting problem and decreasing the computacional cost.
Based on that definition, the proposed method consists of a hybrid intelligent morphological-rank-linear model composed of a MRL filter [31] with a MGA [16], which searches for:

1. The minimum number of time lags to represent the series: initially, a maximum number of time lags (*MaxLags*) is pre-defined and then the MGA will search for the number of time lags in the range [1,*MaxLags*] for each individual of the population;
2. The initial (sub-optimal) parameters of the MRL filter (mixing parameter (λ), rank (r), linear Finite Impulse Response (FIR) filter ($\underline{b}$) and the Morphological-Rank (MR) filter ($\underline{a}$) coefficients.

Then, each element of the MGA population is trained via LMS algorithm [31] to further improve the parameters supplied by the MGA, that is, the LMS is used, for each individual candidate, to perform a local search around the initial parameters supplied by MGA. The main idea used here is to conjugate a local search method (LMS) to a global search method (MGA). While the MGA makes it possible to test of varied solutions in different areas of the solution space, the LMS acts on the initial solution to produce a fine-tuned forecasting model. The proposed method is described in Figure 6.

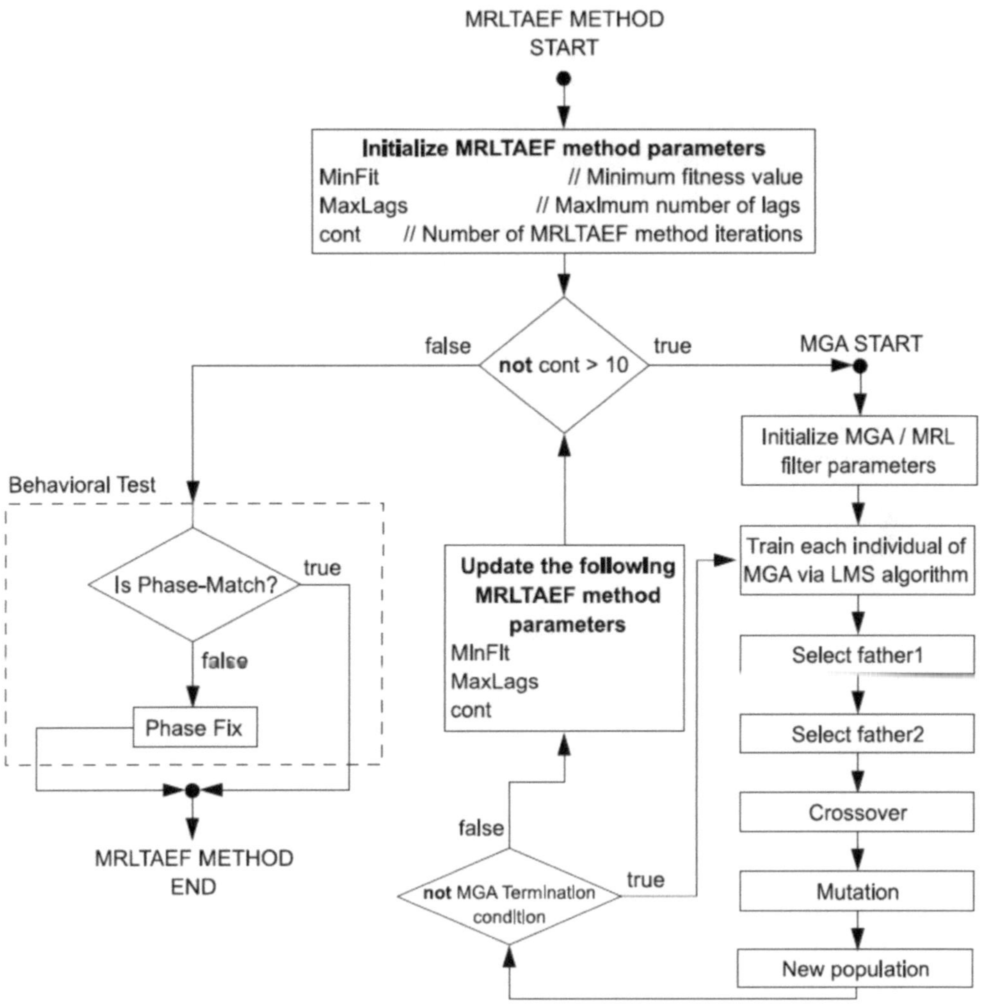

Fig. 6. The proposed method.

Such a process is able to seek the most compact MRL filter, reducing computational cost and probability of model overfitting. Each MGA individual represents a MRL filter, where its input is defined by the number of time lags and its output represents the prediction horizon of one step ahead.

Most works found in the literature have the fitness function (or objective function) based on just one performance measure, like Mean Square Error (MSE). However, Clements et al. [69], since 1993 has shown that the MSE measure has some limitations of availability and comparing the prediction model performance. Information about the prediction, as the absolute percentage error, the accuracy in the future direction prediction and the relative gain regarding naive prediction models (like random walk models and mean prediction) are not described using MSE measure.

In order to provide a more robust forecasting model, a multi-objective evaluation function is defined, which is a combination of five well-known performance measures: Prediction Of Change In Direction (POCID), Mean Square Error (MSE), Mean Absolute Percentage Error (MAPE), Normalized Mean Square Error (NMSE) or U of Theil Statistic (THEIL) and Average Relative Variance (ARV), where all these measures will be formally defined in Section 5. The multi-objective evaluation function used here is given by

$$\text{Fitness Function} = \frac{\text{POCID}}{1 + \text{MSE} + \text{MAPE} + \text{THEIL} + \text{ARV}}. \tag{60}$$

Whereas there are linear and nonlinear metrics in the such evaluation function and each one of these metrics can contribute to different forms for the evolution process, the Equation 60 was built from empirical form to have all information necessary to describe as well as allow the time series generator phenomenon.

After MRL filter adjusting and training, the proposed method uses the phase fix procedure presented by Ferreira [15], where a two step procedure is introduced to adjust time phase distortions observed ("out-of-phase" matching) in financial time series. Ferreira [15] has shown that the representations of some time series (natural phenomena) were developed by the model with a very close approximation between the actual and the predicted time series (referred to as "in-phase" matching), whereas the predictions of other time series (mostly financial time series) were always presented with a one step delay regarding the original data (referred to as "out-of-phase" matching).

The proposed method uses the statistical test (t-test) to check if the MRL filter model representation has reached an in-phase or out-of-phase matching (in the same way of TAEF method [15]). This is conducted by comparing the outputs of the prediction model with the actual series, making use only of the validation data set. This comparison is a simple hypothesis test, where the null hypothesis is that the prediction corresponds to in-phase matching and the alternative hypothesis is that the prediction does not correspond to in-phase matching (or corresponds to out-of-phase matching).

If this test accepts the in-phase matching hypothesis, the elected model is ready for practical use. Otherwise, the proposed method performs a new procedure to adjust the relative phase between the prediction and the actual time series. The phase fix procedure has two steps (described in Figure 7): (i) the validation patterns are presented to the MRL filter and the output of these patterns are re-arranged to create new inputs patterns (reconstructed patterns), and (ii) these reconstructed patterns are represented to the same MRL filter and the output set as the prediction target. This procedure of phase adjustment considers that

the MRL filter is not a random walk model, it just shows a behavior characteristic of a random walk model: the $t + 1$ prediction is taken as the t value (Random Walk Dilemma).
If the MRL filter was like a random walk model, the phase adjust procedure would not work. Such phase fix was originally proposed by Ferreira [15], where he observed the fact that when Artificial Neural Network (ANN - Multilayer Perceptron like) is correctly adjusted (TAEF method), the one step shift distortion in the prediction can be softened.

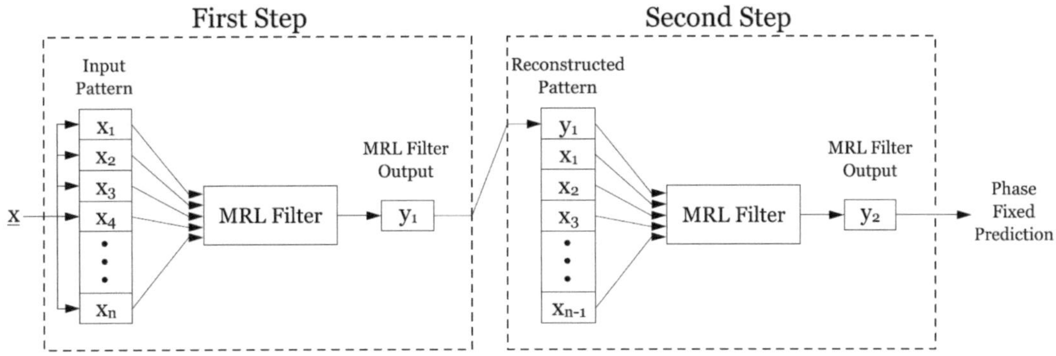

Fig. 7. Phase fix procedure.

The termination conditions for the MGA are:

1. Minimum value of fitness function: $fitness \geq 40$, where this value mean the accuracy to predict direction around 80% ($POCID \gtrsim 80\%$) and the sum of the other errors around one ($MSE + MAPE + THEIL + ARV \cong 1$);
2. The increase in the validation error or generalization loss (Gl) [54]: $Gl > 5\%$;
3. The decrease in the training error process training (Pt) [54]: $Pt \leq 10^{-6}$.

Each individual of the MGA population is a MRL filter represented by the data structure with the following components (MRL filter parameters):

- $\underline{a}$: MR filter coefficients;
- $\underline{b}$: linear FIR filter coefficients;
- ρ: variable used to determine the rank r;
- λ: mixing parameter;
- NLags: a vector, where each position has a real-valued codification, which is used to determine if a specific time lag will be used ($\text{NLags}_i > 0$) or not ($\text{NLags}_i \leq 0$).

5. Performance metrics

Many performance evaluation criteria are found in literature. However, most of the existing literature on time series prediction frequently employ only one performance criterion for prediction evaluation. The most widely used performance criterion is the Mean Squared Error (MSE), given by

$$\text{MSE} = \frac{1}{N} \sum_{j=1}^{N} (\text{target}_j - \text{output}_j)^2, \tag{61}$$

where N is the number of patterns, target_j is the desired output for pattern j and output_j is the predicted value for pattern j.

The MSE measure may be used to drive the prediction model in the training process, but it cannot be considered alone as a conclusive measure for comparison of different prediction models [69]. For this reason, other performance criteria should be considered for allowing a more robust performance evaluation.

A measure that presents accurately identifying model deviations is the Mean Absolute Percentage Error (MAPE), given by

$$\mathrm{MAPE} = \frac{1}{N}\sum_{j=1}^{N}\left|\frac{\mathrm{target}_j - \mathrm{output}_j}{x_j}\right|, \tag{62}$$

where x_j is the time series value at point j.

The random walk dilemma can be used as a naive predictor ($X_{t+1} = X_t$), commonly applied to financial time series prediction. Thus, a way to evaluate the model regarding a random walk model is using the Normalized Mean Squared Error (NMSE) or U of Theil Statistic (THEIL) [70], which associates the model performance with a random walk model, and given by

$$\mathrm{THEIL} = \frac{\sum_{j}^{N}(\mathrm{target}_j - \mathrm{output}_j)^2}{\sum_{j}^{N}(\mathrm{target}_j - \mathrm{target}_{j-1})^2}, \tag{63}$$

where, if the THEIL is equal to 1, the predictor has the same performance than a random model. If the THEIL is greater than 1, then the predictor has a performance worse than a random walk model, and if the THEIL is less than 1, the predictor is better than a random walk model. In the perfect model, the THEIL tend to zero.

Another interesting measure maps the accuracy in the future direction prediction of the time series or, more specifically, the ability of the method to predict if the future series value (prediction target) will increase or decrease with respect to the previous value. This metric is known as the Prediction Of Change In Direction (POCID) [15], and is given by

$$\mathrm{POCID} = \frac{100}{N}\sum_{j=1}^{N} D_j, \tag{64}$$

where

$$D_j = \begin{cases} 1, \text{ if } (\mathrm{target}_j - \mathrm{target}_{j-1})(\mathrm{output}_j - \mathrm{output}_{j-1}) > 0 \\ 0, \text{ otherwise} \end{cases} \tag{65}$$

The last measure used associates the model performance with the mean of the time series. The measure is the Average Relative Variance (ARV), and given by

$$\mathrm{ARV} = \frac{\sum_{j=1}^{N}(\mathrm{target}_j - \mathrm{output}_j)^2}{\sum_{j=1}^{N}(\mathrm{output}_j - \overline{\mathrm{target}})^2}, \tag{66}$$

where, $\overline{target}$ is the mean of the time series. If the ARV is equal to 1, the predictor has the same performance of the time series average prediction. If the ARV is greater than 1, then the predictor has a performance worse than the time series average prediction, and if the ARV is less than 1, the predictor is better than the time series average prediction. In the ideal model, ARV tend to zero.

6. Simulations and experimental results

A set of six real world financial time series (Dow Jones Industrial Average (DJIA) Index, National Association of Securities Dealers Automated Quotation (NASDAQ) Index, Standard & Poor 500 Stock (S&P500) Index and Petrobras Stock Prices, General Motors Corporation Stock Prices and Google Inc Stock Prices) were used as a test bed for evaluation of the proposed method. All time series investigated were normalized to lie within the range [0, 1] and divided into three sets according to Prechelt [54]: training set (50% of the points), validation set (25% of the points) and test set (25% of the points).

For all the experiments, the following initialization system parameters were used: $cont = 1$, $MinFit = 40$ and $MaxLags = 4$. The MGA parameters used in the proposed MRLTAEF method are a maximum number of MGA generations, corresponding to 10^4, crossover weight $w = 0.9$ (used in the crossover operator), mutation probability equals to 0.1. The MR filter coefficients and the linear FIR filter coefficients ($\underline{a}$ and $\underline{b}$, respectively) were normalized in the range [-0.5, 0.5]. The MRL filter parameters λ and ρ were in the range [0, 1] and $[-MaxLags, MaxLags]$, respectively.

Next, the simulation results involving the proposed model will be presented. In order to establish a performance study, results previously published in the literature with the TAEF Method [15] were examined in the same context and under the same experimental conditions. For each time series, ten experiments were done, where the experiment with the best validation fitness function is chosen to represent the prediction model.

In order to establish a performance study, results previously published in the literature with the TAEF Method [15] on the same series and under the same conditions are employed for comparison of results. In addition, experiments with MultiLayer Perceptron (MLP) networks and Morphological-Rank-Linear (MRL) filters were used for comparison with the MRLTAEF method. The Levenberg-Marquardt Algorithm [71] and the LMS algorithm [31] were employed for training the MLP network and the MRL filter, respectively. In all of the experiments, ten random initializations for each architecture were carried out, where the experiment with the best validation fitness function is chosen to represent the prediction model. The statistical behavioral test, for phase fix procedure, was also applied to all the MLP, MRL and TAEF models in order to guarantee a fair comparison among the models.

It is worth mentioning that the results with ARIMA models were not presented in our comparative analysis since Ferreira [15] has shown that MLP networks obtained results better than ARIMA models, for all financial time series used in this work. Therefore, only MLP networks were used in our comparative analysis.

Furthermore, in order to analyze time lag relations in the studied time series, the graphical methodology proposed by [42, 72], referred to as lagplot [72] or phase portrait [42], was employed. This consists of dispersion graph constructions relating the different time lags of the time series (X_t vs X_{t-1}, X_t vs X_{t-2}, X_t vs X_{t-3}, ...), and allow observations of possible relative strong relationships between any pair of time lags (when a structured appearance is shown in the graph). Although such technique is very limited since it depends on human interpretation of the graphs. However, its simplicity is a strong argument for its utilization [15].

6.1 Dow Jones Industrial Average (DJIA) index series

The Dow Jones Industrial Average (DJIA) Index series corresponds to daily records from January 1st 1998 to August 26th 2003, constituting a database of 1,420 points. Figure 8 shows the DJIA Index lagplot.

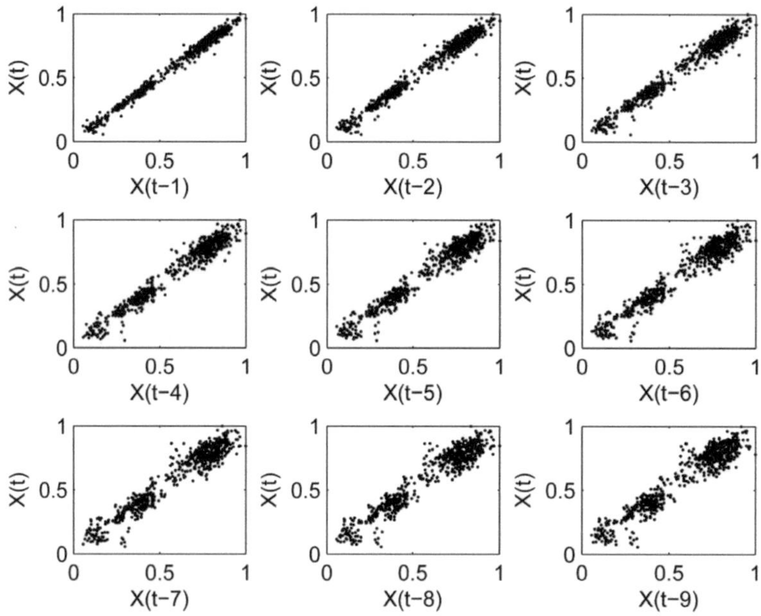

Fig. 8. DJIA Index series lagplot.

According to Figure 8, it is seen that for all the time lags of DJIA Index series there is a clear linear relationship among the lags. However, with the increase in the time lag degree, the appearance of the structure towards the graph center indicates a nonlinear relationship among the lags.

For the DJIA Index series prediction (with one step ahead of prediction horizon), the proposed method automatically chose the lag 2 as the relevant time lag (n = 1), defined the parameters ρ = 1.6374 and λ = 0.0038, and classified the best model as the "out-of-phase" model. Table 1 shows the results (with respect to the test set) for all the performance measures for the MLP, MRL, TAEF and MRLTAEF models.

	MLP		MRL		TAEF		MRLTAEF	
	In-Phase	Out-Of-Phase	In-Phase	Out-Of-Phase	In-Phase	Out-Of-Phase	In-Phase	Out-Of-Phase
MSE	0.0827	0.0830	8.2763e-4	8.2148e-4	8.4183e-4	2.6841e-5	8.4886e-4	4.4636e-6
MAPE	9.3700	9.3788	9.6601	9.6578	10.1529	0.1993	9.6068	0.1833
NMSE	0.9878	0.9885	0.9889	0.9916	1.0006	0.0318	1.0005	0.0053
ARV	3.3877e-2	3.4204e-2	3.4227e-2	3.3981e-2	0.0346	0.0007	3.4685e-2	1.8272e-4
POCID	46.74	46.59	46.71	46.82	47.57	97.14	46.32	99.43
Fitness	4.0734	4.0567	3.9977	4.0071	3.9027	78.8584	3.9784	83.6398

Table 1. Results for the DJIA Index series.

Figure 9 shows the actual DJIA Index values (solid line) and the predicted values generated by the MRLTAEF out-of-phase model (dashed line) for the last 100 points of the test set.

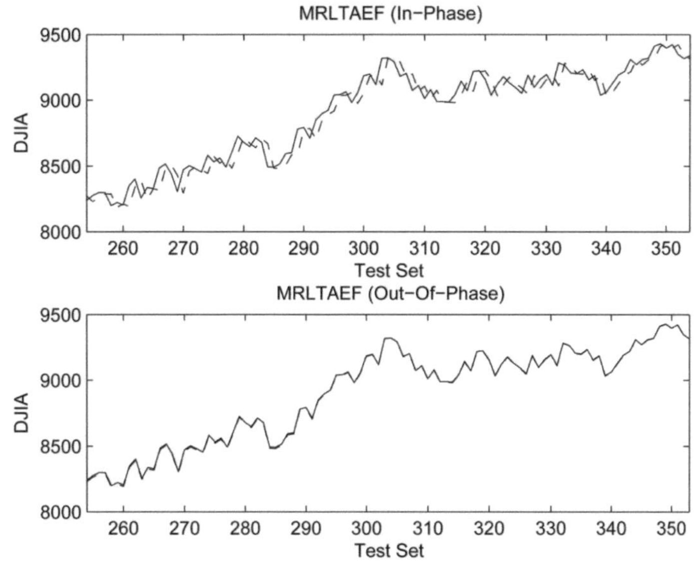

Fig. 9. Prediction results for the DJIA Index series (test set): actual values (solid line) and predicted values (dashed line).

Another relevant aspect to notice is that the MRLTAEF model chose the parameter λ = 0.0038, which indicates that it used 99.62% of the linear component of the MRL filter and 0.38% of the nonlinear component of the MRL filter, supporting the assumption (through lagplot analysis) that the DJIA Index series has a strong linear component mixed with a nonlinear component.

6.2 National association of securities dealers automated quotation (NASDAQ) index series

The National Association of Securities Dealers Automated Quotation (NASDAQ) Index series corresponds to daily observations from February 2nd 1971 to June 18th 2004, constituting a database of 8428 points. Figure 10 shows the NASDAQ Index lagplot.

According to Figure 10, it is seen that the time lags of NASDAQ Index series present a clear linear relationship among them, which, in theory, can contribute to a better forecasting result.

For the NASDAQ Index series prediction (with one step ahead of prediction horizon), the proposed method automatically chose the lag 2 as the relevant time lag (n = 1), defined the parameters ρ = 1.5581 and λ = 0.0005, and classified the model as "out-of-phase" matching. Table 2 shows the results (of the test set) for all performance measures for MLP, MRL, TAEF and MRLTAEF models.

Figure 11 shows the actual NASDAQ Index values (solid line) and the predicted values generated by the MRLTAEF out-of-phase model (dashed line) for the last 100 points of the test set.

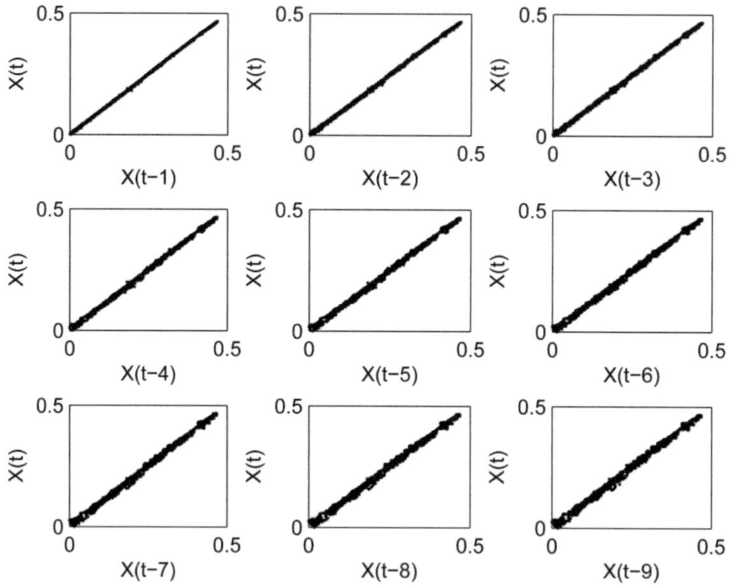

Fig. 10. NASDAQ Index series lagplot.

	MLP		MRL		TAEF		MRLTAEF	
	In-Phase	Out-Of-Phase	In-Phase	Out-Of-Phase	In-Phase	Out-Of-Phase	In-Phase	Out-Of-Phase
MSE	0.0022	0.0023	2.0730e-5	2.0728e-5	2.1449e-5	3.2374e-6	1.8751e-5	1.3003e-10
MAPE	2.6988e-3	2.7001e-3	0.4100	0.4097	0.2012	0.0774	0.3979	1.3350e-3
NMSE	1.1728	1.1759	1.1057	1.1043	1.1441	0.1726	1.0002	6.9324e-6
ARV	3.4977e-3	3.5011e-3	3.3038e-3	3.2912e-3	0.0034	5.1500e-4	2.9884e-3	2.0713e-8
POCID	53.06	53.94	52.89	53.21	52.70	89.63	52.70	99.95
Fitness	24.2123	24.6932	20.9962	21.1376	22.4377	78.8584	21.9482	99.8160

Table 2. Results for the NASDAQ Index series.

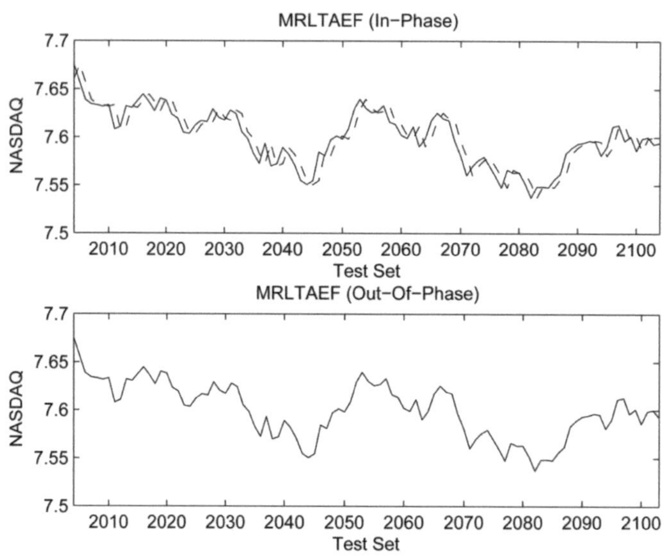

Fig. 11. Prediction results for the NASDAQ Index series (test set): actual values (solid line) and predicted values (dashed line).

It is worth mention that, as the MRLTAEF model chose λ= 0.0005, it used 99.95% of the linear component of the MRL filter and 0.05% of the nonlinear component of the MRL filter. This result can indicate that there is a nonlinear relationship among the time lags, a fact which could not be detected by the lagplot analysis.

6.3 Standard & Poor 500 (S&P500) index series

The Standard & Poor 500 (S&P500) Index is a pondered index of market values of the most negotiated stocks in the New York Stock Exchange (NYSE), American Stock Exchange (AMEX) and Nasdaq National Market System. The S&P500 series used corresponds to the monthly records from January 1970 to August 2003, constituting a database of 369 points. Figure 12 shows the S&P500 Index lagplot.

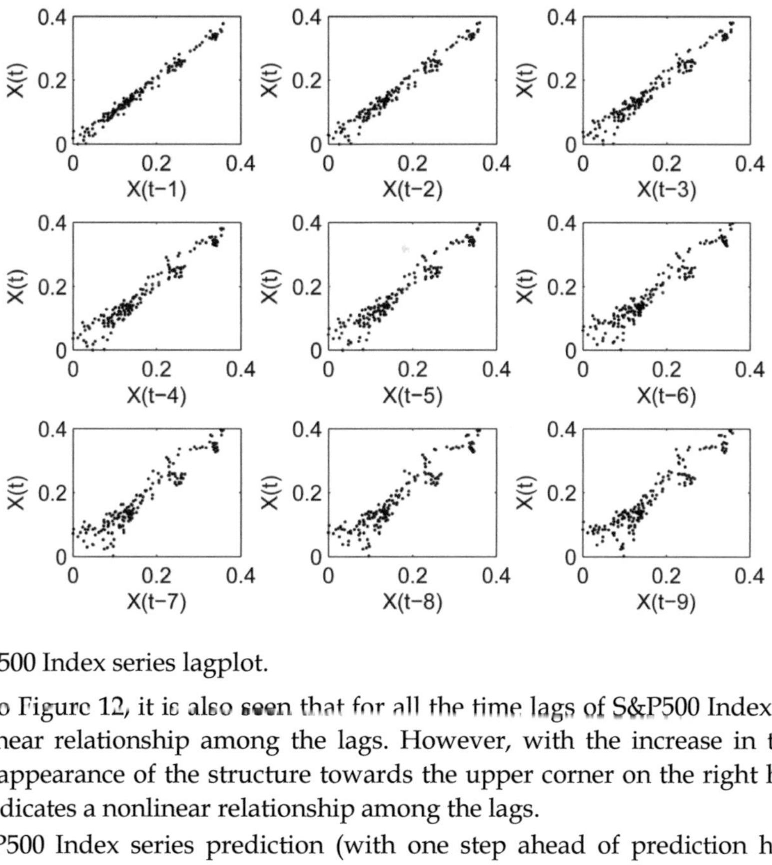

Fig. 12. S&P500 Index series lagplot.

According to Figure 12, it is also seen that for all the time lags of S&P500 Index series there is a clear linear relationship among the lags. However, with the increase in the time lag degree, the appearance of the structure towards the upper corner on the right hand side of the graph indicates a nonlinear relationship among the lags.

For the S&P500 Index series prediction (with one step ahead of prediction horizon), the proposed method automatically chose the lags 2, 3 and 10 as the relevant time lags (n = 3), defined the parameters ρ = 1.2508 and λ = 0.0091, and classified the best model as "out-of-phase" matching. Table 3 shows the results (for the test set) for all the performance measures for the MLP, MRL, TAEF and MRLTAEF models.

Figure 13 shows the actual S&P500 Index values (solid line) and the predicted values generated by the MRLTAEF out-of-phase model (dashed line) for the 90 points of the test set.

	MLP		MRL		TAEF		MRLTAEF	
	In-Phase	Out-Of-Phase	In-Phase	Out-Of-Phase	In-Phase	Out-Of-Phase	In-Phase	Out-Of-Phase
MSE	0.0095	0.0096	9.9894e-5	1.0982e-4	7.4290e-4	8.0263e-4	1.1032e-4	1.3488e-6
MAPE	1.0100	1.0103	0.9400	1.0214	1.0431	1.0228	1.0222	0.0935
NMSE	0.9166	0.9179	0.9590	1.0397	7.2412	7.0883	1.0522	0.0120
ARV	7.2728e-3	7.2875e-3	7.7320e-3	8.4926e-3	0.0100	0.0012	8.6381e-3	1.0690e-4
POCID	51.11	50.98	67.77	52.18	50.54	100.00	50.56	98.86
Fitness	17.3644	17.3101	23.3140	16.9983	5.4373	10.9732	16.3988	89.4168

Table 3. Results for the S&P500 Index series.

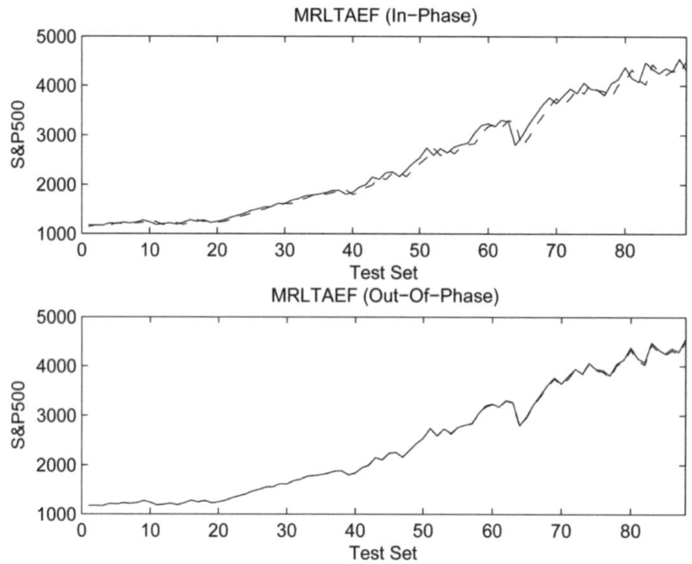

Fig. 13. Prediction results for the S&P500 Index series (test set): actual values (solid line) and predicted values (dashed line).

The proposed MRLTAEF chose λ = 0.0091, implying that it used 99.01% of the linear component of the MRL filter and 0.91% of the nonlinear component of the MRL filter, confirming the assumption (through lagplot analysis) that the S&P500 Index series has a strong linear component mixed with a nonlinear component.

6.4 Petrobras stock prices series

The Petrobras Stock Prices series corresponds to the daily records of Brazilian Petroleum Company from January 1st 1995 to July 3rd 2003, constituting a database of 2,060 points. Figure 14 shows the Petrobras Stock Prices lagplot.

According to Figure 14, it is seen that for all the time lags of the Petrobras Stock Prices series there is a clear linear relationship among the lags. However, with the increase in the time lag degree, the appearance of the structure towards the graph center indicates a nonlinear relationship among the lags.

For the Petrobras Stock Prices series prediction (with one step ahead of prediction horizon), the proposed method chose the lag 3 as the relevant time lag (n = 1), defined the parameters ρ = 1.9010 and λ = 0.0070, and classified the best model as "out-of-phase" matching. Table 4 shows the results (for the test set) of all the performance measures for the MLP, MRL, TAEF and MRLTAEF models.

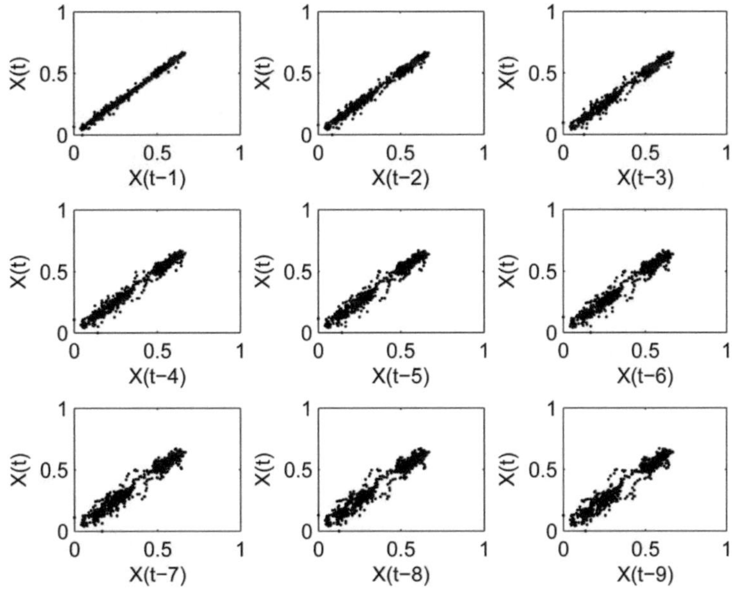

Fig. 14. Petrobras Stock Prices series lagplot.

	MLP		MRL		TAEF		MRLTAEF	
	In-Phase	Out-Of-Phase	In-Phase	Out-Of-Phase	In-Phase	Out-Of-Phase	In-Phase	Out-Of-Phase
MSE	0.0095	0.0095	8.8100e-5	8.8101e-5	7.5951e-5	1.9049e-5	6.6044e-5	2.6435e-6
MAPE	0.5100	0.5101	0.8002	0.8000	0.5480	0.2850	0.6609	0.1722
NMSE	1.5124	1.5130	1.3992	1.3998	1.2077	0.3023	1.0521	0.0419
ARV	0.0890	0.0895	0.0826	0.0829	0.0050	0.0019	0.0618	2.4770e-3
POCID	51.63	51.64	52.02	52.08	52.79	97.68	51.53	99.03
Fitness	16.5433	16.5401	15.8496	15.8645	19.1214	61.4641	18.5702	81.4003

Table 4. Results for the Petrobras Stock Prices series.

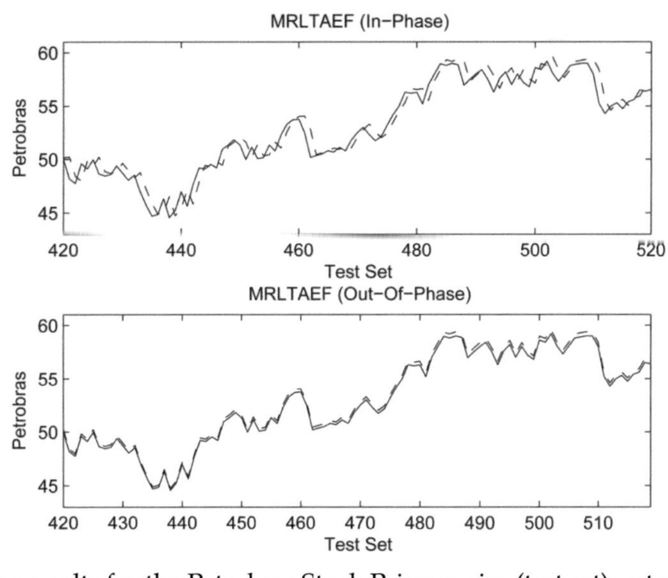

Fig. 15. Prediction results for the Petrobras Stock Prices series (test set): actual values (solid line) and predicted values (dashed line).

Figure 15 shows the actual Petrobras Stock Prices (solid line) and the predicted values generated by the MRLTAEF model out-of-phase (dashed line) for the 100 points of the test set.

For this series the proposed MRLTAEF chose $\lambda = 0.0070$, which means that it used 99.30% of the linear component of the MRL filter and 0.7% of the nonlinear component of the MRL filter, confirming the assumption (through lagplot analysis) that the Petrobras Stock Prices series has a strong linear component mixed with a nonlinear component.

6.5 General motors corporation stock prices series

The General Motors Corporation Stock Prices series corresponds to the daily records of General Motors Corporation from June 23th 2000 to June 22th 2007, constituting a database of 1,758 points. Figure 16 shows the General Motors Corporation Stock Prices lagplot.

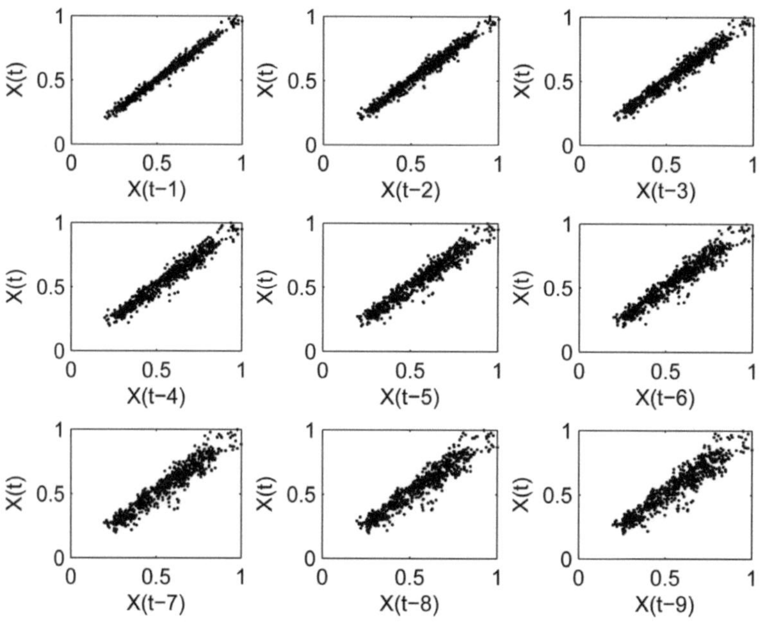

Fig. 16. General Motors Corporation Stock Prices series lagplot.

According to Figure 16, it is virified that for all the time lags of the General Motors Corporation Stock Prices series there is a clear linear relationship among the lags. However, with the increase in the time lag degree, the appearance of the structure towards the upper corner on the right hand side of the graph indicates a nonlinear relationship among the lags.

For the General Motors Corporation Stock Prices series prediction (with one step ahead of prediction horizon), the proposed method chose the lags 2, 4, 5 and 8 as the relevant time lags ($n = 4$), defined the parameters $\rho = 0.0617$ and $\lambda = 0.0011$, and classified the best model as "out-of-phase" matching. Table 5 shows the results (for the test set) of all the performance measures for the MLP, MRL, TAEF and MRLTAEF models.

Figure 17 shows the actual General Motors Corporation Stock Prices (solid line) and the predicted values generated by the MRLTAEF model out-of-phase (dashed line) for the 100 points of the test set.

	MLP		MRL		TAEF		MRLTAEF	
	In-Phase	Out-Of-Phase	In-Phase	Out-Of-Phase	In-Phase	Out-Of-Phase	In-Phase	Out-Of-Phase
MSE	1.8224e-4	1.7033e-4	1.6854e-4	1.6936e-4	1.6987e-4	4.0497e-6	1.6832e-4	2.2979e-6
MAPE	0.1628	0.1448	0.1357	0.1345	0.1511	3.8906e-2	0.1358	8.0446e-3
NMSE	1.0993	1.0273	1.0174	1.0223	1.0250	0.0243	1.0162	0.0137
ARV	2.6998e-2	2.5233e-2	2.4999e-2	2.5121e-2	2.5164e-2	6.0196e-4	2.4968e-2	3.4201e-4
POCID	52.63	52.40	52.50	52.48	53.54	94.26	52.51	99.54
Fitness	22.9897	23.8452	24.1017	24.0503	23.3205	88.6058	24.1188	97.3887

Table 5. Results for the General Motors Corporation Stock Prices series.

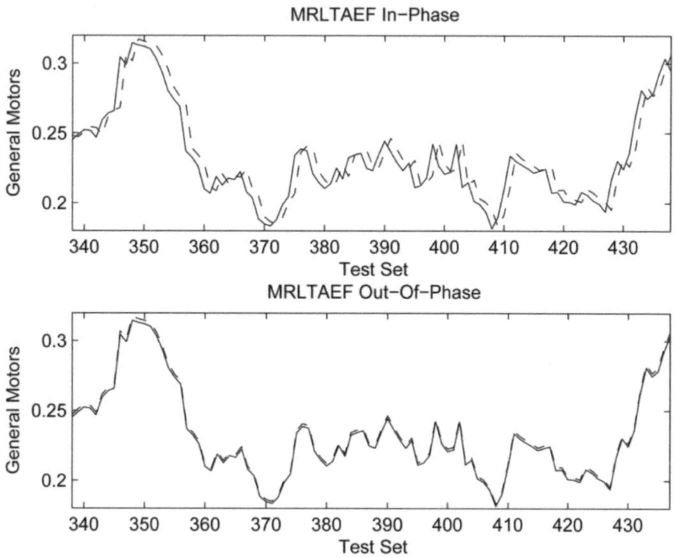

Fig. 17. Prediction results for the General Motors Corporation Stock Prices series (test set): actual values (solid line) and predicted values (dashed line).

For this series the proposed MRLTAEF chose $\lambda = 0.0011$, which means that it used 99.89% of the linear component of the MRL filter and 0.11% of the nonlinear component of the MRL filter, confirming the assumption (through lagplot analysis) that the General Motors Corporation Stock Prices series has a strong linear component mixed with a nonlinear component.

6.6 Google Inc Stock Prices series

The Google Inc Stock Prices series corresponds to the daily records of Google Inc from August 19th 2004 to June 21th 2007, constituting a database of 715 points. Figure 18 shows the Google Inc Stock Prices lagplot.

According to Figure 14, it is seen that for all the time lags of the Google Inc Stock Prices series there is a clear linear relationship among the lags. However, with the increase in the time lag degree, the appearance of the structure towards the graph center indicates a nonlinear relationship among the lags.

For the Google Inc Stock Prices series prediction (with one step ahead of prediction horizon), the proposed method chose the lags 2, 3 and 10 as the relevant time lags ($n = 3$), defined the parameters $\rho = -1.5108$ and $\lambda = 0.0192$, and classified the best model as "out-of-phase" matching. Table 6 shows the results (for the test set) of all the performance measures for the MLP, MRL, TAEF and MRLTAEF models.

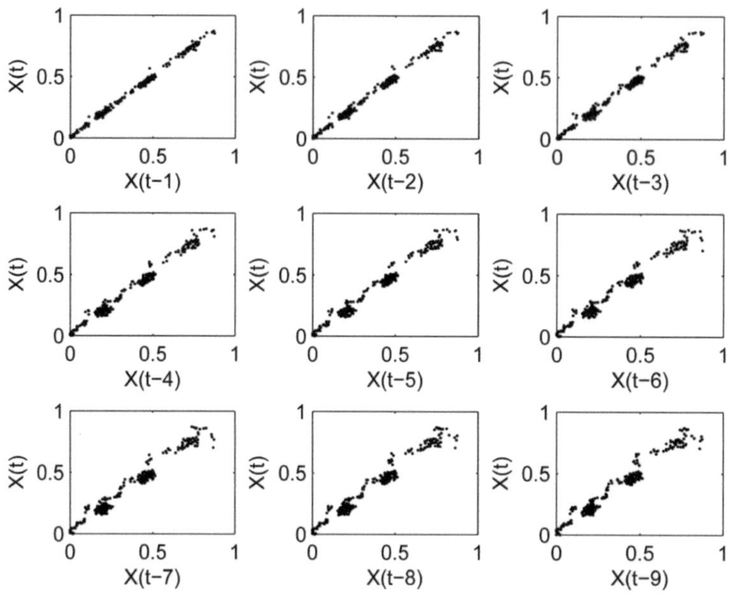

Fig. 18. Google Inc Stock Prices series lagplot.

	MLP		MRL		TAEF		MRLTAEF	
	In-Phase	Out-Of-Phase	In-Phase	Out-Of-Phase	In-Phase	Out-Of-Phase	In-Phase	Out-Of-Phase
MSE	2.8899e-4	3.1912e-4	2.9851e-4	3.1680e-4	3.1500e-4	4.5046e-5	2.8399e-4	5.4079e-6
MAPE	1.4049e-2	1.4549e-2	1.3232e-2	1.4211e-2	1.4257e-2	6.5056e-3	1.3272e-2	2.5518e-3
NMSE	1.0249	1.1271	1.0638	1.1345	1.1117	0.1607	1.0143	0.0195
ARV	0.1210	0.1336	0.1250	0.1259	0.1319	1.9405e-2	0.1189	2.3296e-3
POCID	40.90	43.18	43.75	43.26	42.04	94.85	43.18	99.42
Fitness	18.9330	18.9754	19.8653	19.0159	18.6168	79.9305	20.2266	97.0531

Table 6. Results for the Google Inc Stock Prices series.

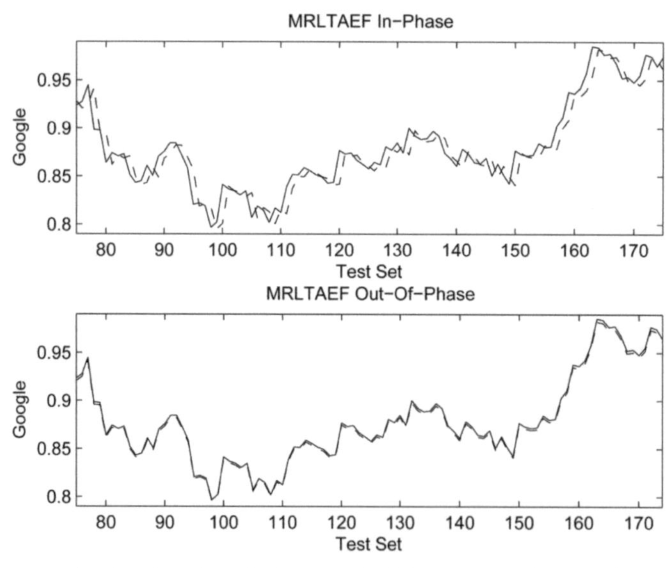

Fig. 19. Prediction results for the Google Inc Stock Prices series (test set): actual values (solid line) and predicted values (dashed line).

Figure 19 shows the actual Google Inc Stock Prices (solid line) and the predicted values generated by the MRLTAEF model out-of-phase (dashed line) for the 100 points of the test set.

For this series the proposed MRLTAEF chose $\lambda = 0.0192$, which means that it used 98.08% of the linear component of the MRL filter and 1.92% of the nonlinear component of the MRL filter, confirming the assumption (through lagplot analysis) that the Google Inc Stock Prices series has a strong linear component mixed with a nonlinear component.

In general, all generated prediction models using the phase fix procedure to adjust time phase distortions shown forecasting performance much better than the MLP model and MRL model, and slightly better than the TAEF model. The proposed method was able to adjust the time phase distortions of all analyzed time series (the prediction generated by the out-of-phase matching hypothesis is not delayed with respect to the original data), while the MLP model and MRL model were not able to adjust the time phase. This corroborates with the assumption made by Ferreira [15], where he discusses that the success of the phase fix procedure is strongly dependent on an accurate adjustment of the prediction model parameters and on the model itself used for prediction.

7. Conclusions

This work presented a new approach, referred to as Morpological-Rank-Linear Time-lag Added Forecasting (MRLTAEF) model, to overcome the RW dilemma for financial time series forecasting, which performs an evolutionary search for the minimum dimension to determining the characteristic phase space that generates the financial time series phenomenon. It is inspired on Takens Theorem and consists of an intelligent hybrid model composed of a Morpological-Rank-Linear (MRL) filter combined with a Modified Genetic Algorithm (MGA), which searches for the minimum number of time lags for a correct time series representation and estimates the initial (sub-optimal) parameters of the MRL filter (mixing parameter (λ), rank (r), linear Finite Impulse Response (FIR) filter ($\underline{b}$) and the Morphological-Rank (MR) filter ($\underline{a}$) coefficients). Each individual of the MGA population is trained by the averaged Least Mean Squares (LMS) algorithm to further improve the MRL filter parameters supplied by the MGA. After adjusting the model, it performs a behavioral statistical test and a phase fix procedure to adjust time phase distortions observed in financial time series.

Five different metrics were used to measure the performance of the proposed MRLTAEF method for financial time series forecasting. A fitness function was designed with these five well-known statistic error measures in order to improve the description of the time series phenomenon as much as possible. The five different evaluation measures used to compose this fitness function can have different contributions to the final prediction, where a more sophisticated analysis must be done to determine the optimal combination of such metrics.

An experimental validation of the method was carried out on four real world financial time series, showing the robustness of the MRLTAEF method through a comparison, according to five performance measures, of previous results found in the literature (MLP, MRL and TAEF models). This experimental investigation indicates a better, more consistent global performance of the proposed MRLTAEF method.

In general, all generated predictive models with the MRLTAEF method using the phase fix procedure (to adjust time phase distortions) showed forecasting performance much better than the MLP model and MRL model, and slightly better than the TAEF model. The MRLTAEF method was able to adjust the time phase distortions of all analyzed time series, while the MLP model and MRL model were not able to adjust the time phase. This fact shows that the success of the phase fix procedure is strongly dependent on the accurate adjustment of parameters of the predictive model and on the model itself used for forecasting. It was also observed that the MRLTAEF model reached a much better performance when compared with a random walk like model, overcoming the random walk dilemma for the analyzed financial times series.

The models generated by the MRLTAEF method are not random walk models. This affirmation is shown with the phase fix procedure. If the MRL filter models were random walk models, the phase fix procedure would generate the same result of the original prediction, since in the random walk model the t+1 value is always the t value.

It is worth mentioning that the first time lag is never selected to predict any time series used in this work. However, a random walk structure is necessary for the phase fix procedure to work, since the key of this procedure is the two step prediction (described by the phase fix procedure) in order to adjust the one step time phase.

Also, one of the main advantages of the MRLTAEF model (apart from its predictive performance when compared to all analyzed models) is that not only they have linear and nonlinear components, but they are quite attractive due to their simpler computational complexity when compared to other approaches such as [33, 34], other MLP-GA models [15] and other statistical models [2-5].

Furthermore, another assumption made by Ferreira [15] was confirmed through the analyzes of the MRL filter mixing parameter (λ). It was argued that through lagplot analysis it is possible to notice in financial time series indicative structures of some nonlinear relationship among the time lags even though they are super-imposed by a dominant linear component. In all the experiments, the MRLTAEF model set a strong linear component mixed with a weak nonlinear component (it uses ~99% of the linear component of MRL filter and ~1% of the nonlinear component of the MRL filter). Since the MRLTAEF method defines a MRL filter like model, which has the ability to select the percentage of use of the linear and nonlinear components, it is believed that it improves the prediction performance through a balanced estimation of the linear and nolinear relationships.

Future works will consider the development of further studies in order to formalize properties of the proposed model using the phase fix procedure. Also, other financial time series with components such as trends, seasonalities, impulses, steps and other nonlinearities can be used for the efficiency confirmation of the proposed method, as well as, further studies, in terms of risk and financial return, can be developed in order to determine the additional economical benefits, for an investor, with the use of the proposed method.

8. Acknowledgements

The authors are thankful to Mr. Chè Donavon David Davis for English support.

9. References

[1] G. E. P. Box, G. M. Jenkins, and G. C. Reinsel. *Time Series Analysis: Forecasting and Control.* Prentice Hall, New Jersey, third edition, 1994.

[2] T. Subba Rao and M. M. Gabr. Introduction to Bispectral Analysis and Bilinear Time Series Models, volume 24 of Lecture Notes in Statistics. Springer, Berlin, 1984.

[3] T. Ozaki. Nonlinear Time Series Models and Dynamical Systems, volume 5 of Hand Book of Statistics. North- Holland, Amsterdam, 1985.

[4] M. B. Priestley. Non-Linear and Non-stationary Time Series Analysis. Academic Press, 1988.

[5] D. E. Rumelhart and J. L. McCleland. Parallel Distributed Processing, Explorations in the Microstructure of Cognition, volume 1 & 2. MIT Press, 1987.

[6] M. P. Clements, P. H. Franses, and N. R. Swanson. Forecasting economic and financial time-series with non-linear models. *International Journal of Forecasting*, 20(2):169-183, 2004.

[7] T. C. Myhre. Financial forecasting at martin marietta energy systems, inc. *The Journal of Business Forecasting Methods & Systems*, 11(1):28-30, April 1992.

[8] M. Crottel, B. Girard, Y. Girard, M. Mangeas, and C. Muller. Neural modeling for time series: a statistical stepwise method for weight elimination. *IEEE Transaction on Neural Networks*, 6(6):1355-1364, 1995.

[9] G. Zhang, B. E. Patuwo, and M. Y. Hu. Forecasting with artificial neural networks: The state of the art. *International Journal of Forecasting*, 14:35-62, 1998.

[10] A. Khotanzad, H. Elragal, and T.-L. Lu. Combination of artificial neural-network forecasters for prediction of natural gas consumption. *Neural Networks, IEEE Transactions on*, 11(2):464-473, Mar 2000.

[11] Renate Sitte and Joaquin Sitte. Neural networks approach to the random walk dilemma of financial time series. *Applied Intelligence*, 16(3):163-171, May 2002.

[12] Marko Hocevar, Brane Širok, and Bogdan Blagojevic. Prediction of cavitation vortex dynamics in the draft tube of a francis turbine using radial basis neural networks. *Neural Computing & Applications*, 14(3):229-234, September 2005.

[13] Arie Preminger and Raphael Franck. Forecasting exchange rates: A robust regression approach. *International Journal of Forecasting*, 23(1):71-84, January-March 2007.

[14] D.M. Zhang, G.P.; Kline. Quarterly time-series forecasting with neural networks. *Neural Networks, IEEE Transactions on*, 18(6):1800-1814, Nov. 2007.

[15] Tiago A. E. Ferreira, Germano C. Vasconcelos, and Paulo J. L. Adeodato. A new intelligent system methodology for time series forecasting with artificial neural networks. In *Neural Processing Letters*, volume 28, pages 113-129, 2008.

[16] F. H. F. Leung, H. K. Lam, S. H. Ling, and P. K. S. Tam. Tuning of the structure and parameters of the neural network using an improved genetic algorithm. *IEEE Transactions on Neural Networks*, 14(1):79-88, January 2003.

[17] T. A. E. Ferreira, G. C. Vasconcelos, and P. J. L. Adeodato. A hybrid intelligence system approach for improving the prediction of real world time series. In *IEEE Proceedings of the Congress on Evolutionary Computation*, volume 1, pages 736-743, Portland, Oregon, 2004. IEEE.

[18] Mariano Matilla-García and Carlos Argüello. A hybrid approach based on neural networks and genetic algorithms to the study of profitability in the spanish stock market. *Applied Economics Letters*, 12(5):303-308, April 2005.

[19] T. A. E. Ferreira, G. C. Vasconcelos, and P. J. L. Adeodato. A new evolutionary method for time series forescasting. In *ACM Proceedings of Genetic Evolutionary Computation Conference - GECCO 2005*, Washington D.C., USA, 2005. ACM.

[20] R. A. Araújo, Germano C. Vasconcelos, and T. A. E. Ferreira. Hybrid differential evolutionary system for financial time series forecasting. In *Proceedings of the IEEE Congress on Evolutionary Computation*, Singapore, 2007.

[21] P. Maragos. A representation theory for morphological image and signal processing. *IEEE Trans. on Pattern Analysis and Machine Intelligence*, 11:586-599, 1989.

[22] J. Serra. *Image Analysis And Mathematical Morphology*. Academic Press, London, 1982.

[23] E. J. Coyle and J. H. Lin. Stack filters and the mean absolute error criterion. *IEEE Trans. Acoust. Speech Signal Processing*, 36:1244-1254, 1988.

[24] S. S. Wilson. Morphological networks. Proceedings of The SPIE Visual Communication and Image Processing IV, 1199:483-493, 1989.

[25] R. P. Loce and E. R. Dougherty. Facilitation of optimal binary morphological filter design via structuring element libraries and design constraints. *Opt. Eng.*, 31:1008-1025, May 1992.

[26] P. Yang and P. Maragos. Character recognition using min-max classifiers designed using an LMS algorithm. *Visual Communications and Image Processing*, 92(1818):674-685, nov. 1992.

[27] J. L. Davidson and F. Hummer. Morphology neural networks: An introduction with applications. *Circuits, System and Signal Process*, 12(2):179-210, 1993.

[28] C. B. Herwing and R. J. Shalkoff. Morphological image processing using artificial neural networks. In C. T. Leondes, editor, *Control and Dynamic Systems, Vol. 67*, pages 319-379. Academic Press, 1994.

[29] P. Salembier. Structuring element adaptation for morphological filters. *Journal for Visual Communication and Image Representation*, 3(2):115-136, June 1992.

[30] P. Salembier. Adaptive rank order based filters. *Signal Process.*, 27(1):1-25, 1992.

[31] L. F. C. Pessoa and P. Maragos. MRL-filters: A general class of nonlinear systems and their optimal design for image processing. *IEEE Transactions on Image Processing*, 7:966-978, 1998.

[32] L. F. C. Pessoa and P. Maragos. Neural networks with hybrid morphological/rank/linear nodes: A unifying framework with applications to handwritten character recognition. *Pattern Recognition*, 33:945-960, 2000.

[33] R. A. Araújo, F. Madeiro, R. P. Sousa, L. F. C. Pessoa, and T. A. E. Ferreira. An evolutionary morphological approach for financial time series forecasting. In *Proceedings of the IEEE Congress on Evolutionary Computation*, Vancouver, Canada, 2006.

[34] R. A. Araújo, R. P. Sousa, and T. A. E. Ferreira. An intelligent hybrid approach for designing increasing translation invariant morphological operators for time series forecasting. In *ISNN (2)*, volume 4492 PART II of *Lecture Notes in Computer Science*, pages 602-611. Springer-Verlag, 2007.

[35] G. Matheron. *Random Sets and Integral Geometry*. Wiley, New York, 1975.

[36] G. J. F. Banon and J. Barrera. Minimal representation for translation invariant set mappings by mathematical morphology. *SIAM J. Appl. Math.*, 51(6):1782-1798, 1991.

[37] F. Takens. Detecting strange attractor in turbulence. In A. Dold and B. Eckmann, editors, *Dynamical Systems and Turbulence*, volume 898 of *Lecture Notes in Mathematics*, pages 366-381, New York, 1980. Springer-Verlag.

[38] R. Savit and M. Green. Time series and dependent variables. *Physica D*, 50:95-116, 1991.

[39] H. Pi and C. Peterson. Finding the embedding dimension and variable dependences in time series. *Neural Computation*, 6:509-520, 1994.

[40] N. Tanaka, H. Okamoto, and M. Naito. Estimating the active dimension of the dynamics in a time series based on a information criterion. *Physica D*, 158:19-31, 2001.

[41] T. C. Mills. *The Econometric Modelling of Financial Time Series*. Cambridge University Press, Cambridge, 2003.

[42] Haolger Kantz and Thomas Schreiber. *Nonlinear Time Series analysis*. Cambridge University Press, New York, NY, USA, second edition, 2003.

[43] Pedro A. Morettin e Clélia M. Toloi. *Modelos para Previsão em Séries Temporias*, volume 1 e 2. IMPA - Instituto de Matemática Pura e Aplicada, São Paulo, 1981.

[44] Pedro A. Morettin e Clélia M. Toloi. *Séries Temporais*. Coleção Métodos Quantitativos. Atual Editora, São Paulo, segunda edition, 1987.

[45] Michalem P. Clements, Philip Hans Franses, Jeremy Smith, and Dick Van Dijk. On setar non-linearity and forecasting. *Journal of Forecasting*, 22(5):359-375, Aug 2003.

[46] J. G. De Gooijer and K. Kumar. Some recent developments in non-linear time series modelling, testing, and forecasting. *International Journal of Forecasting*, 8:135-156, 1992.

[47] R. F. Engle. Autoregressive conditional heteroskedasticity with estimates of the variance of uk onflation. *Econometrica*, 50:987-1008, 1982.

[48] M. P. Clements, P. H. Franses, and N. R. Swanson. Forecasting economic and finalcial time-seires with non-linear models. *International Journal of Forecasting*, 20:169-183, 2004.

[49] Simon Hakykin. *Redes Neurais - Princípos e Prática*. Bookman, Porto Alegre - Brasil, 2a edition, 2002.

[50] T. Kohonen. Self-organized formation of topologically conect feature maps. *Biological Cybernetics*, 43:5-69, 1982.

[51] Teuvo Kohonen. *Self-Organization and Associative Memory*. Springer-Verlog, Berlin, 1984.

[52] J. J. Hopfield. Neural networks and physical systems with emergent coletive computational abilities. In *Proceedings of the National Academy of the Sciences of tha U.S.A.*, volume 79, pages 2554-2558, 1982.

[53] Tom M. Mitchell. *Machine Learning*. WCB McGraw-Hill, Boston, 1997.

[54] Lutz Prechelt. Proben1: A set of neural network benchmark problems and benchmarking rules. Technical Report 21/94, 1994.

[55] John H. Holland. *Adaptation in Natual and Artificial Systems*. University of Michigan Press, Michigan, 1975.

[56] David E. Goldberg. Genetic Algorithms in Search, Optimization, and Machine Learning. Addison-Wesley, 1989.

[57] Charles Darwin. *The origin of species*. United King, 1859.

[58] John H. Holland. Genetic algorithms. *Scientific Amerian*, pages 66-72, july 1992.

[59] M. Mitchell. *A Introduction to Genetic Algorithms*. MIT Press, Canbridge, 1999.

[60] Mitsuo Gen and Runwei Cheng. *Genetic Algorithms and Engineering Design*. John Wiley and sons, New York, 1997.

[61] D. E. Rumelhart and J. L. McClelland. *Parallel Distributed Processing*, volume 1: Foundations. The MIT Press, 1986.

[62] Q. Liang and J. M. Mendel. Interval type-2 fuzzy logic systems: Theory and design. *IEEE Transaction on Fuzzy Systems*, 8(5):535-550, October 2000.

[63] D. Dasgupta. *Artificial Immune System and the Applications*. Springr-Verlog, Berlin, 1999.
[64] Donald Arthur Waterman. *A guide to expert systems*. Addison-Wesley, 1986.
[65] Maria Carolina Monard and José Augusto Baranauskas. *Indução de Regras e Árvores de Decisão*, chapter 5 - Sistemas Inteligentes - Fundamentos e Aplicações, pages 115-139. Malone, São Paulo, 2003.
[66] Suran Goonatilake and Sukhdev Khebbal. *Intelligence Hybrid Systems*. John Wiley & Son, 1995.
[67] H. Minkowski. *Gesammelte Abhandlungen*. Teubner Verlag, Leipzig-Berlin, 1911.
[68] R. P. Sousa. Design of translation invariant operators via neural network training. PhD thesis, UFPB, Campina Grande, Brazil, 2000.
[69] M. P. Clements and D. F. Hendry. On the limitations of comparing mean square forecast errors. *Journal of Forecasting*, 12(8):617-637, Dec. 1993.
[70] T. H. Hann and E. Steurer. Much ado about nothing? exchange rate forecasting: Neural networks vs. linear models using monthly and weekly data. *Neurocomputing*, 10:323-339, 1996.
[71]. M. Hagan and M. Menhaj. Training feedforward networks with the marquardt algorithm. *IEEE Transactions on Neural Networks*, 5(6):989-993, November 1994.
[72] Donald B. Percival and Andrew T.Walden. Spectral Analysis for Physical Applications-Multitaper and Conventional Univariate Techniques. Cambridge University Press, New York, 1998.

4

Evolutionary Logic Synthesis of Quantum Finite State Machines for Sequence Detection

Martin Lukac[1] and Marek Perkowski[2]
[1]Intelligent Integrated Systems Laboratory GSIS, Tohoku University,
[2]Department of Electrical and Computer Engineering, Portland State University
[1]Japan
[2]USA

1. Introduction

Quantum Finite State Machines (QFSM) are a well known model of computation that was originally formalized by Watrous [Wat95a, Wat95b, Wat97], Kondacs [KW97] and more generally Quantum Turing Machines (QTM) have been described by Bernstein [BV97]. In particular the 2-way QFSM have been shown to be more powerful than classical FSM [KW97]. Thus the interest in quantum computational models of automata and machines is not only theoretical but has also possible applications realization of future quantum computer and robotics controllers.
In this chapter we present the evolutionary approach to the synthesis of QFSM's specified by a quantum circuits. This approach was originally proposed by [LP09] and is possible on yet only theoretical basis. In particular this approach requires a selective qubit-initialization in a quantum register. In contrast the current methodology and approaches to practical Quantum Computation, the current practical realization of quantum computation always starts with the initialization of the whole quantum register and terminates by the measurement of either all of the qubits or by the measurement of a given subset of qubits. Moreover in general there is no reuse of any element of the quantum register.
In this text we analyze in details what type of QFSM can be successfully synthesized.
The evolutionary approach will evaluate the results based on both the correctness and the cost of the evolved machines. Multiple parameters such as type of error evaluation, synthesis constraints and evolutionary operators will be discussed when evaluating to the obtained results.
In particular we show how to synthesize QFSMs as sequence detectors and illustrate their functionality both in the quantum world and in the classical (observable) world. The application of the synthesized quantum devices is illustrated by the analysis of recognized sequences.
Finally, we provide analytic method for the used evolutionary approach and we describe the experimental protocol, and its heuristic improvements. We also discuss the results. In addition, we investigate the following aspects of the Evolutionary Quantum Logic Synthesis:

- Quantum probabilistic FSM and Reversible FSM.
- Hardware acceleration for the Fitness evaluation using CBLAS [cbl] and using CUBLAS [cud] (CUDA[cud] implemented Basic Linear Algebra Subprograms (BLAS)[cbl] subroutines).

2. Background in quantum computing

In Quantum Computing the information is represented by a Quantum Bit also called qubit. The wave equation is used to represent a qubit or a set of them. Equation 1 shows a general form in the Dirac notation.

$$\begin{aligned} |\phi\rangle &= e^{i\rho} cos\theta + e^{i(\rho+\psi)} sin\theta \\ &= e^{i\rho}(cos\theta + e^{i\psi} sin\theta) \end{aligned} \tag{1}$$

In Dirac notation $|\cdot\rangle$ represents a column vector, also called a *ket*. The *bra* element denoted $\langle\cdot|$ stands for hermitian conjugate. In this manner a bra-ket $\langle\cdot|\cdot\rangle$ represents the inner, dot-vector product while $|\cdot\rangle\langle\cdot|$ represents the outer vector product. The general equation (1), $e^{i\rho} cos\theta|0\rangle + e^{i(\rho+\psi)} sin\theta|1\rangle$ can be written as $\alpha|0\rangle + \beta|1\rangle$ with $|\alpha|^2 + |\beta|^2 = 1$ and $|\alpha|^2$is the probability of observing the state $|0\rangle$ while $|\beta|^2$ is the probability of observing $|1\rangle$.
In general, to describe basis states of a Quantum System, the Dirac notation is preferred to the vector-based Heisenberg notation. However, Heisenberg notation can be more practical to represent the exponential growth of the quantum register. Let two orthonormal quantum states be represented in the vector (Heisenberg) notation eq. 2.

$$\begin{aligned} |\uparrow\rangle = |0\rangle = \begin{bmatrix} 1 \\ 0 \end{bmatrix} \\ |\downarrow\rangle = |1\rangle = \begin{bmatrix} 0 \\ 1 \end{bmatrix} \end{aligned} \tag{2}$$

Different states in this vector notation are then multiplications of all possible states of the system, and for a two-qubit system we obtain (using the Kronecker product[Gru99, Gra81, NC00]) the states represented in eq. 3:

$$\begin{aligned} |00\rangle = \begin{bmatrix} 1 \\ 0 \end{bmatrix} \otimes \begin{bmatrix} 1 \\ 0 \end{bmatrix} = \begin{bmatrix} 1 \\ 0 \\ 0 \\ 0 \end{bmatrix} \quad |10\rangle = \begin{bmatrix} 0 \\ 1 \end{bmatrix} \otimes \begin{bmatrix} 1 \\ 0 \end{bmatrix} = \begin{bmatrix} 0 \\ 0 \\ 1 \\ 0 \end{bmatrix} \\ |01\rangle = \begin{bmatrix} 1 \\ 0 \end{bmatrix} \otimes \begin{bmatrix} 0 \\ 1 \end{bmatrix} = \begin{bmatrix} 0 \\ 1 \\ 0 \\ 0 \end{bmatrix} \quad |11\rangle = \begin{bmatrix} 0 \\ 1 \end{bmatrix} \otimes \begin{bmatrix} 0 \\ 1 \end{bmatrix} = \begin{bmatrix} 0 \\ 0 \\ 0 \\ 1 \end{bmatrix} \end{aligned} \tag{3}$$

The Kronecker product exponentially increases the dimension of the space for matrices as well:

$$I \otimes X = \begin{bmatrix} 1 & 0 \\ 0 & 1 \end{bmatrix} \otimes \begin{bmatrix} 0 & 1 \\ 0 & 1 \end{bmatrix} = \frac{1}{\sqrt{2}} \begin{bmatrix} 0 & 1 & 0 & 0 \\ 1 & 0 & 0 & 0 \\ 0 & 0 & 0 & 1 \\ 0 & 0 & 1 & 0 \end{bmatrix} \tag{4}$$

This tensor product operation for a parallel connection of to wires is shown in Figure 1.
Assume that qubit a (with possible states $|0\rangle$ and $|1\rangle$) is represented by $|\Psi_a\rangle = \alpha_a|0\rangle + \beta_a|1\rangle$ and qubit b is represented by $|\Psi_b\rangle = \alpha_b|0\rangle + \beta_b|1\rangle$. Each of them is represented by the

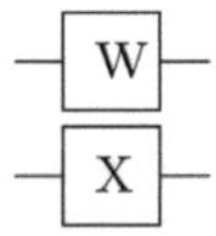

Fig. 1. Circuit representing the $W \otimes X$ operation

superposition of their basis states, but put together the characteristic wave function of their combined states will be:

$$|\Psi_a \Psi_b\rangle = \alpha_a \alpha_b |00\rangle + \alpha_a \beta_b |01\rangle + \beta_a \alpha_b |10\rangle + \beta_a \beta_b |11\rangle \quad (5)$$

with α_a and β_b being the complex amplitudes of states of each EP respectively. As shown before, the calculations of the composed state used the Kronecker multiplication operator. Hence comes the possibility to create quantum memories with extremely large capacities and the requirement for efficient methods to calculate such large matrices.

Quantum Computation uses a set of Quantum properties. These are the measurement, the superposition and the entanglement. First, however, the principles of multi-qubit system must be introduced.

2.1 Multi-Qubit System

To illustrate the superposition let's have a look at a more complicated system with two quantum particles a and b represented by $|\psi_a\rangle = \alpha_0|0\rangle + \beta_a|1\rangle$ and $|\psi_b\rangle = \alpha_b|0\rangle + \beta_b|1\rangle$ respectively. For such a system the problem space increases exponentially and is represented using the Kronecker product [Gru99].

$$|\psi_a\rangle \otimes |\psi_b\rangle = \begin{bmatrix} \alpha_0 \\ \beta_0 \end{bmatrix} \otimes \begin{bmatrix} \alpha_1 \\ \beta_1 \end{bmatrix} = \begin{bmatrix} \alpha_0\alpha_1 \\ \alpha_0\beta_1 \\ \beta_0\alpha_1 \\ \beta_0\beta_1 \end{bmatrix} \quad (6)$$

Thus the resulting system is represented by $|\psi_a \psi_b\rangle = \alpha_a \alpha_b|00\rangle + \alpha_a \beta_b|01\rangle + \beta_a \alpha_b|10\rangle + \beta_a \beta_b|11\rangle$ (5) where the double coefficients obey the unity (completeness) rule and each of their powers represents the probability to measure the corresponding state. The superposition means that the quantum system is or can be in any or all the states at the same time. This superposition gives the massive parallel computational power to quantum computing.

2.2 Entanglement and projective measurements

Assume the above two-particle vector (two-qubit quantum system) is transformed using the quantum circuit from Figure 2.

This circuit executes first a Hadamard transform on the top qubit and then a Controlled-Not operation with the bottom qubit as the target. Depending on the initial state of the quantum register the output will be either $|\psi_a \psi_b\rangle = \alpha_a \alpha_b|00\rangle \pm |\beta_a \beta_b|11\rangle$ or $|\psi_a \psi_b\rangle = \alpha_a \beta_b|01\rangle \pm |\beta_a \alpha_b|10\rangle$. Thus it is not possible to estimate with 100% probability the initial state of the quantum register.

Let $|ab\rangle = |00\rangle$ at level a (Figure 2). The first step is to apply the [H] gate on the qubit-a and the resulting state at level b of the circuit is

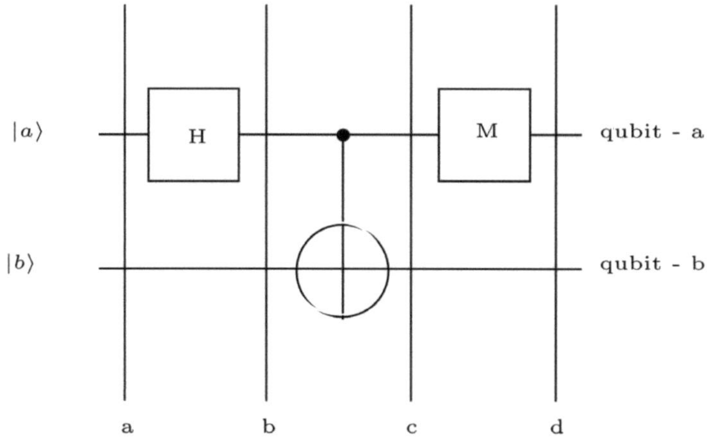

Fig. 2. EPR producing circuit

$$
\begin{aligned}
|ab\rangle &\rightarrow (H \otimes W)|ab\rangle \\
&= \frac{1}{\sqrt{2}}(|0\rangle + |1\rangle)|0\rangle \\
&= \frac{1}{\sqrt{2}}(|00\rangle + |10\rangle) = \begin{bmatrix} \frac{1}{\sqrt{2}} \\ 0 \\ \frac{1}{\sqrt{2}} \\ 0 \end{bmatrix}
\end{aligned} \tag{7}
$$

Next the application of the CNOT gate results in:

$$
|\psi_a\psi_b\rangle = \frac{1}{\sqrt{2}} \begin{pmatrix} 1 & 0 & 0 & 0 \\ 0 & 1 & 0 & 0 \\ 0 & 0 & 0 & 1 \\ 0 & 0 & 1 & 0 \end{pmatrix} \times \begin{pmatrix} 1 \\ 0 \\ 1 \\ 0 \end{pmatrix} = \frac{1}{\sqrt{2}} \begin{pmatrix} 1 \\ 0 \\ 0 \\ 1 \end{pmatrix} = \frac{1}{\sqrt{2}}(|00\rangle + |11\rangle) \tag{8}
$$

For an output 0 (on the qubit-a), the projective measurement of the first (topmost) qubit (qubit-a on Figure 2) on this stage would collapse the global state (with a single measurement) to the state $|00\rangle$:

$$
|ab\rangle \rightarrow \frac{M_0|ab\rangle}{\sqrt{\langle ab|M_0^{\dagger} M_0|ab\rangle}} = \begin{bmatrix} 1 & 0 & 0 & 0 \end{bmatrix}^T = |00\rangle \tag{9}
$$

with

$$
M_0|ab\rangle = \frac{1}{\sqrt{2}} \begin{bmatrix} 1 & 0 & 0 & 0 \\ 0 & 1 & 0 & 0 \\ 0 & 0 & 0 & 0 \\ 0 & 0 & 0 & 0 \end{bmatrix} \begin{bmatrix} 1 \\ 0 \\ 0 \\ 1 \end{bmatrix} = \frac{1}{\sqrt{2}} \begin{bmatrix} 1 \\ 0 \\ 0 \\ 0 \end{bmatrix} \tag{10}
$$

and

$$\begin{aligned}\sqrt{\langle ab|M_0^\dagger M_0|ab\rangle} &= \sqrt{\frac{1}{2}}\begin{bmatrix}1 & 0 & 0 & 1\end{bmatrix}\begin{bmatrix}1 & 0 & 0 & 0\\0 & 1 & 0 & 0\\0 & 0 & 0 & 0\\0 & 0 & 0 & 0\end{bmatrix}\begin{bmatrix}1\\0\\0\\1\end{bmatrix}\\ &= \frac{1}{\sqrt{2}}\begin{bmatrix}1 & 0 & 0 & 1\end{bmatrix}\begin{bmatrix}1\\0\\0\\0\end{bmatrix}\\ &= \frac{1}{\sqrt{2}}\end{aligned} \tag{11}$$

Similarly, the probability of measuring output on the qubit-a in state $|0\rangle$ is:

$$\begin{aligned}p(0) &= \begin{bmatrix}\frac{1}{\sqrt{2}} & 0 & 0 & \frac{1}{\sqrt{2}}\end{bmatrix}\left(\begin{bmatrix}1 & 0 & 0 & 0\\0 & 0 & 0 & 0\\0 & 0 & 0 & 0\\0 & 0 & 0 & 0\end{bmatrix} + \begin{bmatrix}0 & 0 & 0 & 0\\0 & 1 & 0 & 0\\0 & 0 & 0 & 0\\0 & 0 & 0 & 0\end{bmatrix}\right)\begin{bmatrix}\frac{1}{\sqrt{2}}\\0\\0\\\frac{1}{\sqrt{2}}\end{bmatrix}\\ &= \begin{bmatrix}\frac{1}{\sqrt{2}} & 0 & 0 & \frac{1}{\sqrt{2}}\end{bmatrix}\begin{bmatrix}1 & 0 & 0 & 0\\0 & 1 & 0 & 0\\0 & 0 & 0 & 0\\0 & 0 & 0 & 0\end{bmatrix}\begin{bmatrix}\frac{1}{\sqrt{2}}\\0\\0\\\frac{1}{\sqrt{2}}\end{bmatrix}\\ &= \frac{1}{2}\end{aligned} \tag{12}$$

If one would look to the output of the measurement on the second qubit (qubit-b), the probability for obtaining $|0\rangle$ or $|1\rangle$ is in this case the following:

$$\begin{aligned}p(0) &= \begin{bmatrix}\frac{1}{\sqrt{2}} & 0 & 0 & \frac{1}{\sqrt{2}}\end{bmatrix}\left(\begin{bmatrix}1 & 0 & 0 & 0\\0 & 0 & 0 & 0\\0 & 0 & 0 & 0\\0 & 0 & 0 & 0\end{bmatrix} + \begin{bmatrix}0 & 0 & 0 & 0\\0 & 0 & 0 & 0\\0 & 0 & 1 & 0\\0 & 0 & 0 & 0\end{bmatrix}\right)\begin{bmatrix}\frac{1}{\sqrt{2}}\\0\\0\\\frac{1}{\sqrt{2}}\end{bmatrix}\\ &= \begin{bmatrix}\frac{1}{\sqrt{2}} & 0 & 0 & \frac{1}{\sqrt{2}}\end{bmatrix}\begin{bmatrix}1 & 0 & 0 & 0\\0 & 0 & 0 & 0\\0 & 0 & 1 & 0\\0 & 0 & 0 & 0\end{bmatrix}\begin{bmatrix}\frac{1}{\sqrt{2}}\\0\\0\\\frac{1}{\sqrt{2}}\end{bmatrix}\\ &= p(1) = \frac{1}{2}\end{aligned} \tag{13}$$

Thus the expectation values for measuring both values 0 or 1 on each qubit independently are $\frac{1}{2}$.

If however one looks on the second and non-measured qubit (if the qubit-a is measured, it is the qubit-b, and vice versa) and calculates the output probabilities, the output is contradictory to the expectations given by standard probabilistic distribution such as a coin toss $q = 1 - p$. To see this let's start in the state

$$\begin{bmatrix} \frac{1}{\sqrt{2}} \\ 0 \\ 0 \\ \frac{1}{\sqrt{2}} \end{bmatrix} \tag{14}$$

and measure the qubit-a and obtain a result. In this case assume the result of the measurement is given by:

$$|\Psi\rangle \to \frac{M_0|\Psi\rangle}{\sqrt{\langle\Psi|M_0^\dagger M_0|\Psi\rangle}} = \begin{bmatrix} 1 \\ 0 \\ 0 \\ 0 \end{bmatrix} \tag{15}$$

Then measuring the second qubit (qubit-b) will not affect the system because the measurement of the qubit-a has collapsed the whole system into a single basis state:

$$|\Psi\rangle \xrightarrow{M} |00\rangle \tag{16}$$

The probability for obtaining a $|1\rangle$ on the qubit-b is thus 0 and the measurement on qubit-b (after having measured qubit-a) has no effect on the system at all. The states of qubits are thus correlated. This non-locality paradox was first described by Einstein-Podolsky-Rosen work[EPR35] and is known as the EPR paradox. This particular phenomenon is one of the most powerful in quantum mechanics and quantum computing, as it allows together with superposition the speedup of finding solutions to certain types of problems. Finally, it can be noted that mathematically, the entangled state is such that it cannot be factored into simpler terms. For example, the state $\frac{(|00\rangle+|01\rangle)}{\sqrt{2}} \to \frac{1}{\sqrt{2}}(|0\rangle+|1\rangle)|0\rangle$ and thus it can be factored. However, the states as those introduced in eq. 15 cannot be transformed in such a manner and are thus entangled; physically implying that they are related through measurement or observation. □

2.3 Single-Qubit quantum gates

We are now concerned with matrix representation of operators. The first class of important quantum operators are the one-qubit operators realized in the quantum circuit as the one-qubit (quantum) gates. Some of their matrix representations can be seen in equation 17.

$$\begin{array}{lll} a)\ X = \begin{bmatrix} 0 & 1 \\ 1 & 0 \end{bmatrix} & b)\ Y = \begin{bmatrix} 0 & -i \\ i & 0 \end{bmatrix} & c)\ Z = \begin{bmatrix} 1 & 0 \\ 0 & -1 \end{bmatrix} \\ d)\ H = \frac{1}{\sqrt{2}}\begin{bmatrix} 1 & 1 \\ 1 & -1 \end{bmatrix} & e)\ V = \frac{(1+i)}{2}\begin{bmatrix} 1 & -i \\ -i & 1 \end{bmatrix} & f)\ Phase = \begin{bmatrix} 1 & 0 \\ 0 & i \end{bmatrix} \end{array} \tag{17}$$

Each matrix of an Operator has its inputs from the top (from left to right) and the outputs on the side (from top to bottom). Thus taking a state $|\psi\rangle$ (eq.18) and an unitary operator H (eq. 19)

$$|\Psi\rangle = \alpha|0\rangle + \beta|1\rangle \tag{18}$$

$$H = \frac{1}{\sqrt{2}} \begin{bmatrix} 1 & 1 \\ 1 & -1 \end{bmatrix} \quad (19)$$

the result of computation is represented in equation 20.

$$H|\Psi\rangle = \frac{1}{\sqrt{2}} \begin{bmatrix} 1 & 1 \\ 1 & -1 \end{bmatrix} \begin{bmatrix} \alpha \\ \beta \end{bmatrix} = \begin{bmatrix} \frac{\alpha+\beta}{\sqrt{2}} \\ \frac{\alpha-\beta}{\sqrt{2}} \end{bmatrix} \quad (20)$$

$$U = \begin{matrix} \\ \\ 00 \leftarrow \\ 01 \leftarrow \\ 10 \leftarrow \\ 11 \leftarrow \end{matrix} \begin{matrix} 00 & 01 & 10 & 11 \\ \downarrow & \downarrow & \downarrow & \downarrow \\ 1 & 0 & 0 & 0 \\ 0 & 1 & 0 & 0 \\ 0 & 0 & 0 & 1 \\ 0 & 0 & 1 & 0 \end{matrix} \quad (21)$$

Equation 21 shows the inputs (input minterms) on the top of the matrix and the output minterms on the left side. Thus for an input $|10\rangle$ (from the top) the output is $|11\rangle$ (from the side).

2.4 Multi-Qubit quantum gates

The second class of quantum gates includes the Controlled-U gates. Schematic representation of such gates can be seen in Figure 3. Gates in Figure 3a – Figure 3c represent the general structures for single-control-qubit single-qubit gate, two-control-qubit single-qubit gate, single-control-qubit two-qubit gate and two-control-qubit two-qubit gate respectively. The reason for calling these gates *Controlled* is the fact that they are based on two operations: first there is one or more control bits and second there is a unitary transformation similar to matrices from equation 17 that is controlled. For instance the Feynman gate is a Controlled-NOT gate and has two input qubits a and b as can be seen in

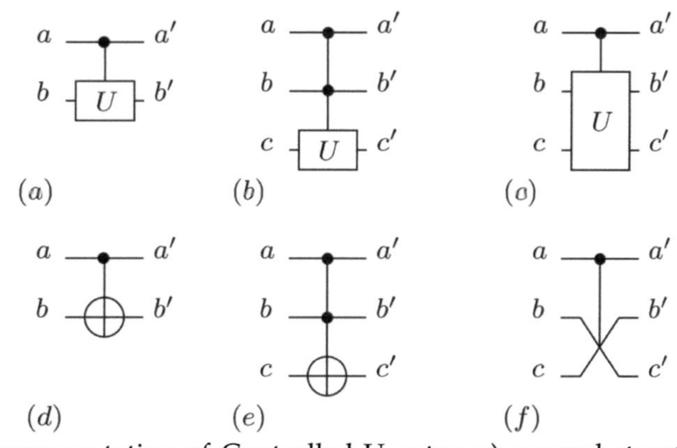

Fig. 3. Schematic representation of Controlled-U gates: a) general structure of single-qubit controlled-U gate (control qubit a, target qubit, b) two-qubit controlled, single-qubit operation, c) single-qubit controlled, two-qubit target quantum gate, d) Feynman (CNOT), e) Toffoli (CCNOT), f) Fredkin. a, b, c are input qubits and a′, b′ and c′ are respective outputs.

Figure 3. Its unitary matrix with input and output minters is shown in eq. (21). Thus qubits controlling the gate are called the control qubits and the qubits on which the unitary transform is applied to are called the target qubits.
Figures 3d - Figure 3f represent special cases where the controlled unitary operator is Not, Not and Swap, respectively. The respective unitary matrices are in equations 21, 22a and 22b.
Equation 21 shows that if the input state is for instance |00⟩ (from the top) the output is given by $U|00\rangle = p_{00}|00\rangle = 1 \times |00\rangle$. Similarly for all other possible input /output combinations.

$$(a) \begin{bmatrix} 1&0&0&0&0&0&0&0\\ 0&1&0&0&0&0&0&0\\ 0&0&1&0&0&0&0&0\\ 0&0&0&1&0&0&0&0\\ 0&0&0&0&1&0&0&0\\ 0&0&0&0&0&1&0&0\\ 0&0&0&0&0&0&\mathbf{0}&\mathbf{1}\\ 0&0&0&0&0&0&\mathbf{1}&\mathbf{0} \end{bmatrix} \quad (b) \begin{bmatrix} 1&0&0&0&0&0&0&0\\ 0&1&0&0&0&0&0&0\\ 0&0&1&0&0&0&0&0\\ 0&0&0&1&0&0&0&0\\ 0&0&0&0&1&0&0&0\\ 0&0&0&0&0&\mathbf{0}&\mathbf{1}&0\\ 0&0&0&0&0&\mathbf{1}&\mathbf{0}&0\\ 0&0&0&0&0&0&0&1 \end{bmatrix} \qquad (22)$$

The *Controlled-U* gate means that while the controlled qubit a is equal to 0 the qubits on output of both wires are the same as they were before entering the gate (a′ = a, b′ = b). Now if qubit a equals to 1, the result is a′ = a and b′ = ¬b according to matrix in equation (17.a). It can be easily verified that the CCNOT (Toffoli) gate is just a Feynman gate with one more control qubit and the Fredkin gate is a controlled swap as shown on Figure 3.
A closer look at equations (21 and 22) gives more explanation about what is described in eq. 21: CNOT, eq. 22*a* : Toffoli and eq. 22*b* : Fredkin gates. For instance, equation 21 shows that while the system is in states |00⟩ and |01⟩ the output of the circuit is a copy of the input. For the inputs |10⟩ and |11⟩ the second output is inverted and it can be seen that the right-lower corner of the matrix is the NOT gate. Similarly in the other two Controlled gates the NOT gate matrix can be found.

2.5 NMR-based quantum logic gates

The NMR (Nuclear Magnetic Resonance) technology approach to quantum computing [Moo65, PW02, DKK03] is the most advanced quantum realization technology used so far, mainly because it was used to implement the Shor algorithm [Sho94] with 7 qubits [NC00]. Yet other technologies such as Ion trap [DiV95], Josephson Junction [DiV95] or cavity QED [BZ00] are being used. The NMR quantum computing has been reviewed in details in [PW02, DKK03] and for this paper it is important that it was so far the NMR computer that allowed the most advanced algorithm (7 qubit logic operation) to be practically realized and analyzed in details. Thus it is based on this technology that the constraints of the synthesis are going to be established for the cost and function evaluation. Some prior work on synthesis has been also already published [LLK+06] and few simple cost functions have been established.
For the NMR-constrained logic synthesis the conditions are:

- Single qubit operations: rotations R_x, R_y, R_z for various degrees of rotation θ. With each unitary rotation (R_x, R_y, R_z) represented in equation 23

$$
\begin{aligned}
R_x(\theta) &= e^{-i\theta X/2} = cos\frac{\theta}{2}I - isin\frac{\theta}{2}X = \begin{pmatrix} cos(\frac{\theta}{2}) & -isin(\frac{\theta}{2}) \\ -isin(\frac{\theta}{2}) & cos(\frac{\theta}{2}) \end{pmatrix} \\
R_y(\theta) &= e^{-i\theta Y/2} = cos\frac{\theta}{2}I - isin\frac{\theta}{2}Y = \begin{pmatrix} cos(\frac{\theta}{2}) & -sin(\frac{\theta}{2}) \\ sin(\frac{\theta}{2}) & cos(\frac{\theta}{2}) \end{pmatrix} \\
R_z(\theta) &= e^{-i\theta Z/2} = cos\frac{\theta}{2}I - isin\frac{\theta}{2}Z = \begin{pmatrix} e^{-i\theta/2} & 0 \\ 0 & e^{i\theta/2} \end{pmatrix}
\end{aligned}
\quad (23)
$$

- Two-qubit operation; depending on approach the Interaction operator is used as J_{zz} or J_{xy} for various rotations θ

Thus a quantum circuit realized in NMR will be exclusively built from single qubit rotations about three axes x,y,z and from the two-neighbor-qubit operation of interaction allowing to realize such primitives as CNOT or SWAP gates. Examples of gates realized using NMR quantum primitives are shown in Figure 5 to Figure 8.

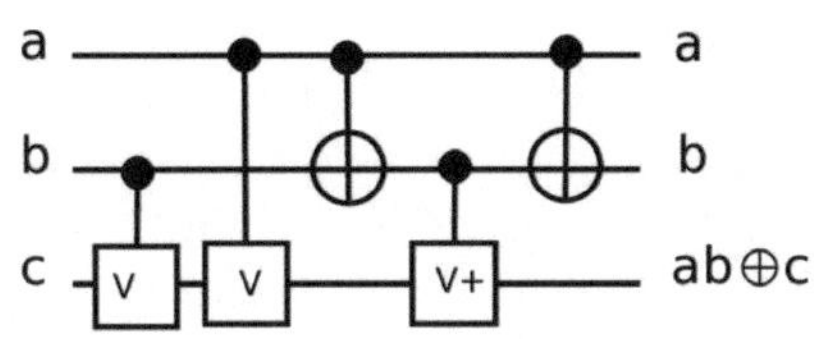

Fig. 4. Structure of the Toffoli gate

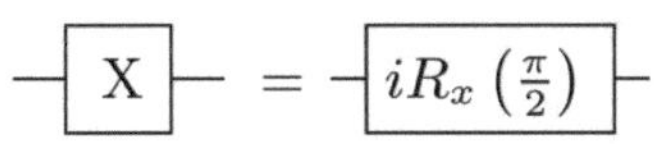

Fig. 5. Single pulse Logic gate - NOT

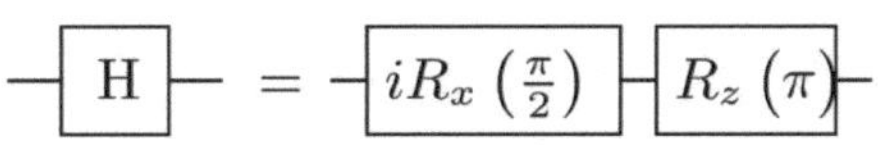

Fig. 6. Two-pulses logic gate - Hadamard

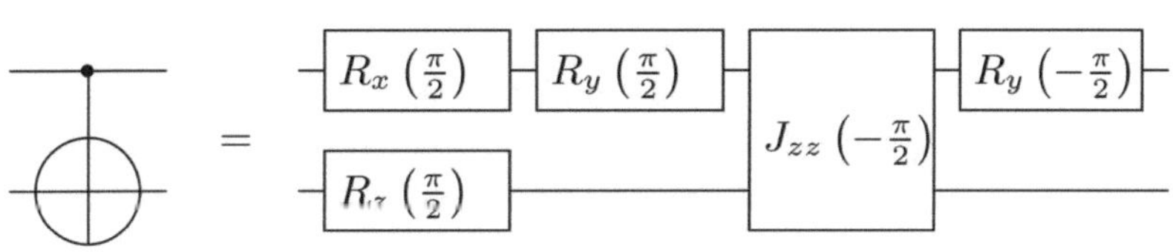

Fig. 7. Detailed Realization of Feynman Gate with five EM pulses.

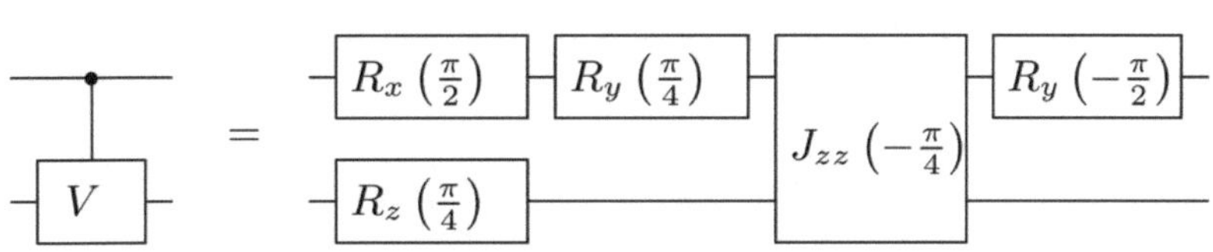

Fig. 8. Five-pulses logic gate - Controlled-V

Also, the synthesis using the NMR computing model using EM pulses, is common to other technologies such as Ion Trap [CZ95, PW02] or Josephson Junction [BZ00]. Thus the cost model used here can be applied to synthesize circuits in various technologies, all of these technologies having the possibility to express the implemented logic as a sequence of EM pulses.

3. Quantum finite state machines

The paradigms of quantum circuits from Section 2 are applied in this paper to the synthesis of computational models such as QFSM as defined in [LPK09]. This section briefly introduces the knowledge about Quantum computational models and their properties as well as specifies the types of devices that are going to be synthesized. We describe the 1-way Quantum Finite State Machines (FSM) from both the theoretical (computational) point of view as well as from the engineering (circuit) point of view. Most of the work in this area is still on the theoretical level but the proofs of concept quantum devices [Dun98, SKT04, MC06, RCHCX+08, YCS09] allow to speculate that such models will be useful for quantum logical devices that will appear in close future.

3.1 1-way quantum finite automata

Quantum Finite State Machines (QFSM) are a natural extension of classical (probabilistic) FSM's. Two main types of QFSM are well known: One-way QFSM (1QFSM) [AF98, MC00] and two-way QFSM (2QFSM)[AW02, KW97]. As will be illustrated and explained the 1QFSM, can accept sequentially classical input, quantize it, process it and measures its quantum memory after each operation (Figure 9). In this work the focus is on the synthesis of the 1QFSM from Figure 9(b). From now on the general designation of QFSM will refer to 1QFSM in this work. Other type of described QFSMs will be specifically named.

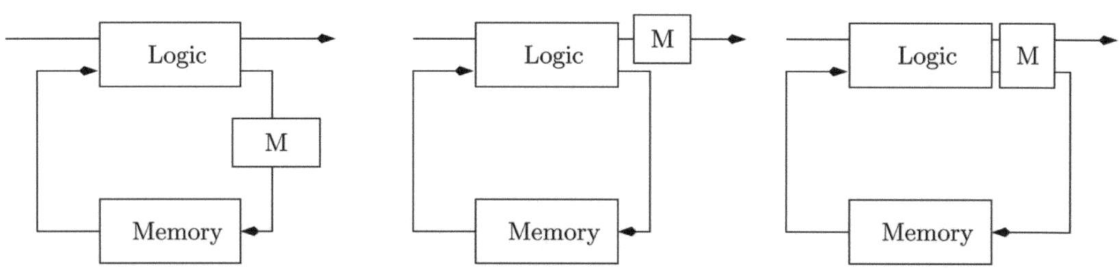

Fig. 9. Schematic representation of a 1QFSM; (a) after each computation step the machine state is measured, (b) after each computation step the output is measured, (c) after each computational step the machine state and the output state are measured.

In contrast to that, the 2QFSM is designed to operate on quantum input data (allowing to put the reading head in superposition with the input tape, and requiring all the input data to be present at once for the maximum efficiency) and the measurement is done only at the end of a whole process.

Definition 3.1

Quantum State Machine - a QFSM is a tuple $\Gamma = \{Q, \Lambda, q_0, Q_{ac}, Q_{rjI}, \delta\}$, where Q is a finite set of states, σ is the input alphabet, δ is the transition function. The states $q_0 \in Q'$, $Q_{ac} \subset Q$ and $Q_{rj} \subset Q$ are the initial states, the set of accepting states and the set of rejected states, respectively. □

The QFSM machine action maps the set of machine states and the set of input symbols into the set of complex machine next states. The computation of such machine is required to be done using unitary operators and is performed on the basis set B^q using unitary operators $U\theta$, $\theta \in \Theta$. In particular the QFSM uses a set of Unitary Operators corresponding to the input of input characters on the input tape. Thus for a given string to be processed and prior to the whole process termination (string either accepted or rejected), the overall processing can be represented as:

$$MU_{\theta_n} MU_{\theta_n - 1} MU_{\theta_n - 2} \dots MU_{\theta_3} MU_{\theta_2} MU_{\theta_1} |q_0\rangle \tag{24}$$

with MU_{θ_n} being the application of the U_{θ_n} operator to the current state and creating the configuration $U_{\theta_n} | q\rangle$ followed by the measurement of the current state M (projecting the state into G).

The 1QFSM was proven to be less powerful or equally powerful to its classical counterpart 1FSM [Gru99, KW97] in that it can recognize the same classes of regular languages as the classical FSM can recognize.

The above described 1QFSM is also called the measure-many quantum finite automaton [KW97]. A model called measure-once quantum finite automata was also introduced and studied by Moore [MC00]. The measure-many 1QFSM is similar to the concepts of the 2QFSM. For comparison we illustrate the main differences between the 1QFSM and 2QFSM below.

Example 3.1.1 1QFSM

Let $Q = \{|q_0\rangle, |q_1\rangle\}$be two possible states (including the accepting and rejecting states) of a single-qubit machine M and with transition functions specified by the transitions defined in eq. 25 corresponding to the state diagram in Figure 10a.

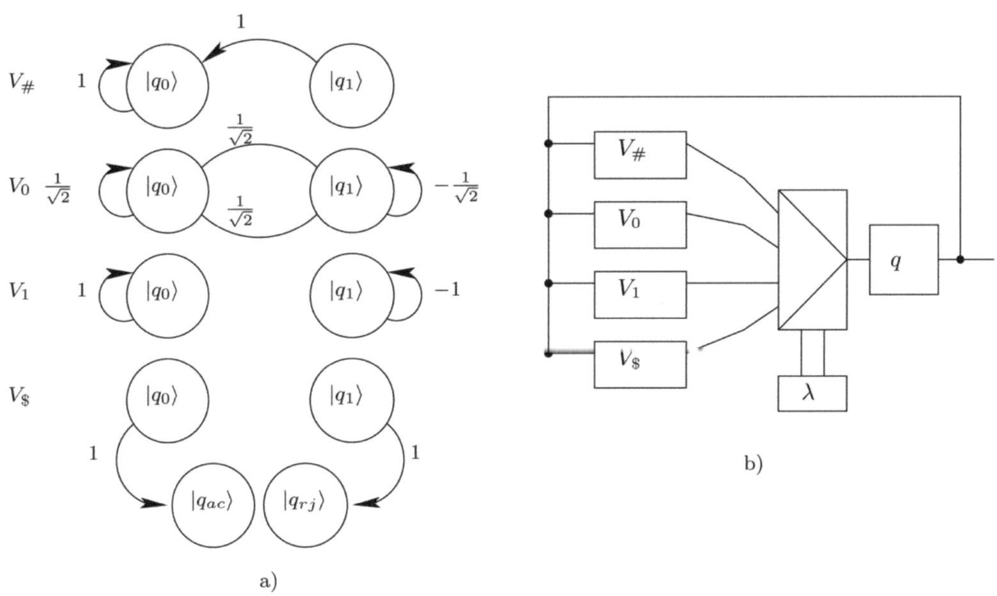

Fig. 10. (a) State transition diagram for the 1QFSM defined by the transition function 25, (b) the representation of the QFSM using quantum multiplexers. Observe two control outputs $| q \rangle$ specifying the machine action/states and the input symbols selecting the appropriate unitary transform V_λ for $\lambda \subset \{\#, \$, 0, 1\}$.

$$
\begin{aligned}
V_{\#}|q_i\rangle &= |q_0\rangle \\
V_{\$}|q_0\rangle &= |q_{ac}\rangle \\
V_{\$}|q_1\rangle &= |q_{rj}\rangle
\end{aligned}
\qquad
\begin{aligned}
V_0|q_0\rangle &= \frac{1}{\sqrt{2}}|q_0\rangle + \frac{1}{\sqrt{2}}|q_1\rangle \\
V_0|q_1\rangle &= \frac{1}{\sqrt{2}}|q_0\rangle - \frac{1}{\sqrt{2}}|q_1\rangle \\
V_1|q_0\rangle &= |q_0\rangle \\
V_1|q_1\rangle &= -|q_1\rangle
\end{aligned}
\tag{25}
$$

The machine M, specified in eq. 25 represents a state machine that uses the H gate when the input is 0 ($V_0 = H$) and the Pauli-Z rotation gate when the input is 1 ($V_1 = Z$). Observe that machine M would have different behavior for measure-once and measure-many implementation. In the measure-many case, the machine generates a quantum coin-flip while receiving input 0 and while receiving input 1 the Pauli-Z rotation is applied. Observe in the measure-once case, that for example for the string input θ = "010" the many-measure machine will implement a NOT using $[H][Z][H]$. □

Note that in this approach to QFSM each input symbol $\lambda \in \{\#, \$, 0, 1\}$ is represented by a unitary transform that can be seen as shown in Figure 10. No measurement is done here on $|q\rangle$ while the sequence of quantum operators is applied to this state. The 2QFSM operates on a similar principle as the 1QFSM model but with the main difference being the application of the measurement. This is schematically shown in Figure 11 for the completeness of explanation.

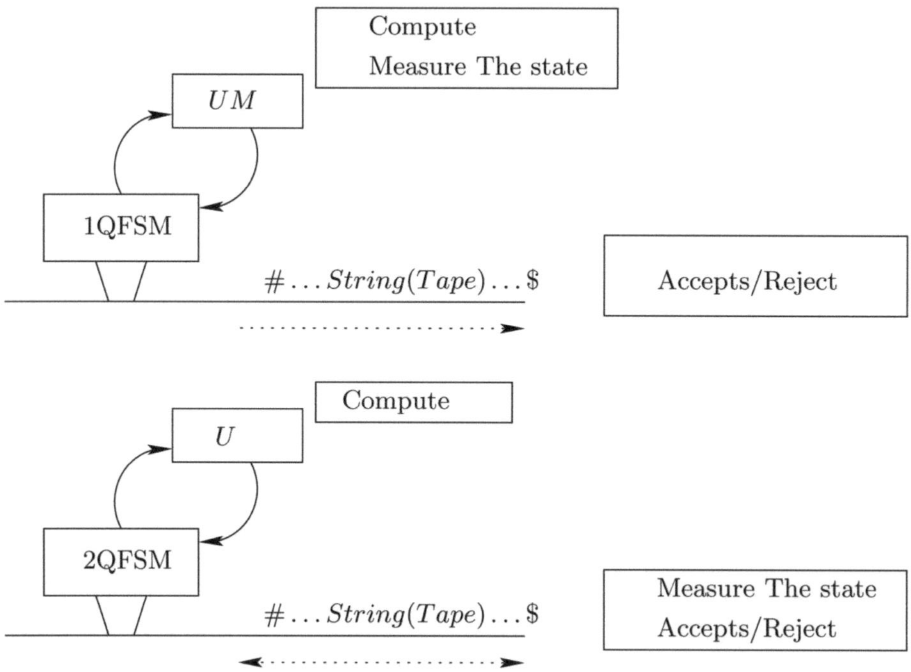

Fig. 11. Schematics representing the difference between the 1QFSM and 2QFSM. On the top, the 1QFSM - for each input character read from left to right from the tape, a unitary transform U is applied on the state and the state is measured. On the bottom, the 2QFSM moves on the input tape left and right, the unitary transform U is applied on the state and only once the computation is terminated the final state is observed/measured.

3.2 Quantum logic synthesis of sequence detectors

The problem to synthesize the QFSM is to find the simplest quantum circuit for a given set of input-output sequences thus letting the state assignment problem for this machine be directly solved by our synthesis algorithm. This direct synthesis approach can be applied to binary, multiple-valued and fuzzy quantum machines with no principle differences - only fitness functions are modified in an evolutionary algorithm [LPG+03, LP05].

Let us assume that there exists a sequential oracle that represents for instance Nature, robot control or robot's environment. In our example this oracle is specified by a state diagram in Figure 12a. This oracle can represent partial knowledge and a deterministic or probabilistic machine of any kind. Assume that there is a clearing signal (denoted by an arrow in Figure 12a) to set the oracle into its initial state. By giving initial signals and input sequences and observing output sequences the observer can create a behavior tree from Figure 12b.

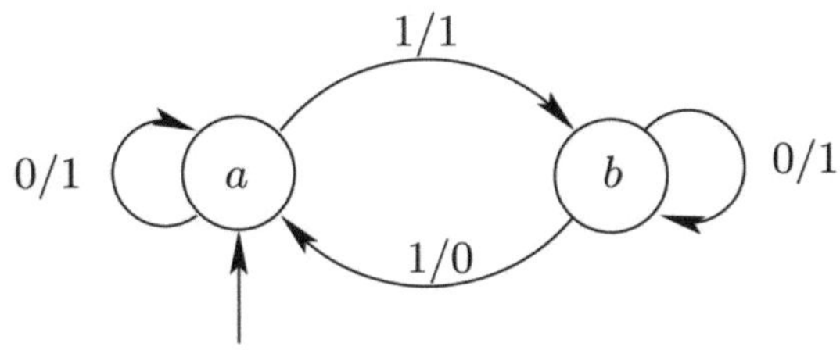

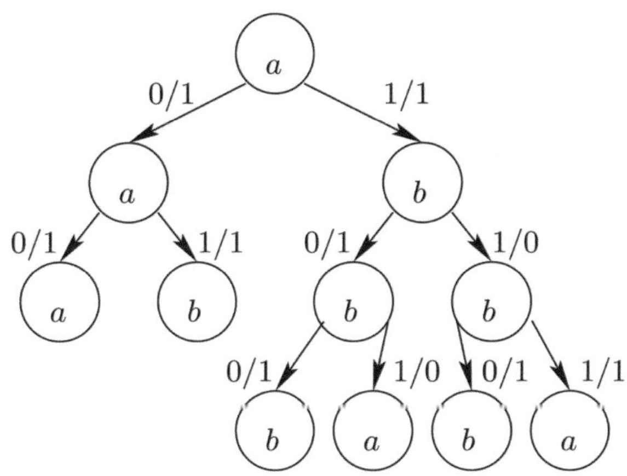

Fig. 12. Example of a deterministic oracle and its diagnostic tree.

As in general this oracle is never fully known, we perform experiments with it to determine some of its input-output behaviors. Assume that the oracle from Figure 12a is represented by the sequences from the experiments. These input-output sequences are shown in eq. 26 with $|iqo\rangle$ represents the input qubit, the state qubit and the output qubit respectively. Observe that the diagnostic tree form Figure 12(b) shows the state with $\{a, b\}$ and the inputs and the outputs as 0 and 1.

$$\begin{aligned}
|iq0\rangle &\rightarrow |iqo\rangle \\
000 &\rightarrow 011 \\
001 &\rightarrow 011 \\
100 &\rightarrow 111 \\
101 &\rightarrow 110 \\
110 &\rightarrow 101 \\
111 &\rightarrow 101
\end{aligned} \tag{26}$$

As the full knowledge of the oracle is in general impossible - the oracle is approximated by sets of input-output sequences and the more such sequences that we create - the more accurate characterization of the oracle as a QFSM can be created.

The overall procedure for the detection of a sequence of length j can be summarized as follows:

1. Initialize all qubits of the quantum register to the initial desired state,
2. repeat j times:
   a. Initialize the input qubit to a desired state and set the output qubit to $|0\rangle$
   b. Apply the quantum operator on the quantum register of the QFSM
   c. Measure the output qubit and observe the result

Using the procedure describe above one can synthesize quantum circuits for oracles being well known universal quantum gates such as Fredkin. The input-output sequences found from this oracle are next used to synthesize the QFSM from Figure 13a. Figure 13b shows the state-diagram of the machine.

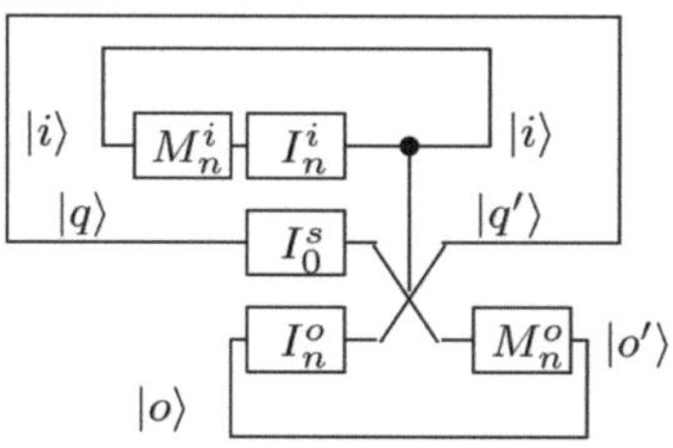

(a)

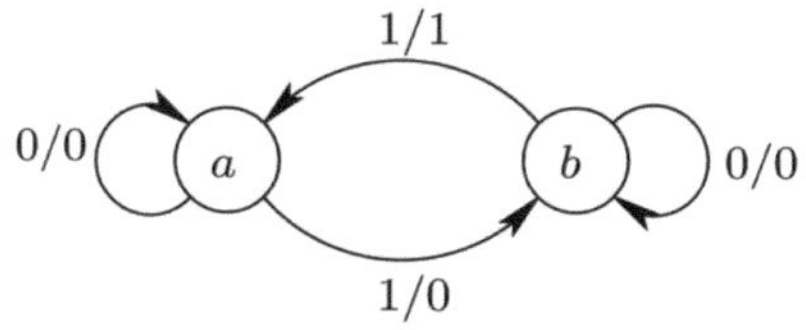

(b)

Fig. 13. Example of implementation of Fredkin gate as a quantum FSM of first class. Observe the notation where $|i\rangle$ is the input, $|q\rangle$ is the machine state and $|o\rangle$ is the machine output.

We will call the machine in Figure 13(a) the QFSM of the first class. This is because both the output and the input qubits are initialized after each computation. Observe that it is represented with feedback lines as in Figure 9 with input and output being initialized for each input and the state initialized only once - at the beginning of the computation. The interested reader can read more on this representation in [LP09], however it is important to

understand that the feedback lines are shown here only as the equivalent notation to the classical FSM as in Figure 9. The circuit-based approach to QFSM does not require this notation as this "loop" is represented by the fact that the quantum qubit preserves its state [LP09].
A set of input-output sequences defining partially the "Fredkin QFSM" is represented in eq. 27.

$$\begin{aligned} |iq0\rangle &\rightarrow |iqo\rangle \\ 000 &\rightarrow 000 \\ 001 &\rightarrow 000 \\ 100 &\rightarrow 100 \\ 101 &\rightarrow 100 \\ 110 &\rightarrow 101 \\ 111 &\rightarrow 101 \end{aligned} \tag{27}$$

A class two QFSM has in turn the initialization I_n applied only to the input qubit. This way the generated sequence is now expressed not only as a function $f(i,q)\oplus|0\rangle$ but rather as $f(i,q)\oplus|o\rangle$. This means that now the output is directly dependent also on the previous output state. This QFSM of the second class is shown in Figure 14. The difference between the QFSM of the first and of the second class can be seen on the output qubit $|o\rangle$ where in the case of the QFSM of the first class the initialization I_n^o means the initialization of the output at each computation step while the class two QFSM uses I_0^o initializes the output only once, at the beginning of the computation.

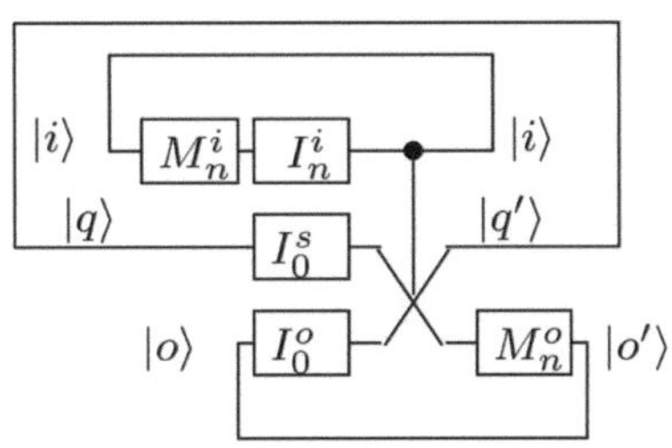

Fig. 14. Example of implementation of Fredkin gate as a quantum FSM of second class where the output is initialized only once and the measurement is done either after each input or only completely at the end.

For instance, a class two QFSM constructed from a "Fredkin oracle" differs from the class by different possible state transition. This is shown in Table 1. The first column represent the current state of the quantum register build from the input, state and output qubits $|iqo\rangle$. The second column shows the state transitions of the class one QFSM. Observe that as the output qubit is always being initialized to $|0\rangle$ only four possible initial states exists (see eq. 27). The third column representing the state transitions of the class two QFSM and as can be seen in this case the state transition function is the full "Fredkin oracle" function.
Moreover, the difference between the first and the second class of these QFSM's has also deeper implications. Observe that the QFSM presented in this paper, if implemented without the measurement on the output and the input qubit (the measurement is executed only after l computational steps) the QFSM becomes the well-known two-way QFSM

PS	NS_{one}	NS_{two}
$\|iqo\rangle$	$\|iqo\rangle$	$\|iqo\rangle$
000	000	000
001	—	001
010	010	010
011	—	011
100	100	100
101	—	110
110	101	101
111	—	111

Table 1. Comparison of the state transition between the class one and class two QFSMs

[KW97] because the machine can be in superposition with the input and the output. This is equivalent to stating that the reading head of a QFSM is in superposition with the input tape as required for the time-quadratic recognition of the $\{a^n b^n\}$ language [KW97].

Observe that to represent the 1-way and the 2-way QFSM in the circuit notation the main difference is in the missing measurement operations between the application of the different *CU* (Controlled-U) operations. This is represented in Figures 15 and 16 for 1-way and the 2-way QFSMs, respectively.

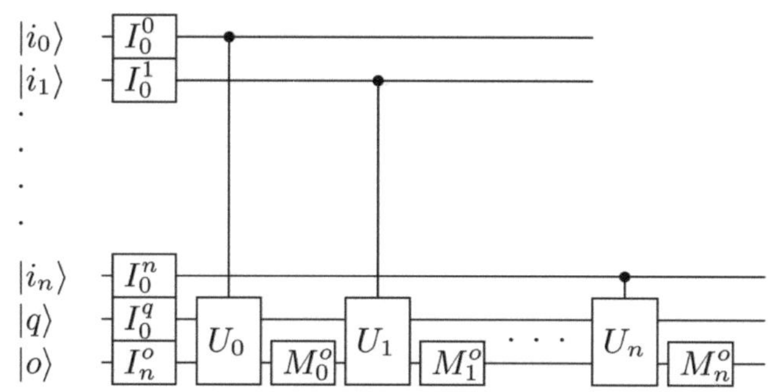

Fig. 15. Example of circuit implementing 1-way QFSM.

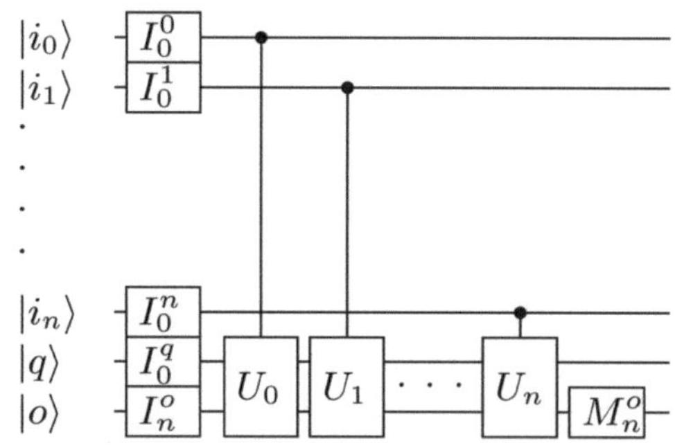

Fig. 16. Example of circuit implementing 2-way QFSM.

An interesting example of QFSM is a machine with quantum controls signals. For instance a circuit with the input qubit in the superposition generating the EPR quantum state [NC00] is shown in Figure 17.

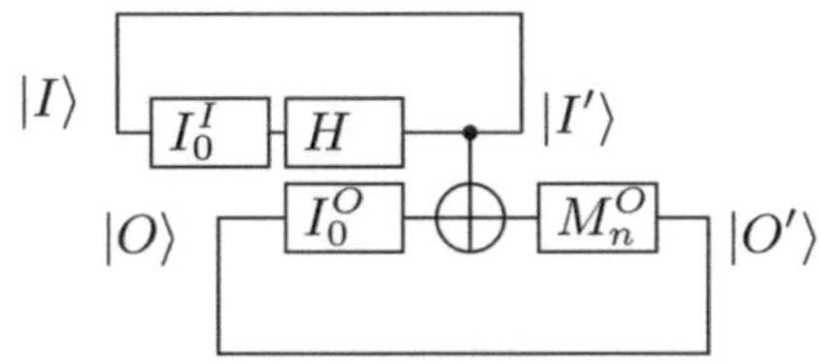

Fig. 17. Example of the EPR circuit used as a QFSM.

Observe the behavior of this QFSM as both class one and class two machine given in Table 2. In this case the distinction between the class one and class two machines is negligible because any measurement of the system collapses the whole system as the result of the entanglement present in it.

PS	NS_{one}	NS_{two}
$\|iqo\rangle$	$\|iqo\rangle$	$\|iqo\rangle$
00	00+11	00+11
01	-	01+10
11	-	00+11
10	01+10	01+10

Table 2. Comparison of the state transition between the class one and class two EPR circuit QFSM

Figure 17 shows that because of the entanglement this machine has two distinct possible recognizable sequences. When the machine uses exclusively the output qubit initialized to $|0\rangle$ the possible initial states are only $|00\rangle$ and $|10\rangle$ because the measurement of the output state resulting in $|11\rangle \xrightarrow{I_n^0} |10\rangle$ and $|01\rangle \xrightarrow{I_n^0} |00\rangle$.

4. Evolutionary algorithms and quantum logic synthesis

In general the evolutionary problem solving can be split into two main categories; not separated by the methods that each of the trends are using but rather by the problem representation and by the type of problem solved. On one hand, there is the Genetic Algorithm (GA) [Gol89, GKD89] and Evolutionary strategies (ES) [Bey01, Sch95] that in general represents the information by strings of characters/integers/floats and in general attempts to solve combinatorial problems. On the other hand the design of algorithms as well as state machines was traditionally done by the Genetic Programming (GP) [Koz94, KBA99] and the Evolutionary Programming (EP) [FOW66, ES03].

Each of this approaches has its particular advantages and each of them has been already more or less successfully applied to the Quantum Logic synthesis. In the EQLS field the main body of research was done using the Genetic Programming (GP) for the synthesis of either quantum algorithms and programs [WG98, Spe04, Lei04, MCS04] or some specific types of quantum circuits[WG98, Rub01, SBS05, SBS08, LB04, MCS05]. While the GP approach has been quite active area of research the Genetic Algorithm approach is less popular and recently only [LP08, YI00] were using a Genetic Algorithm for the synthesis of quantum circuits. However, it was shown in [LP09] that it is also possible to synthesize quantum finite state machines specified as quantum circuit using a GA. The difference between the popularity of the usage between the GP and the GA for EQLS is mainly due to fact that the problem space of quantum computing is not well known and is extremely large. Thus synthesizing quantum algorithms or circuits using the circuit approach (as in GA) can be much harder than using a rule-based or a program based approach (as in GP). Thus one could conclude that the GP approach deals only with the required information (programming, logic rules, relations) while the GA circuit based approach synthesize the overall unitary operator without any regards to the structure of the required information itself.

5. Genetic algorithm

A Genetic algorithm is a set of directed random processes that make probabilistic decisions - simulated evolution. Table 3 shows the general structure of a GA algorithm used in this work and this section follows this structure with the focus on the information encoding in the individuals and on the evaluation of the designed QFSMs that are created by the GA.

```
t ← 0;
initialize(P(t));                               /* initial population */
while (not termination-condition) do
evaluate(P(t));                                 /* evaluate fitness */
t ← t + 1;
Q_s(t) ← select(P(t ← 1));                      /* selection operator */
Q_r(t) ← recombine(Qs(t));                      /* crossover operator */
P(t) ← mutate(Q_r(t));                          /* mutation operator */
end while
```

Table 3. Structure of a Genetic Algorithm

5.1 Encoding/Representation

For quantum logic synthesis the representation that we use is based on the encoding introduced in [LPMP02]. This representation allows to describe any Quantum or Reversible circuit [LPG+03, LP02]. All individuals in the GA are strings of ordered characters (each character representing a quantum gate) partitioned into parallel Blocks (Figure 18). Each block has as many inputs and outputs as the width of the quantum array (five in the case

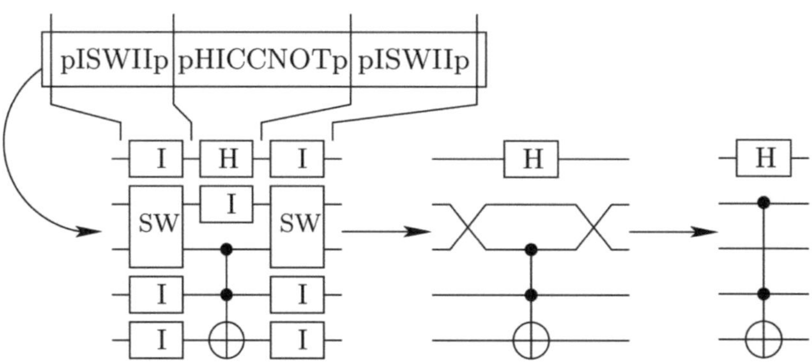

Fig. 18. Transformation of a QC from the chromosome (on the top) encoded string, to a final quantum circuit notation representation of this QC (on the right). Here *SW* is a Swap gate, H is a Hadamard gate and I is a Identity. In the middle there is one *CCNOT* (Toffoli) gate.

of Figure 18). The chromosome of each individual is a string of characters with two types of tags. First a group of characters is used to represent the set of possible gates that can be used in the individual string representation. Second, a single character 'p' is used as a separator between parallel blocks of quantum gates. An example of a chromosome can be seen in Figure 18. In this encoding each space (empty wire or a gate) is represented by a character with appropriate decoding shown. Our problem-specific encoding was applied to allow the construction of as simple genetic operators as possible. The advantage of these strings is that they allow encoding of an arbitrary QL or RL circuit without any additional parameters. Several such parameters were used in previous research [LPG+03, LP05] and using them made the genetic algorithm more complicated. Please note that only the possibility to move gate characters, remove and add them to the chromosome consequently make it possible to construct an arbitrary circuit and also to modify this circuit in order to optimize it.

5.2 Initialization steps of GA

The GA requires an input file (c.f. Pseudo-Code 28 and Pseudo-Code 29) which specifies all input parameters and required settings.

$$\begin{aligned}
&20 : \text{Measurement} : 1\\
&21 : \text{Measured qubits indexes:}0\\
&22 : 16\\
&22 : 0 : (1,0)\\
&23 : 1 : (1,0)\\
&\quad\vdots\\
&38 : 0 : (1,0)
\end{aligned} \tag{28}$$

However, for the clarity of explanation we focus only on particular settings required for the synthesis of the QFSM. The lines (20-38) shows the to search for a QFSM recognizing a sequence, first the measurement is required (line 20), the index of the output qubit is given (line 21) and finally the desired input sequence is given. This is done by both specifying the input value (here 0 or 1) and the probability of detection (here 1). Observe that the probabilities are specified as complex numbers with only the real component defined, e.g. (1,0). The use of complex coefficients for these observation probabilities is due to the fact that as in our previous work [LP05, Luk09] it allows to specify don't cares. For instance the coefficient (0,1) represents a logical don't care.

The GA has several other settings, (common to most of GA methods) but also requires to specify circuit specific parameters. The initial circuits are created with a random size within the interval specified by a maximal (t_{max}) and minimal number of segments (t_{min}) in each individual (chromosome). Thus the size of the chromosome is not limited during the lifetime of an individual to a precise value, rather each individual has a dynamically changing genome within the bounds defined by the above variables. The presented GA is a subclass of the Messy GA [GKD89].

Another important parameter is related to the cost of the implemented Quantum Circuit. Each evolutionary run has specified the minimal cost *MinCost* that represents the known minimum for the target function or device. If such minimal value is not known, a small value is used so that it always underestimates a possible minimal cost of the implementation. This circuit cost value is used in the cost function described in Section 5.4.1.

$$\begin{aligned}
&44 :1\\
&45 :1\\
&46 :\text{wire}\\
&47 :(1,0)(0,0)\\
&48 :(0,0)(1,0)\\
&\quad\vdots\\
&64 :2\\
&65 :1\\
&66 :\text{Controlled_V}\\
&66 :(1,0)(0,0)(0,0)(0,0)\\
&67 :(0,0)(1,0)(0,0)(0,0)\\
&68 :(0,0)(0,0)(0.5,0.5)(0.5,-0.5)\\
&69 :(0,0)(0,0)(0.5,-0.5)(0.5,0.5)
\end{aligned} \tag{29}$$

The input specifications also include the elementary quantum gates to be used as components, like the single qubit H, X, Y, Z or V gates and two qubit operations such as *CNOT* or *CV*, which are the building blocks of the quantum circuits to be found. The quantum gates are represented as quantum unitary (and Hermitian) matrices with the cost specified for each gate. This is shown in eq. 29, where for each input gate the number of wires and its cost is given as well. For instance, lines 66 to 69 in eq. 29 shows the unitary matrix of the *CV* gate[BBC+95], line 64 shows the number of qubits of this gate and the line 65 shows its cost.

Observe that each unitary matrix is specified by complex coefficients with real and imaginary component. For instance (1, 0) represents the real state while (0.5, 0.5) represents a complex state with coefficient $\frac{1+i}{2}$.

In the presented experiments various sets of Quantum gates have been used but only the most succesful runs are presented. In particular only circuits with the most common gates are shown. These gates include single-qubit gates such as Pauli rotations, the V and V† gates, two-qubit gates such as CNOT, CV and CV† and three-qubit macros such as Toffoli gates.

5.3 Evaluation of synthesis errors in sequential quantum circuits

In order to properly evaluate a a QFSM for sequence detection the measurement operation must by applied on several occasions during the detection procedure. As was explained in the section 2, a quantum system must be measured in order for the information to be obtainable and readable in the macro world. Moreover, the measurement is a vital operation if one desires to reuse a quantum state. Recently, it was proven that a unknown quantum state cannot be completely erased [PB99] but is also easily understandable by observing the nature of the quantum computing.

The simplest explanation of the impossibility of completely erase an unknown state is due to the fact that there is no such a reversible quantum operation that would bring any quantum state to let's say the $|0\rangle$ state. This is because every reversible operation is a permutation (even when it contains complex coefficients) and any operation that would achieve such a state reduction is inherently non reversible and by default non-quantum. An example of such non-reversible operation is shown in eq. 30.

$$\Xi|\psi\rangle \rightarrow |0\rangle \Leftrightarrow \Xi = \begin{pmatrix} 1 & 1 \\ 0 & 0 \end{pmatrix} \tag{30}$$

Thus measuring a quantum state allows to determine its observable and consequently allows to apply a Unitary transformation that would generate the desired state. The model of computation for Quantum Finite State Machines proposed in [LPK09] is used here as model. Figure 19 shows steps of evaluation of a sequential Quantum Circuit. Observe that this QFSM has one qubit $|q\rangle$ for state, one qubit $|i\rangle$ for input and one qubit $|o\rangle$ for output. From the classical point of view this can be seen as an instance of a Mealy finite state machine.

The synthesis process generates a unitary transformation matrix U, that during the evaluation is applied to the sequence of quantum states. Observe that both the input qubit and the output qubit must be measured in order to preserve a valid quantum state qubit $|q\rangle$ as well as allow to properly restore both the input and the output qubit. After each iteration of the computation (application of the U operator) the output qubit is set to $|0\rangle$ while the input qubit is set to either $|0\rangle$ or $|1\rangle$ depending on the the user specifications from the input file.

Equation 31 shows the first and the last step of the QFSM evaluation for the detection of the input sequence starting with $s = \{10011001110001\}$. Note that the detection requires that for all the input values but the last one the output qubit is set to $|0\rangle$ and is set to $|1\rangle$ for the last character.

$$\begin{aligned}
|000\rangle &\xrightarrow{I_1^1} |010\rangle \\
|010\rangle &\xrightarrow{U} |\psi\rangle \\
|\psi\rangle &\xrightarrow{M^0} |\rho\rangle \otimes |o\rangle \\
|\rho\rangle \otimes |o\rangle &\rightarrow p^0(0) \\
&\xrightarrow{M^1} |q\rangle \otimes |i\rangle \otimes |o\rangle \\
&\vdots \\
|q00\rangle &\xrightarrow{I_1^1} |010\rangle \\
|q10\rangle &\xrightarrow{U} |\psi\rangle \\
|\psi\rangle &\xrightarrow{M^1} |\rho\rangle \otimes |o\rangle \\
|\rho\rangle \otimes |o\rangle &\rightarrow p^0(1) \\
&\xrightarrow{M^1} |q\rangle \otimes |i\rangle \otimes |o\rangle
\end{aligned} \tag{31}$$

At the end of each evaluation sequence, the state of the output qubit and of the input qubit is determined by the measurement and can be reset with desired Unitary transformation to either $|0\rangle$ or to $|1\rangle$. The machine state qubit $|q\rangle$ is known only at the beginning of each evaluation sequence. This means that the state of the qubit can be in superposition or an orthonormal state. This also means that the machine state can be a multi qubit state that can become entangled between the various state qubits.

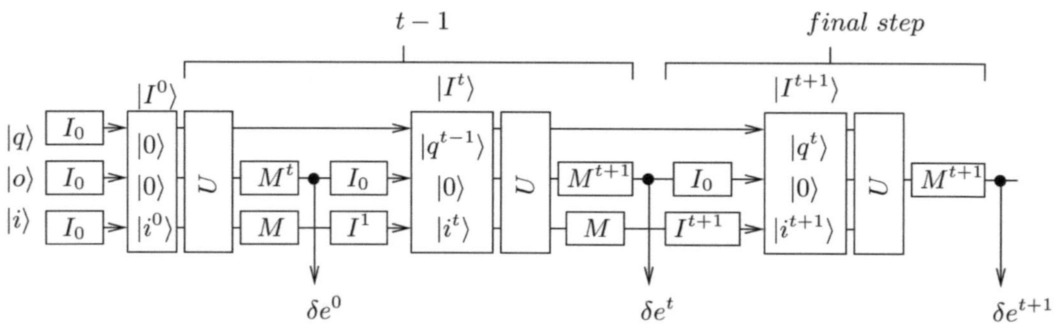

Fig. 19. Schematic representation of the process of evaluation of a QC as a Measure-Many (one-way)QFSM in this work.

Finally, the evaluation process is recored as a set of probabilities denoted as $p^0(0)$ and $p^0(1)$. They represent the probability of observation of the desired output 0 or 1 during the sequence detection. In particular, in this case the overall correctness of the detection can be written as:

$$\begin{aligned} p(s) =& p^0(0) \cdot p^0(0) \cdot p^0(0) \cdot \ldots \cdot p^0(1) \\ =& \left[\prod^{n-2} p^0(0) \right] \cdot p^0(1) \end{aligned} \tag{32}$$

To evaluate the error of the detector either the eq. 32 was used as a direct measure (it represents the correctness of the detection with respect to the selected observables), or a more standard calculation was used. The eq. 33 shows the standard RMS error computation. Both of these error evaluations are compared in the experimental section of this work.

$$p(s) = \frac{1}{n} \left(\left[\sum_{j=0}^{n-2} (1 - p_j^0(0))^2 \right] + (1 - p_{n-1}^0(1))^2 \right) \tag{33}$$

5.4 Fitness functions of the GA

During the search for the QFSM's a parameterized fitness function was used. This was done in order to allow the minimization for both the error and the cost of the synthesized Quantum circuit. This "weighted function" methodology was based on our previous experience in the evolutionary quantum Logic synthesis [LPG+ 03, LP05, LP09].

The parameterization allows to select the weight with which the error of the circuit and the cost of the circuit modifies the overall fitness value. The choice of this weight is left on the user that can decide what criteria of evaluation is more important. However, we experimentally determined some optimal settings that allowed correct circuits with minimal cost to be synthesized.

5.4.1 The cost function

The cost function is based on a parameter known as the *minimum cost* that is provided by the user and that permits to estimate a normalization constant. This means that the cost function acts as a bonus inversely proportional to the size of the circuit to the fitness function for a given estimated and unreachable minimum. In this work the *cost function* is defined by

$$G(c) = exp^{-\frac{(MinCost-Cost)^2}{\frac{Cost}{2}^2}} \tag{34}$$

where *Mincost* is the parameter given by the user and *Cost*, given by $\sum_{j=1}^{k} c_j$, is the sum of costs of all gates in the evolved circuit. Equation 34 was experimentally determined to be sensitive enough to influence both circuits far and close to the optimal cost.

5.4.2 The weighted fitness function

The weighted fitness functions used is shown in eq. 35 and an alternative version is in eq. 36. Both equations calculate the fitness value using the fitness function and the cost function together. In this case, the error of the circuit (QFSM) is calculated with respect to the overall probability of detecting the desired sequence as specified by eq. 32.
Each component of these weighted functions can be adjusted by the values of parameters α and β.

$$f_3 = \alpha\,(1 - e) + \beta G(c) \tag{35}$$

$$f_4 = \alpha\left(\frac{1}{e+1}\right) + \beta G(c) \tag{36}$$

The reasons for these various fitness functions are the following:

- to allow different selection pressures during the individual selection process,
- by calibrating the cost to always underestimate the minimal possible size of the desired circuit it is possible to further manipulate the selection process.
- the parameterization allows in the extreme cases to completely eliminate the cost component and thus also includes fitness functions solely based on the correctness of the circuit.

For instance the fitness function 35 is not equal to one, unless both the cost of the circuit and the error are minimal. Thus a GA using such a weighted function has more freedom for searching a solution, because the fitness function is now optimizing the circuit for two parameters. Similarly in the case of the fitness function 36 which decreases the value of the fitness of longer circuits, therefore preferring the shorter ones. Thus individuals with different circuit properties will have equal fitness value.

5.5 Other evolutionary settings

For the clarity and the focus of this paper we present the rest of the settings in the Table 4. Only the final parameters are shown and in particular only those that were used during the runs that generated the presented results. To sum it up, the SUS[Bak87] selection method was used with n = 4 individuals. The mutation operator was used both on the level of individual quantum gates but also on the level of the parallel blocks. The crossover was a two parent, two point recombination process that preserves the width of the quantum circuit by selecting cut points only between the parallel blocks.

selection	Stochastic Universal Sampling with n = 4 individuals
mutation	Gate level, Segment level
crossover	Two point, two parent
population size	50,90,120
generations	500,900
elitism	yes

Table 4. Parameters of the GA used during the experiments.

5.6 CUDA acceleration

The CUDA framework was developed by NVIDIA for the growing usage of the GPU for computing tasks. The acceleration implemented in the GA is restricted only to the matrix calculation. Figure 20 shows where the CUDA acceleration is used.

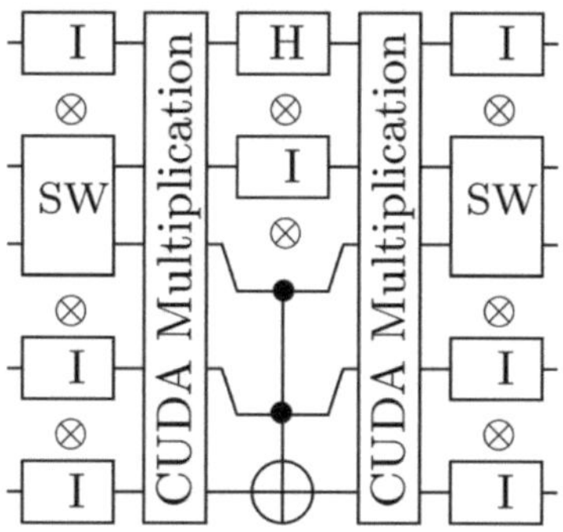

Fig. 20. Schema representing the usage of the CUDA accelerator in the computation of a Quantum Circuit Matrix Representation.

The reason for using the accelerated matrix multiplication only during the matrix multiplication and not for the Kronecker matrix product is the fact that the Kronecker product is less computationally expensive as it requires only $2^n \times 2^n$ multiplications while the matrix product requires $2^n \times 2^n$ multiplications and 2^n additions. Moreover, in order to maximize the CUDA usage it is more optimal to use multiplication on matrices of the same dimensions without requiring to re-parameterize the CUDA device. This is the case in the matrix multiplication between each parallel block in a Quantum Circuit.

6. Experiments and discussion

The experiments carried in this section confirms the possibility to design classical sequence detectors using the 1-way (measure many) circuit-based QFSM's model. The experimentation was done over a set of random sequences of various length. Each sequence was being tested for circuits with different number of state qubits. This was done in order to observe the role of embedding of the non-reversible sequence into a larger, reversible unitary matrix.

The general function that the QFSM generates on the output is described by the eq. 37

$$o(\lambda) = \begin{cases} 1 & ifj < length(s) \\ 0 & o.w. \end{cases} \tag{37}$$

with λ being a symbol read from the input and j is the index of the λ symbol in the sequence. Thus the minimal condition for each sequence to be detected properly is that the amount of the states is large enough to embed all the zero output to one half of the truth table. this is a required consequence because the QFSM must have both the output function and the state transition function reversible.

The experimentation was done for 5 randomly generated binary sequences with 7, 10, 15, 20 and 35 binary digits each. The sequences are shown in eq. 38

$$\begin{aligned} s_7 &= \{\ 0\,1\,0\,1\,1\,1\,1\ \} \\ s_{10} &= \{\ 1\,0\,1\,1\,0\,1\,1\,0\,0\,0\ \} \\ s_{15} &= \{\ 0\,1\,0\,1\,0\,0\,1\,1\,0\,1\,0\,1\,0\,1\,1\ \} \\ s_{20} &= \{\ 0\,1\,0\,1\,1\,1\,1\,1\,0\,0\,0\,1\,1\,1\,1\,0\,0\,1\,1\,1\ \} \\ s_{25} &= \{\ 1\,0\,1\,1\,0\,1\,1\,1\,1\,0\,1\,0\,0\,1\,0\,1\,1\,1\,1\,0\,0\,0\,0\,1\,0\ \} \end{aligned} \tag{38}$$

Each sequence was synthesized using a circuit with 3,4,5 and 6 qubits. The six qubit circuit is large enough to embed even the largest sequence so as a reversible function is synthesizable. Figures 21, 24 and 27 shows some examples of obtained circuits for each of the sequences.

Figure 21 is an example of Quantum Circuit that was used to detect the s_7 sequence and does not use any probabilistic states. For the sake of understanding let us analyze the sequence detection procedure using this circuit. The desired sequence is $s_7 = \{0\,1\,0\,1\,1\,1\,1\}$ thus the set of input states is given by $\{|0^{\otimes^r}\rangle|00\rangle, |\phi 10\rangle, |\phi 00\rangle, |\phi 10\rangle, |\phi 10\rangle, |\phi 10\rangle, |\phi 10\rangle\}$, with $|\phi\rangle$ being the unmeasured component of the automata state. Naturally there are cases where it is going to be determined by the measurement but for the clarity it is left in symbolic form and thus allowing it to be in superposed or entangled state.

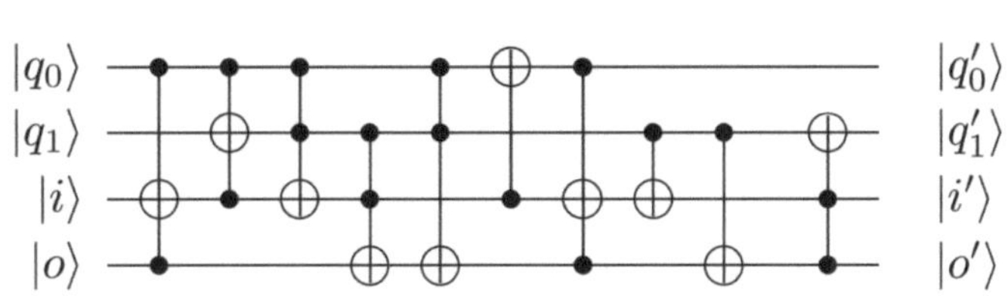

Fig. 21. s_7-sequence exact detector

The size of the QFSM is four qubits with two topmost qubits $|q_0\rangle$, $|q_1\rangle$ are the state qubits, $|i\rangle$ is the input qubit and $|o\rangle$ is the output qubit (Figure 21). Table 22 represents the consecutive states as obtained during the QFSM procedure described in this work (Section 5.3). In particular this QFSM shows that it recognize the given sequence without the use of any probabilistic or superposed states.

This can also be seen on the circuit matrix that can easily be build from the given sequence of gates. For clarity the state transition is also shown in the form of a equation (eq. 39).

I: (1,0)(0,0)(0,0)(0,0)(0,0)(0,0)(0,0)(0,0)(0,0)(0,0)(0,0)(0,0)(0,0)(0,0)(0,0)(0,0) O: (1,0)(0,0)(0,0)(0,0)(0,0)(0,0)(0,0)(0,0)(0,0)(0,0)(0,0)(0,0)(0,0)(0,0)(0,0)(0,0)
I: (0,0)(0,0)(1,0)(0,0)(0,0)(0,0)(0,0)(0,0)(0,0)(0,0)(0,0)(0,0)(0,0)(0,0)(0,0)(0,0) O: (0,0)(0,0)(0,0)(0,0)(0,0)(0,0)(0,0)(0,0)(0,0)(0,0)(0,0)(0,0)(0,0)(0,0)(1,0)(0,0)
I: (0,0)(0,0)(0,0)(0,0)(0,0)(0,0)(0,0)(0,0)(0,0)(0,0)(0,0)(0,0)(1,0)(0,0)(0,0)(0,0) O: (0,0)(0,0)(0,0)(0,0)(0,0)(0,0)(0,0)(0,0)(0,0)(0,0)(1,0)(0,0)(0,0)(0,0)(0,0)(0,0)
I: (0,0)(0,0)(0,0)(0,0)(0,0)(0,0)(0,0)(0,0)(0,0)(0,0)(1,0)(0,0)(0,0)(0,0)(0,0)(0,0) O: (0,0)(0,0)(1,0)(0,0)(0,0)(0,0)(0,0)(0,0)(0,0)(0,0)(0,0)(0,0)(0,0)(0,0)(0,0)(0,0)
I: (0,0)(0,0)(1,0)(0,0)(0,0)(0,0)(0,0)(0,0)(0,0)(0,0)(0,0)(0,0)(0,0)(0,0)(0,0)(0,0) O: (0,0)(0,0)(0,0)(0,0)(0,0)(0,0)(0,0)(0,0)(0,0)(0,0)(0,0)(0,0)(0,0)(0,0)(1,0)(0,0)
I: (0,0)(0,0)(0,0)(0,0)(0,0)(0,0)(0,0)(0,0)(0,0)(0,0)(0,0)(0,0)(0,0)(0,0)(1,0)(0,0) O: (0,0)(0,0)(0,0)(0,0)(0,0)(0,0)(1,0)(0,0)(0,0)(0,0)(0,0)(0,0)(0,0)(0,0)(0,0)(0,0)
I: (0,0)(0,0)(0,0)(0,0)(0,0)(0,0)(1,0)(0,0)(0,0)(0,0)(0,0)(0,0)(0,0)(0,0)(0,0)(0,0) O: (0,0)(0,0)(0,0)(0,0)(0,0)(1,0)(0,0)(0,0)(0,0)(0,0)(0,0)(0,0)(0,0)(0,0)(0,0)(0,0)

Fig. 22. Four qubits s_7-sequence detector with deterministic input and output states

$$
\begin{aligned}
s_0 \Rightarrow 0: &\quad |0000\rangle \xrightarrow{U} |0000\rangle \\
s_1 \Rightarrow 1: &\quad |0000\rangle \rightarrow |0010\rangle \xrightarrow{U} |1110\rangle \\
s_2 \Rightarrow 0: &\quad |1110\rangle \rightarrow |1100\rangle \xrightarrow{U} |1010\rangle \\
s_3 \Rightarrow 1: &\quad |1010\rangle \xrightarrow{U} |0010\rangle \\
s_4 \Rightarrow 1: &\quad |0010\rangle \xrightarrow{U} |1110\rangle \\
s_5 \Rightarrow 1: &\quad |1110\rangle \xrightarrow{U} |0110\rangle \\
s_6 \Rightarrow 1: &\quad |0110\rangle \xrightarrow{U} |0101\rangle
\end{aligned}
\qquad (39)
$$

Observe that two different steps can be clearly distinguished in eq. 39; first a standard step that acts directly on a previously generated machine state such as in steps s_0, s_3, s_4, s_5 and s_6, second a step that requires explicit modification of the previous machine state, in particular a state that requires an initialization of the output and/or the input qubit, such as shown in steps s_1 to s_2. Observe that this particular sequence detector does not requires - for this sequence – any re-initialization of the input qubit as a result of previous step; the input qubit is not modified by the automaton. Also observe that despite the fact that this circuit can generate quantum states, these states are not generated during the sequence s_7. This can be seen on Figure 23.

The states in a circle represent natural states as would be obtained by the cycle of the reversible function, while the states in the hexagons represents forced states that are obtained after modifying the input qubit. The Figure 23 also represents the forced states with one dotted arrow incoming and one outgoing dashed arrows. The arrow incoming to the forced state is indexed with a binary number representing the required input change so that the forced state is obtained. The outgoing arrow represents that the forced state is then used as a normal natural state; i.e. a Unitary transform is applied to it and the result is computed. For instance the s1 character recognition, starts with the machine in the state $|0000\rangle$, which is forced to $|0010\rangle$ and then the Unitary transformation is applied and yields $|1110\rangle$ state. The whole sequence detection can be in this manner analysed from eq. 39 and Figure 23.

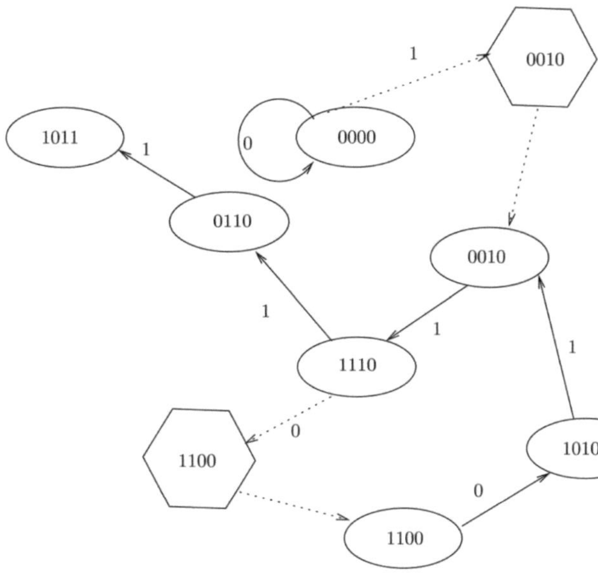

Fig. 23. The cycle of a Reversible Circuit used as a detector for the s_7 sequence

A more interesting example is shown in Figure 24. The displayed circuit also recognizes the same sequence s_7 but in this case the automaton uses probabilistic and superposed quantum states. This can be seen in Table 25; this table has every row split in half so that it fits in size. For more details eq. 40 shows step by step the process of recognition performed by this automaton. Observe that as the result of the last step the output of the circuit is $|o\rangle = |1\rangle$ thus confirming the correct sequence has been detected.

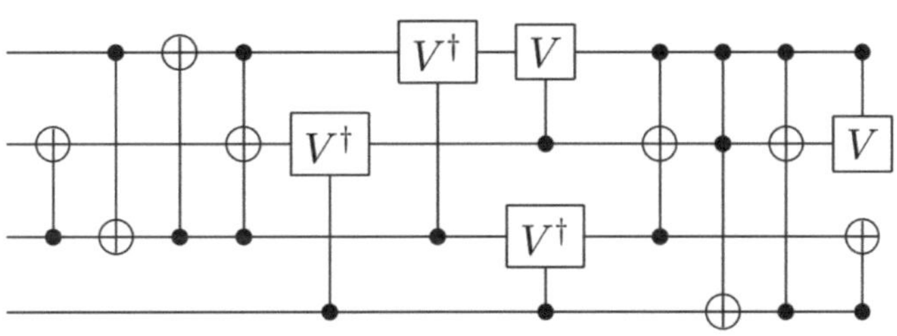

Fig. 24. s_7-sequence detector with probabilistic and superposed states

$$
\begin{aligned}
s_0 \Rightarrow 0: &\quad |0000\rangle \xrightarrow{U} |0000\rangle \\
s_1 \Rightarrow 1: &\quad |0000\rangle \to |0010\rangle \xrightarrow{U} \frac{1+i}{2}|0110\rangle + \frac{1-i}{2}|1000\rangle \\
s_2 \Rightarrow 0: &\quad \frac{1+i}{2}|0110\rangle + \frac{1-i}{2}|1000\rangle \to \frac{1-i}{\sqrt{2}}|1000\rangle \xrightarrow{U} \frac{1-i}{\sqrt{2}}|1010\rangle \\
s_3 \Rightarrow 1: &\quad \frac{1-i}{\sqrt{2}}|1010\rangle \xrightarrow{U} \frac{1-i}{\sqrt{2}}|0010\rangle \\
s_4 \Rightarrow 1: &\quad \frac{1-i}{\sqrt{2}}|0010\rangle \xrightarrow{U} \frac{i}{\sqrt{2}}|0110\rangle + \frac{-i}{\sqrt{2}}|1000\rangle \\
s_5 \Rightarrow 1: &\quad \frac{i}{\sqrt{2}}|0110\rangle + \frac{-i}{\sqrt{2}}|1000\rangle \to |0110\rangle \xrightarrow{U} |1100\rangle \\
s_6 \Rightarrow 1: &\quad |1100\rangle \to |1110\rangle \xrightarrow{U} \begin{array}{l} \frac{1-i}{4}|0011\rangle + \frac{-1-i}{4}|0111\rangle + \frac{1-i}{4}|1001\rangle \\ + \frac{1}{2}|1011\rangle + \frac{1+i}{4}|1101\rangle + \frac{i}{2}|1111\rangle \end{array}
\end{aligned} \tag{40}
$$

I: (1,0)(0,0)(0,0)(0,0)(0,0)(0,0)(0,0)(0,0) (0,0)(0,0)(0,0)(0,0)(0,0)(0,0)(0,0)(0,0) O: (1,0)(0,0)(0,0)(0,0)(0,0)(0,0)(0,0)(0,0) (0,0)(0,0)(0,0)(0,0)(0,0)(0,0)(0,0)(0,0)
I: (0,0)(0,0)(1,0)(0,0)(0,0)(0,0)(0,0)(0,0) (0,0)(0,0)(0,0)(0,0)(0,0)(0,0)(0,0)(0,0) O: (0,0)(0,0)(0,0)(0,0)(0,0)(0,0)(0.5,0.5)(0,0) (0.5,-0.5)(0,0)(0,0)(0,0)(0,0)(0,0)(0,0)(0,0)
I: (0,0)(0,0)(0,0)(0,0)(0,0)(0,0)(0,0)(0,0) (0.707107,-0.707107)(0,0)(0,0)(0,0)(0,0)(0,0)(0,0)(0,0) O: (0,0)(0,0)(0,0)(0,0)(0,0)(0,0)(0,0)(0,0) (0,0)(0,0)(0.707107,-0.707107)(0,0)(0,0)(0,0)(0,0)(0,0)
I: (0,0)(0,0)(0,0)(0,0)(0,0)(0,0)(0,0)(0,0) (0,0)(0,0)(0.707107,-0.707107)(0,0)(0,0)(0,0)(0,0)(0,0) O: (0,0)(0,0)(0.707107,-0.707107)(0,0)(0,0)(0,0)(0,0)(0,0) (0,0)(0,0)(0,0)(0,0)(0,0)(0,0)(0,0)(0,0)
I: (0,0)(0,0)(0.707107,-0.707107)(0,0)(0,0)(0,0)(0,0)(0,0) (0,0)(0,0)(0,0)(0,0)(0,0)(0,0)(0,0)(0,0) O: (0,0)(0,0)(0,0)(0,0)(0,0)(0,0)(0.707107,0)(0,0) (0,-0.707107)(0,0)(0,0)(0,0)(0,0)(0,0)(0,0)(0,0)
I: (0,0)(0,0)(0,0)(0,0)(0,0)(0,0)(1,0)(0,0) (0,0)(0,0)(0,0)(0,0)(0,0)(0,0)(0,0)(0,0) O: (0,0)(0,0)(0,0)(0,0)(0,0)(0,0)(0,0)(0,0) (0,0)(0,0)(0,0)(0,0)(1,0)(0,0)(0,0)(0,0)
I: (0,0)(0,0)(0,0)(0,0)(0,0)(0,0)(0,0)(0,0) (0,0)(0,0)(0,0)(0,0)(0,0)(0,0)(1,0)(0,0) O: (0,0)(0,0)(0,0)(0.25,-0.25)(0,0)(0,0)(0,0)(-0.25,-0.25) (0,0)(0.25,-0.25)(0,0)(0.5,0)(0,0)(0.25,0.25)(0,0)(0,0.5)

Fig. 25. Four qubits s_7-sequence detector with probabilistic input and output states

6.1 Sequence detection

The detection of a given sequence by the here formulated QFSM's can be analyzed starting from Reversible Circuits. Assume, the initial state is 0000 for the rest of this discussion. As example take the reversible (deterministic) detector such as given in figure 21. It is obvious that the power of properly detecting a given sequence; i.e. to generate a sequence $0 \times n + 1 \times 1$ is proportional to the cycle of this detector given by the reversible circuit for a fixed n and to the fact of having the cycle connected to a finish sequence either by a forced change of input or by a natural evolution.

To see this, just assume that the given circuit is specified by the following permutation cycle (0, 4, 8, 12)(2, 6, 10, 14)(1, 3, 5, 7, 9, 11, 13, 15). Clearly, the first cycle (0, 4, 8, 12) represents the states containing the 0 as input and 0 as output, the (2, 6, 10, 14) cycle represents the states having 1 for input and 0 as output and the last cycle represents all outputs having the output bit set to 1. The longest possible sequence this automaton can detect (without using the force states transitions) is of length 0 becausethe detecting cycle is disjoint from both the cycles identifying 0's and 1's.

For illustration assume the Reversible Circuit specifying the automaton be described by (0,6,4,2) (8,12,10,14,1) (3,5,7,9,11,13,15) permutation cycles. This automaton will not detect successfully any sequence if starting from the initial state 0000. This is shown in figure 26. Observe that no matter the input change of any of the state of the cycle (0,6,4,2) will always lead back to a state from the same cycle. Thus such a machine cannot generate a 1 on the output when starting in the state $|0000\rangle$.

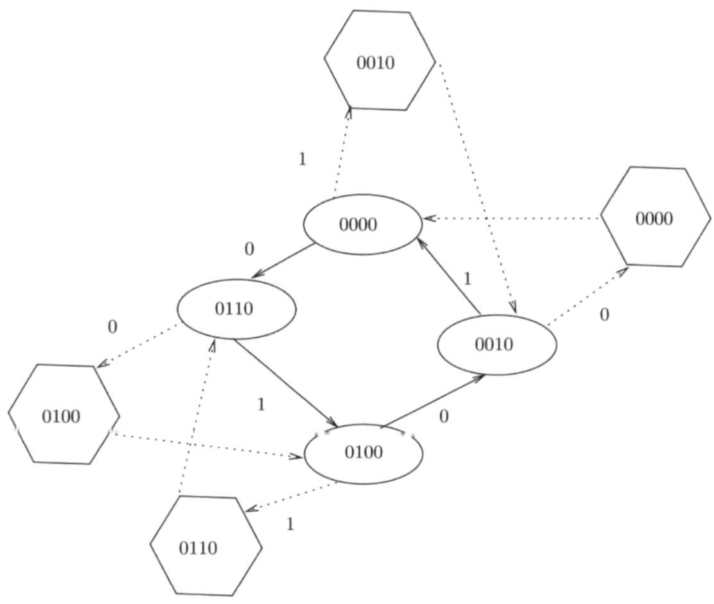

Fig. 26. The cycle of a Reversible Circuit used as a detector

The Figure 26 shows that in order to have a successful detector, at least one natural transition $|\phi\rangle \xrightarrow{U} |\phi'\rangle$ or a forced transition $|\rho\rangle\,|i\rangle\,|o\rangle \rightarrow |\rho\rangle\,|\bar{i}\rangle\,|o\rangle$ must lead to a cycle that allows to generate an output with value 1.

Now consider an Reversible Circuit defined by the permutations given by (0, 4, 8, 12, 3) (2, 6, 10, 14, 1) (5, 7, 9, 11, 13, 15). Such automaton now can detect any sequence that contains at

least four consecutive 0's or four consecutive 1's. To maximize the length of a given sequence it is possible to allow the automaton to modify also its input qubit. In that case, as also seen in the presented protocol in the Section 5.3, the maximal complexity of the detected sequence is still equal to the sequence of maximum four 0's and four 1's.
The important cycles used for detection of the above specified Reversible circuit are shown in Figure 28. Observe that only two out of three cycles are shown as the last cycle contains all minterms that have 1 as output and thus can only be used as the end of sequence indicator. Also the cycles are shown only up to a final state. Thus for instance the state $|0011\rangle$ is not connected back to $|0000\rangle$ because once such state is attained the detection is terminated. Such specified detector will detect any sequence that terminates with four 1's or four 0's.

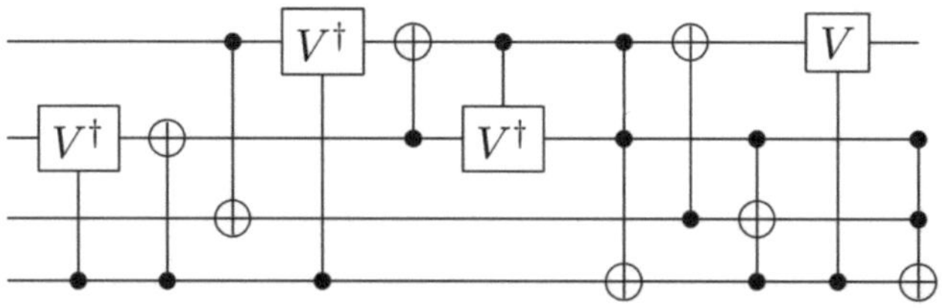

(a) s_{10}-sequence detector with probabilistic and superposed states

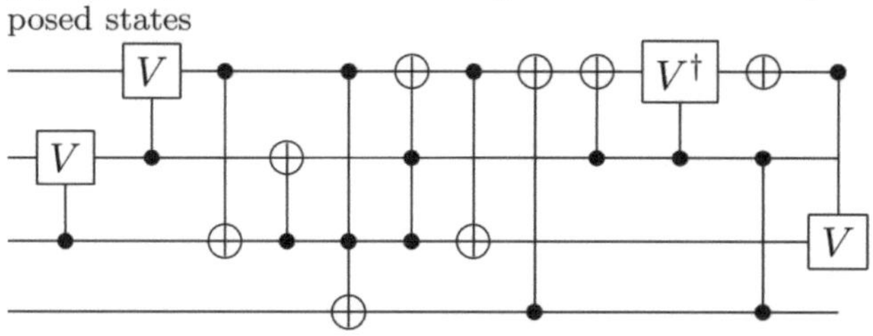

(b) s_{15}-sequence detector with probabilistic and superposed states

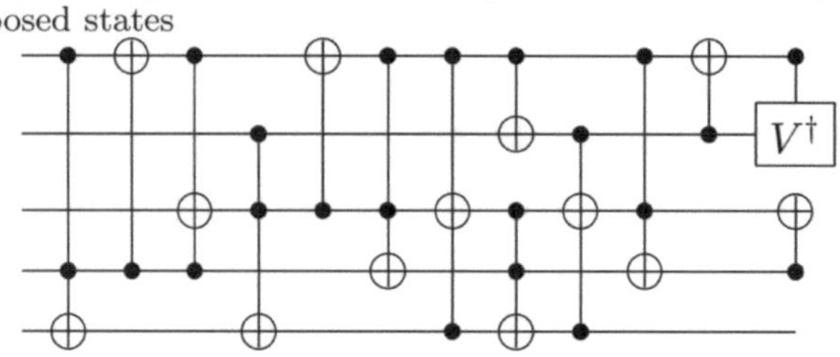

(c) s_{20}-sequence detector with deterministic states

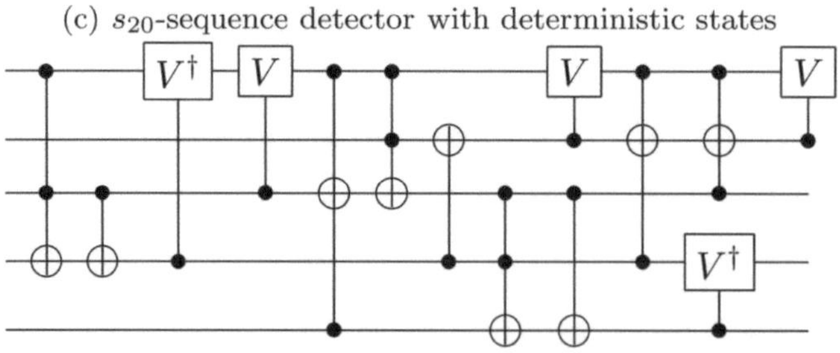

(d) s_{25}-sequence detector with superposed and probabilistic states

Fig. 27. Quantum circuits detecting the sequences s_{10} to s_{25}

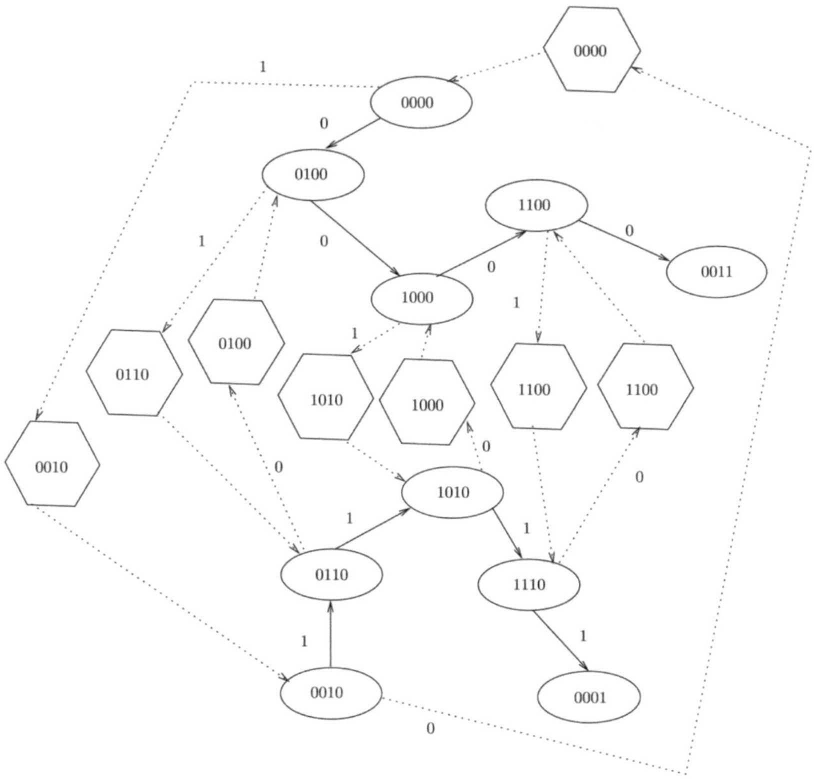

Fig. 28. The Reversible Circuit specified by the cycles (0,4,8,12,3) (2,6,10,14,1) (5,7,9,11,13,15) used as a detector

Finally observe that for a given sequence it is possible to design a detector that is either specified by only natural state transitions - as specified by the cycles of a reversible quantum function or by combining the cycle with forced transitions. The former method will always generate larger circuits while the later will allow more compact designs. However in the framework of the presented Quantum detectors these approaches are equivalent from the point of view of implementation. That is, at the begining of each computation cycle one need to know exactly the input quantum state. Thus the main adavantage in designing detectors with only natural state transitions resides in the fact that no initialization of the input qubit is required because it is set at the output of the previous computational cycle.
To close this discussion about the detectors it is possible to synthesize detectors using both purely Reversible or Quantum Unitary matrix. The size of the required circuit is dependent on the amount of continuous 0's or 1's however it is not restricted by it. It is straight forward to imagine such sequence detector that will have only smaller cycles and still will detect similar sequence. This is because if the unitary transform modifies the input qubit, smaller cycles can be combined to detect these particular sequences. For instance Figure 29 shows a portion of a detector specified by a Reversible circuit. This detector will detect among others the sequences terminating with three 0's or two 1's. Recall that only natural transitions are used for the detection procedure. Thus for instance in figure 29 $|1110\rangle$ changes to state $|1100\rangle$ when the input is changed from 1 to 0 and the consequent application of the Unitary matrix on this state generates an 1 on output. This is the final state, and it indicates that at

least three 0 have been successfully detected before attaining it. The interested reader is encouraged to read more about reversible and quantum sequence detector in [LP09, LPK09]. Table 5 shows the minimum number of qubits that have been experimentally obtained in order to properly detect the sequences studied here. The sequence s_7 has a sequence of four 1's and a set of individual 1 and thus cannot be detected by less than circuit with 4 qubits.

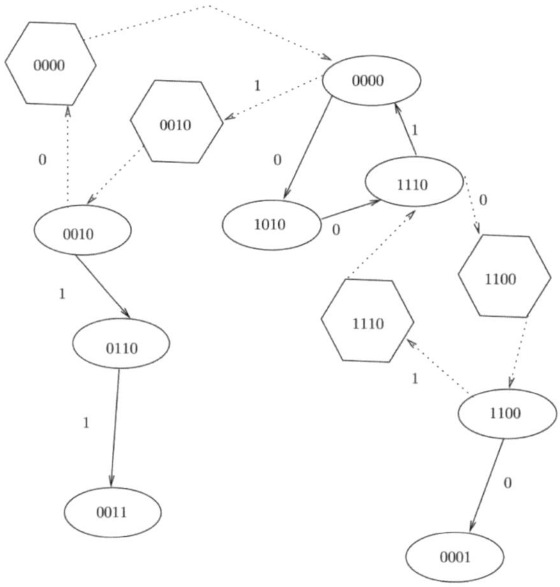

Fig. 29. The Reversible Circuit detecting sequences ending with four 0's or four 1's.

s_7	4
s_{10}	4
s_{15}	4
s_{20}	5
s_{25}	5

Table 5. Minimum number of qubits required to detect a sequence: experimental observations

The sequence s_{10} has two cycles at least: one with a sequence of two 1's followed by a 0 and a sequence of three 0's. It is also not possible to construct such detector on 3 qubits because the number of states required is at least 4 for both sequence and not counting the individual 0's and 1's. Similarly other sequences can be analyzed.
The Genetic Algorithm was run for multiple sizes for each sequence starting with three qubits. The search was terminated when a circuit satisfying the constraints was found and multiple searches were performed at the minimal width. Figure 30 shows the average of the Fitness value for the s_7, s_{10} and s_{15} sequences. The drawings show each curve over 500 generation cycles required for the detection of each of the sequences after which the maximum generation is attained. Each curve is an average of 15 runs and the most interesting feature is that similarly to quantum function logic synthesis the algorithm finds a circuit that is very close to the complete solution and then stagnates before finding a solution. This problem is related to both the difficulty of synthesis as well as the fact that

Quantum circuit are specified by Unitary matrices in which the error is of symmetric nature. Such error can be seen as a step function where with each step a pair of coefficient in the Unitary matrix is corrected.
Also observe how the fitness value stagnates with larger sequences with the presented qubits despite the fact that a solution was found for each sequence for the presented number of qubits. Interestingly, observe that the sequence s_7 to s_{20} are from the same class as they have been identified by detectors of similar size. This goes back to the discussion above about the limits of a Quantum and Reversible circuit to recognize a particular class of sequences.

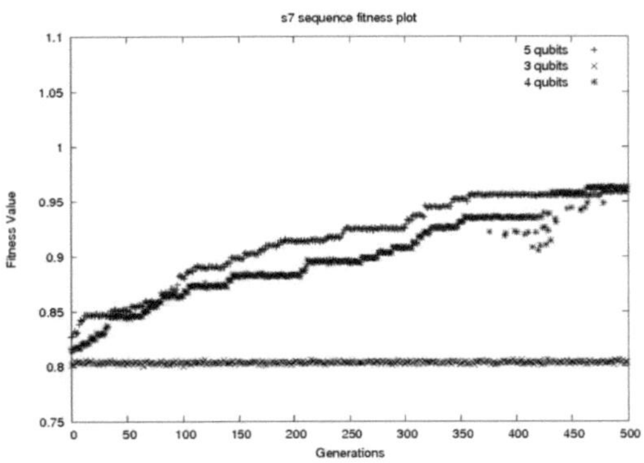

(a) s_7 sequence fitness average

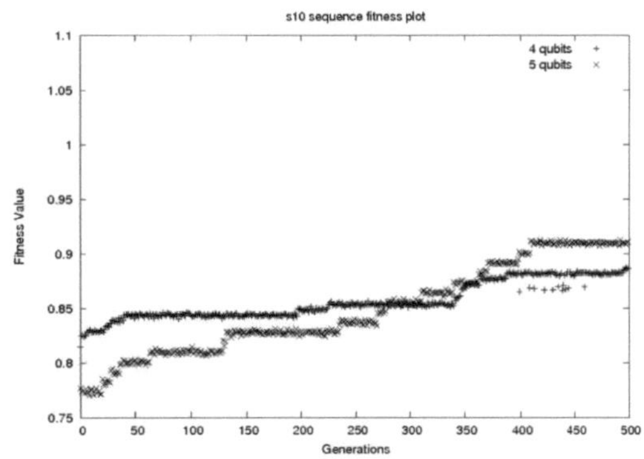

(b) s_{10} sequence fitness average

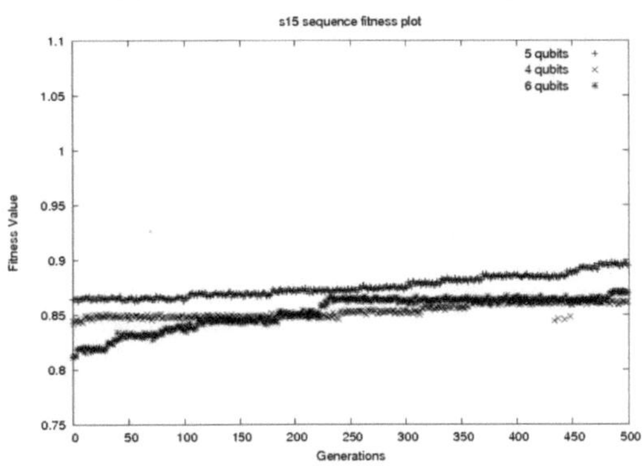

(c) s_{15} sequence fitness average

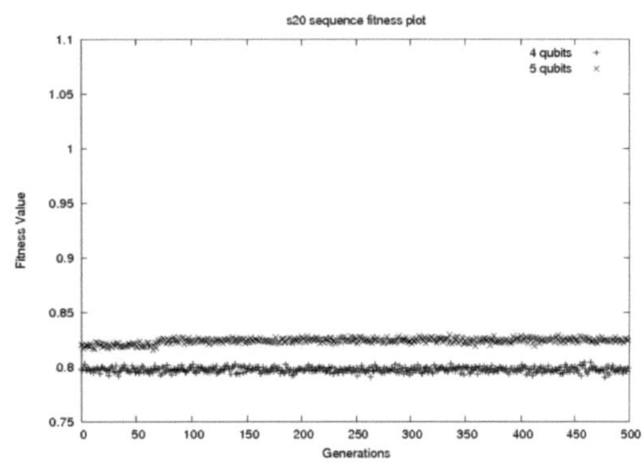

(d) s_{20} sequence fitness average

Fig. 30. Figures capturing the fitness average for four sequence detectors

7. Conclusion

In this paper we presented a methodology and we showed some experimental results confirming that our approach is possible in simulated environment. Also because all simulated elements of the presented experiments are based on existing Quantum operations, the simulated detectors are Quantum-realizable.
It is well known that the state assignment problem is a NP-complete problem [Esc93] and the finding a minimal State Assignment has been solved only for particular subsets of FSM's [LPD95] or using Quantum computing [ANdMM08]. This problem is here naturally solved (without addressing it). The setup of this experimental approach automatically generates a state assignment such that when the detection is successful the state assignment is as well.

This is a natural consequence of both the fact that the machine is reversible and the fact that the sequence is successfully identified.
The presented algorithm proved successful in the design of Quantum detectors. Despite the sequences were randomly generated the proposed approach was possible due to the hardware accelerated computational approach. For more details about this approach the reader can consult [LM09].
The synthesis of quantum detectors has not been completely explored and remains still an open issue mainly because Quantum computing implementation is not a well established approach. Each technology provides different possibilities and has different limitations. In some cases specification using Quantum circuits is the most appropriate in others Hamiltonians must be used. Thus one of the main remaining tasks is to completely describe Quantum detectors and formally define their issues related with implementation and define classes of circuits more approapriate for different technologies.

8. References

[AF98] A. Ambainis and R. Freivalds. 1-way quantum finite automata: strengths, weaknesses and generalizations. pages 332–341, Nov 1998.

[ANdMM08] M.P.M. Araujo, N. Nedjah, and L. de Macedo Mourelle. Quantum-inspired evolutionary state assignment for synchronous finite state machines. Journal of Universal Computer Science, 14(15):2532–2548, 2008.

[AW02] A. Ambainis and J. Watrous. Two-way finite automata with quantum and classical states. Theoretical Computer Science, 287(1):299–311, 2002.

[Bak87] J. E. Baker. Reducing bias and inefficiency in the selection algorithm. In *In Proceedings of the Second International Conference on Genetic Algorithms and their Application*, pages 14–21, 1987.

[BBC+95] A. Barenco, C. H. Bennett, R. Cleve, D. P. DiVincenzo, N. Margolus, P. Shor, T. Sleator, J. A. Smolin, and Weinfurter H. Elementary gates for quantum computation. *The American Physical Society*, 5:3457–3467, 1995.

[Bey01] H.G. Beyer. *The Theory of Evolution Strategies*. Springer, 2001.

[BV97] E. Bernstein and U. Vazirani. Quantum complexity theory. *SIAM Journal of computing*, pages 1411–1473, 1997.

[BZ00] A. Blais and A. M. Zagoskin. Operation of universal gates in a solid state quantum computer based on clean josephson junctions between d-wave superconductors. *Phys. Rev. A*, 61, 2000.

[cbl] *GSL CBLAS*. http://www.gnu.org/software/gsl/manual/html node/GSLCBLAS-Library.html.

[cud] *NVIDIA CUDA*. http://www.nvidia.com/object/cuda learn.html.

[CZ95] J.I. Cirac and P. Zoller. Quantum computation with cold trapped ions. *Physical Review letters*, 74(20):4091, 1995.

[DiV95] P. DiVincenzo. Two-bit gate for quantum computation. *Physical Review A*, 50:1015, 1995.

[DKK03] L.M. Duan, A. Kuzmich, and H.J. Kimble. Cavity QED and quantum-information processing with 'hot' trapped atoms. *Physical Review A*, 67, 2003.

[Dun98] M. R. Dunlavey. Simulation of finite state machines in a quantum computer, 1998.

[EPR35] A. Einstein, B. Podolsky, and N. Rosen. Can quantummechanical description of physical reality be considered complete? *Phys. Rev.*, 47(10):777–780, May 1935.

[ES03] A.E. Eiben and J.E. Smith. *Introduction to Evolutionary Computing*. Springer, 2003.

[Esc93] B. Eschermann. State assignment for hardwired vlsi control units. *ACM Comput. Surv.*, 25(4):415–436, 1993.

[FOW66] L.J. Fogel, A.J. Owens, and M.J. Walsh. *Artificial Intelligence through Simulated Evolution*. John Wiley, 1966.

[GKD89] D.E. Goldberg, B. Korb, and K. Deb. Messy genetic algorithms: Motivation, analysis and first results. *Complex Systems*, 3:493- 530, 1989.

[Gol89] D.E. Goldberg. *Genetic Algorithms in Search, Optimization and Machine Learning*. Addison-Wesley, MA, 1989.

[Gra81] A. Graham. *Kronecker Products and Matrix Calculus With Applications*. Ellis Horwood Limited, Chichester, U.K., 1981.

[Gru99] J. Gruska. *Quantum computing*. Osborne/McGraw-Hill,U.S., 1999.

[KBA99] J.R. Koza, F.H. Bennett, and D. Andre. *Genetic Programming III: Darwinian Invention and Problem Solving*. San Francisco, California: Morgan Kaufmann Publishers, 1999.

[Koz94] J.R. Koza. *Genetic Programming II: Automatic Discovery of Reusable Programs*. MIT Press, 1994.

[KW97] A. Kondacs and J.Watrous. On the power of quantum finite state automata. In *IEEE Symposium on Foundations of Computer Science*, pages 66–75, 1997.

[LB04] A. Leier and W. Banzhaf. Comparison of selection strategies for evolutionary quantum circuit design. In *Proceedings of the Genetic and Evolutionary Computation Conference (GECCO)*, pages 557–568, 2004.

[Lei04] A. Leier. *Evolution of Quantum Algorithms Using Genetic Programming*. PhD thesis, University of Dortmund, 2004.

[LLK+06] S. Lee, S-J. Lee, T. Kim, J-S. Lee, J. Biamonte, and M. Perkowski. The cost of quantum gate primitives. *Journal of Multiple Valued Logic and Soft Computing*, 12(5/6):561–574, 2006.

[LM09] Miller M. Perkowski M. Lukac M., Kameyama M. Evolutionary quantum logic synthesis: Representation vs. micro-parallelism - submitted, 2009.

[LP02] M. Lukac and M. Perkowski. Evolving quantum circuit using genetic algorithm. In *Proceedings of the 2002 NASA/DoD Conference on Evolvable hardware*, pages 177–185, 2002.

[LP05] M. Lukac and M. Perkowski. Combining evolutionary and exhaustive search to find the least expensive quantum circuits. In *Proceedings of ULSI symposium*, 2005.

[LP08] M. Lukac and M. Perkowski. Inductive learning of quantum behaviors. *Facta Universitatis, special issue on Binary and Multiple-Valued Switching Theory and Circuit Design*, 2008.

[LP09] M. Lukac and M. Perkowski. Quantum finite state machines as sequential quantum circuits. In *Proceedings of ISMVL*, 2009.

[LPD95] Shihming Liu, Massoud Pedram, and Alvin M. Despain. A fast state assignment procedure for large fsms. In *DAC '95: Proceedings of the 32nd ACM/IEEE conference on Design automation*, pages 327–332, New York, NY, USA, 1995. ACM.

[LPG+03] M. Lukac, M. Perkowski, H. Goi, M. Pivtoraiko, C. H. Yu, K. Chung, H. Jee, B.-G. Kim, and Y.-D. Kim. Evolutionary approach to quantum reversible circuit synthesis. *Artif. Intell. Review.*, 20(3-4):361–417, 2003.

[LPK09] M. Lukac, M. Perkowski, and M Kameyama. Sequential quantum devices: A circuit-based approach, 2009.

[LPMP02] M. Lukac, M. Pivtoraiko, A. Mishchenko, and M. Perkowski. Automated synthesis of generalized reversible cascades using genetic algorithms. In *Proceedings of Fifth Intern. Workshop on Boolean Problems*, pages 33–45, 2002.

[Luk09] M. Lukac. *Quantum Logic Synthesis and Inductive Machine Learning, Ph.D. dissertation*. PhD thesis, 2009.

[MC00] C. Moore and J.P. Crutchfield. Quantum automata and quantum grammars. *Theoretical Computer Science*, 237:275–306, 2000.

[MC06] Jialin Mi and Chunhong Chen. Finite state machine implementation with single-electron tunneling technology. In *ISVLSI '06: Proceedings of the IEEE Computer Society Annual Symposium on Emerging VLSI Technologies and Architectures*, page 237, Washington, DC, USA, 2006. IEEE Computer Society.

[MCS04] P. Massey, J.A. Clark, and S. Stepney. Evolving quantum circuits and programs through genetic programming. In *Proceedings of the Genetic and Evolutionary Computation conference (GECCO)*, pages 569–580, 2004.

[MCS05] P. Massey, J.A. Clark, and S. Stepney. Evolving of a humancompetitive quantum fourier transform algorithm using genetic programming. In *Proceedings of the Genetic and Evolutionary Computation conference (GECCO)*, pages 1657–1664, 2005.

[Moo65] G.E. Moore. Cramming more components onto integrated circuits. In *Electronics, April 19*, 1965.

[NC00] M. A. Nielsen and I. L. Chuang. *Quantum Computation and Quantum Information*. Cambridge University Press, 2000.

[PB99] Arun Kumar Pati and Samuel L. Braunstein. Impossibility of deleting an unknown quantum state, 1999.

[PW02] J. Pachos and H. Walther. Quantum computation with trapped ions in an optical cavity. *Physical Review Letters*, 89(18), 2002.

[RCHCX+08] Y. Rong-Can, L. Hong-Cai, L. Xiu, H. Zhi-Ping, and X. Hong. Implementing a universal quantum cloning machine via adiabatic evolution in ion-trap system. *Communications in Theoretical Physics*, 49(1):80–82, 2008.

[Rub01] B.I.P. Rubinstein. Evolving quantum circuits using genetic programming. In *Congress on Evolutionary Computation (CEC2001)*, pages 114–121, 2001.

[SBS05] R. Stadelhofer,W. Banzhaf, and D. Suter. Quantum and classical parallelism in parity algorithms for ensemble quantum computers. *Physical Review A*, 71, 2005.

[SBS08] R. Stadelhofer, W. Banzhaf, and D. Suter. Evolving blackbox quantum algorithms using genetic programming. *Artif. Intell. Eng. Des. Anal. Manuf.*, 22:285–297, 2008.

[Sch95] H.P Schwefel. *Evolution and Optimum Seeking*. New York, Wiley & Sons, 1995.

[Sho94] P.W. Shor. Algorithms for quantum computation: Discrete logarithms and factoring. In *Proc. 35nd Annual Symposium on Foundations of Computer Science (Shafi Goldwasser, ed.)*, pages 124– 134. IEEE Computer Society Press, 1994.

[SKT04] A. Sakai, Y. Kamakura, and K. Taniguchi. Quantum lattice-gas automata simulation of electronic wave propagation in nanostructures. pages 241–242, Oct. 2004.

[Spe04] L. Spector. *Automatic Quantum Computer Programming: A Genetic Programming Approach*. Kluwer Academic Publishers, 2004.

[Wat95a] J. Watrous. On one-dimensional quantum cellular automata. In *Proceedings of the 36th Annual Symposium on Foundations of Computer Science*, pages 528–537, 1995.

[Wat95b] J. Watrous. On one-dimensional quantum cellular automata. In *Proceedings of the 36th Annual Symposium on Foundations of Computer Science (FOCS'95)*, pages 528–532, 1995.

[Wat97] J. Watrous. On the power of 2-way quantum finite state automata. Technical Report CS-TR-1997-1350, 1997.

[WG98] C. Williams and A. Gray. Automated design of quantum circuits. In *in Proceedings of QCQC 1998*, pages 113–125, 1998.

[YCS09] A. Yakaryllmaz and A.C. Cem Say. Efficient probability amplification in two-way quantum finite automata. *Theoretical Computer Science*, 410(20):1932 - 1941, 2009. Quantum and Probabilistic Automata.

[YI00] T. Yabuki and H. Iba. Genetic algorithms for quantum circuit design, evolving a simpler teleportation circuit. In *Proceedings of the Genetic and Evolutionary Computation Conference (GECCO)*, pages 421–425, 2000.

5

Conflicting Multi-Objective Compatible Optimization Control

Lihong Xu[1], Qingsong Hu[2], Haigen Hu[1] and Erik Goodman[3]

[1]Tongji University, 1239 Siping Road, Shanghai 200092,
[2]Shanghai Ocean University, 999 Huchenghuan Road, Shanghai 201306,
[3]Michigan State University, East Lansing, MI 48824,
[1,2]P.R.China
[3]USA

1. Introduction

It is clear that there exist many practical control problems in which the consideration of multiple objectives is typically required, and these objectives may conflict with each other. For example, in many practical control systems, control error often conflicts with energy consumption. In the past ten years, we have been studying the greenhouse environment control problem and have gained a considerable understanding of greenhouse dynamics. In a greenhouse, we must keep the temperature and humidity in certain range that is suitable for the plants. However, we are simultaneously required to minimize energy consumption to reduce the cost. The control means include ventilation, heating and spraying, of which heating and spraying are high-energy-consumption methods. In winter, we can improve the temperature by heating and decrease the humidity by heating and ventilating. With the traditional control strategy, we could maintain the temperature and humidity at a very precise point, but the high energy consumption and expensive cost of this strategy would make the greenhouse unprofitable, which implies that this control strategy would not to be chosen by any users. This type of problem is also widely found in industrial control.

There have existed two main traditional methods to solve the above-mentioned multi-objective problem. One is the trade-off weight method (Masaaki, 1997), which translates this multi objective problem into a single-objective one by adding a set of trade-off weights (Masaaki, 1997; Rangan & Poolla, 1997; Eisenhart, 2003). The major advantage of this method is that the translated single-objective control problem is very easy to deal with, but the disadvantage is that the control result will be strongly associated with the trade-off weights chosen, and the controlled objectives may not be satisfactory if we provide bad weights. In addition, the selection of weights is very difficult for users and engineers in the practical situation. Another approach is the constraints method, which optimizes the most important control objective and translates the others into system constraints (Scherer, 1995; Scherer et al, 1997; Sznaier et al, 2000). The advantage of this approach is to satisfy all controlled objectives through constraints; however, the constraint bounds are very difficult for users or control engineers to determine suitably in a practical problem. Bounds that are too tight may bar the existence of a feasible solution for the optimization problem, while too loose bounds may make the optimization problem lose practical significance.

Since the traditional multi-objective control method cannot ensure the existence of a feasible controller in advance, we have adopted a multi-objective coordinated control system in the greenhouse. When these objectives conflict with each other, it is impractical to fix all the objectives at some given optimal "points". To ensure the existence of a feasible controller, we are willing to "back off" on our desire that all the controlled objectives be precisely at their optimal values, relaxing these "point" controlled objectives to some suboptimal "intervals" or "regions," more generally—we call them "compatible objective regions". For example, in the greenhouse, we regulate the temperature objective to be in the interval 24-30°C instead of exactly at 28°C, and the humidity objective to 60%-85% instead of exactly 70%. According to the experts, this greenhouse environment is also very suitable for the plants. Then we design a controller by optimizing the energy consumption objective. This compatible control system can obtain better economic benefit than before and has gained considerable attention from users (Wu, 2003).

Based on the successful application, we have generalized a common compatible control theory framework (Xu et al, 2006) from the practical experience obtained with the compatible objective region used in the greenhouse. We call this method "multi-objective compatible control (MOCC)".

Control of urban traffic flow is also a typical complex multi-objective control problem, evidencing conflict between the main roads and support roads in the saturation state. Intensive research has focused on this problem to improve traffic management. MOCC has also been applied to this traffic flow control problem, including a Ph.D. dissertation written on the subject (Chen et al, 2008).

Considering a general discrete-time system, the multi-objective control problem can be abstracted as

$$x(k+1) = f(x(k), u(k), k) \tag{1}$$

where k denotes the time step, $x(k) \in R^n$ denotes the state, and $u(k) \in R^m$ is the control variable. The state and control variables are required to fulfill the following constraints

$$u(k) \in X \,,\; u(k) \in U \tag{2}$$

where X and U are subsets of R^n and R^m, respectively, containing the origin as an interior point. Then the multi-objective control problem considered here consists in minimizing, at any time step k ,

$$\min_{x(k)\in X, u(k)\in U} J_i\{(k+1)\} = h_i(x(k), x(k-1), \ldots, x(0), u(k), u(k-1), \ldots, u(0)) \tag{3}$$

$$i = 1,2,\ldots,n, k = 1,2,\ldots$$

subject to the system dynamics (1), and

$$x(k-j) \in X, j = 0,1,\ldots,k \,,\; u(k-j) \in U, j = 0,1,\ldots,k \tag{4}$$

It is difficult to obtain the Pareto solutions by traditional optimization methods. A multi-objective evolutionary algorithm (MOEA) is a robust search and optimization methodology that is able to cope with multiple objectives in parallel without translating the multiple objectives into one (see (Fleming & Purshouse, 2002; Goldberg, 1989), and among MOEA algorithms, especially when used for problems with only two objectives, NSGA-II performs

relatively well in both convergence and computing speed, see (Deb et al, 2002; Jensen, 2003)). It permits a remarkable level of flexibility with regard to performance assessment and design specification.
This paper is organized as follows. The second section is the description of two-layer MOCC with the precise model. The third section is the one-layer MOCC combining offline and online parts. A non-even spread reflecting the preference of the user is proposed in this section. The fourth section is the MOCC application to greenhouse environment control. The fifth section is the conclusion.

2. Multi-objective compatible control strategy with a precise model

In this section, we propose a two-layer MOCC framework suitable for a problem with a precise model.

2.1 System description and two-layer MOCC strategy

We first abstract the theoretical multi-objective control problem. Here the controlled system model can be described as follows:

$$x(k+1) = f(x(k), u(k), k) \tag{5}$$

$$y(k) = Cx(k) \tag{6}$$

where $x(k) \in R^n$ denotes the plant states, $y(k) \in R^n$ and $u(k) \in R^m$ are the control outputs and inputs, subject to constraints $\| u(k) \|_\infty \le a$. The aim of control is to make $y(k)|_{k\to\infty} \to y^*$. Taking two objectives as an example, we aim to design controller

$$\pi^p(x(0)) = \{u(0), u(1), ..., u(p-1)\}$$

and to minimize two conflicting objectives: control error, h_1, and control energy consumption h_2, defined as:

$$\begin{aligned} h_1 &= \sum_{k=1}^{p} (y(k) - y^*)^T (y(k) - y^*) \\ h_2 &= \sum_{k=0}^{p-1} u(k)^T u(k) \end{aligned} \tag{7}$$

Then the multi-objective control problem (5)-(7) can be translated into the following multi-objective optimization problem:

$$\min h_1 = \sum_{k=1}^{p} (y(k) - y^*)^T (y(k) - y^*) \tag{8}$$

$$\min h_2 = \sum_{k=0}^{p-1} u(k)^T u(k) \tag{9}$$

$s.t.$ 1. $\pi^p(x(0)) = \{u(0), u(1), ..., u(p-1)\}$

2. $\| u(k) \|_{\infty} \leq a$

3. $h_1 \leq h_1^L$

4. $h_2 \leq h_2^L$

In a practical control system, control error and control energy consumption always lie within an acceptable range; here we denote by h_1^L and h_2^L the maximum acceptable values--which are called the practical objective constraint condition L. Note that h_1^L and h_2^L are only the worst acceptable values and not our control objectives. For example, in a greenhouse, the worst acceptable values h_1^L and h_2^L only ensure that the plants survive, but not that they flourish; our aim is to construct a suitable environment for the plants to grow productively, and not only one in which they can survive.

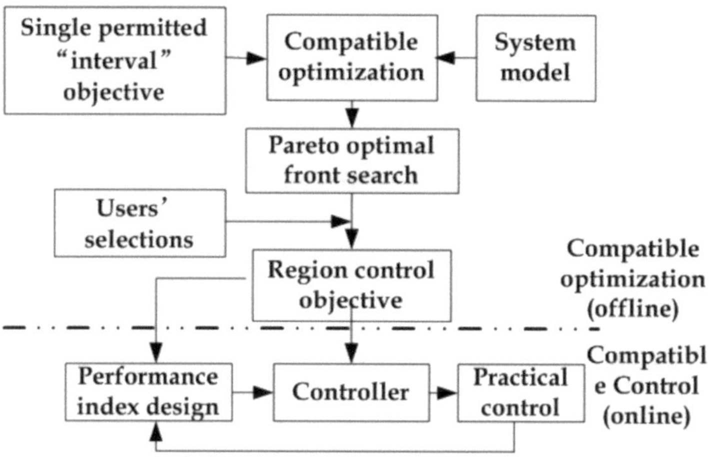

Fig. 1. Two-layer compatible control framework

Next we describe what is meant by a compatible control framework. If the model is precise, the two-layer compatible control framework is as shown in Figure 1. In this section, the uncertainty in the model is all reflected as uncertainty of initial conditions, as will be described more fully in the next subsection. For a two-objective problem, compatible optimization will mean optimization of one of the objectives while maintaining both within an acceptable region of the space identified via the multi-objective search. It differs from the classical method of converting two-objective search to a single-objective search with a constraint on the other, since that approach does not use the Pareto front from the multi-objective search to set the values for the constraints for the measure that is converted from an objective to a constraint.

The first layer is compatible optimization and has the following two requirements:

1. Obtain a compatible (multi-dimensional) controlled objective region
2. The compatible controlled objective region must meet Pareto-optimality and the users' requirements.

The second layer is the compatible control layer and is devoted to satisfy the following requirements:

3. Design a real-time controller to control the system to remain within the (multi-dimensional) objective region determined in the first layer;

4. Optimize further the objective that is most critical to the user to optimize, rather than simply to keep within a specified region.

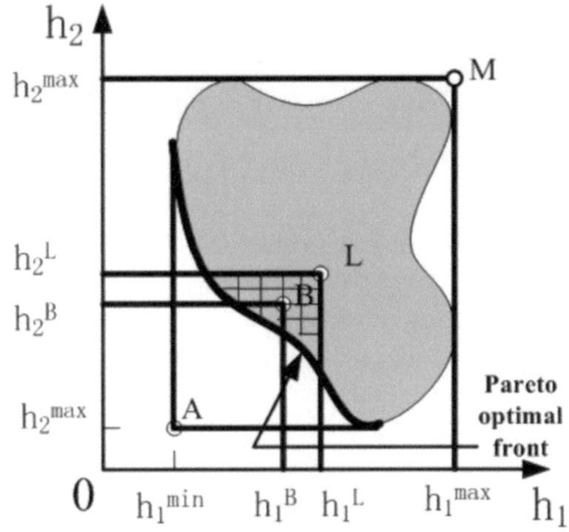

Fig. 2. Space with two conflicting objectives

In Figure 2, the shaded area in rectangle *AM* is the space of objectives in which control solutions exist; the cross-hatched area in rectangle *AL* is the area that meets the constraints of the practical problem; we shall call it the objective region with feasible control solutions; the bold curve is the Pareto optimal front of the objective space with control solutions.

The "optimal point" *A* is not in the subset of the objective space that contains feasible control solutions when the objectives conflict. So *A* is not an optimal point objective that can be attained. This means that there is no controller to realize *A*(*A* is a "Utopia" point). To guarantee the existence of a solution, the point objective *A* will be expanded to a region objective *AB*, where *AB* is a rectangular region (it is an interval for each single objective in *AB*; that is why we have to expand the point objective to an interval objective). To ensure the existence of a solution (i.e., a compatible solution), *B* must be in the region that includes a feasible control solution (the cross-hatched area in Figure 2). Since the selection of *B* would ideally optimize certain of the users' requirements, *B* should be a point on the Pareto optimal front, and included in rectangle *AL* (the bold Pareto front in Figure 2), in order not to be dominated by a better choice of *B*.

To determine the position of *B*, we must have two steps in the first layer algorithm: the first step is to find the Pareto front of the objective space with control solutions--that is, to find multiple, uniformly distributed points on (or approximating) the Pareto front; the second step is, according to the requirements of the users, to select one point *B* on the Pareto front that best defines the users' objective region (that is, the users' desired region for keeping the objectives within). Thus, the compatible objective region is obtained and the first-layer task is finished.

The second layer aims to design a compatible control system to realize the compatible multiple objectives from the first layer. In the controller design, we will not only realize these interval objectives, but also further optimize the objective that users are most concerned to minimize. The discussion above sketches the main ideas of our compatible control methodology.

The detailed algorithm will be introduced in the next section.

2.2 Energy-saving multi-objective compatible control algorithm (Xu, 2006)

Supposing the system model to be precise, an open-loop control method is adopted here. To conveniently illustrate our compatible control algorithm, we use as an example a linear discrete-time system as our controlled model

$$x(k+1) = Ax(k) + Bu(k) \tag{10}$$

$$y(k) = Cx(k) + Du(k) \tag{11}$$

where $x(k) \in R^n$ denotes the plant states, $y(k) \in R^q$ and $u(k) \in R^m$ are the control outputs and inputs, respectively, with constraint $\| u(k) \|_\infty \le a$. Because of different practical situations, the initial conditions may be different. We suppose that the initial conditions lie in some given compact set, *i.e.*, $X_0 = \{(x_1, x_2) \mid x_1 \in [9,11], x_2 \in [9,11]\}$ and the state-space matrices are

$$A = \begin{bmatrix} 0.8 & 0 \\ -0.1 & 0.9 \end{bmatrix}, B = \begin{bmatrix} 1 & 0 \\ 0 & 1 \end{bmatrix}, C = \begin{bmatrix} 1 & 0 \\ 0 & 1 \end{bmatrix}, D = 0.$$

We shall denote this kind of control problem with uncertain initial states as the $I.C. - (X(0))$ problem (namely, control under uncertain initial state).
The control horizon is set $p = 15$ and $y^* = 0$ here. We aim to minimize the following two control performance indexes (control error, h_1 , and energy consumption, h_2).

$$h_1 = \sum_{k=1}^{15} y(k)^T y(k) \tag{12}$$

$$h_2 = \sum_{k=0}^{14} u(k)^T u(k) \tag{13}$$

To reduce computation and ensure control performance, we enforce $u(k) = u(5), k > 5$.

2.2.1 The compatible optimization layer-first layer

The aim of the compatible optimization layer is to find a compatible and relatively optimal objective region. To achieve this, first we should have a method to compare points in the multi-objective space, judging them to be better or worse, or sometimes, neither. It is easy to compare points in a single objective problem. However, it is not so direct in multi--objective problems. In this paper, we adopt Pareto non-domination as the comparison method.
In Figure 3 we assume that every individual i in the population has two attributes: 1) Non-domination rank r_i; 2) Local crowding distance d_i. Here $r(1) = r(3) = r(5) = 1,$, $r(2) = r(6) = 2$, $r(4) = 3$. The next step is to seek a Pareto-optimal set--i.e., a set composed of many non-dominated solutions. In each generation of the GA, popsize offspring and popsize parents are sorted using non-dominated sorting, and the popsize best are retained as parents for the next generation. The non-dominated sorting principle used to select solutions is:

$$i \prec_n j \text{ if } (r_i < r_j) \text{ or } ((r_i = r_j) \text{ and } d_i > d_j) \tag{14}$$

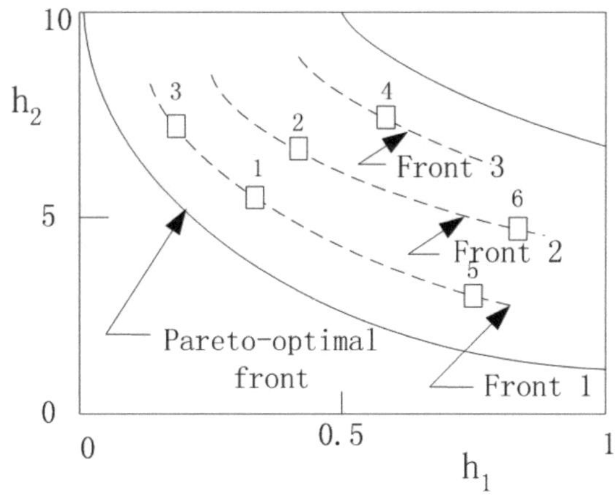

Fig. 3. Three fronts according to non-domination

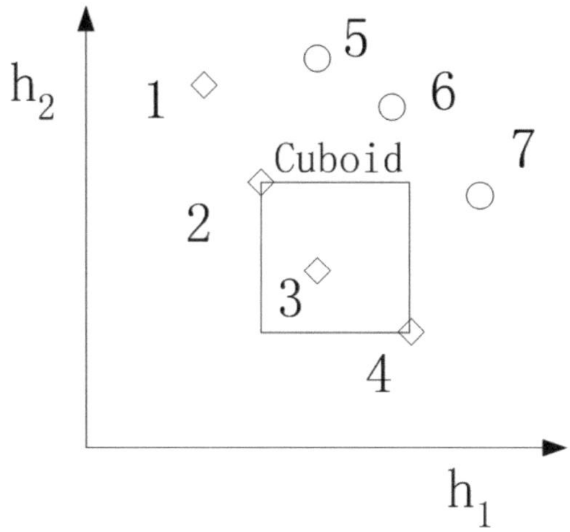

Fig. 4. The crowding distance relationship calculation

Based on the discussion above, and combined with the non-dominated sorting principle of NSGA-II, we propose our MOCC algorithm as follows, to determine the set of control inputs to be applied.

Algorithm 2.1 Robust Multi-Objective Optimization Algorithm

Step 1. Initialize parameters including the population size, *NIND*, the number of generations to calculate, *MAXGEN*, the number of variables *NVAR*, and the binary code length *PRECI* ;

Step 2. For variables $u(k), k = 0, 1, 2, ..., 14$, create a random initial population *Chrom* of candidate control vectors and set generation $gen = 0$;

Step 3. $X(0)$ is the initial region. Calculate the maximum h_1 and h_2 values of the population *Chrom* in the $X(0)$ region;

Step 4. Based on the non-dominated solution definition, separate the population of solutions into consecutively ranked fronts and calculate the individual crowding distances d_i within each front;

Step 5. If $gen \le MAXGEN$, set $Chrom\_f = Chrom$ and store $Chrom\_f$ as the parent population;

Step 6. Selection operation: randomly choose pairs of solutions in the population and subject each pair to a tournament; the total number of tournaments is $NIND$. In each tournament, one solution is selected according to the solution's rank and crowding distance d_i value, and then becomes a breeder in the new population, $Chrom$;

Step 7. Crossover operation: perform crossover on pairs of solutions in population $Chrom$;

Step 8. Mutation operation: mutate the solutions in population $Chrom$; we obtain an offspring population $Chrom$;

Step 9. $X(0)$ is the initial region. Calculate the maximum h_1 and h_2 values of the offspring population $Chrom$ over the $X(0)$ region;

Step 10. Compare the offspring population $Chrom$ and parent population $Chrom\_f$ according to the Pareto non-domination definition and retain $NIND$ Pareto-optimal solutions;

Step 11. Set $gen = gen + 1$; if $gen < MAXGEN$ then return to Step 5; otherwise, stop the loop;

Step 12. Display the Pareto-optimal solutions.

Let $NIND = 80, MAXGEN = 150, NVAR = 12, PRECI = 2$. For the initial region control problem example here, we choose five arbitrary initial states $X(0)$ in the initial state region $X(0)$: [10.9, 10.8], [10.8, 10.9], [10.7, 11], [11, 10], [11, 9.5]; see Figure 5. The computational results of Algorithm 2.1 as a curve are shown in Figure 6.

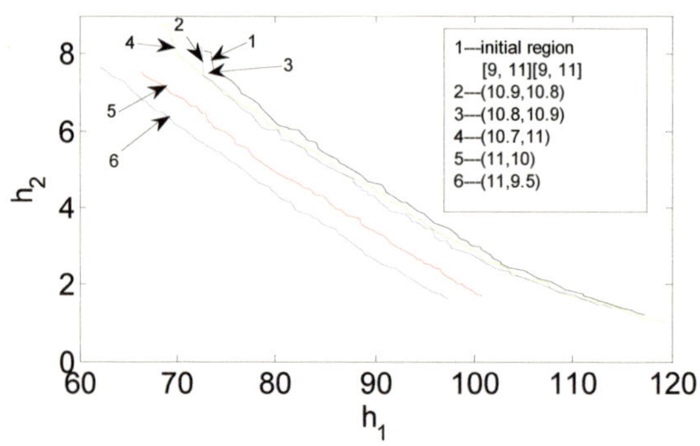

Fig. 5. Pareto fronts for some fixed initial points, namely, [11,10], [11,9.5], [10.7,11], [10.8,10.9] and [10.9,10.8].

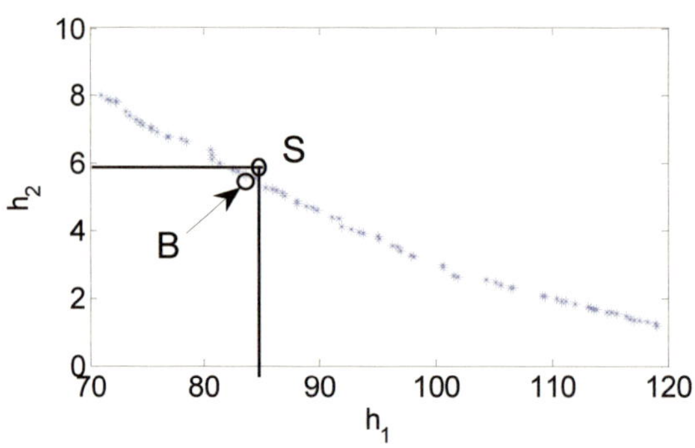

Fig. 6. The upper-right boundary of Pareto band and the user's selection of interval objective

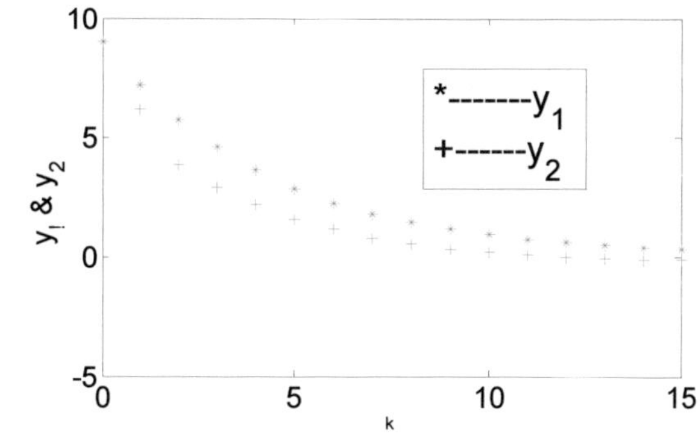

Fig. 7. The control result of the second layer controller

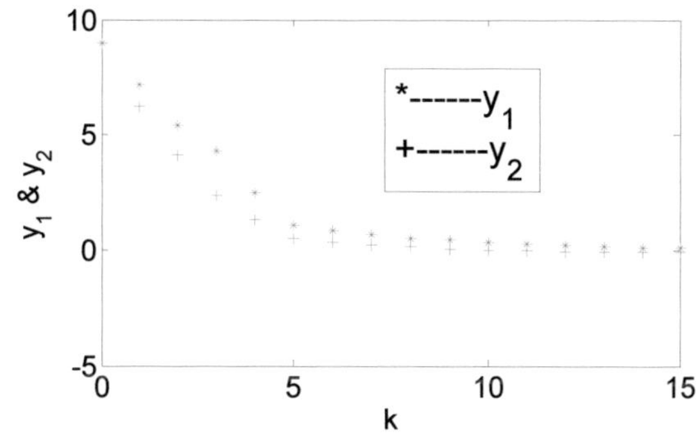

Fig. 8. The control result of the first layer (corresponding to point B in Figure 6)

2.2.2 Compatible control system design — the second layer

The second layer aims to design a multi-objective compatible control system. Assume that we now take energy consumption h_2 as the objective that users are most concerned to minimize.

If we normalize h_1 and h_2 in the intervals $h_1 \in [0,800]$ and $h_2 \in [0,8]$ as $\bar{h}_1$ and $\bar{h}_2$, then the normalized constraints are computed to be $\bar{h}_1 \le 0.66$. We make the interval objective $\bar{h}_1 \in [0, 0.6556]$ from the first layer into a constraint. We now do constrained, single-objective optimization of $\bar{h}_2$ subject to the $\bar{h}_1$ constraint. The online multi-objective compatible control algorithm is now defined as follows:

Algorithm 2.2 (Robust multi-objective compatible controller design)

Step 1. For an arbitrary given initial condition $x(0) \in X(0)$ and randomly created initial values of variable $u(k), k = 0,1,2,...,14$;

Step 2. Determine the control input $u_{best}(k), k = 0,1,2,...,14$ by minimizing the performance index $\bar{h}_2$ with plant performance constraints $\bar{h}_1 \in [0, 0.6556]$ and input constraints $u(k) \le 1, k = 0,1,2,...,14$ by traditional optimal methods with constraints for multiple variables;

Step 3. Implement the control input $u_{best}(k), k = 0,1,2,...,14$.

The system control result for the example with control input $u_{best}(k)$ and $x(0) = [10.8, 10.8]$ is shown as Figure 7.

In order to show that the performance for the primary controlled objective h_2 (i.e., energy consumption) has been improved in the second layer design, the control result of the first layer controller at the same point *B* is shown in Figure 8, and the difference of objective h_2 between the controllers of the first and second layers is quite apparent in Figure 9.

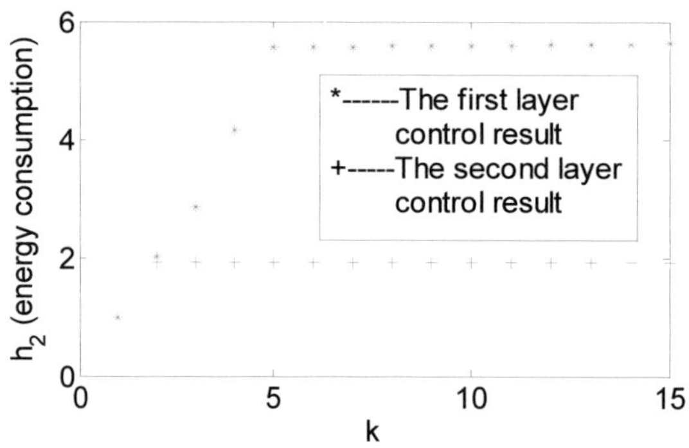

Fig. 9. Comparison of objective h_2 between the controllers of the first and second layers

From Figure 9, compared with the controller obtained by algorithm 2.1 in the first layer at B, the energy consumption h_2 with control input $u_{best}(k)$ obtained by Algorithm 2.2 in the second layer has decreased from 2.338 to 1.5651 (actual energy consumption, not normalized). It indicates that our method not only ensured the robustness of the system but also obviously reduced energy consumption.

3. Iterative MOCC based on preference selection strategy

It is difficult to generate a model that matches the real-world system precisely, so the two-layer method in the previous section is limited in its applicability. Disturbance and model error are usual in control problems. To make the method more usable for real-world problems, an online iterative MOCC algorithm is proposed in this section.

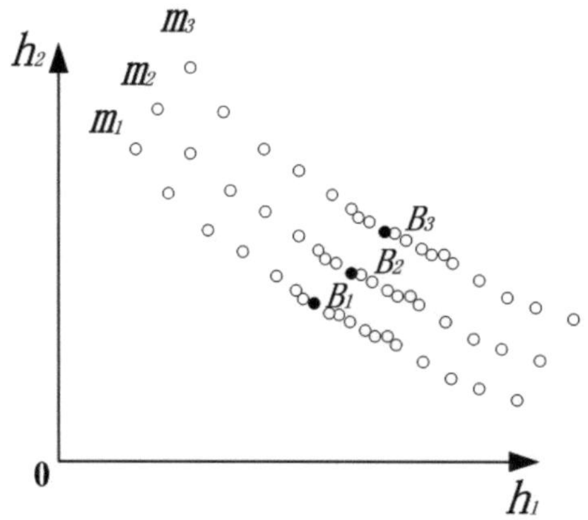

Fig. 10. Control process with non-even staged Pareto front at every control step

The control process can also be explained by figure 10. With the increasing of the time step k, the staged Pareto front will progress from m_3 to m_1 with selecting the control inputs corresponding with B_3, B_2 and B_1 step by step. Note that staged Pareto front m_3, m_2, or m_1 represents an optimization at every time step k, that means the control input is computed by iteratively solving a suitable constrained optimization problem. Since k increases as the control system operates, the Pareto front of the control objective space is related to k, that is, it differs from the ultimate control problem Pareto front, but will converge to it. When the system is stable after certain steps, the Pareto front will also come to be stable.

The multi-objective control problem (MOCP) is different from the pure MOEA because the state variables are time dependent. This is a big challenge because it means that the time to compute a satisfactory solution at each time step must be small, in order to allow for multiple time steps (essentially, allowing for on-line determination of the control.) Population size in the evolutionary algorithm dramatically affects the computation time, but it is necessary to keep a certain population size to make the control process stable. This variety of control problem is different from pure dynamic multi-objective optimization since the states between neighboring time steps are tightly related, which means the neighboring sets in the time series of solution sets are typically relatively close. This is the foundation for taking the evolved population (set of candidate solutions) calculated for any given step as the initial population for the next step, which can obviously decrease the computing load as well as improve system stability. In this section, based on NSGA-II, a multi-objective iterative compatible control algorithm is presented according to the principles above. The iterative MOCC process is as shown in Figure 11.

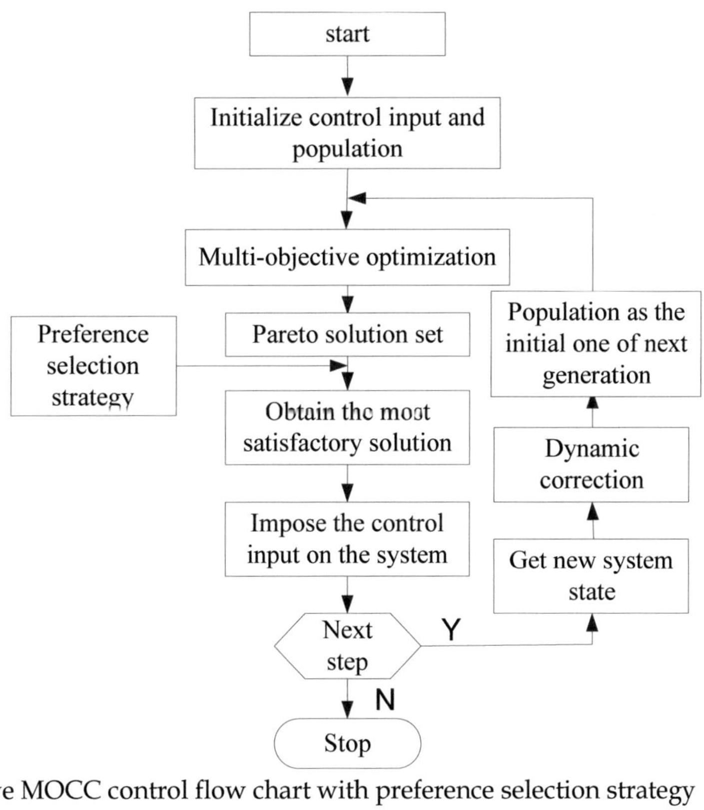

Fig. 11. Iterative MOCC control flow chart with preference selection strategy

3.1 Preference selection strategy and iterative control algorithm (Hu(a) et al, 2009)

Since the control problem is different from the pure optimization problem. For example, it concerns much more about the system stability, even on the sacrifice of losing certain optimal performance. There also exist disturbance and uncertainty in model structure. Therefore, without considering much more about the uniform spread of the solutions on the Pareto front, we take care more about the certain section of the Pareto front. This certain section is named as the optimal control objective area. To realize the non-uniform spread of the staged Pareto front, integrated with the niche technology that maintain the uniform spread of solutions in NSGA-II, an optimal control objective preference selection strategy is proposed which can be explained by the following eq.(15), where the right part is adopted to revise the fitness value of every solution according to its distance to the optimal control objective h_m^C .

$$d_{I_j^m} = d_{I_j^m} + \frac{h_m^{(I_{j+1}^m)} - h_m^{(I_{j-1}^m)}}{f_m^{\max} - f_m^{\min}} \frac{W}{(h_m^{(I_j^m)} - h_m^C)^2} \tag{15}$$

For the convergence of the system, whether or not the system is convergent can be evaluated through state variation, and convergence speed can be improved by selecting suitable individuals from the population. Since the system convergence cannot be judged from one or two steps, certain long step of system state should be tracked to evaluate whether the system is convergent or divergent. Whether a solution in the Pareto front is convergent or divergent is according to its oscillation at this point. The oscillation judgment should be after certain long time from the start of the control process since the system required the time to converge to the objective value. By this method, we can make sure which part in the full Pareto front is convergent. If it is, guide the state to an individual that locates in the nearest non-divergent segment of the Pareto front. The detailed algorithm shown as the flow chart in figure 11 is as follows.

Algorithm 3.1 (Online iterative control process based on preference selection strategy)

Step 1. Initialize parameters including the population size, $NIND$, the number of generations to calculate, $MAXGEN$, the number of variables, $NVAR$ and the binary code length $PRECI$; for variable $u(k), k = 0,1,2,...,14$ (the control vector to be solved for), create a random initial population $Chrom$ and set generation $gen = 0$;

Step 2. Calculate the h_1 and h_2 values of population $Chrom$ based on the initial state $X(0)$; according to the non-dominated sorting relationship, separate the population of solutions into consecutively ranked fronts and calculate the individual crowding distances d_i within each front;

Step 3. Set $Chrom\_f = Chrom$ and store $Chrom\_f$ as the parent population; selection operation: randomly choose pairs of solutions in the population $Chrom$ and subject each pair to a tournament, the total number of tournaments is $NIND$; in each tournament, one solution is selected according to the solution's rank and crowding distance d_i value, and then becomes a breeder in the new population, $Chrom$; crossover operation: perform crossover on the solutions in the population, $Chrom$; mutation operation: mutate the solutions in population $Chrom$; obtain an offspring population $Chrom$; compare the offspring population and parent population

$Chrom\_f$ according to the Pareto non-domination definition and (when applicable) crowding, and retain $NIND$ Pareto-optimal solutions;

Step 4. Set $gen = gen + 1$; if $gen \leq MAXGEN$, then return to Step 3, otherwise, stop the loop; selection strategy: according to the user's preference strategy, however it may be algorithmically captured, select the individual in the population that is most satisfactory, and impose its control input on the system, then get the actual state;

Step 5. Keep population $Chrom$ as the initial population of the online control calculation; initialize the online loop counter $MAXGEN\_Online$ and the initial state with the current state, and replace $X(0)$ with the current system state;

Step 6. For as long as the process is to be controlled, repeat Step3 to Step5, only replace $MAXGEN$ with $MAXGEN\_Online$, otherwise, stop the loop.

3.2 Multi-objective control problem example

This subsection intends to introduce a multi-objective control problem example with an oscillating Pareto front segment.

(a) Control system model:

$$\begin{aligned} x_1(k+1) &= -0.2x_1(k)^2 - 0.2x_1(k)^2 + 0.1 - u_1(k)^2 - u_2(k)^2 \\ x_2(k+1) &= 0.3x_1(k) - 0.3x_2(k) + 0.1 + u_1(k) - u_2(k) \end{aligned} \tag{16}$$

(b) Two Objectives:

$$\min\{h_1(k) = (1 + x_1(k))^2, h_2(k) = (1 + x_2(k))^2\} \tag{17}$$

(c) Constraints:

$$u_1, u_2 \in [-0.2, 0.5] \tag{18}$$

(d) Initial point:

$$x_1(0) = 1, x_2(0) = 1 \tag{19}$$

Since the ε-*constra*int method has the capability to determine non-convex Pareto solutions, it is applied in this section to get the ultimate Pareto front of the control problem. One Pareto solution on the ultimate Pareto front will be obtained with one constraint. The Pareto front will be found by calculating with enough different constraints to fill the possible range. The Pareto front of this control problem is as shown in Figure 12.

The feature of this example is that when 0.95<c<1, objective h_2 is oscillating (see Figure 12). Simulation results of the two-objective variation process are as shown in Figure 13 and Figure 14, where c=0.965. Obviously the system is unstable, from Figure 14. It is easy to find that the oscillation in Figure 14 is the swing between A_1 and A_2 in Figure 12.

In this example, the control result is oscillating if the constraint c is located in 0.95-1.0. This subsection will try to design a selection strategy to judge and jump out if the control system is in the oscillating or divergent state, which can be embedded as the selection strategy in the flow chart shown in Figure 10. With Algorithm 3.1, if first h_1 is set as h_1<0.965, the same value as used in the ε-*constra*int method in the example, the algorithm will find that the state is not stable. A nearest non-divergent state will be found. See Figure 12, where a new suitable solution B is selected, and leads the system into a convergent state (see Figure 15 and the oscillating part and evenly distributed part in Figure 16).

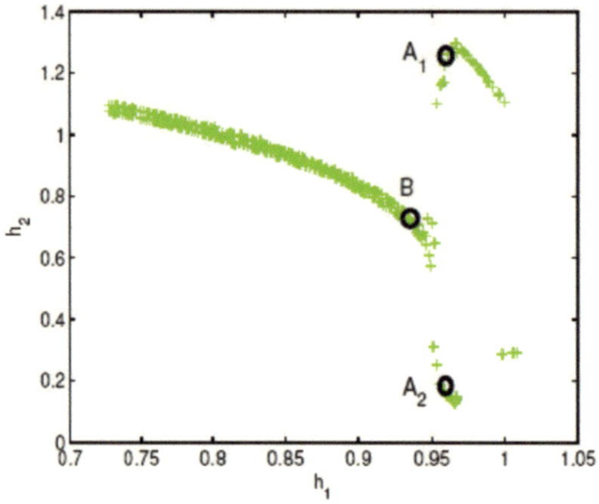

Fig. 12. Ultimate Pareto front of the oscillating multi-objective non-convex control problem example

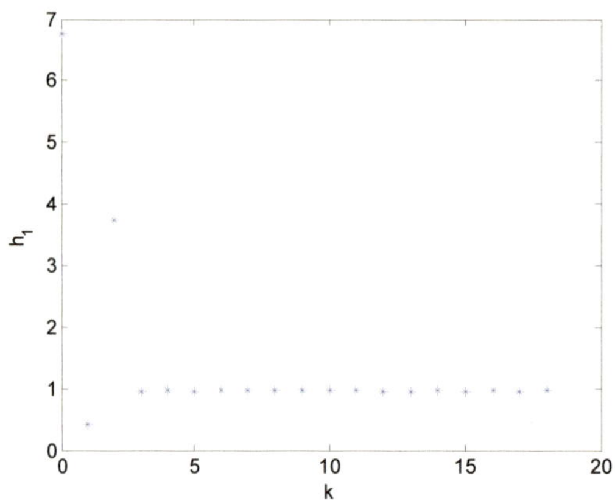

Fig. 13. Variation of h_1 with $\varepsilon - constraint$ method at $c = 0.965$

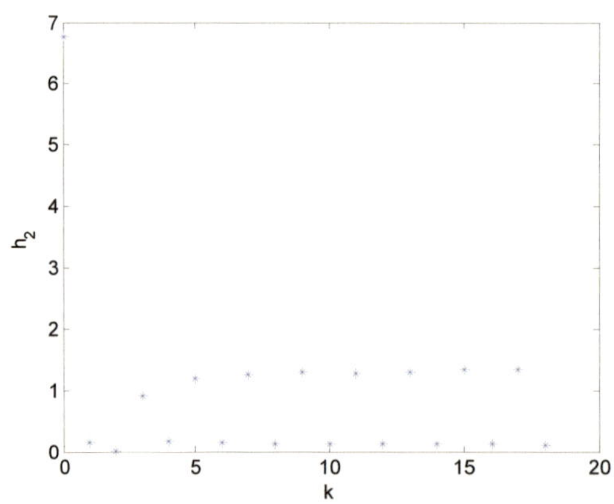

Fig. 14. Variation of h_2 with $\varepsilon - constraint$ method at $c = 0.965$

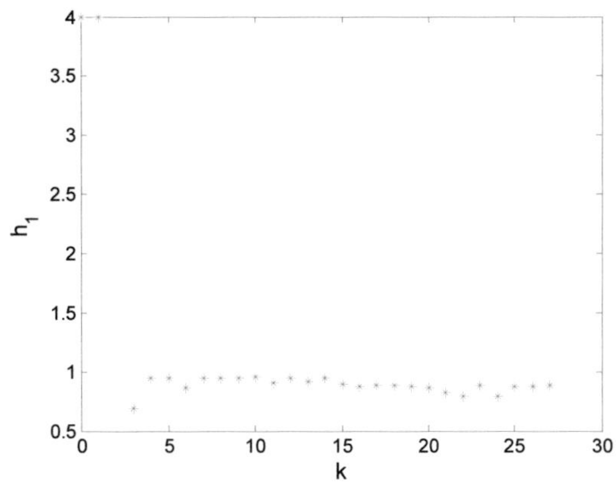

Fig. 15. Variation of h_1 with Algorithm3.1

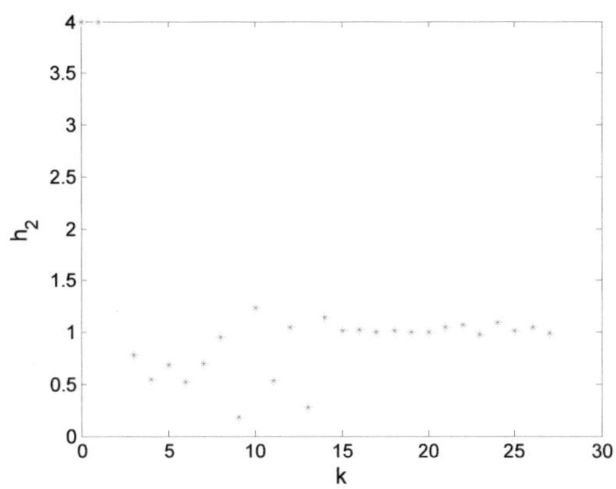

Fig. 16. Variation of h_2 with Algorithm 3.1

4. Application of MOCC to greenhouse environment control

It is well recognized that the greenhouse environment has a great influence on plant growth, production yield, quality, and maintenance processes of the plants. The greenhouse environment differs from a purely physical (non-biological) system, in that the greenhouse system is typically more complex and nonlinear, and the biological system is likely to have significant and numerous effects on its physical surroundings. Greenhouse interior temperature, air humidity and CO_2 concentration are the main control components influencing plant growth and energy usage. These components can be changed through heating, fogging, CO_2 injection, respectively, and ventilation affects all three of these components. Studies and research applications involving environmental control of greenhouses have been performed by many researchers (Pasgianos et al, 2003; Nielsen & Madsen, 1995; Young et al, 2000; Arvanitis et al. 2000; Taylor et al. 2000; Zolnier et al., 2000). These studies and researches are very important to engineering applications in the greenhouse.

There exists a series of dynamic models for greenhouse environments in the literature. The central state variable of greenhouse climate is typically air temperature, with relative

humidity and carbon dioxide concentration also considered. There are many disturbances to the greenhouse climate, which are primarily from solar radiation, outside temperature (conductive heat transfer and ventilation heat transfer) and interactions with occupants (plants), the controlled heating and ventilating equipment, and the floor.
Taking into account these analysis mentioned above, a simple greenhouse heating/cooling/ ventilating model can be obtained from the extant literature as the following differential equations:

$$\frac{dT_{in}(t)}{dt}=\frac{1}{\rho C_p V_T}[Q_{heater}(t)+S_i(t)-\lambda Q_{fog}(t)]-\frac{V_R(t)}{V_T}\cdot[T_{in}(t)-T_{out}(t)]-\frac{UA}{\rho C_p V_T}[T_{in}(t)-T_{out}(t)] \quad (20)$$

$$\frac{dw_{in}(t)}{dt}=\frac{Q_{fog}(t)}{V_H}+\frac{1}{V_H}[E(S_i(t),w_{in}(t))]-\frac{V_R(t)}{V_H}\cdot[w_{in}(t)-w_{out}(t)] \quad (21)$$

$$E(S_i(t),w_{in}(t))]=\alpha\frac{S_i(t)}{\lambda}-\beta_T w_{in}(t)$$

where T_{in}/T_{out} is the inside/outside air temperature(^{o}C), w_{in}/w_{out} is the inside/outside relative humidity(%), UA is the heat transfer coefficient of enclosure (WK^{-1}), V is the geometric volume of the greenhouse (m^3), ρ is the air density ($1.2kgm^{-3}$), C_p is the specific heat of air ($1006Jkg^{-1}K^{-1}$), Q_{heater} is the heat provided by the greenhouse heater(W), Q_{fog} is the water capacity of the fog system (gH_2Os^{-1}), S_i is the intercepted solar radiant energy (W), λ is the latent heat of vaporization (2257 Jg^{-1}), V_R is the ventilation rate (m^3s^{-1}), $E(S_i,w_{in})$ is the evapotranspiration rate of the plants (gH_2Os^{-1}), which is affected by the given solar radiation, α and β_T are scaling parameters, V_T and V_H are the temperature and humidity of the actively mixing air volumes, respectively. Generally, V_T and V_H are as small as 60%-70% of the geometric volume V of the greenhouse.

4.1 Description of the MOCC algorithm based on energy-saving preference

Classical Multi-objective Control Problem methods commonly pursue a precise point as the control objective, and then optimize its tolerance with the reference value. In greenhouse climate, energy consumption and control precision conflict with each other. Low control deviation tolerance is at the cost of high energy consumption. If the greenhouse climate is controlled to a precise point, energy consumption must be high. In practical greenhouse engineering, plants can grow and flourish in some interval or region of humidity and temperature rather than only at one precise point. So it is unnecessary for the greenhouse climate control problem to pursue low control deviation tolerance. Humidity and temperature setpoints can be enlarged to intervals, which can reduce energy consumption while keeping the greenhouse climate suitable for plants to grow and flourish.

4.2 Control objectives

In greenhouse climate, Q_{heater} , Q_{fog} and V_R are the control inputs. In order to save energy, they should be minimized as much as possible. In practical greenhouse engineering, these three inputs have different power requirements. We set these three power ratios as $\lambda_1:\lambda_2:\lambda_3$ respectively. Then the energy objective function can be described as follows:

$$f_1 = \lambda_1 Q_{heart,\%} + \lambda_2 Q_{\%,\text{fog}} + \lambda_3 V_{R,\%}$$
$$(0 \le Q_{heart,\%}, Q_{\%,\text{fog}}, V_{R,\%} \le 1) \qquad (22)$$

In the greenhouse climate model, although energy saving is an optimization objective, the temperature and humidity must also be kept in a range that promotes healthy plant growth. If the interior temperature and humidity of the greenhouse are unfit for plant growth, energy saving loses its practical significance. So energy consumption must be reduced while maintaining a greenhouse climate suitable for plant growth.

According to the analysis above, temperature and humidity objective functions will be cast as tolerances around a pre-set point, shown as:

$$f_2 = abs(T_{in} - T_{set}) \qquad (23)$$

$$f_3 = abs(W_{in} - W_{set}) \qquad (24)$$

T_{set}, W_{set} are the optimal values of the temperature and humidity ranges that will serve as the midpoints of the allowable ranges to be determined as suitable for plant growth. In the control process, if the values of (23) and (24) are within the ranges to be determined, then these objectives will be treated as having the same value, and will allow have no effect on the multi-objective optimization, which will consider only energy consumption.

4.3 The preference interval of energy-saving information (Xu et al, 2009)

In the greenhouse climate control problem, the energy-saving preference information is incorporated into the optimization process. In this situation, solutions with lower energy consumption are superior to others. In standard NSGA-II, the definition of crowding distance is identical except for the extreme points. Crowding distance plays a key role in obtaining well-distributed Pareto optimal solutions. In order to obtain dense Pareto optimal solutions distributed in the preference interval, the crowding definition of standard NSGA-II is modified.

First, the special temperature and humidity intervals that are suitable for plant growth are defined. Second, the minimum energy consumption value J within these special intervals can be obtained in each evolutionary generation. Because J is changed in the evolutionary computation process, adaptation is applied in this algorithm and J is updated in each evolutionary generation. Third, in the evolutionary process, J is set as the preference point. According to the preference point, the preference interval $J \le J_1 \le \theta * J$ (here θ is a constant, $1 < \theta$) is defined. Finally, in each evolutionary generation, if the solution lies within the preference interval, its crowding distances is set to n times that of the standard NSGA-II crowding distance. The time step should be chosen appropriately and carefully. If it is too small, the preference information will lose its power and can't direct the optimization, whereas if it is too larger, it can lead to the phenomenon of premature convergence.

Through modification of NSGA-II, dense Pareto optimal solutions with energy-saving preference information are obtained in the neighborhood of minimum value J, and, to some degree because of the reduction of population diversity, the algorithm can quickly converge to Pareto-optimal solutions.

4.4 Simulation results (Hu(b) et al, 2009)

In order to validate the effectiveness of the algorithm with energy-saving preference information, we use the classical greenhouse climate model mentioned above to illustrate it. Because Q_{heater} , Q_{fog} and V_R are normalized in the energy consumption function (22), coefficients $\lambda_1, \lambda_2, \lambda_3$ are percents of maximum power, respectively. In practical greenhouse engineering, the energy consumption of a heater is higher than that of devices generating fog or ventilation, and ventilation has the lowest energy consumption of these three control inputs.

In most scenarios, in summer, the control inputs used in a greenhouse are only fog and ventilation. So in that case, the energy consumption can be presented as:

$$f_1 = \lambda_2 Q_{\%,\text{fog}} + \lambda_3 V_{R,\%} \tag{25}$$

In simulation, we set $\lambda_2 : \lambda_3 = 20:1$ and $T_{set} = 27,\ W_{set} = 0.7$. Then

$$f_2 = abs(T_{in} - 27) \tag{26}$$

$$f_3 = abs(W_{in} - 0.7) \tag{27}$$

In the greenhouse climate model, the parameters of Table 1 are suitable for summer or winter. Their differences are the initial conditions. For the MOCC method, we set 24°C-30 °C and relative humidity 60%-80% as the control intervals. For the classical control method, we set 27 °C and relative humidity 70% as the control point.

Parameters name	Unit expression	values
C_0	$\min W^0C^{-1}$	-324.67
UA	W^0C^{-1}	29.81
t_v	min	3.41
λ'	W	465
α'	$gm^{-3}\min^{-1}W^{-1}$	0.0033
$1/V'$	$gm^{-3}\min^{-1}$	13.3

Table 1. Identified greenhouse model parameters

Operators and parameters	values
$T_{\text{in}}(0) = C_{T_0}(^0C)$	35
$w_{\text{in}}(0) = C_{w_0}(\%)$	35
$T_{\text{out}}(t)(^0C)$	30
$w_{\text{out}}(t)(\%)$	40
$S_i(t)(W/m^2)$	200

Table 2. Initial parameters of greenhouse in summer

Due to the rapidity of change of outdoor climate, we chose 15 minutes as the control step size and operate the control for 1.5 hours. In Figures 17 and 18, control results of the MOCC method and classical control method (precise point control) in summer are shown. The horizontal axis represents control step and vertical axis is the control result. The total energy consumption is 4.1 for MOCC, and 8 for the precise point control. Because the control point is enlarged to an interval in MOCC, it allows much more room to compromise between control precision and energy consumption. In the greenhouse climate control problem, the requirement for control precision is low, and the control results of MOCC are suitable for plant growth, which allows a large reduction of energy consumption compared to precise point control.

In winter, control inputs are heat, fog and ventilation, and solar radiant energy is weak, so $S_i(t)$ is chosen as 20 rather than 200 in summer. In simulation, the initial conditions are shown in Table 3, and the energy consumption function is described as follows:

$$f_1 = 100Q_{heart,\%} + 20Q_{\%,\text{fog}} + V_{R,\%} \tag{28}$$

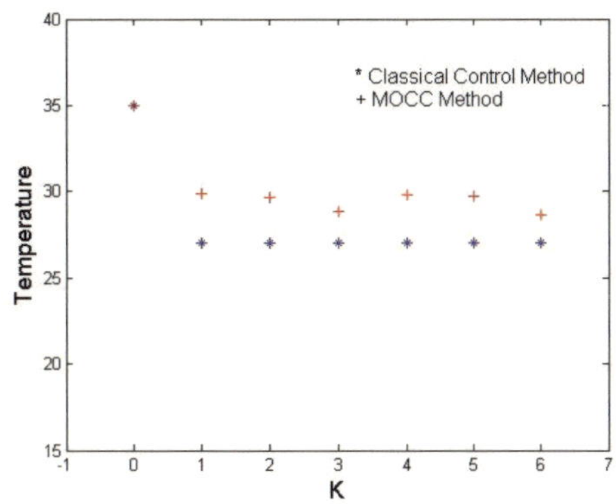

Fig. 17. The control results of Temperature in summer

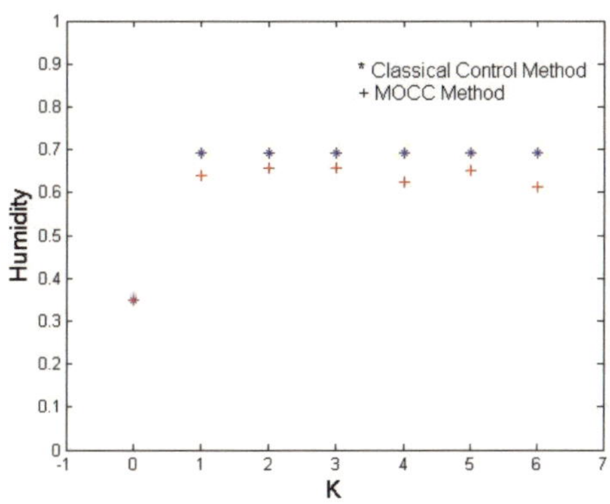

Fig. 18. The control results of Humidity in summer

In Figures 19 and 20, control results of the MOCC method and classical control method (precise point control) in winter are shown. The total energy consumption is 34.8 for MOCC, and 204.5 for precise point control. Comparing the energy consumption of MOCC and the classical control method, the MOCC method has an overwhelming advantage over classical control method with respect to energy saving.

Operators and parameters	values
$T_{in}(0) = C_{T_0}(^0C)$	15
$w_{in}(0) = C_{w_0}(\%)$	40
$T_{out}(t)(^0C)$	-2
$w_{out}(t)(\%)$	20
$S_i(t)(W/m^2)$	20
temperature 'interval' control objective	$24^0C - 30^0C$
Humidity 'interval' control objective	$60\% - 80\%$

Table 3. Initial parameters of greenhouse in winter

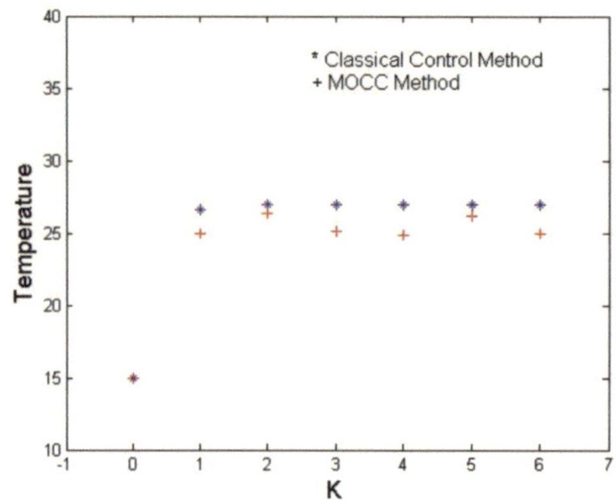

Fig. 19. The control results of Temperature in winter

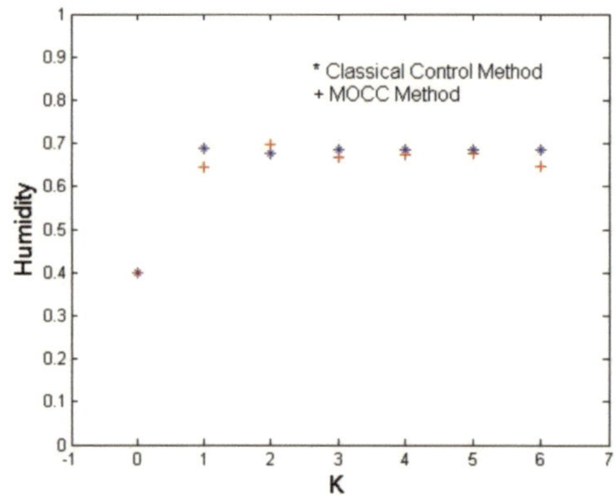

Fig. 20. The control results of Humidity in winter

5. Conclusions

Based on ideas developed in addressing practical greenhouse environmental control, we propose a new multi-objective compatible control method. Several detailed algorithms are proposed to meet the requirements of different kinds of problem: 1) A two-layer MOCC framework is presented for problems with a precise model; 2) To deal with situations including model error and disturbance in the practical problem, a MOCC combining offline and online parts is proposed; 3) MOCC is applied to practical greenhouse control. The result illustrates the validity of the new strategy. The result of applying MOCC to this problem shows that MOCC can be applied widely.

6. Acknowledgement

This paper is supported by NSF (No. 60674070), 863 Plan (No. 2008AA10Z227) and National SCI. & Tech. Support Plan (No. 2008BADA6B01) Of China.

7. References

Arvanitis, K.G., Paraskevopoulos, P.N. & Vernardos, A.A., (2000). Multirate adaptive temperature control of greenhouses. *Computers and Electronics in Agriculture.* 26, 3, 303-320, 0168-1699

Chen, J. (2008). Multi-objective Control Research on Oversaturated Urban transportation, Ph.D dissertation, (Advisor: Xu, L.), Tongji University, Shanghai, China

Deb, K., Agrawal, S., Pratap, A., & Meyarivan, T.(2002). A fast and elitist multi-objective genetic algorithm: NSGA-II, *IEEE Transactions on Evolutionary Computation*, 6, 182-197, 1089-778X

Eisenhart, K. J. (2003). Multiobjective optimal control problems with endpoint and state constraint, Ph.D. thesis, Western Michigan University

Fleming, P.J., & Purshouse, R.C.(2002). Evolutionary algorithms in control systems engineering: a survey, *Control Engineering Practice*, 10, 1223-1241, 0967-0661

Goldberg, D.E.(1989). Genetic Algorithms in Search, *Optimization and Machine Learning*, Addison-Wesley, Reading, MA

Hu(a), Q, Xu, L & Goodman, D E (2009). Non-even spread NSGA-II and its application to conflicting multi-objective compatible control, *2009 World Summit on Genetic and Evolutionary Computation*, June 12-14, 2009, Shanghai, China

Hu(b), H, Xu, L & Hu, Q (2009). Model-based Compromise control of greenhouse climate using Pareto optimization, *2009 World Summit on Genetic and Evolutionary Computation*, June 12-14, 2009, Shanghai, China

Jensen, M.T.(2003). Reducing the run-time complexity of multi-objective EAs: the NSGA-II and other algorithms, *IEEE Transactions on Evolutionary Computation*, 7, 503-515, 1089-778X

Masaaki, I. (1997). Multiobjective optimal control through linear programming with interval objective function, *Proceedings of the 36th SICE Annual Conference*, July 29-31, 1997,Tokushima, 1185-1188.

Nielsen, B. & Madsen, H.(1995). Identifieation of transfer functions for control of greenhouse air temperature. *Journal of agriculture Engineering Research*., 60, 25–34, 1995.

Pasgianos, G., Arvanitis K., Polycarpou P., & Sigrimis N.(2003). A nonlinear feedback technique for greenhouse environmental control, *Computers and Electronics in Agriculture*, 40:153–177, October 2003, 0168-1699

Rangan, S. & Poolla, K.(1997). Weighted optimization for multiobjective full-information control problems, *System & Control Letter*, 31, 207-213, 0167-6911

Scherer, C. W.(1995). Multiobjective $H_2 - H_\infty$ Control, *IEEE Transaction on Automatic Control*, 40, 1054-1061, 0018-9286

Scherer, C., Gahinet P. & Chilali, M.(1997). Multiobjective output-feedback control via LMI Optimization, *IEEE Transactions on Automatic Control*, 42, 896-911, 0018-9286

Sznaier, M., Rotstein, H., Bu, J. Y. & Sideris, A.(2000). An exact solution to continuous-time mixed $H_2 - H_\infty$ control problems, IEEE Transactions on Automatic Control, 45, 2095-2101, 0018-9286

Taylor, C.J., Chotai, A. & Young, P.C. (2000). State space control system design based on non-minimal state variable feedback: further generalizations and unification results. *International Journal of Control*, 73, 1329-1345, 1755-9340

Wu, J. (2003) Research and application of low-cost greenhouse environment control system, March, 2003, Ph.D. thesis (Advisor: Xu L.) of Tongji University, Shanghai, China, 53-58.

Xu, L., Zou, Z. & Hu, Q.(2006). Two-Layer Optimization Compatible Control for Multi-Objective Control Systems, *IEEE International Conference on Networking, Sensing and Control*, 23-25 April, 2006, 658-663.

Xu, L. , Hu, Q. & Goodman E. D.(2007). Two Layer Iterative Multi-Objective Compatible Control Algorithm , *46th IEEE CDC (Conference on Decision and Control)*, USA

Xu, L. , Hu, Q. & Goodman E. D.(2007). A Compatible Energy-saving Control Algorithm for a Class of Conflicted Multi-objective Control Problem , *2007 IEEE CEC (Congress on Evolutionary Computation)*, Singapore

Xu, L, Hu, H. & Zhu, B.(2009). Energy-saving control of greenhouse climate based on MOCC strategy, *2009 World Summit on Genetic and Evolutionary Computation*, June 12-14, 2009, Shanghai, China

Young, L. B. D., Price P.C. & Janssens K.(2000). Recent developments in the modelling of imperfectly mixed irspaces. *Computers and electronics in agriculture*, 26, 239–254, 0168-1699

Zolnier, S., Gates, R.S., Buxton, J. & Mach, C., (2000). Psychrometric and ventilation constraints for vapor pressure deficit control. *Computers and electronics in agriculture*. 26, 343-359, 0168-1699

6

A Multi-Criterion Evolutionary Approach Applied to Phylogenetic Reconstruction

W. Cancino and A.C.B. Delbem
Institute of Mathematics and Computer Sciences
University of São Paulo
Brazil

1. Introduction

Phylogenetic inference is one of the central problems in computational biology. It consists in finding the best tree that explains the evolutionary history of species from a given dataset. Various phylogenetic reconstruction methods have been proposed in the literature. Most of them use one optimality criterion (or objective function) to evaluate possible solutions in order to determine the best tree. On the other hand, several researches (Huelsenbeck, 1995; Kuhner & Felsenstein, 1994; Tateno et al., 1994) have shown important differences in the results obtained by applying distinct reconstruction methods to the same input data. Rokas et al. (2003) pointed out that there are several sources of incongruity in phylogenetic analysis: the optimality criterion employed, the data sets used and the evolutionary assumptions concerning data. In other words, according to the literature, the selection of the reconstruction method has a great inuence on the results.

In this context, a multi-objective approach can be a relevant contribution since it can search for phylogenies using more than one criterion and produce trees which are consistent with all employed criteria. Recently, Handl et al. (2006) discussed the current and future applications of multi-objective optimization in bioinformatics and computational biology problems. Poladian & Jermiin (2006) showed how multi-objective optimization can be used in phylogenetic inference from various conicting datasets. The authors highlighted that this approach reveals sources of such conicts and provides useful information for a robust inference. Coelho et al. (2007) propose a multi objective Artificial Immune System (De Castro & Timmis, 2002) approach for the reconstruction of phylogenetic trees. The developed algorithm, called omniaiNet, was employed to find a set of Pareto-optimal trees that represent a trade-off between the minimum evolution (Kidd & Sgaramella, 1971) and the least-squares criteria (Cavalli-Sforza & Edwards, 1967). Compared to the tree found by Neighbor Joining (NJ) algorithm (Saitou & Nei, 1987), solutions obtained by omni-aiNet have better minimum evolution and least squares scores.

In this paper, we propose a multi-objective approach for phylogenetic reconstruction using maximum parsimony (Fitch, 1972) and maximum likelihood (Felsenstein, 1981) criteria. The basis of this approach and preliminary results were presented in (Cancino & Delbem, 2007a,b). The proposed technique, called PhyloMOEA, is a multi-objective evolutionary algorithm (MOEA) based on the NSGA-II (Deb, 2001). The PhyloMOEA output is a set of distinct solutions representing a trade-off between the criteria considered. Results show the found trees are statistically consistent with the maximum parsimony and maximum likelihood solutions calculated separately. Moreover, the clade supports obtained from the trees found by Phylo-MOEA approximate, in general, the clade posterior probabilities of trees inferred by Bayesian inference methods.

This paper is organized as follows. Section 2. presents a brief introduction to the phylogenetic reconstruction methods. Section 3. introduces the key concepts of genetic algorithms and their application in phylogenetic inference. Section 4. provides background information about multi-objective optimization. Section 5. presents a detailed description of PhyloMOEA. Section 6. discusses the experiment results involving four nucleotide datasets and discusses the main results. Finally, Section 7. presents conclusions and proposes future work.

2. Phylogenetic reconstruction

Phylogenetic analysis studies the evolutionary relationships among species. The data used in this analysis usually come from sequence data (nucleotide or aminoacid sequences), morphological features, or other types of data (Felsenstein, 2004). Frequently, researchers only use data from contemporary species due the information about past species is unknown. Consequently, the phylogenetic reconstruction is only an estimation process since it is based on incomplete information (Swofford et al., 1996).

The evolutionary history of species under analysis is often represented as a leaf-labelled tree, called phylogenetic tree. The actual species (or taxons) are represented by the external nodes of the tree. The past species (ancestors) are referred by internal nodes of the tree. Nodes are connected by branches which may have an associated length value, representing the evolutionary distance between the nodes connected by the branch. It is important to stress that a phylogenetic tree is a hypothesis (of many possible ones) concerning the evolutionary events in the history of species.

A phylogenetic tree can be rooted or unrooted. In a rooted tree, there is a special node called root, which defines the direction of the evolution, determining ancestral relationships among nodes. An unrooted tree only shows the relative positions of nodes without an evolutionary direction.

The main objective of the phylogenetic inference is the determination of the best tree that explains the evolutionary events of the species under analysis. Several phylogenetic reconstruction methods have been proposed in the literature. Swofford et al. (1996) separated phylogenetic reconstruction methods into two categories:

1. Algorithmic methods, which use well-defined steps to generate a tree. An important feature of these methods is that they go directly to the final solution without examining many alternatives in the search space. Consequently, the solutions are quickly produced by these methods. Clustering approaches like NJ (Saitou & Nei, 1987) are in this category.
2. Optimality criterion methods, which basically have two components: an objective function (optimality criterion) and a search mechanism. The objective function is used to score each possible solution. The search mechanism walks through the tree search space in order to find the best scored tree according to the criterion used. Optimality methods are slower than algorithmic methods, however, they often provide more accurate answers (Huelsenbeck, 1995). Examples of optimality criterion methods are

maximum parsimony (Fitch, 1972), maximum likelihood (Felsenstein, 1981) and least squares (Cavalli-Sforza & Edwards, 1967).

One of the main problems in phylogenetic inference is the size of the tree search space which increases exponentially in function of the number of taxons. In the case of optimality criterion methods, this means that the search mechanism requires heuristic techniques, which are able to find adequate solutions in reasonable running time for large or even moderate datasets. Exhaustive and exact search techniques can also be employed, although their use is constrained to problems with a small number of species.

Sections 2.1, 2.2 and 2.3 present a brief review of the criteria employed in this study: maximum parsimony, maximum likelihood and Bayesian inference.

2.1 Maximum parsimony

The parsimony principle states that the simplest hypothesis concerning an observed phenomenon must always be preferred. Parsimony methods search for a tree that minimizes the number of character state changes (or evolutionary steps). This tree, called maximum parsimony tree, refers to the simplest explanation of the evolutionary history for the species in a given dataset (Felsenstein, 2004).

Let D be a dataset containing n species. Each specie has N sites, where d_{ij} is the character state of specie i at site j. Given tree T with node set $V(T)$ and branch set $E(T)$, the parsimony score of T is defined as (Swofford et al., 1996):

$$PS(T) = \sum_{j=1}^{N} \sum_{(v,u)\in E(T)} w_j \cdot C(v_j, u_j), \tag{1}$$

where w_j refers to the weight of site j, v_j and u_j are, respectively, the character states of nodes v and u at site j for each branch (u, v) in T and C is the cost matrix, such that $C(v_j, u_j)$ is the cost of changing from state v_j to state u_j. The leaves of T are labelled by character states of species from D, i.e., a leaf representing k-th species has a character state d_{kj} for position j. The following properties can be noted from Equation (1):

1. Parsimony criterion assumes independence of sites, i.e., each site is evaluated separately;
2. The calculation of the parsimony score only takes into account the tree topology. Thus, the parsimony criterion does not incorporate other information, like branch lengths.

There are several variants of the parsimony criterion. One of the simplest is the Fitch parsimony (Fitch, 1972), which assumes a unitary cost matrix such that $C_{xy} = 1$ if $x \neq y$; otherwise $C_{xy} = 0$. The Fitch and even other more complex variants of parsimony can be even generalized for arbitrary cost matrix and restrictions of state changes (Sankoff, 1985).

Given a tree T, it is necessary to determine the character states of its internal nodes such that $PS(T)$ is minimized. This is also known as the small parsimony problem. In the case of the Fitch parsimony, a post-order traversal in T is enough to minimize $PS(T)$ (this procedure is known as Fitch algorithm (Fitch, 1972)). In the case of generalized parsimony, the small parsimony problem can be solved by applying the Sankoff algorithm (Sankoff, 1985).

Having defined an algorithm to minimize $PS(T)$ for a given tree T, we should determine the tree T^* such that $PS(T^*)$ is the minimum for all tree search space. The problem of finding T^*

is called large parsimony problem, which was proved to be NP-hard (Felsenstein, 2004). However, several heuristic techniques have been proposed to overcome such a difficulty (Goloboff, 1996).

2.2 Maximum likelihood

Likelihood is a widely-used statistical measurement. It evaluates the probability of a hypothesis giving rise to the observed data (Swofford et al., 1996). Thus, a hypothesis with higher probability is preferred to one with lower probability. The likelihood of a phylogenetic tree, denoted by $L = P(D \mid T, M)$, is the conditional probability of the sequence data D given a tree T and an evolutionary model M, which contains several parameters related to tree branch lengths and a sequence substitution model (Felsenstein, 2004). Two assumptions are necessary to compute likelihoods:

1. Evolution at different sites is independent;
2. Evolution from different tree lineages is independent, i.e., each subtree evolves separately.

Given a tree T, $L(T)$ is calculated from the product of partial likelihoods from all sites:

$$L(T) = \prod_{j=1}^{N} L_j(T), \tag{2}$$

where $L_j(T) = P(D_j \mid T, M)$ is the likelihood at site j. The site likelihoods can also be expressed as:

$$L_j(T) = \sum_{r_j} C_j(r_j, r) \cdot \pi_{r_j}, \tag{3}$$

where r is the root node of T, r_j refers to any possible state of r at site j, π_{r_j} is the frequency of state r_j, and $C_j(r_j, r)$ is the conditional likelihood of the subtree rooted by r. More specifically, $C_j(r_j, r)$ is the probability that everything that is observed from node r to the leaves of T, at site j, given r has state r_j. Let u and v be the immediate descendants of r, then $C_j(r_j, r)$ can be formulated as:

$$C_j(r_j, r) = \left[\sum_{u_j} C_j(u_j, u) \cdot P(r_j, u_j, t_{ru})\right] \left[\sum_{v_j} C_j(v_j, v) \cdot P(r_j, v_j, t_{rv})\right], \tag{4}$$

where u_j and v_j refer to any possible state of nodes u and v, respectively. t_{rv} and t_{ru} are the lengths of the branch connecting node r to nodes v and u, respectively. $P(r_j, u_j, t_{ru})$ is the probability of changing from state r_j to state u_j during evolutionary time t_{ru}. Similarly, $P(r_j, v_j, t_{rv})$ is the probability of changing from state r_j to state v_j at time t_{vu}. Both probabilities are provided by the evolutionary model M.

An efficient method to calculate L was proposed by Felsenstein (Felsenstein, 1981) using a dynamic programming approach, where L is obtained by a post-order traversal in T. Usually, it is convenient to work with logarithmic values of L, then Equation (2) results in:

$$\ln L(T) = \sum_{j=1}^{n} \ln L_j(T). \tag{5}$$

The likelihood calculation presented in this section assumes that sites evolve at equal rates. However, this assumption is often violated in real sequence data (Yang, 2006). Several among site-rate variation (ASRV) approaches can be incorporated in model M. One of the most employed ASRV approaches is the discrete-gamma model (Yang, 1994) where variables rates at sites follow a Γ distribution discretized in a number of categories. Several studies (Huelsenbeck, 1995; Tateno et al., 1994) have pointed out that the use of ASRV models can improve the results of the likelihood inference. However, ASRV models also increase the computational cost of the likelihood calculations.

In order to maximize L for a given tree T, it is necessary to optimize the parameters of model M (i.e: branch lengths and parameters of the substitution model chosen), which can be achieved using classical optimization methods (Felsenstein, 2004). Finding the maximum likelihood tree in the search space is a more difficult problem. Moreover, only heuristic approaches (Guindon & Gascuel, 2003; Lemmon & Milinkovitch, 2002; Lewis, 1998; Stamatakis & Meier, 2004) are feasible for large or even moderate datasets.

2.3 Bayesian Inference

Bayesian Inference methods have been more recently applied to phylogenetic inference (Larget & Simon, 1999; Rannala & Yang, 1996). The main objective of these methods is the calculation of the posterior probability of a tree topology and a model given the data.

Let D be a dataset containing n species. Let T_i be the i-th tree topology from N_T tree possible topologies for n species. Let M be the model containing parameters as branch lengths and an sequence substitution model. The posterior probability of tree T_i given D is expressed by:

$$P(T_i/D) = \frac{P(D/T_i, M)P(T_i, M)}{\sum_{j=0}^{N_T} \int P(D/T_j, M)P(T_j, M)dM}, \tag{6}$$

where $P(D|T_i, M)$ is the likelihood of T_i and $P(T_j, M)$ ($P(T_i, M)$) refers to the prior probability of tree T_j (T_i) and the parameters of M. The prior probabilities for tree topologies and parameters of M are specified in advance. Calculating the denominator from Equation 6 involves summing over all tree topologies and integrating over all parameters of M. This calculation is feasible only for small trees. To avoid this problem, the Markov chain Monte Carlo (MCMC) methods have been employed (Yang, 2006).

The MCMC algorithm walks through the tree topology and the parameter spaces. At the end of an MCMC execution, a sample of its iterations can be summarized in a straightforward way (Yang, 2006). For example, the tree topology with the highest posterior probability, called MAP tree, corresponds to the most visited tree during MCMC execution. Posterior probabilities from other tree topologies are calculated in a similar way. Moreover, it is also possible to calculate clade posterior probabilities of the MAP tree. In this case, the clade posterior probability refers to the proportion of visited trees that include the clade. Mr.Bayes (Ronquist et al., 2005) and BAMBE (Larget & Simon, 1998) are programs that implement Bayesian inference applied to phylogenetic reconstruction.

3. Genetic algorithms in phylogenetic inference

Genetic Algorithms (GAs) are metaheuristics (Alba, 2005) that can be used in phylogenetic inference. In the following paragraphs, GAs and their application to phylogenetic analysis are discussed.

Genetic Algorithms are search and machine learning techniques inspired by natural selection principles (Goldberg, 1989). They have been applied to a wide range of problems of science and engineering (Deb, 2001). A GA uses a set of individuals, called population, where each individual represents solutions for a given optimization problem. A fitness value, based on the problem objective function, is associated with each individual in the population. Individuals are internally codified using a data structure that must be able to store all relevant problem variables and represent all feasible solutions.

First, a GA creates an initial population and calculates the fitness of its individuals. Then, a new population is generated using three genetic operators: selection, crossover and mutation (Goldberg, 1989). The selection operator uses individuals'fitness to choose adequate candidates to generate the next population. Features of the selected candidates are combined by the crossover operator and new offspring solutions are created. Then, small modifications are performed in offspring solutions by the mutation operator at a very low rate. The new individuals are stored in the next population. While crossover is useful to explore the search space, mutation can help to escape from local optima. The average fitness of the new population is expected to be better than the average fitness of the previous population. This process is repeated until a stop criterion has been reached. The selection operator leads Gas towards an optimal or near-optimal solution in the fitness landscape. The solutions found by the GA are in the final population.

Various papers have described the application of GAs to the phylogeny problem focused on one optimality criterion. Matsuda (1996) performed the first application of GAs to phylogenetic inference using the maximum likelihood criterion. Lewis (1998) proposed GAML, a GA for maximum likelihood, which introduces a sub-tree swap crossover and mutation operator based on SPR (Sub-tree Pruning and Regrafting (Swofford et al., 1996)) branch swapping. In his study, Lewis used the HKY85 (Hasegawa et al., 1985) evolutionary model whose parameters are included in the encoding of the individual. Thus, GAML optimized the tree topology, branch lengths and parameters of HKY85 model simultaneously.

Katoh et al. (2001) proposed GA-mt, a GA for maximum likelihood, which outputs multiple trees in the final population. These trees include the maximum likelihood tree and multiple alternatives that are not significantly worse compared with the best one. GA-mt also takes into account ASRV in the likelihood calculation. The crossover is a tree swap operator and the mutation is based on TBR (Tree Bisection and Reconnection (Swofford et al., 1996)) topological modifications. GA-mt employs Initial trees taken from bootstrap resampling analysis (Felsenstein, 2004).

Lemmon and Milinkovitch developed METAPIGA (Lemmon & Milinkovitch, 2002), a metapopulation GA (metaGA) for phylogenetic inference using maximum likelihood. In the proposed metaGA, several populations evolve simultaneously and cooperate in the search for the optimal solutions. METAPIGA combines advantages such as fast search for optimal trees, identification of multiple optima, fine control over algorithm speed and accuracy, production of branch support values (Felsenstein, 2004) and user-friendly interface. Another key element proposed by the authors is the consensus pruning mechanism. This procedure identifies the common regions (partitions) that are shared by trees in populations. These regions are protected against changes introduced by topological modifications. Thus, the search is only focused on the unprotected regions until no more changes are allowed. METAPIGA includes a subtree swap crossover operator and several mutation operators based on SPR, NNI (Nearest Neighbor Interchange (Swofford et al., 1996)), taxa swap and subtree swap topological changes. These operators are applied only if they do not destroy any consensus region.

Zwickl (2006) proposed a GA approach called GARLI (Genetic Algorithm for Rapid Likelihood). GARLI was developed in order to find the maximum likelihood tree for moderate and large sequence data (nucleotides, aminoacids and codon sequences). The author introduces several improvements in the topological search and branch length optimization tasks. These novel proposals reduce significantly the computational time required to perform the aforementioned tasks. For example, instead of optimizing all tree branches, GARLI optimizes a branch if the tree likelihood improvement is higher than a predetermined value. Thus, only branches that lead to a significant likelihood gain are considered for optimization. Parallel GARLI versions were also proposed.

GAs and local search were combined by Moilanen (2001) in PARSIGAL, a hybrid GA for phylogenetic inference using the maximum parsimony criterion. PARSIGAL uses a subtree exchange crossover operation and, instead of mutation, a local search approach based on NNI and TBR is employed. Using this hybrid algorithm, the GA defines the promising regions that should contain the global optimum, while the local search quickly reaches such a solution. PARSIGAL also includes heuristics for a fast recalculation of parsimony scores after topological modifications performed by the local search mechanism.

Congdon (2002) proposed a GA, called GAPHYL, which uses the parsimony criterion for the inference of phylogenetic trees. GAPHYL uses several subpopulations to avoid premature convergence, a subtree swap crossover operator and a taxa swap mutation operator. Other applications of GAs for phylogenetic inference employ distance-based optimality criterion (Cotta & Moscato, 2002).

Experimental results from the researches described above have shown that Gas have better performance and accuracy when compared to heuristics implemented in widely-used phylogenetic software, like PHYLIP (Felsenstein, 2000) and PAUP* (Swofford, 2000). Moreover, GAs are also suitable for use with several optimality criteria in order to solve multi-objective optimization problems (MOOP). Section 4. briey describes MOOPs and the application of GAs to them.

4. Multi-Objective Optimization

A MOOP deals with two or more objective functions that must be simultaneously optimized. In this context, the *Pareto dominance* concept is used to compare two solutions. A solution x dominates a solution y if x is not worse than y in all objectives and if it is better for at least one. Solving an MOOP implies calculating the Pareto optimal set whose elements, called Pareto optimal solutions, represent a trade-off among objective functions. Pareto optimal solutions are not dominated by any other in the search space. The curve formed by plotting these solutions in the objective function space is called Pareto front. If there is no additional information regarding the relevance of the objectives, all Pareto optimal solutions have the same importance. Deb (2001) highlights two fundamental goals in MOOP:

1. Finding a set of solutions as close as possible to the Pareto optimal front;
2. Finding a set of solutions as diverse as possible.

Many optimization techniques have been proposed to deal with MOOPs (Deb, 2001). The simplest approach transforms an MOOP into a single optimization problem using a weighted sum of objective functions. This strategy finds a single point in the Pareto front for each weight combination. Thus, several runs using different weight values are required to obtain a reasonable number of Pareto optimal solutions. Nevertheless, this method does not guarantee solution diversity in the frontier. Other classical methods to deal with MOOPs also have limitations, i.e., they need *a priori* knowledge of the problem, for example, target values (which are not always available).

Evolutionary algorithms for multi-objective optimization (MOEAs) have been successfully applied to both theoretical and practical MOOPs (Deb, 2001). In general, the most elaborated MOEAs are capable of finding a distributed Pareto optimal set in a single run. NSGA-II, SPEA2 (Zitzler et al., 2001), PAES (Knowles & Corne, 1999) are some of the most relevant MOEAs available in the literature.

Section 5. describes PhyloMOEA, the proposed MOEA, which is based on the NSGA-II, to solve the phylogenetic inference problem using maximum parsimony and maximum likelihood criteria.

5. PhyloMOEA

In general, optimality criterion methods solve the phylogenetic reconstruction problem as a single objective optimization problem, i.e., only a single optimality criterion (maximum parsimony, maximum likelihood, etc.) is employed to evaluate possible solutions. As a consequence, the results obtained from diverse phylogenetic methods often disagree. A feasible alternative is a multi-objective approach which takes into account several criteria simultaneously. This approach not only enables the determination of the best solution according to each criterion separately, but also finds intermediate solutions representing a trade-off among the criteria used. The following Subsections describe the proposed algorithm.

5.1 Internal encoding

A phylogenetic tree are usually represented using an unrooted tree data structure. An internal node is represented as a circular linked list, where each node has a pointer to its adjacent nodes (Felsenstein, 2004). The degree of an internal node defines the number of elements in the list.

On the other hand, PhyloMOEA employs a standard graph structure provided by the Graph Template Library (GTL) (Forster et al., 2004). GTL facilitates the implementation of genetic operators and the storage of additional information, such as branch lengths. Furthermore, parsimony and likelihood criteria can operate on rooted or unrooted trees.

5.2 Initial solutions

PhyloMOEA uses two populations, a parent population and an offspring population, as NSGA-II does. The parent population is denoted as P_i, where i refers to the i-th generation. In the first generation, solutions from P_1 are created by an initialization procedure. In subsequent generations, P_i stores the best solutions found in the previous i-1 iterations.

Solutions from P_i are also used to create the offspring population, denoted by Q_i, by applying selection, crossover and mutation operators.

PhyloMOEA can generate initial random trees in P_1; however, these trees are poor estimations of the maximum parsimony and likelihood trees. In this case, the PhyloMOEA's convergence is severely affected. In order to overcome this drawback, the initial solutions are provided by maximum likelihood, maximum parsimony and bootstrap analysis, which are performed before PhyloMOEA's execution. This strategy is usually employed by other GA-based phylogenetic programs (Katoh et al., 2001; Lemmon & Milinkovitch, 2002). There

5.3 Objective functions

PhyloMOEA calculates parsimony scores of the unrooted trees using the Fitch algorithm (Fitch, 1972). Several improvements to the original algorithm are detailed in the literature (Goloboff, 1999; Ronquist, 1998). It is possible to quickly recalculate the parsimony score after applying topological changes to the trees. Thus, unnecessary recalculations are avoided and evaluations of solutions are fast. These improvements were not implemented in PhyloMOEA.

The likelihood scores are calculated using the Felsenstein algorithm (Felsenstein, 1981). However, for large datasets, this calculation is time-consuming (Swofford et al., 1996). There are some approaches described in the literature (Larget & Simon, 1998; Stamatakis et al., 2002) in order to overcome this problem.

5.4 Fitness evaluation

The fitness of a solution is obtained using two values: a rank and a crowding distance (Deb, 2001). The rank value is calculated using a non-dominated sorting algorithm applied to $R = P_i \cup Q_i$ (see Section 5.2). This algorithm divides R into several frontiers, denoted by F_1, F_2,..., F_j. The first frontier (F_1) is formed by non- dominated solutions from R. Solutions in F_1 are removed from R and the remaining solutions are employed to calculate the next set of non-dominated solutions, denoted by F_2. This process is repeated in order to find F_3, and so on, until R is empty. The rank value of an individual is the index of the frontier it belongs to.

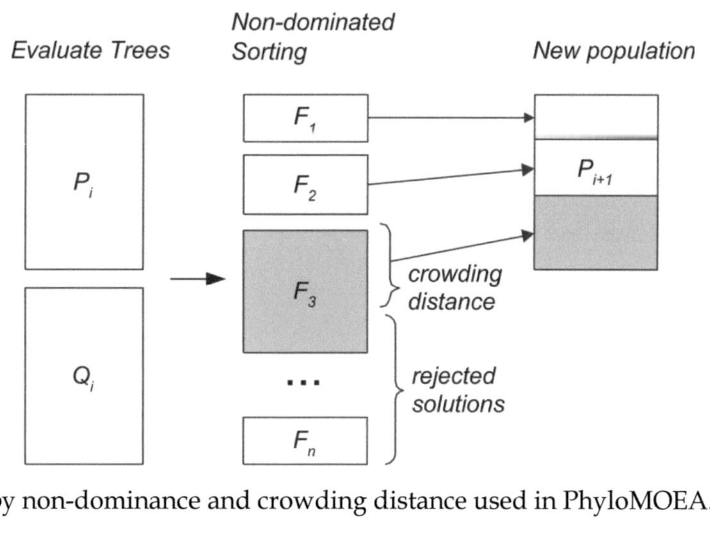

Fig. 1. Sorting by non-dominance and crowding distance used in PhyloMOEA.

Solutions from the frontiers are copied to the next population P_{i+1}. As P_i and Q_i have size N, there are $2N$ solutions which compete for N slots in P_{i+1}. Solutions from frontiers $F_{j=1 \cdots n}$ are copied to P_{i+1} until there are more solutions in frontier F_n than slots in P_{i+1}. In this case, the individuals from F_n with the highest crowding distance values are copied to P_{i+1} until P_{i+1} is fulfilled. The crowding distance is useful to maintain the population diversity. It reflects the density of solutions around its neighborhood. This value is calculated from a perimeter defined by the nearest neighbors in each objective. Figure 1 illustrates the non-dominated sorting algorithm and crowding distance mechanism implemented in PhyloMOEA.

PhyloMOEA uses a tournament selection to choose individuals for reproduction. It randomly picks two individuals from P_i and chooses the best one, which has the lowest rank. If both solutions have the same rank, the solution with the longest crowding distance is preferred.

5.5 Crossover operator

The crossover operator implemented in PhyloMOEA is the same operator proposed in GAML (Lewis, 1998). It combines a subtree from two parent trees and creates two new offspring trees. Given trees T_1 and T_2, this operator performs the following steps:

1. Prune a subtree s from T_1;
2. Remove all leaves from T_2 that are also in s;
3. The offspring subtree T_1' is obtained by regrafting s to an edge randomly chosen from T_2.

The second offspring, denoted as T_2' is created in a similar way: prune a subtree from T_2 and regraft it in T_1. Figure 2 illustrates this operator.

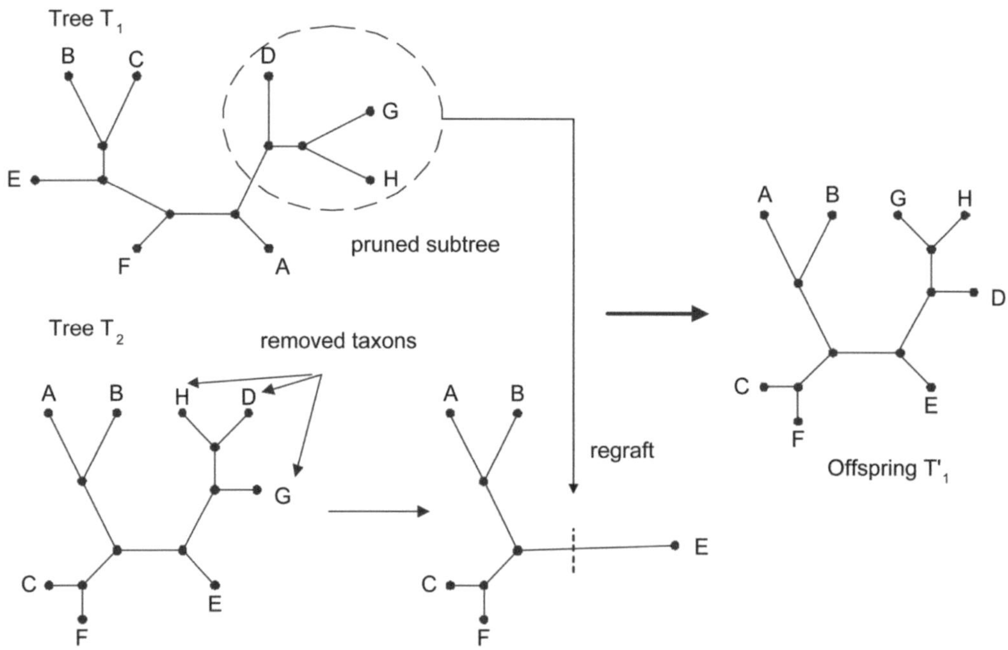

Fig. 2. Example of the crossover operator.

5.6 Mutation operator

There are three well-known topological modifications used in phylogenetic inference: NNI, SPR and TBR (See Section 3.). NNI was employed in PhyloMOEA, since it performs fewer topological modifications than the others. This mutation operator performs the following steps:

1. Choose an interior branch whose connected nodes i, j define two pairs of neighbors: A, B adjacent to i ($A,B \neq j$) and C, D adjacent to j ($C,D \neq i$);
2. Execute a swap of two nodes taken from each pair of neighbors.

Figure 3 illustrates the NNI mutation operator. This operator also modifies branch lengths in order to improve the tree likelihood value. Some branches, chosen at random, have their lengths multiplied by a factor obtained from a Γ-distribution (Lewis, 1998).

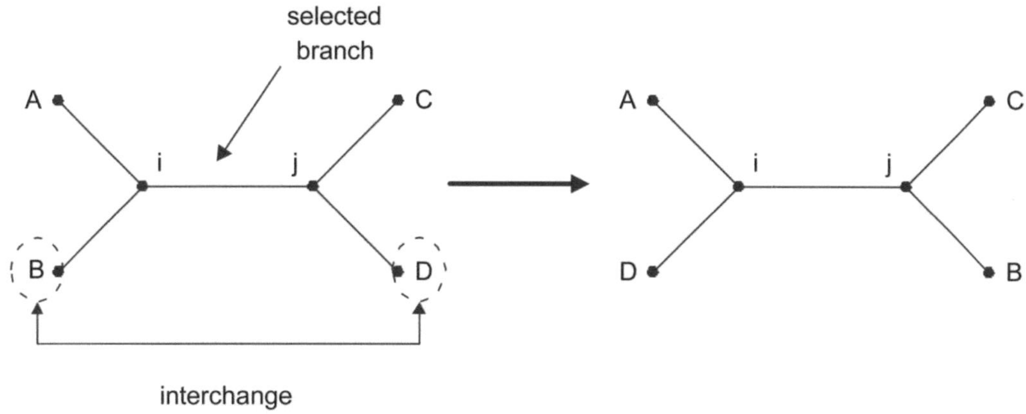

Fig. 3. Example of NNI mutation operator.

Branch lengths from trees in the final population are optimized using a non-decreasing Newton-Raphson method described by Yang (2006). Since this optimization is time-consuming, it is applied only after a PhyloMOEA execution.

6. Results

This section describes the performed tests and analysis of the results. PhyloMOEA was tested using four nucleotide datasets:

1. The *rbcL*_55 dataset comprises 55 sequences (each sequence has 1314 sites) of the rbcL chloroplast gene from green plants (Lewis, 1998);
2. The *mtDNA*_186 dataset contains 186 human mitochondrial DNA sequences (each sequence has 16608 sites) obtained from The Human Mitochondrial Genome Database (mtDB) (Ingman & Gyllensten, 2006);
3. The *RDPII*_218 dataset comprises 218 prokaryotic sequences of RNA (each sequence has 4182 sites) taken from the Ribosomal Database Project II (Cole et al., 2005);
4. Finally, the *ZILLA*_500 dataset includes 500 rbcL sequences (each sequence has 1428 sites) from plant plastids (Guindon & Gascuel, 2003).

The optimization using maximum parsimony was performed by program NONA for the four datasets. Similarly, maximum likelihood analysis was carried out using programs RAxML-V and PHYML. The discrete-gamma HKY85 model (HKY85+Γ) was used to consider ASRV. RAxML-V calculates the likelihood using the HKY85CAT model (Stamatakis, 2006), which is an approximation of the HKY85+Γ. The branch lengths of the tree obtained by RAxML - V and the parameters of the HYK85+Γ model were optimized using PHYML. The aforementioned programs include sophisticated heuristics that produce satisfactory and fast results. Table 1 shows the parsimony and likelihood scores obtained from these programs. Such values represent extreme points of the Pareto front for the two objectives (parsimony and likelihood).

Dataset	NONA		RAxML-V	
	Pars.	Likelihood	Pars.	Likelihood
rbcL_55	4.874	-21.989,580	4.893	-21.889,844
mtDNA_186	2.438	-40.010,941	2452	-39.896,442
RDPII_218	41.534	-147.794,345	42.813	-134.696,535
ZILLA_500	16.219	-81.880,193	16.310	-81.018,060

Table 1. Parsimony and likelihood scores of the phylogenies found by NONA and RAxML-V+PHYML.

The trees in the initial population were generated from a bootstrap analysis applied to each dataset by using software PHYML, which employs the BIONJ algorithm (Gascuel, 1997) to each replication. The parsimony and likelihood scores of solutions obtained by the BIONJ algorithm are close to the scores shown in Table 1. However, for *RDPII*_218 and *ZILLA*_500 datasets, the tree topologies obtained by bootstrap were not close enough to those produced by NONA and RAxML-V+PHYML. Consequently, the PhyloMOEA's convergence is slower in this case. TO mitigate this effect, all solutions from Table 1 were included in the initial population.

Table 2 shows the parameters of PhyloMOEA used for the experiments. The *ZILLA*_500 dataset requires the largest number of generations and population size since it contains a larger number of species.

Parameter	Value
Generations	500 (*rbcL*_55, *mtDNA*_186, and *RDPII*_218) 2000 (*ZILLA*_500)
Population size	50 (*rbcL*_55, *mtDNA*_186, and *RDPII*_218) 100 (*ZILLA*_500)
Crossover rate	0.8
Mutation rate	0.05
Mutation operator	NNI
Substitution model	HKY85

Table 2. Parameters used by PhyloMOEA in the experiments.

Due to the stochastic nature of GAs, PhyloMOEA was run 10 times for each dataset. At the end of each run, the solutions provided by PhyloMOEA could be classified into two types:

1. *Pareto-optimal Solutions* (POS), which are the non-dominated solutions of the final population;

2. *Final Solutions* (FS), which include POS and the trees that have equal parsimony scores and different likelihood scores. These trees are promising from the perspective of parsimony criterion.

Table 3 shows the best score, average score and standard deviation (σ) for the maximum parsimony and maximum likelihood criteria for all executions. The values in bold (Table 3) indicate the parsimony and likelihood scores improved by PhyloMOEA when compared with scores from Table 1. This improvement only occurs in the *mtDNA_186* dataset. On the other hand, the standard deviation of parsimony score for this dataset indicates that the best solutions found by PhyloMOEA can be inferior than the one found by NONA.

The number of FS found for each execution can also be used to evaluate the ability of PhyloMOEA to reproduce results. Table 4 shows the maximum, average and standard deviation of the number of solutions in the two types of solution sets (POS and FS) for all executions. The low standard deviation values indicate the robustness of PhyloMOEA's behavior.

	Parsimony		Likelihood	
Dataset	Best	Average $\pm\sigma$	Best	Average $\pm\sigma$
rbcL_55	4.874	4.874,00 ±0,00	-21.889,844	-21.889,844 ±0,00
mtDNA_186	**2.437**	2.437,90 ±0,32	**-39.896,441**	-39.896,441 ±0,00
RDPII_218	41.534	41.534,00 ±0,00	-134.696,535	-134.696,535 ±0,00
ZILLA_500	16.219	16.219,00 ±0,00	-81.018,060	-81.018,060 ±0,00

Table 3. Summary of the results found by PhyloMOEA for parsimony and likelihood criteria.

	Number of POS		Number of FS	
Dataset	Max.	Average $\pm\sigma$	Max.	Average $\pm\sigma$
rbcL_55	13	10,30 ±1,49	61	52,50 ±5,74
mtDNA_186	10	8,50 ±1,43	59	50,80 ±4,44
RDPII_218	27	23,90 ±1,97	80	77,40 ±3,03
ZILLA_500	26	19,60 ±3,27	71	63,10 ±4,58

Table 4. Summary of experiment results for the number of solutions found by PhyloMOEA.

Figures 4(a), 4(b), 4(c) and 4(d) show the Pareto fronts obtained in one PhyloMOEA execution for *rbcL_55*, *mtDNA_186*, *RDPII_218* and *ZILLA_500* datasets, respectively. Parsimony scores are represented in the horizontal axis while likelihood scores are represented in the vertical one. These Figures also show Final Solutions near the Pareto front. Since the parsimony scores are integer values, the resulting Pareto front is a discontinuous set of points. The two extreme points from the frontier represent the maximum parsimony and maximum likelihood trees found by PhyloMOEA. If both points are close to each other, a reduced number of intermediate solutions is expected. This is the case for *rbcL_55* and *mtDNA_186* datasets, as illustrated in Figures. 4(a) and 4(b). Moreover, Table 3 shows a smaller number of trees in the Pareto front found for both datasets. On the other hand, extreme points in *RDPII_218* and *ZILLA_500* datasets are distant from each other. Consequently, there is a greater number of intermediate solutions, as shown in Figs. 4(c) and 4(d) and in Table 4. Nevertheless, PhyloMOEA was able to find a relatively large number of FS for all datasets.

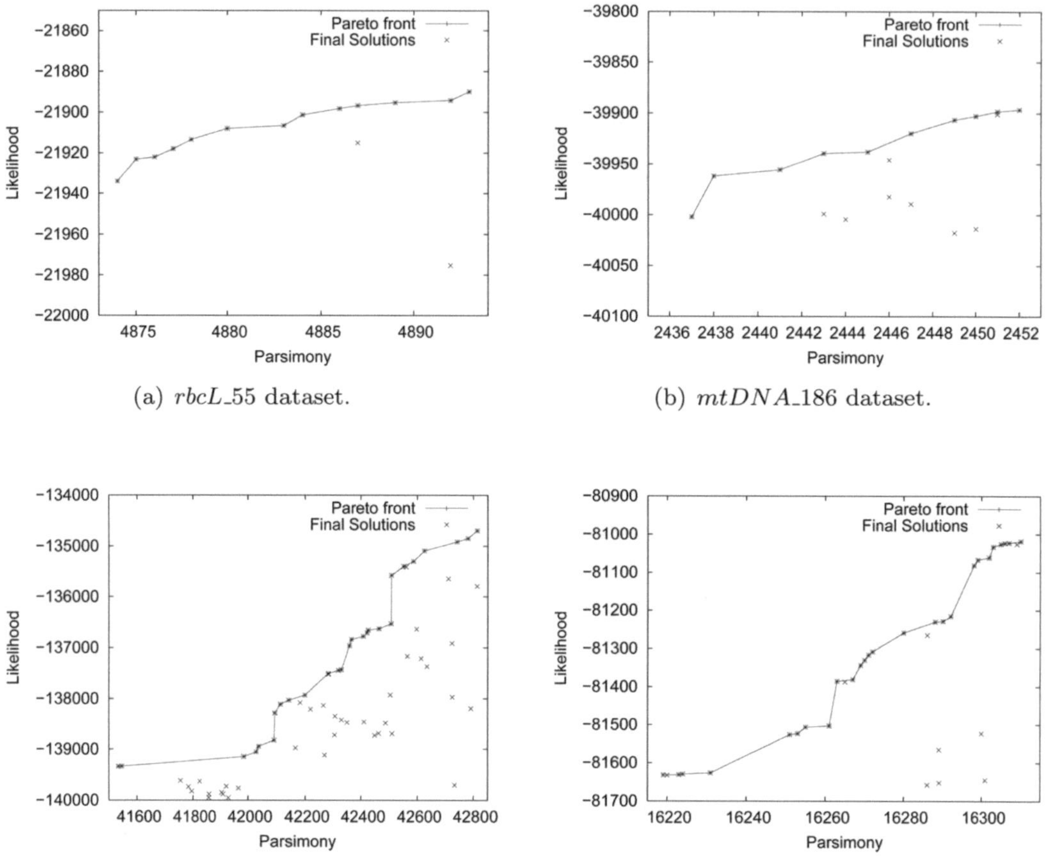

(a) *rbcL_55* dataset. (b) *mtDNA_186* dataset.

(c) *RDPII_218* dataset. (d) *ZILLA_500* dataset.

Fig. 4. POS and FS for the employed datasets.

Solutions from POS and FS were compared using the Shimodaira-Hasegawa test (SH test) (Shimodaira & Hasegawa, 1999). The SH-test calculates a P–value for each solution, which indicates if a tree is significantly worse than the best scored tree according to a criterion. If a tree has a P–value lower than a given bound (usually 0.05), it can be rejected. The SH-test was performed for parsimony and likelihood criteria using PHYLIP and PAML (Yang, 1997), respectively.

Tables 5 and 6 summarize the results from the applications of the SH-test to POS and FS for each dataset showing the number of non-rejected ($P \geq 0.05$) and rejected ($P < 0.05$) trees according to parsimony and likelihood criteria. It can be noted in Table 5 that there are few rejected POS for the *rcbL_55* and *mtDNA_186* dataset in both criteria. This is due to the extreme solutions in the Pareto front having their parsimony and likelihood scores close and, therefore, intermediate solutions cannot be rejected. On the other hand, extreme solution scores for *RDPII_218* and *ZILLA_500* datasets are more distant. Thus, SH-test rejects a larger number of POS for parsimony and likelihood criteria.

In the case of the FS, the SH-test applied to parsimony and likelihood criteria rejects most of the solutions for *rbcL_55*, *RDPII_218* and *ZILLA_500* datasets. On the other hand, the SH-test for parsimony criteria does not reject most of the FS from the *mtDNA_186* dataset. It reveals that parsimony scores for FS are close to the best parsimony score found. The likelihood scores of FS from the *mtDNA_186* dataset are also close to the maximum likelihood score, however, the proportion of rejected solutions is greater in this case.

	SH-test Parsimony		SH-test Likelihood	
Dataset	**Non-Rej.**	**Rej.**	**Non-Rej.**	**Rej.**
rbcL_55	11	2	8	5
mtDNA_186	10	0	9	1
RDPII_218	2	25	4	23
ZILLA_500	9	17	8	18
Total	32	44	29	47

Table 5. Summary of SH-test results for POS.

	SH-test Parsimony		SH-test Likelihood	
Dataset	**Non-Rej.**	**Rej.**	**Non-Rej.**	**Rej.**
rbcL_55	19	40	18	41
mtDNA_186	41	13	29	25
RDPII_218	6	74	5	75
ZILLA_500	16	55	12	59
Total	82	182	64	200

Table 6. Summary of SH-test results for FS.

It can also be noted from Tables 5 and 6 that the number of non-rejected FS is greater than the number of non-rejected POS. In most of the cases, the number of non-rejected solutions is doubled. Thus, the criterion used to maintain relevant solutions for the parsimony criterion was also useful to find alternative solutions according to the likelihood criterion.

We should highlight that the SH-test was designed to be applied for one criterion, i.e. this is not a multi-criteria test. However, the SH-test shows that some of the POS are not significantly worse than the best trees resulting from a separate analysis. Thus, PhyloMOEA was able to find intermediate solutions (distinct trees) that are consistent with the best solutions obtained from the parsimony and likelihood criteria.

Clade supports were calculated using the POS and FS. The support for a clade represents the proportion of trees which include such clade (Felsenstein, 2004). These values were compared with the clade posterior probabilities resulting from a Bayesian inference analysis. This analysis was performed for four datasets using Mr.Bayes. The number of Mr.Bayes iterations was fixed to 1.000.000 for *rbcL_55* and *mtDNA_186* datasets, 1.500.000 for the *RDPII* 218 dataset and 2.000.000 for the *ZILLA_500* dataset. The evolutionary model employed was HKY85+Γ. The default values of the remaining Mr.Bayes'parameters were maintained.

The clades shared by trees found by PhyloMOEA and Mr. Bayes were classified into 7 types in order to facilitate the analysis:

- Type I: clade belongs only to intermediate trees. This type of clade is not present in the maximum parsimony and maximum likelihood trees;
- Type II: clade is only in the maximum parsimony tree;
- Type III: clade belongs to the maximum parsimony tree and intermediate trees;

- Type IV: clade is only in the maximum likelihood tree;
- Type V: clade belongs to the maximum likelihood and intermediate trees;
- Type VI: clade is included in both maximum parsimony and maximum likelihood trees;
- Type VII: clade is contained in maximum parsimony, maximum likelihood and intermediate trees.

Tables 7–10 illustrate the results of the comparison of the clades for *rbcL_55*, *mtDNA_186*, *RDPII_218* and *ZILLA_500* datasets, respectively. These Tables are divided into two parts which show the results for the shared clades of Mr.Bayes trees with PhyloMOEA POS and FS, respectively. The columns of these tables displays the clade type, the number of clades for each type, the PhyloMOEA mean clade support and the Mr.Bayes mean clade posterior probability. The values in bold indicate the highest support by PhyloMOEA and Mr.Bayes.

Results from Tables 7–10 indicate that most of the clades shared between PhyloMOEA and Mr.Bayes trees belong to types I,III,V and VII. However, only clades type V and VII have average clade support larger than 0.5 in most of the cases. This imply that PhyloMOEA and Mr.Bayes support clades that are shared among maximum likelihood and/or maximum

		POS			FS	
Type	Number	PhyMOEA	Mr.Bayes	Number	PhyMOEA	Mr.Bayes
I	1	0,2308	0,3535	18	0,0231	0,1797
III	2	0,6538	0,1471	2	0,5492	0,1471
V	6	0,5897	0,7648	6	0,4912	0,7648
VII	46	**0,9950**	**0,9229**	46	**0,8146**	**0,9229**
Total	55	0,6173	0,5471	72	0,4696	0,5036

Table 7. PhyloMOEA and Mr.Bayes clade support for the *rbcL_55* dataset.

		POS			FS	
Type	Number	PhyMOEA	Mr.Bayes	Number	PhyMOEA	Mr.Bayes
I	10	0,2091	0,1903	101	0,0299	0,1435
II	5	0,0909	0,2148	0	0	0
III	13	0,3776	0,1834	18	0,3002	0,1922
IV	2	0,0909	0,0696	0	0	0
V	35	0,6182	0,3627	37	0,4789	0,3468
VII	138	**0,9960**	**0,8730**	138	**0,9516**	**0,8730**
Total	203	0,3971	0,3156	294	0,4401	0,3889

Table 8. PhyloMOEA and Mr.Bayes clade support for the *mtDNA_186* dataset.

		POS			FS	
Type	Number	PhyMOEA	Mr.Bayes	Number	PhyMOEA	Mr.Bayes
I	15	0,1544	0,3119	48	0,0398	0,3279
III	10	0,4053	0,5405	10	0,4366	0,5405
V	127	0,5864	0,8174	127	0,4830	0,8174
VII	74	**0,9968**	**0,9656**	74	**0,9968**	**0,9656**
Total	226	0,5357	0,6589	259	0,4815	0,6629

Table 9. PhyloMOEA and Mr.Bayes clade support for the *RDPII_218* dataset.

	POS			FS		
Type	Number	PhyMOEA	Mr.Bayes	Number	PhyMOEA	Mr.Bayes
I	14	0,0842	0,1477	113	0,0117	0,1891
III	64	0,3261	0,2820	63	0,3474	0,2764
V	118	0,6554	0,5946	119	0,6128	0,6035
VII	374	**0,9964**	**0,9133**	373	**0,9751**	**0,9113**
Total	570	0,5155	0,4844	668	0,4868	0,4951

Table 10. PhyloMOEA and Mr.Bayes clade support for the *ZILLA*_500 dataset.

parsimony and intermediate trees. Moreover, the difference between PhyloMOEA and Mr.Bayes average support is small for clades type VII; while the same difference for clades type V is greater. On the other hand, most of the clades support values for types I, II, III and VI are low.

Figures 5(a)-5(d) shows the PhyloMOEA and Mr.Bayes clade support values for *rbcL*_55, *mtDNA*_186, *RDPII*_218 and *ZILLA*_500 datasets. Only support values for clades type V and VII are displayed in these Figures. Most of the points for which PhyloMOEA clade supports approximates Mr.Bayes posterior probabilities are located around the [1,1] coordinate. Moreover, these points correspond to type VII clades.

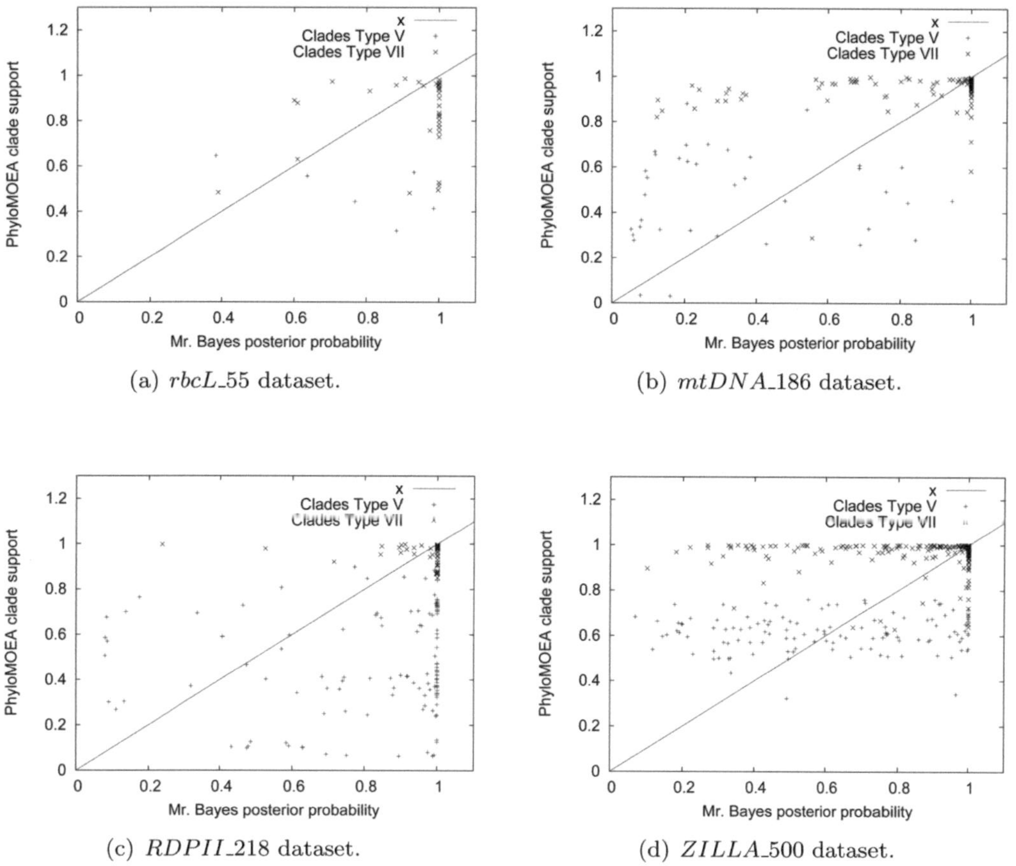

(a) *rbcL*_55 dataset. (b) *mtDNA*_186 dataset.

(c) *RDPII*_218 dataset. (d) *ZILLA*_500 dataset.

Fig. 5. PhyloMOEA clade support vs. Mr.Bayes posterior probability values for the dataset tested.

7. Conclusions

In this paper, we proposed an MOEA approach, called PhyloMOEA which solves the phylogenetic inference problem using maximum parsimony and maximum likelihood criteria. The PhyloMOEA's development was motivated by several studies in the literature (Huelsenbeck, 1995; Jin & Nei, 1990; Kuhner & Felsenstein, 1994; Tateno et al., 1994), which point out that various phylogenetic inference methods lead to inconsistent solutions.

Techniques using parsimony and likelihood criteria yield to different trees when they are applied separately to the four nucleotide datasets used in the experiments. On the other hand, PhyloMOEA was applied to the four datasets and found a set of trees that represents a trade-off between these criteria. POS and FS trees obtained by PhyloMOEA were statistically evaluated using the SH-test. The results of this test suggest that several PhyloMOEA solutions are consistent with the criteria used. It is important to observe that the PhyloMOEA trees are not directly comparable with trees obtained by other phylogenetic reconstruction programs since these programs consider only one optimality criterion.

Moreover, support values for clades included in trees obtained by PhyloMOEA were calculated. The clades were classified into several types according to the type of trees the clade is in: maximum parsimony, maximum likelihood or intermediate trees. Support values were compared with clade posterior probabilities reported by Mr.Bayes for the four test datasets used. The results show that PhyloMOEA clade support closely approximates Mr.Bayes posterior probabilities if the clades found in the set of trees correspond to intermediate and maximum likelihood/maximum parsimony trees.

Despite the relevant results found by PhyloMOEA, there are aspects that could be addressed in order to improve the algorithm and corresponding results:

- PhyloMOEA requires several hours to find acceptable Pareto-solutions if initial trees are poorly estimated. This problem can be improved taking into account local search strategies (Guindon & Gascuel, 2003; Stamatakis & Meier, 2004). PhyloMOEA's performance is also decreased by the likelihood calculation, which is computationally intensive. As mentioned in Section 5.3, there are other techniques that address this problem (Larget & Simon, 1998; Stamatakis & Meier, 2004);
- The proposed algorithm does not optimize parameters of the evolution model employed in the likelihood calculation. These values can be included in each solution such that they can be optimized during the algorithm execution (Lewis, 1998);
- PhyloMOEA uses only Fitch parsimony which has a unitary state change cost matrix. The use of more complex parsimony models or even generalized parsimony can improve the results (Swofford et al., 1996);
- Clade support obtained from PhyloMOEA trees can be also compared with bootstrap support values. A bootstrap analysis, using parsimony and likelihood criteria separately, enables the separation of clades that best support the maximum parsimony and maximum likelihood trees. This could lead to a better comparison between PhyloMOEA and bootstrap clade support values;
- This research has not investigated the metrics for convergence and diversity of the obtained Pareto front. Measurements for convergence are difficult to obtain since the Pareto front is unknown in this case. On the other hand, various diversity metrics found in the literature (Deb, 2001) can be investigated;

The experiments have shown that PhyloMOEA can make relevant contributions to phylogenetic inference. Moreover, there are remaining aspects that can be investigated to improve the current approach.

8. Acknowledgments

The authors would like to acknowledge the State of Sao Paulo Research Foundation (FAPESP) for the financial support provided for this research (Grants N° 01/13846-0 and N° 2007/08655-5)

9. References

E. Alba. *Parallel metaheuristics: a new class of algorithms*. Wiley series on parallel and distributed computing. John Wiley, Hoboken, NJ, 2005. ISBN 0471678066 (cloth).

W. Cancino and A. Delbem. Inferring phylogenies by multi-objective evolutionary algorithms. *International Journal of Information Technology and Intelligent Computing*, 2(2), 2007a.

W. Cancino and A.C.B. Delbem. Multi-criterion phylogenetic inference using evolutionary algorithms. In *Computational Intelligence and Bioinformatics and Computational Biology, 2007. CIBCB '07. IEEE Symposium on*, pages 351 - 358, April 2007b.

L.L. Cavalli-Sforza and A.W.F. Edwards. Phylogenetic Analysis: Models and Estimation Procedures. Evolution, 21(3):550-570, 1967.

G. Coelho, A. Silva, and F. von Zuben. A multiobjective approach to phylogenetic trees: Selecting the most promising solutions from the pareto front. In *7th International Conference on Intelligent Systems Design and Applications*, 2007.

J. Cole, B. Chai, R. Farris, Wang, S. Kulam, D. McGarrell, G. Garrity, and J. Tiedje. The Ribosomal Database Project (RDP-II): Sequences and Tools for High-throughput rRNA Analysis. Nucleic Acids Research, 33:D294-D296, 2005.

C.B. Congdon. GAPHYL: An evolutionary algorithms approach for the study of natural evolution. In *Genetic and Evolutionary Computation Conference (GECCO- 2002)*, 2002.

C. Cotta and P. Moscato. Inferring Phylogenetic Trees Using Evolutionary Algorithms. In J. Merelo, editor, *Parallel Problem Solving From Nature VII*, pages 720-729. Springer-Verlag, 2002.

L. De Castro and J. Timmis. Artificial immune systems: a new computational intelligence approach. Springer, London, 2002.

K. Deb. Multi-Objective Optimization using Evolutionary Algorithms. John Wiley & Sons, New York, 2001.

J. Felsenstein. Evolutionary Trees from DNA Sequences: A Maximum Likelihood Approach. *Journal of Molecular Evolution*, 17:368[376, 1981.

J. Felsenstein. *Inferring Phylogenies*. Sinauer, Sunderland, Massachusetts, 2004.

J. Felsenstein. PHYLIP (Phylogeny Inference Package), 2000. URL http://evolution.genetics.washington.edu/phylip.html.

W.M. Fitch. Toward Defining the Course of Evolution: Minimum Change for a Specific Tree Topology. *Systematic Zoology*, 20(4):406-416, 1972.

M. Forster, A. Pick, M. Raitner, and C. Bachmaier. *GTL – Graph Template Library Documentation*. University of Pasdau, 2004. URL http://infosun.fmi.uni-passau.de/GTL/.

O. Gascuel. BIONJ: An Improved Version of the NJ Algorithm Based on a Sample Model of Sequence Data. *Molecular Biology and Evolution*, 14(7):685-695, 1997.

D.E. Goldberg. *Genetic Algorithms in Search, Optimization, and Machine Learning*. Addison-Wesley Publishing Company, Inc., Reading, MA, 1989.

P. Goloboff. Methods for faster parsimony analysis. *Cladistics*, 12(3):199-220, 1996.

P. Goloboff. Analyzing large data sets in reasonable times: Solutions for composite optima. *Cladistics*, 15(4):415-428, 1999.

S. Guindon and O. Gascuel. A Simple, Fast, and Accurate Algorithm to Estimate Large Phylogenies by Maximum Likelihood. *Systematic Biology*, 5(52):696-704, 2003.

J. Handl, D. Kell, and J. Knowles. Multiobjective Optimization in Computational Biology and Bioinformatics. *IEEE Transactions on Computational Biology and Bioinformatics*, 4(2):289-292, 2006.

M. Hasegawa, H. Kishino, and T.A. Yano. Dating of the Human{Ape Splitting by a Molecular Clock of Mitochondrial DNA. *Journal of Molecular Evolution*, 22: 160-174, 1985.

J. Huelsenbeck. Performance of Phylogenetic Methods in Simulation. *Systematic Biology*, 44:17-48, 1995.

M. Ingman and U. Gyllensten. mtDB: Human Mitochondrial Genome Database, a Resource for Population Genetics and Medical Sciences. *Nucleic Acids Research*, 34:D749-D751, 2006.

L. Jin and M. Nei. Limitations of the Evolutionary Parsimony Method of Phylogenetic Analysis. *Molecular Biology and Evolution*, 7:82-102, 1990.

K. Katoh, K. Kuma, and T. Miyata. Genetic Algorithm-Based Maximum-Likelihood Analysis for Molecular Phylogeny. *Journal of Molecular Evolution*, 53:477-484, 2001.

K. Kidd and L. Sgaramella. Phylogenetic analysis: Concepts and Methods. *American Journal of Human Genetics*, 23(3):235-252, 1971.

J.D. Knowles and D.W. Corne. The Pareto Archived Evolution Strategy: A New Baseline Algorithm for Multiobjective Optimisation. In *1999 Congress on Evolutionary Computation*, pages 98-105, Washington, D.C., 7 1999. IEEE Service Center.

M.K. Kuhner and J. Felsenstein. A Simulation Comparison of Phylogeny Algorithms under Equal and Unequal Evolutionary Rate. *Molecular Biology and Evolution*, 11: 459-468, 1994.

B. Larget and D. Simon. Markov chain monte carlo algorithms for the Bayesian analysis of phylogenetic trees. *Molecular Biology and Evolution*, 16(6):750-759, June 1999.

B. Larget and D.L. Simon. Faster likelihood calculations on trees. Technical report, Department of Mathematics and Computer Science. Duquesne University, 1998.

Alan R. Lemmon and Michel C. Milinkovitch. The Metapopulation Genetic Algorithm: An Efficient Solution for the Problem of Large Phylogeny Estimation. In *Proceedings of the National Academy of Sciences*, volume 99, pages 10516-10521, 2002.

Paul O. Lewis. A Genetic Algorithm for Maximum-Likelihood Phylogeny Inference Using Nucleotide Sequence Data. *Molecular Biology and Evolution*, 15(3):277-283, 1998.

H. Matsuda. Construction of phylogenetic trees from amino acid sequences using a genetic algorithm. In *Pacific Symposium on Biocomputing '96*, pages 512-523. World Scientific, 1996.

A. Moilanen. Simulated evolutionary optimization and local search: Introduction and application to tree search. *Cladistics*, 17:S12-S25, 2001.

L. Poladian and L.S. Jermiin. Multi-Objective Evolutionary Algorithms and Phylogenetic Inference with Multiple Data Sets. *Soft Computing*, 10(4):359-368, 2006.

B. Rannala and Z. Yang. Probability distribution of molecular evolutionary trees: A new method of phylogenetic inference. *Journal of Molecular Evolution*, 43(3): 304-311, SEP 1996.

A. Rokas, B. Wiliams, N. King, and S. Carroll. Genome-Scale Approaches to Resolving Incongrounce in Molecular Phylogenies. *Nature*, 425(23):798-804, 2003.

F. Ronquist. Fast fitch-parsimony algorithms for large data sets. *Cladistics*, 14(4): 386-400, 1998.

F. Ronquist, J. Huelsenbeck, and P. van der Mark. *MrBayes 3.1 Manual*. School of Computer Science. Florida State University, 2005.

N. Saitou and M. Nei. The Neighbor-Joining Method: A New Method for Reconstructing Phylogenetic Trees. *Molecular Biology and Evolution*, 4(4):406-425, 1987.

D. Sankoff. Simultaneous Solution of the RNA Folding, Alignment and Proto- Sequence Problems. *SIAM Journal on Applied Mathematics*, 45(5):810-825, 1985.

H. Shimodaira and M. Hasegawa. Likelihood-Based Tests of Topologies in Phylogenetics. *Molecular Biology and Evolution*, 16(8):1114-1116, 1999.

A. Stamatakis. Phylogenetic models of rate heterogeneity: a high performance computing perspective. In *Parallel and Distributed Processing Symposium, 2006. IPDPS 2006. 20th International*, page 8 pp., April 2006. doi: 10.1109/IPDPS.2006.1639535.

A. Stamatakis and H. Meier. New Fast and Accurate Heuristics for Inference of Large Phylogenetic Trees. In *18th IEEE/ACM International Parallel and Distributed Processing Symposium (IPDPS2004)*, 2004.

A. Stamatakis, T. Ludwig, H. Meier, and M. Wolf. Accelerating parallel maximun likelihood-based phylogenetic tree calculations using subtree equality vectors. In Proceedings on CD, editor, *15th IEEE/ACM Supercomputing Conference (SC2002)*, Baltimore, Maryland,, 11 2002.

D. Swofford. PAUP* Phylogenetic Analisys Using Parsimony, 2000. CSIT Florida State University.

D. Swofford, G. Olsen, P.J. Waddell, and D. Hillis. Phylogeny Reconstruction. In *Molecular Systematics*, chapter 11, pages 407-514. Sinauer, 3 edition, 1996.

Y. Tateno, N. Takezaki, and M. Nei. Relative Efficiences of the Maximum-Likelihood, Neighbor-Joining, and Maximum Parsimony Methods when Substitution Rate Varies with Site. *Molecular Biology and Evolution*, 11:261-267, 1994.

Z. Yang. PAML: A Program Package for Phylogenetic Analysis by Maximum Likelihood. *Computer Applications in Biosciences*, 13(5):555-6, 1997.

Z. Yang. Maximum-likelihood phylogenetic estimation from DNA sequences with variable rates over sites: Approximate methods. *Journal of Molecular evolution*, 39 (3):306-314, 1994.

Z. Yang. *Computational molecular evolution*. Oxford series in ecology and evolution. Oxford University Press, Oxford, 2006.

E. Zitzler, M. Laumanns, and L. Thiele. SPEA2: Improving the Strength Pareto Evolutionary Algorithm. Technical Report 103, Computer Engineering and Networks Laboratory (TIK), Swiss Federal Institute of Technology (ETH) Zurich, Gloriastrasse 35, CH-8092 Zurich, Switzerland, May 2001.

D.J. Zwickl. Genetic Algorithm Approaches for the Phylogenetic Analysis of Large Biological Sequence Datasets under the Maximum Likelihood Criterion. PhD thesis, Faculty of the Graduate School. University of Texas., 2006.

7

New Perspectives in Predicting Membrane Protein-protein Interactions

Kelvin X. Zhang[1,2] and B.F. Francis Ouellette[2]
[1]*University of British Columbia*
[2]*Ontario Institute for Cancer Research*
Canada

1. Introduction

Cells are multi-molecular entities whose biological functions rely on stringent regulations both temporally and specially. These regulations are achieved through a variety of molecular interactions including protein-DNA interactions, protein-RNA interactions and protein-protein interactions (PPIs). PPIs are extremely important in a wide range of biological functions from enzyme catalysis, signal transduction and more structural functions. Owing to advanced large-scale techniques such as yeast two-hybrid and mass spectrometry, interactomes of several model organisms such as *Saccharomyces cerevisiae* (Gavin et al., 2006; Ho et al., 2002; Ito et al., 2001; Krogan et al., 2006; Uetz et al., 2000), *Drosophila melanogaster* (Formstecher et al., 2005; Giot et al., 2003) and *Caenorhabditis elegans* (Li et al., 2004) have recently been extensively studied. Such large-scale interaction networks have provided us with a good opportunity to explore and decipher new information from them. However, there are some limitations of these large-scale data sets: 1) the experimental techniques for detecting PPIs are time-consuming, costly and labor-intensive; 2) the quality of certain datasets is uneven; and 3) technical limitations such as the requirement to tag proteins of interest still exist. As a complementary alternative, computational approaches that identify PPIs have been studied intensively for years and have yielded some interesting results.

Proteins with at least one transmembrane domain constitute 20% to 35% of all known proteins, and therefore account for an important fraction of the proteins involved in biological mechanisms. However, for several reasons, the research on membrane protein interactions has been lagging behind. First, although the current available interactomes contain adequate interactions for analysis, the data sets still have a large amount of false positives. For example, compared to a gold-standard data set, identified protein-protein interactions from three frequently-used high-throughput methods (yeast two-hybrid (Uetz, et al., 2000), tandem affinity purification (TAP) (Gavin, et al., 2006) and high-throughput mass spectrometry protein complex identification (HMS-PCI)) (Ho, et al., 2002) yielded very low accuracy, coverage and overlap (von Mering et al., 2002). Second, some large-scale experimental techniques are biased against membrane proteins. For instance, in order to check whether proteins interact or not, they need to be expressed in the nucleus which may not be their native living environment.

The modified version of the yeast two-hybrid called the split-ubiquitin membrane yeast two-hybrid (MYTH) system (Stagljar et al., 1998) was developed for specially detecting the interactions between membrane proteins. However, it is still time-consuming and labor-intensive, making it infeasible to generate a complete picture of the interactome of membrane proteins at current stage. Several groups have tackled this problem using computational approaches. Miller and colleagues (Miller et al., 2005) worked on identifying interactions between integral membrane proteins in yeast using a modified split-ubiquitin technique. To address the challenges presented in experimental techniques, Xia and colleagues (Xia et al., 2006) developed a computational method to predict the interactions between helical membrane proteins in yeast by integrating 11 genomic features such as sequence, function, localization, abundance, regulation, and phenotype using logistic regression. It however suffers low prediction power and low verifiability with experimental results. In addition to utilizing genomic features to predict protein-protein interactions, graph theory based on the topology of network is an alternative approach to infer protein-protein relationship from protein interaction networks and showing interesting results (Nabieva et al., 2005; Valente & Cusick, 2006). Our group proposed a method to predict interactions between membrane proteins using a probabilistic model based on the topology of protein-protein interaction network and that of domain-domain interaction network in yeast (Zhang & Ouellette, 2008).

The objective of this chapter is to provide an overview focused on recent approaches in predicting membrane proteins by computational methods including a new approach to predict membrane protein-protein interactions developed in our own laboratory. We also discuss the applicability of each computational approach and also the strengths, weaknesses and challenges of all of them.

2. Experimental identification of PPIs between membrane proteins

Currently, the yeast two-hybrid (Y2H) and the tandem affinity purification (TAP) following by mass spectrometry are the two mainstream experimental techniques to identify protein-protein interactions on a large scale. In the yeast two-hybrid system, a bait protein containing a DNA binding domain hybridizes with a prey protein containing an activation domain. If the reporter gene is generated, it means that this pair of proteins interact with each other as the activation domain actives the transcription of the reporter gene. An alternative way is to tag a protein of interest and then express it in cells. The tagged protein and its interacting/binding proteins are purified as it binds to a column or bead. After purification, proteins interacted with the tagged protein are analyzed and identified through SDS-PAGE followed by mass spectrometry. These approaches have provided us with an important amount of valuable protein-protein interactions, which makes it possible to build a more robust interactome of cells.

Besides some intrinsic limitations of these approaches such as high false positives and the requirement to tag proteins of interest, both of them are biased against membrane proteins. In the yeast two-hybrid system, the generation of the reporter gene product indicates an interaction. As the activation of the transcription of the reporter gene takes place in the cell nucleus, participating proteins must be localized to the nucleus. However, membrane proteins usually locate at the cell membrane instead of in the cell nucleus, which makes them excluded from the results of the yeast two-hybrid system. Due to their chemical properties, membrane proteins are difficult to manipulate in protein purification, too.

Therefore, interactions between membrane proteins are less likely to be detected in such approaches.

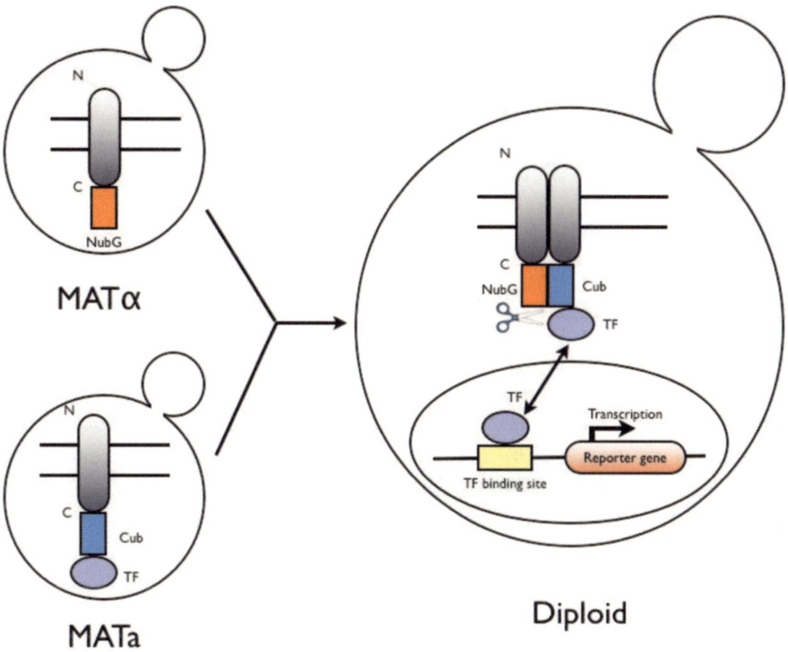

Fig. 1. The split-ubiquitin membrane yeast two-hybrid system. Two membrane proteins are fused to NubG and Cub-TF, respectively. They both are expressed in different mating type. If two membrane proteins interact with each other upon mating as a diploid, the two halves of ubiquitin reconstitute as a quasi-native ubiquitin, a target of ubiqutin-specific proteases that cleave the ubiqutin. The reporter gene is transcribed if two membrane proteins interact with each other as uniqutin-specific proteases release TF into the nucleus and then actives the transcription of the reporter gene.

To overcome the drawback of the above methods, an approach called the split-ubiquitin membrane yeast two-hybrid (MYTH) system was first developed by Stagljar et al. (Stagljar, et al., 1998) and then was further modified in recent years. MYTH is a yeast-based genetic technology to detect detection of membrane protein interactions *in vivo*. This system is based on the split-ubiquitin approach, in which protein-protein interactions can direct the reconstitution of two ubiquitin halves. In such system (Figure 1), individual proteins are simultaneously introduced into the mutant yeast strain. The carboxy-terminal half of ubiquitin (Cub) and a LexA-VP16 transcription factor (TF) are fused onto the N- or C-terminus of a membrane protein while the amino-terminal half of ubiquitin bearing an Ile 13 Gly mutation (NubG-Prey or Prey-NubG) is fused onto the N- or C-terminus of another membrane protein. The protein fused to the Cub and TF can be referred to as the bait protein and is typically a known protein that the investigator is using to identify new binding partners. The protein fused to the NubG-Prey or Prey-NubG can be referred to as the prey protein and can be either a single known protein or a library of known or unknown proteins. If the bait protein interacts with the prey protein, quasi-native ubiquitin is reconstituted. The resultant ubiquitin-specific proteases (UBPs) from the process of ubiquitin can cleave at the C-terminus of the Cub, which releases the TF, so some reporter genes such as HIS3, ADE2 and lacZ can be transcribed in the system.

The split-ubiquitin approach has been widely applied and has yielded interesting results. Thaminy et al. (Thaminy et al., 2003) identified the interacting partners of the mammalian ErbB3 receptor using the split-ubiquitin approach, which proved the effectiveness of such system. Miller et al. (Miller, et al., 2005) further applied this approach to construct an array of yeast expressing the fusion of membrane proteins of interest on a large scale. Recently, more applications of the split-ubiquitin approach have been proposed. For example, novel interactors of the yeast ABC transporter Ycf1p (Paumi et al., 2007) and the human Frizzled 1 receptor (Dirnberger et al., 2008) have been identified using such method.

3. Computational prediction of PPIs between membrane proteins

3.1 Multiple evidence-based

Thanks to current advanced techniques, the relationship between genes can be evaluated based on various types of biological data such as protein-protein interaction data, genetic interaction data, gene co-expression data and phylogenetic profiles. These data sets help us better understand gene functions in the context of specific pathways or biological networks and also enables us to discover gene relationships too weak to be detected in individual data type.

The first attempt to predict interaction between membrane proteins on a large scale started from the work of Miller and colleagues (Miller, et al., 2005). They first generated a set of putative protein-protein interactions between membrane proteins through a modified split-ubiquitin technique. In order to test how reliable these putative protein-protein interactions are, they employed an artificial intelligent approach, support vector machine (SVM), to predict interactions at the different confidence levels. For training purposes, they compiled a positive training set containing 56 protein-protein interactions between membrane proteins from their experimental results and the literatures and a negative training set containing random protein pairs. Besides 10 features derived from experiments such as the number of interactions that the Cub-PLV participates, other 8 genomic features such as Gene Ontology term similarity and co-expression are included as input parameters to the SVM algorithm (Table 1). Finally, they tested 1,985 putative interactions from the experiment using the trained SVM and identified 131 highest confident interactions, 209 higher confident interactions, 468 medium confident interactions and 1,085 low confident interactions.

Xia et al. proposed a prediction method to identify 4,145 helical membrane protein interactions by optimally combining 14 genomic features (Table 1) (Xia, et al., 2006). After the fold enrichment analysis between interacting membrane protein pairs and all membrane protein pairs, they found 11 features are good indicators to predict interactions. Three features (relative protein abundance, relative mRNA expression and relative marginal essentiality) do not demonstrate statistically significant difference between interacting membrane protein pairs and all membrane protein pairs. The authors compiled a gold-standard positive set by selecting all membrane protein pairs in the same MIPS complex and a gold-standard negative set by paring all membrane proteins not in the MIPS complexes. They applied both the logistic regression classifier and the Naïve Bayes classifier on the gold-standard data sets using 11 genomic features. They demonstrated that the integration-based classifier outperforms single evidence-based classifier. Also the logistic regression classifier has higher true positive rate than the Naïve Bayes classifier.

Features	Biological relevance	Ref1	Ref2
The number of interactions that the Cub-PLV participates	A membrane protein was proved to interact with other membrane proteins in the experiment.		*
The number of interactions that the NubG participates	A membrane protein was proved to interact with other membrane proteins in the experiment.		*
Weather both spots for a given NubG were found by the Cub-PLV in either repetition	A membrane protein was proved to interact with other membrane proteins in the experiment.		*
Whether repeated screens by using the same Cub-PLV found this NubG	A membrane protein was proved to interact with other membrane proteins in the experiment.		*
The total number of times that this interaction was observed in the screen	A membrane protein was proved to interact with other membrane proteins in the experiment.		*
Whether a reciprocal interaction is observed	A reciprocal interaction represents the more reliable interaction.		*
Whether the reciprocal interaction was tested	A reciprocal interaction represents the more reliable interaction.		*
The total number of times that this interaction was observed in this orientation or its reciprocal	A reciprocal interaction represents the more reliable interaction.		*
The strength of growth of the yeast in the positive colonies	Stronger interactions result in more growth of the yeast.		*
The relative strength of growth of the yeast in the positive colonies to the controls.	Stronger interactions result in more growth of the yeast.		*
The mutual clustering coefficients, the meet/min coefficient, the geometric coefficient, and the hypergeometric coefficient	High coefficient score indicates interactions.		*
The difference in the codon enrichment correlation (CEC) between the two proteins	Interacting proteins might have comparable codon compositions.		*

GO functional similarity	A pair of membrane proteins tends to interact with each other if they share very similar Gene Ontology (GO) terms.	*	*
MIPS functional similarity	A pair of membrane proteins tends to interact with each other if they share very similar functional categories as defined in the MIPS database.	*	
Membrane co-localization	A pair of membrane proteins tends to interact with each other if they are assigned to the same cellular localization based on the SGD database.	*	*
Total protein abundance	A pair of membrane proteins tends to interact with each other if the sum of their protein abundance is high.	*	
Total mRNA expression	A pair of membrane proteins tends to interact with each other if the sum of their mRNA expression level is high.	*	*
Relative protein abundance	A pair of membrane proteins tends to interact with each other if the absolute difference between their protein abundance is low.	*	
Relative mRNA expression	A pair of membrane proteins tends to interact with each other if the absolute difference between their mRNA expression levels is low.	*	*
mRNA expression correlation	A pair of membrane proteins tends to interact with each other if the correlation of their mRNA expression profiles over time-course experiments is high.	*	*
Transcriptional co-regulation	A pair of membrane proteins tends to interact with each other if they are related by a same transcription factor.	*	
Co-essentiality	A pair of membrane proteins tends to interact with each other if they both are essential genes.	*	*

Total marginal essentiality	A pair of membrane proteins tends to interact with each other if the sum of their marginal essentiality is high.	*	
Relative marginal essentiality	A pair of membrane proteins tends to interact with each other if the absolute difference between their marginal essentiality is low.	*	
Genetic interaction	A pair of membrane proteins tends to interact with each other if they also genetically interact with each other.	*	
Gene fusion, phylogenetic profile, gene neighborhood, gene cluster	A pair of membrane proteins tends to interact with each other if they have high score in the Prolinks database representing functional relatedness.	*	

Table 1. A list of biological features indicating the interactions between membrane proteins. Ref1 represents the method proposed by Xia et al. and Ref2 represents the method proposed by Miller et al. A star sign means this feature has been applied to the corresponding approach.

3.2 Protein primary sequence and structure-based

Helix-helix interactions within a membrane protein or between membrane proteins play a critical role in protein folding and stabilization. Therefore, it has been of great importance to test if a pair of membrane proteins could interact with each other through helix-helix interactions.

Eilers et. al proposed a method to calculate helix-helix packing values at the level of individual atoms, amino acids and entire proteins (Eilers et al., 2002). They found that packing values could be utilized to differentiate transmembrane proteins and soluble proteins as transmembrane helices pack more tightly. Besides packing values, they also demonstrated that helix contact plot, a method to calculate distances between all backbone atoms of each interacting helix pair, is another feature that can be used to classify transmembrane proteins and soluble proteins because the helix contact plot of transmembrane proteins display a broader distribution than that of soluble proteins. This study provides us with a good starting point to predict interactions between membrane proteins using helix packing and interhelical propensity.

Instead of using physical properties between residues, Fuchs et al. developed an approach to predict helical interactions based on the co-evolving mechanism of residues (Fuchs et al., 2007). The underlying hypothesis is that residues within the same particular protein structure tend to be mutated concurrently. They first generated a set of co-evolving residues from seven different prediction algorithms and the helix-helix interactions were then predicted by comparing helix pairs to their structural information in the Protein Data Bank (PDB) combined with this set of co-evolving residues. With this approach, interacting helices could be predicted at the specificity of 83% and the sensitivity of 42%. It is demonstrated that evolutionarily conserved residues are a valuable feature to predict membrane protein interactions.

As more and more structural information related to residues becomes available, more sophisticated computational approaches are needed to improve prediction performance. In a recent publication, a two-level hierarchical method based on support vector machine (SVM) was proposed. In this study, they built two layers of SVMs (Lo et al., 2009). The first layer of SVM was to predict contact residues. Three input features were included at this level: residue contract propensity, evolutionary profile and relative solvent accessibility. The prediction of interactions between contact residues was implemented in the second layer of SVM in which contract residues were used as inputs. They selected five different features in this level: residue pair contact propensities, evolutionary profile, relative solvent accessibility, helix-helix interaction type and helical length. Tested on a set of 85 interacting helical pairs, 768 contact pairs and 939 contact residues, this method reaches to the sensitivity of 67% and specificity of 95%. This approach further proves the notion that the integration of diverse structural and sequence information with residue contact propensities is a good direction to predict helix-helix interactions and membrane protein interactions.

3.3 Network topology-based

A network topology-based approach was proposed by our group (Zhang & Ouellette, 2008). It is able to predict interactions between membrane proteins using a probabilistic model based on the topology of protein-protein interaction network and that of domain-domain interaction network in yeast. It has been demonstrated that the more likely a pair of proteins are functionally related to each other, the more likely they are to share interaction partners (Brun et al., 2003). Moreover, domain-domain interactions have also been shown as indicators of protein interactions due to the binding of modular domains or motifs (Jothi et al., 2006; Pawson & Nash, 2003). Therefore, we sought to examine the hypothesis that two proteins that share same interactors may interact with each other themselves. In order to address this question, we considered the internal protein-protein and domain-domain relationship of a pair of proteins and their protein-protein interaction partners.

Protein-protein interaction and domain-domain interaction data from disparate sources were integrated and then a log likelihood scoring method was applied on all putative integral membrane proteins in yeast to predict all putative integral membrane protein-protein interactions based on a cut-off threshold. It is shown that our approach improves on other predictive approaches when tested on a "gold-standard" data set and achieves 74.6% true positive rate at the expense of 0.43% false positive rate. Furthermore, it is also found that two integral membrane proteins are more likely to interact with each other if they share more common interaction partners. Recently, we proposed an improved approach to predict membrane PPIs by incorporating one more piece of evidence – gene ontology (GO) semantic similarity.

A scoring model can infer how closely a pair of genes is related in a protein-protein interaction network. According to previous research, if two proteins interact with a very similar group of proteins, they are likely to interact with each other (Ho, et al., 2002; Yu et al., 2006), thus, for a given pair of genes, we first mapped them to a pair of proteins, and then found a common set of interactors for this pair of genes and protein-protein interactions within the whole set of common interactors. A scoring method was employed to calculate the likelihood that a group of genes (a pair of query genes) and the whole set of their common interactors are more densely connected (the number of PPIs within a group of proteins) than would be expected at random (Kelley & Ideker, 2005):

$$S_p(S,I) = \log \frac{P(S,I \mid N)}{P(S,I \mid N_{control})} = \log \frac{\prod_{(x,y)\in S\times S} \beta P_I(x,y) + (1-\beta)(1-P_I(x,y))}{\prod_{(x,y)\in S\times S} c_{x,y} P_I(x,y) + (1-c_{x,y})(1-P_I(x,y))} \quad (1)$$

where S is a set of common interactors plus a given pair of genes and I is a set of protein-protein interactions among those genes. $P_I(x, y)$ is an indicator function that equals 1 if and only if the interaction (x, y) occurs in I and otherwise 0. For network N, interactions are expected to occur with high probability for every pair of proteins in S. In our work, we followed the previous knowledge to estimate β and set β to 0.9 (Mewes et al., 2006). For network $N_{control}$, the probability of observing each interaction $c_{x,y}$ was determined by estimating the fraction of all control networks with randomly expected degree distribution which also contain that protein-protein interaction. Comparable control networks were randomly generated by rewiring interaction networks with same node number from the same gene set and same number of degrees, and by repeating the process 100 times.

Should a given pair of proteins has a documented list of domain-domain interactions in iPfam, then we will have two sets of domains corresponding to two proteins. Hence, given a pair of proteins and their common interaction partners, a lot of domain-domain pairs among these sets of domains are possible. A modified model (2) implies dense domain-domain interactions existing in a group of common interactors of a given gene pair. A related log-odds score was used to evaluate the probability that the domain-domain interactions bridging between these two genes and their common interaction partners were denser than random based on the above scoring method:

$$S_d(S,I) = \log \frac{\prod_{(x,y)\in S\times S} \beta \frac{\sum_{(m,n)\in x\times y} D_I(m,n)}{D_x \times D_y} + (1-\beta)(1 - \frac{\sum_{(m,n)\in x\times y} D_I(m,n)}{D_x \times D_y})}{\prod_{(x,y)\in S\times S} c_{x,y} \frac{\sum_{(m,n)\in x\times y} D_I(m,n)}{D_x \times D_y} + (1-c_{x,y})(1 - \frac{\sum_{(m,n)\in x\times y} D_I(m,n)}{D_x \times D_y})} \quad (2)$$

Compared to the previous equation, $D_I(m, n)$ is an indicator function that equals 1 if and only if the domain-domain interaction (m,n) occurs in I and otherwise 0; D_x/D_y is the number of domains in each protein x and y; for network $N_{control}$, the probability of observing each domain-domain interaction $c_{x,y}$ was determined by estimating the fraction of all control networks with randomly expected degree distribution that also contain that domain-domain interactions occurring between two proteins.

In order to measure the functional similarity between a pair of proteins, we developed a new scoring approach based on GO terms. Given two groups of GO terms (M, N) representing two proteins, the functional similarity between a pair of proteins was calculated by the following formula:

$$S_{GO}(M,N) = \frac{\sum_{i=1}^{m} \max_{j=1}^{n}(GO(i,j)) + \sum_{i=1}^{n} \max_{j=1}^{m}(GO(i,j))}{m+n} \quad (3)$$

where M is the set of unique GO terms of the protein x; N is the set of unique GO terms of the protein y; m is the number of GO terms in the set M; n is the number of GO terms in the set N; GO(i,j) is the similarity score between GO term i and GO term j. The similarity scores between a pair of GO terms were computed based on the algorithm G-SESAME, a new advanced method to measure the semantic similarity of GO terms by considering the locations of their ancestor terms of the two specific terms (Wang et al., 2007).
To put the above three types of scores together, the final scoring function for a given pair of proteins was then:

$$S_{final} = S_p + S_d + S_{go} \quad (4)$$

For each possible interaction between integral membrane proteins, we calculated three different scores: PPI score, DDI score and a combined PPI/DDI/GO score according to (1)(2)(3)(4). This generated a table with 996,166 interacting pairs of proteins, each with three interaction probability scores. We compared the performance of our proposed approach by different types of scores: PPI score, DDI score, GO score and the combined score. A ROC curve was plotted by measuring sensitivity and specificity when tested against the gold-standard data set at different cut-off values (Fig. 2). The area under curve is 0.95 for combined score, 0.85 for PPI, 0.74 for DDI and 0.8 fro GO terms, respectively, which indicates the good prediction performance of the proposed scoring method. Better performance can be achieved if we used combined scores rather than using PPI scores or DDI scores alone. It is estimated that there are around 5,000 interactions existing between

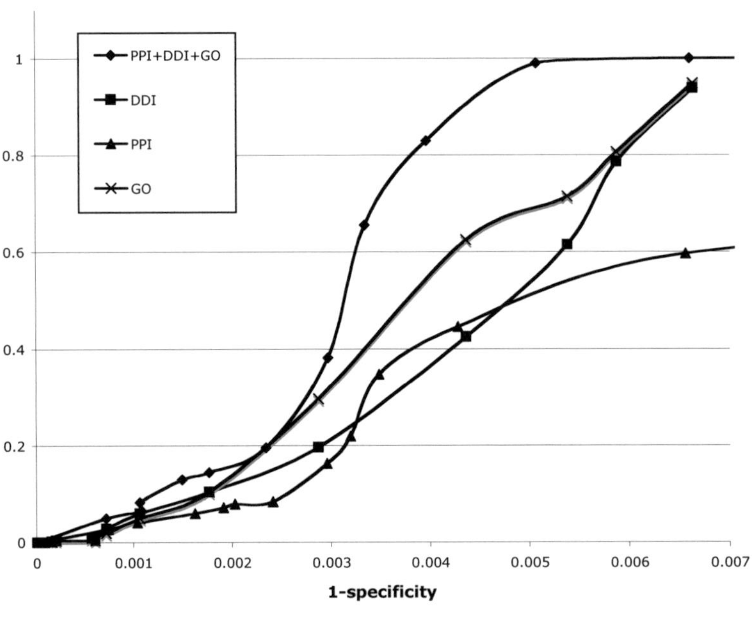

Fig. 2. Curve of receiver operating characteristics (ROC) plotted by the different cut-off values when tested against the gold-standard data set. The area under the curve plotted by PPIs combined with DDIs and GO terms is 0.95, 0.85 for PPI, 0.74 for DDI and 0.8 for GO, respectively.

membrane proteins [12]. Based on that number, we achieved 81.2% true positive rate (sensitivity) at the expense of 0.42% false positive rate (1 - specificity) for a cut-off score of 455, which predicted 4,531 interactions between integral membrane proteins, about 0.61% coverage of all possible interactions among integral membrane proteins.

The map of the interactome of integral membrane protein was built based on 4,531 predicted protein-protein interactions between integral membrane proteins at the cutoff value of 455 (Fig. 3) by Cytoscape (Shannon et al., 2003). 53.4% (281/527) proteins in the interactome map contains at least one transmembrane helix according to the predictions by TMHMM. 80% (392/513) interactions within gold-standard data set overlaps with those within the interactome map but only accounts for 8.4% of the whole interactome of integral membrane proteins. By checking the topology properties of the interactome map, we found that most interactions in the gold-standard data set are in the same complex such as lipid biosynthesis, energy couple proton transport, protein biosynthesis, protein targeting to mitochondria and ATP synthesis coupled electron transport, which reflects the characteristics of performed experiments (detecting protein-protein interactions between same complexes). Our predicted interactions indicates some new members in some complexes such as transport, secretion, vesicle-mediated transport and intracellular transport, which is probably caused by some false negatives from experimental methods.

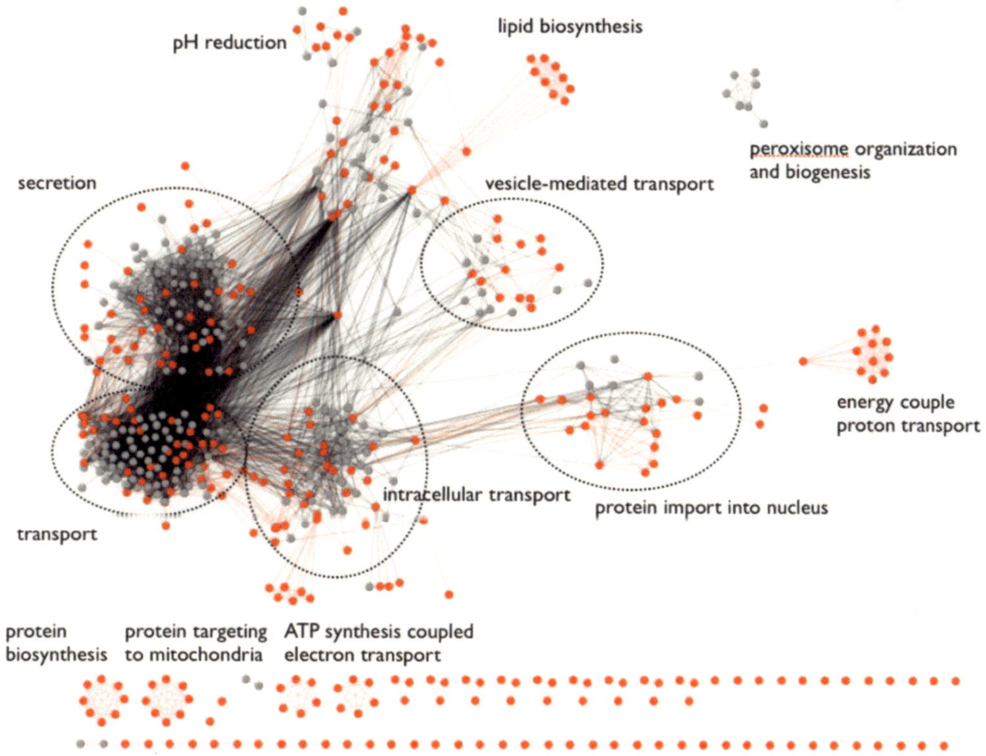

Fig. 3. The interactome map of membrane proteins in yeast. Nodes are represented as membrane proteins, and edges are represented as our predicted interactions between a pair of membrane proteins. Red nodes represent membrane proteins in the gold-standard data set and red edges represent interactions in the gold-standard data set.

One example is that in the group of protein import into nucleus, KAP95 and SSA1 do not interact with other proteins within the group according to the gold-standard data set, however they both play a critical role on nuclear localization signal (NLS)-directed nuclear transport by interacting other proteins to guide transport across the nuclear pore complex (Denning et al., 2001; Liu & Stewart, 2005). Furthermore, observed from the map, some interactions not within the gold-standard data set are found to bridge two complexes. For example, NUP116 and ATP14 are predicted to interact each other connecting two groups: protein import into nucleus and energy couple protein transport. Although there is no evidence demonstrating the direct interaction between NUP116 and ATP14, some research results indicate that ATP14 might be involved in ATP synthesis in the process of protein importing into nucleus (Dingwall & Laskey, 1986; Vargas et al., 2005). Interestingly, we found some new complexes such as peroxisome organization and biogenesis related to the functions of peroxisome membrane proteins such as peroxisome biogenesis and peroxisomal matrix protein import (Eckert & Erdmann, 2003; Heiland & Erdmann, 2005; Honsho et al., 2002).

4. Challenges in predicting membrane PPIs

Complemented by experimental methods, computational approaches provide us with a promising path to reveal a more complete picture of the membrane protein interactome. However, we should be aware of several challenges in predicting membrane PPIs.

First, we are still in lack of reliable membrane PPIs, which results in the difficulty of compiling the gold-standard data set. Currently, positive interaction data is collected from protein pairs in the same protein complex and negative interaction data is derived from those pairs not in the same protein complex. The data quality problem arises as the complex data itself is limited by experimental approaches and contains false positive PPIs. On the other hand, the complex data is biased against membrane proteins, therefore, making it difficult to access the prediction performance of various approaches due to the scarcity of membrane PPIs in the gold-standard data set and the small coverage of membrane interactome. Furthermore, another concern is that large amount of negative data may bring false negatives during the training.

Moreover, it is challenging to interpret the prediction results from different approaches. Inconsistency of predicted membrane proteins has been observed. For example, Miller and colleagues (Miller, et al., 2005) identified 1,949 putative non-self interactions among 705 integral membrane proteins. Xia and colleagues (Xia, et al., 2006) predicted 4,145 helical membrane protein interactions among 516 proteins. Our group recently predicted 4,660 PPIs between integral membrane proteins using the PPIs network and the DDIs data (Zhang & Ouellette, 2008). Interestingly, only 79 protein-protein interactions are overlapped between the results from all three approaches (Figure 4). The reason for these differences among three large-scale sets of membrane protein interactions may be that each approach focuses on different aspects. The experimental result from Miller *et al.* is reliable but probably contains false positives and false negatives due to the intrinsic limitation of experimental techniques they employed. The approach proposed by Xia *et al.* is more focused on the interactions between complexes instead of on binary protein-protein interactions, so the result from Xia *et al.* is prone to predict interactions in the complex. Our approach emphasizes the interactions through the topological properties of PPI and DDI networks and appears to improve on the above methods because these interactions are probably important features for membrane protein interactions. The better prediction accuracy may be achieved by more sophisticated approaches by incorporating various biologically meaningful evidence such as network topological features, protein primary sequences and structures.

Currently, computational membrane protein interaction prediction is intensively studied but focuses only on yeast. Theoretically, methodologies can be applicable to a variety of organisms. However, even with the unprecedented increase of heterogeneous biological data, the data of some organisms such as *Mus musculus, Drosophila melanogaster* and especially *Homo sapiens* is far from complete. Therefore, prediction approaches based on multiple lines of evidence undertake the challenge caused by data incompleteness.

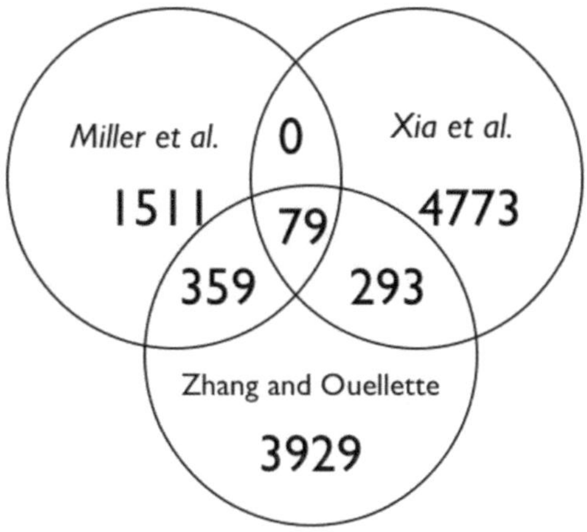

Fig. 4. Comparison of the prediction results from three large-scale methods. There are 438 predicted protein-protein interactions overlapping between data sets from Miller et al. and Zhang and Ouellette, 79 between Miller et al. and Xia et al., 372 between Xia et al. and Zhang and Ouellette, respectively.

5. Conclusions

In this chapter, we reviewed various computational approaches to predict protein-protein interactions between membrane proteins. In spite of some limitations caused by incompleteness of existing experimental data, computational methods have demonstrated reasonable prediction accuracy, which make them to be good resources to provide testable hypotheses for experimental validation. With an emergence of different types of high-throughput data at the systematic level, it prompts us to develop and propose computational methods to identify PPIs between membrane proteins by integrating these data sets. Therefore, complemented with various prediction methods and experimental approaches, such studies lead us to elucidate a cell's interactome.

6. Acknowledgment

The authors are grateful to thank Michelle Brazas and Li Zhang for comments on the manuscripts.

This work was conducted with the support of the Ontario Institute for Cancer Research through funding provided by the government of Ontario. KXZ is supported by the CIHR/MSFHR Strategic Training Program in Bioinformatics. KXZ is also supported by the CIHR Canada Graduate Scholarships Doctoral Award.

7. References

Brun, C., Chevenet, F., Martin, D., Wojcik, J., Guenoche, A., and Jacq, B. (2003). *Genome Biol* 5, R6.

Denning, D., Mykytka, B., Allen, N. P., Huang, L., Al, B., and Rexach, M. (2001). *J Cell Biol* 154, 937-50.

Dingwall, C., and Laskey, R. A. (1986). *Annu Rev Cell Biol* 2, 367-90.

Dirnberger, D., Messerschmid, M., and Baumeister, R. (2008). *Nucleic Acids Res* 36, e37.

Eckert, J. H., and Erdmann, R. (2003). *Rev Physiol Biochem Pharmacol* 147, 75-121.

Eilers, M., Patel, A. B., Liu, W., and Smith, S. O. (2002). *Biophys J* 82, 2720-36.

Formstecher, E., Aresta, S., Collura, V., Hamburger, A., Meil, A., Trehin, A., Reverdy, C., Betin, V., Maire, S., Brun, C., Jacq, B., Arpin, M., Bellaiche, Y., Bellusci, S., Benaroch, P., Bornens, M., Chanet, R., Chavrier, P., Delattre, O., Doye, V., Fehon, R., Faye, G., Galli, T., Girault, J. A., Goud, B., de Gunzburg, J., Johannes, L., Junier, M. P., Mirouse, V., Mukherjee, A., Papadopoulo, D., Perez, F., Plessis, A., Rosse, C., Saule, S., Stoppa-Lyonnet, D., Vincent, A., White, M., Legrain, P., Wojcik, J., Camonis, J., and Daviet, L. (2005). *Genome Res* 15, 376-84.

Fuchs, A., Martin-Galiano, A. J., Kalman, M., Fleishman, S., Ben-Tal, N., and Frishman, D. (2007). *Bioinformatics* 23, 3312-9.

Gavin, A. C., Aloy, P., Grandi, P., Krause, R., Boesche, M., Marzioch, M., Rau, C., Jensen, L. J., Bastuck, S., Dumpelfeld, B., Edelmann, A., Heurtier, M. A., Hoffman, V., Hoefert, C., Klein, K., Hudak, M., Michon, A. M., Schelder, M., Schirle, M., Remor, M., Rudi, T., Hooper, S., Bauer, A., Bouwmeester, T., Casari, G., Drewes, G., Neubauer, G., Rick, J. M., Kuster, B., Bork, P., Russell, R. B., and Superti-Furga, G. (2006). *Nature* 440, 631-6.

Giot, L., Bader, J. S., Brouwer, C., Chaudhuri, A., Kuang, B., Li, Y., Hao, Y. L., Ooi, C. E., Godwin, B., Vitols, E., Vijayadamodar, G., Pochart, P., Machineni, H., Welsh, M., Kong, Y., Zerhusen, B., Malcolm, R., Varrone, Z., Collis, A., Minto, M., Burgess, S., McDaniel, L., Stimpson, E., Spriggs, F., Williams, J., Neurath, K., Ioime, N., Agee, M., Voss, E., Furtak, K., Renzulli, R., Aanensen, N., Carrolla, S., Bickelhaupt, E., Lazovatsky, Y., DaSilva, A., Zhong, J., Stanyon, C. A., Finley, R. L., Jr., White, K. P., Braverman, M., Jarvie, T., Gold, S., Leach, M., Knight, J., Shimkets, R. A., McKenna, M. P., Chant, J., and Rothberg, J. M. (2003). *Science* 302, 1727-36.

Heiland, I., and Erdmann, R. (2005). *Febs J* 272, 2362-72.

Ho, Y., Gruhler, A., Heilbut, A., Bader, G. D., Moore, L., Adams, S. L., Millar, A., Taylor, P., Bennett, K., Boutilier, K., Yang, L., Wolting, C., Donaldson, I., Schandorff, S., Shewnarane, J., Vo, M., Taggart, J., Goudreault, M., Muskat, B., Alfarano, C., Dewar, D., Lin, Z., Michalickova, K., Willems, A. R., Sassi, H., Nielsen, P. A., Rasmussen, K. J., Andersen, J. R., Johansen, L. E., Hansen, L. H., Jespersen, H., Podtelejnikov, A., Nielsen, E., Crawford, J., Poulsen, V., Sorensen, B. D., Matthiesen, J., Hendrickson, R. C., Gleeson, F., Pawson, T., Moran, M. F., Durocher, D., Mann, M., Hogue, C. W., Figeys, D., and Tyers, M. (2002). *Nature* 415, 180-3.

Honsho, M., Hiroshige, T., and Fujiki, Y. (2002). *J Biol Chem* 277, 44513-24.

Ito, T., Chiba, T., Ozawa, R., Yoshida, M., Hattori, M., and Sakaki, Y. (2001). *Proc Natl Acad Sci U S A* 98, 4569-74.

Jothi, R., Cherukuri, P. F., Tasneem, A., and Przytycka, T. M. (2006). *J Mol Biol* **362,** 861-75.

Kelley, R., and Ideker, T. (2005). *Nat Biotechnol* 23, 561-6.

Krogan, N. J., Cagney, G., Yu, H., Zhong, G., Guo, X., Ignatchenko, A., Li, J., Pu, S., Datta, N., Tikuisis, A. P., Punna, T., Peregrin-Alvarez, J. M., Shales, M., Zhang, X., Davey, M., Robinson, M. D., Paccanaro, A., Bray, J. E., Sheung, A., Beattie, B., Richards, D. P., Canadien, V., Lalev, A., Mena, F., Wong, P., Starostine, A., Canete, M. M., Vlasblom, J., Wu, S., Orsi, C., Collins, S. R., Chandran, S., Haw, R., Rilstone, J. J., Gandi, K., Thompson, N. J., Musso, G., St Onge, P., Ghanny, S., Lam, M. H., Butland, G., Altaf-Ul, A. M., Kanaya, S., Shilatifard, A., O'Shea, E., Weissman, J. S., Ingles, C. J., Hughes, T. R., Parkinson, J., Gerstein, M., Wodak, S. J., Emili, A., and Greenblatt, J. F. (2006). *Nature* 440, 637-43.

Li, S., Armstrong, C. M., Bertin, N., Ge, H., Milstein, S., Boxem, M., Vidalain, P. O., Han, J. D., Chesneau, A., Hao, T., Goldberg, D. S., Li, N., Martinez, M., Rual, J. F., Lamesch, P., Xu, L., Tewari, M., Wong, S. L., Zhang, L. V., Berriz, G. F., Jacotot, L., Vaglio, P., Reboul, J., Hirozane-Kishikawa, T., Li, Q., Gabel, H. W., Elewa, A., Baumgartner, B., Rose, D. J., Yu, H., Bosak, S., Sequerra, R., Fraser, A., Mango, S. E., Saxton, W. M., Strome, S., Van Den Heuvel, S., Piano, F., Vandenhaute, J., Sardet, C., Gerstein, M., Doucette-Stamm, L., Gunsalus, K. C., Harper, J. W., Cusick, M. E., Roth, F. P., Hill, D. E., and Vidal, M. (2004). *Science* 303, 540-3.

Liu, S. M., and Stewart, M. (2005). *J Mol Biol* 349, 515-25.

Lo, A., Chiu, Y. Y., Rodland, E. A., Lyu, P. C., Sung, T. Y., and Hsu, W. L. (2009). *Bioinformatics* 25, 996-1003.

Mewes, H. W., Frishman, D., Mayer, K. F., Munsterkotter, M., Noubibou, O., Pagel, P., Rattei, T., Oesterheld, M., Ruepp, A., and Stumpflen, V. (2006). *Nucleic Acids Res* 34, D169-72.

Miller, J. P., Lo, R. S., Ben-Hur, A., Desmarais, C., Stagljar, I., Noble, W. S., and Fields, S. (2005). *Proc Natl Acad Sci U S A* 102, 12123-8.

Nabieva, E., Jim, K., Agarwal, A., Chazelle, B., and Singh, M. (2005). *Bioinformatics* 21 Suppl 1, i302-10.

Paumi, C. M., Menendez, J., Arnoldo, A., Engels, K., Iyer, K. R., Thaminy, S., Georgiev, O., Barral, Y., Michaelis, S., and Stagljar, I. (2007). *Mol Cell* 26, 15-25.

Pawson, T., and Nash, P. (2003). *Science* 300, 445-52.

Shannon, P., Markiel, A., Ozier, O., Baliga, N. S., Wang, J. T., Ramage, D., Amin, N., Schwikowski, B., and Ideker, T. (2003). *Genome Res* 13, 2498-504.

Stagljar, I., Korostensky, C., Johnsson, N., and te Heesen, S. (1998). *Proc Natl Acad Sci U S A* 95, 5187-92.

Thaminy, S., Auerbach, D., Arnoldo, A., and Stagljar, I. (2003). *Genome Res* **13,** 1744-53.

Uetz, P., Giot, L., Cagney, G., Mansfield, T. A., Judson, R. S., Knight, J. R., Lockshon, D., Narayan, V., Srinivasan, M., Pochart, P., Qureshi-Emili, A., Li, Y., Godwin, B., Conover, D., Kalbfleisch, T., Vijayadamodar, G., Yang, M., Johnston, M., Fields, S., and Rothberg, J. M. (2000). *Nature* 403, 623-7.

Valente, A. X., and Cusick, M. E. (2006). *Nucleic Acids Res* 34, 2812-9.

Vargas, D. Y., Raj, A., Marras, S. A., Kramer, F. R., and Tyagi, S. (2005). *Proc Natl Acad Sci U S A* 102, 17008-13.

von Mering, C., Krause, R., Snel, B., Cornell, M., Oliver, S. G., Fields, S., and Bork, P. (2002). *Nature* 417, 399-403.

Wang, J. Z., Du, Z., Payattakool, R., Yu, P. S., and Chen, C. F. (2007). *Bioinformatics* 23, 1274-81.

Xia, Y., Lu, L. J., and Gerstein, M. (2006). *J Mol Biol* 357, 339-49.

Yu, H., Paccanaro, A., Trifonov, V., and Gerstein, M. (2006). *Bioinformatics* 22, 823-9.

Zhang, K. X., and Ouellette, B. F. F. (2008). *IEEE Congress on Evolutionary Computation*, 1801-1806.

8

Evolutionary Computation Applications in Current Bioinformatics

Bing Wang[1,2] and Xiang Zhang[2]
[1]*School of Electrical Engineering & Information, Anhui University of Technology, Ma'anshan, Anhui 243002,*
[2]*Department of Chemistry, University of Louisville, KY 40292,*
[1]*China*
[2]*USA*

1. Introduction

Over the past few decades' rapid development in genomics, proteomics, metabolomics and other types of omics research, a tremendous amount of data related to molecular biology have been produced. Understanding and exploiting these data is now the key to the success of advancing molecular biology, and this requirement has been stimulated the development and expansion of bioinformatics (Altman, 2007; Jones, et al., 2006). As a fast growing interdisciplinary scientific area, bioinformatics can be defined in several ways, but the emphasis is always on the use of information processing methods to manage, analyze and interpret information from biological data, sequences and structures, with promising applications to biomarker discovery and pharmaceutical design. Important sub-disciplines within the field include (Pal, et al., 2006):

a. Development and implementation of tools and databases that enable efficient access, usage and management of various types of information.
b. Analysis and interpretation of various types of data, including nucleotide and amino acid sequences, protein domains, and protein structures.
c. Development of new algorithms to assess relationships among members of large data sets, such as methods for protein family classification, protein structure and function prediction, gene location and correlation networks.
d. Simulation of biological process using computational models to assist experiment design and implementation, such as protein functional site finding, disease biomarker discovery and drug design.

The post-genome era is characterized by a major expansion in the available biological data. Many important bioinformatics problems are so comprehensive that an exhaustive search of all potential solutions is always challenging, and most likely impossible. Yet another approach of using biologists' current library of standard constructive and approximate algorithms is impractical in terms of time, money, and computational power (Fogel & Corne, 2002). The researchers are then either forced to pose a simpler hypothesis which typically leads to wrong understanding of problem, or to attempt to develop computational algorithms which can search large solution spaces in a reasonable time.

Therefore, evolutionary computation algorithms have been gaining the attention of researchers for solving current bioinformatics problems (Fogel, et al., 2008). As a class of randomized search and optimization techniques which inspired by the process of biological evolution, evolutionary computation can be used to search very large and complex spaces effectively and return good solutions in a rapid fashion. The majority of current implementations of evolutionary computation methods descend from three strongly related but independently developed approaches: genetic algorithms (GAs), evolutionary programming (EG) and evolution strategies (ES). In general, an evolutionary computation method first generates an initial population of solutions. It then repeats a simulated natural evolutionary processes which includes reproduction, mutation, recombination, natural selection and survival of the fittest (Eberbach, 2005). In the last decade, evolutionary computation has experienced a tremendous growth in applications for bioinformatics.
The purpose of this chapter is to provide a survey on the role of evolutionary computation methods, especially GAs, in current bioinformatics tasks. Some important bioinformatics topics, such as sequence analysis, protein structure and function prediction, protein-protein interaction prediction and microarray analysis will be explained here. Conclusions and some future research directions are also discussed in this chapter.

2. Sequence analysis

Since the development of high-throughput techniques in biological experimental methods during the last two decades, the rate of addition of new sequences to the database increases continuously. However, such a collection of sequences does not, by itself, help our understanding of the biology of different organisms. Therefore, the multiple sequence alignment (MSA) is of great interest to biologists since it can provide scientific insight of inferring evolutionary history or discovering conserved regions among closely related protein, ribonucleic acid (RNA) or Deoxyribonucleic acid (DNA) sequences (Pei, 2008; Pirovano & Heringa, 2008; Sobel & Martinez, 1986). In many cases, the MSA assumes the target sequences have an evolutionary relationship by which they share a lineage and are descended from a common ancestor. This assumption makes MSA a fundamental and crucial tool in analysis of sequences which come from the same or a close family. MSA is often used to assess sequence conservation of protein domains, secondary and tertiary structures.
MSA is the process of lining up a set of sequences in the "best possible way". Sum-of-pairs score (SP-score) is usually used to determine the "best possible way" to build an alignment. For k sequences of length at most n via dynamic programming, the SP-score can be solved in $\theta(2^k n^k)$ steps. Unfortunately, this method is almost always time-consuming and unpractical even for a small number of sequences. Moreover, MSA is known as NP-hard (Just, 2001; Wang & Jiang, 1994), and hence finding the best solution is intractable. However, it can be solved by treating the MSA problem as an optimization problem and therefore, the evolutionary computation methods can be applied to search the positions of gap for aligning multiple sequences.
Notredame and Higgins proposed a MSA approach based on genetic algorithm and an associated software package called SAGA (sequence alignment by genetic algorithm) (Notredame & Higgins, 1996). This method uses a genetic algorithm to select from an evolving population the alignment which optimizes the COFFEE Objective Function (OF)

(Notredame, et al., 1998). The OF is a measure of the consistency between the multiple alignments and a library of CLUSTALW pairwise alignments (Thompson, et al., 2002). The approach was tested in a set of 13 cases based mainly on alignments of sequences of known tertiary structure. It was claimed by the authors that this method can find globally optimal multiple alignments or very close to it in a reasonable time frame for completely unaligned sequences. But it also has been mentioned that SAGA is still fairly slow for large test cases (e.g. with >20 or so sequences). This genetic algorithm-based method was extended and improved to a new package, named RAGA (Notredame, et al., 1997), for alignment of two homologous RNA sequences whose secondary structure of one of them is known.

A similar work by Zhang et al. (Zhang & Wong, 1997) was described to align sequences in a two-step method. This first step identifies matches whose input is the sequences to be aligned and output is the matched subunits. The matched subunits are organized on a form called pre-alignment. The pre-alignment is the input of the second step, which identifies mismatches (i.e. deletion, insertions and substitutions). The output of the second step is an alignment. In this work, the task of identifying matches is converted into a search problem using a genetic algorithm. To apply GA, each biomolecular sequence was represented by the subunits. The alignment of sequence was converted from characters space to subunits space and therefore, the computational cost was decreased dramatically.

Other relevant researches of solving multiple sequence alignment using evolutionary computation methods can be found in (Fisz, 2006; Gondro & Kinghorn, 2007). Each of these methods relies on the principle similar to SAGA: a population of multiple alignments evolves by selection, combination and mutation. The main difference between these methods and SAGA are the design of better mutation operators that can improve the efficiency and the accuracy of the algorithms.

3. Protein structure prediction

A protein is a chain of amino acid residues that folds into a specific native tertiary structure under certain physiological conditions. There are 20 amino acids which can be divided into several classes based on their size and other physical and chemical properties. Proteins fold into one or more specific spatial conformations that enable the proteins to perform their biological function. In order to understand the functions of proteins at a molecular level, it is often necessary to determine the three dimensional structure of each protein. Protein structure prediction is, therefore, one of the most important research topics in bioinformatics.

A number of studies using the evolutionary computation method for protein structure prediction have been made in the last decades. As the first attempt to predict protein structure using GAs, Dandekar and Argos used a tetrahedral lattice and structural information was encoded as gene (Dandekar & Argos, 1996; Dandekar & Argos, 1997). Each residue has seven possible conformations encoded by three bits. Each gene therefore is encoded with 3×N bits long, where N is the number of residues. The fitness function contains terms that encouraged strand formation and pairing and penalizes steric clashes and nonglobular structures. The function was parameterized on a set of four helix bundle proteins and on one of the β-structure proteins reproduced. The success of this method relies on the correct pre-assignment of secondary structure, and may introduce bias in the potential towards the experimental structure.

Sun et al. (Sun, et al., 1999) reduced the molecular structure of each protein to its backbone atoms and each side chain was approximated by a single virtual united-atom. A statistical potential of mean force derived from known protein structures was used to assess fitness. A conformation library of peptide fragments containing 2-5 amino acid residues was extracted from known protein structures to construct initial conformations. Fragments were selected from the library based on sequence similarity, which appears that it will introduce a strong bias, particularly for the longer fragments. A root mean square error of 1.66Å on average to the crystal structure can be achieved for melittin, a protein of 26 residues. Similar results for avian pancreatic polypeptide inhibitor and apamin were also obtained.

Another earlier work discussing the reduced three-dimensional lattice protein using genetic algorithm was reported by Unger et al. (Unger & Moult, 1993). In this method, each peptide was considered as only single point units without side chains and represented by three bits to encode five degrees of freedom. All residues are divided into two groups: hydrophobic and hydrophilic. The evaluation function scored -1 for each pair of non-bonded hydrophobic neighbors. The algorithm begins with a population of identical unfolded configurations, and the population size is 200. The string of bond angles along the chain was used for describing a conformation. Each generation begins with a series of K mutations being applied to each individual in the population, where K is encoding length. These mutations are filtered using a Monte Carlo step, and mutations resulted in better energy will be accepted. Cross-over sites were selected randomly. Three types of Montel Carlo (MC) methods were applied for comparing the performance of GA. Test data consisted of a series of ten randomly produced 27 length sequences and ten randomly produced 64 length sequences. Experimental results indicted that GA can find the global minimum for all but one sequence. MC also can find the global minimum for short sequences, but it is not for the longer sequences. Although this work demonstrated the potential advantages of GA-base methods for protein structure prediction, this simple model did not test its applicability to real proteins.

Other investigations on protein structure prediction are available in (Arunachalam, et al., 2006; Contreras-Moreira, et al., 2003; Cooper, et al., 2003). These studies show that GAs is superior to MC and other search methods for protein structure prediction.

4. Protein-protein recognition and docking

Protein-protein recognition represents a fundamental aspect of biological function. Although the protein structures are now routinely determined by experimental methods, it is much more difficult to ascertain the structure of protein complexes. When two molecules are in close proximity, it can be energetically favorable for them to bind together tightly. The molecular docking study focuses on the prediction of energy and physical configuration of binding between two molecules. The success of docking and the resulting docked configuration can refine the design of drug molecules. Methods for protein docking, such as DOCK (Kuntz, et al., 1982), FLOG (Miller, et al., 1994), and GOLD (Jones, et al., 1997), are widely used in drug-discovery programs. The principal techniques currently available for protein docking are: molecular dynamics, MC method, genetic algorithms, fragment-based methods, complementarity methods and distance geometry. Here, we will focus on the EC-based protein docking approaches.

GOLD (Genetic Optimisation for Ligand Docking) is a docking program that uses a GA search strategy and includes rotational flexibility for selected receptor hydrogens along with full ligand flexibility (Jones, et al., 1997). For searching the space of available binding modes

efficiently, hydrogen bond motifs have been directly encoded into the GA. The fitness function is the sum of a hydrogen bond term, a 4-8 inter-molecular dispersion potential and a 6-12 intra-molecular dispersion potential for the internal energy of the ligand. Each complex was run using an initial population of 500 individuals into five sub-populations, and migration of individual chromosomes between sub-populations was permitted. The GOLD validation test set is one of the most comprehensive docking methods. It comprises of 100 different protein complexes. This program achieved a 71% of success rate based primarily on a visual inspection of the docked structures. An extension to GOLD can be found in another work (Verdonk, et al., 2003) which included an addition of hydrophobic fitting points used in the least squares fitting algorithm to generate the ligand orientation.
Gardinaer et al. (Gardiner, et al., 2001) described a GA for protein-protein docking method, in which the proteins were represented by dot surfaces calculated using the Connolly program (Connolly, 1986). The GA was used to move the surfaces of one protein relative to the other to locate the area of greatest surface to complementarity between the two. Surface dots were deemed complementary if their normals are opposed, their Connolly shape type is complementary, and their hydrogen bonding or hydrophobic potential is fulfilled. For a possible orientation of the query with respect to the target, the number of matching dots and the number of clashes between query dots and target interior points were counted. If any dots matched, penalty was determined by the number of clashes; otherwise, penalty was set as a very big value (100,000 in the paper). The fitness function was then given by the number of matches subtracted penalty. The algorithm was tested on 34 large protein-protein complexes where one or both proteins had been crystallized separately. Parameters were established for 30 of the complexes that have at least one near-native solution ranked in the top 100.
AutoDock software (Goodsell, et al., 1996) uses a genetic algorithm as a global optimizer combined with energy minimization as a local search method. In this implementation, the ligand is flexible and the receptor is rigid. The ligand-receptor was represented as a grid. The genetic algorithm uses two point crossover and mutation operators. The fitness function comprises five terms: a directional 12-10 hydrogen bond term; a coulombic electrostatic potential; a term proportional to the number of sp^3 bonds in the ligand to represent unfavourable entropy of ligand binding due to the restriction of conformational degrees of freedom; and a desolvation term. This scoring function is based loosely around the AMBER force field from which protein and ligand parameters are taken. The desolvation term is an inter-molecular pairwise summation combining an empirical desolvation weight for ligand carbon atoms, and a pre-calculated volume term for the protein grid. Each of the five terms are weighted using an empirical scaling factor determined using linear regression analysis from a set o 30 protein-ligand complexes with known binding constants. Now the software has been updated to version 4.0.
A number of other investigations can be found in (Gardiner, et al., 2001; Gardiner, et al., 2003; Kang, et al., 2009; Po & Laine, 2008).

5. Conclusions

This chapter provides an overview of some bioinformatics tasks and the relevance of the evolutionary computation methods, especially GAs. There are two advantages of GA-based approaches. One is that GAs are easier to run in parallel than single trajectory search procedures, and therefore allow groups of processors to be utilized for a search. The other is that GAs appear to be more efficient in finding acceptable solutions than other semi-random move methods such as MC (Pedersen & Moult, 1996).

Although the current GA-based methods are very useful and can produce elegant solutions for bioinformatics tasks, there are some general characteristics that might limit the effectiveness of GAs. First, the basic selection, crossover, and mutation operators are common to all applications. Second, a GA requires extensive experimentation for the specification of several parameters so that appropriate values can be identified. Third, GAs involves a large degree of randomness and different runs may produce different results. So it is necessary to incorporate problem specific domain knowledge into GAs to reduce randomness and computational time and current research is going on in this direction also.

However, as an optimization algorithm and an effective searching tool, GAs can be used in other bioinformatics tasks, such as gene expression and microarray data, gene regulatory network identification, construction of phylogenetic trees, protein functional site prediction, characterization of metabolic pathways, and so on.

6. Acknowledgement

This work has been partially supported by National Science Foundation of China (project No. 60803107) and the startup fund of University of Louisville.

7. References

Altman, R.B. (2007) Current progress in bioinformatics 2007, Brief Bioinform, 8, 277-278.

Arunachalam, J., Kanagasabai, V. and Gautham, N. (2006) Protein structure prediction using mutually orthogonal Latin squares and a genetic algorithm, Biochem Biophys Res Commun, 342, 424-433.

Connolly, M.L. (1986) Shape complementarity at the hemoglobin alpha 1 beta 1 subunit interface, Biopolymers, 25, 1229-1247.

Contreras-Moreira, B., Fitzjohn, P.W., Offman, M., Smith, G.R. and Bates, P.A. (2003) Novel use of a genetic algorithm for protein structure prediction: searching template and sequence alignment space, Proteins, 53 Suppl 6, 424-429.

Cooper, L.R., Corne, D.W. and Crabbe, M.J. (2003) Use of a novel Hill-climbing genetic algorithm in protein folding simulations, Comput Biol Chem, 27, 575-580.

Dandekar, T. and Argos, P. (1996) Ab initio tertiary-fold prediction of helical and non-helical protein chains using a genetic algorithm, Int J Biol Macromol, 18, 1-4.

Dandekar, T. and Argos, P. (1997) Applying experimental data to protein fold prediction with the genetic algorithm, Protein Eng, 10, 877-893.

Eberbach, E. (2005) Toward a theory of evolutionary computation, Biosystems, 82, 1-19.

Fisz, J.J. (2006) Combined genetic algorithm and multiple linear regression (GA-MLR) optimizer: Application to multi-exponential fluorescence decay surface, J Phys Chem A, 110, 12977-12985.

Fogel, G. and Corne, D. (2002) Evolutionary computation in bioinformatics. Morgan Kaufmann ; Elsevier Science, San Francisco, Calif. Oxford.

Fogel, G.B., Porto, V.W., Varga, G., Dow, E.R., Craven, A.M., Powers, D.M., Harlow, H.B., Su, E.W., Onyia, J.E. and Su, C. (2008) Evolutionary computation for discovery of composite transcription factor binding sites, Nucleic Acids Res, 36, e142.

Gardiner, E.J., Willett, P. and Artymiuk, P.J. (2001) Protein docking using a genetic algorithm, Proteins, 44, 44-56.

Gardiner, E.J., Willett, P. and Artymiuk, P.J. (2003) GAPDOCK: a Genetic Algorithm Approach to Protein Docking in CAPRI round 1, Proteins, 52, 10-14.

Gondro, C. and Kinghorn, B.P. (2007) A simple genetic algorithm for multiple sequence alignment, Genet Mol Res, 6, 964-982.

Goodsell, D.S., Morris, G.M. and Olson, A.J. (1996) Automated docking of flexible ligands: applications of AutoDock, J Mol Recognit, 9, 1-5.

Jones, D.T., Sternberg, M.J. and Thornton, J.M. (2006) Introduction. Bioinformatics: from molecules to systems, Philos Trans R Soc Lond B Biol Sci, 361, 389-391.

Jones, G., Willett, P., Glen, R.C., Leach, A.R. and Taylor, R. (1997) Development and validation of a genetic algorithm for flexible docking, J Mol Biol, 267, 727-748.

Just, W. (2001) Computational complexity of multiple sequence alignment with SP-score, J Comput Biol, 8, 615-623.

Kang, L., Li, H., Jiang, H. and Wang, X. (2009) An improved adaptive genetic algorithm for protein-ligand docking, J Comput Aided Mol Des, 23, 1-12.

Kuntz, I.D., Blaney, J.M., Oatley, S.J., Langridge, R. and Ferrin, T.E. (1982) A geometric approach to macromolecule-ligand interactions, J Mol Biol, 161, 269-288.

Miller, M.D., Kearsley, S.K., Underwood, D.J. and Sheridan, R.P. (1994) FLOG: a system to select 'quasi-flexible' ligands complementary to a receptor of known three-dimensional structure, J Comput Aided Mol Des, 8, 153-174.

Notredame, C. and Higgins, D.G. (1996) SAGA: sequence alignment by genetic algorithm, Nucleic Acids Res, 24, 1515-1524.

Notredame, C., Holm, L. and Higgins, D.G. (1998) COFFEE: an objective function for multiple sequence alignments, Bioinformatics, 14, 407-422.

Notredame, C., O'Brien, E.A. and Higgins, D.G. (1997) RAGA: RNA sequence alignment by genetic algorithm, Nucleic Acids Res, 25, 4570-4580.

Pal, S., Bandyopadhyay, S. and Ray, S.S. (2006) Evolutionary computation in bioinformatics: a review, IEEE/ACM Trans on Systems, Man, and Cybernetics - Part C, 36, 601-615.

Pedersen, J.T. and Moult, J. (1996) Genetic algorithms for protein structure prediction, Curr Opin Struct Biol, 6, 227-231.

Pei, J. (2008) Multiple protein sequence alignment, Curr Opin Struct Biol, 18, 382-386.

Pirovano, W. and Heringa, J. (2008) Multiple sequence alignment, Methods Mol Biol, 452, 143-161.

Po, M.J. and Laine, A.F. (2008) Leveraging genetic algorithm and neural network in automated protein crystal recognition, Conf Proc IEEE Eng Med Biol Soc, 2008, 1926-1929.

Sobel, E. and Martinez, H.M. (1986) A multiple sequence alignment program, Nucleic Acids Res, 14, 363-374.

Sun, Z., Xia, X., Guo, Q. and Xu, D. (1999) Protein structure prediction in a 210-type lattice model: parameter optimization in the genetic algorithm using orthogonal array, J Protein Chem, 18, 39-46.

Thompson, J.D., Gibson, T.J. and Higgins, D.G. (2002) Multiple sequence alignment using ClustalW and ClustalX, Curr Protoc Bioinformatics, Chapter 2, Unit 2 3.

Unger, R. and Moult, J. (1993) Genetic algorithms for protein folding simulations, J Mol Biol, 231, 75-81.

Verdonk, M.L., Cole, J.C., Hartshorn, M.J., Murray, C.W. and Taylor, R.D. (2003) Improved protein-ligand docking using GOLD, Proteins, 52, 609-623.

Wang, L. and Jiang, T. (1994) On the complexity of multiple sequence alignment, J Comput Biol, 1, 337-348.

Zhang, C. and Wong, A.K. (1997) A genetic algorithm for multiple molecular sequence alignment, Comput Appl Biosci, 13, 565-581.

9

GA-Based Q-Learning to Develop Compact Control Table for Multiple Agents

Tadahiko Murata and Yusuke Aoki
Kansai University
Japan

1. Introduction

Recently reinforcement learning has received much attention as a learning method (Sutton, 1988; Watkins & Dayan, 1992). It does not need a priori knowledge and has higher capability of reactive and adaptive behaviors. However there are some significant problems in applying it to real problems. Some of them are deep cost of learning and large size of action-state space. The Q-learning (Watkins & Dayan, 1992), known as one of effective reinforcement learning, has difficulty in accomplishing learning tasks when the size of action-state space is large. Therefore the application of the usual Q-learning is restricted to simple tasks with the small action-state space. Due to the large action-state space, it is difficult to apply the Q-learning directly to real problems such as control problem for robots with many redundant degrees of freedom or multiple agents moving cooperatively one another.

In order to cope with such difficulty of large action-state space, various structural and dividing algorithms of the action-state space were proposed (Holland, 1986; Svinin et al., 2001; Yamada et al., 2001). In the dividing algorithm, the state space is divided dynamically, however, the action space is fixed so that it is impossible to apply the algorithm to the task with a large action space. In the classifier system, "don't care" attribute is introduced in order to create general rules. But, that causes partially observable problems. Furthermore, an ensemble system of general and special rules should be prepared in advance.

Considering these points, Ito & Matsuno (2002) proposed a GA-based Q-learning method called "Q-learning with Dynamic Structuring of Exploration Space Based on Genetic Algorithm (QDSEGA)." In their algorithm, a genetic algorithm is employed to reconstruct an action-state space which is learned by Q-learning. That is, the size of the action-state space is reduced by the genetic algorithm in order to apply Q-learning to the learning process of that space. They applied their algorithm to a control problem of multi-legged robot which has many redundant degrees of freedom and a large action-state space. By applying their restriction method for the action-state space, they successfully obtained the control rules for a multi-legged robot by their QDSEGA. However, the way to apply a genetic algorithm in their approach seems so straightforward. Therefore we have proposed a crossover for QDSEGA (Murata & Yamaguchi, 2005; Murata & Yamaguchi, 2008). Through their computer simulations on a control problem of a multi-legged robot, they could make about 50% reduction of the number of generations to obtain a target state of the problem.

In this chapter, we apply the QDSEGA with the neighboring crossover to control multiple agents. An application of QDSEGA to multiple agent system has been considered (Ito and Gofuku, 2003; Ito et al., 2004) though, they still applied genetic operators straightforward. We apply the neighboring crossover to Multi Agent Simulations (MAS) problem and show its effectiveness to reduce the number of actions in a Q-table. We also propose a deletion algorithm to make more compact Q-table in MAS problem. We employ the application in Ito et al. (2004) where a Q-table is developed for homogeneous multiple agents. Computer simulation results show that the size of Q-table can be reduced by introducing the proposed neighboring crossover and the deletion algorithm.

2. QDSEGA

In this section, we briefly explain the outline of QDSEGA (Ito & Matsuno, 2002; Ito & Gofuku, 2003; Ito et al., 2004; Murata & Yamaguchi, 2005). QDSEGA has two dynamics. One is a learning dynamics based on Q-learning and the other is a structural dynamics based on Genetic Algorithm. Figure 1 shows the outline of QDSEGA. In QDSEGA, each action is represented by an individual of a genetic algorithm. According to actions defined by a set of individuals, an action-state space called Q-table is created. Q-learning is applied to the created Q-table. Then the learned Q-table is evaluated through simulations. A fitness value for each action is assigned according to Q-table. After that, each individual (i.e., each action) is modified through genetic operations such as crossover and mutation. We show some details in these steps in the following subsections, and show our proposed method for crossover and a deletion algorithm in the next section.

2.1 Action encoding

Each individual expresses a selectable action on the learning dynamics. It means that a set of individuals is selected by genetic operations, and a learning dynamics is applied to the subset. After the evaluation of the subset of actions, a new subset is restructured by genetic operations.

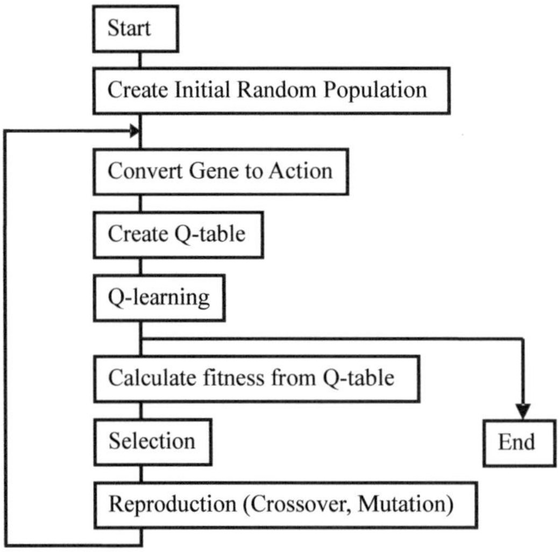

Fig. 1. Outline of QDSEGA

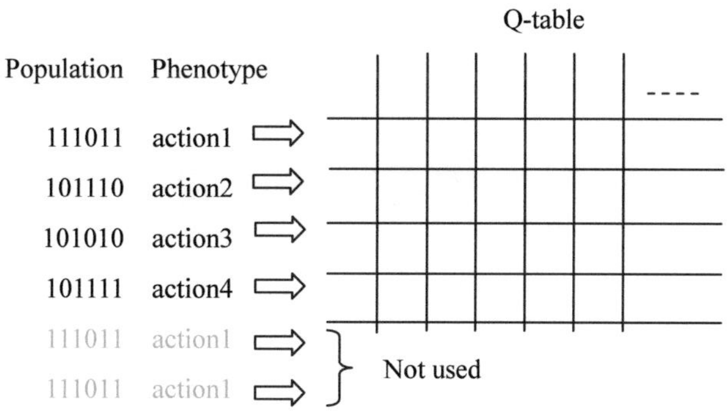

Fig. 2. Q-table created from a set of individuals

2.2 Q-table

An action-state space called Q-table is created from the set of individuals. When several individuals are the same code, only one action is used in the action-state space to avoid the redundancy of actions. Figure 2 shows this avoidance process.

2.3 Learning dynamics

In QDSEGA, the conventional Q-learning (Watkins & Dayan, 1992) is employed as a learning dynamics. The dynamics of Q-learning are written as follows:

$$Q(s,a) \leftarrow (1-\alpha)Q(s,a) + \alpha\{r(s,a) + \gamma \max_{a'} Q(s',a')\}, \tag{1}$$

where $Q(s,a)$ is a Q-value of the state s and the action a, r is the reward, α is the learning rate, and γ is the discount rate.

2.4 Fitness

The fitness $fit(a_i)$ for each action is calculated by the following equation:

$$fit(a_i) = fit_Q(a_i) + k_f \cdot fit_u(a_i), \tag{2}$$

where $fit_Q(a_i)$ is a fitness value for action a_i calculated from Q-table, $fit_u(a_i)$ is a fitness value for action a_i calculated from the frequency of use, and k_f is a non-negative constant value to determine the ratio of $fit_Q(a_i)$ and $fit_u(a_i)$. We show the detail explanation of these factors in this subsection.

(a) Fitness of Q-table

The fitness of Q-table $fit_Q(a_i)$ is calculated from Q-values in the current Q-table. In order to calculate $fit_Q(a_i)$ for each action a_i the following normalization is taken place in advance as for the Q-values in the current Q-table.

First, calculate the maximum and minimum value of each state as follows:

$$V_{\max}(s) = \max_{a'}(Q(s,a')), \tag{3}$$

$$V_{\min}(s) = \min_{a'}(Q(s,a')) \,. \tag{4}$$

Then Q' of the normalized Q-table is given as follows:

$$\text{If } Q(s,a) \geq 0 \text{ Then } Q'(s,a) = \frac{1-p}{V_{\max}(s)} Q(s,a) + p \,, \tag{5}$$

$$\text{Else } (\, Q(s,a) < 0 \,) \text{ Then } Q'(s,a) = -\frac{p}{V_{\min}(s)} Q(s,a) + p \,, \tag{6}$$

where p is a constant value which means the ratio of reward to penalty. After this normalization process, we fix the action a_i and sort $Q'(s,a_i)$ according to their value from high to low for all states. We define the sorted $Q'(s,a_i)$ as $Q'_s(s,a_i)$, and $Q'_s(1,a_i)$ means the maximum value of $Q'(s,a_i)$, and $Q'_s(N_s,a_i)$ means the minimum value of $Q'(s,a_i)$, where N_s is the size of states. Using the normalized and sorted Q-value $Q'_s(s,a_i)$, the fitness of action a_i is calculated as follows:

$$fit_Q(a_i) = \sum_{j=1}^{Ns} (w_j \frac{\sum_{k=1}^{j} Q'_s(k,a_i)}{j}) \,, \tag{7}$$

where w_j is a weight which decides the ratio of special actions to general actions.

(b) Fitness of Frequency of Use

The fitness of frequency of use $fit_u(a_i)$ is introduced to save important actions. That fitness is defined as follows:

$$fit_u(a_i) = N_u(a_i) / \sum_{j=1}^{N_a} N_u(a_j) \,, \tag{8}$$

where N_a is the number of all actions of one generation and $N_u(a_i)$ is the number of times which a_i was used for in the Q-learning of this generation. Important actions are used frequently. Therefore the actions with high fitness value of $fit_u(a_i)$ are preserved by this fitness value.

2.5 Genetic algorithm and neighboring crossover

Ito & Matsuno (2002) says "the method of the selection and reproduction is not main subject so the conventional method is used." They employed a crossover that exchanges randomly selected bits between the parent individuals according to the crossover probability P_c. They mutated each bit according to the mutation probability P_m. They did not replace parent individuals with offspring. Therefore the number of individuals is increased by the genetic operations. As for the elite preserving strategy, they preserve 30% individuals with the highest fitness value.

Since they did not modify genetic operators for QDSEGA, we have proposed a crossover operation for the multi-legged robot control problem (MRC problem) in (Murata & Yamaguchi, 2005; Murata & Yamaguchi, 2008). We developed a neighboring crossover for QDSEGA for MRC problems.

The crossover employed in QDSEGA (Ito & Matsuno, 2002) causes drastic change in the phenotype of a solution since randomly selected bits are changed between two solutions. If the change of solution in phenotype is so drastic, the good part of the solution may be broken. In order to avoid causing such drastic change among solutions, we proposed a crossover between similar parent solutions. We define the similarity by the number of the same genes in the same locus of a chromosome. We introduced a parameter k_{sim} to denote the similarity. Thus, the crossover is applied among individuals that have the same genes more than k_{sim}.

This kind of the restriction for the crossover has been proposed in the research area of distributed genetic algorithms (DGAs). Researches on DGAs can be categorized into two areas: coarse-grained genetic algorithms (Tanese, 1989; Belding, 1995) and fine-grained genetic algorithms (Mandelick & Spiessens, 1989; Muhlenbein et al., 1991; Murata et al., 2000). In the coarse-grained GAs, a population, that is ordinarily a single, is divided into several subpopulations. Each of these subpopulations is individually governed by genetic operations such as crossover and mutation, and subpopulations communicate each other periodically. Algorithms in this type are called the island model because each subpopulation can be regarded as an island. On the other hand, several individuals are locally governed by genetic operations in fine-grained GAs. In a fine-grained GA, each individual exists in a cell, and genetic operations are applied to an individual with individuals in neighboring cells. The DGAs are known to have an advantage to keep the variety of individuals during the execution of an algorithm, and avoid converging prematurely.

While we don't define any solution space such as cells or islands in our proposed crossover, our restriction in crossover operation may have the same effect of keeping variety in a population and attain the effective search.

3. Transportation task using Q-learning

3.1 Transportation task

We consider a transportation task shown in Ito & Gofuku (2003) and Ito et al. (2004). Figure 3 shows a transportation task used in this chapter. There is a world with 25 cells and a goal cell shown in "G" where five agents exist in Cell 0 and Cell 4. The aim of the transportation task is to convey a load shown in "L1" to the goal cell. In order to carry "L1" to "G", the

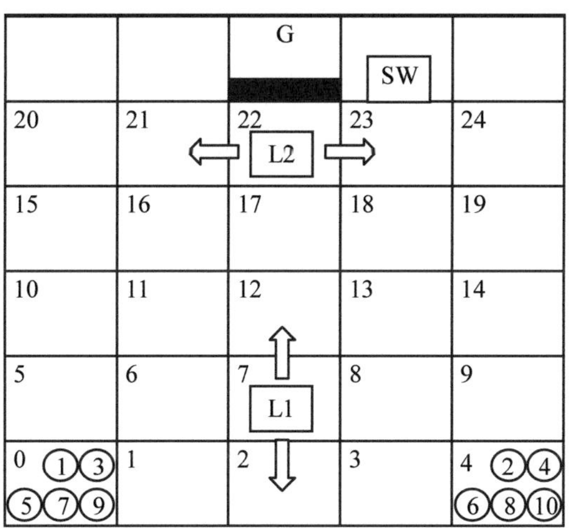

Fig. 3. Transportation task

other load shown in "L2" should be removed from Cell 22. Simultaneously, the door of "G" should be opened before carrying "L1". To open the door, the switch shown in "SW" should be pushed by an agent in Cell 23.

Each load has a mobile direction. As shown in Figure 3, "L1" can be moved only in the vertical direction, and "L2" only in the horizontal direction. To move a load, more than one agent should push it toward the same movable direction. Therefore, to convey "L1" to "G", agents should remove "L2" from Cell 22, open the door, and move "L1" to the goal.

In order to control actions of each agent, Ito & Gofuku, (2003); Ito et al., (2004) employed their QDSEGA where the state of the agent is handled as a chromosome of an individual to which genetic operators are applied. Figure 4 shows the chromosome representation of the agent location in Figure 3. Each chromosome consists of genes with the same number of agents. The figure in each gene shows the identification number of cell where the agent locates. Since the agents with odd number locate in Cell 0, all genes for those agents have 0 as its value.

	1	2	3	4	5	6	7	8	9	10
Chromosome	0	4	0	4	0	4	0	4	0	4

Fig. 4. Chromosome representation for the agents in Figure 3

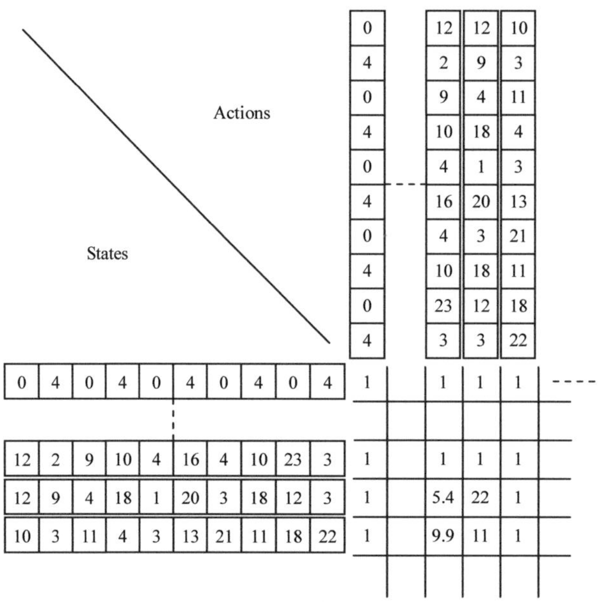

Fig. 5. An example of Q-table with a set of chromosomes

3.2 Q-learning in our simulation

Q-table of the Q-learning is generated using a set of chromosomes. Figure 5 shows an example of Q-table that shows the relations of agent locations.

In Figure 5, each column in the Q-table shows a chromosome generated by genetic operations. Rows of the table consist of the same chromosomes of the columns. That is, the chromosomes in the rows act as states in the Q-table, and the chromosomes in the column act as actions the agent can take in the fired state. When the ten agents locates in the start position (Cell 0 or Cell 4 as in Fig. 3), the current position is shown as (0, 4, 0, 4, 0, 4, 0, 4, 0, 4) in the table. If the target position (10, 3, 11, 4, 3, 13, 21, 11, 18, 22) is selected as an action from the current position, Agent "1" moves from Cell 0 to Cell 10, Agent "2" moves from Cell 4 to Cell 3, and so on.

With this Q-table, Q-learning is applied. In order to move each agent to the target position, Ito & Gofuku, (2003) and Ito et al., (2004) proposed the following rules.

<**R1**: The rule to decide a path to a target position>

If $x(i) \neq x_t$ **Then** $x(i+1) = x(i) - \text{sgn}(x(i) - x_t)\Delta x$, $y(i+1) = y(i)$,

Else if $y(i) \neq y_t$ **Then** $y(i+1) = y(i) - \text{sgn}(y(i) - y_t)\Delta y$, $x(i+1) = x(i)$,

Else $x(i+1) = x(i)$, $y(i+1) = y(i)$.

where x_t, y_t are the coordinates of the target position, and $x(i), y(i)$ are the coordinates of the current position of the agent in time *i*. Using this rule, the agent moves in horizontal direction first, then it moves vertically to the target position.

<**R2**: The rule to avoid a collision>

If *obstacle is on the course that is given by R1* **Then**
  If *the obstacle is load* **Then** *Employ R3*
  Else *Don't move*
Else *Move using R1*

Since the collision between agents is assumed to avoid using traffic rules, Ito & Gofuku, (2003); Ito et al., (2004) considered only the collision between an agent and a load. If the load can not be carried by the agent alone, it should stop until other agents come.

<**R3**: The rule to move the load>

If *Load is on the course that is given by R1* **Then** *Push the Load to the way that the agent has to go*
Else *Move using R1*

If the way that the agent has to go is not the direction to which the load can be moved, the agent should stop beside the load.

<**R4**: The rule to open the door>

If *Switch is in a cell where the agent stops* **Then** *Turn on the switch to open the door*
Else *Nothing is done*

3.3 A deletion algorithm to create more compact control table

When we observe a Q-table developed by QDSEGA, some actions or chromosomes are not used in moving multiple agents. That is, unnecessary actions are generated through genetic operations. In order to make a compact Q-table, we mark the chromosomes that are not used for a prespecified term in Q-Learning process.

4. Computer simulation

4.1 Parameter specifications

In this section, we show the simulation results to compare the conventional QDSEGA and the QDSEGA with the neighboring crossover shown in Subsection 2.5 and the deletion algorithm in Subsection 3.3. The neighboring crossover can be applied to the parent solutions that have the same genes more than k_{sim}. In this paper, we employed $k_{sim} = 0, 2, 4, 6, 8$. Since $k_{sim} = 10$ means the crossover between the same chromosomes, we did not use. When $k_{sim} = 0$, the crossover is applied between any parent solutions. The deletion algorithm is applied when the reward for the developed Q-table becomes larger than 100. This means that the deletion algorithm is applied after attaining the goal by multiple agents.

We employed the same parameter specifications as shown in Ito & Gofuku (2003) and Ito et al. (2004) except the learning rate and the discount rate in Equation (1). We found better specifications for those parameters by preliminary simulations:

[Genetic Algorithm]

The number of individuals: 300,
Selection: Roulette selection,
Type of crossover: uniform crossover,
The probability of crossover: 0.2,
Type of mutation: change the value among valid cell number,
The probability of mutation: 0.001,
The number of generations: 100,
Weights in Equation (2): $k_f = 200$,
Weights in Equation (7): $w_1 = 0.5, w_{N_s} = 0.5$, $w_i = 0\,(i = 2,..., N_{s-1})$.

[Q-learning]

Reward: When "L1" reaches the goal, $r = 100$,
When "L1" moves up or "L2" is removed, $r = 20$,
When "L1" moves down or "L2" blocks the course of "L1", $r = -20$,
When any agent can not move to the target position, $r = -10$,
Learning rate in Equation (1): $\alpha = 0.9$,
Discount rate in Equation (1): $\gamma = 0.1$,
ε-greedy action selection: 10% random action,
The number of trials of each learning dynamics: 10,000.

4.2 Simulation results

Figures 6 and 7 show that the average reward for the obtained Q-table and an average number of actions (or situations) in Q-table. The average reward for Q-table is calculated over the last 100 trials among 10,000 trials. The maximum average reward is 130. These figures show that the proposed QDSEGA with $k_{sim} = 2, 4$ could obtain the better or similar average reward with comparing to the algorithm without the neighboring crossover. As for the number of actions, the larger k_{sim} enables the less number of actions as shown in Figure 7. This shows that a compact Q-table can be obtained using the proposed neighboring crossover. Obtaining a compact Q-table enables users to find important actions to control the multiple agents.

In order to obtain a compact Q-table with high average reward, we apply our proposed neighboring crossover after the average reward becomes larger than 100. Since the neighboring crossover is applied to the similar parent solutions, that crossover often produces the offspring that is the same chromosome. This causes the reduction of the size of Q-table. As shown in Figure 7, the number of actions in the Q-table reduced rather than the previous QDSEGA. However, this reduction may prevent improving the performance in the average reward.

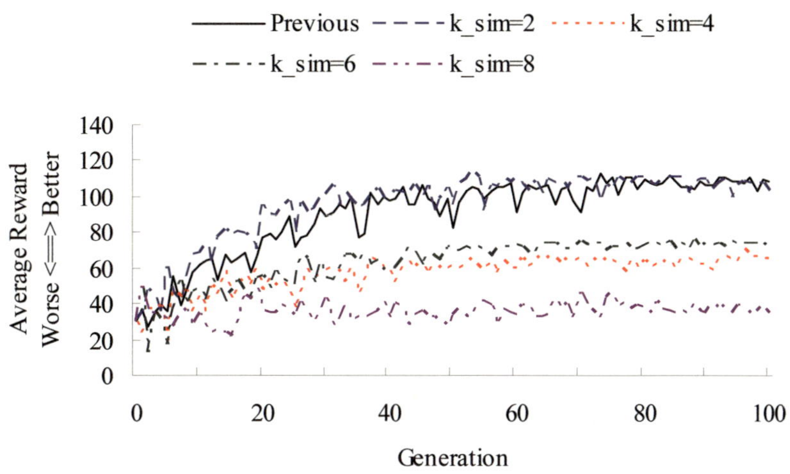

Fig. 6. Gain attained by Q-learning generated by QDSEGA

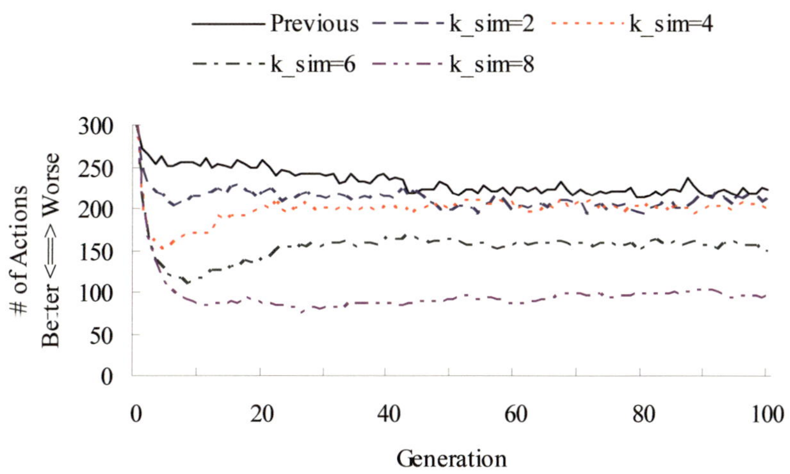

Fig. 7. The number of actions in Q-table generated by QDSEGA

Figures 8 and 9 show that the average reward and the average number of actions in Q-table. From these figures, we can see that the proposed QDSEGA can keep the high average reward with any value of k_{sim}. Figure 9 shows that the large value of k_{sim} enables to reduce the number of actions in Q-table.

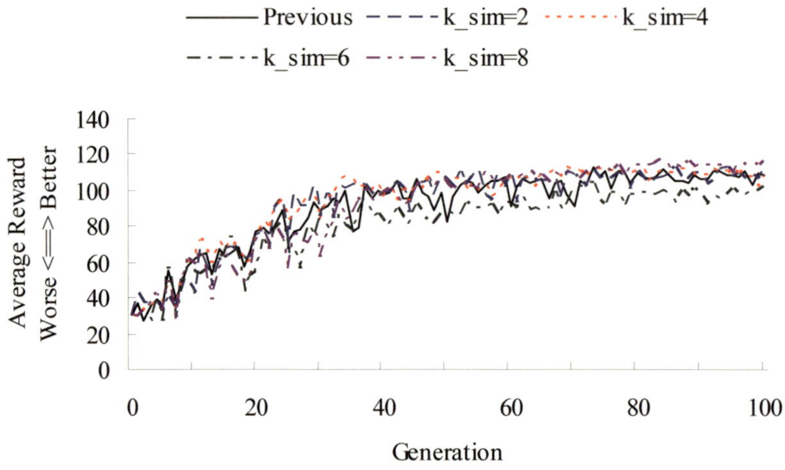

Fig. 8. Gain attained by Q-learning generated by QDSEGA applied the neighboring crossover when obtaining 100 reward

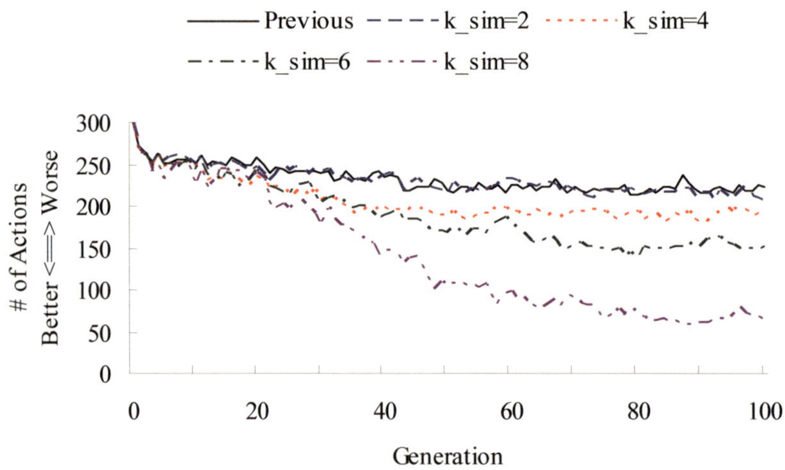

Fig. 9. The number of actions in Q-table generated by QDSEGA applied the neighboring crossover when obtaining 100 reward

Although the neighboring crossover has an effect to reduce the number of actions, there are some actions that are not used in moving agents. Therefore, we apply the deletion algorithm in Subsection 3.3. Figures 10 and 11 show the results of QDSEGA with neighboring crossover and the deletion algorithm. From these figures, we can see that the deletion algorithm does not degrade the performance in the average reward but have a fine effect to reduce the number of actions. By combining the neighboring crossover and the deletion algorithm, we could obtain more compact control table with high performance than using the previous algorithms.

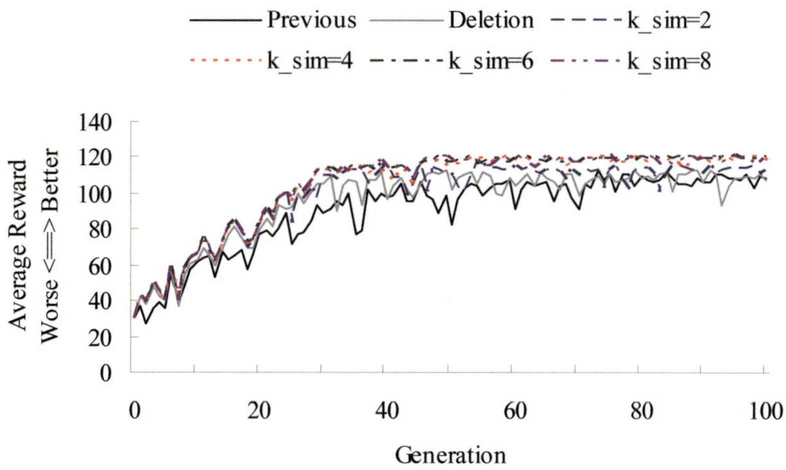

Fig. 10. Gain attained by Q-learning generated by QDSEGA applied the neighboring crossover and the deletion algorithm when obtaining 100 reward

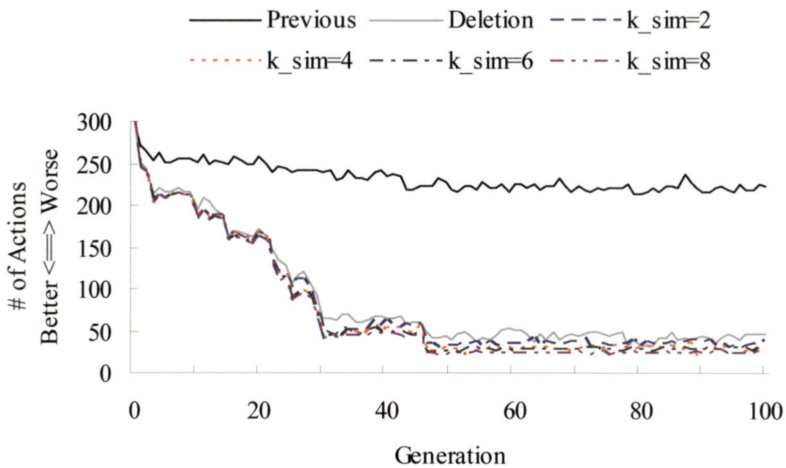

Fig. 11. The number of actions in Q-table generated by QDSEGA applied the neighboring crossover and the deletion algorithm when obtaining 100 reward

Table 1 shows the average number of actions obtained at the final generation. From this table, we can see that the number of actions is reduced by the neighboring crossover and the deletion algorithm. Especially the deletion algorithm could reduce it without degrading the performance of the developed control table using neighboring crossover.

After obtaining a compact control table, we can examine the states and actions that are used to reach the goal. We can see that in order to achieve the task to bring "L1" to the goal, only two actions are required from the initial states shown in Figure 3. For example, the two actions in Figure 12 are enough to convey "L1" to the goal with ten agents. Figure 13 shows the states or positions of the agents according to the obtained states shown in Figure 12.

Without Deletion Algorithm	Previous	2	4	6	8
# of actions	222.2	210.8	196.9	149.2	96.5

With Deletion Algorithm	Previous	2	4	6	8
# of actions	46.6	39.0	28.0	30.2	25.1

Table 1. Size of the Q-table at the final generation

	1	2	3	4	5	6	7	8	9	10
Initial State	0	4	0	4	0	4	0	4	0	4
Transition	23	1	15	7	12	3	24	12	16	19
Final State	21	15	23	22	16	22	16	7	16	21

Fig. 12. Succession of the states to achieve the goal

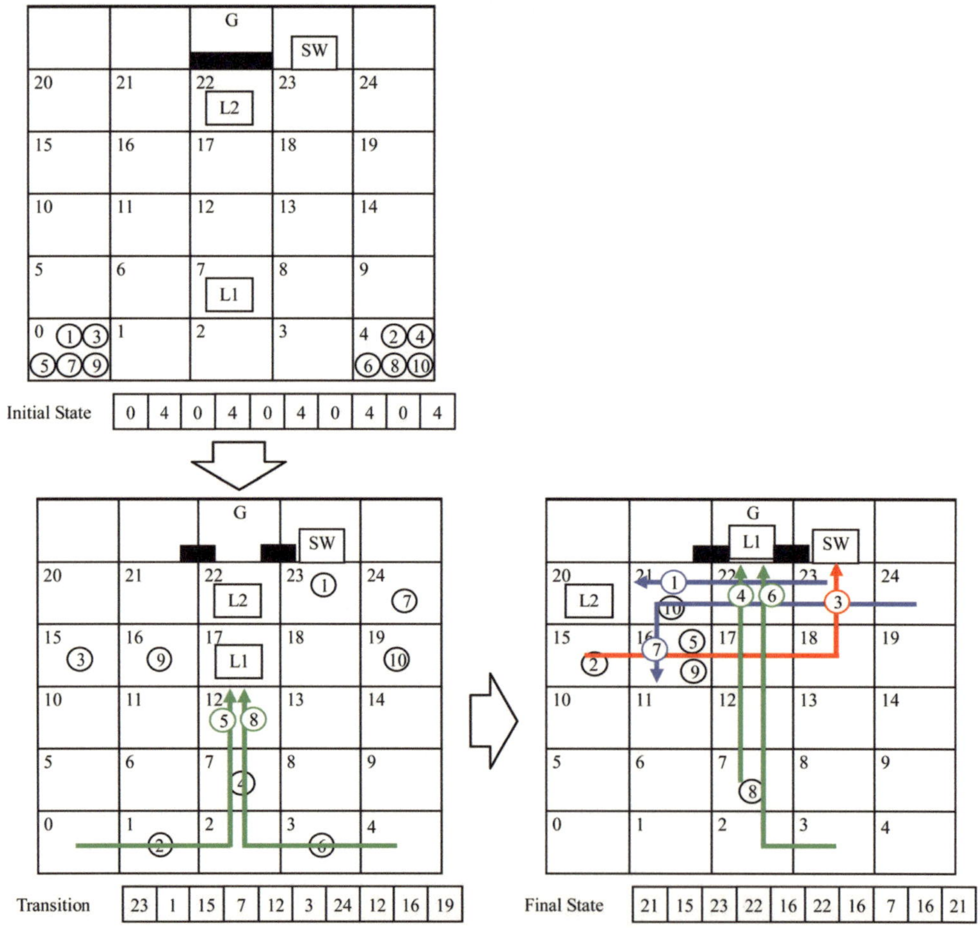

Fig. 13. Achievement of carrying the load to the goal

5. Conclusion

In this chapter, we show the effectiveness of the neighboring crossover and the deletion algorithm especially in reducing the size of the Q-table. By reducing the Q-table, it becomes easy to read the Q-table that is required for attaining the objective to reach the goal and minimizes the memory to store the developed control table.

As for other further study, we can bring other objective functions to achieve the goal. In Figures 6, 8, and 10, we compared the average reward as shown in the previous study (Ito and Gofuku, 2003; Ito et al., 2004). From these figures, we could minimize the total moving cost of all the agents to achieve the goal.

Furthermore, Ito and Gofuku (2003) examined the effectiveness of QDSEGA for multi-agent system with heterogeneous ability. We can show the effectiveness of the neighboring crossover in that problem too.

6. Acknowledgments

This work was partially supported by the MEXT, Japan under Collaboration with Local Communities Project for Private Universities starting 2005.

7. References

Belding, T. C. (1995). The distributed genetic algorithm revisited. *Proceedings of 6th International Conference on Genetic Algorithms*, pp. 114-121, ISBN 1558603700, University of Pittsburgh, July 1995, Morgan Kaufmann Publishers, Inc., San Francisco, USA

Holland, J. H. (1986). Escaping brittleness: the possibilities of general purpose learning algorithms applied to parallel rulebased system, *Machine Learning: An artificial intelligence approach*, Vol. 2, pp. 593-623, Morgan Kaufmann Publishers Inc., ISBN 0934613001, San Francisco, USA

Ito, K. & Matsuno, F. (2002). A study of reinforcement learning for the robot with many degrees of freedom -Acquisition of locomotion patterns for multi legged robot-, *Proceedings of IEEE International Conference on Robotics and Automation*, pp. 392-397, ISBN 0780372727, Washington, D.C., USA, May 2002, Institute of Electrical and Electronics Engineers, Inc., Piscataway, USA

Ito, K. & Gofuku, A. (2003). Hybrid autonomous control for heterogeneous multi-agent system, *Proceedings of 2003 IEEE/RSJ International Conference on Intelligent Robots and Systems*, pp. 2500-2505, ISBN 0780378601, Las Vegas, October 2003, Institute of Electrical and Electronics Engineers, Inc., Piscataway, USA

Ito, K., Gofuku, A. & Takeshita, M. (2004). Hybrid autonomous control for multi mobile robots, *Advanced Robotics*, Vol. 18, No. 1, pp. 83-99, ISSN 01691864

Mandelick, B. & Spiessens, P. (1989). Fine-grained parallel genetic algorithms, *Proceedings of 3rd International Conference on Genetic Algorithms*, pp. 428-433, ISBN 1558600063, George Mason University, June 1989, Morgan Kaufmann Publishers, Inc., San Francisco, USA

Muhlenbein, H., Schomisch, M. & Born, J. (1991). The parallel genetic algorithm as function optimizer, *Proceedings of 4th International Conference on Genetic Algorithms*, pp. 271-

278, ISBN 1558602089, San Diego, July 1991, Morgan Kaufmann Publishers, Inc., San Francisco, USA

Murata, T. & Yamaguchi, M. (2005). Neighboring Crossover to Improve GA-Based Q-Learning Method for Multi-Legged Robot Control, *Proceedings of Genetic and Evolutionary Computation Conference 2005*, pp. 145-146, ISBN 1595930108, Washington, D.C., June 2005, The Association for Computing Machinery, Inc., New York , USA

Murata, T. & Yamaguchi, M. (2008). Multi-Legged Robot Control Using GA-Based Q-Learning Method With Neighboring Crossover, In: *Frontiers in Evolutionary Robotics*, Iba (Ed.), pp. 341-352, I-Tech Education and Publishing, ISBN 9783902613196, Vienna, Austria

Murata, T., Ishibuchi, H. & Gen, M. (2000). Cellular genetic local search for multi-objective optimization, *Proceedings of Genetic and Evolutionary Computation Conference 2000*, pp. 307-314, ISBN 1558607080, Las Vegas, July 2000, The Association for Computing Machinery, Inc., New York, USA

Sutton, R. S. (1988). *Reinforcement Learning: An Introduction*, The MIT Press, ISBN 0262193981, Cambridge, USA

Svinin, M., Ushio, S., Yamada, K. & Ueda, K. (2001). An evolutionary approach to decentralized reinforcement learning for walking robots, *Proceedings of the 6th International Symposium on Artificial life and Robotics*, pp. 176-179, Tokyo, January 2001

Tanese, R. (1989). Distributed genetic algorithms, *Proceedings of 3rd International Conference on Genetic Algorithms*, pp. 434-439, ISBN 1558600063, George Mason University, June 1989, Morgan Kaufmann Publishers, Inc., San Francisco

Watkins, C.J.C.H. & Dayan, P. (1992). Technical note q-learning, *Machine Learning*, Vol. 8, pp. 279-292

Yamada, K., Ohkura, K., Svinin, M. & Ueda, K. (2001). Adaptive segmentation of the state space based on bayesian discrimination in reinforcement learning, *Proceedings of the 6th Int. Symposium on Artificial life and Robotics*, pp. 168–171, Tokyo, January 2001

10

Genetic Programming in Application to Flight Control System Design Optimisation

Anna Bourmistrova and Sergey Khantsis
Royal Melbourne Institute of Technology
Australia

1. Introduction

1.1 Evolutionary algorithms

EAs are often considered as an example of *artificial intelligence* and a *soft computing* approach. Their unique ability to search for complete and global solutions to a given problem makes EAs a powerful problem solving tool which combine such important characteristics as robustness, versatility and simplicity.

Historically, there exist several branches of EAs, namely Genetic Algorithms, Genetic Programming, Evolutionary Programming and Evolutionary Strategies. Their development started independently in the 1960s and 70s. Nevertheless, all of them are based on the same fundamental principle - evolution. 'Evolution' is used here in its Darwinian sense, the advance through 'survival of the fittest'.

Despite of a remarkable simplicity, EAs have proven to be capable of solving many practical tasks. The first and obvious application is numerical optimisation (minimisation or maximisation) of a given function. However, EAs are capable of much more than function optimisation or estimation of a series of unknown parameters within a given model of a physical system. Due to, in a large part, their stochastic nature, EAs can *create* such complex structures as computer programs, architectural designs and neural networks. Several applications of EAs have been known to produce a patentable invention (Koza et al., 1996, Koza et al., 1999 and Koza et al., 2003).

Unfortunately, such a truly intelligent application of EAs is rarely used for practical purposes. GP and similar algorithms often require a supercomputing power to produce an optimal solution for a practical task. This may be overcome, at least partially, by narrowing the search space.

A general engineering design practice is to propose a new design based on existing knowledge of various techniques (not uncommonly even from other fields) and no less important, intuition. Following this, the proposal is analysed, tried on a real system or its mathematical model, findings and errors are analysed again, the design is modified (or rejected) and the process continues until a satisfactory solution is found.

EAs work basically on the same principle, although, obviously, using less analytical analysis but more trial-and-error approach. It was found, however, that the process of selecting the most suitable solutions at each stage and producing the next iteration variants is, overall, largely intelligent and heuristic. EAs are capable to answer not only the question *how to do* something (how to control, in particular), but also the question *what to do* in order to meet

the objective. It is therefore appealing to apply such a promising automated technique to a problem with no general solution at hand.
The guidance and flight control is not a totally unstudied area where no convincing guesses can be made and where no parallels with the existing solutions are possible. This fact allows to watch, understand and guide, to a certain extent, the process of evolution. It also enables to optimise the EA for the purposes of control design.
The latter is especially useful because there are still very little research done on artificial evolution of structures of controllers in particular. An overwhelming majority of EA applications is concerned with numeric optimisation. A few proponents of a more advanced use (e.g. Koza et al., 2000, De Jong & Spears, 1993) are keen to show the real scope of possible applications, including controller design.

1.2 Unmanned aerial vehicles and shipboard recovery

Over the past two decades, the use of UAVs is becoming a well accepted technique not only for the military applications but also in the civilian arena. Typical applications of UAVs range from such traditional military missions as battlefield surveillance, reconnaissance and target acquisition to atmospheric research, weather observation, coastal and maritime surveillance, agricultural and geological surveying, telecommunication signals retranslation, and search and rescue missions.
The critical parts of a UAV mission are the launch and recovery phases. Although some UAVs can be conventionally operated from runways, the ability of UAVs to be operated from confined areas, such as remote land sites, ships and oil rigs, greatly increase their practical applications. Such operations generally require the aircraft to either have Vertical Take- Off and Landing (VTOL) capability or some form of launch and recovery assistance.
Unlike launch, the ways of UAV recovery are numerous. Probably the most widely used method, apart from runway landing, is the parachute assisted recovery. Unfortunately, parachute recovery can hardly be used when the landing area is extremely limited (for example, a ship's deck) and in the presence of high winds and strong gusts.
The first practicable and widely used solution for shipboard recovery of a fixed-wing UAV was capturing by an elastic net. This method has been employed for the USN *RQ-2 Pioneer* UAV, first deployed in 1986 aboard the battleship USS *Iowa*. The recovery net is usually stretched above the stern of the ship and the aircraft is flown directly into the net. A serious disadvantage of this method is that it is quite stressful for the aircraft. Nevertheless, due to simplicity of the recovery gear and reasonably simple guidance and flight control during the approach, this technique is still very popular for maritime operations.
Other methods include such techniques as deep stall and perched recovery and various forms of convertible airframes. However, these methods often imply very specific requirements to the UAV design and high complexity of control.
In this work a novel recovery method is proposed. This method, named *Cable Hook Recovery*, is intended to recover small to medium-size fixed-wing UAVs on frigate size vessels. It is expected to have greater operational capabilities than the *Recovery Net* technique, which is currently the most widely employed method of recovery for similar class of UAVs, potentially providing safe recovery even in very rough sea and allowing the choice of approach directions.
There are two distinct areas in recovery design: design of the recovery technique itself and development of a UAV controller that provides flight control and guidance of the vehicle in

accordance with the requirements of this technique. The controller should provide autonomous guidance and control during the whole recovery process (or its airborne stage). It should be noted that there exists a number of control design techniques applicable to the area of guidance and flight control. They all have different features and limitations, producing the controllers with different characteristics. It is expected that linear control techniques will not be sufficient for control of the aircraft through the whole recovery stage due to large atmospheric disturbances, ship motion and aircraft constraints.

Under these conditions when so many factors remain uncertain during the process of development, even the very approach to the control problem is unclear. It is desirable that the controller design methodology allow to produce an optimally suitable controller even when faced with such uncertainties and that could be done with application of EAs.

2. Evolutionary algorithms

Over the hundred years of aviation history, various linear control methods have been successfully used in the aerospace area due to their simplicity and analytical justifiability. Despite their natural limitations, linear control techniques still remain as one of the most accepted design practices. However, growing demands to the performance of aircraft, and on the other hand, a remarkable increase in available computation power over the past years have led to significant growth if the popularity of nonlinear control techniques.

A principal difficulty of many nonlinear control techniques, which potentially could deliver better performance, is the impossibility or extreme difficulty to predict theoretically the behaviour of a system under all possible circumstances. Therefore, it becomes a challenging task to verify and validate the designed controller under all real flight conditions. There is a need to develop a consistent nonlinear control design methodology that enables to produce a required controller for an arbitrary nonlinear system while assuring its robustness and performance across the whole operational envelope at the same time.

The Evolutionary Algorithms (EAs) is a group of such stochastic methods which combine such important characteristics as robustness, versatility and simplicity and, indeed, proved the success in many applications, such as neural network optimisation (McLean &. Matsuda, 1998), finance and time series analysis (Mahfoud & Mani, 1996), aerodynamics and aerodynamic shape optimisation (McFarland & Duisenberg, 1995), automatic evolution of computer software and, of course, control (Chipperfield & Flemming, 1996).

2.1 Introduction to evolutionary algorithms

Evolutionary algorithm is an umbrella term used to describe computer-based problem solving systems which employ computational models of evolutionary processes as the key elements in their design and implementation. All major elements found in natural evolution are present in EAs. They are:

- Population, which is a set of individuals (or members) being evolved;
- Genome, which is all the information about an individual encoded in some way;
- Environment, which is a set of problem-specific criteria according to which the fitness of each individual is judged;
- Selection, which is a process of selecting of the fittest individuals from the current population in the environment;
- Reproduction, which is a method of producing the offspring from the selected individuals;

- Genetic operators, such as mutation and recombination (crossover), which provide and control variability of the population.

The process of evolution takes a significant number of steps, or generations, until a desired level of fitness is reached. The 'outcome' should not be interpreted as if some particular species are expected to evolve. The evolution is not a purposive or directed process. It is expected that highly fit individuals will arise, however the concrete form of these individuals may be very different and even surprising in many real engineering tasks. None of the size, shape, complexity and other aspects of the solution are required to be specified in advance, and this is in fact one of the great advantages of the evolutionary approach. The problem of initial guess value rarely exists in EA applications, and the initial population is sampled at random.

The first dissertation to apply genetic algorithms to a pure problem of mathematical optimisation was Hollstien's work (Hollstien, 1971). However, it was not until 1975, when John Holland in his pioneering book (Holland, 1975) established a general framework for application of evolutionary approach to artificial systems, that practical EAs gained wide popularity. Until present time this work remains as the foundation of genetic algorithms and EAs in general.

Now let us consider the very basics of EAs. A typical pseudo code of an EA is as follows:

```
Create a {usually random} population of individuals;
Evaluate fitness of each individual of the population;
until not done {certain fitness, number of generations etc.}, do
Select the fittest individuals as 'parents' for new generation;
Recombine the 'genes' of the selected parents;
Mutate the mated population;
Evaluate fitness of the new population;
end loop.
```

It may be surprising how such a simple algorithm can produce a practical solution in many different applications.

Some operations in EAs can be either stochastic or deterministic; for example, selection may simply take the best half of the current population for reproduction, or select the individuals at random with some bias to the fittest members. Although the latter variant can sometimes select the individuals with very poorly fitness and thus may even lead to temporary deterioration of the population's fitness, it often gives better overall results.

2.2 Evolutionary algorithm inside

There are several branches of EAs which focus on different aspects of evolution and have slightly different approaches to ongoing parameters control and genome representation.

In this work, a mix of different evolutionary methods is used, combining their advantages. These methods have the common names: Genetic Algorithms (GA), Evolutionary Programming (EP), Evolutionary Strategies (ES) and Genetic Programming (GP).

As noted above, all the evolutionary methods share many properties and methodological approaches.

2.2.1 Fitness evaluation

Fitness, or objective value, of a population member is a degree of 'goodness' of that member in the problem space. As such, fitness evaluation is highly problem dependent. It is implemented in a function called fitness function, or more traditionally for optimisation methods, objective function. The plot of fitness function in the problem space is known as fitness landscape.

The word 'fitness' implies that greater values ('higher fitness') represent better solutions. However, mathematically this does not need to be so, and by optimisation both maximisation and minimisation are understood.

Although EAs are proved themselves as robust methods, their performance depends on the shape of the fitness landscape. If possible, fitness function should be designed so that it exhibits a gradual increase towards the maximum value (or decrease towards the minimum). In the case of GAs, this allows the algorithm to make use of highly fit building blocks, and in the case of ESs—to develop an effective search strategy quickly.

In solving real world problems, the fitness function may be affected by noise that comes from disturbances of a different nature. Moreover, it may be unsteady, that is, changing over time. Generally, EAs can cope very well with such types of problem, although their performance may be affected.

It is accepted that the performance of an optimisation algorithm is measured in terms of objective function evaluations, because in most practical tasks objective evaluation takes considerably more computational resources than the algorithm framework itself. For example, in optimisation of the aerodynamic shape of a body, each fitness evaluation may involve a computer fluid flow simulation which can last for hours. Nevertheless, even for simple mathematical objective functions EAs are always computationally intensive (which may be considered as the price for robustness).

The computation performance may be greatly improved by parallelisation of the fitness evaluation. EAs process multiple solutions in parallel, therefore they are extremely easily adopted to parallel computing.

Another useful consequence of maintaining a population of solutions is the natural ability of EAs to handle multi-objective problems. A common approach - used in this work - to reduce a multiobjective tasks to a single-objective one, by summing up all the criteria with appropriate weighting coefficients, is not always possible. Unlike single point optimisation techniques, EAs can evolve a set of Pareto optimal solutions simultaneously. A Pareto optimal solution is the solution that cannot be improved by any criterion without impairing it by at least one other criterion, which is a very interesting problem on its own.

2.2.2 Genome representation

In EA theory, much as well as in natural genetics, genome is the entire set of specifically encoded information that fully defines a particular individual. This section focuses only on numeric genome representation. However, EAs are not limited to numeric optimisations, and for more 'creative' design tasks a more sophisticated, possibly hierarchical, genome encoding is often required. In fact, virtually any imaginable data structure may be used as a genome. This type of problem is addressed in Section 2.5 Genetic Programming.

A commonly used genome representation in GAs is a fixed length binary string, called chromosome, with real numbers mapped into integers due to convenience of applying genetic operators, recombination (crossover) and mutation.

Accuracy is a common drawback of digital (discrete) machines, and care should be taken when choosing appropriate representation. For example, if *8* bit numbers are used and the problem determines the range of *[-1.0; 1.0]*, this range will be mapped into integers *[00000000; 11111111]* (*[0; 255]* decimal)1. As *255* corresponds to *1.0*, the next possible integer, *254*, will correspond to *0.99215686*, and there is no means of specifying any number between *0.99215686* and *1.0*.

The required accuracy is often set relative to the value, not the range. In this case, linear mapping may give too low accuracy near zero values and too high accuracy towards the end of the range. This was the reason for inventing the so called floating point number representation, which encodes the number in two parts: mantissa, which has a fixed range, and an integer exponent, which contain the order of the number. This representation is implemented in nearly all software and many hardware platforms which work with real numbers.

Another type of genome encoding which should be mentioned is the permutation encoding. It is used mostly in ordering problems, such as the classic Travelling Salesman Problem, where the optimal order of the given tokens is sought after. In this case, a chromosome can represent one of the possible permutations of the tokens (or rather their codes), for example, '*0123456789*' or '*2687493105*' for ten items. When this type of encoding is used, special care should be taken when implementing genetic operators, because 'traditional' crossover and mutation will produce mostly incorrect solutions (with some items included twice and some items missing).

Finally, a vector of floating point real values can be used as a chromosome to represent the problem that deals with real values. However, domain constraints handling should be implemented in most cases, as the floating point numbers, unlike integers, have virtually no highest and lowest values (in a practical sense). Moreover, special recombination and mutation operations should be used in this case.

2.2.3 Selection

Selection is the key element of all evolutionary algorithms. During selection, a generally fittest part of the population is chosen and this part (referred as mating pool) is then used to produce the offspring.

The requirements for the selection process are somewhat controversial. On the one hand, selection should choose 'the best of the best' to increase convergence speed. On the other hand, there should be some level of diversity in the population in order to allow the population to develop and to avoid premature convergence to a local optimum. This means that even not very well performing individuals should be included in the mating pool.

This question is known as the conflict between exploitation and exploration. With very little genetic diversity in a population, new areas in the search space become unreachable and the process stagnates. Although exploration takes valuable computation resources and may give negative results (in terms of locating other optima), it is the only way of gaining some confidence that the global optimum is found (Holland, 1975).

It should be noted that the optimal balance between exploitation and exploration is problem dependent. For example, real-time systems may want a quick convergence to an acceptable sub-optimal solution, thus employing strong exploitation; while engineering design which uses EAs as a tool is often interested in locating various solutions across the search space, or may want to locate exactly the global optimum. For the latter tasks, greater exploration and thus slower convergence is preferred.

Balance between exploitation and exploration can be controlled in different ways. For example, intuitively, stronger mutation favours greater exploration. However, it is selection that controls the balance directly. This is done by managing the 'strength' of selection. Very strong selection realises exploitation strategy and thus fast convergence, while weak selection allows better exploration.

A general characteristic that describes the balance between 'perfectionism' and 'carelessness' of selection is known as selection pressure or the degree to which the better individuals are favoured. Selection pressure control in a GA can be implemented in different ways; a very demonstrative parameter is the size of the mating pool relative to the size of the population. As a rule, the smaller the mating pool, the higher the selection pressure.

A quantitative estimation of the selection pressure may be given by the take-over time (Goldberg & Deb, 1991). With no mutation and recombination, this is essentially the number of generations taken for the best member in the initial generation to completely dominate the population.

The efficiency of one or another selection method used in EAs largely depends on population properties and characteristics of the whole algorithm. A theoretical comparison of the selection schemes may be found in (Goldberg & Deb, 1991).

First, all selection methods can be divided into two groups: stochastic and deterministic. Deterministic methods use the fitness value of a member directly for selection. For example, the best half of the population may be selected or all individuals with the fitness better than a given value may be included in the mating pool. In contrast, stochastic selection methods use fitness only as a guide, giving the members with better fitness more chances to be selected allowing greater exploration. However, deterministic methods can also be tuned to allow greater exploration. For example, every second member in a sorted by fitness list can be taken for reproduction instead of the best half of the population.

One of the simple ways to reduce the possible impact of stochastic sampling errors is to guarantee that the best, or elite, member(s) is always selected for reproduction. This approach is known as Elitism. In effect, elitism is the introduction of a portion of deterministic selection into a stochastic selection procedure. In most cases, elitism assumes that the elite member is not only selected, but also propagated directly to the new population without being disrupted by recombination or mutation. This approach ensures that the best-so-far achievement is preserved and the evolution does not deteriorate, even temporarily.

Another feature which may be applied to any selection scheme is population overlapping. The fraction of the old population which is replaced with the fresh members is called a generation gap (De Jong, 1975). Nothing particularly advantageous is found in overlapping schemes, although they may be useful for some problems, in particular for steady and noiseless environments (Goldberg & Deb, 1991).

It should be also noted that some reproduction schemes allow multiple selection of one member, while others do not. The former case (also referred to as replacement) means that the selected member is returned back to the mating pool and thus may be selected again in the same generation. This feature is often used in stochastic selection methods such as fitness proportional selection and tournament selection.

2.2.3.1 *Deterministic selection*

All members are straightforwardly sorted according to their fitness value and some of the best members are picked up for reproduction. A certain number of members (or population percentage) is usually chosen, or the members may be selected one by one and reproduced until the next generation population is filled up.

As noted before, deterministic methods are more suitable for the algorithms with small populations (less than about *20–40* members). They are therefore used in the areas where small populations are desirable (e.g. when fitness evaluation is extremely costly) or where it is traditionally adopted (in particular in Evolutionary Strategies, see Section 2.4).

2.2.3.2 *Fitness proportional selection and fitness scaling*

In fitness proportional selection, all individuals receive the chances to reproduce that are proportional to their objective value (fitness). There are several implementations of this general scheme which vary in stochastic properties and time complexity: roulette wheel (Monte Carlo) selection, stochastic remainder selection and stochastic universal selection. The roulette wheel method is described here in more detail.

The analogy with a roulette wheel arises because one can imagine the whole population forming a roulette wheel with the size of any individual's slot proportional to its fitness. The wheel is then spun and the 'ball' thrown in. The probability of the 'ball' coming to rest in any particular slot is proportional to the arc of the slot and thus to the fitness of the corresponding individual (Coley, 1999).

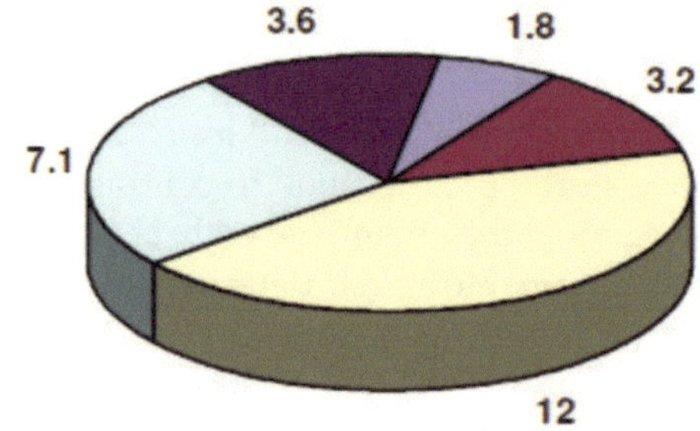

Fig. 1. Roulette wheel selection

There are no means to control the selection pressure and the convergence speed: they are determined entirely by the fitness of each individual.

However, such a control is often necessary. If for example, a fit individual is produced, fitness proportional selection with replacement can allow a large number of copies of this individual to flood the subsequent generations.

One of the methods intended to overcome this problem and to maintain a steady selection pressure is linear fitness scaling (Coley, 1999). Linear fitness scaling works by pivoting the fitness of each individual about the average population fitness. The scale is chosen so that an approximately constant proportion of copies of the best members is selected compared to the 'average member'.

There are some more sophisticated scaling techniques, such as sigma scaling (Coley, 1999), in which the (expected) number of trials each member receives is adjusted according to the standard deviation of the population fitness.

2.2.3.3 *Ranking selection*

This is a development of the fitness proportional selection, aimed to achieve greater adaptability and to reduce stochastic. The idea represents the combination of fitness proportional and deterministic selection. The population is sorted according to the fitness, and a rank is assigned to each individual. After assigning the rank, a proportionate selection is applied as described in the previous section, using rank values instead of fitness.

Ranking has two main advantages before fitness proportional selection (even that with fitness scaling). First, the required selection pressure can be controlled more flexibly by applying a specific rank assignment function. Second, it softens stochastic errors of the search, which can be especially destructive for the fitness functions affected by noise. If a particularly fit member is generated that stands well off the whole population. Even if the proportionate selection is constrained by fitness scaling, this best member will be greatly favoured, whilst the rest of the population will receive very low selection pressure because the differences between their fitness values are insignificant as compared to the 'outlier'. In contrast, ranking will establish a predefined difference between the neighbouring members, ensuring an adequate selection pressure for the whole population.

2.2.3.4 *Tournament selection*

Tournament selection is a simple yet flexible stochastic selection scheme. Choose some number s of individuals randomly from a population and then select the best individual from this group. Repeat as many times as necessary to fill up the mating pool. This somewhat resembles the tournaments held between s competitors. As a result, the mating pool, being comprised of tournament winners, has a higher average fitness than the average population fitness.

The selection pressure can be controlled simply by choosing appropriate tournament size s. Obviously, the winner from a larger tournament will, on average, have a higher fitness than the winner of a smaller tournament. In addition, selection pressure can be further adjusted via randomisation of the tournament.

2.2.4 Recombination

Recombination allows solutions to exchange the information in a way similar to that used by a biological organism undergoing sexual reproduction. This effective mechanism allows to combine parts of the solution (building blocks) successfully found by parents. Combined with selection, this scheme produces, on average, fitter offspring. Of course, being a stochastic operation, recombination can produce 'disadvantaged' individuals as well; however, they will be quickly perished under selection.

Recombination is usually applied probabilistically with a certain probability. For GAs, the typical value is between *0.6* and *0.8*; however, the values up to *1.0* are common.

2.2.4.1 *Alphabet based chromosome recombination*

In essence, recombination is 'blending' the information of two (or more) genomes in some way. For typical GAs, an approach from natural genetics is borrowed. It is known as crossover. During crossover, chromosomes exchange equal parts of themselves. In its simplest form known as single-point crossover, two parents are taken from the mating pool. A random position on the chromosome (locus) is chosen. Then, the end pieces of the chromosomes, starting from the chosen locus, are swapped.

Single-point crossover can be generalised to k-point crossover, when k different loci are chosen and then every second piece is swapped. However, according to De Jong's studies (De Jong, 1975) and also (Spears & Anand, 1991), multi-point crossover degrades overall algorithm performance increasingly with an increased number of cross points.

There is another way of swapping pieces of chromosomes, known as uniform crossover. This method does not select crossover points. Instead, it considers each bit position of the two parents one by one and swaps the corresponding bits with a probability of *50%*. Although the uniform crossover is, in a sense, an extreme case of multi-point crossover and can be considered as the most disruptive its variant, both theoretical and practical results (Spears & Anand, 1991) show that uniform crossover outperforms k-point crossover in most cases.

2.2.4.2 *Real value recombination*

Real-coded EAs require a special recombination operator. Unlike bit strings, real parameters are not deemed as strings that can be cut into pieces. Instead, they are processed as a whole in a common mathematical way. Due to rather historical reasons, real-coded EAs were mostly developing under the influence of Evolutionary Strategies and Evolutionary Programming (see Section 2.4). As a result, real-value recombination has not been properly considered until the fairly recent past ('90s). Nevertheless, a number of various recombination techniques have been developed. Detailed analysis of them is available in (Beyer & Deb, 2001, Deb et al., 2001 and Herrera et al., 1998).

The simplest real-value recombination one can think of is the averaging of several parents, which is known as arithmetic crossover. This method produces one offspring from two or more parents. Averaging may be weighted according to parents' fitness or using random weighting coefficients.

Self-adaptive recombination create offspring statistically located in proportion to the difference of the parents in the search space. These recombination operators generate one or two children according to a probability distribution over two or more parent solutions where if the difference between the parent solutions is small, the difference between the child and parent solutions should also be small.

The most popular approach is to use a uniform probability distribution—the so called 'blend crossover', *BLX*. The *BLX* operator randomly picks a solution in the range

$$\left[x_1 - \alpha\left(x_2 - x_1\right); x_2 + \alpha\left(x_2 - x_1\right)\right] \tag{1}$$

for two parents $x_1 < x_2$. is the parameter which controls the spread of the offspring interval beyond the range of the parents' interval $[x_1; x_2]$.

Other approaches suggest non-uniform probability distribution. The Simulated Binary Crossover (*SBX*) uses a bimodal probability distribution with its mode at the parent solutions. It produces two children from two parents. This technique has been developed by K. Deb and his students in 1995. As the name suggests, the *SBX* operator simulates the working principle of the single-point crossover operator on binary strings.

A different approach is demonstrated by the Unimodal Normal Distribution Crossover (*UNDX*) (Ono & Kobayashi, 1997). It uses multiple (usually three) parents and create offspring solutions around the centre of mass of these parents. *UNDX* uses a normal probability distribution, thus assigning a small probability to solutions away from the centre of mass. Another mean-centric recombination operator is the Simplex Crossover (*SPX*). It differs from *UNDX* by assigning a uniform probability distribution for creating offspring in a restricted region marked by the parents.

Although both mean-centric and parent-centric recombination methods were found to exhibit self-adaptive behaviour for real-coded GAs similar to that of ESs (see Section 2.4), in a number of reports parent-centric methods were found generally superior (Deb et al., 2001).

2.2.5 Mutation

Mutation is another genetic operator borrowed from nature. However, unlike recombination, which is aimed at producing better offspring, mutation is used to maintain genetic diversity in the population from one generation to the next in a explorative way.

Not unlike recombination, mutation works differently for alphabet-based chromosomes and real-coded algorithms. However, in both cases it is merely a blind variation of a given individual.

2.2.5.1 *Bit string mutation*

In nearly all ordinary GAs, mutation is implemented as variation of a random bit in the chromosome. Each bit in the chromosome is considered one by one and changed with certain probability P_m. Bit change can be applied either as flipping (inverting) of the bit or replacing it with a random value. In the latter case, the actual mutation rate will be twice as low, because, on average, half of the bits are replaced with the same value.

In GAs, mutation is usually controlled through mutation probability P_m. As a rule, Gas put more stress on recombination rather than on mutation, therefore typical mutation rates are very low, of the order of *0.03* and less (per bit). Rates close to *0.001* are common. Nevertheless, mutation is very important because it prevents the loss of building blocks which cannot be recovered by recombination alone.

Mutation probability can be supressed in a number of ways. However, this may easily have an adverse effect—mutation is known for the ability to 'push' the stagnated process at the later stages.

Another technique to avoid stagnation is so called 'hypermutation'. Hypermutation is a method in which mutation probability is significantly (*10–100* times) increased for a small number of generations (usually one) during the run, or such a high rate is applied constantly to a certain part of the population (e.g. *20%*). Both hypermutation and random immigrants techniques are especially effective for dynamic environments, where the fitness landscape can change significantly over time (Grefenstette, 1999).

The above mutation control methods have a common drawback: they are not selective. Sometimes an individual approach may be desirable. In particular, stronger mutation might be applied to the weakest members, while less disruptive mutation to the best individuals. Alternatively, some more sophisticated methods can be developed. Such fine tuning is a more common feature of Evolutionary Strategies (see section 2.4) and real-coded GAs.

Some more direct control methods utilise additional bits in the genotype which do not affect the phenotype directly. However, these bits control the mutation itself. In the simplest case, a single flag bit can control the applicability of mutation to the respective parameter when zero value disables mutation and unity enables it.

2.2.5.2 *Real value mutation*

Implementation of a real-value mutation is rather more straightforward than that of alphabet strings. Unlike the latter, it is not an operation directly inspired by nature; however, as the real-coded algorithms generally do not use tricky encoding schemes and have the same problem-space and genotype values of the parameters, real-value mutation can be considered as the operation working on a higher level, up to direct phenotype mutation for function optimization problems.

Mutation to a real value is made simply by adding a random number to it. It is evident that the strength of real-value mutation can be controlled in a very convenient way, through the variance of the distribution (or the window size for the uniform distribution). Like with the common GAs that operate string-type chromosomes, mutation strength can be adapted using many different techniques, from simple predefined linear decrease to sophisticated adaptation strategies

2.2.6 Measuring performance

Performance of an EA is the measure how effective the algorithm is in search of the optimal solution. As evolutionary search is a stochastic and dynamic process, it can hardly be positively measured by a single figure. A better indicator of the performance is a convergence graph, that is, the graph 'fitness vs. computation steps'.

This figure presents two typical convergence graphs of two independent runs of the same GA with different sets of parameters. It can be seen that although the first run converges faster, it stagnates too early and does not deliver the optimal solution. Therefore, not the convergence speed nor time to reach a specified value, nor any other single parameter can be considered as a sole performance measure.

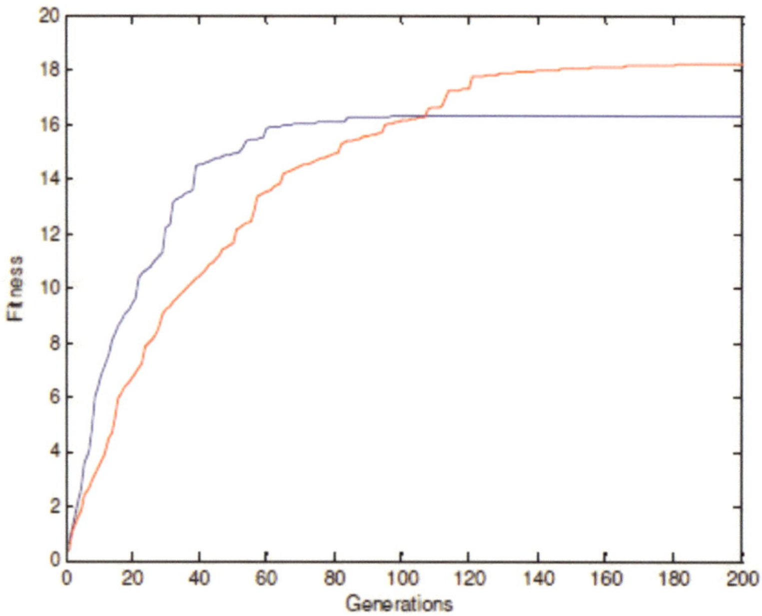

Fig. 2. Typical convergence graphs

De Jong in (De Jong, 1975) used two measures of the progress of the GA: the off-line performance and the on-line performance. The off-line performance is represented by the running average of the fitness of the best individual, f_{max}, in each population:

$$f_{off}(g) = \frac{1}{g}\sum_{i=1}^{g} f_{\max}(g) \tag{2}$$

where g is the generation number. In contrast, the on-line performance is the average of all fitness values calculated so far:

$$f_{on}(g) = \frac{1}{g}\sum_{i=1}^{g} f_{avg}(g) \tag{3}$$

The on-line performance includes both good and bad guesses and therefore reflects not only the progress towards the optimal solution, but also the resources taken for such progress.

Another useful measure is the convergence velocity:

$$V(g) = \ln \sqrt{\frac{f_{\max}(g)}{f_{on}(1)}} \tag{4}$$

In the case of a non-stationary dynamic environment, the value of previously found solutions is irrelevant at the later steps. Hence, a better measure of optimisation in this case is the current-best metric instead of running averages.

When comparing the performance of different algorithms, it is better to use the number of fitness evaluations instead of the number of generations as the argument for performance characteristics.

2.2.7 The problem of convergence and genetic drift

Usually, the progress of EAs is fast at first and then loses its speed and finally stagnates. This is a common scenario for optimisation techniques. However, progressing too quickly due to greedy exploitation of good solutions may result in convergence to a local optimum an thus in low robustness. Several methods that help to control the convergence have been described in the above sections, including selection pressure control and adaptation of recombination and mutation rates.

However, it is unclear to which degree and how in particular to manage the algorithm's parameters. What is 'too fast' convergence? Unfortunately, the current state of EA theory is inadequate to answer this question *before* the EA is initiated.

For the most of the real-world problems, it takes several trial runs to obtain an adequate set of parameters. The picture of convergence process, as noted before, is not a good indicator of the algorithm's characteristics. In contrast, the plot of genetic diversity of the population against generation number (or fitness function evaluations) gives a picture which can explain some performance problems. If the population quickly loses the genetic diversity, this usually means a too high initial selection pressure. The further saturation may be attributed to reduction of selection pressure at the later stages. The loss of genetic diversity is known as genetic drift (Coley, 1998).

2.2.8 Schema theory

Schema theory has been developed by John Holland (Holland, 1975) and popularised by David Goldberg (Goldberg, 1989) to explain the power of binary-coded genetic algorithms. More recently, it has been extended to real-value genome representations (Eshelman & Schaffer, 1993) and tree-like *S*-expression representations used in genetic programming (Langdon & Poli, 2002, O'Reilly & Oppacher, 1995). Due to the importance of the theory for understanding GA internals, it is mentioned here, though it is not within the scope of this work to discuss it in details.

2.3 Genetic algorithms

Genetic algorithms are one of the first evolutionary methods successfully used to solve practical problems, and until now they remain one of the most widely used EAs in the engineering field. John Holland in (Holland, 1975) provided a general framework for GAs and a basic theoretical background, much of which has been discussed in the former sections. There are more recent publications on the basics of GA, for example (Goldberg, 1989). The basic algorithm is exactly as in the Section 2.1; however, several variations to this scheme are known. For example, Koza (Koza, 1992) uses separate threads for asexual reproduction, crossover and mutation, chosen at random; therefore, only one of these genetic operators is applied to an individual in each loop, while classical GA applies mutation after crossover independently.

One of the particularities of typical GAs is genome representation. The vast majority of GAs use alphabet-based string-like chromosomes described in Section 2.2.2, although real coded GAs are gaining wider popularity. Therefore, a suitable mapping from actual problem space parameters to such strings must be designed before a genetic search can be conducted.

The objective function can also have the deceptive properties as in most practical cases little is known about the fitness landscape. Nevertheless, if the fitness function is to be designed for a specific engineering task (for example, an estimate of the flight control quality, as will be used in this study later), attention should be paid to avoiding rugged and other GA-difficult fitness landscapes.

Of the two genetic operators, recombination (crossover) plays the most important role in Gas. Typical probability of crossover is *0.6* to *0.8* and even up to *1.0* in some applications. On the contrary, mutation is considered as an auxiliary operator, only to ensure that the variability of the population is preserved. Mutation probabilities range from about *0.001* to *0.03* per bit.

Population size is highly problem dependent; however, typical GAs deal with fairly large or at least moderate population sizes, of the order of *50* to *300* members, although smaller and much larger sizes (up to several thousands) could be used.

Although by far the largest application of GAs is optimisations of different sorts, from simple function optimisations to multi-parameter aerodynamic shape optimisation (McFarland & Duisenberg, 1995) and optimal control (Chipperfield & Flemming, 1996), GAs are suitable for many more tasks where great adaptation ability is required, for example, neural networks learning (Sendhoff & Kreuz, 1999) and time series prediction (Mahfoud & Mani, 1996). The potential of GA application is limited virtually only by the ability to develop a suitable encoding.

2.4 Evolutionary strategies and evolutionary programming

Evolutionary Programming was one of the very first evolutionary methods. It was introduced by Lawrence J. Fogel in the early 1960s (Fofel, 1962), and the publication (Fogel et al., 1966) by Fogel, Owens and Walsh became a landmark for EP applications. Originally, EP was offered as an attempt to create artificial intelligence. It was accepted that prediction is a keystone to intelligent behaviour, and in (Fogel et al., 1966) EP was used to evolve finite state automata that predict symbol strings generated from Markov processes and non-stationary time series.

In contrast, Evolutionary Strategies appeared on the scene in an attempt to solve a practical engineering task. In 1963, Ingo Rechenberg and Hans-Paul Schwefel were conducting a series of wind tunnel experiments in Technical University of Berlin trying to optimise aerodynamic shape of a body. This was a laborious intuitive task and the students tried to work strategically. However, simple gradient and coordinate strategies have proven to be unsuccessful, and Rechenberg suggested to try random changes in the parameters defining the shape, following the example of natural mutations and selection.

As it can be seen, both methods are focusing on behavioural linkage between parents and the offspring rather than seeking to emulate specific genetic operators as observed in nature. In addition, unlike GAs, natural real-value representation is predominantly used. In the present state, EP and ES are very similar, despite their independent development over 30 years, and the historical associations to finite state machines or engineering field are no longer valid. In this study, ES approach is employed, so further in this section Evolutionary Strategies are described, with special notes when the EP practice is different.

2.4.1 Self-adaptation

One of the most important mechanisms that differs ES from the common GAs is endogenous control on genetic operators (primarily mutation). Mutation is usually performed on real-value parameters by adding zero mean normally distributed random values. The variance of these values is called step size in ES.

The adaptation of step size rules can be divided into two groups: pre-programmed rules and adaptive, or evolved, rules. The pre-programmed rules express a heuristic discovered through extensive experimentation. One of the earliest examples of pre-programmed adaptation is Rechenberg's (1973) *1/5* rule. The rule states that the ratio of successful mutations to all mutations should be *1/5* measured over a number of generations. The mutation variance (step size) should increase if the ratio is above *1/5*, decrease if it is below and remain constant otherwise. The variance is updated every k generations according to:

$$\sigma^{(g)} = \begin{cases} \sigma^{(g-k)} / c & n_s > 1/5 \\ \sigma^{(g-k)} \cdot c & n_s < 1/5 \\ \sigma^{(g-k)} & n_s = 1/5 \end{cases} \qquad (5)$$

where n_s is the ratio of successful mutations and $0.817 \; c < 1$ is the adaptation rate. The lower bound $c = 0.817$ has been theoretically derived by Schwefel for the sphere problem (Ursem, 2003). The upper index in parenthesis henceforth denotes the generation number.

The other approach is the self-adaptive (evolved) control where Schwefel (Schwefel, 1981) proposed to incorporate the parameters that control mutation into the genome. This way, an individual $\boldsymbol{a} = (x, \sigma)$ consists of *object variables* (sometimes referred as *describing parameters*) x and *strategy parameters* σ. The strategy parameters undergo basically the same evolution as object variables: they are mutated and then selected together, though only on the basis of objective performance, on which strategy parameters have indirect influence. The underlying hypothesis in this scheme is that good solutions carry good strategy parameters; hence, evolution discovers good parameters while solving the problem.

2.5 Genetic programming

Genetic programming (GP) is an evolutionary machine learning technique. It uses the same paradigm as genetic algorithms and is, in fact, a generalisation of GA approach. GP increases the complexity of the structures undergoing evolution. In GP, these structures represent hierarchical computer programs of varying size and shape.

GP is a fairly recent EA method compared to other techniques discussed before in this chapter. The first experiments with GP were reported by Stephen Smith (Smith, 1980) and Nichael Cramer (Gramer, 1985). However, the first seminal book to introduce GP as a solid and practical technique is John Koza's 'Genetic Programming', dated 1992.

In GP, each individual in a population is a program which is executed in order to obtain its fitness. Thus, the situation is somewhat opposite to GAs: the individual is a 'black box' with

an arbitrary input and some output. The fitness value (often referred to as *fitness measure* in GP) is usually obtained through comparison of the program's output with the desired output for several input test values (*fitness cases*). However, fitness evaluation in GP is problem dependent and may be carried out in a number of ways. For example, the fitness of a program controlling a robotic animal may be calculated as the number of food pieces collected by the animal minus resources taken for search (e.g. path length). When seeking a function to fit the experimental data, the deviation will be the measure of fitness.
One of the characteristics of GP is enormous size of the search space. GP search in the space of possible computer programs, each of which is composed of varying number of functions and terminals. It can be seen that the search space is virtually incomprehensible, so that even generation of the initial random population may represent some difficulties. Due to that, GP typically works with very large populations of hundreds and even thousands of members. Two-parent crossover is usually employed as the main genetic operator, while mutation has only a marginal role or is not used at all.

2.5.1 Genome representation in GP and S-expressions

Unlike linear chromosomes in GAs, genomes in GP represent hierarchical, tree-like structures. Any computer program or mathematical expression can be depicted as a tree structure with functions as nodes and terminals as leaves. For example, let us consider an expression for one of the roots of a square equation $ax^2 + bx + c = 0$:

$$\frac{-b+\sqrt{b^2-4ac}}{2a}$$

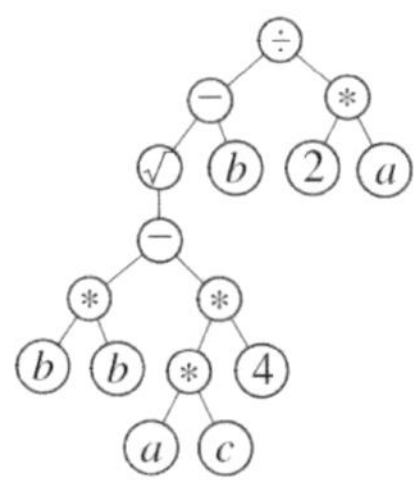

Fig. 3. Tree-like representation of an expression

The convenience of such tree-like structures is that they can be easily modified on the sub-tree level. Any sub-tree can be taken out and replaced with another one, preserving syntax validity of the expression.
However, the trees such as shown in Fig. 3 should be encoded in some computer-readable form for actual GP implementation. This can be done in a number of ways. Some systems (e.g. MATLAB) provide built-in mechanisms for storage and operation on hierarchical structures. If this is not available, string representations are employed. An expression or a program can be encoded in a common for imperative languages way; for example, the formula for the root of a square equation from Fig. 3 can be written as

$$\left(sqrt\left(b*b-4*a*c\right)-b\right)/\left(2*a\right) \tag{6}$$

Unfortunately, such representation, although being mathematically readable, is inconvenient to handle in a GP way. It has to be parsed to the tree-like form for every operation. Therefore, another syntax is traditionally used.
One can note that in the trees such as the ones above, an operation always precedes its arguments on the branch, e.g. instead of 'a + b' it reads '+ a b'. This notation is known as

prefix notation or Polish notation. It is used in the programming language LISP and its derivatives— certainly not the most human-friendly language but very flexible and useful in many areas, and is one of the most popular languages in GP field.

There are extensions to the tree-based GP. Most of them employ decomposition of the programs into sub-trees (modules) and evolving these modules separately. One of the most widely used methods of this kind is Koza's Automatically Defined Functions (ADF) (Koza, 1994). In ADF approach, the program is split into a main tree and one or more separate trees which take arguments and can be called by the main program or each other. In another approach, code fragments from successful program trees are automatically extracted and are held in a library, and then can be reused in the following generations by any individual via library calls.

However, tree-based GP is not the only option. It is possible to express a program as a linear sequence of commands. One of the examples of linear GP systems is stack-based GP (Perkins, 1994). In stack-based languages (such as Forth) each program instruction takes its arguments from a stack, performs its calculations and then pushes the result back onto the stack. For example, the sequence *1 2 +* . pushes the constants *1* and *2* onto the stack, then '+' takes these values from the stack, performs the addition and pushes the result *3* back. The final dot extracts and prints out the result. The notation such as '*1 2 +*' is the opposite to that used in LISP and is called *reverse Polish notation* (or *postfix notation*).

2.5.1.1 *Function set and terminal set*

When designing a GP implementation, proper care should be taken for choosing the function and terminal sets. The function set $F = \{f_1, f_2,\ldots,f_{nf}\}$ is the set of functions from which all the programs are built. Likewise, the terminal set $T = \{a_1, a_2,\ldots,a_{nt}\}$ consists of the variables available for functions. In principle, the terminals can be considered as functions with zero arguments and both the sets can be combined in one set of primitives $C = F \cup T$.

The choice of an appropriate set of functions and variables is crucial for successful solution of a particular problem. Of course, this task is highly problem dependent and requires significant insight. In some cases, it is known in advance that a certain set is sufficient to express the solution to the problem at hand.

However, in most practical real-world problems the sufficient set of functions and terminals is unknown. In these cases, usually all or most of the available data is supplied to the algorithm or iterative design is employed when additional data and functions are added if the current solution is unsatisfactory. As a result, the set of primitives is often far from the minimal sufficient set.

The effect of adding extraneous functions is complex. On the one hand, an excessive number of primitives may degrade performance of the algorithm, similar to choosing excessive genome length in GA. On the other hand, a particular additional function or variable may dramatically improve performance of both the algorithm and solution for a particular problem. For example, addition of the integral of error $\int(H - H_{set})dt$ as an input to altitude hold autopilot allows to eliminate static error and improve overall performance. Alternatively, the integrator function may be introduced along with both the current altitude reading H and the desired altitude H_{set}.

2.5.2 Initial population

Generation of the initial population in GP is not as straightforward as it usually is in conventional GAs. It has been noted above that the shape of a tree has (statistically) an

influence on its evolution and that both sparse and bushy trees should be presented in the initial population. To this end, a so called 'ramped half-and-half' method, suggested by Koza (Koza, 1992), is typically used in GP. In this method, half of the trees in the population are generated as full trees and another half as random trees.
The 'ramped half-and-half' method employs two techniques for random tree generation: the 'full' method and the 'grow' method. Both of them start from choosing one of the functions from the function set F at random. It becomes the root of the new tree. Then, for each of the inputs of this function, a new primitive is selected with uniform probability. If the path from the root to the current point is shorter than the specified maximum depth, the new primitive is selected from the function set F for the 'full' method and from the union set C for the 'grow' method. If the path length reaches the specified depth, a terminal from the set T is selected at random for both methods. The process continues until the tree is complete, i.e. all the inputs are connected.

2.5.3 Genetic operators

2.5.3.1 *Crossover*

Crossover is usually the most important genetic operator in GP. Its classic variation (Koza, 1992) produces two children trees from two parent trees by exchanging randomly selected sub-trees of each parent. Both parents are selected using one of the stochastic selection methods such as fitness proportional selection and tournament selection. The crossover operation begins by choosing, using a uniform probability distribution, one random point in each parent independently to be the crossover point for that parent. The point may be a node as well as a leaf. Then, the sub-trees that have roots at the crossover points are removed from the parents, and the sub-tree from the second parent is inserted in place of the removed sub-tree of the first parent.
In terms of S-expressions, the sub-tree crossover is equivalent to exchanging the sublists of the parental lists. Considering the example from Fig. 3, the parental solutions are

$$\left(-\left(*\ \ x\ \ x\right)\ \left(*\left(*\ \ x\ \ y\right)2\right)\right) \text{ and } \left(/\ \ \left(+\ \ \left(*\ \ x\ \ x\right)\ \ y\right)\ \ 2\right) \tag{7}$$

The sub-lists corresponding to the selected crossover fragments are emphasized. These sublists are swapped between the parents and the following offspring are produced:

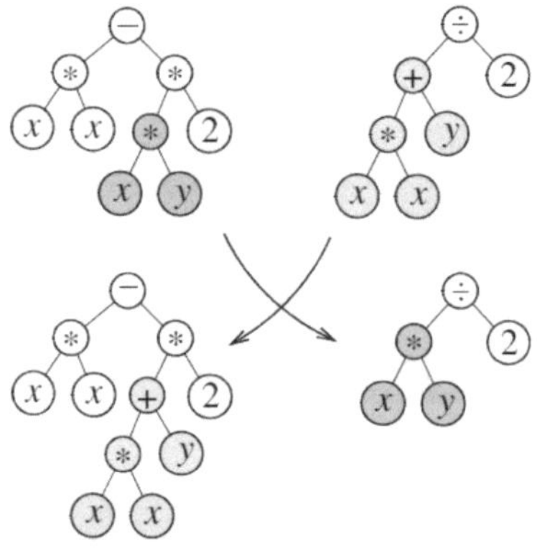

Fig. 4. Sub-tree crossover: $x^2 - 2xy$ crossed with $(x^2 + y)/2$ to produce $x^2 - 2(x^2 + y)$ and $xy/2$

$$\left(-\left(* \quad x \quad x\right) \quad \left(*\left(+ \quad \left(* \quad x \quad x\right) \quad y\right) 2\right)\right) \text{ and } \left(/ \quad \left(* \quad x \quad y\right) \quad 2\right) \tag{8}$$

It can be noted that in such a simple operation, syntactic validity of the resulting expressions is always preserved.

To avoid excessive growth of the branches of the program trees, a maximum depth value is usually established. If the crossover operation produces an offspring of impermissible depth, this offspring is disregarded and its parent is reproduced as is. Koza (Koza, 1992) uses the default maximum depth of *17*. Even such a modest value allows creation of the trees of enormous size, up to $2^{17} - 1 = 131071$ (for binary trees).

2.5.3.2 *Other genetic operators*

Reproduction as such is simply copying of the selected individual into the next generation population. In classical GP (Koza, 1992), about *10%* of the population is selected for simple reproduction and *90%* is reproduced through crossover.

Mutation is typically a replacement of a randomly selected sub-tree of an individual with a new randomly generated sub-tree. A special case is point mutation, when a single random terminal is inserted in place of a sub-tree. In fact, point mutations sometimes happen during crossover operation. In general, mutation is less needed for GP than for GAs, because crossover alone can reintroduce genetic diversity. In many practical applications, mutation is not used at all.

Permutation is changing of the order of arguments of a randomly selected function. The effect and usefulness of permutation is roughly the same as that of mutation.

Editing is changing the shape and structure of a tree while maintaining its semantic meaning. Usually this implies a mathematical simplification of the expression. For example, the sub-trees which can be immediately evaluated may be replaced with a corresponding terminal, e.g. the expression (+ *2 3*) may be replaced with (*5*).

Simplification of the solutions may reduce (sometimes significantly) their length and thus reduce the computation time needed for their evaluation. In addition, shorter expressions are less vulnerable to disruption caused by crossover and mutation as there are fewer chances that they will be torn apart.

2.5.4 Convergence in GP

The question of convergence in GP is more complicated than in GAs. Generally, it is assumed in EA theory that the population converges when it contains substantially similar individuals (Langdon & Poli, 1992). Unlike conventional GAs, which have one-to-one mapping between genotype and phenotype, this rarely happens in GP. The search space in GP is essentially bigger than the phenotypic search space of the problem at hand. Any solution to the problem may be represented in an infinite number of ways.

Therefore, the population in GP may contain significantly different individuals (in terms of size and shape) and continue to evolve while yielding practically similar solutions to the problem.

However, the genotype cluster does not stabilise and continues to evolve. Since then, most of the highly fit individuals are produced by adding relatively insignificant branches to the successful core that came from the common ancestor. Therefore, each descendant genotype tends to be bigger than its parents. This results in a progressive increase in size known as bloat.

2.5.5 Bloat

The rapid growth of programs produced by GP is known since the beginning (Koza, 1992). As already noted, this growth need not to be correlated with increase of fitness because it consists of the code that does not change the semantics of the evolving programs. The rate of growth varies depending upon the particular GP paradigm being used, but usually exponential rates are observed (Nordin & Banzhaf, 1995).

For greater detail of different theories of bloat the reader is referred to (Langton, 1999) or (Langton & Poli, 2002). Generally, it should be noted that GP crossover by itself does not change the average program size. Bloat arises from the interaction of genetic operators and selection, i.e. selection pressure is required.

The most commonly (if not always) used restrictive technique is size and depth limits. Its implementation is already described in Section 2.5.3.1. It should be noted that the actual experiments (Langton & Poli, 2002) indicate that the populations are quickly affected by even apparently generous limits. Another commonly used approach is to give some preference to smaller solutions. The 'penalty' for excessive length may be included in fitness evaluation. However, in order not to degrade the performance of the algorithm, this component should be small enough so that it would have effect only for the solutions with identical phenotypic performance.

3. Aircraft flight control

Not unlike the generic control approach, aircraft flight control is built around a feedback concept. Its basic scheme is shown in Fig. 5. The controller is fed by the difference between the commanded reference signal r and the system output y. It generates the system control inputs u according to one or another algorithm.

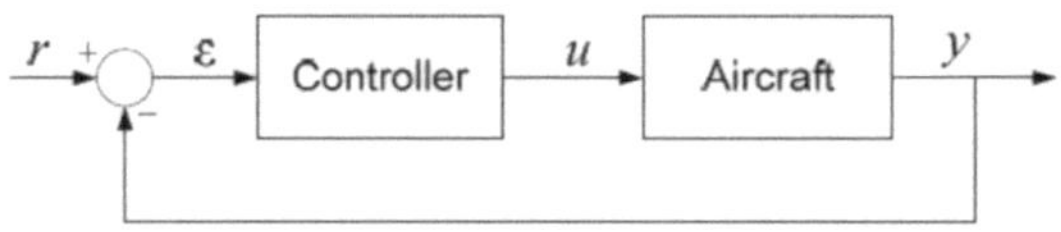

Fig. 5. Feedback system (one degree of freedom)

One of the main tasks of flight control as an engineering discipline is design of the controllers which enable a given aircraft to complete a defined mission in the most optimal manner, where optimality is based on mission objective.

3.1 Intelligent control

Intelligent control is a general and somewhat bold term that describes a diverse collection of relatively novel and non-traditional control techniques based on the *soft computing* approach. These include neural networks, fuzzy logic, adaptive control, genetic algorithms and several others. Often they are combined with each other as well as with more traditional methods.

Evolutionary and *genetic algorithms* (EAs, GAs) are global optimisation techniques applicable to a broad area of engineering problems. They can be used to optimise the parameters of various control systems, from simple PID controllers (Zein-Sabatto & Zheng, 1997) to fuzzy logic and neural network driven controllers (Bourmistrova, 2001; Kaise & Fujimoto, 1999). Another common design approach is evolutionary optimisation of trajectories, accompanied by a suitable tracking controller (e.g. (Wang & Zalzala, 1996)). An elaborated study of applications of EAs to control and system identification problems can be found in (Uzrem, 2003). As discussed above, Genetic Algorithms (in the form of *Genetic Programming*) are able to evolve not only the parameters, but also the *structure* of the controller.

In general, EAs require substantial computational power and thus are more suitable for offline optimisation. However, online evolutionary-based controllers have also been successfully designed and used. The *model predictive control* is typically employed for this purpose, where the controller constantly evolves (or refines) control laws using an integrated simulation model of the controlled system. A comprehensive description of this approach is given in (Onnen et al., 1997).

3.2 Flight control for the UAV recovery task

Aircraft control at recovery stage of flight can be conventionally separated into two closely related, but distinctive tasks: guidance and flight control. Guidance is the high-level ('outer loop') control intended to accomplish a defined mission. This may be path following, target tracking or various navigation tasks. Flight control is aimed at providing the most suitable conditions for guidance by maintaining a range of flight parameters at their optimal levels and delivering the best possible handling characteristics.

The landing of an aircraft is a well established procedure which involves following a predefined flight path. More often than not, this is a rectilinear trajectory on which the aircraft can be stabilised, and the control interventions are needed only to compensate disturbances and other sources of errors.

The position errors with respect to the ideal glidepath can be measured relatively easily. Shipboard landing on air carriers has tight error tolerances and absence of flare manoeuvres before touchdown. The periodic ship motion does have an effect on touchdown; however, it does not affect significantly the glidepath, which is projected assuming the average deck position.

Ship oscillations in high sea cause periodic displacement of the recovery window makes it impossible to project an optimal flight path when the final approach starts. Therefore, it turns out that the UAV recovery problem resembles that of homing guidance rather than typical landing. While stabilisation on a known steady flight path can be done relatively easy with a PID controller, homing guidance to a moving target often requires a more sophisticated control.

3.3 UAV controller structure

The objective is to synthesise such guidance strategy that enables reliable UAV recovery, and to produce a controller that implements the target tracking guidance strategy.

The evolutionary design (ED) method applied for this task allows to evolve automatically both the structure and the parameters of the control laws, thus potentially enabling to generate a 'full' controller, which links available measurements directly with the aircraft control inputs (throttle, ailerons, rudder and elevator) and implements both the guidance strategy and flight control (Fig. 6):

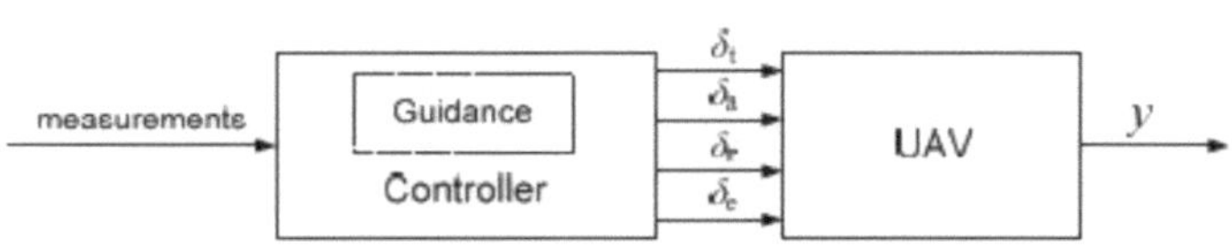

Fig. 6. Full controller with embedded guidance strategy

However, this approach, even though appealing at first and requiring minimum initial knowledge, proves to be impractical as the computational demands of the evolutionary algorithms (EAs) soar exponentially with the dimensionality of the problem. It is therefore desirable to reduce complexity of the problem by reducing the number of inputs/outputs and limiting, if appropriate, possible structures of the controllers.

Also it is highly desirable to decompose the complex control task into several simpler problems and to solve them separately. A natural way of such decomposition is separating the trajectory control (guidance) and flight control. The guidance controller issues commands u_g to the flight controller, which executes these commands by manipulating the control surfaces of the UAV (Fig. 7). These two controllers can be synthesised separately using appropriate fitness evaluation for each case.

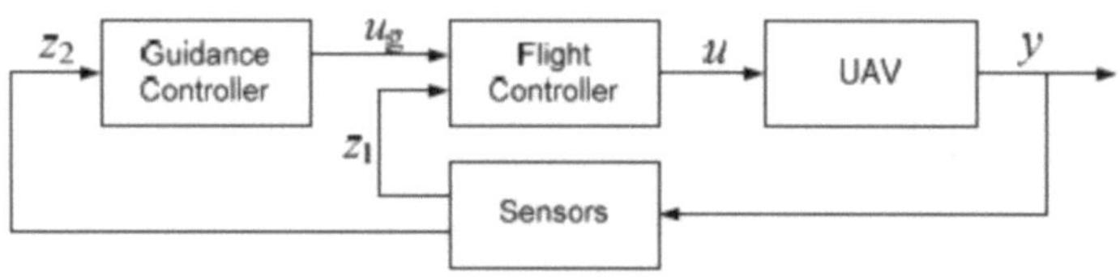

Fig. 7. UAV recovery control diagram

The internal structure of the controller is defined by the automatic evolutionary design based on predefined set of inputs and outputs. As an additional requirement is that the outputs u_g should represent a group of measurable flight parameters such as body accelerations, velocities and Euler angles, which the flight controller can easily track.

The structure of the output part of the guidance controller is as shown in Fig. 8 which allows to evolve the horizontal and vertical guidance laws separately, which may be desirable due to different dynamics of the UAV's longitudinal and lateral motion and also due to computational limitations.

Input measurements to the guidance controller should be those relevant to trajectory like positioning information, pitch and yaw angles and airspeed.

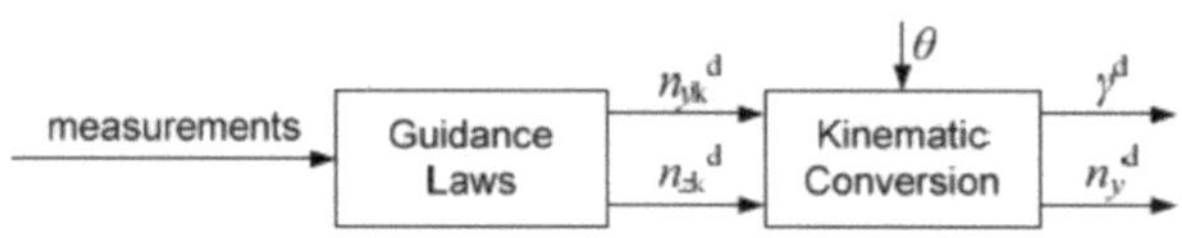

Fig. 8. Guidance controller

The derived quantities from raw measurements are the vertical and lateral velocity components with respect to the approach ground reference frame.

The system is based on radio distance metering and provides ten independent raw measurements (Fig. 9): three distances d_1, d_2 and d_3 from the UAV to the radio transmitters located at both ends of the recovery boom which supports the arresting wire and at the base of recovery mast; three rates of change of these distances; distance differences (d_1 - d_2) and (d_3 - d_2); and rates of change of the differences.

The guidance laws evolution process is potentially capable to produce the laws directly from raw measurements, automatically finding necessary relationships between the provided data and the required output.

Flight controller receives two inputs from the guidance controller: bank angle demand γ^d and normal body load factor demand n_y^d. It should track these inputs as precisely as possible by manipulating four aircraft controls: throttle, ailerons, rudder and elevator.

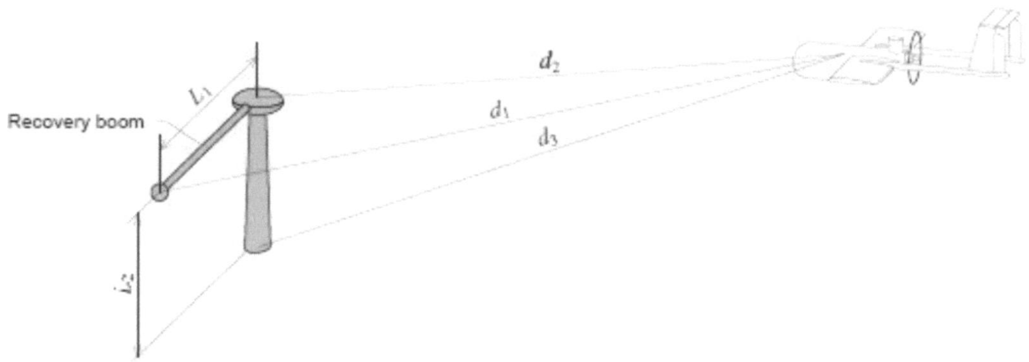

Fig. 9. Positioning scheme

The available measurements from the onboard sensors are body angular rates ω_x, ω_y, ω_z from rate gyros, Euler angles γ, ψ, θ, body accelerations n_x, n_y, n_z from the respective accelerometers, airspeed V_a, aerial angles a and β, actual deflection of the control surfaces δ_a, δ_r, δ_e, and engine rotation speed N_{rpm}.

For simplicity of design, the controller is subdivided into independent longitudinal and lateral components. In longitudinal branch, elevator tracks the input signal n_y^d, while throttle is responsible for maintaining a required airspeed. In lateral control, naturally, ailerons track γ^d, while rudder minimises sideforce by keeping n_z near zero.

4. Evolutionary Design

The Evolutionary Design (ED) presented in this section, generally, takes no assumptions regarding the system and thus can be used for wide variety of problems, including nonlinear systems with unknown structure. The core of evolutionary design is a specially tailored evolutionary algorithm (EA) which evolves both the structure and parameters of the control laws.

Parallel evolution can be implemented in a variety of ways. One of the few successfully employed variants is the *block structure controller evolution* (Koza et al., 2000).

In this work the ED algorithm enables to evolve suitable control laws within a reasonable time by utilising gradual evolution with the principle of strong casualty. This means that structure alterations are performed so that the information gained so far in the structure of the control law is preserved. Addition of a new block, though being random, does not cause disruption to the structure. Instead, it adds a new dimension and new potential which may evolve later during numerical optimisation.

The addition of new points or blocks is carried out as a separate dedicated operation (unlike sporadic structure alterations in the sub-tree crossover), and is termed *structure mutation*. Furthermore, in this work structure mutation is performed in a way known as *neutral structure mutation*. That's when the new block should be placed initially with zero coefficient. The usefulness of neutral mutations has been demonstrated for the evolution of digital circuits (Van Laarhoven & Aarts, 1987) and aerodynamic shapes (Olhofer et al., 2001). As a result, the ED algorithm basically represents a numerical EA with the inclusion of structure mutations mechanism.

Control laws are represented as a combination of static functions and input signals, which are organised as a dynamic structure of *state equations* and *output equations* in form of continuous representation.
The controller being evolved has m inputs, r outputs and n states. So, the controller comprises of n state equations and r output equations:

$$\begin{matrix} \dot{x}_1 = g_1(x,u) & & y_1 = f_1(x,u) \\ \dot{x}_2 = g_2(x,u) & \text{and} & y_2 = f_2(x,u) \\ \vdots & & \vdots \\ \dot{x}_n = g_n(x,u) & & y_n = f_n(x,u) \end{matrix} \tag{9}$$

where $\boldsymbol{u}$ is size m vector of input signals, $\boldsymbol{x} = [x_1,x_2,\ldots x_n]$ is size n vector of state variables, $y_{1\ldots r}$ are controller outputs. Initial value of all state variables is zero. All $n+r$ equations are built on the same principle and are evolved simultaneously. For structure mutations, a random equation is selected from this pool and mutated.
Input signals delivered to each particular controller are directly measured signals as well as the quantities derived from them. Within each group, inputs are organised in the subgroups of 'compatible' parameters. Compatible parameters are those which have close relationship with each other, have the same dimensions and similarly scaled. The examples of compatible parameters are the pairs (n_x, n_{xg}), (ω_y, $\dot{\psi}$), (V_a, V_{CL}).
Therefore, every controller input may be represented by a unique *code* consisting of three indices: the number of group a, the number of subgroup b and the number of item in the subgroup c. The code is designated as u(a,b,c).
Each of the control equations (9) is encoded as described above. To this end, only one single output equation of the form $y = f(\boldsymbol{u})$ will be considered in this section.
The encoding should allow a simple way to insert a new parameter in any place of the equation without disrupting its validity and in a way that this insertion initially does not affect the result, thus allowing neutral structure mutations. Conceptually, the equation is a sum of input signals, in which:

- every input is multiplied by a numeric coefficient or another similarly constructed expression;
- the product of the input and its coefficient (whether numeric or expression) is raised to the power assigned to the input;
- a free (absolute) term is present.

The simplest possible expression is a constant:

$$y = k_0 \tag{10}$$

A linear combination of inputs plus a free term is also a valid expression:

$$y = k_2u_2 + k_1u_1 + k_0 \tag{11}$$

Any numeric constant can be replaced with another expression. An example of a full featured equation is

$$y = ((k_4u_4 + k_3)u_3)^{-0.5} + k_2u_2 + (k_1u_1)^2 + k_0 \tag{12}$$

This algorithm can be illustrated by encoding the example (12). The respective internal representation of this expression is:

- Equation: $y = ((k_4u_4 + k_3)u_3)^{-0.5} + k_2u_2 + (k_1u_1)^2 + k_0$
- Expression: { u(3,-0.5) u(4) 1 2 *u*(2) 3 u(1,2) 4 5 }
- Object parameters: [k_4 k_3 k_2 k_1 k_0]
- Strategy parameters: [s_4 s_3 s_2 s_1 s_0]

This syntax somewhat resembles Polish notation with implicit '+' and '*' operators before each variable. The representation ensures presence of a free term in any sub-expression, such as k_3 and k_0 in the example above.

The algorithm of structure mutation is presented below.

1. Select an input (or a state variable) at random: u(a,b,c).
2. Obtain the initial values of the numeric coefficient and the strategy parameter
3. Append the object parameters vector with the initial coefficient, and the strategy parameters vector with the initial step size.
4. Form a sub-expression consisting of the selected variable code and the obtained index: { u(a,b,c) *n* }.
5. With 40% probability, set the insertion point (locus) to 1; otherwise, select a numeric value in the expression at random with equal probability among all numeric values present and set the locus to the index of this value.
6. Insert the sub-expression into the original expression at the chosen locus (*before* the item pointed).

This procedure may produce redundant expressions when the selected variable already exists at the same level. Thus an algebraic simplification procedure is implemented.

Fitness evaluation of a controller can be divided into two main stages. First is the preparation of the sample task and simulation of the model with the controller in the loop. The second stage is analysis of the results obtained from the simulation and evaluation of the fitness as such.

Other parameters of flight taken into account is control usage (or control effort): it is desirable to keep control usage at minimum.

The total fitness value is calculated as the weighted sum of all estimates:

$$F = W_c C_c + W_f C_f + W_e C_e + \ldots \tag{13}$$

The exact value of the weighting coefficients *W*, as well as the number of estimates taken into account, is individual for each controller. As a rule, the weighting coefficients are chosen empirically.

Several steps of design algorithm need further clarification.

Initial population is initialised with the control laws of the form $y = const$ with randomly chosen constants.

The *selection* is performed deterministically. The populations used in this study were of moderate size, usually 24 to 49 members. Selection pressure is determined by the number of the offspring *n* of each individual. The smaller *n*, the lower the selection pressure. For nearly all runs in this work $n = 2$, which means that half of the population is selected. This is a rather mild level of selection pressure.

The parameters determining *structure mutation* occurrence, k_s and P_s, both change during the evolution. The probability of structure mutation P_s is normally high in the beginning (0.7 to 1.0) and then decrease exponentially to moderate levels (0.4 to 0.6) with the exponent 0.97 to the generation number. In the beginning of evolution, k_s is reduced by half until the generation 20 and 100 respectively.

Reproduction is performed simultaneously with mutation, as it is typically done in ES, with the exception that this operation is performed separately for each selected member.

5. Controller synthesis and testing

The UAV control system is synthesised in several steps. First, the flight controller is produced. This requires several stages, since the flight controller is designed separately for longitudinal and lateral channels. When the flight controller is obtained, the guidance control laws are evolved.

Application of the ED algorithm to control laws evolution is fairly straightforward: 1) preparation of the sample task for the controller, 2) execution of the simulation model for the given sample task and 3) analysis of the obtained performance and evaluation of the fitness value. For a greater detail of control system design reader is referred to (Bourmistrova & Khantsis, 2009). When both the model and fitness evaluation are prepared, the final evolution may be started. Typically, the algorithm is run for 100–200 generations (depending on complexity of the controller being evolved). The convergence and the resulting design is then analysed and the evolution, if necessary, is continued.

Step 1. *PID autothrottle* - Initially a simple PID variant of autothrottle is evolved - to ensure a more or less accurate airspeed hold. At the next stage, its evolution is continued in a full form together with the elevator control law. The PID structure of the controller may be ensured by appropriate initialisation of the initial population and by disabling structure mutations. Therefore, the algorithm works as a numerical optimisation procedure. The structure of the autothrottle control law is following:

$$\begin{aligned} \dot{x}_1 &= k_1 x_1 + k_2 \Delta V_a \\ \delta_t &= k_3 x_1 + k_4 \Delta V_a + k_5 \dot{V}_a + k_6 \end{aligned} \tag{14}$$

where $\Delta V_a = V^d - V_a$ is the airspeed error signal, δ_t is the throttle position command and $k_{1...6}$ are the coefficients to be optimised.

Step 2. *Longitudinal control* - With a simple autothrottle available, elevator control can be developed to provide tracking of the normal body load factor demand n_y^d. Altogether, the reference input signal is

$$n_y^d(t) = 0.03\left(H^d - H(t)\right) + \cos\theta(t) + 0.2c(t) \tag{15}$$

Elevator control law is initialised as follows:

$$\begin{aligned} \dot{x}_2 &= 0 \\ \delta_e &= k_1 x_2 + k_2 \Delta n_y + k_3 \end{aligned} \tag{16}$$

where $\Delta n_y = n_y^d - n_y$ is the load factor error and the coefficients $k_{1...3}$ are sampled at random for the initial population.

Step 3. *Lateral control* - Lateral control consists of two channels: ailerons control and rudder control. As a rule, for an aerodynamically stable aircraft such as the *Ariel* UAV, lateral control is fairly simple and is not as vital for flight as longitudinal control. For this reason, both control laws, for ailerons and rudder, are evolved simultaneously in one step.

Both ailerons and rudder control laws are initialised in a similar manner to (16):

$$\begin{aligned} \dot{x}_3 &= 0 \\ \dot{x}_4 &= 0 \\ \delta_a &= k_{11}x_3 + k_{12}\Delta\gamma + k_{13} \\ \delta_r &= k_{21}x_4 + k_{22}n_z + k_{23} \end{aligned} \tag{17}$$

Step 4. *Guidance* - At this point, flight controller synthesis is completed and guidance laws can be evolved. Guidance controller comprises two control laws, for the vertical and horizontal load factor demands, n_{yk}^d and n_{zk}^d respectively. This is equivalent to acceleration demands

$$a_{yk}^d = gn_{yk}^d \text{ and } a_{zk}^d = gn_{zk}^d \tag{18}$$

These demands are passed through the kinematic converter to form the flight controller inputs n_y^d and γ^d.

In the guidance task, the random factors include initial state of the UAV; Sea State, atmospheric parameters, and initial state of the ship.

Fitness is calculated as follows:

$$F_g = 40\Delta h_1^2 + 20\Delta z_1^2 + 50|\psi_1| + 25|\gamma_1| + 500C_c(n_{yk}^d) + 500C_c(n_{zk}^d) + 100C_f(n_{zk}^d) \tag{19}$$

where Δh_1 and Δz_1 are vertical and horizontal miss distances, and ψ_1 and γ_1 are final yaw and bank angles. Greater weight for vertical miss than that for horizontal miss is used because vertical miss allowance is smaller (approximately 3–4 m vs. 5 m) and also because vertical miss may result in a crash into the boom if the approach is too low.

Algorithm initialisation is the same as for longitudinal flight control laws evolution, except that elitism is not used and the population size is 48 members. The initial population is sampled with the control laws of the form

$$\begin{aligned} \dot{x}_6 &= 0 \\ \dot{x}_7 &= 0 \\ a_{yk}^d &= k_{11}x_6 + k_{12} \\ a_{zk}^d &= k_{21}x_7 + k_{22} \end{aligned} \tag{20}$$

where all coefficients k are chosen at random. For convenience, the control laws are expressed in terms of accelerations, which are then converted to load factors according to (18). Since these control laws effectively represent 'empty' laws $y = const$ (plus a low-pass output filter with randomly chosen bandwidth), structure mutation is applied to each member of the initial population.

From the final populations, the best solution is identified by calculating fitness of each member using N = 25 simulation runs, taking into account also success rate. As an eample the best performing controller is the following (unused state variables are removed) with 100% success rate in the 25 test runs with average fitness 69.52:

$$\dot{x}_6 = -3.548\omega_v$$
$$a_{yk}^d = 0.916x_6 - 54.3\omega_v - 0.1261 \quad (25)$$
$$a_{zk}^d = -107.68\omega_h + 0.0534V_{zT} + 0.4756$$

The other attempted approach is the pure proportional navigation (PPN) law for recovery which was compared with the obtained solutions (Duflos et al., 1999; Siouris & Leros, 1988). The best PN controller have been selected using the fitness values of each member of the final population averaged over 100 simulation runs. It is the following:

$$a_{yk}^d = -3.27V_{CLa}\omega_V$$
$$a_{zk}^d = -3.18V_{CLa}\omega_h \quad (26)$$

This controller received the fitness 88.85 and showed success rate 95%.

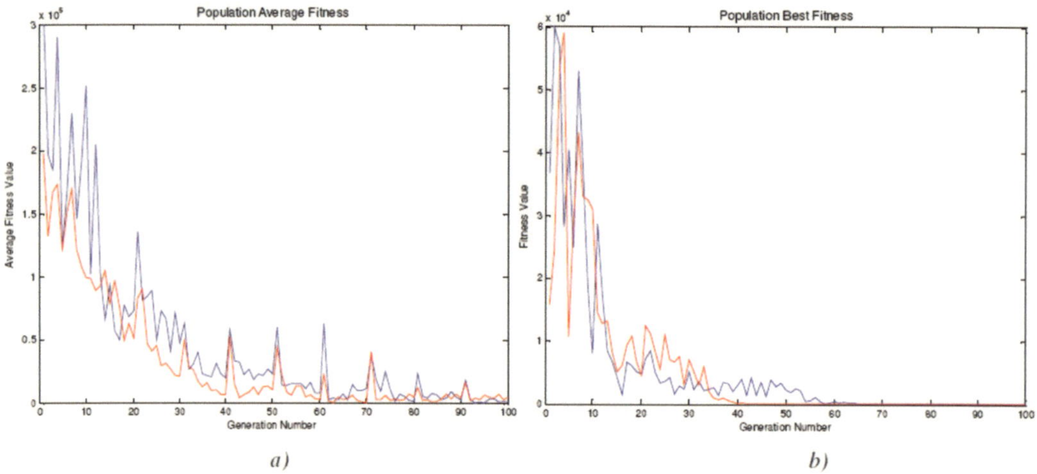

Fig. 12. Population average fitness (a) and best fitness (b) for two independent evolutions of guidance controller

5.1 Controller testing

In this work, two main types of simulation tests are conducted - robustness and performance. Results are presented for robustness test, which is aimed at ensuring the controller has good robustness to modelling uncertainties and to test whether the controller is sensitive to specific perturbations.

Perturbations were introduced in two ways - in form of variation of physical quantities and by introducing additional dynamic elements and by changing internal variables such as aerodynamic coefficients. For a realistic test, all perturbations should be applied simultaneously to identify the worst case scenario. However, single perturbation tests (the *sensitivity analysis*) allow to analyse the degree of influence of each parameter and help to plan the robustness test more systematically.

In this type of test, a single model variable is perturbed by a set amount and the effect upon the performance of the controller is determined. Performance evaluation can be measured in a manner similar to fitness evaluation of the guidance controller (equation (19)).

The additional parameters taken into account in performance measurement are impact speed V_{imp} and minimum altitude $H_{\min}$ attained during the approach.
Altogether, the performance cost (PC) is calculated as follows:

$$PC = 40\Delta h_1^2 + 20\Delta z_1^2 + 50|\psi_1| + 25|\gamma_1| + 50 f_V + 20 f_H + 10C_c(\delta_a) + 10C_c(\delta_r) + C_c(\delta_e) + \ldots \\ + 200C_f(\delta_a) + 200C_f(\delta_r) + 200C_f(\delta_e) \quad (21)$$

where

$$f_V = \begin{cases} V_{imp} - 30, & V_{imp} > 30 \\ 0, & V_{imp} \le 30 \end{cases}, \quad f_H = \begin{cases} 10 - H_{\min}, & H_{\min} > 10 \\ 0, & H_{\min} \le 10 \end{cases}. \quad (22)$$

Impact speed V_{imp} and minimum altitude $H_{\min}$ are measured in m/s and metres respectively. Other designations are as in (19). Unlike fitness evaluation in the flight controller evolution, the commanded control deflections δ_a, δ_r and δ_e are saturated as required for control actuators.
The environment delivers a great deal of uncertainty. The range of disturbances and the initial ship phase are chosen to provide a moderately conservative estimation of controller performance. Results for different dynamic scenarios are presented in (Bourmistrova & Khantsis, 2009).
The parameters corresponding to aircraft geometry and configuration are tested in a similar manner. The range is increased to the scale factors between 0 and 10 (0 to 1000%) with step 0.05. The allowable perturbations (as factors to the original values) are summarised in Table 1, where * denotes the extreme value tested.

Parameter	Lower limit factor		Upper limit factor	
	Controller 1	Controller 2	Controller 1	Controller 2
Empty mass (m_{empt})	0.50*	0.50*	1.54	1.52
Rolling moment of inertia (I_x)	0.20	0.20	10*	2.43
Yawing moment of inertia (I_y)	0*	0*	10*	10*
Pitching moment of inertia (I_z)	0*	0*	2.17	1.91
xy cross product of inertia (I_{xy})	0*	0*	10*	10*
Wing area (S)	0.74	0.87	1.55	1.60

Table 1. Allowable perturbations of UAV inertial properties and geometry

Example in Fig. 13 demonstrates results for varying empty mass. Dashed cyan and green lines on the trajectory graphs represent the 'unrolled' along the flight path traces of the tips of the recovery boom (lateral position on the top view and vertical position on the side view). The bar on the right hand side illustrates the size of recovery window.
For some parameters, no noticeable drop in performance is experienced within the testing limits. These limits indicate quite large perturbations that can reasonably be expected. The main perturbations that cause a performance degradation are those that affect the physically attainable trajectory and not the operation of the controller, e.g. increasing weight and decreasing wing area. However, as follows from the above analysis, careful adjustment of elevator efficiency and/or horizontal stabiliser incidence may help to increase the tolerance to increased weight. There is still sufficient margin in angles of attack and engine power.

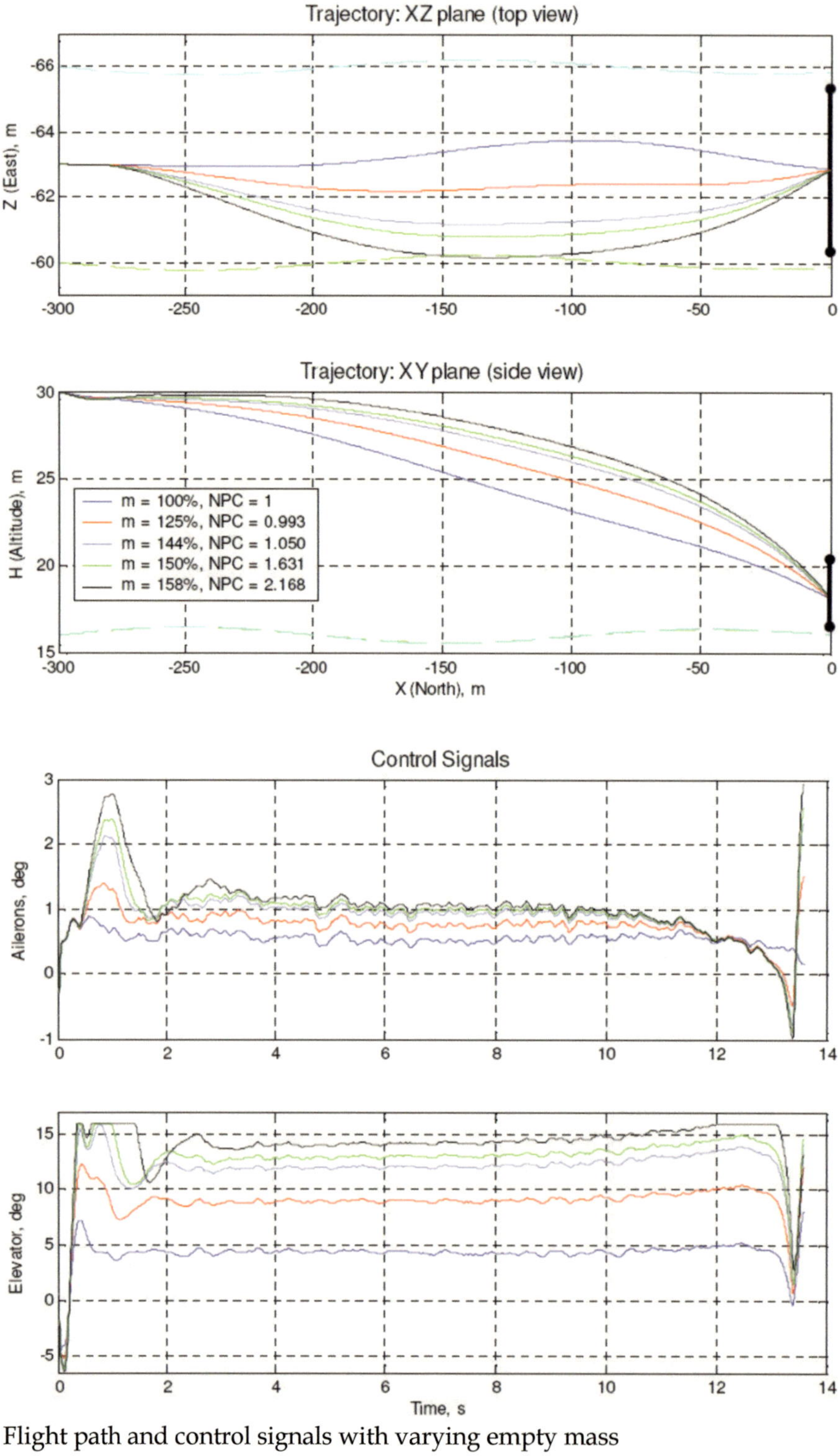

Fig. 13. Flight path and control signals with varying empty mass

The other parameters evaluated in this research were the perturbations of the power unit parameters, the aircraft aerodynamics parameters and sensor noise (Khantsis, 2006).

Overall, these tests have not exposed any significant robustness problems within the controllers. Large variations in single aircraft parameters caused very few control problems. However, such variations cannot realistically judge the performance of the controllers under simultaneous perturbations of multiple parameters.

6. Conclusions

In this chapter, an application of the Evolutionary Design (ED) is demonstrated. The aim of the design was to develop a controller which provides recovery of a fixed-wing UAV onto a ship under the full range of disturbances and uncertainties that are present in the real world environment.

Evolutionary computation is an attractive and quickly developing technique. Methodological shortcomings of the early approaches and lack of intercommunication between different EA schools contributed to the fact that evolutionary computation remained relatively unknown to the engineering and scientific audience for almost three decades. Despite computational demands, evolutionary methods offer many advantages over conventional optimisation and problem solving techniques. The most significant one is flexibility and adaptability of EAs to the task at hand.

In this study, a combination of the EA methods is used to evolve a capable UAV recovery controller. An adapted GP approach is used to represent the control laws. However, these laws are modified more judiciously (yet stochastically) than commonly accepted in GP and evolved in a manner similar to ES approach.

One of the greatest advantages of developed methodology is that minimum or no a priori knowledge about the control methods is used, with the synthesis starting from the most basic proportional control or even from 'null' control laws. During the evolution, more complex and capable laws emerge automatically. As the resulting control laws demonstrate, evolution does not tend to produce parsimonious solutions.

The method demonstrating remarkable robustness in terms of convergence indicating that a near optimal solution can be found. In very limited cases, however, it may take too long time for the evolution to discover the core of a potentially optimal solution, and the process does not converge. More often than not, this hints at a poor choice of the algorithm parameters.

The simulation testing covers the entire operational envelope and highlights several conditions under which recovery is risky. All environmental factors—sea wave, wind speed and turbulence—have been found to have a significant effect upon the probability of success. Combinations of several factors may result in very unfavourable conditions, even if each factor alone may not lead to a failure. For example, winds up to *12* m/s do not affect the recovery in a calm sea, and a severe ship motion corresponding to Sea State 5 also does not represent a serious threat in low winds. At the same time, strong winds in a high Sea State may be hazardous for the aircraft.

On the whole, Evolutionary Design is a useful and powerful tool for complex nonlinear control design. Unlike most other design methodologies, it tries to *solve* the problem at hand automatically, not merely to optimise a given structure. Although ED does not exclude necessity of a thorough testing, it can provide a near optimal solution if the whole range of conditions is taken into account in the fitness evaluation. In principle, no specific knowledge about the system is required, and the controllers can be considered as 'black boxes' whose internals are unimportant. Successful design of the controller for such a challenging task as shipboard recovery demonstrates great potential abilities of this novel technique.

7. References

Beyer, H.-G. & Deb, K. (2001). On self-adaptive features in real-parameter evolutionary algorithms, Proceedings on *IEEE Transactions on Evolutionary Computation*, pp. 250-270 vol. 5(3), ISBN 1089-778X, Germany, June 2001

Bourmistrova, A. (2001). Knowledge based control system design for autonomous flight vehicle, *PhD thesis*, RMIT University: Melbourne, September 2001

Bourmistrova, A. & Khantsis, S. (2009). Flight control system design optimisation via Genetic Programming, in *Recent advances in signal processing*, IN-TECH, ISBN: 978-953-7619-41-1

Chipperfield, A. & Fleming, P. (1996). Systems integration using evolutionary algorithms, Proceedings of *UKACC International Conference on Control '96*, pp. 705- 710 vol.1, October 1996

Coley, D. A. (1998). *An Introduction to Genetic Algorithms for Scientists and Engineers.* University of Exeter, ISBN 9810236026, 9789810236021, Published by World Scientific, 1999

K. A. De Jong, W. M. Spears. *On the state of evolutionary computation*, ed. S. Forrest, in *5th International Conference on Genetic Algorithms* proceedings. San Mateo, CA, Morgan Kaufmann: p. 618, 1993.

Cramer, N. L. (1985). A representation for the adaptive generation of simple sequential programs, Proceedings on *International Conference on Genetic Algorithms and their Applications*, pp. 183- 187, ed. J. J. Grefenstette, Carnegie-Mellon University, Pittsburgh May 1985

Deb, K., Joshi, D. & Anand, A. (2001). Real-coded evolutionary algorithms with parentcentric recombination, *KanGAL Report 2001003*, Indian Institute of Technology.

Duflos, E., Penel, P. & Vanheeghe, P. (1999). 3D guidance law modelling, IEEE Transactions on Aerospace and Electronic Systems, Vol. 35, No 1, page numbers (72-83), (January 1999), ISSN: 0018-9251

Eshelman, L. J. & Schaffer, J. D. (1993). Real-coded genetic algorithms and interval schemata, in *Foundations of Genetic Algorithms 2*, page numbers (187-202), ed. L. D. Whitley, Morgan Kaufmann: San Mateo, CA, 1993

Fogel, D. B. (1962). Autonomous automata, *Industrial Research*, Vol. 4, page numbers (14-19), 1962

Fogel, D. B., Owens, A. J. & Walsh, M. J. (1966). *Artificial intelligence through simulated evolution.* New York: Wiley, 1966

Goldberg, D. E. (1989). *Genetic Algorithms in search, optimisation and machine learning.* Addison-Wesley, 1989

Goldberg, D. E. & Deb, K. (1991). A comparative analysis of selection schemes used in genetic algorithms, Foundations of Genetic Algorithms, page numbers (69-93), ed. G. J. E. Rawlins. Morgan Kaufmann, San Mateo, CA, ISBN-10: 1558601708

Grefenstette, J. J. (1999). Evolvability in dynamic fitness landscapes: A genetic algorithm approach, Proceedings on *Congress of Evolutionary Computation*, IEEE Press, pp. 2031–2038 vol. 3, Washington, ISBN: 0-7803-5536-9

Herrera, F., Lozano, M. & Verdegay, J. L. (1998). Tackling real-coded genetic algorithms: Operators and tools for behavioural analysis, *Artificial Intelligence Review*, page numbers (265-319), Vol. 12, No 4, Springer, ISSN 0269-2821

Holland, J. H. (1975). *Adaptation in Natural and Artificial Systems.* University of Michigan Press

Hollstien, R. B. (1971). Artificial genetic adaptation in computer control systems, *Doctoral dissertation*, University of Michigan

Kaise, N. & Fujimoto, Y. (1999). Applying the evolutionary neural networks with genetic algorithms to control a rolling inverted pendulum, *Lecture Notes in Computer Science : Simulated Evolution and Learning*, Volume 1585/1999, (January 1999), page numbers (223-230), Springer Berlin / Heidelberg, ISBN 978-3-540-65907-5

Khantsis, S., (2006). Control System Design Using Evolutionary Algorithms for Autonomous Shipboard Recovery of Unmanned Aerial Vehicles, *PhD thesis*, RMIT University: Melbourne, 1992

Koza, J. R. (1992). *Genetic Programming: On the programming of computers by means of natural selection*, Cambridge, Massachusetts: MIT Press, December 1992 (6th ed. 1998), ISBN-10:0-262-11170-5

Koza, J. R. (1994). *Genetic Programming II: Automatic discovery of reusable programs.* Cambridge, Massachusetts: MIT Press, May 1994, ISBN-10:0-262-11189-6

Koza, J. R., Bennett III, F. H., Andre D. & Keane, M. A. (1996). Four problems for which a computer program evolved by genetic programming is competitive with human performance, Proceedings on *IEEE International Conference on Evolutionary Computation*, Nagoya, Japan, May 1996, ISBN: 0-7803-2902-3

Koza, J. R., Bennett III, F. H., Andre, D. & Keane, M. A. (1999). *Genetic Programming III: Darwinian Invention and Problem Solving.* Kluwer Academic Publishers, ISBN 1-55860-543-6

Koza, J. R., Keane, M. A., Yu, J., Bennett III, F. H. & Mydlowec, W. (2000). Automatic creation of human-competitive programs and controllers by means of genetic programming, *Genetic Programming and Evolvable Machines*, Vol. 1, No 1, page numbers (121-164), (January 2000), ISSN: 1389-2576

Koza, J. R., Keane, M. A., Streeter, M. J., Mydlowec, W., Yu, J. & Lanza G. (2003). *Genetic Programming IV: Routine Human-Competitive Machine Intelligence.* Kluwer Academic Publishers

Langdon, W. B (1999). The evolution of size and shape, in *Advances in genetic programming 3*, ed. L. Spector, W. B. Langdon and et al, MIT Press, page numbers (163-190), July 1999, ISBN-10:0-262-19423-6

Langdon, W. B. & Poli, R. (2002). *Foundations of genetic programming.* Berlin: Springer-Verlag, ISBN 978-3-540-42451-2

Mahfoud, S. W. & Mani, G. (1996). Financial forecasting using genetic algorithms. *Applied Artificial Intelligence*, page numbers (543-565), Vol 10, November 1996, ISSN: 1087-6545

McFarland, R. E. & Duisenberg, K. (1995). Simulation of rotor blade element turbulence, *Technical Memorandum 108862*, Acc. No. NASA TM-108862, NASA, January 1995

McLean, D. & Matsuda, H. (1998). Helicopter station-keeping: comparing LQR, fuzzy-logic and neural-net controllers, *Engineering Applications of Artificial Intelligence,* page numbers (411- 41811), Vol. 11, November 1998, ISSN 0952-1976

Nordin, P. & Banzhaf, W. (1995). Complexity compression and evolution, ed. L. J. Eshelman, Proceedings on *6th International Conference on Genetic Algorithms,* pp. 310-317, Pittsburgh, PA, Morgan Kaufmann, July 1995

Olhofer, M., Jin, Y. & Sendhoff, B. (2001). Adaptive encoding for aerodynamic shape optimization using Evolution Strategies, Proceedings of *Congress on Evolutionary Computation,* pp. 576-583 vol. 1, Seoul, South Korea, 2001, ISBN:1-59593-010-8

Onnen, C., Babuska, R., Kaymak, U., Sousa, J. M., Verbruggen, H. B. & Isermann, R. (1997). Genetic algorithms for optimization in predictive control, *Control Engineering Practice,* Vol. 5, No 10, page numbers (1363-1372), (October 1997), ISSN: 0967-0661

Ono & Kobayashi, S. (1997). A real-coded genetic algorithm for function optimisation using unimodal normal distribution crossover, ed. T. B$ck, Proceedings on *7th International Conference on Genetic Algorithms,* pp. 246-253, San Mateo, CA, Morgan Kauffman, 1997

Perkins, T. (1994). Stack-based genetic programming, Proceedings on *IEEE World Congress on Computational Intelligence,* pp. 148-153 vol 1, Orlando, Florida, IEEE Press, 27-29 June 1994

Schwefel, H.-P. (1981). *Numerical optimisation of computer models.* New York: Wiley

Sendhoff, B. & Kreuz, M. (1999). *Variable encoding of modular neural networks for time series prediction,* ed. V. W. Porto, Proceedings on *Congress on Evolutionary Computation,* pp. 259-266, IEEE Press, Piscataway, NJ, July 1999

Siouris, G. M., Leros, P. (1988). Minimum-time intercept guidance for tactical missiles, *Control Theory and Advanced Technology,* Vol. 4, No 2, page numbers (251-263), (February, 1988), ISSN 0911-0704

Smith, S. F. (1980). A learning system based on genetic adaptive algorithms, *PhD dissertation,* University of Pittsburgh

Spears, W. M. & Anand, V. (1991). A study of crossover operators in genetic programming, ed. Z. W. Ras, M. Zemankova, Proceedings on *International Symposium on Methodologies for Intelligent Systems,* pp. 409-418, Berlin: Springer-Verlag, 542., 1991, ISBN:3-540-54563-8

Ursem, R. K. (2003). Models for evolutionary algorithms and their applications in system identification and control optimization, *PhD dissertation,* Department of Computer Science, University of Aarhus, Denmark, 2003

van Laarhoven, P. J. M. & Aarts, E. H. L. (1987). *Simulated annealing: theory and applications.* Dordrecht, The Netherlands: D. Reidel, ISBN-10: 9027725136

Wang, Q. & Zalzala, A. M. S. (1996). Genetic control of near time-optimal motion for an industrial robot arm, Proceedings of *IEEE International Conference on Robotics and Automation,* pp. 2592-2597 vol. 3, ISBN: 0-7803-2988-0, Minneapolis, MN, April 1996

11

Efficient Estimation of Distribution Algorithms by using the Empirical Selection Distribution

S. Ivvan Valdez[1], Arturo Hernández[2] and Salvador Botello[2]
[1]*Universidad del Papaloapan (UNPA),*
[2]*Centre for Research in Mathematics A.C. (CIMAT),*
México

1. Introduction

Estimation of Distribution Algorithms (EDAs) (Mühlenbein et al., 1996; Mühlenbein & PaaB, 1996) are a promising area of research in evolutionary computation. EDAs propose to create models that can capture the dependencies among the decision variables. The widely known Genetic Algorithm could benefit from the available dependencies if the building blocks of the solution were correlated. However, it was proved that the building blocks of a genetic algorithm have a limited capacity for discovering and using complex relationships (correlations) among variables. EDAs instead, focus on learning probability distributions which serve as the vehicle to capture the data dependencies and the data structure as well.
In order to show how the proposed method unifies the theory for infinite sized population with the finite sized population case of practical EDAs, we explain them first. An EDA with infinite sized population would perform the steps shown in the algorithm in Table 1.

EDA with an infinite size population	
1	$t=0$
2	Initialize a probability model $p(x,t)$ (usually a uniform distribution).
3	Generate an infinite sized sample X_t from $p(x,t)$.
4	Evaluate X_t in the objective function(s) and constraint(s).
5	**Compute the selection distribution** $p^S(x,t)$, **and use it as the new search distribution. Then:** $p(x,t+1) = p^S(x,t)$. **(Selection and model rcomputation step)**
6	$t=t+1$
7	If the stop criterion is not reached go to Step 3

Table 1. The estimation of distribution algorithm with an infinite size population: the selection distribution is equal to the search distribution.

The selection method introduces the search bias necessary to improve the current best solution, and in fact, "pushes" the population towards the optimum. For this case where the population is infinite, imagine a probability value could be computed for every point in the search space. Therefore, the "exact" probability distribution of the selected individuals (which is also an infinite set), can be used to sample the new population. Such distribution, the **selection distribution**, is the probability of any point in the search space of being selected. Four selection distribution formulas for an infinite population are shown in Table

2, left column: Truncation, Boltzmann, Proportional, and Binary Tournament selections. In the same table but right column, we show the proposed empirical selection distributions studied in this paper. The first objective of this paper is to show that the proposed distributions converge to the theoretical ones as the population grows. The second objective is to apply the empirical distributions in practical EDAs, and to compare their performance through the analysis of several experiments. It has been proved that the ideal EDAs with any of the four selection distributions shown, converges to the optimum after a large number of generations (Zhang & Mühlenbein, 2004).

Selection Model	Empirical Selection Distribution
Truncation $p^S(x,t)=\begin{cases}\frac{p(x,t)}{\alpha(t)} & \text{if } f(x)\geq\theta_t \\ 0 & \text{otherwise}\end{cases}$	$\hat{p}^S(x_i,t)=\begin{cases}\frac{1}{\lvert X_t^S\rvert} & \text{if } f(x_i)\geq\theta_t \\ 0 & \text{otherwise}\end{cases}$
Boltzmann $p^S(x,t)=\frac{e^{\beta(t)f(x)}p(x,t)}{Z(t)}$	$\hat{p}^S(x_i,t)=\frac{e^{\beta(t)f(x)}}{\sum_{j=1}^{\lvert X\rvert}e^{\beta(t)f(x_j)}}$
Proportional $p^S(x,t)=\begin{cases}\frac{p(x,t)}{\alpha(t)} & \text{if } f(x)\geq\theta_t \\ 0 & \text{otherwise}\end{cases}$	$\hat{p}^S(x_i,t)=\frac{f(x_i)}{\sum_{j=1}^{\lvert X\rvert}f(x_j)}$
Binary Tournament $p^S(x,t)=2p(x,t)\int_{f(y)\leq f(x)}p(y,t)dy$	$\hat{p}^S(x_i,t)=\frac{\sum_{j=1}^{\lvert X\rvert}I(i,j)}{\sum_{i=1}^{\lvert X\rvert}\sum_{j=1}^{\lvert X\rvert}I(i,j)}$. Where $I(i,j)=1$, if $f(x_j)<f(x_i)$, and 0 otherwise.

Table 2. Left: Selection models for the EDA with an infinite sized population. Right: the respective **empirical selection distribution**.

Let us now contrast the infinite sized population case with the standard practical EDA, thereby, with a finite sized population. The practical EDA is presented in the algorithm in Table 3. Notice the selection operator returns a selected set X_t^S whose size is a fraction of the total population. In the next step the standard EDA seeks to approximate the distribution of the selected set via a parametric distribution. The distribution parameters, and in some cases the data structure, are learned from the selected set. Such distribution, the **search distribution**, is the model (with a predefined structure), used for learning the underlying joint probability density of the selected set, $p(x,t+1)\approx p(X_t^S,t)$. Also, note that the next population is simulated from the search distribution. The search distribution and its learning algorithm are so important for an EDA that, in fact, gives name to the EDA version.

Examples of search distributions are: Bayesian networks (Pelikan et al.., 1999), Polytrees (Soto & Ochoa, 2000), and Dependency Trees in discrete spaces. Also, Gaussian univariate and multivariate models (Bosman & Thierens, 2000; Larrañaga et al., 1999) in the continuous case, among others (Larrañaga & Lozano, 2001; Lozano et al., 2006; Pelikan et al., 2006).

	Standard EDA with a finite size population
1	$t=0$
2	Initialize a probability model $p(x,t)$ (**search distribution**).
3	Generate an infinite sized sample X_t from $p(x,t)$.
4	Evaluate X_t in the objective function(s) and constraint(s).
5	**$S_t \leftarrow$SELECTION(X_t) (selection step)**
6	**Recompute the search distribution model $p(x,t+1)$, such that, $p(x,t+1) \approx p(S_t)$ (parametercomputation step).**
7	$t=t+1$
7	If the stop criterion is not reached go to Step 3

Table 3. The estimation of distribution algorithm with a finite size population: the search distribution is computed by learning parameters from the selected set.

The approach introduced in this work is shown in the algorithm in Table 4. No selection operator is used, our approach firstly calculates the proposed **empirical selection distribution** to approximate to the theoretical selection distribution. The empirical selection distribution, $\hat{p}^S(x_i,t)$, is the exact selection distribution when the population is thought as a model of the whole search space. Then, the search distribution model is created directly using the information from the empirical selection distribution, and used to simulate the new population. Remember, the empirical selection distribution equations are presented in Table 2, right column. The calculation of the empirical selection distribution is easy (as we shall explain later), however, its main advantage is to carry all the information needed to build the best approximating search distribution.

	EDA with the Empirical Selection Distribution
1	$t=0$
2	Initialize a probability model $p(x,t)$ (**search distribution**).
3	Generate an infinite sized sample X_t from $p(x,t)$.
4	Evaluate X_t in the objective function(s) and constraint(s).
5	**Compute the empirical selection distribution $\hat{p}^S(x,t)$ (selection step)**
6	**Recompute the search distribution model $p(x,t+1)$, with $\hat{p}^S(x,t)$ (parametercomputation step).**
7	$t=t+1$
7	If the stop criterion is not reached go to Step 3

Table 4. The estimation of distribution algorithm with a finite size population: the search distribution is computed by learning parameters from the selected set.

The chapter is presented as follows: Section 2 briefly reviews the most common selection methods used in EDAs. Section 3 discusses about the convergence of the empirical selection distribution to the exact selection distribution. Section 4 introduces the general method to approximate the search distribution to the selection model. Section 5 is a comparison with related work. Section 6 presents well known EDAs, which have been modified to apply the proposed method. A set of experiments is presented in Section 7 and discussion about the performance of different selection methods. Finally, Section 8 shows the perspectives of future work and concludes.

2. Selection methods

The main goal of a selection operator is to bias the population towards promising regions of the search space. Truncation, Boltzmann, Proportional and Tournament selection operators discussed in this paper are introduced through an example. Assume the following objective function and an infinite sized population whose elements have as fitness the function value at $(x,y) = \exp(|x|-2)^2 + 4\cos(20x) + \exp(|y|-2)^2 + 4$. The plot of this function is shown in Figure 1(a). Most of the EDAs draw the initial population from a uniform distribution, which is shown in Figure 1(b). Hence, during the first iteration any point has the same sampling probability. Assuming an infinite sized population, the rest of the figures show the selection distribution function.

- The **Truncation selection** is shown in Figure 1(c). This selection is widely used by many EDAs. Here the select set would be the best population above a function threshold of $\theta = 30$. The probability density of the truncation selection is shown in Figure 1(c). Observe the flat area; it means the selection probability for the population above the threshold value is the same. The truncation selection hides the roughness of the objective function above the threshold value by assigning to such area the same selection probability.
- The **Boltzmann selection** is shown in Figure 1(d). This operator exponentially favors the most promising regions (the zones with high function value), as shown in Figure 1(d). Most of the probability mass is condensed on a single peak which corresponds to the function optimum. Since the remaining region is quite flat, the Boltzmann selection will deliver a selected set clustered on the peak region.
- The **Proportional selection** is shown in Figure 1(e). This operator, proposed by John Holland for the standard genetic algorithm, selects points with some probability directly proportional to its objective value. The resulting probabilistic model of this method, shown in Figure 1(e), is very similar to the objective function (although in a different scale).
- The **Tournament** selection is shown in Figure 1(f). The tournament selection picks the best point found in a randomly chosen subset of the population. The usual size of the subset is 2. Figure 1(f) shows that the resulting probabilistic model acquires the roughness of the objective function. A larger subset would increase the selection pressure on the winning individual, therefore, flatting the density function shown.

Zhang and Mühlenbein have shown the selection models just illustrated can drive the population to the function optimum (Zhang & Mühlenbein, 2004). The main factor that makes convergence possible is the bias the selection operator introduces into the population. In the following section we provide simple proofs of the convergence of the empirical selection distribution to the selection distribution.

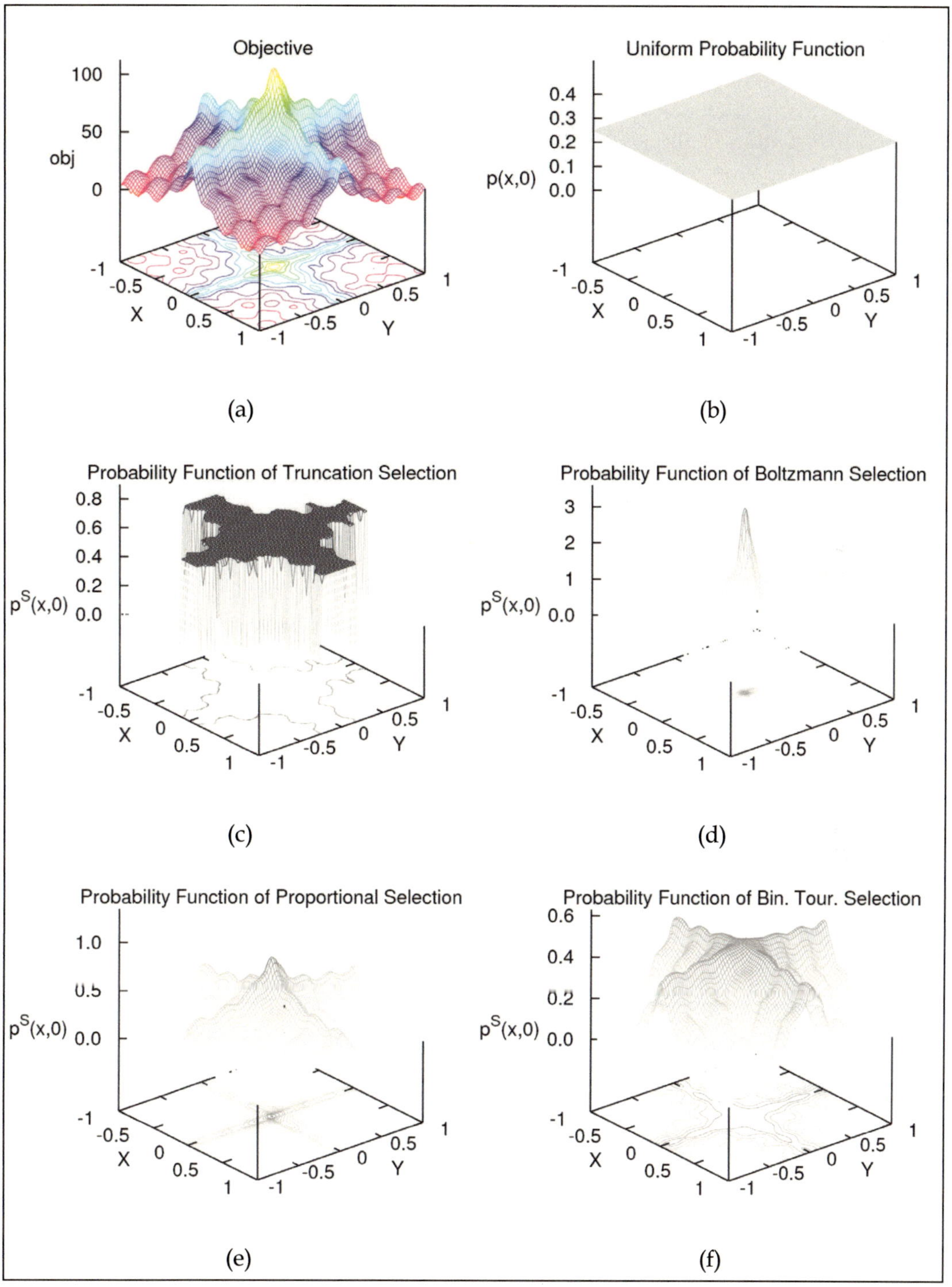

Fig. 1. a) Objective function example, b) uniform distribution, c) to f) probability densities of the most widely used selection methods.

3. Convergence of the empirical selection distribution to the selection distribution

The empirical selection distribution equations for the four selection methods are shown in Table 2. In this section we provide simple proofs on the convergence of the empirical selection distribution to the selection distribution with large population size. In fact, the larger the population size, the better the approximation of the empirical selection distribution to the selection distribution.

3.1 Discrete variables

Assume an EDA with discrete variables and a search distribution denoted by $p(x,t)$ (the continuous case will be further tackled).

Truncation selection. Say the search space is described by m binary variables, $\{y_1, y_2, ..., y_m\}$. There are $n = 2^m$ combinations, and denote by x_i, $i = \{1,2,...,n\}$ to each combination. Then, for a large sample X with size $|X| >> n$, every combination x_i receives a frequency $freq_i$ of instances. The empirical selection distribution at generation t is given by:

$$\hat{p}^S(x_i, t, \theta_t) = freq_i \cdot \frac{1}{|S_t|} \tag{1}$$

Being $|S_t|$ the number of instances of X such that $f(x) > \theta_t$. Now recall that for a infinite sample $freq_i / |X| = p(x_i, t)$, then for $\alpha(t) = |S_t| / |X|$ the empirical selection distribution is given by:

$$\hat{p}^S(x_i, t, \theta_t) = \frac{p(x_i, t)}{\alpha(t)}, \tag{2}$$

which is exactly the expression given in Table 2 for the infinite sized population. The $\alpha(t)$ value is the proportion of truncated solutions.

Boltzmann selection. The empirical selection model is given by:

$$\hat{p}^S(x_i, t) = \frac{e^{\beta(t) f(x_i)}}{\sum_{j=1}^{|X|} e^{\beta(t) f(x_j)}}, \tag{3}$$

then, in an analogous way to the truncation method:

$$\hat{p}^S(x_i, t) = \frac{freq_i \cdot e^{\beta(t) f(x_i)}}{\sum_{j=1}^{|X|} freq_k \cdot e^{\beta(t) f(x_k)}}, \tag{4}$$

Substituting $freq_i = |X| \cdot p(x_i, t)$, and $freq_i = |X| \cdot p(x_i, t)$, $Z(t) = \sum_{k=1}^{n} p(x_k, t) \cdot e^{\beta(t) f(x_k)}$, then:

$$\hat{p}^S(x_i,t) = \frac{p(x_i,t)\cdot e^{\beta(t)f(x_i)}}{Z(t)}, \tag{5}$$

So, we have the exact Boltzmann selection distribution.
Proportional selection. The empirical selection model is given as follows:

$$\hat{p}^S(x_i,t) = \frac{f(x_i)}{\sum_{k=1}^{|X|} f(x_k)}, \tag{6}$$

then:

$$\hat{p}^S(x_i,t) = \frac{freq_i f(x_i)}{\sum_{k=1}^{|X|} freq_k f(x_k)}, \tag{7}$$

Substituting, $freq_i = |X| \cdot p(x_i,t)$ then:

$$\hat{p}^S(x_i,t) = \frac{p(x_i,t) f(x_i)}{\sum_{k=1}^{|X|} p(x_k,t) f(x_k)}, \tag{8}$$

and $E(t) = \sum_{k=1}^{n} p(x_k,t)\cdot f(x_k)$, then the empirical selection for such large sample X is given by:

$$\hat{p}^S(x_i,t) = \frac{p(x_i,t) f(x_i)}{E(t)}, \tag{9}$$

which is exactly the expression in Table 2.
Binary tournament selection. For the tournament selection method the exact selection distribution for the discrete case is given by:

$$\hat{p}^S(x_i,t) = \frac{p(x_i,t) \sum_{f(y)<f(x_i)} p(y,t)}{C}, \tag{10}$$

being C the normalization constant, the number 2 in Table 2 is also a constant, so it is absorbed by C. Then the empirical selection distribution is given by:

$$\hat{p}^S(x_i,t) = \frac{\sum_{j=1}^{|X|} I(i,j)}{\sum_{i=1}^{|X|}\sum_{j=1}^{|X|} I(i,j)}, \tag{11}$$

Where $I(i,j)=1$, if $f(x_j)<f(x_i)$ and 0 otherwise. The term $\sum_{i=1}^{|X|}\sum_{j=1}^{|X|} I(i,j)$ is a normalization constant. Then, considering that for any y value the number of instances in the large population X are $freq_y = |X| \cdot p(y,t)$, and the number of instances of a variable (vector) value x_i is $freq_i = |X| \cdot p(x_i,t)$, then substituting:

$$\hat{p}^S(x_i,t) = \frac{p(x_i,t) \sum_{f(y)<f(x_i)} p(y,t)}{C}, \tag{12}$$

which is the exact selection distribution for $C = \sum_{i=1}^{|X|} p(x_i,t) \cdot \sum_{f(y)<f(x_i)} p(y,t)$.

3.2 Continuous variables

For the continuous case, consider a univariate search space with domain in the interval *[a,b]*, then a set of points x_i for *i=1,2,...,* $|X|$ define partitions. If we use these points as possible instances of a discrete variable, then, we have the equivalence with the discrete selections distribution previously shown. The partition size is $\Delta_i = x_{i+1} - x_i$, if $\Delta_i < \varepsilon$, the sums in Equation 8 can be written as Riemann sums. Even though this is not a proof for continuous cases, it is a strong argument to explain the convergence of the empirical selection distribution to the selection distribution. Figure 2 shows the similarities between the exact selection density function and the empirical selection distributions.

4. Computing the search distribution

Following the usual steps of an EDA, an arbitrary large sample should be obtained from the empirical selection distribution, and then used to learn the search distribution parameters. In our approach, sampling the empirical selection is avoided without diminishing the advantages of using all the information at hand. It is known that the relative frequency of a point x_i for an infinitely large sample is equal to the probability $\hat{p}^S(x_i,t)$. Thus, the sampling process can be avoided and $\hat{p}^S(x_i,t)$ can be used as the frequency of the point x_i.

For example, suppose that the search distribution is a Gaussian with mean μ and variance *v*. These parameters must be computed to get the best approximation of the Gaussian to the selection model. Assume (for a moment) that a sample $\hat{S}$ of size $|\hat{S}|$ is obtained from the empirical selection distribution. The only possible values sampled from the empirical selection distribution are those in the population. Hence, most of the points x_i would get more than one instance in the sample $\hat{S}$. Denote the number of instances of a point x_i as $freq_i$, the estimator of the mean is:

$$\mu = \frac{\sum_{i=1}^{|X|} freq_i \cdot x_i}{|\hat{S}|}, \tag{13}$$

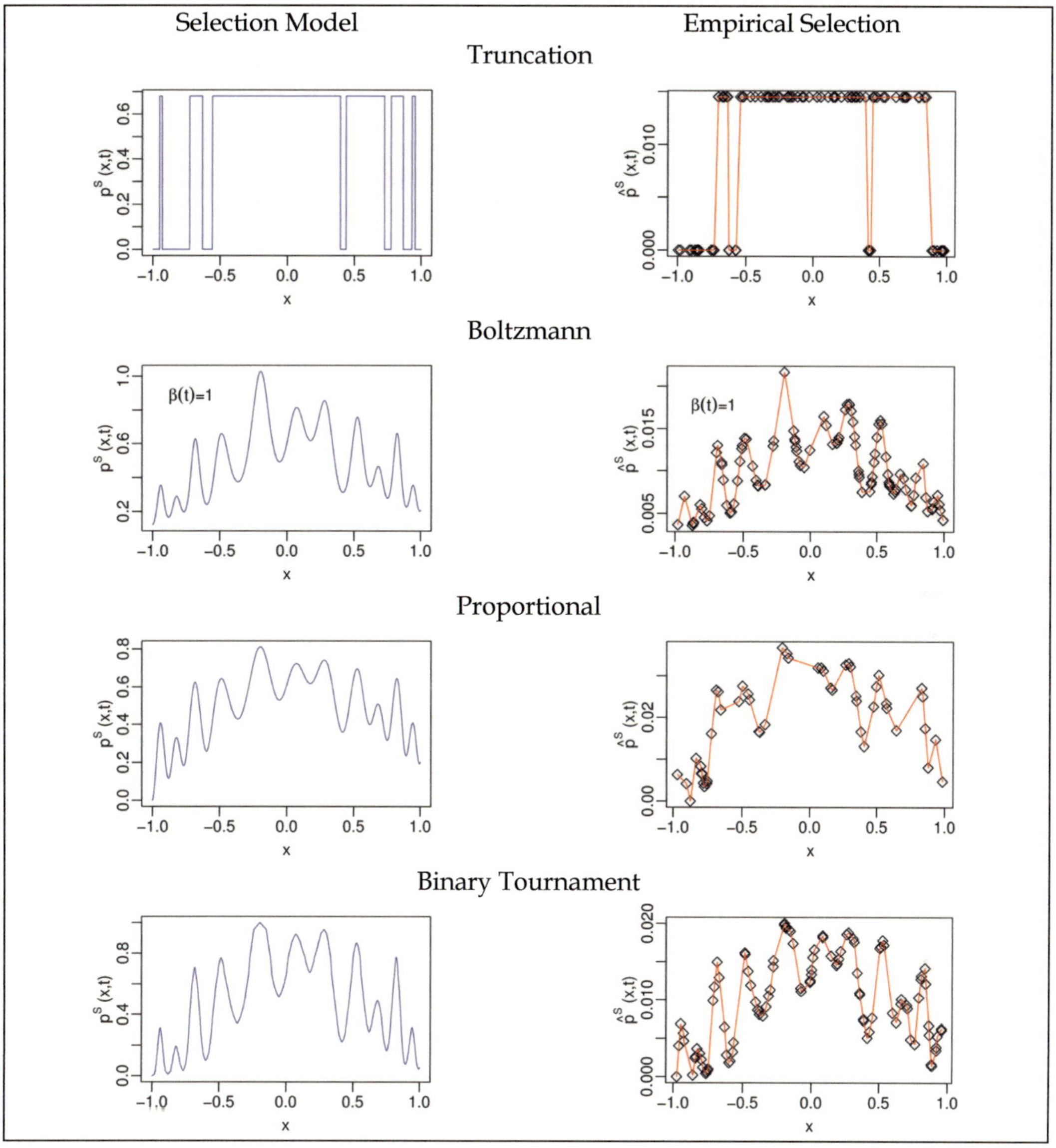

Fig. 2. Left: Selection model plot. Right: empirical selection distribution plot.

Let us denote $\hat{p}_i^S = \hat{p}^S(x_i,t)$. We know that when $|\hat{S}| \to \infty$, then, $\frac{freq_i}{|\hat{S}|} = \hat{p}_i^S$. Substituting this term in Equation 13, the mean is simply computed as follows:

$$\mu = \sum_{i=1}^{|X|} \hat{p}_i^S \cdot x_i \,, \tag{14}$$

where $\hat{p}_i^S$ is the probability of a point computed with the empirical selection distribution. Therefore, sampling the empirical distribution is not necessary. Also important, note that the computation of the probabilities $\hat{p}_i^S$ is independent of the search distribution parameters. This allows us to easily adapt an EDA to any of the four selection models. These models cover most EDA implementations and other selection methods can be also expressed as distributions. In addition, the computational cost of $\hat{p}_i^S$ in most of the cases is lower or equal to that of applying a selection operator. For example, the Proportional and Boltzmann selections must calculate the probabilities in Table 2 in order to obtain a sample which becomes the selected set. This sample is not necessary for the empirical selection distribution based EDA (ES-EDA). For the truncation method in the standard EDA as well as the ES-EDA, it is only necessary to know the individuals whose objective function is greater than θ_t, thus, the computational cost is the same. The binary tournament selection requires comparisons of the order of the selected set size, while the empirical selection distribution requires comparisons of order $|X|(|X|-1)/2$, hence, it is the unique case in which an ES-EDA has a greater cost than the standard EDA. The parameter computation in the ES-EDA in general increases its computational cost only by multiplying each individual value x_i by its corresponding frequency $\hat{p}_i^S$, which is a minimal cost.

5. Related work

In order to show that this work is an extension of previous but less general approaches, we will show the equivalence of the resulting formulae when applying frequencies from the empirical selection distribution. Yunpeng et al. (Yunpeng et al., 2006) approximate the Boltzmann distribution with a Gaussian model by minimizing the Kullback-Leibeler divergence. The computation of the Gaussian distribution parameters is presented in Equations 15 and 16. Note that this approach which requires costly analytical work, gives exactly the same formulae as the Boltzmann empirical selection distribution presented in Table 2 with the $UMDA_c$ and the $EMNA_{global}$.

$$\mu = \frac{\sum_{i=1}^{|S|} e^{\Delta\beta f(x_i)} \cdot x_i}{\sum_{i=1}^{|S|} e^{\Delta\beta f(x_i)}}, \tag{15}$$

$$\Gamma = \frac{\sum_{i=1}^{|S|} \left[e^{\Delta\beta f(x_i)} \cdot (x_i - \mu)(x_i - \mu)^T \right]}{\sum_{i=1}^{|S|} e^{\Delta\beta f(x_i)}}, \tag{16}$$

6. Modifying successful EDAs with the empirical selection distribution

This section presents several successful EDAs which have been modified to accept the relative frequencies given by the empirical selection distribution. Continuous and discrete EDAs with univariate and multivariate models are presented. Table 5 presents the notation used.

$p(x,t)$	Search distribution in generation t.
n	Number of variables.
X_t	Population.
$\lvert X \rvert$	Population size.
$\hat{p}_j^S$	Frequency of x_i, according to $\hat{p}^S(x_i,t)$ in Table 2.
F_t	Population objective values.
X_{best}	An optimum approximation.
$I(x,k)$	Indicator, 1 if $x_i = k$, and 0 otherwise.

Table 5. Notation used for the empirical selection based EDAs.

A practical EDA based on the empirical selection distribution is presented in Table 6. Since the parameter computation in line 8 is the only section that should be changed according to the particular search distribution, a pseudo-code is separately presented for each algorithm. The selection procedure in line 6 must be understood as the computation of the empirical selection distribution (according to Equations in Table 2).

	Practical EDA based on the Empirical Selection Distribution
1	Initialize the search distribution model $p(x,0)$
2	Sampling(X_t ,$p(x,0)$)
3	Evaluation(F_t , X_t)
4	**While** the stopping criterion is not met **do**
5	Selection($\hat{p}^S(x,t)$, X_t, F_t)
6	Parameter_Computation($p(x,t)$, $\hat{p}^S(x,t)$, X_t, F_t)
7	Sampling(X_{t+1}, $p(x,t)$)
8	Evaluation(F_t, X_{t+1})
9	Elitism(X_{best}, F_{t+1}, X_{t+1})
10	**End While**
Ensure: An optimum approximation X_{best}.	

Table 6. Pseudo-code a practical EDA based on the empirical selection distribution.

For (i=1 to n) {

    For (k=1 to m_i) {

$$b_{i,k} = \sum_{j=1}^{|X|} I(x_j,k) \cdot \hat{p}_j^S$$

    }

}

Table 7. Pseudo-code for the ES-UMDA parameter computation.

6.1 UMDA

The Univariate Marginal Distribution Algorithm (UMDA) was introduced by Mühlenbein and PaaB (Mühlenbein & PaaB, 1996). It is based on the estimation of univariate marginal probabilities. This model considers that all variables are statistically independent. It uses the simplest model for discrete distributions. Each variable x_i has attached a probability

vector $b_{i,k}$, that is, the probability of x_i taking the value *k*, is: $b_{i,k} = p(x_i = k)$. Note that in the original UMDA the computation of the parameter $b_{i,k}$ is basically done by counting bits of a variable of the selected set.
The UMDA is quite simple to adapt to the relative frequencies given by the empirical selection distribution. The pseudo-code of the ES-UMDA (ES=Empirical Selection) parameter computation is shown in Table 7.

6.2 UMDA$_c$

The Univariate Marginal Distribution Algorithm for continuous domains (UMDA$_c$) was introduced by Larrañaga et al. (Larrañaga et al., 1999). It uses a univariate model, in the specific case of UMDA$^G{}_c$, there are *n* univariate Gaussian distributions (for a *n*-dimensional problem). Two parameters are needed for the Gaussian at each dimension *i*, the mean μ_i and the standard deviation σ_i. The computation of both parameters is simply done by weighting each point by its corresponding relative frequency (probability) as shown in Table 8.

For (*i=1* to *n*) {

$$\mu = \sum_{j=1}^{|X|} \hat{p}_i^S \cdot x_{j,i}$$

$$\sigma_i^2 = \sum_{j=1}^{|X|} \hat{p}_i^S \cdot (x_{j,i} - \mu_i)^2$$

}

Table 8. Pseudo-code for the ES-UMDA$_c$ parameter computation.

6.3 K2-Bayesian-network based EDA

Bayesian networks have been successfully used in EDAs, for instance the Bayesian Optimization Algorithm (BOA) introduced by Pelikan et al. (Pelikan et al., 1999). A BOA-like algorithm based on the K2 algorithm (Cooper & Herskovits, 1992) is presented. The parameter computation has been modified to use the empirical selection distribution. The K2 is a greedy heuristic search method, for maximizing the probability $P(B_S,D)$ of the structure B_S and the data *D*. For maximizing $P(B_S,D)$ the K2 maximizes $g(i,\pi_i)$, which is a measure related with the probability of x_i given a set of parents π_i.

$$g(i,\pi_i) = \prod_{j=1}^{q_i} \frac{(r_i - 1)}{(N_{ij} + r_i - 1)} \prod_{k=1}^{r_i} N_{ijk}!, \tag{17}$$

where x_i has r_i possible discrete values. Each variable x_i in B_s has a set of parents, which are represented by a list of variables π_i. N_{ijk} is the number of cases in *D* in which the variable x_i has the value v_{ik}, and π_i is instantiated as w_{ij}. w_{ij} denotes the *j*-th unique instantiation of π_i relative to *D*, and q_i is the number of such unique instantiations of π_i. $N_{ij} = \sum_{k=1}^{r_i} N_{ijk}$. For a deeper explanation of the K2 algorithm the reader is directed to (Cooper & Herskovits, 1992).

Learning a Bayesian network with the K2 is a counting process of point instances. Then, in order to compute Equation 17 an integer frequency for each point is needed. For obtaining an integer frequency, let us define a sample size for the selection method, say $|\hat{S}|$. When using the empirical selection distribution we have a relative frequency $\hat{p}_l^S$ associated with a point x_l, if that point is such a case for N_{ijk}, then, instead of summing a single case we will sum integer($|\hat{S}| \cdot \hat{p}_l^S$). As $|\hat{S}|$ grows, the approximation of the K2 Bayesian network to the empirical selection distribution will be more accurate, but the computational cost of Equation 17 increases as well. Once the K2 Bayesian network structure has been learned, the frequencies $|\hat{S}| \cdot \hat{p}_l^S$ must be used to compute the conditional probabilities.

6.4 EMNA$_{global}$

The EMNA$_{global}$ was introduced by Larrañaga et al. (Larrañaga et al., 2001). It is based on the estimation of a multivariate normal density function. This model can represent linear dependencies between normal variables in the covariance matrix. The pseudo-code of the ES-EMNA$_{global}$ parameter computation is shown in Table 9. Note that it is quite easy to insert the empirical selection distribution in univariate as well as multivariate algorithms, also it is inserted in discrete and continuous domains with a minimum analytical and computational effort.

For (i=1 to n) {

$$\mu = \sum_{j=1}^{|X|} \hat{p}_i^S \cdot x_{j,i}$$

For (k=1 to i) {

$$\sigma_{i,k} = \sum_{j=1}^{|X|} \hat{p}_i^S \cdot (x_{j,i} - \mu_i)(x_{j,k} - \mu_i)$$

$$\sigma_{k,i} = \sigma_{i,k}$$

}

}

Table 9. Pseudo-code for the ES-EMNA$_{global}$ parameter computation.

7. Experiments and performance analysis

This section provides a set of experiments to address the performance and advantages of the empirical selection distribution. Two kinds of experiments are presented:

1. Graphically we show that the search distribution based on the empirical selection distribution constitutes a robust and better approximation to the selection model.
2. Using the EMNA$_{global}$ (Larrañaga et al., 2001) and the BMDA (Pelikan & Mühlenbein, 1999), we show the impact of the empirical selection distribution on the EDA performance.

7.1 Graphical comparison

For better plots, the unidimensional objective function shown in Figure 3 is used. This analysis contrasts the three concepts discussed in the introduction: the ideal EDA, the standard EDA, and the EDA with the empirical selection distribution, combined with the four discussed selection methods.

Even though the exact selection distribution can be computed for the ideal EDA, to perform the correct comparison we use a predefined Gaussian model for the three approaches. We show the Gaussian approximation with a very large population (considered as infinite), contrasted with the approximation computed by using the selected set from a standard sized population, and the approximation computed by using the empirical selection distribution. The experiments are designed as follows:

- **The ideal EDA**. A very large population (10^4 individuals) equally spaced is used, then, a larger selected set (10^5) is extracted using the selection method. Using the huge selected set (10^5 individuals) the parameters of the search distribution are computed. This approximation will be called the exact approximation. A special case is the truncation method which uses the same population size, but a smaller selected set is obtained by truncating at $\theta = 0.9$.
- **The standard EDA**. A relatively small population (30 individuals) is randomly drawn, the selection method is applied delivering the selected set used to compute the search distribution. Most of the selection methods add randomness to the procedure (except the truncation method which delivers a deterministic selected set), as a consequence the search distributions could differ after applying the selection method to the same population several times. Thus, we present the different search models computed when selecting 10 selected sets of 15 individuals from the same population.
- **The EDA with the empirical selection distribution**. Using the same population of 30 individuals used by the standard EDA, the empirical selection distribution is used to compute the search distribution parameters. Notice that the empirical selection distribution is unique for a given population as well as the search model delivered by this method.

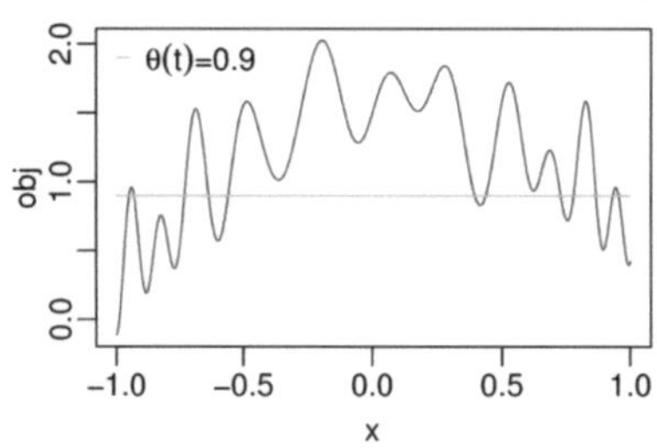

Fig. 3. Unidimensional objective function used for the graphical experiments.

Truncation selection. The truncation method shown in Figure 4(a) is basically the same for the standard EDA and the empirical selection distribution, because the points used are the same in both approximations. Thus, in this case the empirical selection performs at least as well as the standard selection method.

Boltzmann selection. As shown in Figure 4(b), the empirical selection method delivers a very good approximation to the exact model. The search models computed by the standard EDA approximation are a belt of Gaussians. The empirical selection approximation is at the middle of this belt, it is less affected by a single point or small set of points (robustness). It is possible that the randomness of the standard selection method guides the search to a better optimum approximation. In general, it is not the expected behaviour, given its difference with the exact model, the small size of the selected set (usually 50% of the population) and the consequent loss of information which favors the tendency of being biased to sub-optimal regions. Also, it is expected that the behaviour of the Boltzmann selection varies according to the β value. The empirical selection computes the same search model from the same population, thus, a more stable behaviour is expected in contrast with the standard EDA. This could be especially useful when designing annealing schedules, because with the empirical selection distribution a similar performance under similar conditions is expected.

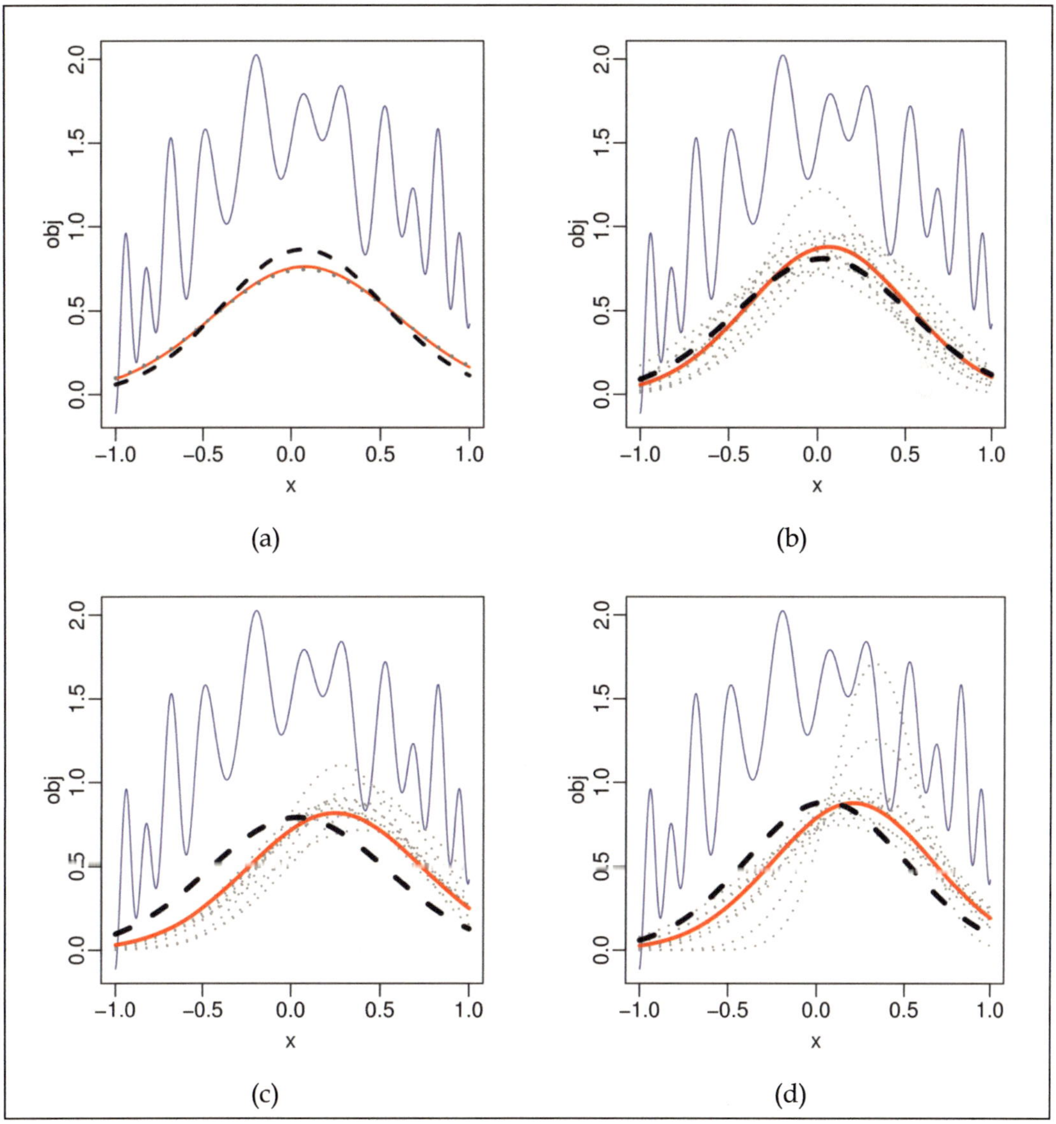

Fig. 4. Selection methods: (a) truncation, (b) Boltzmann, (c) proportional and (d) tournament. Search distributions for: 1) The exact approximation with dashed line, 2) the standard EDA approximation with doted lines, and 3) the empirical selection approximation with solid line. The objective function (solid line), and the population used for practica EDAs (circles).

Proportional selection. The proportional selection does not use extra parameters, therefore, no expensive parameter tuning is required. At the same time, however, there is no way to control the high selection pressure exerted over the fittest individuals that usually lead the population to premature convergence. Thus, a search distribution which better represents the selection method could be useful, also a more predictable search model is useful when tuning other controls such as the population size, because the expected behaviour could be better inferred. Figure 4(c), shows the search densities (points) computed when applying the selection method 10 times on the same population. Notice that these models are easily biased to different regions, most of them suboptimal.
Binary tournament selection. The binary tournament selection seems to be the most robust selection method according to Figure 4(d). The plot shows that this selection delivers Gaussians more similar than those delivered by other selection methods. This selection can be used as a reference for the expected performance of an EDA, considering the robustness, and the good performance of this selection according to the experiments in the next section. The parameter tuning for other selection methods can be done trying to obtain at least the same performance as the binary tournament selection. It is parameter free, and it is less sensible to large objective values in the population. As shown in Figure 4(d) the empirical selection distribution computes an accurate approximation when compared with the exact method.

7.2 Performance comparison

It has been previously shown that the estimation of the search distribution according to the empirical selection distribution accurately approximates the exact search distribution. Other claim is that the empirical selection distribution preserves some building blocks that can not be preserved by the standard EDA, due to the fact that the last one only uses a part of the population, while the empirical selection based EDA use the whole population in most of the cases. To support these arguments, we present experiments using the bivariate marginal distribution algorithm (BMDA) (Pelikan & Mühlenbein, 1999), and the $EMNA_{global}$ (Larrañaga et al., 2001), as well as the counterparts based on the empirical selection distribution: the ES-BMDA and ES-$EMNA_{global}$.

7.3 Test 1. The $EMNA_{global}$

We present a comparison using the $EMNA_{global}$ and three problems widely used to test EDAs performance (Larrañaga et al., 2001): Sphere, Griewangk and Rosenbrock. In order to maximize the functions and convert them to have positive objective values, an objective function $g(x)$ is adjusted as: $f(x)=-g(x)+1.8e7$, and $f(x)$ is used as the fitness function.
Experiments description: 30 independent runs are performed with 50 variables, the domain for all variables is [-600,600], the population size is 2000, selecting 1000 individuals for the standard EMNA. Truncation is 50% of the population, and elitism according to the general EDA in Table 6. The annealing schedule for the Boltzmann selection is fixed by initializing $\beta_0 = 0$, $\Delta\beta = 100/n$, and $\beta_t = \beta_{t-1} + \Delta\beta$. For the Rosenbrock function $\Delta\beta = 50/n$. For the Boltzmann and proportional selections the objective function is normalized by applying $f(x)=g(x)-g^{min}/(g^{max}-g^{min}+1)$, in order to avoid numerical problems.
Stopping criterion: 300 000 function evaluations.
Results: Table 10 compares the results obtained by the standard EMNA (denoted by St.), and the Empirical Selection based EMNA (denoted by ES). We report the mean and standard deviation of the objective function as well as the result of a hypothesis test based

n		Truncation	Boltzmann	Proportional	Binary Tournament
Sphere					
10	St	5.048e-9 (1.158e-9)	2.168e-6 (7.745e-7)	7.703e-2 (2.666e-2)	6.219e-9 (1.234e-9)
	ES	5.159e-9 (1.105e-9)	2.370e-6 (5.901e-7)	6.738e-2 (2.347e-2)	5.762e-9 (1.395e-9)
	Hyp. Test	N	N	N	N
20	St	3.767e-8 (7.306e-9)	9.924e-1 (1.356)	7.365 (2.314)	6.607e-8 (1.166e-8)
	ES	3.790e-8 (6.003e-9)	1.092 (2.298e+0)	6.661 (1.071)	7.628e-8 (1.074e-8)
	Hyp. Test	N	N	N	St
30	St	1.093e-7 (1.123e-8)	2.725e+1 (1.804e+1)	2.018e+2 (1.524e+2)	1.660e-5 (1.914e-6)
	ES	1.091e-7 (7.991e-9)	1.726e+1 (1.503e+1)	5.549e+1 (1.005e+1)	3.520e-5 (3.874e-6)
	Hyp. Test	N	ES	ES	St
40	St	2.213e-7 (1.673e-8)	1.060e+2 (4.624e+1)	1.283e+3 (6.554e+2)	1.889e-3 (2.983e-3)
	ES	2.239e-7 (1.682e-8)	6.394e+1 (4.757e+1)	2.142e+2 (2.060e+1)	1.094e-3 (1.099e-4)
	Hyp. Test	N	ES	ES	ES
50	St	1.999e-6 (2.266e-7)	4.289e+2 (1.779e+2)	4.735e+3 (1.379e+3)	3.543 (5.801)
	ES	1.712e-6 (2.082e-7)	1.826e+2 (9.569e+1)	5.357e+2 (6.471e+1)	1.111e-2 (1.032e-3)
	Hyp. Test	ES	ES	ES	ES
Griewnagk					
10	St	9.356e-10 (2.077e-10)	0.36098 (0.18955)	0.3194 (0.05671)	1.062e-9 (3.608e-10)
	ES	9.231e-10 (2.251e-10)	0.17173 (0.09324)	0.3343 (0.06324)	1.114e-9 (2.647e-10)
	Hyp. Test	N	ES	N	N
20	St	4.921e-9 (5.351e-10)	0.19738 (0.19323)	0.6325 (0.07413)	1.003e-8 (1.788e-9)
	ES	4.968e-9 (6.329e-10)	0.06382 (0.08591)	0.6553 (0.04763)	1.207e-8 (1.526e-9)
	Hyp. Test	N	ES	ES	St
30	St	1.044e-8 (1.007e-9)	0.13667 (0.11265)	1.0302 (0.06677)	1.125e-6 (1.846e-7)
	ES	1.004e-8 (9.885e-10)	0.03527 (0.05150)	0.9466 (0.03131)	2.223e-6 (3.029e-7
	Hyp. Test	N	ES	ES	St
40	St	1.817e-8 (1.357e-9)	0.26945 (0.12897)	1.3946 (0.19001)	6.056e-4 (2.088e-3)
	ES	1.809e-8 (1.694e-9)	0.05683 (0.05088)	1.0543 (0.00679)	4.868e-5 (5.506e-6)
	Hyp. Test	N	ES	ES	ES
50	St	7.568e-8 (1.352e-8)	0.54303 (0.24312)	2.3571 (0.46186)	1.036e-1 (1.265e-1)
	ES	6.852e-8 (1.364e-8)	0.17259 (0.07979)	1.1365 (0.02057)	3.899e-4 (3.021e-5)
	Hyp. Test	ES	ES	ES	ES
Rosenbrock					
10	St	9.292 (7.714)	6.795 (0.5562)	1.125e+05 (65566)	7.647 (0.2958)
	ES	8.929 (3.113)	6.862 (0.4907)	1.133e+05 (56613)	7.880 (0.7487)
	Hyp. Test	N	N	N	St
20	St	20.131 (5.753)	19.404 (2.4900)	1.313e+07 (7154997)	17.915 (0.9468)
	ES	19.339 (4.762)	18.386 (1.1359)	9.138e+06 (2823051)	17.657 (0.8191)
	Hyp. Test	N	ES	ES	N
30	St	28.865 (1.218)	35.728 (7.9373)	1.656e+08 (154793875)	31.681 (8.1603)
	ES	30.695 (6.149)	35.246 (5.2851)	5.800e+07 (16388688)	27.852 (0.6024)
	Hyp. Test	N	ES	ES	ES
40	St	42.413 (4.465)	71.699 (18.6654)	5.469e+08 (269436266)	84.128 (52.2806)
	ES	41.709 (3.324)	53.984 (8.8081)	1.845e+08 (53383769)	40.544 (3.1687)
	Hyp. Test	N	ES	ES	ES
50	St	65.604 (13.422)	1109.840 (3713.7494)	1.183e+09 (641262869)	2594.724 (3675.9199)
	ES	60.987 (9.248)	93.034 (16.7544)	3.695e+08 (82888904)	61.753 (4.9202)
	Hyp. Test	N	ES	ES	ES

Table 10. Performance comparison between the standard $EMNA_{global}$ (St) and the empirical selection distribution based $EMNA_{global}$ (ES).

on the Bootstrap methodology with a significance of 5% (Efron & Tibshirani, 1993). We test that the mean of the ES-based $EMNA_{global}$ is less than the mean of the standard $EMNA_{global}$, and vice versa. An **N** below the mean and standard deviation means that neither is better, **St** means that the standard $EMNA_{global}$ is the best, an ES that the empirical selection based $EMNA_{global}$ is the best. The conditions of the experiment are maintained while the dimensions are growing, the purpose is to show that the empirical selection in general performs better, and can use the information efficiently. Note that the standard EDA (St-EDA) and the Empirical Selection EDA (ES-EDA) are very similar in lower dimensions, but for higher dimensions the ES-EDA clearly outperforms the St-EDA. The explanation is that the population size is not growing with the dimensions, thus, for lower dimensions the selected set size is enough to adequately estimate the search distribution, but for higher dimensions the information is not sufficient, or it is not efficiently used. The runs where the St-EDA outperforms the ES-EDA (tournament 20 and 30 variables), can be explained by selection pressure issues. The St-EDA uses a subset of the best individuals in the population, no matter which selection method is used. On the other hand, the ES-EDA uses all the points, so for the same parameters the variance of the ES-EDA will be greater than the St-EDA, because the whole population covers a wider region than the selected set. So, the convergence of the St-EDA is faster, and the exploration is concentrated in a smaller region, resulting in a poor performance for higher dimensions as shown in Table 10. Notice that even the hypothesis test says that the St-EDA is better in 4 cases, the ES-EDA finds solutions very close to the optimum in all cases.

7.4 Test 2. The BMDA

The BMDA works in discrete domains, in this case a binary domain. It builds a graphical model with bivariate dependencies, the dependencies are considered according a χ^2 hypothesis test. The χ^2 computation uses empirical probabilities, thus, the ES-BMDA computes these empirical probabilities by summing the relative frequencies $\hat{p}_i^S$ given by the empirical selection distribution formulae. For example, if we need to compute the marginal probability of the variable x_j takes the value of 1, say $p(x_j = 1)$, if an individual i in the population is an instance of $x_j = 1$ then we sum $\hat{p}_i^S$, the standard procedure at the end divides the sum over the total number of individuals, when using the empirical selection this normalization is not necessary. This test is performed by using the deceptive function of order 3 shown in Equation 18, which was also used for the experiments in the original paper of the BMDA (Pelikan & Mühlenbein, 1999).

$$f_{3deceptive}(x, \pi_i) = \sum_{i=1}^{\frac{n}{3}} f_3(x_{\pi(3(i-1)+1)} + x_{\pi(3(i-1)+2)} + x_{\pi(3(i-1)+3)}), \tag{18}$$

where x is a bit string, π is any permutation of order n, and f_3 is defined in Equation 19.

$$f_3(u) = \begin{cases} 0.9 & \text{if } u = 0 \\ 0.8 & \text{if } u = 1 \\ 0 & \text{if } u = 2 \\ 1 & \text{otherwise} \end{cases}, \tag{19}$$

For n = 30 we use π = { 6, 27, 18, 20, 28, 16, 1, 23, 24, 3, 2, 13, 8, 5, 17, 11, 29, 15, 30, 9, 25, 12, 19, 22, 4, 10, 14, 21, 26). For n = 60, π = { 49, 31, 40, 59, 5, 23, 57, 37, 47, 19, 27, 30, 8, 56, 3, 36, 45, 17, 41 , 33, 21, 53, 39, 51, 50, 29, 16, 10, 24, 55, 15, 32, 7, 13, 2, 52, 14, 60, 12, 22, 34, 25, 35, 1, 28, 18, 20, 9, 38, 26, 46, 58, 42, 43, 44, 48, 6, 4, 11}. The deceptive function correlates subsets of 3 variables. Pelikan and Mühlenbein (Pelikan & Mühlenbein, 1999) shown that the BMDA is capable of solving this problem that can not be solved by the simple GA. Our purpose is to show that the ES-BMDA is more efficient than the standard BMDA and can use the information in the whole population, thus it is capable of finding and using more correlations to approximate the optimum.

Experiments description: We reproduce the settings of the original BMDA paper (Pelikan & Mühlenbein, 1999). 30 independent runs are performed with 30 and 60 variables, the population size is 1300, selecting 1000 individuals for the standard EDA. 50% of the best individuals are preserved no matter which selection is used (as in the original paper) for the BMDA and the ES-BMDA. Truncation is 50% of the population, and elitism according to the general EDA in Table 6. The annealing schedule for the Boltzmann selection is fixed by initializing $\beta_0 = 0$, $\Delta\beta = 1$, and $\beta_t = \beta_{t-1} + \Delta\beta$. For the Boltzmann and proportional selections the objective function is normalized by applying $f(x)=g(x)-g^{min}/(g^{max}-g^{min}+1)$, in order to avoid numerical problems.

Stopping criterion: To reproduce the results of the original BMDA we use the ordering parameter as stopping criterion (Pelikan & Mühlenbein, 1999). The ordering parameter is defined in Equation 20, where p is the vector of univariate marginal frequencies $p_i(1)$. When $\chi(p) > 0.95$ we stop the algorithm that means that the univariate probabilities are almost 1 or 0.

$$\chi(p) = \sum_{i=1}^{n} \left(p_i(1) - \frac{1}{2} \right)^2 , \qquad (20)$$

Results: Table 11 compares the results obtained by the standard BMDA (denoted by St.), and the Empirical Selection based BMDA (denoted by ES). We report the mean and standard deviation of the evaluations and objective function, as well as the result of a hypothesis test based on the Bootstrap methodology with a significance of 5% (Efron & Tibshirani, 1993). We test that the mean of the ES-BMDA is less than the mean of the standard BMDA, and vice versa, for 30 and 60 variables. For the evaluations test we only use the runs in which the optimum is found. The evaluations comparison is not perform for 60 variables, because most of the runs did not find the optimum. The results bring out evidence about the arguments that the empirical selection based EDAs are more efficient, and that the use of the information in the whole population is an advantage to build optimal solutions, because as shown the ES-BMDA needs less evaluations than the St-BMDA, also, the ES-BMDA is more effective to find the optimum in the 60 dimension runs, so, with the same resources (population size) the ES-BMDA can deliver better results.

8. Perspectives, future work and conclusions

EDAs researchers have approximated the selection distribution since the first approaches (Mühlenbein, 1997; Bosman & Thierens, 2000). This chapter proposes a general method for this purpose. Most of the search distributions used by EDAs are parametric, and the

n		Truncation	Boltzmann	Proportional	Bin.ary Tournament
Deceptive Function of Order 3,Objective Function					
30	St	10 (0)	9.993333(0.02537081)	9.997 (0.01825742)	9.997 (0.01825742)
	ES	10 (0)	10 (0)	9.997 (0.01825742)	9.997 (0.01825742)
	Hyp. Test	N	N	N	N
60	St	19.79 (0.1213431)	19.73 (0.1368362)	19.60667 (0.1818171)	19.81 (0.1028893)
	ES	19.84 (0.1101723)	19.85(0.1252584)	19.80667(0.1080655)	19.85333(0.1166585)
	Hyp. Test	N	ES	ES	N
Evaluations					
30	St	14841.67(783.7887)	14300(482.8079)	24526.67(1497.223)	15925(609.5151)
	ES	14755(619.0023)	14148.33(441.2919)	22923.33(869.2777)	15578.33(578.4467)
	Hyp. Test	N	N	ES	ES
Number of times the optimum was reached (in 30 runs)					
30	St	30	28	29	29
	ES	30	30	29	29
60	St	3	2	0	3
	ES	6	9	3	7

Table 11. Performance comparison between the standard BMDA (St) and the empirical selection distribution based BMDA (ES).

parameters are learned from a sample by counting frequencies. Thus, in addition to the presented algorithms, any other search distribution which uses frequencies can be modified to use the empirical selection distribution. For instance bivariate models (Pelikan & Mühlenbein, 1999) and histograms (Tsutsui et al., 2001) are completely based on frequencies. Another important line of study are clustering based algorithms (Larrañaga & Lozano, 2001), for example the k-means algorithm is based on distances. When using the empirical selection distribution in clustering, instead of using a single point in the position x_i, we use its relative frequency $\hat{p}^S(x_i,t)$. This measurement will move the mean of the cluster to the regions with highest fitness values, helping to perform a better search.
Important issues in EDAs such as diversity and premature convergence can be tackled using the empirical selection distribution. Studies on convergence phases (Grahl et al., 2007) have shown that the maximum likelihood estimated variance might not be the best to perform an optimum search. Thus, a possible line of work is: how to favor diversity using the empirical selection distribution? A possibility is by simply modifying the fitness function into the empirical selection distribution formulae. This line of work may be an alternative to recent proposals on variance scaling (Grahl et al., 2006; Bosman et al., 2007).
Multi-objective applications and how to insert the Pareto dominance in the selection distribution is another possible research line. With respect to this topic the Pareto ranking seems to be the most natural way of tackling this important issue.
Ever since the very first proposed EDAs (Baluja, 1994) to the most recent works (Pelikan et al., 2008), incremental learning has been applied to the learning distribution phase. Future work must contemplate how to insert the empirical selection distribution into incremental approaches, or how to use historical or previous empirical selection distributions.

The selection methods presented are just a sample of the possibilities, other methods such as combined truncation-proportional, truncation-Boltzmann, 3-tournament, etcetera must be explored.

Finally, the advantages of the presented method are summarized as follows:

- it is easy to implement.
- It has a wide range of applications.
- It has low computational as well as analytical cost.
- It avoids being wrongly biased by a single solution or a small set.
- It uses all the information from the population to accurately approximate the selection distribution.
- The perspectives, future use and applications are promising, and the possible lines of work are really extensive.

9. References

Baluja , S. (1994). Population-Based Incremental Learning: A Method for Integrating Genetic Search Based Function Optimization and Competitive Learning. *Technical report, Carnegie Mellon University*, Pittsburgh, PA, USA, 1994.

Bosman, P. A. N.; Grahl, J. & Rothlauf, F. (2007). SDR: A Better Trigger for Adaptive Variance Scaling in Normal EDAs. *In GECCO '07: Proceedings of the 8th annual conference on Genetic and evolutionary computation*, pp. 516-522, ISBN 978-1-59593-697-4, London, UK. July, 2007, ACM.

Bosman, P. A. N. & Thierens, D. (2000). Expanding from Discrete to Continuous Estimation of Distribution Algorithms: The IDEA. *In PPSN VI: Proceedings of the 6th International Conference on Parallel Problem Solving from Nature*, pp. 767-776, ISBN 3-540-41056-2, Paris, France, 2000. Springer-Verlag.

Cooper, G. & Herskovits, E. (1992). A Bayesian Method for the Induction of Probabilistic Networks from Data. *Machine Learning*, Vol. 9, No. 4, (october, 1992), pp. 309-347, ISSN:0885-6125.

Efron, B. & Tibshirani, R.J. (1993). *An Introduction to the Bootstrap*. Chapman and Hall, Monographs on Statistics and Applied Probability, ISBN-13: 9780412042317, New York, 1993.

Grahl, J.; Bosman, P.A. & Rothlauf, F. (2006). The Correlation-Triggered Adaptive Variance Scaling IDEA. *In GECCO '06: Proceedings of the 8th annual conference on Genetic and evolutionary computation*, pp. 397-404, ISBN 1-59593-010-8, Seattle, Washington, USA, July, 2006. ACM.

Grahl, J.; Bosman, P. A. N. & Minner, S. (2007). Convergence Phases, Variance Trajectories, and Runtime Analysis of Continuos EDAs. *In GECCO'07: Proceedings of the 8th annual conference on Genetic and evolutionary computation*, pp. 516-522, ISBN 978-1-59593-697-4, London, UK. July, 2007, ACM.

Larrañaga, P.; Etxeberria, R.; Lozano, J. & Peña, J. (1999). Optimization by Learning and Simulation of Bayesian and Gaussian Networks. *Technical Report EHU-KZAA-IK-4/99*, Department of Computer Science and Artificial Intelligence, University of the Basque Country, 1999.

Larrañaga, P. & Lozano, J. A. (2001). *Estimation of Distribution Algorithms: A New Tool for Evolutionary Computation*. Kluwer Academic Publishers, ISBN 978-0-7923-7466-4, Norwell, MA, USA, 2001.

Lozano, J. A.; Larrañaga, P.; Inza, I. & Bengoetxea, E. (2006). Towards a New Evolutionary Computation, *Studies in Fuzziness and Soft Computing*. Vol. 192, ISBN 978-3-540-29006-3, Springer, 2006.

Müehlenbein, H.; Bendisch, J.; & Voight, H.M. (1996). From recombination of genes to the estimation of distributions II. Continuous parameters. *In PPSN IV: Proceedings of the 4th International Conference on Parallel Problem Solving from Nature*, pp. 188-197, ISBN 978-3-540-61723-5, Berlin, Germany, September, 1996, Springer-Verlag.

Mühlenbein, H. (1997). The Equation for Response to Selection and Its Use for Prediction. *Evolutionary Computation*, Vol. 5, No. 3, September, 1997,pp. 303-346, ISSN 1063-6560.

Mühlenbein, H. & PaaB, G. (1996). From Recombination of Genes to the Estimation of Distributions I. Binary Parameters. *In PPSN IV: Proceedings of the 4th International Conference on Parallel Problem Solving from Nature*, pp. 178-187, ISBN 978-3-540-61723-5, Berlin, Germany, September, 1996. Springer-Verlag.

Pelikan, M.; Goldberg, D. E.; & Cantú-Paz, E. (1999). BOA: The Bayesian Optimization Algorithm. In W. Banzhaf, J. Daida, A. E. Eiben, M. H. Garzon, V. Honavar, M. Jakiela, and R. E. Smith, editors, *Proceedings of the Genetic and Evolutionary Computation Conference GECCO-99*, Vol. I, pp. 525-532, Orlando, FL, USA, 1999. Morgan Kaufmann Publishers, San Fransisco, CA.

Pelikan, M. & Mühlenbein, H. (1999). The Bivariate Marginal Distribution Algorithm. *Advances in Soft Computing Engineering Design and Manufacturing*, pp. 521-535, 1999.

Pelikan, M. ; Sastry, K. & Cantu-Paz, E. (2006). Scalable Optimization via Probabilistic Modeling, *Studies in Computational Intelligence*. Vol. 33, Springer, ISBN: 978-3-540-34953-2.

Pelikan, M.; Sastry, K. & Goldberg, D. E. (2008). iBOA: The Incremental Bayesian Optimization Algorithm. *In GECCO '08: Proceedings of the 2008 Conference on Genetic and Evolutionary Computation*, pp. 455-462, ISBN 978-1-60558-131-6, Atlanta, USA, July, 2008, ACM.

Soto, M. & Ochoa, A. (2000). A Factorized Distribution Algorithm based on Polytrees. *In Proceedings of the 2000 Congress on Evolutionary Computation (CEC 2000)*, pp. 232-237, ISBN: 0-7803-6375-2, La Jolla, CA, USA, July, 2000, IEEE.

Tsutsui, S.; Pelikan, M.; & Goldberg, D. E. (2001). Evolutionary Algorithm using Marginal Histogram Models in Continuous Domain. *Technical Report 2001019, Illinois Genetic Algorithms Laboratory*, 2001.

Yunpeng, C.; Xiaomin, S. & Peifa, J. (2006). Probabilistic Modeling for Continuous EDA with Boltzmann selection and Kullback-Leibeler Divergence. *In GECCO '06: Proceedings of the 8th annual conference on Genetic and evolutionary computation*, pp. 389-396, ISBN 1-59593-010-8, Seattle, Washington, USA, July, 2006. ACM.

Zhang, Q. & Mühlenbein, H. (2004). On the Convergence of a Class of Estimation of Distribution Algorithms. *IEEE Transactions on Evolutionary Computation*, Vol. 8, No. 2, (April, 2004), pp. 127-136, ISSN: 1089-778X.

12

Solving Combinatorial Problems with Time Constrains using Estimation of Distribution Algorithms and Their Application in Video-Tracking Systems

Antonio Berlanga, Miguel A. Patricio, Jesús García, and José M. Molina
Applied Artificial Intelligence Group. Universidad Carlos III de Madrid
Colmenarejo, Madrid,
Spain

1. Introduction

EDAs (Estimation of Distribution Algorithms) present the suitable features to deal with problems requiring a very efficient search: small populations and a few iterations, compared with the more classic approaches to Evolutionary Algorithms (EAs). The fundamental difference of EDAs with classical EAs is that the formers carry out a search of the probability distribution describing the optimal solutions while EAs directly make the search and provide the solutions to the problem with the solutions itself. They share the necessity of codification of solutions by means of binary chains, in the EA terminology they are the "individuals" and the definition of a merit measurement that allows to orient the search direction, the so called "fitness function". In the case of EDAs, operators to manipulate individuals in the search, such as mutation, selections, and crossover, are not needed, since the search is performed directly on the distribution which describes all possible individuals.
In this chapter, authors will evaluate the efficiency of EDAs to solve combinatorial problems with time constrains. Specifically, authors will model the visual data association for real-time video tracking problem as a combinatorial problem. Before the application of EDAs to this real-life combinatorial problem, the authors will discuss the application of EDAs algorithms to a classical combinatorial problem, such as the 0/1 knapsack problem, in order to know the complexity degree of the association problem and to find out the most suitable parameters for real-time video tracking problem [1].
The outline of the chapter will be as follows. First, several EDA algorithms will be presented and their evaluation using the theoretical combinatorial problem of 0/1 knapsack problem, which has similar complexity to the association problem in video tracking systems. Next, the mathematical formulation of the Data Association Problem will be shown. Then, the applications of EDA to data association problem, defining the heuristic and the codification, will be presented. Finally, the authors will show the experiments compare the behaviour of several algorithms, taking the advanced Particles-MS tracking as benchmark, in three scenarios taken from two different sources: the publicly available CVBASE [2] and a DV camcorder.

2. Estimation of Distributions Algorithms (EDAs)

The Estimation of Distribution Algorithms (EDAs) [3] are a family of evolutionary algorithms which represents an alternative to the classical optimization methods. Algorithmically, a Genetic Algorithm and an EDA only differ in the procedure to generate new individuals. EDAs replace the use of an evolving population by a vector that directly codifies the joint probability distribution of vectors corresponding to the best solutions. The crossover and mutation operators are replaced by rules that update the probability distribution. A great advantage of the EDAs on the evolutionary algorithms is that they allow expressing the interactions between variables of the problem by means of the associated joint probability distribution. In addition, they improve the time of convergence and the necessary space of memory for its operation. The algorithm of an EDA is sketched in the following graph.

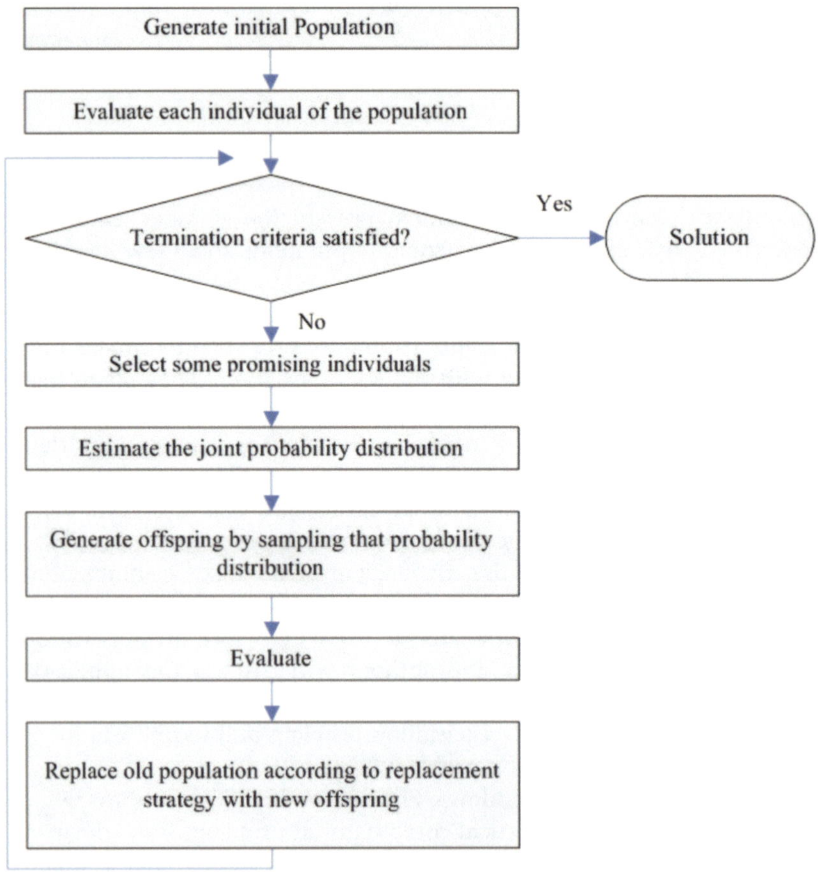

Fig. 1. High level outline of EDA steps

The key point of the use of EDAs is in the estimation of the joint probability distribution. The simplest situation is that in which the joint probability distribution factorizes as a product of univariate and independent distributions, that is to say, there is no dependency between the variables. In this situation the estimation of the probability distribution is made using the marginal frequencies. The problem of association exposed in this work allows this treatment and bases the use of EDAs by the characteristic that allows solving an optimization problem quickly [4], [5]. In the next section, we describe the EDAs more studied and applied to univariate problems and in the appendix the code of each EDA is detailed.

2.1 Description of EDAs algorithms

In this section, we depict the several concepts on the algorithm used in our work. These algorithms are UMDA (Univariate Marginal Distribution Algorithm) [6], PBil (Population-Based Incremental Learning) [7] and cGA (The Compact Genetic Algorithm) [8].

2.1.1 UMDA. Univariate Marginal Distribution Algorithm

In the UMDA [6] the joint probability distribution is estimated as the relative frequencies of the variables' values stored in a data set. Independence between the variables is assumed and theoretically it has been demonstrated that UMDA works almost perfectly with linear problems and rather well when the dependencies are little significant.

In UMDA can appear some problems associated to the genetic drift, and some modifications have been proposed such as the correction of Laplace to the calculation of the relative frequency [9]. In this case the relative frequency is estimated as:

$$p_l(x) = \prod_{i=1}^{n} \frac{\sum_{j=1}^{N} \delta_j\left(X_i = x_i \mid D_{l-1}^{Se}\right) + 1}{N + r_i}, \qquad r_i \text{ different values of } X_i \tag{1}$$

There are theoretical evidences that demonstrate that UMDA approximates their behaviour to a canonical genetic algorithm (GA) with uniform crossover.

2.1.2 PBIL. Population-Based Incremental Learning

The PBIL (Population-Based Incremental Learning) [7] mixes the search applied by genetic algorithms with the competitive learning, applying a Hebbian rule to update the vector of probabilities. It has been empirically demonstrated that PBil works equal or better than GA in problems in which GA works well and fails in the problems that GA fails. The main difference with GA is that PBIL does not use a population of solutions that evolves, replacing it by a vector of probabilities. This change presents some advantages:

- The algorithm is simpler, for example it does not require arrangements.
- The capacity of representation by means of a vector of probabilities in PBIL is minor who the one of a population of solutions in GA, therefore the convergence is faster. Search in exploration is sacrificed to have a higher rate of convergence.

In order to apply the PBil algorithm it is necessary to give value to four parameters: population size, learning rate, probability of mutation and mutation rate. To the association problem the probability of mutation is set to zero with the purpose of accelerating the convergence of the algorithm.

The main parameter that will affect the speed of convergence is the learning rate, whichever greater is its value, more quickly finalizes the search, losing, of course, quality in the solutions. The PBil algorithm originally was oriented to functions optimization, but has been efficient treating combinatorial optimization problems of complexity NP, in terms to find solutions of the same quality that GA needing smaller number of function evaluations.

2.1.3 CGA. The Compact Genetic Algorithm

The cGA [8] simulates the performance of a canonical genetic algorithm with uniform crossover. It is the simplest EDA, and only needs a parameter, the population size that has the effect of a learning rate.

As the authors of CGA suggest, this algorithm has an important additional utility, allows discriminating quickly when a problem is easy to be treated by means of evolutionary algorithms.

3. Adjustment of the EDA parameters using KP0/1 problem

In order to fit the parameters of each one of EDAs applied to tracking systems, we evaluated them using a theoretical combinatorial problem with similar complexity and well-known optimal solution. The objective for these theoretical experiments is two-fold:

- Compare the number of function evaluations that needs each algorithm to obtain solutions of a given quality. This efficiency metric allows us choose the suitable algorithm for the real-time video association problem
- Fit the parameters of each algorithm to obtain the best relation between the quality of solutions and speed of execution

It has been taken three KP0/1 problems [10] with increasing difficulty (10, 20 and 40 objects). These sizes correspond with the practical problem dealt since the codification of the association matrix will be, in the cases of higher-density also around 40. The size of the search space scales with 2^n. For the three problems, the optimal solution is known and not exist correlation between the variables; this is the worst case. The knapsack 0/1 problem of (KP0/1) is a NP-complete combinatorial optimization problem and, for example, the difficulty to be solved was used to make the first algorithm of generalized public key encryption [11]. The knapsack 0/1 problem is defined as:

$$
\begin{aligned}
&\text{Maximize} \sum_{j=1}^{n} c_j x_j \\
&\text{Subject to} \sum_{j=1}^{n} a_j x_j \le b \qquad (2) \\
&x_j \in \{0,1\}, \forall j, c_j > 0, a_j > 0, \sum_j c_j > b, \max_j \{a_j\} \le b
\end{aligned}
$$

The following figures contain the comparison of performances by UMDA, PBIL, CGA and the canonical GA with uniform applied in this work. The number of evaluations of fitness necessary to obtain a certain probability of success has been plotted. An algorithm is successful when it finds the optimal solution and the success probability is calculated with the frequency of success in 50 executions with different random seeds. The parameters of the different algorithms are obtained by trail-and-error treating to diminish the number of fitness evaluations.

The graphs show, for all the algorithms and problems, the exponential growth of the number of evaluations when it is wanted to reach great percentage of success. In the three KP0/1 the UMDA has obtained better results, it needs fewer evaluations than the rest to obtain solutions of the same quality. The PBIL has a behaviour similar to the UMDA treating

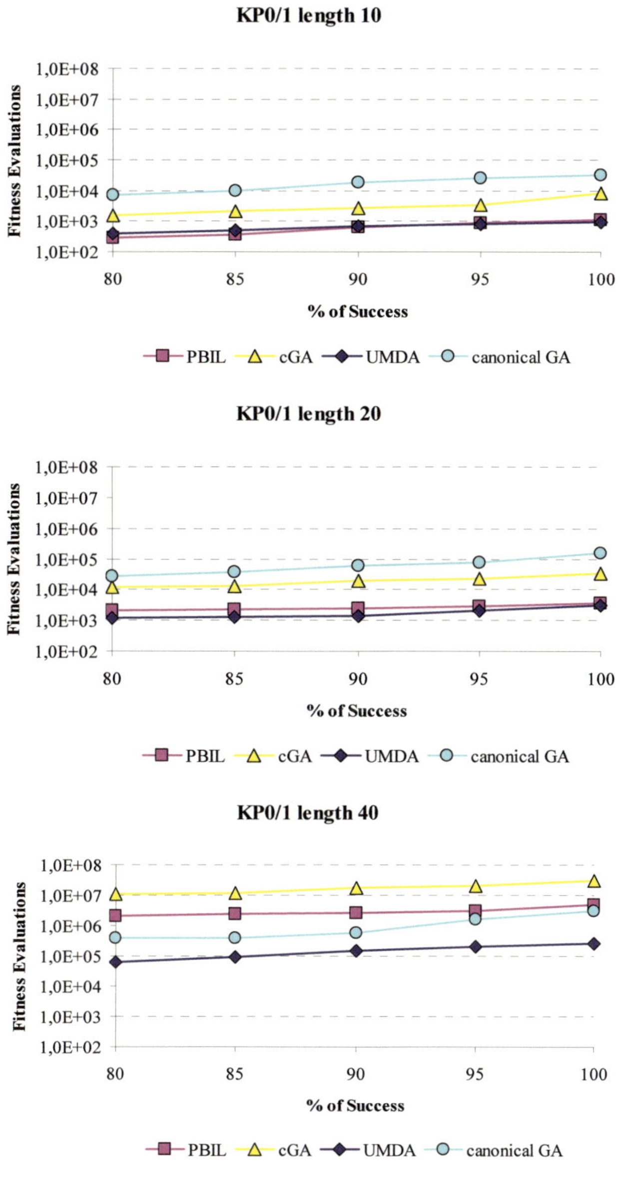

Fig. 2. Comparison of the number of fitness evaluations versus the probability of success of the EDAS and canonical GA to solve several KP0/1 of different complexity

the simplest problems but it behaves worse than the canonical GA when it is applied to the most difficult problem. The CGA shows the worse behaviour, if for the two simpler problems has an intermediate behaviour between UMDA and the canonical GA, for the KP0/1 of 40 objects has instability respect to the parameter that represents the size of the population, N.

In the following figure, the variation of the number of evaluations of fitness based on the difficulty of the problem when the percentage of success is the 100% has been plotted.

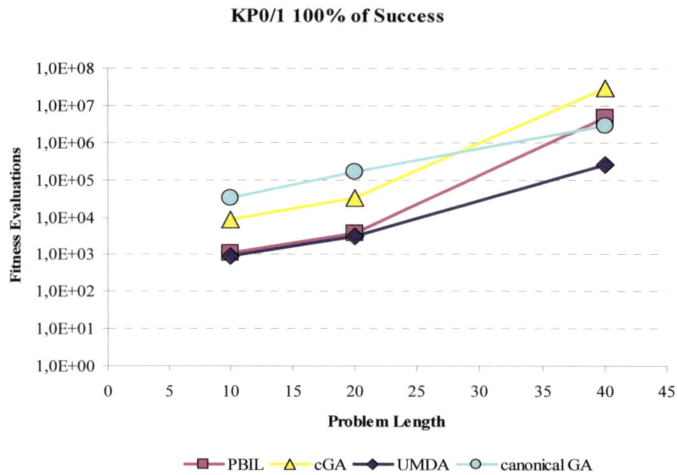

Fig. 3. Evolution of the number of evaluations of fitness based on the length of the problem.

It is observed that the UMDA is the algorithm with smaller number of evaluations of fitness needs to reach the 100% of success. The behaviour of the canonical GA is remarkable, it scales an order of magnitude whenever the difficulty of the problem is duplicated, while this increase is greater for the rest of algorithms. However, for simpler problems the canonical GA needs almost two orders of magnitude more evaluations of fitness to obtain the same quality.

As it has been previously indicated, the objective of this work is to solve the combinatorial optimization problem that appears in the association problem from blobs to tracks for real-time video tracking. The analysis of the EDAs and canonical GA on KP0/1 has allowed us to discriminate the algorithm that presents greater potential of application and its parameters. These parameters are in Table 1 and will be used later to solve the association problem. In section 5, the results of these algorithms applied to the association problem will be presented.

	Parameters that were applied in KP0/1		
	Length 10	**Length 20**	**Length 40**
PBIL	N=1 M=9 LR=0.05	N=1 M=20 LR=0.05	N=8 M=1000 LR=0.05
CGA	N=50	N=200	N=20000
UMDA	N=1 M=9	N=8 M=50	N=8 M=250
GA	M=100 $P_{mutation}$=0.01 $P_{crossover}$=0.9 Elitism=20%	M=200 $P_{mutation}$=0.01 $P_{crossover}$=0.9 Elitism=20%	M=800 $P_{mutation}$=0.01 $P_{crossover}$=0.9 Elitism=20%

Table 1. Values of the parameters of the EDAs and GA that allow to obtain a 100% of success in the problem of the KP0/1

4. Formulation of data association problem

The data association problem, also known as motion correspondence in the case of video analysis, is the most important challenge in multi-target video tracking systems. The complexity of scenarios, expressed in the number of interacting targets, irregular motion, presence of background noise, etc., presents a collection of problems that must be solved to guarantee a robust performance and so reliable output with a certain level of accuracy and stability.

Among alternative approaches, Bayesian inference methods have gained a high reputation for visual processing and estimation [12], [13], [14], due the potential to provide a solution as close to the theoretically optimal as possible. Closeness to theoretical optimum will depend on the computation capability to execute numeric approximations and also on the reliability of statistical models for target appearance, dynamics, likelihoods, a priori densities, etc. It usually becomes an intractable approach for most realistic situations and it is necessary the use of heuristic approaches and simplifications.

4.1 Problem statement. Motion correspondence as a search

The visual tracking problem involves an environment that changes with time [15]. The estimation of the number of objects in a scene, together with their instantaneous location, cinematic state and additional characteristics (shape, colour, identification, etc.) is the problem addressed by a visual tracker. The objects in the scene can be defined as a set of entities described by a set of characteristics that evolve in time (position, velocity, colour, shape, temperature, etc.). In this sense, environment could be defined in an instant as a set of objects, where each object is defined by a set of characteristics in this instant:

$$E[k]= \{O_1[t],\ldots, O_N[t]\} \tag{3}$$

So there are N[k] real objects moving in the covered area at time instant t[k].

The description of the objects is expressed in a vector state space, $x_i \in \Re^d$. For instance a common simplified representation of objects in 2D camera plane contains position of object centroid, together with bounds (width and length) and their velocity and scale derivatives: $x_i = [x \quad y \quad vx \quad vy \quad w \quad h \quad vw \quad vh]^t$ (d=8).

In the case of visual sensor, the phase of image preprocessing acquires some characteristics of the objects (observation), perturbed by the measurement process. The acquisition process is related with the digital image acquisition and the detection process. The first one defines the resolution in pixels and frames by second of the sequence of captured images; the second one defines the objects in the captured image. In the case of visual sensor, observed characteristic are more complex than conventional sensors, for example: color (or gray level), the shape, the skeleton, the contour, etc. and the position is an estimation from the detected object (typically the centroid). We will consider in this work as preprocessing phase the background subtraction to detect moving objects in monocular images [12]. After background subtraction and thresholding, we have a binary image where a detected object is observed through a set of compact regions (blobs), where a blob is a set of adjacent binary detected pixels in this instant:

$$Z^i[k] = \{b_1^i[k],\ldots,b_{M^i}^i[k]\} \tag{4}$$

where M^i is the number of blobs that are due to i-th object (unobservable).
The problem is that both N[k] and i superindex in observations are hidden, they must be deduced from the data. The only observable amount is the global set of blobs appearing in the foreground binary image: $Z[k]=\{b_1[k],\ldots b_M[k]\}$. So, the basic problem in video data association is the re-connection of blobs to be used to update tracks, searching the collection of blobs corresponding to each track $x_i[k]$, $Z^i[k]$. The final object characteristics result from the combination of the blob characteristics that belong to the object
As mentioned in the introduction, target splitting and merging is a distinguishing problem in video data association with respect to other sensors. With other sensors such as radar, each acquired data, a plot, comes from a single object but, in visual sensor, acquired data, a blob, could be the result of several objects (merging), and several blobs can be originated by the same object (split). Blobs corresponding to separate objects can be merged when they come close together in the image, splitting again when they separate. The problem gets more complex since the image may contain false observations due to noise or target fragmentation, so that the total observations may be some arbitrarily large set of observations. This makes it difficult to provide unique track labels for different interacting objects, which is a fundamental capacity required for the usual applications of machine vision such as surveillance, scene analysis (sports), automatic annotation, etc. The problem would be aminorated by using a camera installed in a pole high enough so objects are viewed from near vertical geometry but this is often not possible in practical surveillance configurations (for instance, indoor scenes)
A Bayesian framework to determine the best estimation, X[k], inferred from available measurements, Z[k], is the one targeted at obtaining the maximum a posteriori probability of estimated state, conditioned to the whole set of observations:

$$\hat{X}[k] = \underset{X[k]}{\arg\max}\, P(X[k] \mid Z[k], Z[k-1], \ldots, Z[0]) \quad (5)$$

Where $\hat{X}[k]$ denotes both the number of targets and their state in the scene at time instant t[k],

$\hat{X}[k] = \hat{x}_{1\ldots N_k}[k] = \{\hat{x}_1[k], \ldots, \hat{x}_{N_k}[k]\}$, where $\hat{x}^i[k] \in \Re^d$, in our case d=8 as indicated above. Notice that objects forming state X[k] have a set structure instead of array, since the order in X[k]to represent the real objects is irrelevant.
So a joint estimation problem appears about the number of objects, N[k], and their parameters, $\hat{x}_i[k]$. A complete problem formulation for the multi-target joint estimation problem would take into account the different configurations in the number of objects and their characteristics (shape and motion state). The classical inference formulation applies the Bayes theorem to rearrange the problem in a recursive formulation:

$$\begin{aligned} &P(X[k] \mid Z[k], Z[k-1], \ldots, Z[0]) = \\ &\frac{1}{c} P(Z[k] \mid X[k]) \int \left[P(X[k] \mid X[k-1]) P(X[k-1] \mid Z[k-1], \ldots, Z[0]) \right] dX[k-1] \end{aligned} \quad (6)$$

where the integral in the joint problem would extend over the whole space of predicted state, P(X[k] | X[k-1]) considering both the number of objects and their corresponding states, and c is the normalization constant to guarantee the result is a probability density. In this formulation, and dropping time index for simplicity, P(Z | X) is the probability of observing a particular image Z given a certain current state X. It is the likelihood function and has a fundamental impact in the result. In our case we will particularize the observation process to the analysis of the binarized image resulting from the background subtraction and thresholding, so that

$$Z[k]=\{b_1,\ldots,b_{Mk}[k]\} \tag{7}$$

This multiple-target tracking problem can be split into two interdependent problems, data association (or motion correspondence) between measurements and objects, and state estimation, to update vectors $\hat{x}_j[k],\ j \in \{1,\ldots,N[k]\}$ with the assigned measurements.

Data association is the sequential decision process which takes, for each frame, the available measurements and assigns to the tracked targets up to that time instant. The assignment problem can be considered as part of the maximization of a posteriori likelihood of observations. So, if we consider a particular configuration of X[k] with N[k] tracks, its likelihood will depend on the sequential series of data assignments:

$$P(Z[k] \mid X[k]) = P(Z[k] \mid A[k], Z[k-1], A[k-1], Z[k-2], \ldots, A[0], Z[0]) \tag{8}$$

where the assignment matrix $A[k] = \{a_{ij}[k]\}$ is defined as $a_{ij}[k]=1$ if blob $b_i[k]$ is assigned to track $\hat{x}_j[k]$; and $a_{ij}[k]=0$ otherwise. In k-th frame there are M[k] blobs extracted to be assigned, $b[k]=\{b_1[k],\ldots,b_{Mk}[k]\}$, and the objects tracked up to them (last assignment of blobs was at frame k-1) are: $X[k-1]= \{O_1[k-1],\ldots,O_{Nk-1}[k-1]\}$.

The size of matrix A[k], (1+N[k])xM[k], changes with time, since i=1,…,M[k] represents the blobs extracted from the k-th frame, whose number depends on the variable effects mentioned above during the detection process. Furthermore, N[k] represents the objects in the scene, whose number may also dynamically change when objects appear and disappear in the scene. Special case j=0 is considered to represent assignment of blobs to "null track" at current time, which are used to initialize new objects or are discarded.

5. Multi-blob data association with EDAs

The association problem has been defined as a search over possible blob assignments. This problem could be defined as minimizing a heuristic function to evaluate blob assignments by an efficient algorithm (Estimation of Distribution Algorithm). The heuristic function takes a Bayesian approach to model the errors in observations. The formulation of data association as a minimization problem solved by a genetic technique is not a handicap with respect to the required operation in real time. A worst-case number of operations can be fixed and bound the time consumed by the algorithm, if we restrict the maximum number of evaluations. Then, given a certain population size, the algorithm will run a number of generations limited by this bound on the number of evaluations. The most important aspect is that the EDA should converge to acceptable solutions with these conditions of limited population size and number of generations.

5.1 Encoding and efficient search with EDA algorithms

In the mathematical formulation defined in section 2, the association consists of finding the appropriate values for assignment matrix **A**, where element **A**(i, j) is 1 if blob i is assigned to object j and 0 in the opposite case. In order to be able to use the techniques of evolutionary algorithms, the matrix **A** is codified in a string of bits, being the size of matrix **A** NxM, with N the number of extracted blobs and M the number of objects in the scene. A first possibility for problem encoding was tried with a string of integer numbers representing the possible M objects to be assigned for each blob, including the "null" track 0, as shown in Figure 4:

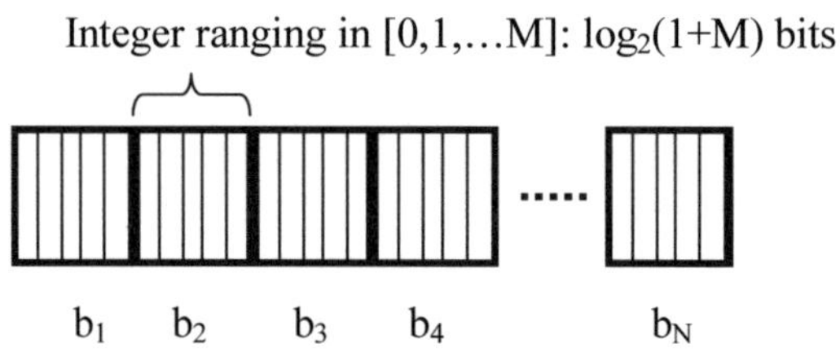

Fig. 4. Simple encoding for blob assignment

This encoding requires strings of $N\log_2(1+M)$ bits and has the problem of constraining search to solutions in which each blob can belong to one object at most. This could be a problem in situations where images from different objects get overlapped and may leave some tracks unassigned and lost.

Then, a direct encoding of A matrix was used for general solutions, where the positions in the string represent the assignations of blobs to tracks. With this codification, where individuals need $N(1+M)$ bits, a blob can be assigned to several objects:

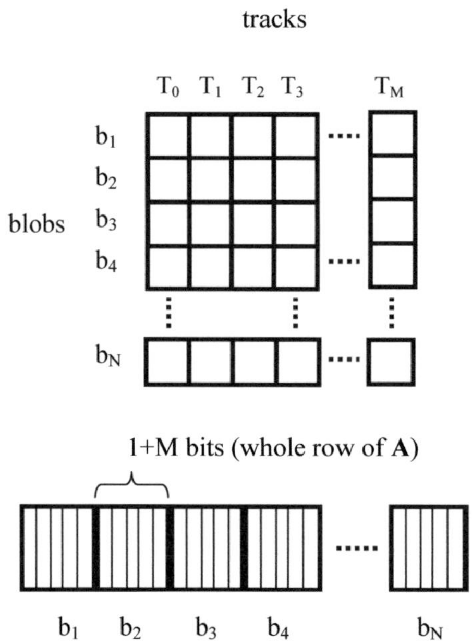

Fig. 5. Direct encoding for whole A matrix

Finally, in order to allow and effective search, the initial individuals are not randomly generated but they are fixed to solutions in which each blob is assigned to the closest object. So, the search is performed over combinations starting from this solution in order to optimize the heuristic after changing any of this initial configuration. Besides, for the case of EDA algorithms, the vector probabilities are constrained to be zero for the case of very far pairs (IF dCentroid(i,j)>GATE_THRESHOLD0=> p_{ij}=0) and those blobs which fall in spatial gates of more than one track have a non-zero change probability.

5.2 Description of the fitness function

Fitness function supplies to the evolutionary algorithms with a score to evaluate the assignment of grouping blobs to active tracks. In this case, the potential assignments explored by EDA algorithms are qualified following the heuristic described in this section. The tracking system keeps information about the centroid position, rectangle bounds and velocity for each track by means of a Kalman filter updating a track state vector, $\hat{x}^i[k]$, adapted to the dynamics of interesting objects. Therefore, we are able to evaluate the similarity between the potential assignment explored by evolutionary algorithm and the prediction of target accordingly to Kalman filter in every frame. Moreover, the fitness function should consider those assignments that leave confirmed tracks with no updating blobs.

Let $O_i[k+1]$ be the set of blobs assigned to track *j* by an individual in evolutionary algorithm for k+1 frame. This set of blobs are represented by its bounding box, specifically by its centroid pixel coordinates, width and height (x_j^e, y_j^e, w_j^e and h_j^e). They are those blobs corresponding to indexes i such that **A**ij[k+1]=1. Track *j* contains the prediction provided by Kalman filter, $\hat{x}_j[k+1|k]$, represented by its centroid pixel coordinates, width and height i (x_j^u, x_j^u, w_j^u and h_j^u).

Let d_j be the normalized distance between the evolutionary proposal and predicted track *j*:

$$d_j = \frac{|x_j^u - x_j^e|}{w_j^u} + \frac{|y_j^u - y_j^e|}{h_j^u} \tag{9}$$

Let s_j be the normalized size similarity between the evolutionary proposal and predicted track *j*:

$$s_j = \frac{|w_j^u - w_j^e|}{w_j^u} + \frac{|h_j^u - h_j^e|}{h_j^u} \tag{10}$$

Let I be the foreground image that we are processing. We define $I(x,y)$ as true, if and only if the pixel (x,y) is in the bounding box of the evolutionary proposal for track *j*. We define the Density Ratio, dr_j, of track *j* as:

$$dr_j = \frac{Card\{I(x,y)\}}{x_j^e * y_j^e} \tag{11}$$

The fitness function, F_i, of an assignment *i* that we have to minimize is:

$$F_i = \sum_{j=1}^{M} (d_j + s_j - dr_j) + ap + lt \tag{12}$$

where, M represents the number of tracks in the frame. So, we incorporate besides two penalization ratios to the fitness function, corresponding to the probabilities of false positive detection (PFA), and probabilities of true positive missing (PD):

- *ap* (assignment penalization). A penalization value is added to the fitness function every time a blob is assigned to a distant track.
- *lt* (lost track). A high value is added every time no blob is assigned to one track.

6. Results

In this section we present the comparison between EDA algorithms presented in this work and a benchmark algorithm based on a combination of Particle Filter [16], [17] and Mean Shift [18], [19] algorithms.

6.1 Video data set definition

The datasets used throughout this paper are employed with three different scenes. These datasets are from two different sources: the publicly available CVBASE dataset [2] and a DV camcorder. The datasets are quite diverse in their technical aspects and the quality of the image sequences radically differ from poor to excellent along with their pixel resolutions.

The following will describe the 3 datasets to gain an understanding of its scene characteristics:

- **Maritime scenes (BOAT).** The videos were recorded in an outdoor scenario using a DV videorecorder. The videos have a high quality with a resolution of 720x480 pixels with 15 fps. The videos feature several boats in an outdoor environment lit by the sun. The videos are very interesting due to the complex segmentation of maritime scenes. The sea has continuous movement, which contributes to the creation of a great amount of noisy blobs.
- **Squash tournament (SQUASH).** The videos are from the CVBASE dataset and were taken on a tournament of recreative players. The videos were recorded in S-VHS videorecorder, using a birds-eye view with wide angle lens. The videos were digitized to digital video format with 25 fps, resolution 384x576 and M-JPEG compression. The selected video is a zenithal record of two players playing squash. They are with close proximity to each other, similar modality of dress, slightly faster movements and constant crossings between players, which make for a challenging sequence.
- **Handball match (HANDBALL).** The videos are also from the CVBASE dataset and have the same characteristics than the squash tournament sequences. Players do not leave the court during the match, there are constant crossings among players with occlusions and disocclusions and the number of objects (players) to track is quite high. These conditions make also for a challenging sequence.

6.2 Evaluation metric definition

Before comparing the obtained results of algorithms used for visual tracking accomplishment, the first step is to determine the metric that allows making the comparisons of the algorithms behaviour. A specific quality measurement of the association has not been used and the global behaviour has been observed. In the analysis, a special emphasis in the speed of algorithms convergence is made in order to evaluate the application of the proposal development in real-time video tracking. The measures taken into account are: Tracks per Frame, Frames per Second and Time per Track.

Measurement TPF (Tracks per Frame) is used to compare the behaviour of the tracking algorithms in terms of continuity of the tracks. An optimal tracker would have to obtain the value referred as "ideal". When the obtained value is below to this "ideal" value, it means the tracker lost in the continuity of the tracks (merge effect) and, conversely, when it is over of "ideal" value, the tracker had an excess of tracks (split effect). The standard deviation of TPF allows discriminating between the behaviours with very similar averages but worse quality (greater deviation). FPS (Frames per Second) is the rate of processed images having applied the tracking algorithms; high values imply a capacity of greater processing. Column TPT (Time per Track) shows the time in milliseconds that the updating algorithm of tracks uses in the association logic, in this case the association is solved by EDAS and GA. The particles filter algorithm incorporates its own strategy of association. The rest of the time necessary to make the tracking (detection and filtrate) is common for all and therefore is not compared.

Besides, in order to grasp the algorithms' behaviour regarding convergence, bi-dimensional histograms with the number of evaluations necessary to obtain the solution and final fitness values are also presented. They have been computed depending on the size of combinatorial search space of data association hypotheses. This size is given, accordingly to encoding in section 4.4 and for each frame processed, by $2^{N(1+M)}$, being N the number of blobs and M the number of active tracks. The relative frequencies are indicated with levels of grey: black is 100%, white is 0%. It is expected that the size of search space makes more difficult the convergence, requiring more evaluations and/or converging to worse solutions.

6.3 Results and discussion

In the following tables the quality measurements of the EDAs, GA and particles filter applied to BOAT, SQUASH and HANDBALL sequences are presented. The parameters of the algorithms, size of the population, number of iterations, rate of variation, etc. have been set corresponding to the problem KP0/1 of length 20.

Recording BOAT displays a scene in the sea with three objects that remain visible in all the frames. Table 2 shows the values of the quality parameters and standard deviations obtained for this scenario.

	mean TPF (ideal=3)	sd TPF	FPS	mean TPT (millisecond)	sd TPT
CGA	2.98	0.07	4.29	2.22	0.08
UMDA	2.93	0.17	4.26	4.16	0.75
PBIL	2.98	0.07	4.04	9.14	1.93
MSPF	2.98	0.07	2.33	67.93	0.78
GA	2.93	0.17	2.21	79.37	18.23

Table 2. Measures of quality of the algorithms applied to BOAT

The results obtained for sequence BOAT show clearly the advantage of the EDAS on GA and particle filter. Observing the referring columns TPF, the quality of the tracking is the same for all the algorithms, very close to the ideal value. UMDA and GA are slightly less stable compared to the rest, but the difference is negligible. The speed that the EDAS solve the combinatorial problem of the association of blobs to tracks is quite superior (50%) to GA and particles filter.
In the following test video, SQUASH, given the normal dynamics of game, there are many situations in which the players move very close and with abrupt movements, which suppose an increase of the complexity of the association problem. The results of the quality measures are in the following table.

	mean TPF (ideal=2)	sd TPF	FPS	mean TPT (millisecond)	sd TPT
CGA	1.88	0.24	14.22	0.78	0.15
UMDA	1.87	0.25	14.40	1.04	0.18
PBIL	1.89	0.23	12.31	4.02	1.48
MSPF	1.90	0.24	5.74	53.22	2.86
GA	1.87	0.26	6.64	37.65	13.58

Table 3. Measures of quality of the algorithms applied to SQUASH

The quality of the tracking has descended due to the increase in the complexity of the scene. The best quality is obtained with the particle filter but all the values are very close. The required time to process the scene continues being very advantageous for the EDAS, superior to the double that the time obtained with the particle filter. Again, have been used the parameters of the algorithms (see Table 1) that were fit when solving the problem of the KP0/1 of length 20.
Finally we show the results on an extraordinarily complex scene. A zenithal camera records a handball match (HANDBALL). In the sequence, there are seen 14 players and 2 referees. Due to the great number of players the accumulations of several of them in small regions of the field are frequent. And the size of space search is in the best case, when only there is a blob to assign by track, of $2^{14x14} = 2^{196}$ different hypotheses. Compared with the previous scenes this is 100 greater orders of magnitude. In this case, the parameters of the algorithms corresponding to the problem of the KP0/1 of length 40 have been applied.

	mean TPF (ideal=16)	sd TPF	FPS	mean TPT (millisecond)	sd TPT
CGA	10.77	1.10	0.81	109.59	9.78
UMDA	7.35	1.01	0.31	1554.12	974.84
PBIL	11.64	1.22	0.66	17.20	13.23
MSPF	12.92	0.52	0.56	160.18	1.21
GA	12.40	1.82	0.04	43202.27	9343.08

Table 4. Measures of quality of the algorithms applied to HANDBALL

In Table 4 it can be noticed that the reduction in the quality of the tracking is very high. The value obtained in FPS implies that these algorithms cannot be used in these conditions to make real-time video tracking.

7. Conclusions

In this chapter, the association problem for real-time tracking in video was formulated as search in a hypotheses space. It is defined as a combinatorial problem, constraining the computational load to allow image processing in real time of the sequence of frames.
Evolutionary Computation techniques have been applied for solving this search problem, in particular Estimation Distribution Algorithms (EDA) that shows an efficient computational behaviour for real-time problems. The authors have done an exhaustive analysis of EDAs algorithms using several KP0/1 problems. These experimentations help the authors to know the complexity degree of the association problem and to find out the most suitable parameters for real-time video tracking problem.
From the parameters obtained in analyzing the KP0/1 problems, the author have been carried out a wide comparison among standard Genetic Algorithm, Particle Filtering based on Mean-Shift weight and several EDA algorithms: CGA, UMDA and PBIL. Three video recordings of different complexity and problematic characteristics have been used to analyze the algorithms performance. Results show the efficiency of EDA algorithms to solve the combinatorial problem in real time and the capacity to be applied in video tracking systems.

8. Acknowledgements

This work was supported in part by Projects CICYT TIN2008-06742-C02-02/TSI, CICYT TEC2008-06732-C02-02/TEC, SINPROB, CAM MADRINET S-0505 /TIC/0255 and DPS2008-07029-C02-02.

9. References

[1] M.A. Patricio, Castanedo, F., Berlanga, A., Perez, O., Garcia, J., & Molina, J. (2008). Computational Intelligence in Multimedia Processing: Recent Advances, chap. Computational Intelligence in Visual Sensor Networks: Improving Video Processing Systems, pp. 351-377. Springer Verlag.

[2] Machine Vision Group, University of Ljubljana: Cvbase '06 workshop on computer vision based analysis in sport environments, found at url: http://vision.fe.uni-lj.si/cvbase06/ (2006)

[3] P. Larrañaga and J. A. Lozano, "Estimation of Distribution Algorithms: A New Tool for Evolutionary Computation". Kluwer Academic Publishers, 2001.

[4] M. Pelikan, D. E. Goldberg and E. Cantú-paz, "Linkage Problem, Distribution Estimation and Bayesian Networks", *Evolutionary Computation* 8(3):311-340, 2000.

[5] P. Bosman, T. Alderliesten, "Evolutionary Algorithms for Medical Simulations - A Case Study in Minimally-Invasive Vascular Interventions", in *Proc. of the 7th Int. Conf. on Genetic and Evolutionary Computation* GECCO '05, 2005.

[6] H. Mühlenbein, "The equation for response to selection and its use for prediction", *Evolutionary Computation*, 5:303–346, 1998.

[7] S. Baluja, "Population based incremental learning: A method for integrating genetic search based function optimization and competitive learning", Technical Report No. CMU-CS-94-163, Carnegie Mellon University, Pittsburgh, Pennsylvania, 1994.

[8] G. Harik, F. Lobo and D. Goldberg, "The Compact Genetic Algorithm", *IEEE Transactions on Evolutionary Computation*, vol. 3, no. 4, 1999.

[9] B. Cestnik, "Estimating probabilities: A crucial task in machine learning", in L. C. Aiello, ed. *Proc. of the 9th European Conference on Artificial Intelligence*, pp. 147-149. Pitman Publishing, 1990.

[10] D. Pisinger, "Where are the hard knapsack problems?", *Computers & Operations Research*, vol. 32, issue 9, pp. 2271-2284, 2005.

[11] R. Merkle and M. Hellman, "Hiding and signatures in trapdoor knapsacks", *IEEE Trans. Information Theory*, 24:525-530, 1978.

[12] Francois Fleuret, Jerome Berclaz, Richard Lengagne, and Pascal Fua. "Multicamera People Tracking with a Probabilistic Occupancy Map" IEEE Transactions on Pattern Analysis and Machine Intelligence, VOL. 30, NO. 2, FEBRUARY 2008, pp 267-282

[13] C. Rasmussen and G. D. Hager, "Probabilistic data association methods for tracking complex visual objects," IEEE Transactions on Pattern Analysis and Machine Intelligence, vol. 23, no. 6, pp. 560–576, June 2001.

[14] I. J. Cox and S. L. Hingorani. "An efficient implementation of reid's multiple hypothesis tracking algorithm and its evaluation for the purpose of visual tracking. IEEE Transaction on Pattern Analysis and Machine Intelligence, 18(2) Feb 1996. pp 138–150.

[15] A. Loza A, Miguel A. Patricio M A, J. Garcia J, J.M. Molina. "Advanced algorithms for real-time video tracking with multiple targets". 10th International Conference on Control, Automation, Robotics and Vision, ICARCV 2008. Hanoi, Vietnam. Dec 17-20, 2008.

[16] M. S. Arulampalam, S. Maskell, N. Gordon, and T. Clapp, "A tutorial on particle filters for online nonlinear/non-gaussian bayesian tracking", *IEEE Transactions on Signal Processing*, vol. 50, no. 2, pp. 174–188, 2002.

[17] S. A. Branko Ristic and N. Gordon, "Beyond the Kalman Filter: Particle Filters for Tracking Applications", Artech House Publishers, 2004.

[18] D. Comaniciu, V. Ramesh and P. Meer, "Real-time tracking of non-rigid objects using mean shift" in US Patent and Trademark Office, 2000.

[19] D. Comaniciu and P. Meer, "Mean shift: A robust approach toward feature space analysis", *IEEE Trans. Pattern Analysis and Machine Intelligence*, vol. 24, pp. 603-619, 2002.

13

Artificial Societies and Social Simulation using Ant Colony, Particle Swarm Optimization and Cultural Algorithms

Alberto Ochoa[1,ض], Arturo Hernández[2], Laura Cruz[3], Julio Ponce[4], Fernando Montes[5,ض], Liang Li[6] and Lenka Janacek[7]
[1]University of Juarez City,
[ض] ISTC-CNR,
[2]CIMAT,
[3]ITCM,
[4]Aguascalientes University,
[5,ض] Veracruzana University,
[6]University of Singapore,
[7]Zilina University
[1,2,3,4,5]México,
[ض]Italy,
[6]Singapore
[7]Slovak Republic

1. Introduction

The proposal of this chapter is to explain the implementation of collective intelligent techniques to improve results in artificial societies and social simulation using diverse concepts such as argumentation, negotiation and reputation models to improve social simulation of artificial societies implementing dioramas, and multivariable analysis in different application domains for example Logistics. These techniques will be useful for answering diverse queries after gathering general information about a given topic. This kind of collective intelligence will be characterized by: ant colony, particle swarm optimization, and cultural algorithms, each one of these implementing diverse models or agents for simulate a social behaviour. Intelligent agents are used to obtain information to take decisions that try to improve the heuristic optimization needed in different application and fields of knowledge.

First, in section 1 of this paper, we approach different concepts related with Artificial Societies and Social Simulation using different strategies to analyze and model the necessary information to support the correct decisions of the evolving models. In other sections we explain the way to generate a specific behaviour with collective-intelligence techniques –ant colony (section 2), particle swarm optimization (section 3), and cultural algorithms (section 4). In section 5 we apply this knowledge in diverse fields and application domains that needs a heuristic optimization and the more innovative perspectives of each technique. In section 6 we analyse three cases of study: Logistics using a point of view of each one of these techniques (Ant Colony, Particle Swarm Optimization and Cultural Algorithms); Stratagems in an intelligent game board (Cultural Algorithms), and a Friendship Algorithm to demostrate the concept of Six Degrees of Separation in Societies of Memory-Alpha (Cultural Algorithms). Finally, in section 7 we provide our conclusions and our main future research in each technique.

2. Social simulation: basic concepts.

Social simulation is the modeling or simulation, usually with a computer, of social phenomena (e.g., cooperation, competition, markets, social networks dynamics, among others). A subset within social simulations are Agent Based Social Simulations (ABSS) which are an amalgam of computer simulations, agent-based modeling, and the social sciences.

History and Development

The birth of agent based model as a model for social systems was primarily brought by computer scientist (Reynolds, 1994). (Epstein and Axtell, 1996) developed the first large-scale agent model, the Sugarscape, to simulate and explore the role of social phenomena such as seasonal migrations, pollution, sexual reproduction, combat, transmission of diseases, and even culture, more recently.

Types of Simulation and Modeling

Social simulation can refer to a general class of strategies for understanding social dynamics using computers to simulate social systems. Social simulation allows for a more systematic way of viewing the possibilities of outcomes. There are four major types of social simulation:

1. system level simulation.
2. agent based simulation.
3. system level modeling.
4. agent based modeling.

A social simulation may fall within the rubric of computational sociology which is a recently developed branch of sociology that uses computation to analyze social phenomena. The basic premise of computational sociology is to take advantage of computer simulations in the construction of social theories. It involves the understanding of social agents, the interaction among these agents, and the effect of these interactions on the social aggregate. Although the subject matter and methodologies in social science differ from those in natural science or computer science, several of the approaches used in contemporary social simulation originated from fields such as physics and artificial intelligence.

System Level Simulation

System Level Simulation (SLS) is the oldest level of social simulation. System level simulation looks at the situation as a whole. This theoretical outlook on social situations uses a wide range of information to determine what should happen to society and its members if certain variables are present. Therefore, with specific variables presented, society and its members should have a certain response to the situation. Navigating through this theoretical simulation will allow researchers to develop educated ideas of what will happen under some specific variables (Chira et al, 2008).

Agent Based Modeling

Agent based modeling (ABM) is a system in which a collection of agents independently interact on networks. Each individual agent is responsible for different behaviors that result in collective behaviors. These behaviors as a whole help to define the workings of the network. ABM focuses on human social interactions and how people work together and communicate with one another without having one, single "group mind". This essentially means that it tends to focus on the consequences of interactions between people (the agents) in a population. Researchers are better able to understand this type of modeling by modeling these dynamics on a smaller, more localized level. Essentially, ABM helps to better understand interactions between people (agents) who, in turn, influence one another (in response to these influences). Simple individual rules or actions can result in coherent group behavior. Changes in these individual acts can affect the collective group in any given population.

Agent-based modeling is simply just an experimental tool for theoretical research. It enables one to deal with more complex individual behaviors, such as adaptation. Overall, through this type of modeling, the creator, or researcher, aims to model behavior of agents and the communication between them in order to better understand how these individual interactions impact an entire population. In essence, ABM is a way of modeling and understanding different global patterns.

Current Research

There are two current research projects that relate directly to modeling and agent-based simulation the following are listed below with a brief overview.

- Agent based simulations of Market and Consumer Behavior, is another research group that is funded by the Unilever Corporate Research. The current research that is being conducted is investigating the usefulness of agent based simulations for modeling consumer behavior and to show the potential value and insights it can add to long-established marketing methods.
- Agent based modeling is most useful in providing a bridge between micro and macro levels, which is part of what sociology studies. Agent based models are most appropriate for studying processes that lack central coordination, including the emergence of institutions that, once established, impose order from the top down. The models focus on how simple and predictable local interactions generate familiar but highly detailed global patterns, such as emergence of norms and participation of collective action. (Macy & Willer, 2002) researched a recent survey of applications and found that there were two main problems with agent based modeling the self-organization of social structure and the emergence of social order. Below is a brief description of each problem Macy and Willer believe there to be;

1. "*Emergent structure*. In these models, agents change location or behavior in response to social influences or selection pressures. Agents may start out undifferentiated and then change location or behavior so as to avoid becoming different or isolated (or in some cases, overcrowded). Rather than producing homogeneity, however, these conformist decisions aggregate to produce global patterns of cultural differentiation, stratification, and hemophilic clustering in local networks. Other studies reverse the process, starting with a heterogeneous population and ending in convergence: the coordination, diffusion, and sudden collapse of norms, conventions, innovations, and technological standards."

2. "*Emergent social order*. These studies show how egoistic adaptation can lead to successful collective action without either altruism or global (top down) imposition of control. A key finding across numerous studies is that the viability of trust, cooperation, and collective action depends decisively on the embeddedness of interaction."

These examples simply show the complexity of our environment and that agent based models are designed to explore the minimal conditions, the simplest set of assumptions about human behavior, required for a given social phenomenon to emerge at a higher level of organization (see Figure 1).

Fig. 1. Social Simulation using agents in an environment related with a wedding.

Researchers working in social simulation might respond that the competing theories from the social sciences are far simpler than those achieved through simulation and therefore suffer the aforementioned drawbacks much more strongly. Theories in social science tend to be linear models that are not dynamic and which are inferred from small laboratory experiments. The behavior of populations of agents under these models is rarely tested or verified against empirical observation.

3. Behaviour in group intelligent techniques – ant colony.

This section describes the principles of any Ant System (AS), a meta-heuristic algorithm based on the ant food-search metaphor. The description starts with the ant metaphor, which is a model of real ants. Then, it follows a discussion of how AS has evolved. The section ends with the explanation of ACS, the most common AS version. ACS Algorithm is the base of the logistic application explained in a later section.

3.1 A metaphor of real ants

The AS was inspired by collective behavior of certain real ants (forager ants). While they are traveling in search of food, they deposit a chemical substance on the traversed path. This substance, called pheromone, is detected with their antennae. The Pheromone communication is an effective way of coordinating the activities of these insects. For this reason, pheromone rapidly influences the behavior of the ants: they will tend to take those paths where there is a larger amount of pheromone.

The behavior followed by real ants is modeled as a probabilistic process. Without any amount of pheromone, the ant explores the neighboring area in a totally random way. In presence of an amount of pheromone, the ant follows a path in a controlled random way. With crossed paths, the ant will follow the trail with the largest amount of pheromone with a higher probability. ***All ants deposit additional pheromone during the*** traveling, then the food-search process evolves with positive feedback. Since the pheromone evaporates, the non-used trails tend to disappear slowly, increasing the positive feedback effect. In this stochastic process, the best ***ant*** receives reward with the highest amount of pheromone, while the worst ***ant*** is ***punished with the lowest amount of pheromone.***

3.2 Artificial ant colony

The AS is inspired in the natural optimization process followed by real ants. The algorithm is a general frame than can be applied to the solution of many combinatorial optimization problems. The artificial society, formed by ants, repeats the food-search process. Each ant builds a solution to the optimization problem. The ants share a pheromone structure, which is a common memory (global information) that can be accessed and updated simultaneously.

The AS is a multi-agent system where low level interactions between single ant-agents result in a complex behavior of the whole ant colony. Each ant-agent has incomplete information or insufficient skill to solve a problem. They need the whole colony to get the final objective. To optimize this kind of collaboration, there is not global control, data is decentralized, and the computation is asynchronous. Besides, the ant colonies exhibit an emergent behavior. This emergent conduct happens because they build their result in an incremental manner. As a consequence, the ant colonies are adaptive, complex and distributed multi-agent systems. The AS was originally proposed to solve the Traveling Salesman Problem (TSP), and the Quadratic Assignment Problem (QAP). Now exist a lot of applications like scheduling, machine learning, data mining (Ponce et al., 2009), and others. There are several variants of AS designed to solve specific problems or to extend the characteristics of the basic algorithm. The next paragraph describes the most important variants in order of appearance. Ant Colony Optimization (ACO) was introduced initially by Dorigo (Dorigo, 1991). ACO use two main characteristics: η_{rs} and τ_{rs}. The heuristic information η_{rs} is used to measure the predilection to travel between a pair of nodes (r,s). The trails of artificial pheromone τ_{rs} is used to compute the learned reference of traveling in a determined arc (r,s). It is formed by three algorithms: Ant-density, Ant-quantity and Ant-Cycle. Ant-density and Ant-quantity use the update of pheromone trails in every step of the ants, while Ant-Cycle makes updates after a complete cycle of the ant. A study of the correct configuration of AS for solving TSP concludes that the main parameter is β, the relative importance of the heuristic information. The study establishes that the optimal number of ants is equivalent to the number of nodes of the problem.

Gambardela and Dorigo (Gambardela, 1995) designed the Ant-Q algorithm, which is based on the principles of Q-learning. It was applied for solving the TSP and Asymmetric TSP (ATSP). Ant-Q uses a table of values Q to indicate how good a determined movement from node r to s is. It applies a rule to choose the next node to be visited and uses reinforcement learning to update Q with the best tour of the ants. Max-Min Ant System algorithm (MMAS) was developed by Stützle and Hoose (Stützle, 1996). It uses the elements of AS. However, it modifies three aspects: updating rule, pheromone values, and the next movement. The updating rule was modified to choose the best tour in every cycle, increasing the probability of early stagnation. Maximum and minimum limits for the pheromone trails were established. These limits avoid repeated movements: bounding the influence of the trail intensity, and leading to a higher degree of exploration.

Other variant of AS, named ASrank, was developed by Bullnheimer, Hartl and Strauss. (Bullnheimer et al., 1997). All solutions are ranked according to their fitness. The amount of deposited pheromone is weighted for each solution, such that the best result deposits more pheromone than bad solutions. This algorithm was tested with TSP and VRP instances. The developed technique is based on the Distributed Q-Leaning algorithm (DQL).

3.3 Ant Colony System (ACS)

Dorigo and Gambardela (Dorigo & Gambardela, 1996) improved AS with an algorithm named Ant Colony System (ACS). It presents three main differences with regard to AS:

transition rule, global updating and local updating. The transition-state rule is modified to establish a balance between the exploration of new arcs and the priority exploitation of a problem. The global updating rule is applied only to the arcs of the best ant tour. A local updating of the pheromone is done while ants build a solution. ACS was applied to TSP and ATSP with the addition of a local search based on a 3-opt scheme. Figure 2 shows a general scheme of the ACS algorithm.

```
Ant_Colony_System ( )
Initialize Data Structures
Do
   For each ant: initialize its solution
   Do
       For each ant:
         Pseudo-random-rule(η_rs, τ_rs) is applied to build a solution
           Local-update(τ_rs)
   Until all ants have completed their solutions
   Global-update(τ_rs)
Until stop criteria is reached
```

Fig. 2. The ACS algorithm.

It is well known that ACS is one of the best ant algorithms. ACS has the best performances and the majority of references (Asmar, 2005). This algorithm was adapted to solve the logistic problem approached in a section 6.1.

4. Behaviour in group intelligent techniques – particle swarm optimization.

The Particle Swarm Optimization (PSO) algorithm is a population-based optimization technique inspired by the motion of a bird flock (Kennedy, J. & Eberhart R., 1995). In the PSO model, every particle flies over a real valued n-dimensional space of decision variables $\vec{X}$. Each particle keeps track of its position $\vec{x}$, velocity $\vec{v}$., and remembers the best position ever visited, P_{Best}. The particle with the best P_{Best} value is called the leader, and its position is called global best, G_{Best}. The next particle's position is computed by adding a velocity term to its current position, as follows:

$$\vec{x}_{t+1} = \vec{x}_t + \vec{v}_{t+1} \tag{1}$$

The velocity term combines the local information of the particle with global information of the flock, in the following way.

$$\vec{v}_{t+1} = w * \vec{v}_t + \phi_1 * (P_{Best} - \vec{x}_t) + \phi_2 * (G_{Best} - \vec{x}_t) \tag{2}$$

The equation above reflects the socially exchanged information. It resumes PSO three main features: distributed control, collective behavior, and local interaction with the environment (Eberhart et al., 1996). The second term is called the cognitive component, while the last term is called the social component. w is the inertia weight, and $\phi 1$ and $\phi 2$ are called acceleration coefficients. The inertia weight indicates how much of the previous motion we want to include in the new one. When the flock is split into several neighborhoods the particle's velocity is computed with respect to its neighbors. The best P_{Best} value in the neighborhood is called the local best, L_{Best}.

$$\vec{v}_{t+1} = w * \vec{v}_t + \phi_1 * (P_{Best} - \vec{x}_t) + \phi_2 * (L_{Best} - \vec{x}_t) \quad (3)$$

Neighborhoods can be interconnected in many diferent ways, some of the most popular are shown in Fig. 3. The star topology is, in fact, one big neighborhood where every particle is connected to each other, thus enabling the computation of a global best. The ring topology allows neighborhoods therefore it is commonly used by the PSO with local best.
PSO is a fast algorithm whose natural behavior is to converge to the best explored local optima. However, attainting flock's convergence to the global optimum with high probability implies certain adaptations (Garro, 2009). The approaches range from modifications to the main PSO equation, to the incorporation of reproduction operators. PSO algorithm has been extended in several directions; in a latter section we show a multiobjective optimization approach to solve a logistic problem, the vehicle routing problem with time windows.

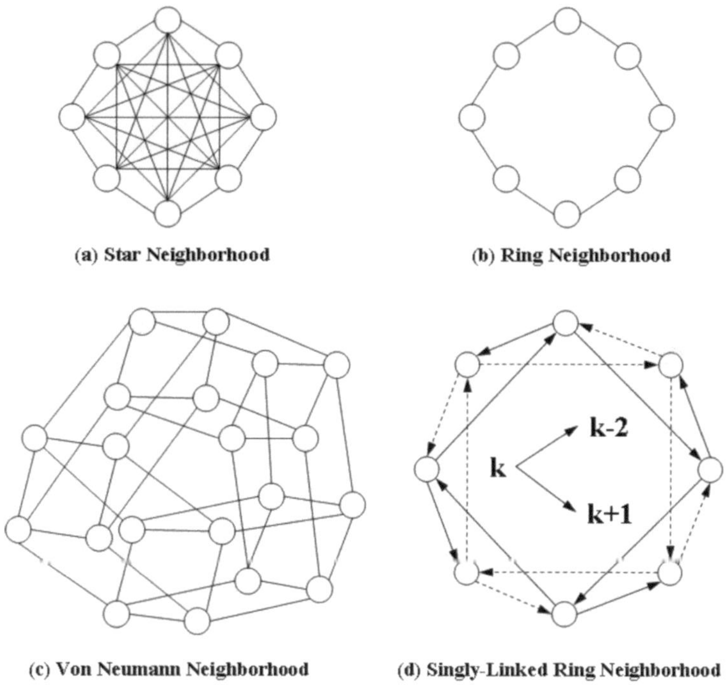

Fig. 3. Neighborhood structures for PSO

5. Behaviour in group intelligent techniques – cultural algorithms.

Cultural algorithms were developed by Robert G. Reynolds in 1994 as a complement to the evolutionary algorithms, this algorithms are bio-inspired in the Cultural Evolution of the Societies, and were focused mainly on genetic and natural selection concepts (Reynolds, 1994). Cultural algorithms operate at two forms: (1) a micro-evolutionary form, which consists of the genetic material that an offspring inherits from its parents (children, grandsons, greats-grandchild, etc), and (2) a macro-evolutionary level, which consists of the knowledge acquired by the individuals through generations (Culture). This knowledge is used to guide the behavior of the individuals that belong to a certain population. Figure 4 illustrates the basic framework of a cultural algorithm. A cultural algorithm operate in two spaces: Population Space and Belief Space. The most of computational problems found at real World, do not have a definitive (final) solution (Desmond & Moore, 1995). Cultural Algorithms uses the culture like a vehicle to store accessible relevant information to the population's members during many generations, and were developed to model the evolution of the cultural component over time and to demonstrate how this learns and acquires knowledge.

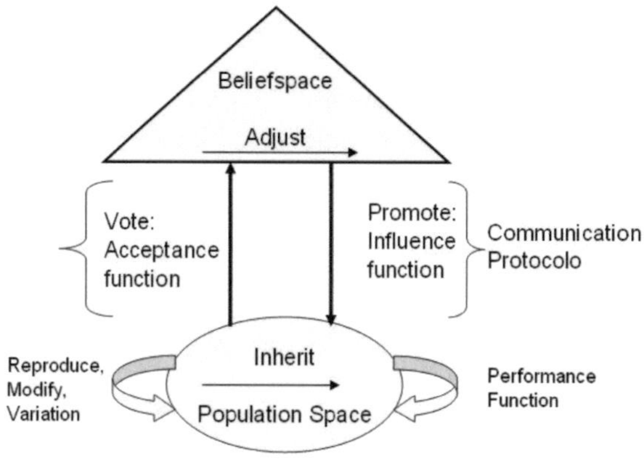

Fig. 4. Conceptual Diagram of Cultural Algorithms.

The Population Space are evaluated with a performance function obj(), and an acceptance function accept() can help to determine which individuals are introduce in the Belief Space. Experiences of those chosen elites will be used to update the knowledge / beliefs of the Belief Space via function update(), this function represents the evolution of beliefs in the population. Next, the beliefs are used to influence the evolution of the population. New individuals are generated under the influence of beliefs in the time that were crates. The two feedback paths of information, one through the accept() and influence() functions, and the other through individual experience and the obj() function create a system of dual inheritance of both population and belief. The population component and the belief space interact with and support each other, in a manner analogous to the evolution of human culture (Wu & Hsiao, 2008).

List of belief space categories

Normative knowledge A collection of desirable value ranges for the individuals in the population eg. acceptable behavior for the agents in population.

Domain specific knowledge Information about the problem domain where cultural algorithms are applied.

Situational knowledge Specific examples of important events - eg. succesful/unsuccesful solutions

Temporal knowledge History of the search space - eg. the temporal patterns of the searching process

Spatial knowledge Information about the topography of the search space

6. Use of collective intelligence techniques in diverse heuristics optimization.

The use of collective intelligence is found in different areas ranging from biology, sociology, and business to computer science. However, a common definition looks for the identification of certain "intelligence" derived from the efforts of joined entities. The aforementioned entities range from bacteria, animals, human to computer processes. Furthermore, the same definition can be applied, in a broad sense, to action selection and evolutionary robotics.

Evolutionary Robotics employs a quasi-optimal approach to develop autonomous controllers for different kinds of robots. The use of genetic algorithms and neural networks are natural candidates, as the preferred methodology, for developing single evolved neural controllers. These controllers are the result of testing populations of adapted individuals during a refinement process through series of computer-program iterations. Next, pairs or groups of individuals can be evolved together. Following this approach a change in the evolution of one individual can be affected by the change of other related individuals in the group. The latter approach has been identified, as its biological counterpart, as co-evolution that can be cooperative or competitive. A cooperative strategy can be developed to achieve a common task (e.g. pushing objects, solving a common task), whereas in a competitive strategy individuals have to struggle to assimilate some scarce resources (e.g. prey and predator, securing of food stashes). In biology diffuse co-evolution has been referred to species evolving in response to a number of other species, which in turn are also evolving in response to a set of species. Consequently, the identification of collective intelligence is more evident when coevolving cooperative groups.

The development of collective behavior in simulation can be achieved by simple scalable control systems as a form of decentralized control. Therefore, the work of (Kube, 1993) exhibited group behavior without the use of explicit communication. A more recent approach by (Marroco & Nolfi, 2007) set a collective task where a group of four robots developed the ability to reach two different target areas and to group in pairs at each different location. Elementary communication skills were evolved alongside the abilities to reach target areas. In this way, coordination is achieved through stigmergy; nevertheless more elaborated communication can be implemented (Mitri, 2006). On the whole, the individual ability to communicate may be one of the requirements for the development of collective intelligence.

The evolutionary approach has been sufficient to solve problems were cooperation and communication skills are necessary for solving a particular task; in contrast communication arises as a deceptive feature within a competitive scenario. In this scenario a common setting is that of the prey and the predator where both individuals are competing for scoring points either for escaping or capturing each other. The experiment can be expanded to add more preys and predators. It is important to notice that the prey/predator sees the other as a source that needs to be secured/avoided making this an instance of the 'action selection' problem (Ochoa et al., 2008).

The action selection problem is related, to the behavior-based approach, and particularly to decision-making when a module takes control of the available actuators until is completed or proves ineffective. In the vertebrate brain, at specific loci, specialized centers of selection can be identified. One of them are the basal ganglia, and recent works support the idea of these nuclei playing an important role in action selection (Prescott et al., 2006). The basal ganglia act as a relay station in the planning and the execution of movements (behavior);

hence gathering information from the cortex and motor cortex. The basal ganglia are able to mediate cognitive and muscular processes. Not only the basal ganglia serves as an important center of action selection; in cooperation with the cerebellum and the sensory cerebrum, all them are able to veto muscular contraction by denying the motor areas sufficient activation. In turn, these individual motor elements form more complex patterns, which can be thought as essential elements in the development of intelligence. The development of intrinsic basal ganglia circuitry with evolvable behavioral modules has already been implemented (Montes et al., 2007). Cooperative individuals not only require a society interaction, but the existence of an internal mechanism (e.g. the basal ganglia) that is able to mediate amongst various sensory processes. Nonetheless, these sensory processes need to be augmented when possible. Therefore, individuals need to build up unified internal perceptions based on their available sensory capabilities in order to produce specialized behavior. The work of (Montes et al., 2008) shows how non-standard avoidance can be achieved by extending sensory information through an evolutionary refinement.

The emergence of collective intelligence based on the behavior-based approach requires stepping out from the modeling of selfish solitary individuals to social organisms. Therefore, we need to group our robots and expose them to numerous interactions to assure complex performances at the level of the group. Here, we have identified some common elements in collective robotics: cooperation, intelligence, communication skills, and the integration of sensory information with action selection. All of those accomplished with the use of the evolutionary robotics approach. As a consequence, we believe that we may contribute to the development of robotic collective intelligence by way of social experiments using the artificial evolutionary method.

7. Cases of studies related to cultural algorithms

Many applications inspired in evolving compute have a great value in Logistics. In this section, we present five in special to compare their contributions, the first is related with Ant Colony in Logistic (6.1 Subsection), another is the use of Particle Swarm Optimization in Logistics (6.2 Subsection), the last three are related with Cultural Algorithms (6.3 Subsection) whih is used to improve Bin Packing Algorithm in a problem of Logistics, another is focused in an interactive game board using the problem of negotiation for obtaining a best situation in the game; in the other way is showed the anlysis of a social networking represented with a Dyoram to determine Six degree of separation in a graph.

7.1 Ant colony in logistic

Many manufacturing companies need merchandise delivered with the minimum quantity of resources and in due time. An optimal solution to this logistic problem could save between 5 to 20 % of the total cost of the products (Toth, 2002). However, this is a high-level complex problem. This type of word problem, named recently *rich problem*, includes several NP-hard sub-problems with multiple interrelated variants. To contribute to this area we approach the bottled-products distribution in a Mexican company. Our proposal includes an innovative ACS solution.

The Routing-Scheduling-Loading Problem (RoSLoP)

RoSLoP involves three tasks: routing, scheduling and loading. They are formulated with two well-known classical problems: Vehicle Routing Problem (VRP) and Bin Packing

Problem (BPP). The routing and scheduling tasks are defined through VRP, while the loading task is stated through BPP. Fig. 5 shows this formulation.

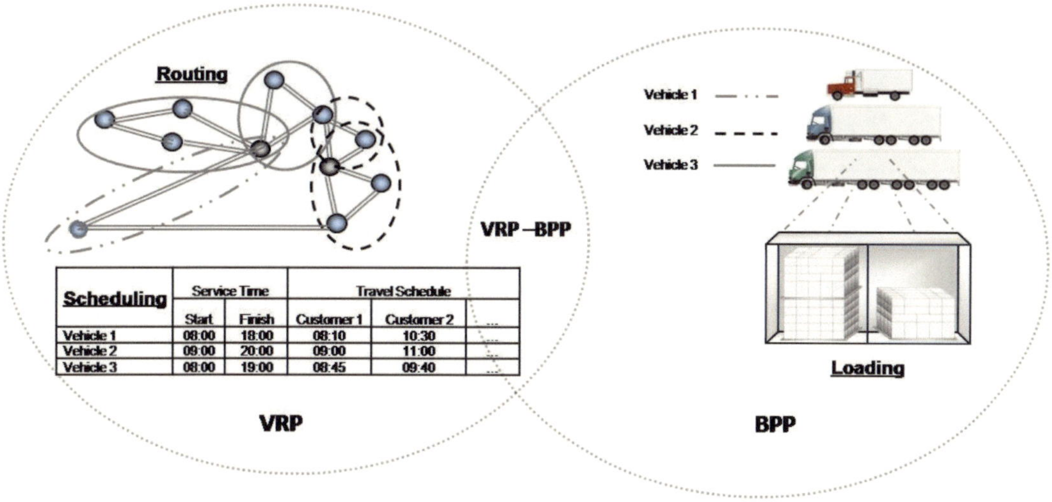

Fig. 5. Routing-Scheduling-Loading Problem (RoSLoP)

RoSLoP includes constrains not considered in VRP and BPP. Previous work approached separately at the most, three variants of BPP (Chan et al., 2005), and five variant of VRP (Pisinger, 2005). Commercial applications have incorporated up to eight variants of VRP without available scientific documentation (OR/MS, 2006). To overcome these limitations, our research tries simultaneously with eleven variants of VRP (Cruz et al., 2008) and five variants of BPP (Cruz et al., 2007).

In order to generalize this problem, RoSLoP is formulated as follows: Given a set of customers with a demand to be satisfied, a set of depots that are able to supply them, and a set of BPP and VRP variants that restrict them, the routes, schedules and loads for vehicles needs to be designed. The Customer demands must be completely satisfied, so the total cost is minimized and the constraints are satisfied.

Methodology of Solution

The assignment of routes and schedules is solved by an ACS algorithm. Three elements complement this algorithm: an auto-adaptive constrained list; an initial search, implemented with the Nearest Neighborhood; and a local search, implemented with 3-opt and Cross-Exchange. The loads are assigned by DiPro algorithm (Cruz et al., 2007). Fig. 6 shows the interaction between the components of ACS and DiPro.

The ACS algorithm in Fig. 7 begins creating an initial solution (line 1). After, it creates an ant colony to minimize the number of vehicles used (lines 3 to 17). In this process, each ant builds a local solution sailing through the adjacent states of the problem. The election of the nodes is done through a pseudo-random selection rule (line 6 to 13). The local solution is compared with respect to the best global solution (line 18) and the updates are done (line 19-20). The stop conditions of lines 17 and 21 are specified with respect to the number of iterations and time of execution respectively. A description of equation and techniques used by ACS are given below.

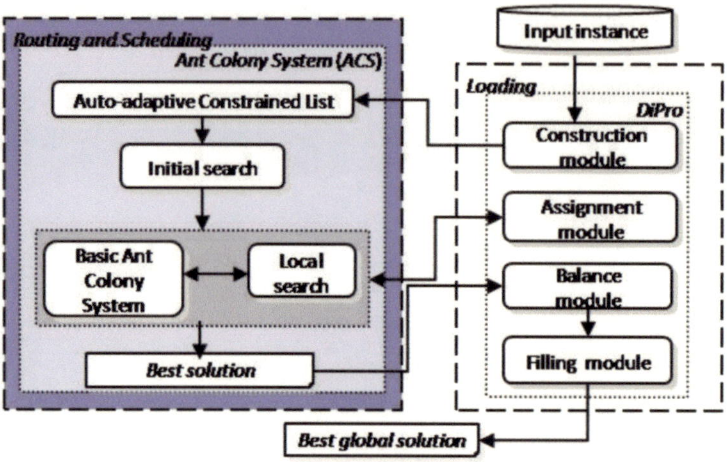

Fig. 6. ACS-DiPro: a solution Methodology of RoSLoP

```
ACS_RoSLoP ( )
Create a feasible global solution
repeat
   repeat /*build an initial local solution*/
      Initialize a local solution and get its number of vehicles t
      for each ant:
         repeat /*build a new local solution */
            Select a vehicle with the Pseudo-random-rule(η_v,τ_v)
            repeat
              Select a customer with the Pseudo-random-rule(η_rs,τ_rs)
              Customer-Local-update(τ_rs)
            until no customer can be visited
            Vehicle-Local-update(τ_v)
         until the demand is satisfied or t is reached
         local_search(new local solution)
         Update the local solution if a better solution is found
      end for each
   until stop criteria is reached
   if the local solution is feasible and better than the global
      Update the global solution
      Customer-Global-update(τ_rs)and Vehicle-Global-update(τ_v)
until stop criteria is reached
```

Fig. 7. The ACS algorithm for RoSLoP

Pheromone Update: Global update of the pheromone trail for customers is done over the best solution. Eq. 4 evaporates the pheromone in all the edges used for the best ant; the evaporation rate is $\rho \in [0,1]$. It also adds a reward using the increment $\Delta\tau_{rs}$, which is the inverse of the length of the best global solution. Local update (Eq. 5) is applied every time that one ant travels from node *r* to node s. It uses τ_0, which is the inverse of the product of the length of the shortest global solution, and the number of visited nodes. Similar equations are used for the vehicle pheromone trail.

$$\tau_{rs} \leftarrow (1-\rho)\tau_{rs} + \rho\Delta\tau_{rs} \tag{4}$$

$$\tau_{rs} \leftarrow (1-\rho)\tau_{rs} + \rho\tau_0 \quad (5)$$

Heuristic Information for Customers: The Eq. 6 determines the heuristic information η_{rs} used in the customer selection. In this equation, Δt_{rs} is the difference between the current time of node r and the arrival time to the node s, ws_s is the remaining size of the time window in s, st_s is the service time in s, and tc_{rs} is the travel cost from r to s.

$$\eta_{rs} = \left(\Delta t_{rs} \cdot (ws_s + st_s) \cdot tc_{rs}\right)^{-1} \quad (6)$$

Heuristic Information for Vehicles: The Eq. 7 calculates the heuristic information η_v used in the selection of the vehicles. In this equation, nv_v is the quantity of trips required by the vehicle v to supply all the demands, $\overline{TM_v}$ is the average of the service time of a vehicle v, $\overline{TR_v}$ is the average travel time of a vehicle v, tr_v is the available service time of the vehicle v, tt_v is the total service time of the vehicle v, and $idpref_v$ is the predilection-of-use grade of a vehicle v.

$$\eta_v = \left(nv_v \cdot (\overline{TM_v} + \overline{TR_v}) \cdot \frac{tr_v}{tt_v} \cdot idpref_v \right)^{-1} \quad (7)$$

Pseudo-random selection rule: An ant k located in node r selects the next node s to move. The selection is made using the pseudo-random selection rule defined in Eq. 8. When a balancing condition is satisfied, the ant selects the best node exploiting the heuristic information and the trails of pheromone. Otherwise, a proportional random exploration is applied. In this equation, q_0 is a parameter of balancing between exploitation and exploration, q is a random value in [0,1], β is the relative importance of the heuristic information, $N_k(r)$ is the set of available nodes for r.

$$\begin{array}{lll} \text{if } q \le q_0 & s = \underset{s \in N_k(r)}{\arg\max}\{\tau_{rs}\eta_{rs}^{\beta}\} & \text{Si } s \in N_k(r) \\ \text{else} & p_{rs}^{x} = \begin{cases} \dfrac{\tau_{rs}\eta_{rs}^{\beta}}{\sum_{s \in N_k(r)} \tau_{rs}\eta_{rs}^{\beta}} & \text{Si } s \in N_k(r) \\ 0 & \text{otherwise} \end{cases} & \end{array} \quad (8)$$

***Auto-adaptive Constrained List* (ACL):** The ACL characterizes the instance graph into subsets that have similar conditions. First, a Minimum Spanning Tree (MST) is generated. When the variability of the cost associated to each path in MST is small, all the nodes form a single conglomerate. Otherwise, it forms conglomerates through a hierarchical grouping. The value of the heuristic information η_{rs} is modified with a factor, which is a ratio of the cardinality of the groups of r and s.

Experimentation

A sample of three real instances and its solution is shown in Table 1. The database contains 312 instances classified by date order, and 356 products. The algorithm was coded in c# and set with 10 ants, 5 colonies, 40 generations, q_0 = 0.9; β = 1; ρ = 0.1. The results show that

ACS_DiPro uses an average of 5.66 vehicles. According with our industrial partner, it represents approximately an average saving of 11% in comparison with the manual solution. Besides, the algorithm execution takes 55.27 s. In contrast, a human expert is dedicated on doing this activity all working day.

Instance	*ORDERS*	ACS_DiPro		
		Distance Traveled	Vehicles Used	Time (s)
13/02/2006	208	1980	5	55.57
06/03/2006	224	1960	5	32.16
09/03/2006	269	2570	6	76.18
...	...	...	...	...
Average	**238.83**	**2245.16**	**5.66**	**55.27**

Table 1. Solution of real instances of RoSLoP

7.2 Logistic application: solving the vehicle routing problem with time window using PSO.

In transportation management, there is a requirement to provide goods and/or services from a supply point to various geographically dispersed points with significant economic implications. The vehicle routing problem (VRP), which was first introduced by (Dantzig & Ramser, 1959), is a well-known combinatorial optimization problem in the field of service operations management and logistics.

The Vehicle Routing Problem concerns the transport of items between de-pots and customers by means of a fleet of vehicles. In the VRP, the decisions to be made define the order of the sequence of visits to the customers; they are a set of routes. A route departs from the depot and it is an ordered sequence of visits to be made by a vehicle to the customers, fulfiing their orders. A solution must be verified to be feasible, checking that it does not violate any constraint, such as the one stating that the sum of the demands of the visited vertices shall not exceed the vehicle capacity.

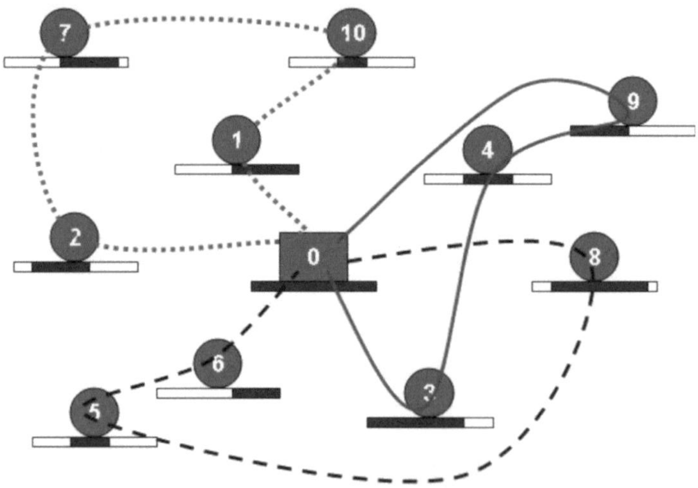

Fig. 8. VRPTW example

The Vehicle Routing Problem (see Figure 8) with Time Windows (VRPTW), is a variant of the VRP which considers the available time window in which either customer has to be supplied. The VRPTW is commonly found in real world applications and is more realistic than the VRP that assumes the complete availability over time of the customers.

Each customer requests a given amount of goods, which must be delivered or collected at the customer location. Time intervals during which the customer is served can be specific. These time windows can be single or multiple. A vehicle can not arrive later than a given time, but it can wait if arriving early. In such a case, the goal of the objective function is to minimize the distance travelled and the waiting time. (Salvelsberg, 1985) proved that even finding a feasible solution to the VRPTW when the number of vehicles is fid is itself a NP-complete problem. An overview on the VRPTW formulation and approaches can be found in (Cordeau et al., 2002).

VRPTW Formulation

The VRPTW is represented by a set of identical vehicles denoted by K, and a directed graph G, which consist of a set of customers and a depot. The nodes 0 represents the depot. The set of n vertices denoting customers is denoted N. The arc set A denotes all possible connections between the nodes (including the node denoting depot). All routes start at node 0 and end at node 0. We associate a cost c_{ij} and a time t_{ij} with each arc (I,j) ε A of the routing network. The travel time t_{ij} includes service time at customer *i*. Each vehicle has a capacity limit q_k and each customer *i*, a demand d_i, *i* ε N. Each customer *i* has a time window, $[a_i, b_i]$, where a_i and b_i are the respective opening time and closing times of *i*.

No vehicle may arrive past the closure of a given time window, b_i. Although a vehicle may arrive early, it must wait until the start of service time a_i is possible. It generates a waiting time w_k for the route. Vehicles must also leave the depot within the depot time window $[a_0, b_0]$ and must return before or, at time b_0. For eliminating any unnecessary waiting time (Russell, 1995), we assume that all routes start just-in-time $w_k = 0$, that is, we adjust the depot departure time of each vehicle $t_k = max(0, a_i - t_{0i})$, i ε N.

Multi-Objective Optimization

In Multi-Objective Optimization (MOO), two or more conflicting objectives contribute to the overall result. These objectives often affect one another in complex, nonlinear ways. The challenge is to find a set of values for them which yields an optimization of the overall problem at hand.

A MOO problem is defined as follows:

$$min_{\vec{x}} \quad \vec{f}(\vec{x}) = [f_1(\vec{x}), f_2(\vec{x}), \ldots, f_n(\vec{x})] \tag{9}$$

subject to

$$g_i(\vec{x}) \leq 0 \quad i = 1, 2, \ldots, m \tag{10}$$

$$h_j(\vec{x}) = 0 \quad j = 1, 2, \ldots, p \tag{11}$$

where $\vec{x} = [x_1, x_2, \ldots, x_d]$ is the vector of decision variables.

The notion of "optimum" in MOO problems difers from that of a single function in global optimization. Having several objective functions the aim is to find good compromises, rather than a single solution.

In 1896, Vilfredo Pareto, an Italian economist, introduced the concept of Pareto dominance (Pareto, 1896). A vector $\vec{x}$ is preferred to (dominates) a vector if each parameter of $\vec{x}$ is no greater than the corresponding parameter of $\vec{y}$ and at least one parameter is less.

Definition 1 *A vector $\vec{x}$ is said to dominate vector $\vec{y}$,*

$$\vec{x} \preceq \vec{y} \tag{12}$$

if and only if $\vec{x}$ is partially less than $\vec{y}$.

$$\forall i \in \{1,2,\ldots,n\}, \vec{x}_i \leq \vec{y}_i \wedge \exists i \in \{1,2,\ldots,n\} : \vec{x}_i < \vec{y}_i \tag{13}$$

Figure 9 shows an example of the Pareto dominance concept between solution vectors *B* and *C*; $B \preceq C$ due because *B* is less than *C* in the two objective functions f_1 and f_2.
A useful concept in MOO, related with Pareto dominance, is the Pareto front. The Pareto front is composed by a set of non-dominated vectors. Figure 9 shows a comparison between two individuals of the Pareto Front, where A is less than B in objective function f_1, but *B* is less than *A* in objective function f_2; therefore both solution vectors are non-dominated.
The Pareto front is particularly useful in engineering: by restricting attention to the set of solutions that are non-dominated, a designer can make tradeoffs within this set, rather than considering the full range of every parameter.

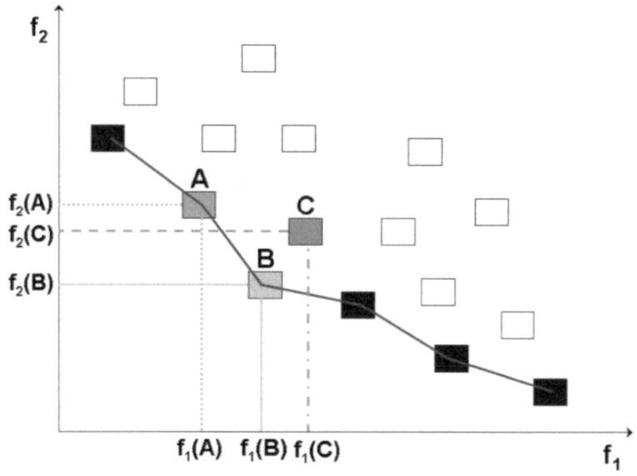

Fig. 9. Pareto Front

Multiobjective approaches to VRPTW

The three objectives of the VRPTW were presented: total distance travelled, number of vehicles, and total waiting time. Many existing VRPTW techniques, however, are single objective-based heuristic methods that incorporate penalty functions, or combine the different criteria via a weighting function (Hasnah, 2002; Li & Lim, 2003). However, in the last five years, some hybrid algorithms have been proposed to solve the VRPTW as a MOO problem. (Tan, 2006), and (Ombuki, 2006), employed the travel distance and the number of vehicles to be minimized. (Chitty & Hernandez, 2004), tried to minimize the total mean transit time and the total variance in transit time. (Murata & Itai, 2005) consider to minimize the number of vehicles and the maximum routing time among the vehicles in order to minimize the active duration of the central depot. (Saadah et al., 2004), minimize the number of vehicles and the total distance travelled. This work proposes a hybrid particle swarm MOO algorithm that incorporates perturbation operators for keeping diversity in the evolutionary search and the concept of Pareto optimality for solving the VRPTW as a MOO problem with 3 objectives: minimize total travel distance, minimize number of vehicles and minimize total waiting time.

Tackling Solomon's logistic problem with MO-PSO

Our Multiobjective PSO (MO-PSO) uses a flock size of 100 members,applies a PSO with parameters $c_1 = 1$ and $c_2 = 1$, and $w = U(0.5, 1)$. Total number of function evaluations is

1,000,000. A PC computer with Windows XP and C++ Builder Compiler, Pentium-4 processor at 3.00GHz, 1.00 GB of RAM was used for all experiments. A well-know problem set proposed by (Solomon, 1987) is used to test our model. In these problems, the travel times are equal to the corresponding Euclidean distances. One problems is chosen for the experiment: problem C101 in dimensions 25.

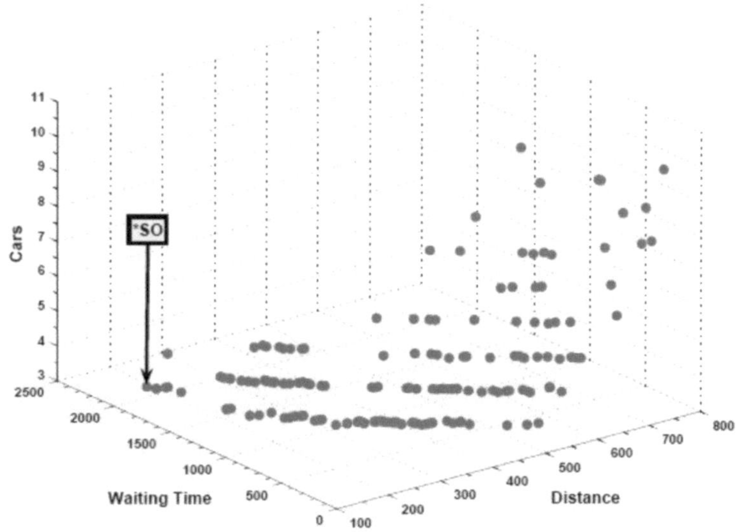

Fig. 10. Pareto front for problem C101 with 25 customers

Figure 10 shows the Pareto front obtained by 10 runs of MO-PSO for the problem C101 with 25 customers. The optimal route obtained by single objective approaches is marked with ***SO** in the figure. The Pareto front obtained by MO-PSO evidenced the huge waiting time accumulated by the optimal solution reported in the literature with single objective (total distance) approaches. The vector reports a total distance of 191.813620 units attained with only 3 cars, and a total waiting time of 2133.144826 units. As we mentioned above, in this problem, the travel times are equal to the corresponding Euclidean distances. Then, the total waiting time is at least 10 times greater than the total travel time performed for all routes. The total waiting time represents the 57.53% of the total available time (3708 units) of the 3 vehicles, if the depot's window time [0; 1236] is taken as reference. Before, we explained that for eliminating any unnecessary waiting time, we assume that all routes start just-in-time w_k = 0, that is, we adjust the depot departure time of each vehicle $t_k = \max(0, a_i - t_{0i})$, $i \in N$. Therefore, there is no waiting times at the beginning of the route.

Table 2 presents some solutions of the Pareto front found by MO-PSO for the problem C101 with 25 costumers. For example, the solution vector (215.703725, 1584.387467, 4) presents a significant reduction in the total waiting time, but, the total distance and number of vehicles increased respect the solution vector (191.813620, 2133.144826, 3). The solution vector (359.85828, 963.12288, 3) has a waiting time of only 25.9% of the total available time (3708 units) of the three vehicles. Finally, the last solution vector (748.901755, 100.252129,10) presents a reduction of 20 times the waiting time of the solution vector (191.813620, 2133.144826, 3), and it represents the 2.7% of the total available time. Although this solution vector increase at least 3 times the total distance and the number of vehicles of the solution vector (191.813620, 2133.144826, 3).

Distance	Waiting Time	Vehicles
191.813620	2133.144826	3
197.256586	2077.701861	3
215.703725	1584.387467	4
276.183581	1293.765800	3
359.858288	963.122881	3
443.570466	744.983131	3
511.430115	478.360000	4
526.659555	466.430155	3
589.610396	276.000750	4
609.975206	199.124629	5
673.520691	172.003649	6
748.901755	100.252129	10

Table 2. Points in the Pareto front of problem C101 with 25 customers

The empirical results show that reducing the total distance often results in an increment of the total waiting time and vice versa. This happens when two customers that are geographically close may not necessarily be close from the temporal point of view. For the 3 dimensions of the problem C101, the total waiting time is over 50% of the available time of all vehicles occupied in each solution. In real-world problems, this levels of waiting times are not conforming to standard usage. Thereby, placing more emphasis on the distance travelled will often result in unnecessary waiting time.

7.3 Cultural algorithms to improve problems of logistics and combinatorial optimization.

Different problems related with Combinatorial problem son explained in this section, the first is related with Logistics in special with the Bin Packing Problem, the second with the concept of Negotiation in many societies and finally the analysis of six degree of separation in a Social Networking each one implement different strategies to improve the problem and using from different point of view Culturaal Algorithms (CAs).

In the fist problem CAs relies on a communication protocol that makes possible to gain access to the belief space. In relation with the evolutionary component of the cultural algorithm, either a Genetic or an Evolutionary Programming algorithm can be indistinctively used. The cultural algorithm operates at two different levels by means of inheritance: at the belief space at a macro-evolutive manner, whereas at a micro-evolutive sense at the very own population space. Once certain beliefs are acknowledged, this 'new knowledge' are assimilated by the population and passed to the belief space (Ochoa, 2008). As a consequence, having an impact on the development of generation of new individuals through posterior epochs.

The use of five particular kinds of knowledge is employed by the cultural algorithm to find, in the search space, a possible solution for a specific problem. This knowledge can be identified as: normative knowledge (acceptable behavior), circumstantial knowledge (successful and disastrous experiences), domain knowledge (objects and their relation in a given domain), historical knowledge (timed behavioral patterns), and topographically knowledge (spatial behavioral patterns) (Reynolds et al., 2005). The implementation of the cultural algorithm was carried out in a standard manner as shown in figure 11.

```
Begin
  Generate a random initial population.
  Calculate the fitness of the initial population.
  Repeat
    Apply to the entire population mutation to create offspring.
    Evaluate each descendant  Select by 7 tournament
    (usually probabilistic) individuals who survive.
  Until a stopping condition is satisfied.
End
```

Fig. 11. Pseudocode for a standard cultural algorithm.

The main contribution of the cultural algorithm to the evolutionary methods is the use of a belief space, and its cultural influence in the population for finding adequate solutions for problems that employ this knowledge space.

Implementation

The prototype is a hybrid intelligent system developed in Matlab 7.6.0, using cultural algorithms. We started by measuring available free space in a standard distribution vehicle. Also we measured the various presentations in cubic centimeters and their volume in liters. We also took into account the demand of the different available presentations, in order to determine the income utility.

PRODUCT	CAPACITY	DEMAND PERCENTAGE	VOLUME	UTILITY
1	20 liters	45 %	36500cm^3	$ 10.00 MXP
2	1.5 liters	15 %	26731cm^3	$ 26.50 MXP
3	1 liter	15 %	18435cm^3	$ 21.60 MXP
4	0.500 liters	25 %	18177cm^3	$ 38.50 MXP

Table 3. Description of the product.

Once the measurements were made, it was necessary to create an algorithm capable of finding the right selection, in terms of the freight, to optimize income utility and reduce costs of transportation (equation 14). Then the population and the belief space were initialized. The demand of the product is calculated based on their volume and income utility (Table 3). Next, the initial population is evaluated based on the restrictions shown in the same table.

$$\text{Max } r_2m_2 \ z = r_1m_1 + + + rnmn \ldots$$

$$V_2m_2 \text{ subject to } v_1m_1 + + + \ldots v_nm_n <= V \tag{14}$$

$$m_1, m_2 \ldots mn> = 0 \text{ and integer}$$

$$V = 1138425\text{cm}^3$$

where:
r: Value per unit.
v: Volume of each unit.
m: are the units of each product type.
V: Maximum capacity in volume.

Any violation of the restrictions will be penalized in such a way that only the best combinations will be obtained. As a result, an average result is obtained and the best individuals are able to influence the next generation based on average individuals. The resultant epoch is a proposed solution for the problem, the halt condition is reached when seven consecutive epochs reach the same result. The result (Time) is the proposed solution, the condition of unemployment is from the recurrence of 7 times without change, ie = or> to the previous ones.

Results

Our initial results are based in a cultural algorithm with an initial population of one hundred individuals. Also, a belief space was created with the same number of individuals. The system was initialized with this population and belief space, and then Variation Operators were applied. The system was iterated until the halt condition was reached producing a nearly optimal solution. The program was used to determine a proper combination of the truckload to maximize profits. The selection of the truckload was based on the volumes of the various water containers and the freight capacity of the truck. In table 4 we observe that after the epoch fifteen the algorithm found a steady solution after eight epochs without improvement.

CAPACITY	20 ltrs	1.5 ltrs	1 liter	0.500 ltrs
Quantity	16	6	6	9
UTILITY $848.00 MXP				

Table 4. Results obtained.

A comparison with the Simplex Method reveals that still this method performs better at this stage in the implementation of our cultural algorithm. In table 5 we notice the maximum utility suggested by following this approach is $771.00 MXP, which is $ 77.00 MXP less than in our algorithm.

	14:37:33		Friday	April	17	2009		
	Decision Variable	Solution Value	Unit Cost or Profit c(j)	Total Contribution	Reduced Cost	Basis Status	Allowable Min. c(j)	Allowable Max. c(j)
1	X1	0.0225	10.0000	0.2250	0	basic	0	M
2	X2	0.1000	26.5000	2.6500	0	basic	0	M
3	X3	0.1500	21.6000	3.2400	0	basic	0	M
4	X4	0.5000	38.5000	19.2500	0	basic	0	M
	Objective	Function	(Max.) =	25.3650				
	Constraint	Left Hand Side	Direction	Right Hand Side	Slack or Surplus	Shadow Price	Allowable Min. RHS	Allowable Max. RHS
1	C1	0.4500	<=	0.4500	0	0.5000	0	615.8346
2	C2	0.1500	<=	0.1500	0	17.6667	0	63.1710
3	C3	0.1500	<=	0.1500	0	21.6000	0	61.0709
4	C4	0.2500	<=	0.2500	0	77.0000	0	31.1428
5	C5	15,348.1000	<=	1,138,425.0000	1,123,077.0000	0	15,348.1300	M

Table 5. Results using the Simplex Method.

As a result of our research we develop a hybrid intelligent system that employs a cultural algorithm with artificial evolution for the optimization of space in the delivery of purified water. Here we demonstrated that is feasible to use a cultural algorithm in problems such as the one described here. Our main contribution resides in a real application of the cultural algorithm, which few years ago exist only at the theoretical level.

In the second problem, we focus our attention on a practical problem adapted from the related literature within the Modelling Societies, "the negotiation toward a common well-being" for a set of societies: to find a safe place (a place where attacks don't exist) in an unknown place, inside a hostile environment with unknown dimensions and populated by attackers in unknown locations.

This type of optimization problem can be represented by a two-dimensional matrix, called "dimension", like is shown in the Figure 12, where A represents the group of societies, M and B the Goal and the attackers (both unknown for the societies) respectively, and the numbers in the dimension represent the experimentation cost for each space. The objective of the cultural algorithm is to find the goal in the minimum number of steps while the spaces are sorted where "attacks" can exist, characterized by penalties of anxiety and uneasiness.

The solution to this problem will be given by a sequence of agents' generations, denoted as "community." The agents can only know the adjacent spaces to them, like in the colonies carried out by a society that only knows finite distances. The group of spaces around the agent is denominated "quadrant." From the agent's point of view, this optimization problem is absolutely complex, because we don't know the location of the goal - or if some exists - and it cannot see the world beyond its quadrant. Besides doesn't have any previous heuristic to try to improve the optimization. For better understanding of the selected cultural algorithm used to solve the optimization problem, now we introduce some basic concepts and representations of the artificial culture related to this problem. These representations are abstraction levels located between (the unknown part of the agent), the domain problem (dimension) and the agents. In the algorithm of cultural change, the space of beliefs (beliefspace) by means of the best paradigm (BestParadigm) are set to zero, representing the fact that the culture increases the quantity of pleasure associated with such spaces, giving an incentive to the behavior associated with the best paradigm (BestParadigm).

Agents

The agents are the actors those that will be able to experience each space in the dimension to what Freud refers as the "principle of satisfaction", according to this, the agent will be able to select the spaces with the lower experimentation cost.

Paradigm

The paradigm is the agents' personal representation for the space of beliefs (beliefspace) or its personal interpretation of the cultural references. According to Gessler, this is the agent's cognition and its private vision of the cultural interpretation of the World. The paradigm could represent the best solution for the problem denoted as the best paradigm (BestParadigm).

Space of beliefs (Beliefspace)

The space of beliefs is the collective representation of the real World. In other words, this is the world as it is interpreted by one culture of the community, where the agents find the way to interact and moral values.

Dimension

The dimension is the real world, which never can be entirely known by the agent. This contains the experimentation cost and on which the agents are able to live when the optimization is improved.

Exploration

The agents belonging to one community search inside the dimension for the most appropriated place to be developed (goal). The obtained solution for the agents whom find the goal in the lesser number of steps could be considered as the community "model", or the best paradigm (BestParadigm). According Geertz, this model or ideology is a "diagram of the psychological and social processes". The culture could then try to lead the behavior of the new generations of agents by means of this best solution. The best solution for the optimization problem will be given by the agent's sequence of movements that find the totality of the optimum number of steps. Each agent in the community is leaded by one function that allows it to select the spaces with the lower quantity of anxiety. It can be observed that the satisfaction principle does not affect the strategy for the global resolution of the problem at collective level (culture). To the contrary, this links the agent with an autonomous entity. The culture controls the behavior to be adopted as model, creating a strategy of global action -an ideology- regarding the given problem domain.
The agent selects the cell with the minimum anxiety, as the indicated for the space of beliefs (Beliefspace) adding to this the cultural value, as:

$$\text{beliefspace}(x) = \text{beliefspace}(x) + \text{dimension}(x) \tag{15}$$

Where x is a set of spaces in the dimension
In this research the functions represent the agent-culture interaction and are selected according with the adopted problem.
Therefore, we cannot try to establish a mathematical model of how the cultural process occurs in the real world. Adopting a random function as was shown previously to explain how we insert, into the process, a system of multiple interactions between the agent and the culture. We try to analyze other mathematical representations in our future work.

1	1	1	1	1	1	1
1	1	1	1	1	1	1
1	1	1	1	1	1	1
1	1	B	3	1	1	1
1	B	B	B	1	1	1
1	B	1	1	1	1	1
1	1	1	2	1	M	1
1	1	A	1	1	1	1

Fig. 12. Representation of the Dimension in a game board

Cultural Algorithms Simulator

To prove and validate the theoretical concepts previously presented, we developed a cultural algorithm simulator (Baharastar). Initially our intention was only to create an environment able to carry out analysis and experiments. When cultural algorithms are used, it becomes more difficult of understanding the peculiarities proposed for each solution. Each time that the system has a precise answer, the obtained solution can hardly being duplicated exactly. This property of the evolutionary algorithms in general and of the cultural algorithms in particular, has been little explored or discussed in the literature. The creation of systems with an individuality or "soul", are our contribution in the area. For such purpose, we select 27 societies described in (Memory Alpha, 2009) and we characterize their behavior using seven base attributes (agility, ability to fight, intelligence, forces, stamina, speed and emotional control), those which allowed describe as well to the society as to the individual.

The development of Baharastar is based on our desire of sharing an intuitive understanding about the treatment for a new class of systems, individuals able to possess unexpected creativity, typical characteristic of living entities. Baharastar is shown in the figure 10, the user has the possibility to choose the starting point and the goal to reach, joined to the places where one can receive an attack by part of the enemy, and the quantity of anxiety associated to each space of the dimension where the societies reside in (agents' communities). Our prototype was developed using JBuilder X platform (see Figure 14).

Experiments

We describe the developed experiments using Baharastar which to contribute in the sense of making evident the importance of the creation of a new methodology to prove and to analyze the obtained results. This was not a trivial task, considering the diversity of behaviors of the provided solutions by Baharastar because it resembles more than a descriptive anthropology than a simple software test. In the first experiment, we compared the performance of 27 communities of 50 agents, and on the other hand 27 communities of 500 agents each one. The associated points to the beginning and goal are shown in the figure 13. The optimal number of steps from the beginning to the goal is 12.

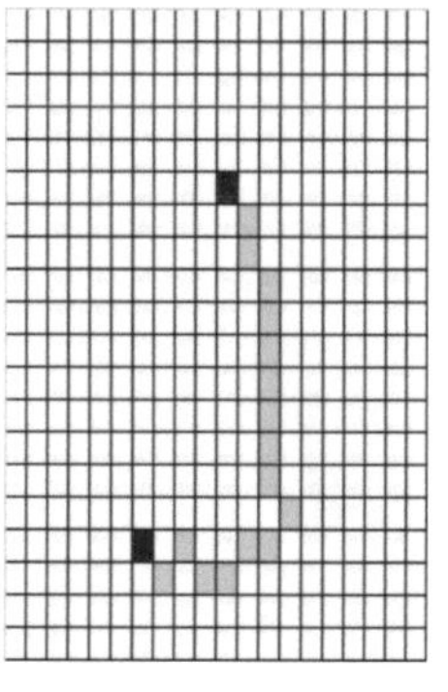

Fig. 13. Evaluation of a optimization problem using Baharastar

One of the most interesting characteristics observed in this experiment is the diversity of cultural patterns established for each community. For the solutions with the same number of steps the provided result for the "beliefspace" is entirely different. The structured scenarios associated to the agents cannot be reproduced in general due they belong to a given instant in the time and space. They represent a unique, precise and innovative form of adaptive behavior which solves a computational problem followed by a complex change of relationships. The generated configurations can be metaphorically related to the knowledge of the community behavior regarding to an optimization problem (to make alliances, to defend from a possible invasion), or a tradition with which to emerge from the experience and with which to begin a dynamics of the process. Comparing the 50 agents of the first community regarding the 500 agents community, this last obtained a better performance in terms of the average number of steps from the beginning to the goal (13.05 versus 14.30), as well as a smaller standard deviation (1.96 versus 2.64). They also had a greater average number of changes in the paradigm (5.85 versus 4.25), which indicates that even the "less negotiating" generations, that explored less interesting parts of the dimension, could optimize their search to achieve better results. In the second experiment, we consider the same scenario for the experiment one, except that after having obtained a solution from a community of 50 agents, we place five near spaces to the goal and we begin with a new community of 500 agents. The new community was informed of the previous cultural configurations but should take into account the new scenario. The comparison among both solutions is not immediate, from the point of view that try to solve different problems. In this experiment, it was surprising to see initially how the community of 500 agents uses the solution offered by the 50 agents, whenever these solutions were close the optimal grade, instead of finding entirely complete new solutions. These results make evident the conservation of a global action strategy which regulates the agents. This can be compared metaphorically with the concept of culture mentioned in the introduction (Suarent & Ochoa et al., 2008).

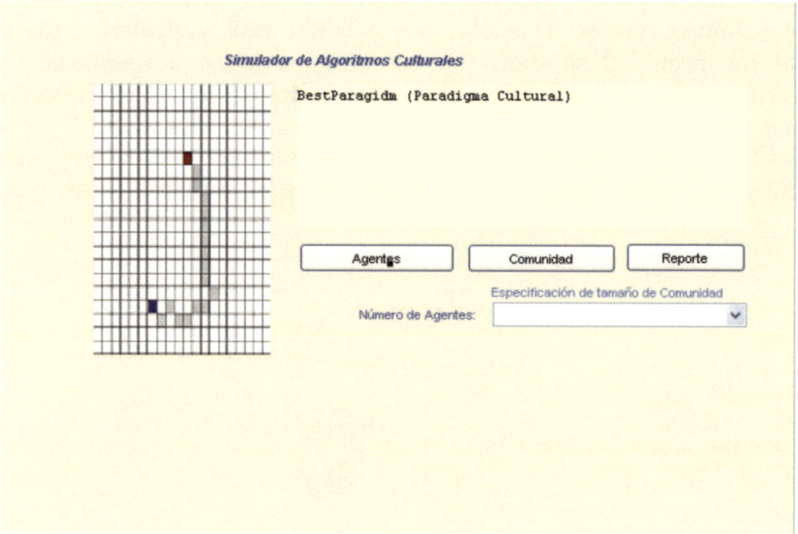

Fig. 14. Developed tool called Baharastar.

In the third Combinatorial problem, we focused our attention on an adapted practical problem of the Literature related to the Society Modelling, "the friendship relationships" of a set of societies (127 societies represented by one issue - 57 Males & 70 Females) characterized in (Memory Alpha, 2009). The solution to this problem will be given by a sequence of generations of agents, denoted like "community". The agents can only select a set of possible friends based on previous behaviors of theirs societies (Beliefspaces). The ratings in Belief space are normalized associated to popularity of a friend (a society which has weighting qualities), this potential friend receive 12 points, the next one 10, and then 8, 7, 6, 5, 4, 3, 2 and 1 (the graph is built using these relations). This allows each person (society) voting to give positive ratings to ten other people (societies). Each individual (society) cannot vote for itself. The order in which the people (societies) generate points is randomly drawn before the beliefs space of each society starts. After their obtained a group of friends, the graph drawn this friendship links, finally the diorama is built. Results are puts in a scoreboard society by society and represented as an adjacency matrix which is analyzed for determining six degrees of separation, in the same order in which societies established friendship, and ranked according to their aggregate score.

The dynamics of social relationship is a highly complex field to study. Even though it can be found many literature regarding friendship networks, weak links / acquaintances, relationship evolution and so on, we are still far from understanding all the process involved. Social research has shown that people use numerous criteria when they consider the possibility of turning an acquaintance into a friend. But this research considers only two: cultural and technological characteristics of people (society) that determine the emergence and evolution of friendship. After studying the theory available, we have decided to use "Six degrees of separation" in order to model the friendship dynamics and determine the concept of *popularity*. This principle assesses that the more similar cluster formed by several people are, the stronger their chances of becoming a group of friends. Thus, we attempt to model the processes in which people of different societies turn to be acquaintances, those turn into friends, and some friends into couples, and some couples in a group of friends (more of 4). Select a friend is among the most personal of human choices, and thus it is not surprising that friendship groups tend toward cultural homogeneity. People with the same preferences usually associate with other similar persons, in our case people represented different societies from different quadrants select people with interesting features and similar profiles to become theirs friends with base in its own preferences.

A preliminary step to constructing a friendship modeling is adequate the relationships of people as a graph. A *graph* (or *network*) *G* is defined by a set of *N* vertices (or nodes) *V ={v1, v2,...,vN}* and a set of *L* edges (or links), *E ={e1, e2, ...,eL}*, linking the nodes. Two nodes are linked when they satisfy a given condition, such as two persons participating in the same reaction in a social network. The graph definition does not imply that all nodes must be connected in a single component (friendship relation). A *connected component* in a graph is formed by a set of elements so that there is at least one path connecting any two of them. Additionally, graphs can also be *weighted* when links have values according to a certain property. This is the case for social networking, where weights indicate the strength and direction of regulatory interactions. Although graphs are usually represented as a plot of nodes and connecting edges, they can also be defined by means of the so-called *adjacency matrix*, i.e., an array *A* of *NxN* elements *aij*, where *aij*=1 if *vi* links to *vj* and zero otherwise. Figure 15 summarizes the different ways of representing a graph.

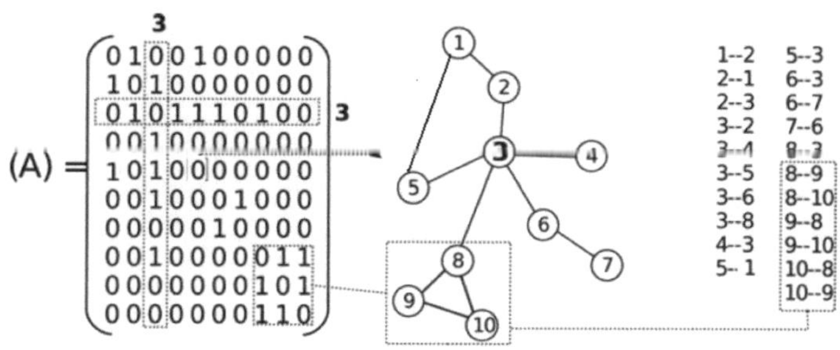

Fig. 15. Different ways of representation for a directed and unweighted graph. Left: Adjacency matrix (A). Centre: Drawn graph. Right: List of pairs (edge list). The triangle motif (in dashed box) is indicated for the three representations. The friendship couple concept is represented in the vertex 5 with 1. Some examples of *k*, *C* and *b* values: for *v3, k3=5, C3=0, b3=0.69; v8, k8=3, C8=0.33, b8=0.36; v10, k10=2, C10=1,b10=0*. Whit all this fundaments is possible determine that exists the concept of Six *degrees of separation* in a Social Networking.

Six degrees of separation (also referred to as the "Human Web") refers to the idea that, if a person is one step away from each person they know and two steps away from each person who is known by one of the people they know, then everyone is no more than six "steps" away from each person on Earth. The easier way to understand this is that person A only needs a maximum of five people in between to connect to person B. (Supposing person A and B don't know each other, see right side of Figure 17).

Experiments

We simulated by means of the developed tool the expectations that propagation of friendship and interests of obtain a friend with specific features (see Figure 16). One of the observed most interesting characteristics in this experiment were the diversity of the cultural patterns established by each community because the selection of different attributes in a potential friend: Musical ability, Logical ability, Understanding emotion, Creativity, Narrative ability, spatial awareness & Physical ability. The structured scenes associated the agents cannot be reproduced in general, so that the time and space belong to a given moment. They represent a unique form, needs and innovator of adaptive behavior which solves a followed computational problem of a complex change of relations. Using Cultural Algorithms implementing with agents is possible simulate the behavior of many people in the selection of a group of friends and determinate whom people support this social networking.

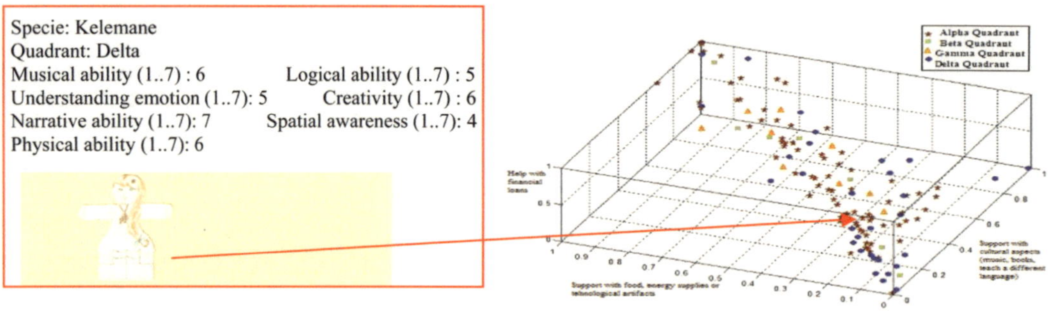

Fig. 16. Individual features of an element and classification of friendship preferences of a sample of societies (127 societies) obtained with Cultural Algorithms.

We first observe that valued friendship (support in troubles related with financial, cultural or energy supplies situations are considered) always plays a very significant role, which should of course not be surprising. Hidden patterns observed in the agents are related with linguistic and cultural distances, and the expectative of selection of a friend whit specific attributes. The nodes with more value in their degree are considered more popular and support the social networking. To get some insight, we run 100 regressions on 100 random samples of half the number of observations, and count the number of times each parameter affect the graph built. *Kelemane Society* was selected as the most popular by the majority of societies because the attributes offered by it are adequates for others. In Figure 17 is shown the seven societies whom demonstrate the concept of Six degrees of separation.

8. Conclusions.

Evolving Compute offer a powerful alternative for optimization problems including Logistics, a real problem in our times. Nowadays all the societies try to improve Intelligent Systems of Logistics.

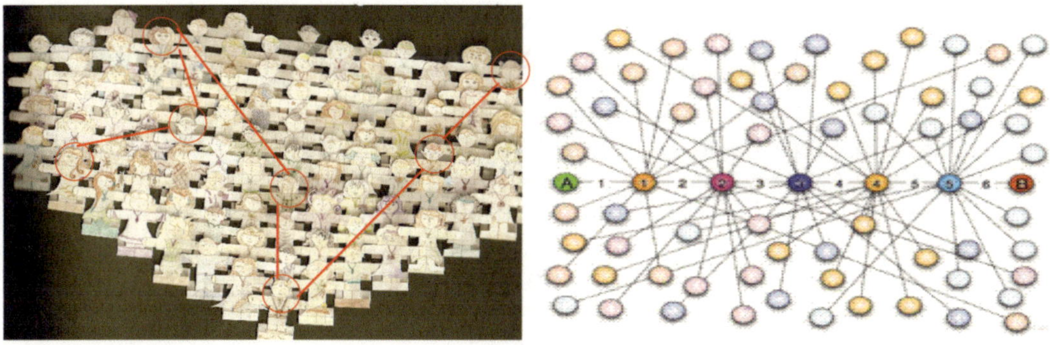

Fig. 17. Diorama obtained with Cultural Algorithms which show the clusters of preferences to become friendships, and an example of six degrees of separation.

Many approaches exist to improve the solution of a real problem using ACs System algorithm, which builds solutions of good quality in a short time. This shows the viability of the development of complex applications based on collaborative intelligent techniques. Specifically, in the logistic of companies which need to distribute their products to obtain significant savings in transportation. This will allow companies to increase their utilities and offer their products in smaller prices.

PSO studies the VRPTW as a tri-objective optimization problem. Specifically, the three dimensions of the problem to be optimized are considered to be separate dimensions of a multi-objective search space: total distance travelled, total cumulated waiting time and number of vehicles engaged. There are a number of advantages in using this MO-PSO model to solve the VRPTW. First, by treating the number of vehicles, total distance, and total waiting time as separate entities, search bias is not introduced. Second, there is a strong philosophical case to be made for treating the VRPTW as a MOO problem. It is not necessary to numerically reconcile these problem characteristics with each another. In other words, we do not specify that either the number of vehicles or the total distance travelled take priority.

CAs provide a comprehensible landscape of the cultural phenomenon. This technology leads to the possibility of an experimental knowledge discovering, created by the community of agents for a given application domain. How much this knowledge is cognitive for the community of agents is a topic for a future work. The answer can be similar to the involved in the hard work of communication between two different cultures. The cultural algorithms offer a long-range alternative for the problems of optimization and redistribution of clusters. For that reason, this technique provides a comprehensible panorama of the cultural phenomenon represented (Ochoa, 2007).

Logistics requiere of the solution propose by many evolving compute techniques (Ant Colony, PSO, and Cultural Algorithms) proportioned knowledge by obtain the best solution in the search space. There are an important number of questions that deserve additional research (Mendoza et al., 2009).

9. References

Asmar D.C., Elshamli A. and Areibi S.: A comparative assessment of ACO algorithms within a TSP environment. Dynamics of Continous Discrete and Impulsive Systems-Series B-Applications & Algorithms, vol. 1, pp. 462-467, 2005

Bullnheimer, B., Hartl, R. F. and Strauss C.: A New Rank Based Version of the Ant System: A Computational Study, Technical report, Institute of Management Science, University of Vienna, Austria, 1997.

Chan W., et al.: Online Bin Parking of Fragile Objects with Application in Cellular Networks. Tech. report, Hong Kong RGC Grant HKU5172/03E. (2005)

Chira, C.; Gog, A.; Dumitrescu, D.: Exploring population geometry and multi-agent systems: a new approach to developing evolutionary techniques. GECCO (Companion) 2008: 1953-1960

Chitty, D. and Hernandez. M. A hybrid ant colony optimisation technique for dynamic vehicle routing. In *Proceedings of Genetic and Evolutionary Computation 2004 (GECCO 2004)*, pages 48{59. ACM, June 2004.

Cordeau, J. ; Desaulniers, G. ; Desrosiers, J. ; Solomon, M. and Soumis, F.. *The VRP with time windows*, pages 157{193. SIAM, Monographs on Discrete Mathematics and Applications. Society for Industrial and Applied Mathematic, 2002.

Cotterill, R. MJ, 2001, Cooperation of the basal ganglia, cerebellum, sensory cerebrum and hippocampus: possible implications for cognition, consciousness, intelligence and creativity, Progress in Neurobiology, Vol. 64, Issue 1, May 2001, Pags 1-33.

Cruz R. L., et al.: DiPro: An Ant Colony System Algorithm to Solve Routing Problems Applied to the Delivery of Bottled Products. Springer-Verlag Berlin Heidelberg, pp. 329-338. (2008)

Cruz R. L. et al. : DiPro: An Algorithm for the Packing in Product Transportation Problems with Multiple Loading and Routing Variants. Springer-Verlag Berlin Heidelberg, pp. 1078-1088. (2007)

Dantzig, G. and Ramser, R. The truck dispatching problem. *Management Science*, 6(1):80{91, October 1959.

Desmond, A. & Moore J. (1995). "Darwin – la vida de un evolucionista atormentado". Generación Editorial, São Paulo, Brazil.

Dorigo, M.: Positive Feedback as a Search Strategy. Technical Report. No. 91-016. Politecnico Di Milano, Italy, 1991.

Dorigo, M. and Gambardella L. M.: Ant Colony System: A Cooperative Learning Approach to the Traveling Salesman Problem. Technical Report TR/IRIDIA/1996-5, IRIDIA, Université Libre de Bruxelles, 1996.

Eberhart, R.; Dobbins, R. and Simpson, P. Computational Intelligence PC Tools. Academic Press Professional, Boston, USA, 1996.

Epstein, J. & Axtell R. *Growing Artificial Societies*. MIT Press/Brookings Institue, Cambridge, MA, 1996.

Gambardella, L.M. and Dorigo M.: Ant-Q: A Reinforcement Learning Approach to the Traveling Salesman Problem. Proceedings of ML-95, Twelfth International Conference on Machine Learning, Tahoe City, CA, A. Prieditis and S. Russell (Eds.), Morgan Kaufmann, pp. 252-260, 1995

Garro, B.; Sossa, H. and Vázquez, R. Design of Artificial Neural Networks using a Modified Particle Swarm Optimization Algorithm. International Joint Conference on Neural Networks (IJCNN 2009). June 14-19, 2009. Atlanta, Georgia, USA.

Hasnah, N. Hybrid genetic algorithms for vehicle routing problems with time windows. *International Journal of the Computer, the Internet and Management*, 10(1):51{67, January 2002.

Kennedy, J. and Eberhart, R. Particle swarm optimization. In *Proceedings of IEEE International Conference On Neural Networks*, pages 1942-1948. IEEE, November 1995.

Kube, R., 1993, Collective Robotics: From Social Insects to Robots, Adaptive Behavior, Vol. 2, No. 2, 189-218.

Li, H. and Lim, A. Local search with annealing-like restarts to solve the vrptw. *European Journal of Operational Research*, 150(1):115{127, October 2003.

Macy, M. W. & Willer, R. From Factors to Actors. Annual Review of Sociology, 28; England; 2002.

Marocco D. & Nolfi S. (2007). Emergence of communication in embodied agents evolved for the ability to solve a collective navigation problem. Connection Science, 19(1): 53-74.

Memory Alpha. memory-alpha.org (Star Trek World), 2009.

Mendoza, R., Vargas, M.; Muñoz, J.; Álvarez F. & Ochoa A. Web Service-Security Specification based on Usability Criteria and Pattern Approach, Special Issue of JSP, Journal of computer, Finland; May 2009.

Mitri, S. and P. Vogt. Co-evolution of Language and Behaviour in Autonomous Robots. In The sixth international conference on the Evolution of Language (Evolang6), World Scientific, pages 428-429, 2006.

Montes F., Prescott, T. J., and Negrete J. (2007) 'Minimizing human intervention in the development of basal ganglia-inspired robot control', Applied Bionics and Biomechanics, 4:3, 101-109.

Montes F., Flandes D. and Pellegrin L. (2008), Action Selection and Obstacle Avoidance using Ultrasonic and Infrared Sensors. In Frontiers in Evolutionary Robotics, Book edited by: Hitoshi Iba, pp. 327-340, April 2008, I-Tech Education and Publishing, Vienna, Austria.

Murata, T. and Itai, R. Multi-objective vehicle routing problems using two-fold emo algorithms to enhance solution similarity on non-dominated solutions. In *Proceedings of Third International Conference on Evolutionary Multi-Criterion Optimization (EMO 2005)*, pages 885{896. Springer, March 2005.

Ochoa A., Ponce J. et al. Baharastar – Simulador de Algoritmos Culturales para la Minería de Datos Social. In Proceedings of COMCEV'2007, México, 2007.

Ochoa, A. "Algoritmos Culturales" Gaceta Ide@s CONCYTEG, Año 3. Núm. 31, 2008.

Ochoa A.; Quezada S.; Ponce J.; Ornelas F.; Torres D.; Correa C.; de la Torre J. & Meza M.(2008). *From Russia with Disdain: Simulating a Civil War by Means of Predator/Prey Game and Cultural Algorithms,* Artificial Intelligence for Humans: Service Robots and Social Modeling, Grigori Sidorov (Ed.), ISBN: 978-607-00-0478-0, pp. 137-145, October 2008, Mexico.

Ombuki, B.; Ross, B. and Hanshar, F. Multi-objective genetic algorithms for vehicle routing problem with time windows. *Applied Intelligence*, 24(1):17-30, February 2006.

OR/MS Today: Vehicle Routing Software Survey. Institute for O. R. and the Manag. Sciences, www.lionhrtpub.com/orms/surveys/Vehicle_Routing/vrss.html. (2006)

Pareto, V. *Cours d'Economie Politique*. Lausanne, Paris, France, 1896.

Pisinger D. and Ropke S.: A General Heuristic for Vehicle Routing Problems. Technical report, Department of Computer Science, Univ. Copenhagen. (2005)

Ponce J.; Padilla F.; Ochoa A.; Padilla A.; Ponce de León E. & Quezada F.(2009). *Ant Colony Algorithm for Clustering through of Cliques,* Artificial Intelligence & Applications, A. Gelbukh (Ed.),ISBN: 978-607-95367-0-1, pp. 29-34, November 2009, Mexico.

Prescott, T. J., Montes F. M., Gurney K., Humphries M. D. & Redgrave P. (2006). A robot model of the basal ganglia: Behavior and intrinsic processing. Neural Networks 19 (2006), pp. 31-61.

Reynolds, R. G. An introduction to cultural algorithms. *Proc. Conf. on Evolutionary Programming,* 1994, pp. 131C139.

Reynolds, R.; Peng B. & Whallon, R." Emergent Social Structures in Cultural Algorithms", 2005

Russell, R. Hybrid heuristics for the vehicle routing problem with time windows. *Transportation Science,* 29(2): 156-166, May 1995.

Saadah, S.; Ross, P. and Paechter, B.. Improving vehicle routing using a customer waiting time colony. In *Proceedings of 4th European Conference on Evolutionary Computation in Combinatorial Optimization (EVOCOP'2004),* pages 188-198. Springer, April 2004.

Salvelsberg, M. Local search in routing problems with time windows. *Annals of Operations Research,* 4(1):285-305, December 1985.

Solomon, M. Algorithms for the vehicle routing and scheduling problems with time window constraints. *Operations Research,* 35(2):254-265, March 1987.

Stützle, T. and Hoos H. H.: Improving the Ant System: A detailed report on the MAXMIN Ant System. Technical report AIDA-96-12, FG Intellektik, FB Informatik, TU Darmstadt; 1996.

Suarent A.; Ochoa A.; Jons S.; Montes F. & Spianetta A. (2009). Evolving Optimization to Improve Dioram's Representation using a Mosaic Image, journal of computers, august 2009, vol. 4, number 8, ISSN 1796-203x. pp. 734-737, ed. Academy publisher, Oulu Finland.

Tan, K.; Chew. Y, and Lee, L. A hybrid multiobjective evolutionary algorithm for solving vehicle routing problem with time windows. *Computational Optimization and Applications,* 34(1):115{151, May 2006.

Toth P., Vigo D, editors. The vehicle routing problem. Monographs on Discrete Mathematics and Applications. SIAM. pp. 363. (2002)

Wu W. and Hsiao M. S. Efficient Design Validation Based on Cultural Algorithms 2008 EDAA

14

Particle Swarm and Ant Colony Algorithms and Their Applications in Chinese Traveling Salesman Problem

Shuang Cong, Yajun Jia and Ke Deng
University of Science and Technology of China
P. R. China

1. Introduction

Intelligent heuristic optimization methods have increasingly attracted the attentions and interests of many scholars in recent years. Such as genetic algorithm, ant colony algorithm, particle swarm optimization, simulated annealing, *etc*.. They have become effective tools to solve the TSP and other NP-hard combinatorial optimization problems. The particle swarm optimization (PSO) algorithm is a population-based evolutionary algorithm which was proposed by Eberhart and Kennedy in 1995 (Eberhart & Kennedy, 1995). The PSO simulates the behaviors of bird flocking. Suppose the following scenario: a group of birds are randomly searching food in an area. There is only one piece of food in the area being searched. No bird knows where the food is. But they know how far the food is in each iteration. So what's the best strategy to find the food? An effective one is to follow the birds which are nearest to the food. The PSO firstly generates a random initial population, the population contains numbers of particles, each particle represents a potential solution of system, each particle is represented by three indexes: position, velocity, fitness. Firstly endows each particle a random velocity, in flight, it dynamically adjusts the velocity and position of particles through their own flight experience (personal best position), as well as their companions' (global best position). The evolutions of particles have a clear direction, the whole group will fly to the search region with higher fitness through continuous learning and updating. This process will be repeated until reach the default maximum iterations or the predetermined minimum fitness. The PSO is therefore in essence a fitness-based and group-based global optimization algorithm, whose advantage lies in the simplicity of algorithm, easy implementing, fast convergence and less parameters. Presently, the PSO has been widely applied in function optimization, neural network training, pattern classification, fuzzy system control and other applications. Whereas, like other intelligent optimization algorithms, the PSO may occur the phenomenon that particle oscillates in the vicinity of optimal solution during searching in the search space, therefore the entire particle swarm performs a strong "convergence", and it is easily trapped in local minimum points, which makes the swarm lose diversity. Thus it has the weakness of solving complex problems, and it is difficult to obtain a more accurate solution in the late evolution. Many scholars proposed some improved algorithms (Yuan et al., 2007; Xu *et al.*, 2008; Lovbjerg, 2001), which improve the search capabilities of the elementary PSO in different aspects.

Bionics appeared in the mid 50's in 20th century, people were inspired from the mechanism of organic evolution, and put forward many new methods to solve complex optimization problems. In these methods, the evolutionary computation including evolution strategies, evolutionary programming, and genetic algorithms is the most remarkable. With people's research to biological group behavior and bio-social, algorithms based on swarm intelligence theory have appeared including Ant Colony Optimization (ACO). Since the Ant System (AS) which is the first algorithm in line with the ACO framework was put forward, the researchers have begun their attempts to improve the design. The first one is Elitist Strategy for Ant System (EAS). The EAS mainly gives special pheromone deposit to the artificial ants, which perform so far the best in constructing solutions followed by the Ant-Q algorithm which combines ant colony algorithm with the Q learning algorithm, uses the synergies of artificial ants. Then there appears the Ant Colony System (ACS), Rank based version AS (AS_{rank}) and Max-Min Ant System (MMAS). These three improvements have greatly improved the performance of AS, in particular the MMAS gets a lot of expansion and becomes an algorithm of highly practical application and one of the best ACO algorithms at present. In recent years, there have been some new improvements of ACO such as Approximate Nondeterministic Tree Search (ANTS). The ANTS is extended to a deterministic algorithm later, and it has a good performance in solving the Quadratic Assignment Problem (QAP); Another new improved algorithm is the Hyper-Cube Framework for ACO, and its purpose is automatically adjusting the value of pheromone trails to ensure that the pheromone trails lie always in the interval [0,1]. The current study for ACO has extended from TSP range to many other fields, and it has developed into solving the multi-dimensional and dynamic combinatorial optimization problems instead of the static one-dimensional optimization problem. The research of ACO has also developed from discrete domain into continuous domain. It has got fruitful research results in improving the performance of the ACO and grafting on bionic natural evolutionary algorithms or local search algorithms.

This chapter is divided into three parts. In part one, in order to solve the shortcoming of easily being trapped in local minimum points, we respectively introduced mutation and simulated annealing (SA) algorithm (Kang *et al.*,1998) to the PSO, and proposed a hybrid algorithm by combined with the advantages of the strong global search ability of PSO and good local search ability of SA. The hybrid algorithm proposed was applied to solve the Chinese Traveling Salesman Problem with 31 cities (C-TSP). The comparative study on the experimental results with SA, elementary PSO (Zhong *et al.*, 2007; Xiao *et al.*, 2004; Li *et al.*, 2008) and PSO with mutation were given. In part two, the mechanisms and properties of the five ant colony algorithms were synthesized, compared and analyzed including basic ant colony algorithm (ant system, AS), elitist strategy of ant system (EAS), a new rank-based version of the ant system (AS_{rank}), max-min ant system (MMAS) and ant colony system (ACS). The efficiency of five algorithms was also compared through their applications in the C-TSP. The investigations of the performances were done in the aspects of the effects of different parameters and the relations between parameters of the algorithms. The third part is conclusions.

2. PSO and its application in C-TSP

2.1 PSO with mutation

In the PSO, each single solution is a "bird" in the search space. The particles fly through the problem space by following the current optimum particles. In every iteration, each particle is updated by following two "best" values. The first one is the best solution it has achieved so far, it is a *personal best position* denote by p_{ib}. Another "best" value, which is tracked by the particle swarm optimizer, is the best value obtained so far by any particle in the population, it is a *global best position* and defined as p_{gb}. All of particles have fitness values which are evaluated by the fitness function to be optimized. Each particle updates according to those two best values, and then a new generation of population is created.

Suppose that the searching space is D dimensional with m randomly initialized particles in it, the particle swarm can be indicated by following parameters: $x_i = (x_{i1}, x_{i2}, ..., x_{iD})$ stands for the location of particle i in the D dimensional space and it is also regarded as a potential solution, $v_i = (v_{i1}, v_{i2}, ..., v_{iD})$ stands for the flight velocity of particle i in the D dimensional space, $p_i = (p_{i1}, p_{i2}, ..., p_{iD})$ stands for the personal best position of particle i, $p_i = (p_{g1}, p_{g2}, ..., p_{gD})$ stands for the global best position in the whole swarm. The particle updates its velocity and position with the following rules:

$$v_{id}^{k+1} = \omega v_{id}^{k} + c_1 rand()(p_{ib} - x_{ib}^{k}) + c_2 rand()(p_{gb} - x_{ib}^{k}) \tag{1}$$

$$x_{ib}^{k+1} = x_{ib}^{k} + v_{ib}^{k+1} \tag{2}$$

in which, i = 1 ,2 ...,m; d = 1 ,2 ,...,D; k is iteration number; c_1, c_2 are called *acceleration coefficients*, which are used to adjust the maximum flight step of personal best value and global best value, *rand*() returns a random number between (0,1); ω is inertia weight which affects the balance of global search ability and local search ability.

In Zhong *et al.* in 2007 a large number of experiments proved that once ω decreases linearly with the iteration, the convergence of algorithm would be significantly improved. Therefore here we let $\omega = \omega_{\max} - \frac{(\omega_{\max} - \omega_{\min}) * k}{K}$, where k is the current iteration number, K is the maximum iteration number, $\omega_{\max}$ is the maximum inertia weight, $\omega_{\min}$ is the minimum inertia weight. The basic principles of Eq. (1) is that the velocity achieves information from the original velocity, personal best value and global best value, the number of information depends on ω, c_1 and c_2. The first part of Eq. (1) is called *memory term*, which denotes the impact of velocity and direction of previous iteration. The second part (the distance between current position of particle i and the personal best position) is called *self-awareness term*, which denotes the information that comes from its own experience. The third part (the distance between current position of particle i and the global best position) is called *population-awareness term*, which denotes the information that comes from another particles of the whole swarm, which reflects the knowledge sharing and cooperation. The PSO algorithm can be implemented in the following 6 steps:

Step 1. Initialize generation and all particles, viz. set the initial position X of each particle and the initial velocity V randomly.

Step 2. For each particle, calculate the fitness value.

Step 3. For each particle, if the fitness value is better than the best fitness value $f(p_{ib})$ in history, set current value as the new p_{ib}.

Step 4. Choose the particle with the best fitness value of all the particles as p_{gb}.

Step 5. For each particle, calculate the particle velocity according to Eq. (1), and update particle position according to Eq. (2).

Step 6. If the maximum iteration or the minimum error criteria is not attained, return to *Step 2*; otherwise end the iteration.

The PSO has been successfully applied in many continuous optimization problems. The Traveling Salesman Problem (TSP) is a typical discrete combinatorial problem. If one wants to solve the TSP with PSO, some improvements of basic PSO must be done. In Huang *et al.*, in 2003 the concept of swap operator and swap sequence were introduced for solving the TSP. Suppose that the solution sequence of the TSP with n nodes is $S=(a_i), i=1,\dots,n$. The definition of *swap operator* $SO(i_1,i_2)$ is the points a_{i_1} and a_{i_2} in the solution sequence S. *Swap sequence* is an orderly sequence with one or more swap operators, meanwhile the order between swap operators is meaningful. Different swap sequence operate on the same solution may generate the same new solutions, the equivalent set of swap sequence is the set of swap sequence which has the same effect. Among all the equivalent sets of swap sequence, the swap sequence with least swap operators is called *basic swap sequence.* An array with N cities denotes the particle's position X, All the possible arrays compose the state space of the problem. Based on vectors, functions and operations defined above, the traditional updating equations will be changed in the following versions (Huang et al., 2003):

$$v_{id}^{k+1} = \omega v_{id}^{k} \oplus \alpha(P_{id} - X_{id}) \oplus \beta(P_{gd} - X_{id}) \tag{3}$$

$$x_{ib}^{k+1} = x_{ib}^{k} + v_{ib}^{k+1} \tag{4}$$

in which, $\alpha, \beta(\alpha,\beta) \in [0,1]$ are random numbers. $\alpha(P_{id} - X_{id})$ denotes that all the swap operators in the basic swap sequence $(P_{id} - X_{id})$ are reserved with a probability of α, similarly, $\beta(P_{gd} - X_{id})$ denotes that all the swap operators in the *basic swap sequence* $(P_{gd} - X_{id})$ are reserved with a probability of β. Thus the greater the value of α is, the more swap operators that $(P_{id} - X_{id})$ will be reserved, and the greater the impact of P_{id} is. Similarly, the greater the value of β is, the more swap operators that $(P_{gd} - X_{id})$ will reserve, and the greater the impact of P_{gd} is. The definition of operator "$\oplus$" is the merger operator of two swap sequences. Operator "+" denotes the implementation of swap operation, operator "-" denotes to obtain the basic swap sequence of two sequences. For example : *A* = *(*1 2 3 4 5*)*, *B* = *(*2 3 1 5 4*)*, as can be seen that *A(*1*)* = *B(*3*)* = 1, so the first swap operator is *SO*(1,3), *B1* = *B* + *SO* (1,3), so one gets that *B1*: (1 3 2 5 4), *A*(2) = *B*1(3) = 1, so the second swap operator is *SO*(2,3), *B* = *B1* + *SO*(2,3), so one gets that *B*2: (1 2 3 5 4). Similarly, the third swap operator is *SO*(4,5), *B*3 = *B*2 + *SO*(4,5) = *A*, thus one gets a basic swap sequence: *SS* = *A* – *B* = (*SO*(1,3), *SO*(2,3), *SO*(4,5)).

The steps of the PSO algorithm for solving the TSP can be described as follows:

Step 1. Initialize generation and all the particles, set each particle a random initial solution and a random swap sequence.

Step 2. If the maximum iteration or the minimum error criteria is met, turn to *Step 5*.

Step 3. According to the particle's current position X_{id}^{k}, calculate the next position X_{id}^{k+1}, namely the new solution.

1. Calculate the difference between P_{id} and X_{id}, $A = P_{id} - X_{id}$, in which A is a basic swap sequence.

2. Calculate the difference between P_{gd} and X_{id}, $B = P_{gd} - X_{id}$, in which B is a basic swap sequence.
3. Calculate the velocity v_{id}^{k+1} according to Eq. (3), and convert the swap sequence v_{id}^{k+1} to a basic swap sequence.
4. Calculate the new solution x_{ib}^{k+1} according to Eq. (4).
5. If x_{ib}^{k+1} is better than P_{id}, set a new solution x_{ib}^{k+1} as new P_{id}.

Step 4. Choose the particle with the best fitness value of all the particles as P_{gd}, turn to *Step* 2.

Step 5. Show the result that obtained.

In the settlement of solving TSP, basic PSO generates new individual through Eq. (3) and Eq.(4), from which one can see that a basic swap sequence generated by Eq. (3) is in fact equivalent to the swap operator to a route, but the route between the two swap cities do not change, so it is easy to generate cross route which is illegal solution. To deal with the problem, inspired by the mutation operator in evolutionary algorithm, we add the mutation operator to the PSO. The specific approach is: after generating a new route by basic PSO approach during each iteration one does the mutation operator to the new route. More specific, change *Step 4* as follows:

Step 4: Generate two mutate cities randomly, then reverse the order of all the cities between two mutate cities. If the length of new route is less than the original route, set the new route as x_{ib}^{k+1}. Otherwise, maintain the original route unchanged.

2.2 A hybrid algorithm of PSO and SA

The SA algorithm derived from the principle of solid annealing. Firstly, heat the solid to a sufficiently high temperature, and then cool it slowly. This process is based on an analogy from thermodynamics where a system is slowly cooled in order to achieve its lowest energy state. According to Metropolis criteria, the probability of particles balance at temperature T is $e^{-\Delta E/(kT)}$, where E is the internal energy at temperature T; ΔE is the increment of internal energy; k is the Boltzmann constant. Once one converts the internal energy E to the objective function value, and the temperature T to control parameter t, the SA algorithm of solving combinatorial optimization problems may be obtained with the initial solution i and initial control parameter t by repeating the iteration of "generate new solution $\rightarrow$ calculate the difference of objective function $\rightarrow$ accept or discard" to the current solution, and gradually reduce the value of control parameter t. The current solution is the approximate to the optimal solution when algorithm is terminated. It is a stochastic heuristic search process based on Monte Carlo iterative method. The process is controlled by *Cooling Schedule*, which includes initial control parameter t, attenuation factor Δt, iteration number for each t and the termination condition .

The SA algorithm used to solve the TSP can be described as follows:

1. *Solution spaces* : Solution spaces are all the routes of visiting each city once. The solution can be denoted as $\{\omega_1, \omega_2, \ldots \omega_n\}$. $\omega_1, \ldots, \omega_n$ in an array that is composed of 1 to n, which denotes one walks to start from the city ω_1, and visits along with the cities $\omega_2, \ldots, \omega_n$ orderly, then returns to the city ω_1.
2. *Objective function*: Objective function is the total distance length of the route pass through all the cities. The objective function value of the optimal route is the least one. Objective function is also called fitness function.

3. *Criteria of new solution generation and acceptance*: Here we use reverse operator to generate new solution, more specifically, choose two different number *k* and *m* between 1 to *n* randomly, moreover, *k* is smaller than *m*, then one swaps the cities between *k* to *m*, that is to convert $\{\omega_1, \omega_2, ... \omega_k, \omega_{k+1}, ..., \omega_m, ..., \omega_n\}$ into $\{\omega_1, \omega_2, ... \omega_m, \omega_{m+1}, ..., \omega_{k+1}, \omega_k, ..., \omega_n\}$. Once the new route is generated, calculate the difference of distance length between new route and current route, if the length of new route is smaller, that is, $\Delta f = f(x_j) - f(x_i) \le 0$, set the new route as x_{ib}^{k+1}, if the length of new route is bigger, but $\exp(-\Delta f / t) > random(0,1)$, still set the new route as x_{ib}^{k+1}, otherwise maintain the current route unchanged.

The SA algorithm in hybrid algorithm of PSO and SA proposed calculates alternately by two steps:

1. Generate a new solution by stochastic perturbation and calculate the change of the objective function.
2. Decide whether the new solution is accepted or not. In the case at a high temperature, the solution that increases the objective function may be accepted by means of decreasing the temperature slowly, which may avoid to trap in local minima. In such a way the algorithm can converge to the global best solution.

The nature of basic PSO is the use of individual and global maximum to guide the position of the next iteration, which can converge fast at the early iteration. But, after several iterations current solution, personal best value and global best value tend to the same, which leads to the loss of population diversity, and makes the solution be trapped in local minima. In order to avoid this phenomenon, inspired by the SA algorithm, we redesign the algorithm's framework: when basic PSO converges to a solution p_g, use the solution p_g as the initial solution of SA, accept the new solution in accordance with the Metropolis criteria. If there is such a solution *y* satisfies $f(y) < f(p_g)$, that is, the solution calculated by basic PSO is not the global optimal solution. Then a new solution *y* can be used to randomly replace a particle in the swarm, and the evolution of PSO continues, which can increase the population diversity as well as retain the previous operation procedure. If there is not such a solution *y*, then let $f(y) < f(p_g)$, that is, no better solution than p_g has been found until the convergence of SA, which indicates that p_g is the global optimal solution.

2.3 The C-TSP application and results analysis

The TSP is a well-known combinatorial optimization problem with typical NP-hard and is often used to verify the superiority of some intelligent heuristic algorithm. The mathematical description of the TSP is: Given a list of *n* cities in order of visiting as $X = \{x_1, x_2, ..., x_n\}$ and $x_{n+1} = x_1$, the task is to find the shortest possible tour distance of

$\min \sum_{i=1, x \in \Omega}^{n} d_{x_i x_{i+1}}$ that visits each city exactly once. The TSP can be modeled as a graph: the graph's vertices correspond to cities and the graph's edges correspond to connections between cities, the length of an edge is the corresponding connection's distance. A TSP tour is now a Hamiltonian cycle in the graph, and an optimal TSP tour is the shortest Hamiltonian cycle.

Chinese Traveling Salesman Problem (C-TSP) is a typical symmetric TSP problem. Its simple description is: Given a list of 31 Chinese capital cities and their pairwise distances, the task is to find the shortest possible tour that visits each city exactly once. The C-TSP is a medium-scale TSP problem, which has $(31-1)!/2 = 1.326*10^{32}$ possible routes.

The algorithms of solving TSP problem are divided into two categories: Exact algorithms and approximation algorithms. The exact algorithms used frequently includes branch and bound algorithms, linear programming and exhaustion method, *etc.*. The running time for this approach lies within a polynomial factor of $O(n!)$, the factorial of the number of cities, so this solution becomes impractical even for only 20 cities. Approximation algorithm is divided into tour route construction algorithm, tour route optimization algorithm and heuristic algorithm, in which heuristic algorithm is the most spectacular including genetic algorithm, ant colony algorithm, particle swarm optimization, simulated annealing, differential evolution, *etc.*. Currently, to C-TSP problem, simulated annealing, improved genetic algorithm, differential evolution all achieve the optimal solution of 15404 *km*. The SA has the advantages of high, quality, robust, easy to achieve but with slow convergence.

The hybrid algorithm proposed is applied into the C-TSP. At the same time, basic PSO, SA and PSO with mutation are also applied to do the comparisons. The programming language is Matlab 7.0, and it runs on Win XP with Intel Core2 Duo 2.10 GHz CPU. We use the discrete PSO (DPSO) that proposed by Huang *et al.* in 2003 as the basic PSO, parameter settings are as follows: Particle number m = 200, maximum inertia weight $w_{\max}$ = 0.99, minimum inertia weight $w_{\min}$ = 0.09, acceleration coefficient $c1$ = 0.8, $c2$ = 0.4, iteration number k = 2000. The parameters of mutation in the PSO are the same as in DPSO. The parameter settings of SA are as follows: Initial temperature T_0 = 5000, termination temperature T_f = 1, cycle constant L = 31000, attenuation factor α = 0.99. The parameter settings of the hybrid algorithm are as follows : Particle number m = 200, maximum inertia weight $w_{\max}$ = 0.99, minimum inertia weight $w_{\min}$ = 0.09, acceleration coefficients $c1$ = 0.8, $c2$ = 0.4, initial temperature T_0 = 5000, termination temperature T_f = 1, cycle constant L = 31000, attenuation factor α = 0.95. Each algorithm has been run for 20 times, the numerical results of four algorithms are listed in Table 1, in which "Worst" denotes the worst solution in 20 runs, "Best" represents the best solution in 20 runs, "Average " is the average fitness in 20 runs, "Optimal rate" denotes the rate that gets the times of the optimal solution (15404) over 20 times runs.

One can see from Table 1 that the result obtained by DPSO is not satisfactory. It is unable to find the optimal solution of 15404, and its average value of solutions is also away from the optimal solution, which is because current solution X_{id}, personal best value p_{ib} and global best value p_{gb} tend to the same after several iterations. The DPSO is difficult to get new effective edge and new effective route, and it is easy to be trapped in local minima. On the other hand, the SA, PSO with mutation and the hybrid algorithm can obtain the optimal solution. The average and worst distances of hybrid algorithm proposed are 15453.4 and 15587, respectively, which are the smallest in all those of the four algorithms. The solutions obtained by the hybrid algorithm proposed are the best and its optimal solution rate is 20%, which is the highest. In order to further compare SA, PSO with mutation and the hybrid algorithm, we have studied the three algorithms in the fitness curve when finding the optimal solution. The results are shown in Figures 1-3, in which the x axes is the iteration number in unite of times, and the y axes is the global best route distance which is just the solution of C-TSP.

Algorithm	Worst	Best	Average	Optimal rate
DPSO	20152	16665	18035.3	0
PSO With Mutation	16194	15404	15662.3	0.1
SA	15606	15404	15467.8	0.15
Hybrid Algorithm	15587	15404	15453.4	0.2

Table 1. Experiment Results

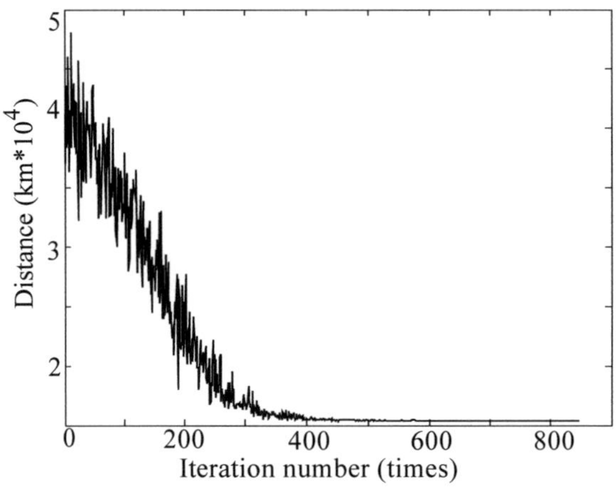

Fig. 1. The C-TSP optimization procedure of SA

From Figure 1 it is clear that SA converges to the optimal solution in about 500 iterations. Figure 2 indicates that PSO with mutation algorithm has oscillation at the early iteration, and it converges to the optimal solution in about 1000 iterations. From Figure 3 one can see that the hybrid algorithm converges to the optimal solution in about 100 iterations. The

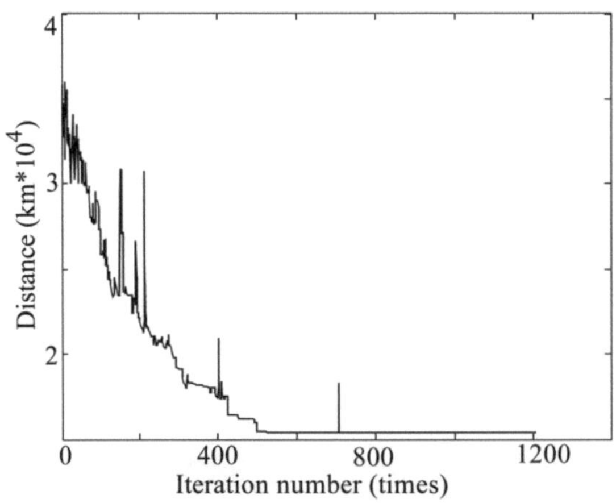

Fig. 2. The C-TSP optimization procedure of PSO with mutation

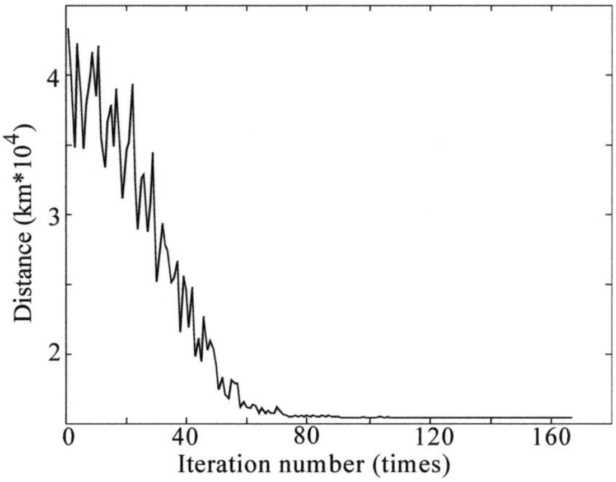

Fig. 3. The C-TSP optimization procedure of hybrid algorithm proposed

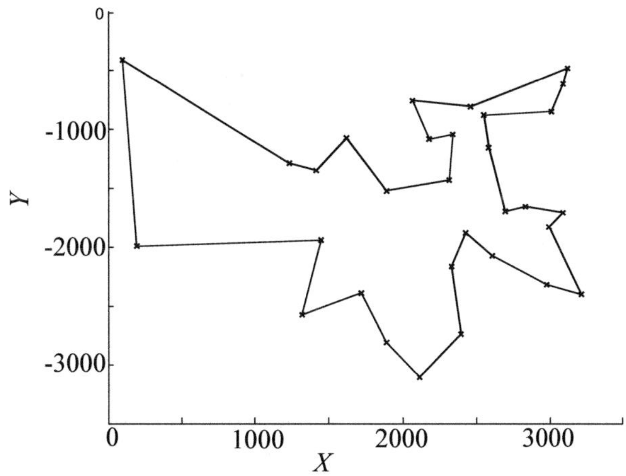

Fig. 4. Optimal route of C-TSP

problem of local optimal solution is not only been solved, but also the convergence speed is greatly decreased. Figure 4 is the optimal route made by the hybrid algorithm for C-TSP problem. The optimal route is: Beijing - Harbin - Changchun - Shenyang - Tianjin - Jinan - Hefei - Nanjing - Shanghai - Hangzhou - Taipei - Fuzhou - Nanchang - Wuhan - Changsha - Guangzhou - Haikou - Nanning - Guiyang - Kunming - Chengdu - Lhasa - Urumchi - Xining - Lanzhou - Yinchuan - Xian - Zhengzhou - Shijiazhuang - Taiyuan - Hohhot – Beijing. The total distance length of the optimal route is 15404 *km*.

3. Ant colony optimization algorithms and their improvements to the C-TSP application

3.1 Ant colony optimization algorithms

Artificial ants of the ACO algorithms build solutions by performing random walk which use a certain stochastic rules on a completely connected graph $G_C = (C, L)$ whose nodes are the components *C*, and the set *L* fully connect the components *C*. Each connection of the map

$G_C = (C, L)$ can be associated pheromone trail τ_{ij}, and heuristic information η_{ij} (The subscripts *i* and *j* are labeling of the nodes on the map).

It is important to note that artificial ants are in parallel movement independently. Although each ant is complex enough to find a (probably poor) solution to the problem under consideration, good-quality solutions can only emerge as the result of the collective interaction among the ants. This collaborative interaction is obtained via indirect communication mediated by the information ants read or write in the variables storing pheromone trail values. To some extent, this is a distributed learning process in which the single ant is not self-adaptive but, on the contrary, it can modify adaptively the way represented and perceived by other ants. Informally an ACO algorithm can be imagined as the interplay of three procedures (Dorigo & Stützle, 2004): Construction of Ants Solutions, Pheromone updating, and Daemon Actions.

1. Construction of Ants Solutions manages a colony of ants that concurrently and asynchronously visit adjacent states of the problem considered by moving through neighbor nodes of the problem's construction graph G_C. They move by applying a stochastic local decision policy that makes use of pheromone trails and heuristic information. In such a way, ants incrementally build solutions of optimization problem. Once an ant has built a solution, the ant evaluates the solution that will be used by the Pheromone updating procedure to decide how much pheromone to deposit.
2. Pheromone updating is the procedure in which the pheromone trails are modified. The trails' values move either increase, as ants deposit pheromone on the components or connections they use, or decrease due to pheromone evaporation. From a practical point of view, the deposit of new pheromone increases the probability whose components/ connections are used by either many ants or at least one ant. A very good solution produced will be used again in future ants. Differently, pheromone evaporation carries out a forgetting factor in order to avoid a too rapid convergence to a sub-optimal region, so pheromone evaporation has the advantage of generating new search areas.
3. Daemon Actions procedure is used to centralize the actions which can not be performed by single ants. Examples of daemon actions are the activation of a local optimization procedure, or the collection of global information used to decide whether it is useful or not to deposit additional pheromone to update the search process.

These three procedures should interact and take into account the characteristics of the problem considered. The TSP can be represented by a complete weighed graph $G_C = (C, L)$ with *C* being the set of nodes representing the cities, and *L* being the set of arcs. Each arc $(i, j) \in L$ is assigned a value d_{ij}, which is the distance between cities *i* and *j*. In the symmetric TSP, $d_{ij} = d_{ji}$ holds for all the arcs in *L*; but in the general case of the asymmetric TSP, the distance between a pair of nodes *i, j* is dependent on the direction of traversing the arc, that is, there is at least one arc (*i, j*) for which $d_{ij} \neq d_{ji}$. More formally, TSP is described as: A finite set $C\{c_1, c_2, \cdots, c_N\}$ of components is given, where *N* is the number of components. Set $L = \{l_{ij} \mid c_i, c_j \in C\}$ fully connects the components C. $d_{ij}(i, j = 1, 2, \cdots n)$ is the Euclid distance of arc l_{ij}:

$$d_{ij} = \sqrt{(x_i - x_j)^2 + (y_i - y_j)^2}, \qquad \forall (i, j) \in L \tag{5}$$

In the TSP, $G = (C, L)$ is a directed graph and the goal is to find a minimum length Hamiltonian circuit of the graph, where a Hamiltonian circuit is a closed path visiting each of the n nodes of G exactly once. In another way, an optimal solution to the TSP is a permutation R of the node indices $\{c_1, c_2, \cdots, c_n\}$ such that the length $F(R)$ is minimal, where $F(R)$ is given by

$$F(R) = \sum_{i=1}^{n-1} d_{R(i)R(i+1)} + d_{R(n)R(1)} \quad (6)$$

The ACO can be applied to the TSP in a straightforward way. The construction graph $G_C = (C, L)$, where the set L fully connects the components C, is identical to the problem graph; the set of states of the problem corresponds to the set of all possible partial tours; and the constraints Ω enforce that the ants construct only feasible tours that correspond to permutations of the city indexes. In all available ACO algorithms for the TSP, the pheromone trails are associated with arcs, so the τ_{ij} refers to the desirability of visiting city j directly after city i. The heuristic information is chosen as $\eta_{ij} = 1/d_{ij}$ thus the heuristic desirability of going from city i directly to city j is inversely proportional to the distance between the two cities. If there is the length of arc (i, j) equal to 0, then put the η_{ij} set to a very small value. For implementation purposes, pheromone trails are usually collected into a pheromone matrix whose elements are the arcs' pheromone trails. This can be done analogously for the heuristic information. Tours are constructed by applying the following simple construction procedure to each ant (Dorigo & Stützle, 2004): (1) choose a initial city according to some criterion. (2) make use of pheromone and heuristic values to probabilistically construct a tour by iteratively adding cities, to which the ant has not visited yet, until all cities have been visited; (3) go back to the initial city. After all ants have completed their tours, they may deposit pheromone on the tours they have followed. Sometimes, adding Daemon Actions such as the local search will improve the performance of algorithm.

3.2 Ant System (AS)

Ant System is created by Marco Dorigo and others in 1991 (Dorigo & Stützle, 2004; Dorido *et al.*, 1991; Colorini *et al.*, 1992; Dorigo 1992), and it is the first algorithm which is in line with the ACO algorithm framework. Initially three different versions of AS were proposed which are called *ant-density*, *ant-quantity*, and *ant-cycle*. These three versions are different on pheromone updating. Whereas in the ant-density and ant–quantity versions the ants update the pheromone directly after a move from one city to an adjacent city. In the ant-cycle version the pheromone deposited by each ant is set to be a function of the tour quality. The version of ant-cycle considers the quality of complete solution and uses pheromone updating method which has overall mechanism. Ant-cycle is better than the other two versions which just consider the single-step path information. Nowadays, when referring to AS, one actually refers to ant-cycle (AS described in this chapter also refers the ant-cycle version). The principle of AS is introduced as follows.

3.2.1 Tour construction

In AS, m artificial ants concurrently build a tour of the TSP. First, the m ants are put on randomly n chosen cities, which is also known as the scale of the problem. At each construction step, ant k applies a probabilistic action choice rule to decide which city to visit next. Evidently the next visit city j must be in the feasible neighborhood of ant k. Due to visit each city only once, so this neighborhood structure N_i^k is restricted by M^k which is used to store information of ant k about the path it followed so far. The following is the path chosen by the probability formula:

$$P_{ij}^k = \begin{cases} \dfrac{[\tau_{ij}]^{\alpha}[\eta_{ij}]^{\beta}}{\sum_{l \in N_i^k} [\tau_{il}]^{\alpha}[\eta_{il}]^{\beta}}, & \text{if } j \in N_i^k; \\ 0, & \text{otherwise}; \end{cases} \quad (7)$$

By this probabilistic rule, the probability of choosing a particular arc(i, j) increases with the value of the associated pheromone trail τ_{ij} and of the heuristic information value η_{ij}. The heuristic information value $\eta_{ij} = 1/d_{ij}$ represents a pre-given inspiration information which describes the objective conditions of the path outside. Pheromone trail τ_{ij} is the key factor in the tour construction and it represents experience which comes from the previous generation. Last, α and β are two parameters which determine the relative influence of the pheromone trail and the heuristic information. Each ant k has a memory storage M^k and it records in accordance with the order in which they visit all the cities visited. This M^k is used to define the feasible neighborhood N_i^k in the construction rule. In addition, the memory M^k allows ant k both to compute the length of the tour T^k it generated and to retrace the path to deposit pheromone. Although the solution of the whole construction is parallel, there are two different ways of implementing it: parallel and sequential solution construction. In the parallel implementation, at each construction step all the ants move from their current city to the next one, while in the sequential implementation an ant builds a complete tour before the next one starts to build another one. These two methods are equivalent in AS, because the pheromones are released only after m ants constructing a complete solution, they do not significantly influence the algorithm's behavior. However, in every step of ants moving if the local pheromone updating is added, then the effect of these two methods is different, such as ACS.

3.2.2 Pheromone trails updating

After all the m ants have constructed their tours, the pheromone trails are updated. First step is pheromone evaporation, and each edge of the pheromone is to evaporate according to pheromone evaporation rate ρ. Pheromone evaporation is implemented by

$$\tau_{ij} \leftarrow (1-\rho) * \tau_{ij} \quad , \quad \forall (i,j) \in L \quad (8)$$

The parameter ρ ($0 \le \rho \le 1$), which represents the pheromone evaporation rate, is used to avoid unlimited accumulation of the pheromone trails and it enables the algorithm to forget bad decisions previously taken. Actually if an arc is not chosen by the m ants then its associated pheromone value decreases exponentially in the number of iterations.

After pheromone evaporation, all the m ants deposit pheromone on the arcs they have crossed in their tours:

$$\tau_{ij} \leftarrow \tau_{ij} + \sum_{k=1}^{m} \Delta\tau_{ij}^{k} , \qquad \forall (i,j) \in L \tag{9}$$

where $\Delta\tau_{ij}^{k}$ is the amount of pheromone ant k deposits on the arcs it has visited. It is defined as:

$$\Delta\tau_{ij}^{k} = \begin{cases} Q / C^{k} , & \text{if arc } (i,j) \text{ belongs to } T^{k}; \\ 0 \quad , & \text{otherwise}; \end{cases} \tag{10}$$

where C^k, the length of the tour T^k built by the k-th ant, is computed as the sum of the lengths of the arcs belonging to T^k. By means of Eq. (10), the better an ant's solution is, the more pheromone the arcs belonging to this tour receive. This ensures the probability of choosing good path.

3.3 Elitist Ant System (EAS)

Elitist Ant System is the first improvement on the initial AS, which is called elitist strategy for Ant system (EAS) (Dorigo & Stützle, 2004; Dorido *et al.*, 1991; Colorini *et al.*, 1992; Dorigo, 1992). EAS gives the ant which has constructed so far the best path solution the elite logo, sets the so far the best path T^{bs}, and provides strong additional reinforcement to the arcs that is belong to the best tour T^{bs} found since the start of the algorithm.

In tour construction, the methods in EAS is the same as the methods in AS. In pheromone updating, the pheromone evaporation formula is the same as (3.4).The additional reinforcement of tour T^{bs} is achieved by adding a quantity e / C^{bs} to its arcs, where e is a parameter that defines the weight given to the best-so-far tour T^{bs}, and C^{bs} is its length. The following is the equation for the pheromone deposit:

$$\tau_{ij} \leftarrow \tau_{ij} + \sum_{k=1}^{m} \Delta\tau_{ij}^{k} + e * \Delta\tau_{ij}^{bs} , \qquad \forall (i,j) \in L \tag{11}$$

where $\Delta\tau_{ij}^{k}$ is defined as in Eq. (10) in AS and $\Delta\tau_{ij}^{bs}$ is defined as follows:

$$\Delta\tau_{ij}^{bs} = \begin{cases} 1 / C^{bs}, & \text{if arc } (i,j) \text{ belongs to } T^{bs}; \\ 0 \ , & \text{otherwise}. \end{cases} \tag{12}$$

The key is that the EAS has adopted a daemon action, which is the additional incentive of the elite ants. Although this operation belongs to the pheromone updating steps, it is a kind of additional guidance to the overall operation. One can image like this: After all the ants including the elite ant depositing pheromone on the arcs they have crossed over their tour, the elite ant give the T^{bs} additional release of pheromones.

Compared with EAS, the pheromone updating mechanism in the AS is weak indeed. Sometimes, the optimal path may be with a very small difference between the paths which are not so satisfactory, and the mechanism in the AS can not make a good distinction between them. This is because of the simple form of the pheromone depositing formula which allows all ants use the same weight for depositing pheromone. Usually, the level for the algorithm to explore the overall optimal solution is not enough. The EAS with the parameter e determining the weight gives the best-so-far tour, that is, the best-so-far solution has been improved in the course of the search status, and the algorithm attempts to search a better solution which around the best-so-far solution. From the other side of the coin, the EAS concentrates a smaller search space which is compressed from original search space. Such a smaller search space may have better solutions. The mechanism increases the probability for finding overall optimal solution, and at the same time it also speeds up the convergence. Experiments later in this chapter show that parameter e needs to be selected with a reasonable value: an appropriate value for parameter e allows EAS to both find better tours and have a lower number of iterations. If parameter e is too small, the elitist strategy will not have much effect because of the low discrimination for better ants, while if the parameter e is too large, the algorithm will be too dependent on the initial best-so-far tour, and have rapid convergence to a small number of local optimal solutions, which weaken algorithm's ability of exploration.

3.4 Rank-Based Ant System (AS_{rank})

Another improvement over AS is the rank-based version of AS (Dorigo & Stützle, 2004; Bullnheimer *et al.*, 1997): AS_{rank}. In AS_{rank}, before updating the pheromone trails, the ants are sorted by increasing tour length and the quantity of pheromone deposited by an ant is weighted according to the rank of the ant. Usually in each iteration, only the (w-1) best ranked ants and the ant produced the best-so-far tour (this ant is not necessarily is belong to the set of ants of the current algorithm iteration) are allowed to deposit pheromone. The best-so-far tour gives the strongest feedback, with weight w; the *r-th* best ant in the current iteration contributes the pheromone updating with the value $1/C^r$ multiplied by a weight given by max {0, w-r}.

In tour construction, the methods in AS_{rank} are the same as the methods in AS. In pheromone updating, the pheromone evaporation formula is the same as in Eq. (8). The AS_{rank} pheromone update rule is:

$$\tau_{ij} \leftarrow \tau_{ij} + \sum_{r=1}^{w-1}(w-r)\Delta\tau_{ij}^{r} + w\Delta\tau_{ij}^{bs}, \qquad \forall(i,j) \in L \tag{13}$$

where $\Delta\tau_{ij}^{r} = 1/C^{r}$ and $\Delta\tau_{ij}^{bs} = 1/C^{bs}$; C^r is the length of *r-th* solution and C^{bs} is the same as in Eq. (12)

Compared with AS the AS_{rank} selects w ants to deposit pheromone according to the rank of solutions' quality, which is a new improved formula. It completely abolishes the *national pheromone deposit* mechanism, in other word, only the ant who has constructed a good enough solution can deposit pheromone and the amount of pheromone to deposit is decided by the rank. It can reduce the operation of the pheromone and get rid of bad solutions directly. The pheromone depositing mechanism in AS_{rank} is a group of elite ants award, and it is better than the mechanism in AS which just depends on the reciprocal of the tours. Totally, the performance of AS_{rank} is much better than AS.

AS_{rank} and EAS are different on the reward strategy of elitist ants. EAS just give the best-so-far solution an additional incentive, although it can find the good solutions, indirectly it is greatly weakened or even abandoned the second-best-so-far solutions whose neighborhood may have better solutions. In AS_{rank}, the algorithm gives a group of elitist ants award, but the award is according to the rank of solutions. On the one hand the mechanism takes into account the importance of the best-so-far solution, which ensures that the experience of the leading elitist ant is retained; on the other hand it considers the neighborhood of sub-optimal solutions, that is, it increases ability to explore the optimal solution.

3.5 MAX-MIN Ant System (MMAS)

Max-Min Ant System is a constructive amendment to AS (Dorigo & Stützle, 2004; Stützle & Hoos, 1996; Stützle & Hoos, 1997; Stützle & Hoos, 2000). It is one of the best ACO algorithms. There are four main modifications with respect to AS:

1. It strongly exploits the best tours found: only either the iteration-best ant, that is, the ant produced the best tour in the current iteration, or the best-so-far ant is allowed to deposit pheromone.
2. It limits the possible range of pheromone trail values in the interval $[\tau_{\min}, \tau_{\max}]$.
3. The pheromone trails are initialized to the upper pheromone trail limit together with a small pheromone evaporation rate.
4. Pheromone trails are reinitialized when the system approaches are stagnated or when no improved tour has been generated for a certain number of consecutive iterations.

The first point strongly exploits the best tours found, but may lead to a stagnation situation in which all the ants follow the same tour. To increase the effect, the second modification is introduced by MMAS. It makes that the pheromone in each arc does not accumulate too large or consume too small, so that it could ensure the sustainability of exploration. The third point makes MMAS have a stronger ability to explore at the initial stage. The fourth point introduces a new mechanism which can be applied to all the ACO algorithms, that is, through the resumption of initial pheromone and re-search thus it increases the possibility of finding the optimal solution.

Since only the optimal solution is allowed to deposit pheromones, the formula about pheromones depositing is very concise:

$$\tau_{ij} \leftarrow \tau_{ij} + \Delta\tau_{ij}^{best}, \qquad \forall (i,j) \in L \tag{14}$$

where $\Delta\tau_{ij}^{best} = 1 / C^{best}$. C^{best} is the length of optimal tour. It can be the best-so-far tour or iteration-best tour.

In general, in MMAS implementations both the iteration-best and the best-so-far updating rules are used, in an alternate way. Obviously, the choice of the relative frequency with which the two pheromone updating rules are applied has an influence on how greedy the search is: When pheromone updating is always performed by the best-so-far ant, the search focuses very quickly around the best-so-far solution, whereas when it is the iteration-best ant that updates pheromones, the number of arcs received pheromone is larger and the search is less directed.

In MMAS, there are two default daemon actions. One is the pheromone trails limits, the other one is the pheromone trails re-initialization. In MMAS, lower and upper limits $\tau_{\min}$ and $\tau_{\max}$ on the possible pheromone values of any arc are imposed in order to limit the probability p_{ij} of selecting a city *j* when an ant is in city *i* in the interval $[P_{\min}, P_{\max}]$, so that it could avoid searching stagnation and enhance the ability to explore. In the long run, the upper pheromone trail limit on any arc is bounded by $1/\rho C^*$, where C^* is the length of the optimal tour. Based on this result, MMAS uses an estimate of this value of $1/\rho C^{bs}$, to define

$\tau_{\max}$: each time a new best-so-far tour is found, the value of $\tau_{\max}$ is updated. The lower pheromone trail limit is set to $\tau_{\min} = \tau_{\max} / a$, where a is a parameter which decides the proportion of upper limit and lower limit. In MMAS, in order to avoid stagnation, the lower pheromone trail limits play a more important role than upper limits. Pheromone trail re-initialization is typically triggered when the algorithm approaches the stagnation behavior or if no improved tour of a given number of algorithm iterations is found. It can increase the exploration of paths that have only a small probability of being chosen. By the way, the pheromone trail re-initialization also increases the probability of finding the global optimal solution (equivalent to cumulative probability).

3.6 Ant Colony System (ACS)

Ant Colony System (ACS) is an extension of AS (Dorigo & Stützle, 2004; Dorigo & Gambardella, 1997). The ACS exploits the search experience accumulated by the ants more strongly than AS. The rule is called pseudorandom proportional rule. When located at city *i*, ant *k* moves to a city *j*, the rule is given by

$$j = \begin{cases} \arg \max\limits_{l \in N_i^k} \{\tau_{il}[\eta_{il}]^{\beta}\}, & \text{if } q \le q_0; \\ J, & \text{otherwise;} \end{cases} \tag{15}$$

where q is a random variable uniformly distributed in $[0,1]$, J is a random variable selected according to the probability distribution given by Eq.(5) with $a = 1$. $q_0 (0 \le q_0 \le 1)$ is a parameter with which the ant makes the best possible move as indicated by the learned pheromone trails from the heuristic information, while with probability $(1 - q_0)$ it performs a biased exploration of the arcs.

This pseudorandom proportional has strong artificial operability because the parameters q_0 can be set to guide the algorithm's preference. By tuning the parameter q_0, it is allowed to modify the degree of exploration and to select whether to concentrate the search of the system around the best-so-far solution or to explore other tours.

In ACS only the best-so-far ant is allowed to update pheromone after each iteration including the pheromone deposit and pheromone evaporation. In each time an ant uses an arc to move from city i to city j, which is called the local pheromone updating to remove some pheromone from the arc to increase the exploration of alternative paths. The global pheromone trail updating is described as the following equation:

$$\tau_{ij} \leftarrow (1-\rho)\tau_{ij} + \rho \Delta\tau_{ij}^{bs}, \qquad \forall (i,j) \in T^{bs} \tag{16}$$

where $\Delta\tau_{ij}^{bs} = 1 / C^{bs}$. C^{bs} is the length of the best-so-far tour T^{bs} . It is worth to note that the deposited pheromone is discounted by a factor ρ, which results in the new pheromone trail becoming a weighted average between the old pheromone value and the amount of pheromone deposited.

The local pheromone trail updating is described as the following equation:

$$\tau_{ij} \leftarrow (1-\varepsilon)\tau_{ij} + \varepsilon\tau_0, \qquad \forall (i,j) \in L \tag{17}$$

where ε, $0 \le \varepsilon \le 1$, ε is the local pheromone evaporation rate and the τ_0 is the initial pheromone. The effect of the local updating rule is to reduce pheromone trail of an ant in some arc so that the arc becomes less desirable for the following ants. The role of local updating is to strengthen the capacity of artificial ant exploration.

3.7 Application of five ACO algorithms in C-TSP and results analysis

In order to demonstrate and verify the properties of five ACO algorithms mentioned above, in this section, we'll apply them in the Chinese TSP with 31 capital cities, and compare their advantages and disadvantages in the medium-scale discrete optimization problem.

The important parameters of Ant System are as follows. *N*: the number of cities; *m*: the number of artificial ants; α: the parameter that controls the relative importance of pheromone trail; β: the parameter that controls the relative importance of heuristic information; ρ: pheromone evaporation rate; *q*: a constant represents the weight of the deposited pheromone; τ_0: initial pheromone trail; NC: preset number of iterations. In addition, in its improved algorithms the addition parameters are as follows. The *e* in EAS : a parameter that defines the weight given to the best-so-far tour. The *w* in AS_{rank}: the number of the artificial ants who are allowed to add pheromone. The *τ_proportion, τ_max, τ_min* and *nowbest_p* in MMAS: *τ_proportion* is a parameter which decides the proportion of upper limit and lower limit; *τ_max* is the upper limit of pheromone; *τ_min* is the lower limit of pheromone; *nowbest_p* is the frequency of selecting best-so-far tours rule of depositing pheromone. The *pbest* and *local_p* in ACS: *pbest* is a probability of choosing right path; *local_p* is the local pheromone evaporation rate.

A candidate list is first built to restrict the number of available choices considered at each construction step. In general, candidate lists contain a number of the best rated choices according to some heuristic criterion. First, configure for each city a nearest neighbor list which records the other cities sorted in ascending order by distance; Second, build the candidate lists for each city and set the parameter $nn(0 \le nn \le n)$ which decides the number of the nearest neighbors needed; Last, get the cities which are previous *nn* cities in the nearest neighbor list into the candidate list for each city. When an ant constructs solution, it gives priority to the candidate list of cities. In fact, the ant usually considers from the first city in the candidate lists that has not been visited and selects with random probability rule. When all the cities in the candidate list have been visited by an ant, the ant will consider other cities and select the city which has a maximum value of $[\tau_{ij}]^{\alpha}[\eta_{ij}]^{\beta}$, that is, the ant selects the city which is the best experience-oriented one. Set the parameter *nn* to a constant which is below the number of cities *n*, especially for a small value, the algorithm's speed will be improved significantly. The mechanism is feasible, because in TSP a good path can not appear a city *i* connects another city *j* which has a long distances from city *i*. In other words, the ant in city *i* should choose the city *j* which nears the city *i*. It is worth to note that the parameter *nn* is important for candidate list. If the value of *nn* is too large, the effect of speeding up algorithm will be weakened. On the other hand, a too small *nn* will make the performance of algorithm very poor. However, it should be noted that the use of truncated nearest-neighbor lists can make it impossible to find the global optimal solution. The global optimal solution does not mean to be the combination of cities in the candidate lists. Perhaps in order to achieve the best, ants in some cities should choose far way cities to go and these cities are not in departure cities' candidate lists.

The steps of Ant System (AS) algorithm is as follows (in the case no candidate lists):

Step 1. Enter an actual TSP, get the scale n of the problem, and transform the instance into a symmetric distance matrix distance (set the diagonal elements with small values to prevent the situation of NAN.)

Step 2. Initialize all the parameters, including m, α, β, ρ, q, τ_0 and NC. Set the iteration number to 0.

Step 3. Initialize storage variable including best-so-far solution *nowbest_opt* = 2 * *vicinity* (*vicinity* is the solution comes form the nearest algorithm), best-so-far path *nowbest_path* = zeros (1, n), pheromone tails matrix τ = ones(n) * τ_0 , and the matrix which describes the importance of heuristic information τ_β = dist.^(- β).

Step 4. Begin to circulate, and set the iteration number $nc = nc + 1$.

Step 5. The starting cities of ants are randomly distributed as begin_city = randperm (n); initialize tabu list *tabu* = ones (m, n) and taboo the starting city; initialize path matrix *path* = zeros (m, n) and add the starting city into the first column; build the matrix that describes the importance of pheromone $\tau_\alpha = \tau.\hat{}\ \alpha$; build the comprehensive weight matrix $\tau_d = \tau_\alpha .* \tau_\beta$.

Step 6. Ant walking steps *step*=*step*+1 (initialize *step* = 0 , and $step \le n-1$).

Step 7. Artificial ants' label $k = k + 1$ (initialize $k = 0$, and $k \le m$)

Step 8. Choose the next city in accordance with the probability formula, taboo the selected city in the ant taboo list *tabu* (k, :), and add this chosen city into the ant path sequence *path* (k, *step* +1).

Step 9. If $k < m$, then turn to step 7; otherwise turn to step 10.

Step 10. If $step \le n-1$, then turn to step 6; otherwise turn to step 11.

Step 11. According to the pheromone updating formula of AS, update the pheromone trails τ, and update the optimal solution as best-so-far solution *nowbest_opt* and the optimal path as best-so-far tour *nowbest_path* which includes the cities of the best-so-far tour.

Step 12. If the iteration number nc < NC, then turn to step 4; otherwise end the operation, export the data and image results.

Remark: The steps described above are just the AS algorithm. The improved algorithms mentioned above should have some changes, which are mainly in the steps of the parameter settings, constructing solutions and pheromone updating. In the process of building a solution, they use parallel mechanism. To add the candidate lists to the algorithm, first of all one needs to add a step in one of the first two steps in the algorithm: list the neighbor cities in ascending order by distance and configure nearest neighbor list for each city, set the parameter *Neighbor_num* of the candidate list, and then get the candidate list *Neighbor_list* from the nearest neighbor list; followed by modifying the step 8: first of all, begin to consider the first city in the candidate list that does not be visited, and select the target city of the next step with probability rules. When the cities of the candidate list have all been visited one compares the values $\tau_d = \tau_\alpha .* \tau_\beta$ of all the other remaining cities, and select the largest one as the next target city; taboo the selected city in the ant taboo list *tabu* (k,:), and add this city into the ant path sequence *path* (k, step +1).

Table 2 is the summary of the experimental results of the five ACO algorithms including adding the mechanism of the candidate list and pheromone re-initialization, *etc.*. Each system runs for 100 times. In Table 2, the algorithm with "_C" has the mechanism of candidate list, the algorithm with "_R" has the mechanism of pheromone re-initialization, Best or Worst mean the best or worst solution of the 100 solutions. "Opt. rate" is the rate of global optimal solution, Average is the average solution of all solutions. "Average converg." is the average convergence iteration number, and Average time is the average time in 100 running solutions. Relative error is described as follows:

$$relative\ error = \frac{|\,average\ \ solution - global\ optimal\ solution\,|}{global\ optimal\ solution} \tag{18}$$

where the *global optimal solution* = 15404, and the average solution is the average solution in 100 running solutions.

Algorithm	Best	Worst	Opt. rate	Average	Relative error	Average converg.	Itera. No.	Average time
AS	15420	15669	0	15569.05	1.071%	1405.95	3000	12.221
AS_C	15420	15620	0	15548.3	0.937%	1380.11	3000	6.044
EAS	15404	15625	48%	15447.4	0.282%	1620.48	4000	16.409
EAS_C	15404	15593	52%	15437.62	0.218%	1606.95	4000	7.954
AS_{rank}	15404	15593	63%	15413.74	0.063%	1857.19	4000	16.662
AS_{rank}_C	15404	15520	65%	15408.05	0.026%	1747.07	4000	8.349
MMAS	15404	15593	55%	15428.54	0.159%	2371.96	5000	20.386
MMAS_C	15404	15593	57%	15424.32	0.132%	2166.56	5000	10.384
MMAS_R	15404	15593	68%	15418.48	0.094%	2984.5	8000	23.951
MMAS_C_R	15404	15520	73%	15418.75	0.096%	2655.68	8000	10.799
ACS	15404	15779	40%	15442.42	0.249%	2889.67	10000	5.546
ACS_C	15404	15745	40%	15445.51	0.269%	2708.9	10000	4.817

Table 2. The summary of the test results when ACO algorithms are applied to the C-TSP

One can obtain from Table 2 the following results:

1. In the test of all 12 kinds of algorithms, from the column "Best" solutions one can see except AS and AS_C which add the mechanism of candidate list to AS, the other 10 kinds of algorithms can detect the global optimal solution 15404.
2. Along all the algorithms, from the column "Opt. rate" one can see max-min ant system which has the mechanisms of the candidate list and pheromone initialization added in MMAS_C_R owns the highest rate of excellent, that is 73%, followed by MMAS_R;

Except AS and AS_C, ACS and ACS_C which add the mechanism of candidate list to ACS have the worse performance, that is 40%.

3. Compare these five algorithms without any mechanism, from the "Opt. rate " one can also see that rank based version AS, AS_{rank} has the highest rate of excellent, that is 63%, followed by MMAS, EAS, ACS, and AS.
4. Compare these five algorithms without any mechanism to those five algorithms with mechanisms of the candidate list respectively, that is, compare XXX with XXX_N, one can see from the optimal rate and average running time except ACS and ACS_C are not obvious, the mechanism of the candidate list slightly improves the performance of the algorithms and greatly reduces the running time.
5. Compare the four cases of MMAS, that is, MMAS, MMAS_C, MMAS_R and MMAS_C_R, one can see from the optimal rate that every mechanism can improve the performance of algorithms, and max-min ant system only with the mechanisms of pheromone initialization the candidate list has a better performance than only with the mechanisms of the candidate list. Of course, max-min ant system with two mechanisms at the same time has the best performance.

4. Conclusions

This chapter has analyzed the characteristics of the SA and PSO for solving the C-TSP problem. Combined the fast convergence speed of PSO with the good local search ability of SA, a hybrid algorithm has been proposed. Numerical simulations show that the proposed algorithm is more efficient in C-TSP than single PSO and SA, respectively. Generally speaking, when ACO algorithms are applied to the TSP instance C-TSP, elitist strategy for ant system, rank based version AS, max-min ant system, ant colony system show better performance, they have a certain percentage to find the global optimal solution, but ant system fails to find global optimal solution. In all these systems, max-min ant system which has the mechanisms of the candidate list and pheromone initialization added in shows the best performance in the C-TSP.

5. Acknowledgement

This work was supported by the National Natural Science Foundation of China under Grant No. 60774098.

6. References

Eberhart, R. C. & Kennedy, J. (1995). A New Optimizer Using Particles Swarm Theory. *Proceedings of the 6th Int'1 Symposium of Micro Machine and Human Science*, pp. 39-43, 0-7803-2676-8, Nagoya, Oct. 4-6

Yuan, Z. L.; Yang, L. L. & Liao, L. (2007). Chaotic Particle Swarm Optimization Algorithm for Traveling Salesman Problem. *Proceedings of the IEEE International Conference on Automation and Logistics*, pp.1121-1124, 978-1-4244-1531-1, Jinan, China, Aug. 18-21

Xu, Y. H., Wang, Q. W. etc. (2008). An Improved Discrete Particle Swarm Optimization Based on Cooperative Swarms. *International Conference on Web Intelligence and*

Intelligent Agent Technology, pp. 79-82, 978-0-7695-3496-1, Sydney, Australia, Dec. 9-12

Lovbjerg, M.; Rasmussen, T. K. & Krink, T. (2001). Hybrid Particle Swarm Optimizaters with Breeding and Subpopulations. *Proc of the Third Genetic and Evolutionary Computation Conference,* Vol. 24, pp. 469-476, San Francisco, USA

Kang, L. H. & Xie,Y.(1998). Non-numerical Parallel Algorithms—Simulated Annealing Algorithm, Science Press, 703003736, Beijing

Zhong, W. L.; Zhang, J. & Chen, W. N.(2007). A Novel Discrete Particle Swarm Optimization to Solve Traveling Salesman Problem. *IEEE Congress on Evolutionary Computation,* pp. 3283-3287, 978-1-4244-1339-3, Singapore, Sept. 25-28

Xiao, J.M.; Li, J.J. & Wang, X.H. (2004). A Modified Particle Swarm Optimization for Travelings Salesman Problems. *Computer Engineering and Applications,* Vol. 40, No. 35: pp. 50-52

Li, L. L.; Zhu, Z. K. & Wang, W.F. (2008). A Reinforced Self-Escape Discrete Particle Swarm Optimization for TSP. *Second International Conference on Genetic and Evolutionary Computing,* pp. 467-470, 978-0-7695-3334-6, Jinzhou, China, Sept. 25-26

Huang, L.; Wang, K. P. & Zhou, C.G.(2003). Particle Swarm Optimization For Traveling Salesman Problems. *journal of JiLin university (science edition),* Vol. 41, No.10: pp. 477-480

Dorigo, M.; & Stützle, T.(2004). Ant Colony Optimization. MIT Press, 978-0-262-04219-2 Boston

Dorigo, M.; Maniezzo, V. & Colorni, A.(1991). Positive feedback as a search strategy. Technical report, *Dipartmento di Elettronica,* Politecnico di Milano, Milan, pp. 91-96

Colorini, A.; Dorigo, M. & Maniezzo, V.(1992). Distributed optimization by ant colonies. In F.J. Varela&P.Bourgine (Eds), *Proceedings of the First European Conference on Artificial Life,* pp.134-142. Cambrige, MA, MIT Press

Dorigo, M. (1992) Optimization, Learning and Natural Algorithms [in Italian].PhD thesis, *Dipartimento di Elettronica,* Politecnico di Milano, Milan

Bullnheimer, B.; Hartl, R.F. & Strauss, C. (1997) A new rank based version of the Ant System: A computational study. *Central European Journal for Operations Research and Economics,* Vol. 7, No. 1: pp. 25-38

Stützle, T. & Hoos, H. H. (1996). Improving the Ant System: A detailed report on the MAX-MIN Ant System. *Technical report AIDA-96-12*, FG Intellektik, FB Informatik, TU Darmstadt, Germany

Stützle, T. & Hoos, H. H.(1997). The MAX-MIN Ant System and local search for the traveling salesman problem. In T.Bäck, Z.Michalewicz, & X.Yao (Eds.), *Proceedings of the 1997 IEEE International Conference on Evolutionary Computation (ICEC'97),* pp.309-314, Piscataway, NJ, IEEE Press

Stützle, T. & Hoos, H. H. (2000). MAX-MIN Ant System. *Future Generation Computer Systems*, Vol. 16, No. 8: pp. 889-914

Dorigo, M. & Gambardella, L. M. (1997). Ant colonies for the traveling salesman problem. *BioSystems*, Vol. 43, No.2: pp. 73-81

Dorigo, M. & Gambardella, L. M. (1997). Ant Colony System: A cooperative learning approach to the traveling salesman problem. *IEEE Transactions on Evolutionary Comtutation*, Vol. 1, No. 1: pp. 53-66